BVR's Guide to Business Valuation Issues in Estate and Gift Tax

2010 Edition

Linda Trugman
CPA/ABV,CBA,ASA,MBA

Published by

BVR
What It's Worth

Business Valuation Resources, LLC
1000 SW Broadway, Suite 1200
Portland, OR 97205
(503) 291-7963 • Fax (503) 291-7955 • www.BVResources.com

BVR
What It's Worth

Managing Editor: Colin Murcray
Chair and CEO: David Foster
President: Lucretia Lyons
Sales: Linda Mendenhall
Customer Service Manager: Stephanie Crader
ISBN: 978-1-935081-29-6

Table of Contents

Section 2: Conference & Teleconference Transcripts & Presentations

Section 3: Court Case Abstracts

Section 1

A Collection of Articles on Estate and Gift Tax Issues

Introduction to *BVR's Guide to Business Valuation Issues in Estate and Gift Tax*

Linda Trugman, CPA/ABV, CBA, ASA, MBA

Another year has passed and while things always seem to stay the same, they often change as well. Since last year's guide was published, practitioners have had the opportunity to hear numerous speakers on the Pension Protection Act and the various penalties that may ultimately be applied to both valuation analysts and preparers by the Internal Revenue Service at conferences, as well as webinars and teleconferences.

In March 2009, Robert Cimasi, MHA, ASA, CBA, AVA, CM&AA; William Forsberg, Esq.; Michael Gregory, ASA, AVA, MBA, PE; and Howard Lewis, MS, AVA participated in a BVR teleconference entitled *IRS New Rules: Pension Protection Act and Beyond*. The panel began with Howard Lewis, the former IRS National Program Manager for Engineering and Valuation Program, who provided a timeline describing how Congress went from Code Section 6701, which included penalties for appraisers who aided and abetted in understating taxes; to Circular 230, which provided guidance for professional responsibility for professionals including appraisers; to the passage of the Pension Protection Act of 2006 that enacted Code Section 6695A, which added appraiser penalties for misstatements and understatements.

William Forsberg, Esq. provided further insight into the Code Section itself. The transcript of the teleconference is included in this *Guide*. One of the major issues that Mr. Forsberg points out is that the statute "requires the penalty to be imposed. There is no discretion, at least the way I read it, that the IRS can have with regard to whether or not a penalty is imposed." A number of other issues regarding this Code Section were also discussed before Michael Gregory of the Internal Revenue Service joined the call. Of course, Mr. Gregory does not represent the service when he speaks on these matters, but it became clear from his comments that he takes issue with the new Code Section as enacted. He gave some perspective on several issues about which the IRS and appraisers but heads (at least through May 2008).

There are a number of interesting pieces of information in the teleconference transcript that affect all of us who work in the estate and gift tax arena. It is definitely worth taking the time to review the transcript and develop an understanding of the Pension Protection Act and how it may affect appraisers.

Approximately one year later, Jay Fishman, FASA; Chris Treharne, ASA, MCBA; and I participated in a teleconference called *Valuation Issues in Estate & Gift Tax*. In the year since the previous teleconference, the appraiser community is still asking a lot of questions about Code Section 6695A, as well as an additional penalty section, 6694, which applies to tax preparers. Jay Fishman has been working on appraisal issues with the IRS for approximately 10 years, so he was able to provide us with an update on Code Sections 6694 and 6695A.

Code Section 6694 is a tax preparer penalty. It is important for appraisers to be aware of Code Section 6694 because the IRS has determined that appraisers are now considered to be non-signing preparers. This penalty is not automatic, and will not be combined with the 6695A penalty. To avoid this penalty, the appraiser must show that the position has substantial authority—although the IRS has not yet defined the term substantial authority.

The discussion then moved on to Code Section 6695A. There have been major concerns about this penalty since its enactment, but in August 2009, the IRS Office of Small Business/Self Employed issued an internal memo to its personnel explaining that the Code Section was designed for implementation on a case by case basis. Of course, this memo was obtained by the public. The policy was called "penalty for valuation misstatements attributable to incorrect appraisals" and is discussed in detail in the transcript included in the *Guide*. Mr. Fishman also discussed the safe harbor rule built into the penalty, which states that if the appraiser can determine that his or her value is "more likely than not" the correct value, then the penalty will not be assessed. However, to date, the IRS has not defined "more likely than not."

On February 18, 2010, representatives from the Internal Revenue Service's Office of Service Wide Penalties met with representatives from the American Society of Appraisers, The Institute of Business Appraisers, the American Institute of Certified Public Accountants, the National Association of Certified Valuation Analysts, the American Bar Association, the National Association of Independent Fee Appraisers, the Appraisal Institute, and the American Society of Farm Managers and Rural Appraisers to offer testimony about Code Section 6695A. These organizations are concerned with three main areas: the percentage tests, the lack of a definition for "more likely than not," and the IRS's implementation memo—particularly the Form 4477 appointment letter.

As part of the IRS's implementation memo, an appointment letter was included. Essentially, if after an audit the IRS personnel believes that there is a case for a 6695A penalty against a preparer, the IRS employee would issue this letter, stating that a valuation misstatement case has been opened and that the appraiser should come to an appointment to discuss his or her appraisal with the appropriate party (e.g., the examiner, the appellate division, or the estate and gift tax lawyer). At this point, the penalty case has already begun. One of the problems with this situation is that the appraiser is now in a position where he or she does not know what has happened during the audit, but might have to disclose that the IRS has started some type of action against him. All of the organizations seem to agree that this is a lack of due process for the appraiser, and hopefully the IRS will reassess the use of this letter.

Of course, all appraisers are concerned with potential penalties, but this is not the only topic that was discussed on the call. Chris Treharne mentioned several technical topics that practitioners deal with on a daily basis,whivh includes defining the valuation subject for transfer (estate and gift) tax purposes. Since these transactions are transfers, the valuation subject is the interest that is being transferred; in other words if a 100 percent interest is owned and a 25 percent interest is the gift, we should concentrate on the 25 percent interest. Chris reminded the audience that the standard of value is fair market value, which means that the buyers and sellers are hypothetical.

The panel also discussed tax-effecting S corporations. BVR has an entire guide on this issue, as it comes up regularly in estate and gift tax transfers. Chris discussed how tax effecting using a 40 percent tax rate may create a penalty for both the analyst and the taxpayer when the IRS says a tax-effect should not have been used. This is not to say that we should ignore this issue and never tax effect, but the analyst should consider the issue and be prepared to defend his position.

Valuation analysts never fail to discuss discounts, and we dealt with a number of questions regarding discounts for lack of control and marketability. Of course, and perhaps ironically, the panelists all agreed that there is no agreed upon methodology for calculating discounts.

One issue that we did not discuss on the teleconference was the current status of family limited partnerships (FLPs). The IRS and taxpayers continue to take FLP issues to court, some successfully and some not. A very brief summary of some of the most recent cases follows. Detailed abstracts and copies of the actual cases can be located in the *Guide.* However, if you are a valuation analyst, please remember not to rely on these cases in your reports. Brief the attorneys and let them make the legal arguments. This especially pertains to the discount area. Often, the discounts pass muster because they do not become part of the legal arguments. If the IRS thinks that they will prevail on the legal issues, they might not argue that the discounts are too high. However, this does not mean that the discount was accepted.

Estate of Jorgensen (TCM 2009-66): When will taxpayers learn that if you do not dot the "i's" and cross the "t's," you will not prevail in court? This is what is known as a bad facts case; nothing was done right and there was no business purpose for the creation of the FLPs. Needless to say, this was a slam dunk for the IRS.

Miller v. Commission (TCM 2009-119): This case involved the creation of an FLP and a subsequent gift; it then dealt with the remaining limited partnership units owned by the decedent at her date of death. In the gift tax portion, the court accepted the validity of the entity because:

- There was active management of the partnership's assets by the decedent's son as general partner;
- There was a change in the investment activity after the formation of the FLP; and
- The decedent retained sufficient living expenses.

Unfortunately, before Mrs. Miller passed away the family transferred all of the rest of her assets to the FLP. These assets were all included in Mrs. Miller's estate under Code Section 2036.

Linton v. U.S. (No 2:08-cv-00227, W.D. Wash.) and *Heckerman v. Commissioner (2009 WL2240326: W.D. Wash.)*: These two cases, both heard by the Western District Court in Washington, were bad facts cases. Although the details of the two cases differ, both involved a similar fact pattern—LLC units were transferred to the LLC before the assets. In both cases, the taxpayers tried to twist the facts to fit what they meant to do, but it did not work.

Keller v. U.S. (2009 WL 2601511, S.D. Tex.): The most interesting detail in this case is that when the Keller family filed the original estate tax return it did not include the FLP in its assets since it had not been fully formed and funded. However, one year later, the estate discovered that another taxpayer had prevailed with a similar set of facts, so it amended the estate tax return and filed for a refund. In court, the taxpayer was able to prevail that the FLP had a legitimate business purpose and the appraiser's combined discount of 47.5 percent on a marketable security (bonds) FLP was accepted.

Estate of Malkin v. Commissioner (TCM 2009-212): Unfortunately, it did not take long before the court was faced with another bad facts case. The decision in this case was quite lengthy because of the various financial maneuverings that the decedent tried before he passed away. Unfortunately for the estate, the judge saw through all of it. He determined that some of the transfers were not bona fide transfers under Code Section 2036 and that they should be included in the estate. Other transfers were indirect gifts to the decedent's children, not gifts of FLP interests.

Murphy v. U.S. (2009 WL 3366099, W.D. Ark.): This was another good facts case and the taxpayers prevailed, first on the 2036 issue and then on the valuation issue. The court listed the following non-tax, legitimate business reasons for the existence of the FLP:

- Pool the family assets for investment according to the father's philosophy;
- Pass the management responsibility to the next generation;
- Enable the father to make lifetime gifts of interests in the FLP while ensuring that the voting of the underlying assets stayed under central management;
- Educate the father's descendants about wealth acquisition, management, and preservation; and
- Protect the family assets from creditors, failed marriages, and dissipation by future generations.

The assets in the FLP included publicly traded stock in Murphy Oil (thinly traded), as well as holdings in a timber company (thinly traded), banking securities, and real estate holdings. Overall, the court adopted the taxpayer's various discounts, believing him to be more credible, which reduced the decedent's pro rate interest of approximately $126 million to $74.5 million, a combined discount of approximately 40 percent.

Estate of Black v. Commissioner (133 T.C. 15): This was another good facts case, where the taxpayers followed all the rules and prevailed on a 2036 challenge. The court cited the following non-tax purposes:

- The FLP adhered to Mr. Black's buy-and-hold investment philosophy, increasing its net asset value nearly fourfold;

- The transfer restrictions prevented Mr. Black's son from selling or encumbering his contribution of $11 million in Erie stock, and they prevented his grandsons from reaching their stock, even when their trusts terminated;
- The Black family's consolidated position allowed it to maintain a seat on the Erie board of directors; and
- The FLP protected the son's stock during a costly divorce, during which his wife received only the 125,000 shares the son had pledged for a personal loan.

Walter M. Price and Sandra K. Price v. Commissioner (TCM 2010-2) and *John W. Fisher v. U.S. (No. 1:08-cv-00908, S.D. Ind.)*: In 2002, the Tax Court (which was affirmed by the 7th Circuit Court of Appeals in 2003) ruled on the *Hackl* case. Essentially, the judge in *Hackl* ruled that annual exclusion gifts were gifts of future interests and therefore did not qualify for the annual gift tax exclusion. The judges in these two cases ruled similarly early in 2010. *Price*, which is appealable to the 8th circuit, and *Fisher*, which is appealable to the 7th circuit, seem to be raising the bar in the taxpayer's ability to use the annual gift tax exclusion for interests in FLPs and LLCs.

Holman v. Commissioner (No. 08-3774, 8th Circuit Court of Appeals): The Holman FLP was funded solely with Dell stock. The Holmans were able to prevail on the legitimacy of the FLP in the original Tax Court hearing, but they lost on the Code Section 2703 issue concerning restrictions in the agreement. The majority of the 8th circuit agreed with the Tax Court but one judge dissented vigorously, arguing that the Tax Court did not look at the entire Code Section and therefore stopped its analysis too quickly. This could be the start of more Code Section 2703 arguments in gift tax cases.

Although it seems that most of the court cases we are aware of deal with transfers of interests in FLPs and LLCs, once in a while another issue will wind its way through the court system.

In January 2009 *Litchfield v. Commissioner (TCM 2009-21)* was decided. This case involved two S corporation holding companies that had not yet existed for 10 years when the decedent passed away. In addition to discounts for lack of control and marketability, the issue of built-in gains taxes was considered. The differences between the two appraisals were substantial, but the taxpayer's expert prevailed due to his thoughtfully considered analysis. A note to appraisers: Although this case involved two S corporations, the issue was not tax-affecting an S corp. (i.e., it was not a progeny of *Gross, Wall, etc.).*

The last issue that surfaced before the courts dealt with defined value clauses was *Estate of Christiansen v. Commissioner (2009 WL 3789908, CA 8)* and *Estate of Petter v. Commissioner (TCM 2009-280).* There are two types of defined value clauses. Both are formulas that put limits on amounts that will be transferred to beneficiaries. The IRS has vehemently opposed these clauses, but was ruled against in both cases.

Overall it was an interesting year for estate and gift taxes. The *Guide* provides the details behind all of the summaries.

IRS Challenges to FLPs and Family LLCs

By Chris Mellen

BUSINESS VALUATION UPDATE™ OCTOBER 2003

Family limited partnerships and family limited liability companies (collectively referred to as "FLPs") have been used for several years now as a tool to simplify the gifting of property interests to family members. Internal Revenue Code (IRC) §7701(a)(2) requires the assets held by a partnership to be related to a trade or business, investment, or income-producing venture. As such, an FLP may: (i) conduct an active trade or business; (ii) own assets requiring some activity; (iii) hold investment assets; or (iv) combine any of the above.

FLPs afford participants many benefits. They allow parents to give children an interest in valuable assets (e.g., real estate, marketable securities, intellectual property, and company stock) without relinquishing control. They serve as a protective shield against creditors. They maintain family control and protect against the disruption that can result from a divorce. For real estate holdings, FLPs simplify property management and avert partition risks by avoiding fractionalization of title.

On the flip side, they are costly to set up and maintain, they restrict liquidity, and they can stir up family issues that may cause discord. Last, but certainly not least, they are likely to invoke IRS scrutiny. The focus of this article is on 10 areas in which the IRS has attacked FLPs, as seen in the plethora of Tax Court cases over the past few years. This is not a complete list of possible IRS attacks, and any partners or members of these entities should seek legal counsel and valuation advice.

1. ***Retained Enjoyment***—The IRS has had success in forcing the assets contributed to the FLP to be included in the decedent's estate under IRC §2036(a) when the decedent did not give up control of the assets after they were contributed to the FLP. As a result, the only discounts allowed when §2036 applies are for fractional interests in the underlying assets; no discounts are allowed for the applicable partnership interest. Ownership or enjoyment of transferred property is retained for purposes of §2036(a)(1) when there is express or implied understanding to that effect among the parties at the time of the transfer, even if the retained interest is not legally enforceable. As such, the court (as in *Church*[1], *Dailey*[2], *Harper*[3], *Kimbell*[4], *Reichardt*[5], *Schauerhamer*[6], *Strangi*[7], and *Thompson*[8]) will look to the actions of the parties after the partnership has been formed to determine whether there was an implied retention of economic benefits. Generally speaking, it is imperative to treat the FLP as a legitimate business by strictly complying with the requirements of the partnership agreement and applicable state law.

2. ***Restrictions on Right to Use***—IRC §2703 was designed to prevent the use of buy sell agreements to artificially depress transfer tax (i.e., gift, generation-skipping, and estate tax) in family situations. This code section generally provides that the value of a property is to be determined for transfer tax purposes without regard to any option, agreement, or the right to acquire or use the property at a price less than fair market value, or without regard to any restriction on the right to sell or use the property unless: (i) the restriction is a bona fide business arrangement; (ii) the restriction is not a device to transfer property to members of the decedent's family for less than full and adequate consideration; and (iii) at the time the restriction or agreement is created, its terms are comparable to similar arrangements entered into by people in arm's-length transactions.

The IRS has attempted to use §2703 to invalidate the entire FLP agreement. Having failed, they have turned their attention to disregarding provisions in the agreement that specifically relate to the right to use the partnership interest. The problem, however, is that the IRS has too broad an interpretation of "use."

Generally, the IRS has been unsuccessful in attacking FLPs under §2703(a). In both *Hall*[9] and *Strangi*, the court said that "mere suspicion and speculation about a -decedent's estate planning and testamentary objectives are not sufficient to disregard an agreement in the absence of persuasive evidence that the agreement is not susceptible of enforcement or would not be enforced by the parties of the agreement." This challenge arose in several other cases including *Church, Jones*[10], *Kerr*[11], *Knight*[12], *and Reichardt.*

3. ***Applicable Restrictions***—IRC §2704(b)(2) provides that, if there is a transfer of an interest in a corporation or partnership to a member of the transferor's family, and the transferor and members of the transferor's family hold, immediately before the transfer, control of the entity, any "applicable restrictions" shall be disregarded in determining the value of the transferred interest. "Applicable restrictions" refers to any restriction that effectively limits the ability of the *partnership* to liquidate in certain situations. The IRS has been unsuccessful in attacking FLPs under §2704(b). Not to be confused, a restriction on *limited partners*' "right to withdraw" is not an applicable restriction (*Kerr*). In several cases, the court (see *Harper, Jones, Kerr, Knight, Reichardt, and Strangi*) has ruled that the partnership agreements were not more restrictive than state law (i.e., applicable restrictions were not present) and recognized the partnership entity.

4. ***Gift of Future Interest***—In *Hackl*[13], the court said that to be a present interest, the gift must convey substantial present economic benefit by reason of use, possession, or enjoyment of either the property itself or income from the property. To ascertain whether income qualified as a present interest, the court employed a three-part test: receipt of income, steady flow to beneficiaries, and determination of the value of that flow. Due in part to the lack of current income, and in part to the unusual restrictions of the agreement, the court ruled that the gifts to the LLC did not qualify for exclusion under IRC §2503(b) because their advantages and enjoyment could not be immediately realized.

5. ***Assignee Interests***—Taxpayers generally have been unsuccessful in trying to take even larger-than-normal discounts under the assignee interest theory. This theory states that, because a willing buyer of an LP interest could buy only the economic rights of the FLP and not the voting and participation rights, the buyer would not get the full bundle of rights of the LP interest without the consent of the other partners. As such, the interest being valued is really an assignee interest, entitled to larger discounts than an LP interest.

The assignee interest theory has failed because: (i) the partners were inconsistent in referring to the interest as an assignee interest (vs. a partnership interest) in the documents; (ii) the appraisal report characterized the interest as a limited partner rather than an assignee; and/or (iii) the parties' actions were inconsistent with the document. Attorneys must give proper guidance to their clients and the appraisers to ensure consistency. The Tax Court has accepted this argument in some cases (e.g., *Adams*[14], *Church, McCord*[15], and *Nowell*[16]) but has rejected it in others (e.g., *Dailey, Jones, and Kerr*). Landmark cases involving assignee interests include *Harrison*[17], *McCord, McLendon*[18], *and Novak*[19].

6. ***Gift on Formation***—There are two types: gift of a partnership interest and gift of capital contributions. As seen in *Church*, to uphold valuation discounts, the facts must demonstrate that the gift is a partnership interest rather than a capital contribution, as the restrictions justifying such a discount would not apply to an outright gift of the underlying assets.

In *Shepherd*[20], the Tax Court determined that the children received an indirect gift upon formation because they did not contribute any funds to the partnership. To avoid this problem, children should contribute something to the FLP on formation and receive ownership percentages equal to their consideration. If they lack the funds, the spouse or some third party can be the partner. Once these steps are accomplished, gifts can be made. In addition, the valuation should be performed as of the date of contribution.

7. ***Aggressive Valuation Adjustments***—Valuation adjustments (e.g., discounts for lack of marketability [DLOM] or lack of control [DLOC]) are one of the most beneficial aspects of establishing an FLP as a vehicle to minimize gift, generation-skipping transfer, and estate taxes. Discounts that are "too high" may catch the attention of the IRS. IRC §6662 also provides for undervaluation penalties. That said, a "high" DLOM or DLOC may be perfectly acceptable if the particular facts and circumstances warrant it (e.g., the IRS's position for a 70% discount in *Robertson*).

Several years ago, author Thomas Solberg aptly stated: "An appraiser should be able to provide an expert opinion as to the value of an asset, not to guess what a potentially adversarial entity will tolerate. The valuation of restricted securities is not a numbers game, and each case must stand on its own facts as presented to the court. Legal precedent, in terms of discounts granted in cases previously decided, is not as important as the nature, quality, and quantity of the evidence and the skill with which that evidence is marshaled and presented. The cases indicate that the courts, if provided with the factual basis to do so, are willing to grant significant discounts for restricted securities to properly reflect the economic realities of the marketplace."[21]

8. ***No Appraisal***—As Steven M. Pack, JD, author of *Family Limited Partnerships: Practical Strategies & Solutions*[22], notes: "Anyone contemplating the planning and implementation of a FLP and subsequent gifting of interest in the FLP is *urged* to spend a little (relatively speaking) to engage qualified, credible and independent business and asset appraisers, to 'save a lot.'" The absence of an appraisal could result in overvaluation (§6662(e)) or undervaluation (§6662(g)) financial penalties, which could ultimately unravel an entire estate plan.

9. ***A "Weak" Appraisal Report***—An appraisal report of an FLP interest should demonstrate the appraiser's understanding of the partnership agreement by including portions of that agreement that are relevant to the determination of the discount. It must connect the empirical market evidence and the subject FLP interest and thus cannot be a "one size fits all" report. The IRS is aggressively challenging appraisals in which the expert has taken average discounts from empirical evidence without considering interest-specific factors.

To start the running of the general three-year statute of limitations for the valuation of any gift, the appraisal report also must meet the "adequate disclosure" requirements of Treasury Regulation §301.6501(c)-1(f).[23] Gifts that do not meet these requirements: (i) are not adequately disclosed; (ii) may not comply with applicable appraisal standards; and (iii) may be exposed to attack indefinitely (as opposed to just three years). The court has addressed this general issue of "weak" appraisal reports in *Berg*[24], *Knight, Mandelbaum*[25], and several other cases.

10. ***Use of an Outdated Appraisal***—Technically speaking, an appraisal of a limited partnership interest in an FLP should be updated whenever any change takes place (e.g., a key partner steps down, voting parameters change, or multiple annual exclusion gifts are made even a day or two prior to the valuation date –12/31/0x to 1/2/0y). Updating is especially important after significant developments that might impact the value of the FLP interest (e.g., material changes in the applicable real estate market or in the stock market). As Steven Pack notes, "Since the taxpayer and/or estate bears the burden of substantiating fair market value where valuation adjustment factors impact on value, appraisal reports prepared at the time a gift is made or immediately following death may save the taxpayer or estate from a costly lesson."

Conclusion

The IRS is also asserting several other methods of attack, seeking out FLP cases it believes it can win in the Tax Court. Keep in mind that the trier of fact (usually a judge in tax cases) can consider only the evidence placed before him or her. Therefore, bad facts make bad law. The IRS frequently takes a "hard line" position to force compromise, knowing that the threat and cost of litigation can be onerous to the taxpayer, and hoping that the attorney is not a skillful negotiator. The taxpayer's attorney, on the other hand, is weighing the costs to the taxpayer of a negotiated settlement versus litigation.

The FLP is a form of business and should be treated as such. It facilitates bringing the younger generation into the decision-making process without turning over total control. It also protects assets and can prevent partition of real property. Emphasis on these nontax benefits, coupled with a delay in gifts and a well-written valuation report that is reasonably consistent with established methodologies, consisting of explicit analysis of marketplace facts, partnership financial characteristics, and agreement structures, should go a long way in mitigating, or possibly even avoiding, IRS attacks.

---

1. *Church v. United States*, 2000 U.S. Dist. LEXIS 714 (W.D. Texas 2000), aff'd, 268 F.3d 1063 (5th Cir. 2001)(unpub).
2. *Estate of Dailey v. Commissioner*, T.C. Memo 2001-263 (2001); costs proceeding at T.C. Memo 2002-301 (2002).
3. *Estate of Harper v. Commissioner*, T.C. Memo 2000-202 (2000); later proceeding at T.C. Memo 2002-121 (2002).
4. *Kimbell v. United States*, 2003 U.S. Dist. LEXIS 523 (N.D. Texas 2003).
5. *Estate of Reichardt v. Commissioner*, 114 T.C. 144 (2000).
6. *Estate of Schauerhamer v. Commissioner*, T.C. Memo 1997-242 (1997).
7. *Estate of Strangi v. Commissioner*, 115 T.C. 478 (2000); aff'd in part, rev'd in part, remanded by *Gulig v. Commissioner*, 2002 U.S. App. LEXIS 11920 (5th Cir. 2002).
8. *Estate of Thompson v. Commissioner*, T.C. Memo 2002-246 (2002).
9. *Estate of Hall v. Commissioner*, 92 T.C. 312 (1989).
10. *Estate of Jones v. Commissioner*, 116 T.C. 121 (2001).
11. *Kerr v. Commissioner*, 113 T.C. 449 (1999), aff'd, 2002 U.S. App. LEXIS 10965 (5th Cir. 2002).
12. *Knight v. Commissioner*, 115 T.C. 506 (2000).
13. *Hackl v. Commissioner*, 118 T.C. 279 (2002), aff'd, 2003 U.S. App. LEXIS 13936 (7th Cir. 2003).
14. *Adams v. United States*, 2001 U.S. Dist. LEXIS 13092 (N.D. Texas 2001).
15. *McCord v. Commissioner*, 120 T.C. No. 13 (2003).
16. *Estate of Nowell v. Commissioner*, T.C. Memo 1999-15 (1999).
17. *Estate of Harrison v. Commissioner*, T.C. Memo 1987-8 (1987).
18. *Estate of McLendon v. Commissioner*, 1995 U.S. App. LEXIS 41277 (5th Cir. 1995), rev'g and remanding T.C. Memo 1993-459 (1993).
19. *Novak v. United States*, 87-2 USTC 13,728 (June 29, 1987).
20. *Shepherd v. Commissioner*, 115 T.C. 376 (2000), aff'd, 2002 U.S. App. LEXIS 3165 (11th Cir. 2002).
21. Thomas A. Solberg, "Valuing Restricted Securities: What Factors Do the Courts and the Service Look For?", *Journal of Taxation* (September 1979): 150-154.
22. Steven M. Pack, *Family Limited Partnerships: Practical Strategies & Solutions*, 2003. Tel. (949) 859-1065.
23. The purpose of the "adequate disclosure" requirements are to apprise the IRS of the nature of the gift and the basis for the value so reported (i.e., valuation discounts). If any discount is taken for lack of control or lack of marketability, these requirements must be met to set the statute of limitations in motion. This includes even those gifts to which the annual exclusion applies (i.e., for gifts under $11,000 in 2003)! Many are not aware, or do not believe, that these requirements apply to annual exclusion gifting where discounts are taken, when in fact they do.
24. *Estate of Berg v. Commissioner*, T.C. Memo 1991-279 (1991), aff'd in part, rev'd in part, 1992 U.S. App. LEXIS 24735 (8th Cir. 1992).
25. *Mandelbaum v. Commissioner*, T.C. Memo 1995-255 (1995) aff'd, 91 F.3d 124 (3d Cir. 1996).

Pass-through Entity Discounts for Built-in Capital Gains Taxes

*By Michael Paschall, ASA, CFA**
First published in *Business Valuation Update*™ May 2004

In *Estate of Dunn v. Commissioner*,[1] the Court of Appeals allowed a dollar-for-dollar reduction in value of a C corporation due to the built-in capital gains evident in that case. While it thus appears that we now have some clarification and solidification on the built- in gains issue for C corporations, this still leaves a major unanswered question: what to do about appreciated assets in pass-through tax entities such as partnerships, LLCs, and S corporations?

In contrast to corporations, owners of partnerships, LLCs, and S corporations have no entity-level tax and are taxed only at the personal level. Despite this difference, the built-in gains issue can still exist with a tax-advantaged entity.

This raises a choice for the hypothetical willing buyer: (1) purchase an asset (such as marketable securities or real estate) outright and get a basis equal to the purchase price, or (2) purchase an interest in a Partnership, LLC, or S corporation, and take a potentially low inside basis on the appreciated assets of that entity. Under scenario (2), the sale of an appreciated asset can mean the pass-through of capital gains liability to the owners of the entity. Although this can result in an increased basis, the benefits of which may be realized upon the later sale of the entity, it also may result in immediate tax liability on the capital gain. If scenario (2) is therefore relatively unattractive to scenario (1), wouldn't the hypothetical willing buyer demand some discount on the purchase of an interest in such an entity?

Recent Tax Court cases of *W.W. Jones II Est.*,[2] and *E.M. Dailey Est.*,[3] may help shed some light on this situation. Both *Jones* and *Dailey* involved gifts of partnership interests. In *Jones*, no discount for built-in gains was allowed on the two gifts made. In *Dailey*, a discount for built-in capital gains was recognized as valid by experts for both the taxpayer and the IRS.

Keeping up with the Joneses

In *Jones*, the decedent formed family partnership A with his son as each party contributed assets to the partnership. The son was the sole general partner and the decedent was a limited partner. The decedent then transferred an 83.03% limited partnership interest to his son.

The decedent also formed family partnership B with his four daughters as each person contributed assets to the partnership. Two of the daughters were general partners. The decedent and the other two daughters were limited partners. The decedent then transferred 16.915% limited partnership interests to each of his four daughters (or 67.66% total).

There were significant built-in gains at both partnerships, $11.1 million in Partnership A and $5.9 million in Partnership B.

The discount battle

The decedent's appraiser applied discounts for lack of control, lack of marketability, and built-in gains, totalling a 66% discount for the partnership A gift and a 58% discount for the partnership B gifts. The appraiser for the IRS opined that no discount was appropriate on either gift.

The Tax Court allowed only an 8% discount for lack of marketability on the gift of the 83.03% interest for partnership A. A key reason for the Tax Court's decision in this matter was the fact that the partnership agreement for Partnership A required a 75% limited partnership vote to remove the general partner or liquidate the partnership. Consequently, the buyer of an 83.03% interest could immediately remove the general partner, install himself as general partner, and liquidate the partnership.

The Tax Court's analysis of Partnership B was different. Because the gifted interests in Partnership B were true minority interests, the Tax Court allowed a 40% discount for lack of control and 8% discount for lack of marketability on the gifts of the 16.915% interests.

Built-in gains and the 754 election

Both parties agreed that the tax on the built-in gains could be avoided by use of a section 754 election.

1. Partnership A

Although the taxpayer's expert acknowledged that there was a 75% to 80% chance that the 754 election would be made and that the election would not create any adverse consequences or burdens on Partnership A, taxpayer's expert nonetheless believed that a discount for built-in gains was appropriate due to the fact that the decedent's son (the sole general partner of Partnership A) stated that he might refuse to cooperate with an unrelated buyer of the 83.03% interest. The Tax Court rejected the opinion of the taxpayer's expert as an "attempt to bootstrap the facts to justify a discount that is not reasonable under the circumstances."

The expert for the IRS argued that no discount for built-in gains was warranted for Partnership A. The expert for the IRS argued that:

> a hypothetical willing seller of the 83.03% interest would not accept a price based on a reduction for built-in capital gains. The owner of that interest has effective control, as

discussed above, and would influence the general partner to make a section 754 election, eliminating any gains for the purchaser and getting the highest price for the seller. Such an election would have no material or adverse impact on the preexisting partners.

2. Partnership B

The Tax Court also did not allow a discount for built-in gains for the gifts of the limited partnership interests in Partnership B. The Tax Court relied primarily on the assumption that a 754 election would not cause a significant burden on Partnership B.

Where do we go from here?

In trying to read between the lines to apply the rationale of this case in future situations, it appears the Tax Court placed weight on the following issues as concerns the ability to take a discount for built-in gains in a partnership scenario:

1. Influence that the transferred interest has over the ability to make the 754 election.

As noted earlier, the Partnership A interest transferred was an 83.03% limited partner interest that had the unilateral ability to direct key actions of that partnership (due to the 75% majority vote required to remove the general partner, sell the partnership assets, etc.). It is easier to see how a discount for built-in gains would be disallowed on such an interest as it represents a controlling interest that presumably can make (or at least heavily influence) the 754 election. On the other hand, the interests being valued in Partnership B were minority 16.915% limited partner interests that did not have any ability to influence key actions of the partnership. It is far less clear in this situation that the buyer of a 16.915% interest would be able to force or heavily influence the 754 election and therefore far more reasonable that some discount for built-in gains should be considered.

2. Resulting detriment or hardship to the partnership or other partners following the 754 election.

About the only real peg that the Tax Court hangs its hat on as concerns the Partnership B gifts was the assumption that a 754 election "would not cause any detriment or hardship to the partnership or the other partners." Although this is a factor that should be considered, this should not be a determinative factor in not allowing a discount for built-in gains, particularly when there are other compelling factors that argue for at least the consideration of a discount for built-in capital gains.

There are several characteristics about the 754 election that suggest its careful use. Among these characteristics are the fact that the election can be made only once, the election can be very difficult to revoke, the election is not necessarily beneficial to the other partners, and there are additional (and perhaps significant) administrative and accounting costs associated with the election.

The Tax Court notes that "the only situation identified in the record where a section 754 election would not be made by a partnership is...a publicly syndicated partnership with 'lots of partners... and a lot of assets' where the administrative burden would be great if an election were made." Unfortunately for the rest of us, we are left to wonder just how many partners constitute "lots of partners," how many assets are "a lot of assets," and the exact location of the line where administrative burden crosses from moderate to great. Based on our conversations with a number of estate planning attorneys, the 754 election is rarely made in the real world due to the disadvantage of additional accounting and tax preparation fees that arise from the election. Due to this increase in compliance costs, a very significant step-up in basis is usually required to make the 754 election worthwhile.

3. Resulting detriment or hardship to the partnership or other partners following the 754 election.

The court's assumption that the hypothetical seller and buyer would negotiate over a 754 election is unconvincing. It is unlikely that a hypothetical willing buyer of a 16.915% limited partnership interest would be successful in negotiating a 754 election, no matter how light the administrative burden of such an election would be.

In *Jones*, then, we are left with a useful framework for analysis of the built-in capital gains issue; however, the logic and reasoning surrounding the failure to allow a discount for built-in capital gains on the Partnership B gifts are less than compelling.

The *Dailey* case

In *Dailey* the Tax Court approves a discount for built-in gains in a partnership; however, the Court does not quantify the discount or give appraisers any guidelines to follow. In *Dailey* the decedent made two separate gifts of limited partnership interests in a family limited partnership that held highly-appreciated marketable securities (primarily Exxon stock).

Even the IRS expert recognizes discounts for built-in gains

The taxpayer's expert in *Dailey*, "citing published data, opined that the aggregate discount is 40% for lack of marketability, control, and liquidity." The taxpayer's expert further "testified that he considered the significant amount of unrealized capital gains relating to the Exxon stock." The expert for the IRS argued for aggregate discounts of 13% and 16% on the two gifts.

However, at trial, he admitted he had not reviewed the partnership agreement, and stated that unrealized capital gains are "an important source of discounts."

The Tax Court ultimately affirmed the 40% discount taken by the taxpayer, finding that the testimony of the expert for the IRS was "contradictory, unsupported by the data, and inapplicable to the facts." The Tax Court, in a sense, was choosing between the lesser of two evils, stating that "neither expert was extraordinary." As a result, it is difficult to have much faith in the conviction of the Tax Court's decision.

Lessons from *Dailey*

The important thing to glean from the *Dailey* case is that the Tax Court gives credit to both experts' statements that unrealized capital gains are an important issue to consider and actually sides with the expert who considered the unrealized capital gains in determining his discount. The unfortunate aspects of the *Dailey* case are that neither expert was particularly compelling and the Tax Court did not quantify the particular discount for unrealized capital gains.

Conclusion

In summary, the *Jones* and *Dailey* cases have at least addressed the issue of built-in capital gains in pass-through entities such as partnership, LLCs, and S corporations. Part of the *Jones* decision makes sense and part of it doesn't. The *Dailey* case offers hope that the courts are moving towards the recognition of the reality of the impact of built-in capital gains on value.

***The 754 election** refers to an election that can be made under IRC section 754. It is a means by which, in an FLP or other limited partnership, the transferee or the substituted limited partner can write up the cost basis of the limited partnership interest transferred to him to what he paid for it as opposed to inheriting the cost basis of the previous owner of the interest. This is particularly important to the acquirer of a partnership interest where the cost basis of the selling partner is very low. Without the election, the new owner assumes the cost basis of his predecessor and is saddled with any capital gains liability. As the 745 election is not mandated, the decision to grant or withhold the election is normally at the total discretion of the general partner. Accordingly, there is an element of uncertainty as to whether or not the general partner will provide the election when a limited partnership interest is transferred. When valuing an FLP or limited partnership, the valuation expert should factor in the probability that one would or would not be granted a 754 election.*

*__Michael A. Paschall__, ASA, CFA, is a Managing Director of Banister Financial, Inc. (Charlotte, NC) and is co-author (along with George B. Hawkins, ASA, CFA) of the CCH Business Valuation Guide. This article is excerpted from the Summer 2003 issue of *Fair Value*™ and is reprinted with permission.

1. *Estate of Dunn v. Commissioner*, 301 F.3d 339 (5th Cir. 2002)
2. *W.W. Jones II Est.*, 116 TC 121, Dec. 54,263 (2001)
3. *E.M. Dailey Est.*, 82 TCM 710, Dec. 54,506(M), TC Memo 2001-263

Abraham and Hillgren: Different Approaches to Section 2036(a) Valuation

By Owen Fiore, JD, CPA
First published in *Business Valuation Update*™ May 2004

Beginning with the 1997 *Schauerhamer*[1] case, and continuing through *Harper*, *Thompson*, *Strangi I* and *Strangi II*,[2] appraisers and tax advisors have witnessed increasingly rapid development of the Tax Court's views on pass-through entity reality and federal transfer tax valuation issues based upon recognition or non-recognition of the entity. In essence, the courts appear to be using IRC Section 2036(a) in estate tax cases as an economic substance approach.

Increased role for business appraisers

While lawyers and other tax advisors have the primary burden to properly structure FLPs and LLCs to minimize the risk of 2036(a) destruction of the entity for estate tax purposes, appraisers can contribute significantly by reviewing entity documents and being an integral part of the planning team. Further, as the *Lappo*[3] and *Peracchio*[4] cases illustrate, pass-through entities are real and viable for gift tax purposes.

This article first reviews the impact of *Estate of Ida Abraham*[5] and *Estate of Lea Hillgren*,[6] two recent Tax Court decisions. These cases suggest an increasingly important role for business valuation appraisers, including consultation with taxpayers and their tax advisors on effective planning of FLPs and LLCs. Appraisers also are key players in gift and estate tax compliance efforts, ultimately supporting valuation adjustments or "discounts" before the IRS and in the courts. In fact, the IRS national compliance program focuses us on the need for greater cooperation among tax advisors and appraisers.

Abraham and *Hillgren*—more guidance?

In *Estate of Ida Abraham*, the court found a fatally defective FLP plan that resulted from tension between a court-supervised guardianship for the decedent, Ida Abraham, and the use of FLPs to shift wealth to heirs. Code Section 2036(a) was applied in full force as a broad estate includability provision. On the other hand, in the *Estate of Lea Hillgren*, the combination of good lawyering and excellent valuation analysis by the estate's appraiser saved the day!

Abraham—another 2036(a) Tax Court opinion

While appearing to apply only the "retained right of enjoyment" provision, namely, Code Section 2036(a)(1), *Estate of Abraham*[7] illustrates the mandate that estate planners and their clients truly must understand the purpose and scope of Section 2036(a). Here, a Massachusetts probate court approved the family's petition in a guardianship proceeding for Ida Abraham to establish a multi-entity estate plan that included real estate trusts, FLPs, and corporate general partners owned by decedent's revocable trusts.

The court authorized gifts and other transfers of partnership interests to family members; however, to protect Mrs. Abraham's financial security, her limited guardian ad litem had *sole discretion* to direct use of up to all of the FLPs' income to satisfy Abraham's medical, support and maintenance needs. That is, this was an overriding requirement and power—possessed by decedent's fiduciary—that could be utilized to prevent otherwise specified pro rata income distributions based on capital interests of the partners. Further, at trial before Tax Court Judge Ruwe, testimony given by the limited guardian ad litem and certain of decedent's children showed that the FLP would be used to satisfy Mrs. Abraham's needs first and foremost.

Essentially, rather than carving out assets not needed or to be relied upon for the decedent's lifetime support, the documentation and testimony made clear that Mrs. Abraham's needs were paramount and that her limited guardian ad litem would be the sole person to determine what portion of the FLP income, up to 100% thereof, would be distributed to her or for her benefit. Further, based upon testimony of decedent's children, the court found the "implied agreement" prohibited by 2036(a)(1) (as was the case in *Schauerhamer*[8]). The court concluded, "...the structure that decedent employed through her legal representatives was merely a testamentary vehicle employed to shift her assets to future generations while maintaining her continued right to benefit from the FLP interests transferred."

Abraham's lesson—don't use FLP for decedent's support

What are we to conclude from the Abraham case? It is not uncommon that the court-appointed guardian or conservator will obtain authority to make gifts from the estate or even to develop an estate plan, including use of entities for both tax and non-tax purposes. However, *Abraham* teaches that the needs of the person under the guardianship or conservatorship must be satisfied out of his or her own assets, including partnership interests and income therefrom, and not from assets (FLP or LLC interests) ostensibly gifted or otherwise transferred to heirs.

In addition, given the emphasis in some of the 2036(a) cases, including *Estate of Stone*,[9] on having sufficient assets outside the FLP to meet expected support needs, again the danger of transferring virtually all assets into the entity—even if pro rata income distributions are mandatory—is very clear.

Hillgren—2036(a) applies, but taxpayer still wins!

Tax Court Judge Cohen, author of the *Strangi I* and *Strangi II* opinions, decided *Estate of Lea K. Hillgren.*[10] This case deals with both the viability of an FLP under 2036(a), and the impact on valuation of the partnership assets (because Judge Cohen determined 2036(a) eliminated the FLP as an entity for estate tax purposes) of a Business Loan Agreement (BLA) between siblings.

Lea Hillgren, active in business and real estate investments, unfortunately suffered from mental illness. She was not married, had no children, and relied heavily upon her brother Mark. Ultimately, Mark and his children became her heirs. Mark facilitated real estate financing and otherwise assisted his sister for a number of years, providing substantial financial support for her real estate. Judge Cohen commented that "when one sibling needed money, the other would lend money." The 1994 BLA substantially encumbered four of decedent's properties, including giving her brother sole discretion for 29 years over any sale, naming him as decedent's attorney-in-fact under the BLA, and granting him a 25% interest in all net cash sales and certain refinancing proceeds. This agreement, found enforceable by the Tax Court, encumbered four of the seven parcels of real estate allegedly placed in the FLP formed January 1,1997.

Since 1984 Lea had suffered from mental illness, attempted suicide in October, 1996, and in early 1997, shortly after the FLP was set up, Lea was hospitalized. She died June 5, 1997, taking her own life.

In spite of the estate's assertions that the FLP was an "asset protection device", the court rejected the estate's claims that the partnership agreement changed any real relationship between Mark and decedent or that it changed decedent's interest in the properties. It was clear from the record that the FLP assets were used to support the decedent and that the entity was not properly respected. In fact, as the court noted, the FLP was kept "invisible" as to outsiders and the certificate of limited partnership was not filed until after commencement of the estate tax examination!

All of taxpayer's discounts upheld—thanks to appraiser

Nonetheless, Judge Cohen, having ruled at the conclusion of the trial that the BLA was a valid and enforceable agreement, proceeded to the question of the valuation of the four properties subject to the BLA. Taxpayer's appraiser, Carsten Hoffmann of FMV Opinions, Inc., was considered credible by the court, his appraisal essentially developing value conclusions by reference to the secondary market in syndicated real estate partnerships. Due to the BLA, the hypothetical buyer of the decedent's interest in the real estate lacked control and marketability.

The IRS appraisers, Ray Klaris and John Thompson, of Klaris, Thomson & Schroeder, Inc. suffered from having been given "instructions" by the Service to disregard the BLA, largely, it appears, due to the forceful position of the IRS Estate Tax Attorney. As Judge Cohen stated, "[a]lthough respondent's experts were qualified, they were hindered in their valuation by respondent's incorrect instructions regarding the effect of the BLA."

Carsten Hoffmann's appraisal was accepted fully. Lack of control and marketability discounts thus were allowed by the court, aggregating 50% as to one property, and as to the three others, from 35% to 40%, plus an additional 5% for each property due to lack of voting rights.

Hillgren's lesson—fully develop and support all valuation issues

As we saw in the *Estate of Stone*,[11] 2036(a) is no "slam dunk" for IRS, if the taxpayer has good facts and documentation, especially if the "bona fide sale" exception to 2036(a) application can be asserted, as was done successfully in *Stone*. What the *Hillgren* case teaches us is that, even if 2036(a) applies to eliminate the FLP or LLC entity, other valuation issues are important and can save the day. Here the impact of an enforceable business loan agreement was significant, and the combination of effective lawyering and excellent appraisal work resulted in a clear taxpayer victory! This type of restriction on property can provide back-up basis for discounts in an FLP/LLC situation.

Effective entity and valuation planning

Even though the future of the federal transfer tax is in doubt and the estate tax exemption equivalent level will continue to rise under current law to as high as $3.5 million, estate planners and tax advisors regularly are called upon to consider FLP/LLC plans for various tax and nontax purposes. Note that the gift tax exemption level is "frozen" at $1 million under current law— another reason for quality discount appraisals. Given the 2036(a) uncertainty (which may well not be cleared up by the ultimate outcome of the *Strangi II*, *Thompson* and *Kimbell* appeals), consider the following two questions:

1. What are the alternatives to FLPs?

Where real estate is the business or investment asset involved, certainly co-tenancy transfers, with or without a co-tenancy management agreement, are worthy of consideration. In fact, even for marketable securities, co-tenancy ownership of the portfolio may allow for some valuation discounts due to shared control.[12]

In the case of a married couple, of course, the "Mellinger principle"[13] can be applied, i.e., the QTIP trust interest in property and the surviving spouse's own interest therein, while both includable in the survivor's gross estate, are to be valued separately for estate tax purposes. On the death of the first spouse, setting up the FLP or LLC at that time may maximize the current law step-up in income tax basis while developing a true "pooling of interests" considered critical in several of the 2036(a) judicial decisions.

Increased use of irrevocable trusts, including "dynasty trusts", GRATs and intentionally defective grantor trusts (IDGTs), should be considered. Further, the irrevocable trust as the FLP/LLC manager is attractive as it can be structured to bring the FLP plan closer to *Byrum*[14] and partially counter a Section 2036(a)(2) argument.

Finally, *timing* is important—consider, as always, "opportunity shifting" as the "transfer" of something not as yet rising to the level of "property."

2. Can Sections 2036(a)(1) and 2036(a)(2) be avoided?

Here we clearly need to audit existing FLP/LLC plans, determining 2036(a) risks for past plan documentation and operation. Both in *Abraham* and *Hillgren*—and certainly in earlier cases—many of the negative factors in such cases could have been avoided, and even now the 2036(a) exposure might be lessened.

For example, transfer of all the senior person's FLP/LLC units should start the 3-year Section 2035 period, so that the transferor at death may well have survived for three years following transfer and 2036(a) will not apply. In addition, perhaps, consideration could be given to an income tax-free liquidation of the tainted FLP or LLC, followed by formation and funding—with some differences—of a new pass-through entity. These present additional opportunities for appraisal engagements.

Other concepts involve revising the FLP agreement or LLC operating agreement as follows: (a) clarify and reinforce fiduciary duties of managers (and track compliance), and/or (b) set forth in the operative documents mandatory income distribution standards.

Of course, such changes can have significant impacts on valuation, and the appraiser should be involved at the onset.

In auditing existing plans, look for and correct obvious mistakes, such as funding delays, statelaw compliance failure, failure to make pro rata distributions to partners or members, or other failures to operate under the applicable contractual agreements. Finally, keep in mind the income tax requirements for FLP/LLC recognition under Code Section 704(e).

Recent IRS estate tax exams generally have called for a comparison between the *Harper*, *Thompson*, and *Strangi* line of cases and the fact pattern of the taxpayer involved in the 706 exam. We have found that examiners and Appeals Officers often are willing to resolve cases without litigation based upon a realistic litigation analysis. Further, if such an analysis is to produce a settlement opportunity, it is quite important to have a complete and credible valuation report. Therefore, estate planners and advisors need to work closely with their business valuation appraisers, providing proper legal and tax assumptions upon which the professional valuation is based.

---

1. *Estate of Schauerhamer v. Comm'r*, T.C. Memo. 1997-242.
2. *Estate of Harper v. Comm'r*, T.C. Memo. 2002-121; *Estate of Thompson v. Comm'r*, T.C. Memo. 2002-246, on appeal to 3rd Cir.; *Estate of Strangi v. Comm'r*, 115 T.C. 478 (2002) (Strangi I) aff'd, except reversed on 2036(a) issue; *Stran-*

gi v. Comm'r, T.C. Memo. 2003-145 2036(a) opinion (Strangi II), on appeal to 5th Cir.; see also *Estate of Kimbell v. U.S.*, 244 F. Supp. 2d 700 (2003), on appeal to 5th Cir.

3. *Lappo v. Comm'r*, T.C. Memo. 2003-258.
4. *Peracchio v. Comm'r*, T.C. Memo. 2003-280.
5. *Estate of Ida Abraham v. Comm'r*, T.C. Memo. 2004-39.
6. *Estate of Lea Hillgren v. Comm'r*, T.C. Memo. 2004-46.
7. Supra, at note 5.
8. Supra, at note 1.
9. *Estate of Stone v. Comm'r*, T.C. Memo. 2003-309.
10. Supra, at note 6.
11. Supra, at note 9.
12. *Brocato v. Comm'r*, T.C. Memo. 1999-424; *Baird v. Comm'r*, T.C. Memo. 2001-258.
13. *Estate of Mellinger*, 112 T.C. 26 (1999), Acquiescence On Decision, A.O.D. 1999-006.
14. *Byrum v. U.S.,* 408 US 125 (1972).

After McCord: The Future of FLP Valuations and Discount Determinations

By William Frazier, ASA
Originally published in *Business Valuation Update*™ November 2006

Some in the business appraisal community have publicly noted that the Fifth Circuit's recent reversal of *McCord v. Commissioner* (Tax Court, 2003) sheds no light on the valuations of family limited partnership interests. They are simply wrong. While it is clear the Fifth Circuit did not directly endorse my valuation conclusions—or repudiate Dr. Bajaj's—the Court did make specific valuation pronouncements.

First, and most important, the Fifth Circuit held that the Tax Court valuation methodology in *McCord* was erroneous and should be disregarded:

> ...the values ascribed by the Majority, being derived by its use of its own imaginative but flawed methodology, may not be used in any way in the calculation of the Taxpayer's gift tax liability.

The major "flaw" relates to the dispute regarding my original valuation under the Assignment Agreement (in which the taxpayers assigned the interests to the donees); and the Tax Court's independent (and "imaginative") valuation under the Confirmation Agreement, which took place two months later, by and among the donees. However, the holding bears repeating, as the Fifth Circuit clearly states that the Tax Court opinion "may not be used *in any way* in the calculation of...gift tax liability" (emphasis added).

Cite *McCord* at your peril

This is about as clear and unambiguous as it gets. Henceforth, no one may rely on the Tax Court's methodology in *McCord* to support any valuation position. Of course, appraisers should never rely on a rejected Tax Court case to support their positions; nevertheless, I see it all of the time.

In the future, some may try to "nuance" the Fifth Circuit's language by saying that the heart of its decision was not about valuation methodology, and therefore, the valuation aspects of *McCord* are still valid precedent. My layman's view is that anyone who asserts this argument does so at his or her peril, for the logical foundation is a very thin sheet of ice.

In addition, the Fifth Circuit did not limit its opinion to the Confirmation Agreement and the "defined gift value" aspects of the case. Most importantly, it gave the Bajaj opinion no weight whatsoever. That is, the Tax Court had rejected the Bajaj opinion (but not his study), and the Fifth Circuit confirmed that this rejection was not erroneous:

> ...given the Majority's non-erroneous rejection of the Commissioner's expert's values...

To be sure, the Fifth Circuit said nothing about the Bajaj opinion—either positive or negative. But its decision renders the Bajaj opinion moot; that is, not part of the valuation record from *McCord*.

While I would like to see the Fifth Circuit's decision as a vindication for my longheld valuation analysis and conclusions, that would be an overstatement. The taxpayers "won" by default—and not entirely due to the adjudicated merits of my methodology:

> [T]he fair market values applicable in this case are, by a process of elimination, those determined by the Frazier report.

But I'll take the win anyway: Had Judge Foley been allowed to keep the case as the bench trial judge, the result would have the same as the Fifth Circuit's decision. That is, the IRS did not meet its burden of proof; and so the Tax Court never would have reached the issue of fair market value. The taxpayers' values would have stood as filed, and the Government's valuation arguments ignored.

Further discussion forthcoming

In my view, two of the most mistaken notions which sprang from *McCord* are: (1) the "Bajaj method" for determining marketability discounts; and (2) the use of REITs (Real Estate Investment Trusts) to determine minority interest discounts for non-distributing FLPs holding real estate.

Given the space limitations here, these are the issues that John Porter, Esq., the taxpayers' attorney on the *McCord* appeal, and I presented during the BVR telephone conference on October 18, 2006. [Editor's Note: Excerpts from this telephone conference are available in this special report.]

New 2036(a) Opinion Emphasizes Criteria for FLP Valuation Benefits

By Owen Fiore, JD, CPA
Originally published in *Business Valuation Update*™ July 2007

After ten years of judicial decisions construing the valuation and estate planning benefits of family limited partnerships (FLPs), Section 2036 of the *Internal Revenue Code* (IRC) has become a formidable weapon for the IRS. If applicable to a particular estate tax case, §2036 could make valuations of FLP or limited liability company (LLC) interests irrelevant. Further, IRS attention to recently enacted appraiser penalty provisions of the IRC underscores the need for heightened due diligence by BV appraisers in FLP cases.

The good news: BV appraisers can provide value-added services by being attentive to "entity reality" issues for FLPs in the gift and estate tax context. They can also work with legal counsel to make sure reasonable assumptions of value become part of the estate's plan in establishing these still-viable entities.

In the beginning, there was *Schauerhamer*

Over the past decade, the IRS has achieved substantial success applying IRC §2036(a) to mostly "bad facts" cases, evidencing the Service's concentrated focus on any perceived estate tax avoidance or similar "abuse."

The first Tax Court decision was *Estate of Schauerhamer*, T.C. Memo. 1997-242 (note: the author was lead trial counsel on this case). After learning that she was suffering a terminal illness, Dorothy Schauerhamer established three partnerships with real estate and other assets; she then gifted limited partnership interests to family members, but stayed on as co-general partner and managing partner of each entity. During the eleven months from the FLP formation to Schauerhamer's death, all income from partnership assets were deposited in her personal bank accounts.

Despite a special partnership agreement permitting the managing partner to hold assets in her name, subject to fiduciary obligations, the Court found this continued relationship to the assets (control and ownership) sufficient to bring §2036(a)(1) into play. By bringing the FLPs back into the gross estate, the Court didn't need to consider the estate's appraisal, including valuation discounts.

Now *Erickson*—another 'bad facts' case

In *Erickson v. Commissioner*, 2007 Tax Ct. Memo LEXIS 108 (April 30, 2007),we have the latest example of the broad reach of §2036(a)(1). The case also reviews the requirements for the "bona fide sale for a full and adequate consideration" exception.

Having suffered from severe Alzheimer's for several years, Hilde Erickson—on advice of counsel and with considerable efforts by one daughter—formed an FLP with real estate and other assets worth over $2 million. A second daughter joined the first as general and limited partners. The FLP wasn't entirely funded, however, until two days before Erickson died at age eighty-eight, at which time substantial gifting of the partnership interests to grandchildren was also accomplished.

Numerous "bad facts" existed in *Erickson*, and in light of the prior Tax Court decisions, one might wonder whether the estate should have pursued the litigation at all. These facts included:

- No separate legal representation of the various partners.
- The lack of understanding of the plan by the younger daughter.
- The age and poor health of the decedent.
- Transfer of virtually all decedent's assets to the FLP (and gifts to grandchildren's trust) were completed only two days before her death.

Given the ten-year precedent, the Tax Court (Judge Kroupa) had little difficulty concluding that §2036(a)(1) applied. The Court also held that the "bona fide sale" exception did not apply, as there was no credible evidence the FLP had any substantial, non-tax business or investment purpose. In fact, here the FLP served as "just a vehicle for changing the form of the investment in the assets, a mere asset container."

Five key factors to support FLP/LLC viability

From this and the long history of FLP cases, we can develop key factors to support the continued viability of a pass-through entity plan using either an FLP or an LLC, or both, as follows:

1. *Plan design.* Rather than merely tax avoidance, plan the entity with non-tax business and/or investment purposes.

2. *Structure.* Pay attention to the guidance on structure, implementation, and operation of FLP/LLC plans that the judicial opinions provide. The IRS *Appeals Settlement Guidelines for FLPs* (October 2006), although heavily redacted, also provides guidance.[1]

3. *Entity formalities.* Consider proper document drafting, timely funding with asset transfers, and operational integrity of the plan.

4. *Utilize appraisers.* Valuation specialists can develop, based on counsel-provided assumptions of value, a credible, well-supported, fair market value appraisal of entity fractional interests upon gift, sale, or death.

5. *Avoid red flags.* The Service (with support of the courts) considers these elements, in combination, as fatal to the entity:

    - Entity formation near taxpayer's death.
    - Transfer to the entity of all (or nearly all) of taxpayer's assets.
    - Funding the entity with personal assets—e.g., taxpayer's home.
    - Absence of active involvement or understanding of the FLP (or LLC) plan by some or all of the younger generation family members.
    - No change in investment or business strategy occasioned by the plan.
    - Non pro-rata distributions from the entity to family members, especially in support of the taxpayer senior person; or to pay estate tax liabilities after death of the taxpayer.

Appraisers be wary—but a team approach works

The ten-year litigation history of FLPs, bracketed by *Schauerhamer* and *Erickson*, should give BV appraisers some pause in valuing fractional FLP/LLC equity interests for transfer tax purposes (gift, estate, and GST taxes). Certainly, appraisers may not provide legal advice, and have no affirmative duty to deal with the details of tax law. However, analysts can provide value-added service to clients and their legal or financial advisors by being attentive to issues of fact, law, and tax that might impinge upon, or even destroy, the usefulness of the business valuation report in a given situation.

Although the IRS "attack mode" is likely to continue, many cases—some ending in published court decisions—have respected the pass-through entity and recognized the beneficial valuation efforts of the appraiser. So the message for BV analysts in the FLP arena is to: 1) be aware; 2) insist on full knowledge and vetting of the facts; and 3) participate actively in a team approach that will, in many cases, help preserve the entity for estate tax purposes and keep it from reaching the courts.

---

1. See *http://www.irs.gov/pub/irsutl/asg_penalties_family_limited_pships_finalredacted10_20_06.pdf.*

Business Valuation Recent Cases, Rulings and Interpretations

By William F. Chandler, JD, CPA/ABV, ASA, CFA

First presented at the New York Society of CPA's Business Valuation Committee on May 21, 2007.

The following discussion of selected case law on family limited partnerships is an extract of a section of an outline that Will Chandler has maintained for the last several years and used in presenting annual valuation update speeches to the AICPA and New York State Society of CPAs valuation section.

Use of the family limited partnership (FLP) and other flow-thru entities have become popular in wealth succession planning because of the opportunity to discount the value of the limited partnership interests. Since a limited partner cannot control the affairs of the partnership, and may be "locked in" to the partnership by restrictions on liquidation and redemption, the value of the limited partnership interest may be substantially discounted from its proportionate share of the entity value. A determination of the fair market value of a limited partner's interest first requires a determination under state law of the legal rights inherent in the interest. For example, value will be affected if the transferee is entitled to become a partner/member or is limited to the status of a mere assignee with no rights to participate in management, and no liquidation or withdrawal rights.[1] Second, federal tax law must be considered. IRC 2704(a) provides that the lapse of a voting or liquidation right will be treated as a transfer of such right for gift or estate tax purposes where the entity is family controlled. IRC 2704(b) provides that restrictions on liquidation rights in a family controlled entity will be ignored for estate and gift tax purposes when such restriction can be removed by family action and the restriction is not one provided by applicable State and Federal law. IRC 2703 generally provides that value is to be determined without regard to any option, agreement or other right to acquire or use the property at a price less than the fair market value of the property determined without such option, agreement or right. Section 2703 also ignores any restriction on the right to sell or use such property.[2]

Beginning in 1997, the IRS issued a series of Technical Advice Memorandums (the "Sham Tams") in an effort to disregard the partnership for valuation purposes[3] relying on its success in *Estate of Murphy* (TCM 1990-472).[4] The Service has been largely unsuccessful in several recent Court decisions in its economic substance and IRC 2703 arguments.

The IRS has, however, achieved success in the courts finding that the value of the underlying partnership assets are included in a decedent's estate under IRC 2036(a) where there is an express or implied agreement at the time of the transfer of the decedent's property to the partnership that he or she will retain the right to the continued enjoyment of the property, even if that retained right is not legally enforceable.

Gift on Formation, IRC 2703, IRC 2704, disregard of partnership arguments largely unsuccessful:

In *Church v. United States*, 85 AFTR 2d 2000-804 (W.D. Tex. January 18, 2000), decedent, two days prior to her death, created a limited partnership with her two children. She conveyed her interest in a ranch with a fair market value of $380,000 and marketable securities worth about $1 million. The District Court recognized the partnership, holding that the objectives of centralized management and creditor protection provided non tax bona fide business objectives.[5] The Court also rejected the IRS argument that the term "property" in IRC 2703 refers to the property transferred to the partnership rather than the partnership interests actually owned, finding that 2703 deals with below-market buy-sell agreements and options that artificially reduce the value of the property subject to the tax (that is, the partnership interests) and are not inherent components of the property interest itself. The Court also rejected the IRS gift on formation argument emphasizing that the partnership was a pro rata entity (each partners' interest was in proportion to his/her capital account). The Court found that no one benefited from the decline in value and that, therefore, there was no donative transfer.

In *Knight v Commissioner*, 115 TCM 36 (November 30, 2000) the Court refused to disregard a limited partnership since it was legally formed under State law and had "no reason to conclude from this record that a hypothetical buyer or seller would disregard it." It also failed to look through the partnership to value the underlying assets (rejecting the IRS' economic substance argument) despite the fact that the partnership kept no records, had no employees, held no meetings, held personal assets (two houses and a ranch) that continued to be used without rent for personal purposes, and conducted minimal investment activities. Nevertheless, the Court rejected the claimed 10% portfolio discount and reduced the claimed 30% DLOM and 10% DLOC discounts to a combined 15% discount.

In *Estate of Strangi*, (115 TC 478 (2000)) a divided Court rejected the IRS gift on formation,[6] IRC 2703, and lack of economic substance arguments.[7] Decedent's son–in-law acting under a power of attorney created a family limited partnership SFLP[8] (and corporate general partner, Stranco, Inc.) funded with cash, marketable securities, real estate, insurance policies, annuities, and other partnership interests with an aggregate value of about $10 million. The corporate general partner was owned 47% by the decedent and 53% by the decedent's children.[9] The partnership was created approximately one year after the decedent had undergone cancer surgery. After decedent's death, the partnership made substantial proportionate cash distributions to the partners and extended lines of credit to the decedent's children giving them access to the partnership funds. Within several years following decedent's death the partnership divided the remaining securities into separate accounts so that each child had access to his/her proportionate share of partnership assets. Although the Tax Court rejected the nontax motives for formation of the partnership as "mere window dressing to conceal tax motives," it did not disregard the partnership under the economic substance doctrine.[10] The Court also rejected the IRS 2703 arguments. However, the Court did reduce the claimed valuation discounts (25% DLOC and 25% DLOM or 43.75% combined) to a combined 31% discount (8% DLOC and 25% DLOM). The Fifth Circuit overruled the Tax Court's denial of IRS' request for leave to amend its petition to include an argument based on IRC 2036(a). On remand, the IRS successfully argued that IRC 2036 should be applied.

The Tax Court has also rejected the IRS' 2704(b) argument. In *Kerr v. Commissioner*, 113 TC 449 (December 23, 1999)), the transferor claimed 50% discounts in two Texas family limited partnerships that held marketable securities, bonds, life insurance policies and real estate. Each partnership agreement provided that no limited partner could withdraw from the partnership or demand the return of his or her capital account prior to the termination of the partnership (generally 50 years). On motion for summary judgment, the Tax Court held that the partnership provisions restricting liquidation and withdrawal were not applicable restrictions, and that the partnership agreement liquidation and withdrawal provisions were comparable to those under state law default rules. Citing *Kerr*, the Court also rejected the IRS' 2704(b) argument in *Knight*. The 5th Circuit affirmed the Tax Court (114 TC 144; 2000) noting that there are three requirements for 2704 to apply. The restriction must 1) effectively limit the ability of the partnership to liquidate; 2) be removable by the family after transfer; and 3) be more restrictive than state law. The Appeals Court held that even if a third party owner is likely to consent to removal of the restriction (and then receive fair market value for its interest) it is not considered removable by the family. In order for the restriction to be removable by the family, the court stated that the "transferor or any member of the transferor's family, either alone or collectively, must have the right to remove the restriction. And that "the probable consent....of a non-family partner, cannot fulfill the requirement that the family be able to remove the restriction on its own."

In *Estate of Jones v. Commissioner* 116 T.C. No. 11, March 6, 2001, the Tax Court relying on *Kerr*, denied IRS argument to find a gift on formation of an FLP. (Decedent and his family transferred assets to form FLP.) Immediately after formation, the decedent gifted his LP interests to members of his family. The Court allowed DLOM's for LP interests gifted.

IRC 2036. TRANSFERS WITH RETAINED LIFE ESTATE

A. General Rule. The value of the gross estate shall include the value of all property to the extent of any interest therein of which the decedent has at any time made a transfer (except in the case of a bona fide sale for an adequate and full consideration in money or money's worth), by trust or otherwise, under which he has retained for his life or for any period not ascertainable without reference to his death or for any period which does not in fact end before his death

1. the possession or enjoyment of, or the right to the income from, the property,

2. or the right, either alone or in conjunction with any person, to designate the persons who shall possess or enjoy the property or the income therefrom.

Regulations provide that the gross estate includes the value of transferred property if the decedent retained the "use, possession, right to the income, or other enjoyment of the transferred property." (20.2036-1(a)(I)). The possession or enjoyment is retained for purposes of 2036(a)(1) where there is an express or implied understanding to that effect among the parties at the time of the transfer, even if the retained interest is not legally enforceable. The existence or nonexistence of such an understanding is determined from all of the facts and circumstances surrounding both the transfer itself and the subsequent use of the property.

An exception to inclusion under 2036(a) exists where the facts establish "a bona fide sale for an adequate and full consideration in money or money's worth." IRS has argued that decedents have effectively retained the possession or enjoyment of, or the right to the income from, the property transferred to the FLP. When successful, the IRS has caused the value of the property held by the estate to be included in the decedent's estate (thereby disallowing the discounts applicable to interests in the partnership). There are generally two issues considered by the courts: 1) whether the creation of the FLP and transfer of assets to it was a "bona fide sale for full and adequate consideration," and, if not, 2) whether the decedent retained the possession or enjoyment of, or the right to the income from, the partnership property.

In *Estate of Harper v. Commissioner*, TCM 2002-121 (May 15, 2002) the Tax Court held that the property contributed by the decedent to the Harper FLP (HFLP) was includable in his gross estate under IRC 2036(a). HFLP was formed in 1994 and was capitalized with substantially all of the decedent's assets. The assets consisted of marketable securities, other securities and a note comprising 94% of decedent's total net worth. Initially, he became the sole limited partner (99%) and his two children were designated as general partners (1%). Decedent subsequently gifted 60% to his children and owned 39% at his death on February 1, 1995.

In finding IRC 2036(a) applicable, the court recognized that the statute "describes a broad scheme of inclusion in the gross estate, not limited by the form of the transaction, but concerned with all inter vivos transfers where outright disposition of the property is delayed until the transferor's death." The court found the facts here to be similar to the facts in *Estate of Reichert v. Commissioner*, 114 T.C. 144 (2000), and *Estate of Schauerhamer v. Commissioner*, TCM 1997-242 where 2036(a) was found to apply. In *Reichert*, the decedent had formed a FLP in which his revocable trust was the general partner. The Court found that the decedent had transferred substantially all of his property to the FLP,[11] was the only trustee who performed any meaningful functions,[12] commingled personal and FLP funds, and lived rent free in the residence transferred to the FLP such that "nothing but legal title had changed in the decedent's relationship to his assets after he transferred them to the partnership." In *Schauerhamer*, the decedent had deposited income earned on partnership accounts in her personal checking account where the funds were commingled and wrote personal checks for partnership items.

In *Harper*, the Court focused on the commingling of funds, the history of disproportionate distributions, and the fact that each partnership was essentially a testamentary plan. The court found that these facts supported a finding that an implied agreement existed such that the decedent would retain the economic benefit of the assets transferred to HFLP. The court found the two part test of the exception were not met, since the decedent's children transferred nothing to him or to the partnership in exchange for their interests (arms length bona fide sale and consideration both lacking). The Court did, however, state that HFLP is to be distinguished from the formation of a partnership in which all contributing partners contribute more than a deminimis amount in exchange for proportionate partnership interests thereby representing a true pooling of interests of the partners (citing *Estate of Harrison* and *Estate of Church*). In Harper, the Court saw the facts as a mere unilateral value recycling and not a legitimate pooling.[13]

On remand, the Tax Court in *Strangi* found IRC 2036 applied to include the value of SFLP's underlying assets in the value of the decedent's estate. Decedent's son-in-law, pursuant to a power of attorney, created the Strangi FLP funded with substantially all of Mr. Strangi's property including his residence, securities and insurance policies. The court determined that the formation was not arms length because of a lack of any negotiations. Moreover, it found a recycling of the decedent's property for partnership interests and a lack of true pooling of assets.

Although SFLP had a short history (decedent died 2 months after formation), the Court found that decedent, as a practical matter, retained the same relationship to his assets that he had before formation of SFLP and Stranco. The Court stated that the following factors may support a finding of an implicit retained interest:

- transfer of a majority of the decedent's assets
- nature of the assets transferred (ie. personal items)
- continued occupation of the transferred property (residence)
- commingling of the entity and personal assets
- disproportionate distributions
- use of entity funds for personal expenses
- testamentary characteristics of the arrangement

The Court looking at the totality of the circumstances further concluded that there was an implied understanding that the decedent's access to the property would not be restricted. In addition, it found that Decedent (through his attorney in fact) retained the right to designate the persons who shall possess or enjoy the property or its income and therefore was includable under 2036(a)(2).

The 5th Circuit affirmed the decision of the Tax Court in *Strangi* (417 F. 3d 468; 2005 U.S. App. LEXIS 14497) finding that the benefits retained by Strangi were "substantial and present" consisting of periodic cash payments, continued use of the transferred house, and post death payments of debts and expenses of his estate. Since these benefits were not "speculative or contingent," the Court examined whether the benefits were available to Strangi pursuant to an implied agreement (all parties acknowledged that no express agreement existed). The Court found nothing clearly erroneous in the Tax Court's decision that the cash distributions (even though proportionate), continued use of the residence (even though accrued rent was charged but not paid), and failure to retain sufficient liquid assets supported a finding that an implied agreement existed. It therefore sustained the TC decision that the decedent retained enjoyment of the transferred assets and that IRC 2036(a) applied.

The Estate argued that even if IRC 2036(a)(1) applied, the partnership assets should not be included in the estate based on the bona fide sale exception. Citing *Kimbell*, the Court stated that the "adequate and full consideration" requirement will generally be satisfied where assets are transferred into a partnership for a proportional interest in the partnership (and the partnership formalities are respected). The IRS conceded that the "adequate and full consideration" requirement was met here since Strangi transferred property for a proportionate interest in the partnership.[14] The Court noted, however, that the exception contains two discrete requirements ((1) a bona fide sale, and (2) for "adequate and full consideration") that must each be satisfied. Because the Tax Court rejected the estate's non-tax business reasons, the 5th Circuit sustained its finding that the sale was not bona fide.

In *Kimbell v. United States* 371 F.3d 257; 2004 U.S. App. LEXIS 9911, (5th Cir.) decedent (age 96) created a FLP two months prior to her death by having her trust contribute property for a 99% LP interest and a LLC (owned by her trust and her son and daughter in law) contribute property for a 1% GP interest. The District Court found that neither prong of the 2036(a) exception was met finding that since family members were on both sides of the transaction it was not at arms length and that the trusts transfer of 99% of the assets for a 99% interest (although pro- rata) was not adequate consideration. The 5th Circuit vacated and remanded the case finding that receipt of a pro-rata interest was adequate and full consideration (and that the government failed to counter taxpayers evidence that there were substantial business reasons for the FLP). The Court found that the taxpayer established that the formation was not a disguised gift or a sham. Thus, the 5th Circuit concluded that adequate and full consideration is received where an actual transfer has occurred even where the value of the partnership interests received are less than the value of the contributed assets.

The 3rd Circuit in *Thompson v. Commissioner*, 382 F. 3d 367; 2004 U.S. App. LEXIS 18473, disagreed with the 5th Circuit's finding of what constitutes full and adequate consideration. Thompson (age 97) transferred assets (primarily marketable securities) to two FLPs for LP interests. The 3rd Circuit found that there could not be full and adequate consideration where the value of the estate is depleted as a result of the transfer (that is, even if the FLP interests received are proportionate to the value of the assets transferred, the consideration could not be adequate and full if those interests are worth less than the value of the assets transferred). The 3rd Circuit also found that there can be no bona fide sale within the meaning of IRC 2036 unless there is a valid non-tax purpose for the transfer.

In *Estate of Bongard v. Commissioner*, 124 T.C. 95; 2005 U. S. Tax Ct. LEXIS 8, the full Tax Court formulated a new and unique test for meeting the bona fide sale exception. The Court held that the adequate and full consideration exception is met if the transferors received partnership interests proportionate to the value of the property transferred provided that the transferor (or his estate) establishes that there was "a legitimate and significant non-tax reason for creating a family limited partnership."

Bongard (age 56), and his irrevocable trust, were the sole shareholders of Empak. At the suggestion of the Board of Directors and advisors, Bongard and the trust (on December 28, 1996) transferred all of their Empak stock to WCB Holdings, LLC (WCB) and received class A (voting) and class B (nonvoting) membership units. The reason for the transfer was to consolidate the holdings to better position Empak for a corporate liquidity event needed to raise capital and remain competitive. One day later, on December 29, 1996, Bongard and the Trust formed BFLP funded with all of Bongard's class B WCB Units for a 99% LP interest and the Trust transferring some of its class B WCB Units for a 1% GP interest (the interest each received was proportionate to the value of the property transferred). In December 1997 Bongard gifted an 8% interest in BFLP to his wife.[15] Bongard died unexpectedly on a trip to Austria on November 16, 1998.

The Tax Court found that Bongard's transfer of his Empak stock to WCB satisfied the bona fide sale exception because there was a "legitimate and significant non-tax reason for the transfer" but that the transfer of his class B WCB Units to BFLP failed to satisfy the bona fide sale exception. The Court found that there was an implied agreement pursuant to which Bongard had retained an IRC 2036(a) interest in the WCB class B Units he transferred to BFLP.

In its analysis of the case, the Court provides a concise summary of the case law beginning with the *Estate of Harrison v. Commissioner,* T.C. Memo. 1987-8, which found in favor of the estate (that decedent met the bona fide sale exception) because the partnership interests received were proportionate to the assets contributed and the formation of the FLP was necessary for the proper management of the decedent's properties (oil and gas properties requiring active management. In contrast, the Court discussed its contrary finding in *Estate of Harper v. Commissioner*, T.C. Memo. 2002-121 where decedent contributed all the property to the FLP but his children received a combined 1% GP interest (failing the adequate and full consideration test because the interests received were not proportionate to the assets transferred). The properties consisted of marketable securities but the decedent did not discuss with his children (the GPs) how the partnership was to be operated or structured and no new investment strategies were employed. The Court found this to be a gratuitous recycling of property and not a true pooling of assets (there was no change in the contributed assets). The Court next discussed its holding in *Estate of Thompson v. Commissioner*, T.C. Memo. 2002-246, where the decedent formed two FLP's funded with cash and securities (with corporate GP's owned 49% by decedent and 51% by his children). Prior to formation of the FLPs, the decedent and his children agreed that he would continue to be taken care of financially and the FLPs provided him with access to the cash to, among other things, continue to make gifts. The Court found that the transfer failed the adequate and full consideration test because there was no true pooling (the assets remained unchanged, there was no change in investment strategy, and the income from FLP assets was specially allocated to contributing partners). The Court found that the lack of a business reason for formation supported its finding.

The Court next discusses the decisions in *Estate of Strangi v. Commissioner*, T.C. Memo. 2003-145, where it found that the formation of SFLP was not an arms length transaction since decedent's son-in-law (Gulig) established and operated SFLP without any meaningful negotiations and essentially recycled the value of decedent's assets through SFLP. Unlike in Harrison, none of the assets were found to qualify SFLP as a "functioning business enterprise." (See also *Estate of Hillgren v. Commissioner*, T.C. Memo. 2004-46). The Court did find that the decedent in *Estate of Stone v. Commissioner*, T.C. Memo. 2003-309, met the bona fide sale exception since the FLPs (five of them) were created to resolve "significant intra-family disputes" and the active management by the Stone's children "qualified [the FLPs] as legitimate business concern[s]." The Stone's determined the assets that would be contributed and retained sufficient assets to meet their liquidity needs. The adequate and full consideration test was met since each partner received assets in proportion to the value of the assets contributed (and capital accounts were properly maintained). The Court found that there was a "genuine pooling of property and services."

The Tax Court considered the two Bongard transactions separately. First, it addressed whether the exception was met with respect to Bongard's formation of WCB. It stated that the bona fide sale exception can only apply where there is an arms length transaction. Although it found that intra-family transactions are subjected to a higher level of scrutiny, it rejected IRS' argument that intra-family transactions can not satisfy the arms length test (provided it was carried out in a way that "ordinary parties to a business transaction would deal with each other"). It found that unrelated parties would have negotiated a similar transaction and noted a lack of evidence to contradict this finding. It rejected IRS' arguments that there was no true pooling finding that the formation of WCB was to "attract potential investors or to stimulate a corporate liquidity event to facilitate Empak's growth." To support its finding of a true pooling, it found that WCB's members capital accounts were properly credited and maintained, its funds were not commingled with decedent's and all distributions were pro rata.[16] Although it found the fact that interests received were proportionate to the assets contributed it stated that this fact alone "may not be sufficient evidence to meet the adequate and full consideration requirement." However, it found the addition of two additional facts allowed Bongard to meet this requirement: 1) that distributions were properly credited to capital accounts (capital accounts were subsequently properly maintained), and 2) most importantly, the existence of a "legitimate and significant non-tax business reason for engaging in this transaction."

The Court reached a contrary conclusion when evaluating the transfers to BFLP. The Court found that BFLP failed to meet the bona fide sale exception since it never diversified its assets, never had an investment plan, and never functioned as a business enterprise or otherwise engaged in any meaningful economic activity. It found the estate's argument that BFLP provided credit protection unpersuasive since WCB accomplished that objective. Having found that the exception did not apply, the Court found that decedent retained ownership of 91% of his BFLP interest and controlled whether BFLP could liquidate its WCB class B interests. In his capacity as CEO and sole member of the Board of Directors of Empak, he determined when Empak redeemed its stock but did not cause BFLP's class B Units to be redeemed. The Court found that decedent "exercised practical control over BFLP" and limited its function to simply holding WCB class B Units (rather than seeking to diversify its investments). It found that "an implied agreement existed that allowed decedent to retain the enjoyment of the property held by BFLP."

---

1. If the partner/member interest has liquidation rights or rights to withdraw and receive a proportionate share of the entity value, little or no valuation discounts may be available.
2. The IRC 2703 valuation rules do not apply if the taxpayer establishes that the option, agreement, right or restriction is a bona fide business arrangement, is not a device to transfer property to members of the transferor's family for less than full and adequate consideration, and its terms are comparable to similar arrangements entered into by persons in an arm's length transaction (2703(b))
3. TAMs 97-19-006 (1/14/97); 97-23-009 (2/24/97); 97-25-002 (3/3/97); 97-30-004 (4/3/97); 97-35-003 (5/8/97); 98-42-003 (7/2/98)
4. In *Murphy* the Court disallowed a minority interest discount where the decedent transferred a 1.76% interest (bringing the date of death interest to 49.65%) 18 days before death.
5. The Court recognized the partnership despite the fact that the corporate general partner had not been formed under Texas law until five months after the decedent's death and the Certificate of Limited Partnership had not been filed with the Texas Secretary of State until after the date of death.
6. Five dissenting Judges would have held that a gift occurred on formation.
7. The economic substance doctrine seeks to disregard transactions entered into solely to avoid taxes. Although not finding much substance beyond tax avoidance, the Tax Court recognized that a willing buyer would not disregard the FLP. Thus, the willing buyer – willing seller test provides some insurance against this attack even where the non tax motivations are weak.
8. Strangi Family Limited Partnership
9. One child had advanced funds on behalf of her siblings. Each had issued a promissory note in her favor for the amount of funds she transferred on their behalf.
10. In a concurring opinion, Judge Wells and Judge Foley found it inconsistent that the Court would reject the business purpose underlying the formation of the partnership and not disregard the partnership for valuation purposes. They stated their belief that the economic substance doctrine generally does not apply to disregard a validly formed entity in transfer tax cases.
11. He retained his car, some personal effects, and a small amount of cash in his checking account.
12. He was the only trustee to have signed the FLP agreement, to open brokerage accounts, or to sign checks.
13. In *Harper*, the Tax Court advanced its "recycling of value" theory where it finds that a transaction is not bona fide if the transferor is also the controlling partner. The transfer effects a mere change in the form of ownership (and is effectively "recycled").
14. Citing *Kimbell*, the Court focused on the three requirements to find "adequate and full consideration" included a finding that 1) the interest credited to each partner was proportionate to the fair market value of the assets each partner contributed to the partnership, 2) the assets contributed were properly credited to each partner's capital account, and 3) a partner's entitlement to distributions on termination or dissolution was equal to their respective capital accounts.
15. In March 1997, Bongard also transferred Class A WCB Units to three trusts f/b/o his family members.
16. It rejected IRS' argument that decedent should have obtained a control premium finding that he had retained "effective control" after the transaction.

Chapter 7

Using Empirical Data to Value Family Limited Partnerships

By Bruce A. Johnson, ASA and James R. Park, ASA

When valuing limited partnership interests, it continues to be common practice for many appraisers to simply derive the Net Asset Value (NAV) of the partnership and then apply discounts for lack of control and lack of marketability based upon average discounts found in various published studies. The Tax Court has been particularly critical of this methodology for several reasons including:

- the wide range of discounts observed in the studies,
- the lack of supporting data on the entities contained within the studies,
- the inability of the appraiser to make adequate comparisons between the partnership being valued and the entities contained in the studies,
- the subjectivity involved in determining the discounts for lack of control and lack of marketability.

For example, in *Knight v. Commissioner*, the Court rejected the appraiser's calculation of a discount for lack of control because its derivation was unsupportable. In *Estate of Weinberg v. Commissioner*, the Court rejected the determination of a discount for lack of marketability citing that the appraiser "failed to adequately take into account certain characteristics of the subject limited partnership interest...."

Because a limited partnership interest is noncontrolling, a limited partner typically cannot exercise control over the sale of the assets of the partnership. Rather, the limited partner looks primarily to the income-generating ability of the partnership and the possible sale of assets at a future point in time to realize a return on their ownership interest. To adequately take into consideration the primary factors that influence the value of a limited partnership interest, appraisers should consider the use of both the Income Approach and Market Approach. The Income Approach allows the appraiser to give consideration to the income generating and distribution-paying capacity of the interest. The Market Approach offers a look at alternative investments with similar characteristics in terms of income generating ability and capital structure that can be purchased instead of the subject limited partnership interest.

Empirical Methodology

The Income and Market Approaches offer a reliable way to value an interest in a family limited partnership by quantifying risk and return using empirical data. For example, using the Income Approach, an appraiser can forecast available cash flow generated by the investment and discount it to present value using a discount rate that reflects the risk of the limited partnership. As we know from basic financial theory, the discount rate increases as the risk of the investment increases.

The Market Approach is useful to determine the value of a privately held interest by using pricing ratios of comparable, but publicly held investments. Revenue Ruling 59-60 states that the sale transactions for publicly held interests should be considered when valuing privately held interests. This is noted as follows:

> As generalization, the prices of stocks which are traded in volume in a free and active market by informed persons best reflect the consensus of the investing public as to what the future holds for the corporations and industries....

Various sources of data frequently used by appraisers to obtain comparative Price to NAV ratios includes, but is not limited to:

- Closed-End Funds, and
- Publicly Held Limited Partnerships

Closed-end fund data can be obtained from sources such as *The Wall Street Journal*, Barrons, Morningstar, and Partnership Profiles, Inc. Comparative data and Price to NAV ratios on a wide variety of publicly held limited partnerships is available through information published by Partnership Profiles, Inc. (*www.PartnershipProfiles.com*), a research company that provides transaction information on limited partnership interests that trade in the informal secondary market.

It is important to note that the Income and Market Approaches are regularly used by appraisers to value privately held noncontrolling interests in operating companies. In addition, these are the methodologies typically used by investors in the capital market.

Discount for Lack of Control

In recent years, the Tax Court has expressed a preference for the use of analytical techniques for the valuation of family limited partnership interests and the determination of discounts for lack of control and marketability at which an interest would trade from its pro rata share of NAV. Using the Income Approach, an estimate of value and the effective discount at which the interest would trade can be determined using projections of net cash flow that are discounted to present value using an appropriate rate of return. Use of the Market Approach results in effective discounts using pricing ratios from comparable publicly held entities.

For example, when a family limited partnership holds real estate, discounting the expected net cash flow using rates of returns from REITs and publicly held limited partnerships results in a noncontrolling, marketable value. Applying Price to NAV ratios from publicly held limited partnerships to the NAV of a privately held limited partnership also results in a noncontrolling, marketable value. For family limited partnerships that invest in marketable securities, practitioners can use Morningstar's (formerly Ibbotson Associates) rate of return data for the Income Approach, and closed-end fund data for the Market Approach.

As more and more appraisers have begun using empirical data in the Income and Market Approach to value interests in limited partnerships, as opposed to average discounts based upon published studies, new information is being published to support the derivation of rates of return for the Income Approach and the determination of pricing ratios for the Market Approach. Partnership Profiles, Inc. is a frequently used source of information. For the Income Approach, they provide an annual Rate of Return Study for real estate limited partnership interests purchased in the secondary market. For the Market Approach, their Guideline Reports reflecting data on actual trades of publicly held limited partnership interests, and their closed-end fund reports reflecting the Price to NAV ratio at which interests in various types of closed-end funds trade, provide the empirical data needed to value most family limited partnerships.

Discount for Lack of Marketability

Once a noncontrolling, marketable value has been determined, practitioners can determine a discount for lack of marketability by examining studies that measure the increased return demanded by investors in third party transactions for the risk of holding an illiquid investment. The three studies are published in the *Comprehensive Guide for the Valuation of Family Limited Partnerships* and provide an indication of the increased return independent investors require over comparable marketable interests.[1] The three studies that measure the increased return demanded by investors are:

1. Private Equity vs. Public Equity Investments

2. Restricted Stock vs. Publicly Traded Stock

3. Long Term vs. Short Term Bond Returns

In general, the studies reflect that on average, investors have required a 30% increase in the rate of return required on noncontrolling, marketable basis. By applying a discount for lack of marketability, the subject interest's rate of return is increased to a level that achieves a rate of return that is sufficient to offset the risk of illiquidity. The rate of return calculation can be determined using the IRR function in MS Excel along with the forecast of net cash flow from the Income Approach.

Conclusion

Typically, investors in third party transactions do not use the Cost Approach by applying general discounts to an investment's net asset value to determine the market value of an interest. Rather, investors seek an appropriate return on their investment (Income Approach) or compare the subject interest to alternative investments (Market Approach) to determine a reasonable value.

Discounts from net asset value can be used to check the reasonableness of the resulting value and are helpful in conveying a value to the client, but it should be noted that the discount is a result of a financial calculation and not a means to determine value.

Appraisers basing their valuations solely on the Cost Approach by primarily using discounts from net asset value run the risk of not being able to adequately support the discount taken. When the focus of a family limited partnership appraisal is on the resulting rate of return to the investor, the appraiser can estimate a value that is supported based on market based rates of return and pricing ratios of third-party transactions of alternative investments.

---

1. *Comprehensive Guide for the Valuation of Family Limited Partnerships* – 3rd Edition, (Dallas, Texas: Partnership Profiles, Inc., 2006), pgs 127-134.

Chapter 8

Non-marketable Investment Company Evaluation (NICE) Method

By William H. Frazier, ASA

The NICE method is a valuation system under the Income Approach to value. It is designed especially to determine the fair market value of equity interests in closely held investment entities, such as family limited partnerships, "S" corporations and limited liability companies. In this article, we will refer to such entities as private investment companies (PICs). In the traditional Market Approach to valuing equity interests in investment entities, the major objectives are to determine the appropriate discounts for lack of control and lack of marketability. These discounts, when applied to net asset value (NAV) determine fair market value. NICE does not use discounts in its operation. Lack of control and lack of marketability are, rather, viewed as investment risks that are embodied into the required rate of return for the subject interest.

The NICE method is not a replacement for the more traditional PIC valuation methodology. However, neither is it merely a corroboration or "sanity check." It is a stand-alone methodology. Its use should result in a fair market value reasonably close to values determined by the traditional method under the Market Approach if the latter was properly applied. Whereas the traditional method uses investment analysis in a general and indirect manner, in NICE, investment returns serve as the engine for calculating results.[1]

King Solomon said "There is nothing new under the sun." And so it is with NICE. The methodology does not espouse any novel theories and relies wholly on well-known investment analysis and theory. Business appraiser readers may also see a similarity to Mercer's QMDM[2] which played no small part in the inspiration for this model. However, NICE operates differently than QMDM. First, QMDM requires that the user assume a specific holding period and a relatively short one at that.[3] We do not believe there is any sound basis for making such an assumption in most cases involving the valuation of an interest in a PIC. Secondly, QMDM has been criticized because it does not provide the user with any guidance as to the additional required return necessary to compensate the investor for lack of control and illiquidity.[4] This is, after all, the crux of the valuation assignment. NICE provides the means for deriving what the incremental required rate of return needs to be for each entity based on its component assets.

The Private Investment Company

PICs usually hold investment assets such as stocks, bonds, and real estate. Occasionally, these entities will own an operating business. For purposes of this article, however, we will be concentrating on PICs with only traditional investment asset classes. Further, since a primary business purpose for most PICs is intergenerational asset appreciation, we are making the simplistic assumption that the PIC will be making distributions only for purposes of satisfying the equity holders' tax obligations arising from entity income such as dividends, interest, and capital gains. The true economic return to the equity holders is derived from the liquidation of the entity. As we will later explain, the liquidation date can be a very distant event, with a practical range of no less than ten years from the formation of the PIC and ending with the stated entity termination date—most often fifty years.

The value of an interest in a PIC is based entirely upon the rates of return (ROR) required by both the buyer and the seller. In the case of the buyer, the required rate of return (RROR) will be the expected (ex ante) ROR from the investment. In the case of the exiting seller, the price at which he is willing to sell will be influenced by the historical or realized ROR from the investment (ex post), available reinvestment rates of return in the marketplace, and, of course, the expected ROR if he chooses not to sell and continue to hold the investment.

Because of lack of control and the unfamiliarity with the operating and entity management of the PIC, a reasonable investor will require a ROR higher than could be otherwise obtained in the public marketplace by investing directly in similar assets to those held by the entity. If the PIC has a portfolio that can be constructed by an investor buying and owning those assets directly, in order for her to prefer to invest in the PIC, she is going to require a ROR higher than that available in the marketplace because of the inherent lack of control and illiquidity of a PIC investment.

The degree of the ROR enhancement will vary based on the asset class. Generally speaking, the safer (less volatile) the asset class, the lower the required adjustment. The reason for this is relatively straightforward, as less volatile assets have a lower requirement for management intensity and, therefore, lower monitoring costs. Conversely, assets that are volatile, illiquid, or volatile and illiquid tend to have high monitoring costs.

The availability of expected return data will also vary based on the asset class. For example, data on publicly traded securities, such as stocks and bonds is plentiful. However, reliable, published return data on investment types such as private equity, real estate, or timberland is relatively thin. However, this does not mean return estimates for these asset classes cannot be postulated—after all, these assets are bought and sold every day by investors who have no better information. What is required is for the appraiser or analyst to build a solid, reasonable case based on the same information available to these risk-taking investors.

The RRORs the hypothetical buyer and seller would reasonably require during a lengthy but uncertain holding period will be expressed by a range or "spread." Furthermore, since the holding period of the investment in the PIC is an uncertainty, a static ROR applicable to all possible future time periods, is a mathematical impossibility. Primarily because of mean reversion, the expected ROR will vary over long periods.

We will determine two "paths" of possible annual returns representing the minimum and maximum reasonable returns for the PIC based on the assets it holds. While the range of the holding period is a lengthy uncertainty, we do know that if we can determine a price or a range of prices that, at any given time of the holding period, point to a rate of return that satisfies both the seller's objectives and the buyer's objectives, we have identified fair market value.

Relationship Between Holding Period and Value

Pratt states, "...value...depends upon an estimate of the future benefits and the required rate of return at which those future benefits are discounted back to the valuation date."[5] Fair market value, then, is the price a hypothetical buyer would pay (and at which a hypothetical seller would sell) based on (1) the expected economic returns to the interest, (2) the expected risks of realizing those expected returns, and (3) consideration of alternative investments and rates of return available in the marketplace.

The length of the holding period is critical to the determination of fair market value under the Income Approach. In all financial calculations time is an essential element. One cannot calculate the interest cost of a loan, the present value of an annuity, or the future value of an investment without the element of time. To ignore the time element in the valuation calculus violates the primary principal of the time value of money.

If we are going to make an issue of the concept of the holding period, then we must examine further what we mean when we say "holding period." What do we mean when we say "short holding period" or "long holding period?" Is there a typical or "average" holding period that can be used as a measuring stick? You probably will not be shocked to learn that there is no definite answer to this question. However, the norm of a holding period is heavily dependent on the type of asset and the type of investors who prefer such investments.

For example, banks seeking a yield on some idle deposits might purchase overnight funds and hold them, literally, overnight. These funds are characterized by very low returns, virtually no risk and high liquidity. On the other end of the spectrum, venture capital investors will invest in highly speculative ventures wherein the return may not be realized for at least five to seven years. These investments are highly illiquid. These funds are expected to realize a very high rate of return.

The concepts of holding period and liquidity, while not synonymous, are highly interrelated. Investors gravitate to investments whose economic return patterns best fit their particular needs. This phenomena was noted and analyzed by Amihud and Mendelson in the *Journal of Financial Economics* [1986].[6]

> Illiquidity can be measured by the cost of immediate execution. An investor willing to transact faces a tradeoff: He may either wait to transact at a favorable price or insist on immediate execution at the current bid or ask price. The quoted ask (offer) price

> includes a premium for immediate buying, and the bid price similarly reflects a concession required for immediate sale...Our model predicts that higher-spread assets yield higher expected returns, and that there is a clientele effect whereby investors with longer holding periods select assets with higher spreads. The resulting testable hypothesis is that asset returns are an increasing and concave function of the spread.

Thus, the authors show that the more illiquid an asset (or asset class) is, the higher the required rate of return, although this rate of return increases at a decreasing rate, i.e., the relationship of return and illiquidity is not a linear one. Also, the paper does not focus on how the return on a specific asset class might change over varying holding periods. Rather, what the paper addresses is that in considering the pricing of assets (stocks in this case) there are groups of investors (clients) with varying degrees of risk tolerance and investment horizons. Assets with poor liquidity will be rejected by most investors but there is a grouping of investors seeking such investments for the higher returns to be realized (the "clientele effect").

It stands to reason that, if a specific asset has additional trading restrictions placed on it above its normal relative level of liquidity (or lack thereof), its rate of return will rise by some marginal function. That is, the "clients" willing to accept a five-year holding period may be unwilling to wait ten years. To attract the ten-year client, the rate of return will have to be increased.

The illiquidity of the PIC investment is not in its assets but in the timing of the economic return. In this way, the value of an interest in a PIC is more like an option or a zero coupon bond. Perhaps the leading research related to this notion has been performed by Francis Longstaff wherein the author looks at the opportunity cost, using options analysis, of being unable to trade an asset during a given period of illiquidity.[7]

Private Investment Companies Are Very Long-Term Investments

In the first place, the fundamental assumption of NICE is that the length of the holding period in most PICs is unknown and not reasonably ascertainable. In those cases where the holding period is known or reasonably predictable, the NICE method is not needed. Value can be calculated by a simple discounted cash flow analysis. In this writer's experience in hundreds of PIC valuations, having a predictable holding period is the rare exception.

Given the considerable variance in the definition of "long-term" in the investment world, it should be clear that what we are contemplating is a method of calculating the value of an investment in a very long-term investment vehicle. Investment analysis for the very long term is somewhat more complicated than the normal investment analysis used for merely "long-term" investments. In the first place, what is meant by the concept of long-term?

A debt with a maturity of greater than one year is considered "long-term debt". Long-term capital gains, for tax purposes, are gains realized on the sale of investments held more than one year. Steven Sharp of the Federal Bureau of Statistics states, "The long-term growth forecasts of equity analysts do not have well-defined horizons, an ambiguity of substantial import for many applications...The estimated coefficients on consensus long-term growth forecasts suggest that the market applies these forecasts to an average horizon somewhere in the range of five to ten years."[8]

What we want to be clear about is that NICE, designed to value investments in PICs, assumes a very long-term and illiquid investment. The term of the majority of PICs we have seen is 50 years. PICs are established, among many other reasons, as a very long-term vehicle to provide for long-term intergenerational capital appreciation. An investment horizon of less than ten years would certainly not represent an investment entity with the foregoing characteristics.

One of the important characteristics of a PIC, then, is that its investment horizon exceeds that of any generally available investment product. There are a number of available investment products in the marketplace with expected holding periods of as much as ten years. The most common types seen are private real estate partnerships, private equity funds, and some hedge funds. However, ten years is generally the maximum term of these funds. Most have a much shorter "duration" as periodic distributions of harvested gains shortens the weighted average holding period to much less than ten years.

The expected minimum holding period of the PIC, however, begins in year ten in our view. In fact, it is this very long-term nature of the PIC that might attract some potential buyers. The hypothetical buyer of such an investment would be those investors with a desire to accept the long-term, illiquid structure as a trade-off for the enhanced return potential above shorter duration and more liquid investments.

The primary reason to exclude the first ten years of the PIC's life from the investment analysis is the presumed extreme unlikelihood of the PIC's liquidation during this period. The expectation is that the possibility of a return within this time frame is about zero. That is, if we accept that the PIC is a very long-term investment vehicle and ten years is more or less the absolute minimum time period to "qualify" for this status, the entity must exist for more than ten years.

Perhaps, most importantly, if the PIC liquidated sooner than the tenth year, one could make the argument that it would be a violation of the purpose of setting up the entity in the first place. While we cannot guarantee that the management of an entity will not violate this premise, it must be our expectation that there is a clear and unambiguous intent to maintain the operations until the end of its stated term. Having said that, we understand that no family has a crystal ball, and therefore, there is a significant probability that the entity will be liquidated before the fiftieth year. However, given that the intent of the PIC is truly to create an intergenerational vehicle for fostering capital appreciation, it is logical to assume that the existence of the entity will be for the very long term. Since the stated liquidation date is year fifty, unless there is evidence to the contrary, the stated liquidation date is the date presumed to have the highest probability of being the actual liquidation date.[9] For this reason, year 49 would have a higher probability of being the liquidation date than year 48 and so on. The date with the lowest significant probability of liquidation is year ten.

While it is certainly possible that the PIC would liquidate in, say, year five, an investor would not include this in his pricing analysis. The reason is that if this was the intent of the insiders, the willing seller's pricing would reflect this information resulting in an asking price far higher than the buyer would be willing to pay. Furthermore, if this was management's intention, it would violate the business purpose of the entity. While there have been (and always will be, we presume) instances of purposeful deception, particularly to achieve a tax avoidance objective, one would hope these are the exceptions and not the norm. In short, our investment model assumes the founders of the PIC have honest intentions and that these intentions will be carried out by management.

In fact, the very long-term nature of the PIC investment may be what attracts hypothetical buyers. There are few, if any, investment products available to those investors seeking excess returns via investing in illiquid, long-lived investment vehicles. While the universe of potential buyers would be small for an investment in a PIC, this type of investment could represent an attractive investment for an institutional investor with a perpetual time horizon. Most likely, this buyer would be a foundation, endowment, or charity which allocate small portions of their portfolios for alternative investments. David F. Swensen, Yale University's Chief Investment Officer, puts it this way "Active [investment] managers pursuing inefficiencies frequently gravitate toward relatively illiquid markets, since rewarding investments tend to reside in dark corners, not in the glare of the floodlights...By avoiding the highly liquid securities favored by market players, serious active investors focus on much more interesting opportunities. In embracing less liquid assets, investors often identify opportunities to establish positions at meaningful discounts to fair value."[10]

Which Holding Period Is It?

It has been argued by some that the holding period of a PIC is not terribly relevant since there is no legal restriction preventing a holder of an equity interest in a PIC from selling the interest privately whenever they so choose.[11] While there may be no such legal restrictions, there are massive practical and financial constraints that are inescapable. First, finding a buyer for the interest will be difficult. As mentioned previously, the only logical "clientele" for such an investment in a very long-term investment will be an investor with a similar very long expected existence. Individuals cannot be reasonably presumed to be likely candidates. Even if the hypothetical buyer was 30 years old, he may not receive the sought after return on his investment until age 80! So, as mentioned previously, the most likely candidate will be an institution with an infinite time horizon, willing to forego liquidity for a higher return.

Selling such an investment to an institution would be a process similar to an equity private placement conducted by an investment banking firm. The process is lengthy and expensive requiring detailed documentation of all facets of the management of the entity and its assets. There are also securities laws that have to be complied with as most investment of this type rely on a section 4.(2) exemption of the Securities Act of 1933. Private placement fees are also often in the range of six to ten percent of the amount invested.

More importantly, however, is the fact that the buyer will be simply stepping into the shoes of the seller. Whatever holding period the seller had, the buyer now has. If the economic return from the ownership of the investment is to come from the liquidation of the PIC, the fact that the new holder of the interest can sell it is of no real benefit. Subsequent buyer would just step in to the shoes of the previous holder, ad infinitum.

An investor buying the PIC interest and re-selling it before the PIC's liquidation would earn a miniscule or possibly even negative return when transaction expenses are taken into account. The desire return on the investment does not come until the receipt of the economic bolus of liquidation. The only holding period that is relevant then is measured by the length of time between entering the investment and liquidation.

Mean Reversion

The ability of any investment manager of a given asset to outperform the benchmark associated with that asset class (his "alpha") declines over time. Thus, the minimum return threshold is the highest it will ever be at the beginning of the PIC measurement period (year ten) and the lowest it will ever be at the last period examined.

The acceptable ROR for an investment in a small, closely held investment entity is actually a reasonable range within the bounds of the minimum and the maximum return thresholds. The magnitude (width) of the range will decline each year due to a well-documented phenomenon known as "mean reversion."

Evidence of mean reversion can be seen in the spread between the yield on commonly used corporate bond indexes and comparable maturity treasury bonds.[12] In addition, a rationale for equity to be more suited for investors with longer horizons is the tendency for stock prices to revert toward their longterm trend.[13]

Since equity returns are mean-reverting, it becomes increasingly difficult for investment managers to outperform the average as time goes by. For example, at any given point in time, many investment advisors or mutual funds will tout their out-performance of the S&P 500 over the past quarter, year, or three-year period. However, as the time horizon lengthens, the list of firms able to boast about outperforming the benchmark grows ever smaller. For example, from Morningstar data we can see that the large-cap value mutual funds that were in the group representing the "Top 40" (about four percent of the total funds covered) of reported returns in that segment outperformed the average by 780 basis points. The same data for the previous five years revealed an excess of 557 basis points. A look at the previous ten years of returns shows that the "top performers" earned a return of just 390 basis points over the average for the segment.

The implication here is that, in order to attract the hypothetical buyer, the investment in the PIC must offer the prospect of above-average returns. In the early years of the investment, the amount by which these unrealized returns exceeds the weighted benchmark returns for the PIC may be significant. However, over time, this margin will shrink. At the maximum time period for the PIC the margin should be quite small. The magnitude will vary by asset class and, therefore, risk.

Lack of Marketability

Unlike equity returns, the additional ROR required for illiquidity is not mean reverting. It will increase over time, although it increases at a decreasing rate.

Fujimoto and Watanabe assert that the risk associated with illiquidity does vary with time:

> Specifically, we find that returns of illiquid stocks tend to continue themselves after large volume-accompanied liquidity shocks, while those of liquid stocks reverse themselves... the dynamic relation between liquidity and return has a practical implication on risk management. The ability to swiftly disengage from financial markets before a liquidity crisis occurs is of importance to investors and financial managers.[14]

In the context of determining the appropriate ROR for an investment in an interest in a PIC, a critical distinction with the concept of illiquidity as discussed in the financial literature must be made. The root cause of illiquidity in an asset and in a PIC are only indirectly related. They are not the same.

The Damodaran article, "Marketability and Value: Measuring the Illiquidity Discount," provides an excellent overview of many scholarly works on this subject. In it he describes the components of illiquidity:

1. Market maker inventory costs or constraints,

2. Processing costs, and

3. Market signaling (adverse selection)[15]

Inventory costs seem to be the largest factor in the cost of illiquidity since this includes the price impact (or "blockage") problem created when large block trades are introduced into the marketplace. The other significant cost is the opportunity cost of waiting. In other words, if the market maker withholds shares from the market for fear of creating an adverse price impact, he runs the risk of the market price moving away from him and leaving him with an inventory loss.[16]

Two important questions for us to answer are:

1. Does the cost of illiquidity change over time? and

2. Does the cost of illiquidity vary with the riskiness of the asset?

The answer to both of the questions above is "yes." The cost of illiquidity, for a given asset, increases with time, although at a decreasing rate. This can be seen in the typical treasury bond yield curve. There is no default risk imbedded in the yield, but it does go up over time. This is referred to as the "Liquidity Preference Theory."

The liquidity preference is explained by the fact that investors require higher returns the longer they have to wait for the return on their investment. However, government securities are freely marketable, and the buyers of long-term T-bonds can sell them at any time. Nevertheless, a change in interest rates could easily mean an investor wishing to sell prior to the end of the term of the bond would realize a loss. So, from a practical standpoint, there is an element of illiquidity associated with even government bonds. Another example of this is the fact that debt issued by U.S. agencies and backed by the full faith and credit of the U.S. government often trades at a yield premium of 50 to 100 basis points to the far more liquid U.S. treasury bonds.[17]

The riskier the asset class, the higher the cost of illiquidity. One observable, market-derived measure of excess rates of return created by lack of marketability of riskier securities can be drawn from the examples of the restricted stock studies. Most of the studies are based on transactions involving either small-capitalization or micro-capitalization common stocks. The long-term rates of returns of these stocks range from 13 percent to 16 percent, based on geometric averages. We have determined that the required ROR of these investors in restricted stocks was about 20 percent. Using the midpoint of the range (14.5 percent), the increase in the ROR for lack of marketability was about 550 basis points for this asset class. This excess ROR requirement relates to a time period of less than ten years.[18] While more research needs to be done on this topic, a reasonable case for illiquidity costs can be inferred by interpolating around and between the two concrete examples given. Thus, the 50 to 100 basis point range sets the floor for illiquidity on riskless investments with a term of ten years and 550 basis points is an approximate measure for a ten-year period on small-cap common stocks.

PIC Expected Return

This is the benchmark against which the investor will be measuring, so this is the starting point for the valuation analysis. If the PIC's historical and expected future investment returns are above average for the asset classes owned, then the excess return required by the hypothetical buyer will be proportionately lower than they would be if the PIC's returns were below average. Theoretically, under the right circumstances, an investor would even be willing to pay a premium to invest. Conversely, if the PIC's returns have lagged the market benchmarks and this trend is expected to continue, then the RROR will exceed the expected future PIC returns by a wide margin. If there is no discernable record of the PIC, it would seem appropriate to assume an average market return.

Benchmark Returns – Ex Post or Ex Ante?

Grabowski, in an article on the equity risk premium, stated, "One needs to consider a variety of alternative sources including examining realized returns over various periods and employing forward-looking estimates such as those implied from projections of future prices, dividends and earnings."[19]

Since value is the present worth of expected future economic returns, it is most logical to assume that any buyer or seller will base his opinion of returns in relation to what he expects is most likely to occur in the future (ex ante). That is, if returns in a certain asset class over the past ten years have been, say, 12 percent but the preponderance of estimates from market analysts for the next ten years is 9 percent, the asset pricing for the next ten years should be based on the market's expectations and not past results.

Application of Benchmark Data

Once the weighted average expected return of the PIC portfolio is determined, enhancements to the required return are necessary because of the lack of control and lack of marketability inherent with the interest. That is, a hypothetical investor would not invest in the PIC without such an enhanced return because he could duplicate, or at least closely replicate, the PIC's portfolio himself while maintaining absolute control and the ability to sell and liquidate the portfolio when he deemed propitious. The critical question becomes: How much additional ROR is required to compensate the investor for the twin risks of lack of control and lack of marketability?

Minimum RROR

The minimum acceptable rate of return for the interest represents the floor or lower parameter of our seller's side of the pricing equation. This is determined for each asset class held by the PIC. The first step is to determine how the PIC performs in this asset class relative to the market. If the performance has been, or is expected to be in the future, average, then an increment needs to be added to this as the seller's offered ROR to the buyer. Whatever the increment is, it must be reasonable and based on some objective measure. Thus, if large-cap value common stocks are the asset class under consideration, the seller may offer a price that would result in the buyer receiving an ROR that was equal to the average of the top performing mutual funds of the same category. Since such objective data is rarely available for time periods beyond ten years, future periods should probably revert to the long-term average. A suggestion might be to gradually adjust the expected ten-year return annually to the long-term average for years 20 and beyond.

To this amount, the illiquidity cost of the asset class must be added. On a combined basis, the adjusted market returns and the illiquidity cost will create the RROR for that asset class over the possible future life of the PIC.

This same step will be repeated for all asset classes held. The resulting Minimum RROR (MIN RROR) profile over the life of the PIC is determined by calculating a weighted average of the indicated RORs of the various asset classes held by the PIC.

Maximum RROR

This is the "bid" response to the seller's asking price. It is performed in exactly the same manner as described above for the MIN RROR. The difference here is that there is a wider spread between the RROR and the PIC expected ROR. The buyer wants a better deal or a lower price than that offered by the seller. Like the MIN RROR, the Maximum RROR (MAX RROR) must be reasonable and based upon objective data. For example, if the Wall Street consensus average expected returns for large-cap value stocks over the next ten years are 9 percent, it would be unreasonable for a buyer to require an average return of 20 percent for this asset class over the life of the PIC. We know that is unreasonable, because we can see the "best-of-the-best" large-cap fund managers were unable to exceed the ten-year benchmark in this category by more than 435 basis points.

MAX RROR is determined for year ten by adding the weighted average results for the marginal increases due to lack of control (295 basis points) and illiquidity (220 basis points). The resulting MAX RROR seen in Table 4 for year ten is 12.95 percent. Due to mean reversion and the progressive shortening of the holding period, year ten is the highest the MAX RROR will ever be.

Lack of Persistence in Mutual Fund Returns

At this point, these questions might be asked: If we can identify specific mutual funds with returns far above the benchmark, why wouldn't the investor invest in these funds rather the PIC? Why would an investor subject herself to long periods of illiquidity when the same returns offered by the PIC can be obtained in a fully marketable mutual fund? The answer is that while we can observe the historical returns of mutual funds, we do not know with any degree of confidence that a specific fund will continue its above-average performance in the future. Numerous scholars, including Malkiel[20] and Porter and Trifts[21] have documented the lack of persistence in mutual fund returns. Thus, the MIN and MAX RRORs cited previously are relative measures to historical market returns in a general sense.

Illustration of NICE Mechanics

In our example, the PIC we will be dealing with is a family limited partnership (the "Partnership"). The Partnership is an investment-holding entity. The Partnership has total assets of $10,000,000 and owns equal amounts of long-term government bonds and large-cap U.S. equities (a blend of growth and value stocks). We are valuing a ten percent limited partnership interest (the "Interest"). The marketable securities are held in a brokerage account and managed by an account executive.

The expected growth in NAV was based on the average rates of returns of government bonds and large-cap equities. The Partnership has a life of 50 years. The limited partnership interest which is the subject of this exercise is being valued at the inception of the Partnership. We are also assuming that the PIC will not be making any distributions except to provide for the equity holders' federal tax liability created by their ownership in the PIC.

MIN RROR

As shown in Tables 1 and 2, Morningstar data tells us that the average returns for mutual funds covered as of April 30, 2006 were 7.96 percent for a large-cap blend of growth and value funds (422 funds) and 6.55 percent for government bond funds (18 funds). We place the minimum reasonable required return enhancement at 189 basis points for the large-cap common stock funds. This increment increases the ROR of this asset class to an amount equal to the lower quartile of the large-cap Top Performers for ten years (9.85 percent). The minimum reasonable required return enhancement for the long-term government bond funds was determined to be 25 basis points. (There are no Top Performers for long-term government bond funds since the entire Morningstar universe is only 18 funds.) As can be seen by looking at Table 3, the minimum marginal RROR for both asset classes declines over time.

Table 2
Morningstar Top Performing Fund Analysis Government Bonds - Long Term

Ticker	Name	10-Year Total Return
BTTRX	American Century Target Mat 2025 Inv	10.29%
BTTTX	American Century Target Mat 2015 Inv	9.89%
BTFTX	American Century Target Mat 2020 Inv	9.04%
PGOVX	PIMCO Long-Term U.S. Government Instl	8.21%
BTTNX	American Century Target Mat 2010 Inv	7.81%
VUSTX	Vanguard Long-Term U.S. Treasury	7.45%
WHOSX	Wasatch-Hoisington U.S. Treasury	7.45%
PRULX	T. Rowe Price U.S. Treasury Long-Term	6.78%
FEDBX	Federated U.S. Government Bond	6.66%
DRGBX	Dreyfus U.S. Treasury Long-Term	5.83%
TRUSX	ISI Total Return U.S. Treasury	5.83%
RYGBX	Rydex Govt Long Bond Advantage Inv	5.72%
ABUSX	AllianceBernstein Bond U.S. Govt A	4.97%
PADGX	Pacific Advisors Government Secs A	4.32%
	75th Percentile of Top 40 Performers	**8.11%**
	Category Average of 18 funds	**6.55%**
	Minimum Marginal RROR	**0.25**
	Maximum Marginal RROR	**1.56**

Table 1 Morningstar Top Performing Fund Analysis Large-Cap Blend		
Ticker	**Name**	**10-Year Total Return**
FEXPX	Fidelity Export & Multinational	15.04%
SACPX	Salomon Brothers Capital O	14.61%
HIACX	Hartford Capital Appreciation HLS IA	14.39%
LMVTX	Legg Mason Value Prim	14.12%
MPGFX	Mairs & Power Growth	13.65%
VPMCX	Vanguard PRIMECAP	13.23%
TVAFX	Thornburg Value A	13.13%
LLPFX	Longleaf Partners	13.03%
THPGX	Thompson Plumb Growth	12.81%
SLASX	Selected American Shares S	12.32%
SEQUX	Sequoia	12.30%
CENSX	Century Shares Trust Instl	11.61%
NYVTX	Davis NY Venture A	11.59%
SRVEX	Victory Diversified Stock A	11.50%
EXTAX	Exeter Tax Managed A	11.29%
GTVLX	AIM Basic alue A	11.20%
AHDEX	AHA Diversified Equity I	11.04%
FLEPX	DWS Equity Partners A	10.93%
TORYX	Torray	10.66%
PRBLX	Parnassus Equity Income	10.64%
TOCQX	Tocqueville	10.46%
PMEIX	Allianz PEA Equity Premium Strategy I	10.41%
LSCGX	Loomis Sayles Tax-Managed Equity Inst.	10.39%
VADBX	Morgan Stanley Equally-Wtd S&P 500 B	10.36%
ANDEX	Old Mutual Analytic Defensive Equity Z	10.17%
FDGFX	Fidelity Dividend Growth	10.07%
PIODX	Pioneer A	9.98%
FSCGX	Fidelity Select Industrial Equipment	9.88%
PBDEX	Analytic Disciplined Equity PBHG	9.87%
SHFVX	Legg Mason Partners Fundamental Value A	9.85%
TRSGX	T. Rowe Price Personal Strat Growth	9.84%
ITVAX	GE Value Equity A	9.70%
OBDEX	Old Mutual Analytic U.S. Long/Short Z	9.70%
LRLCX	Lord Abbett Large-Cap Core A	9.67%
CAPEX	Eaton Vance Tax-Mgd Growth 1.0	9.66%
BEQGX	American Century Equity Growth Inv	9.64%
FEDEX	Federated Capital Appreciation A	9.61%
RIMEX	Rainier Core Equity	9.57%
GMCTX	GMO U.S. Core III	9.55%
NEFGX	IXIS CGM Advisor Targeted Equity A	9.54%
	Average of Top 40 Performers	**11.18%**
	25th Percentile of Top 40 Performers	**9.85%**
	75th Percentile of Top 40 Performers	**12.31%**
	Category Average of 422 funds	**7.96%**
	Minimum Marginal RROR	**1.89%**
	Maximum Marginal RROR	**4.35%**

Table 3 NICE Summary of Minimum ROR Differential						
1. Average Expected Returns by Asset Class						
	LT Ave	10 yr	20 yr	30 yr	40 yr	50 yr
Govt Bonds	5.90	5.90	5.90	5.90	5.90	5.90
Large Cap	10.25	9.70	10.25	10.25	10.25	10.25
Weighted Average ROR of Partnership		**7.80**	**8.08**	**8.08**	**8.08**	**8.08**
II. Minimum Marginal Required Return Component for Lack of Control						
		10 yr	20 yr	30 yr	40 yr	50 yr
Govt Bonds		0.25	0.21	0.18	0.14	0.10
Large Cap		1.89	1.51	1.12	0.74	0.35
Weighted Average Lack of Control Component		**1.07**	**0.86**	**0.65**	**0.44**	**0.23**
III. Minimum Marginal Required Return Component for Illiquidity						
		10 yr	20 yr	30 yr	40 yr	50 yr
Govt Bonds		0.67	0.66	0.63	0.50	0.00
Large Cap		2.52	2.50	2.40	2.00	0.00
Weighted Average Illiquidity Component		**1.60**	**1.58**	**1.51**	**1.25**	**0.00**
Minimum Required Return (I. + II. + III.)						
		10 yr	20 yr	30 yr	40 yr	50 yr
Govt Bonds		6.82	6.78	6.70	6.54	6.00
Large Cap		14.11	14.25	13.77	12.99	10.60
Weighted Average RROR of Interest		**10.47**	**10.51**	**10.24**	**9.76**	**8.30**
Differential		2.67	2.44	2.16	1.69	0.23

The MIN RROR is also increased for lack of marketability. We have previously stated that for a ten-year holding (illiquid) period the increased rate of return would be 50 to 100 basis points for government bonds and 500 to 600 basis points for small cap common stock. As has also been previously discussed, the RROR for lack of liquidity is lower as the holding period shortens. Thus, in the first year of the Partnership, the ROR increment necessitated by illiquidity will be at its highest point. At the end of the term of the Partnership the ROR increment due to illiquidity will be zero. Based on the foregoing, we have selected an increment of 200 basis points for the lack of marketability associated with the common stock portfolio (in year 40, or with a remaining holding period of ten years). The selection is somewhat subjective but is governed by some fairly tight restraints. The primary determinants of the ROR component needed for illiquidity for any investment is related to risk (volatility) and the holding period (length of time the investment is subject to the volatility). In our view, large-cap common stocks are near the midpoint of the range described above for government bonds and small-cap common stocks. In the MIN RROR case, then, we are using an RROR component for illiquidity of slightly below the mid-point of the range.

Table 4 NICE Summary of Maximum ROR Differential						
1. Average Expected Returns by Asset Class						
	LT Ave	10 yr	20 yr	30 yr	40 yr	50 yr
Govt Bonds	5.90	5.90	5.90	5.90	5.90	5.90
Large Cap	10.25	9.70	10.25	10.25	10.25	10.25
Weighted Average ROR of Partnership		**7.80**	**8.08**	**8.08**	**8.08**	**8.08**
II. Maximum Marginal Required Return Component for Lack of Control						
		10 yr	20 yr	30 yr	40 yr	50 yr
Govt Bonds		1.56	1.36	1.16	0.95	0.75
Large Cap		4.35	3.63	2.92	2.21	1.50
Weighted Average Lack of Control Component		**2.95**	**2.50**	**2.04**	**1.58**	**1.13**
III. Maximum Marginal Required Return Component for Illiquidity						
		10 yr	20 yr	30 yr	40 yr	50 yr
Govt Bonds		1.26	1.25	1.20	1.00	0.00
Large Cap		3.14	3.12	3.00	2.50	0.00
Weighted Average Illiquidity Component		**2.20**	**2.18**	**2.10**	**1.75**	**0.00**
Maximum Required Return (I. + II. + III.)						
		10 yr	20 yr	30 yr	40 yr	50 yr
Govt Bonds		8.72	8.51	8.26	7.85	6.65
Large Cap		17.19	17.00	16.17	14.96	11.75
Weighted Average RROR of Interest		**12.95**	**12.75**	**12.21**	**11.41**	**9.20**
Differential		5.15	4.68	4.14	3.33	1.13

The MAX RROR is increased by 250 basis points for the lack of marketability associated with the common stock portfolio and 100 basis points for the government bonds' illiquidity. Again, these amounts are inserted ten years prior to the scheduled termination of the Partnership (or expected liquidation date, if it were known this would occur prior to the stated termination date). These amounts can be seen to slightly increase over time to the present. The illiquidity ROR enhancement is higher than the MIN RROR case since this case represents the buy-side and reflects the natural tendency of the buyer to want as low a price (high ROR) as is reasonably possible.

In Figure 1, the MAX RROR scenario is seen where the implied ROR of the Interest (concave dashed) coincides with the MAX RROR (short-long dashed line) in year ten. The indicated fair market value of the MAX RROR case is a price of $630.

Figure 1: Maximum RROR

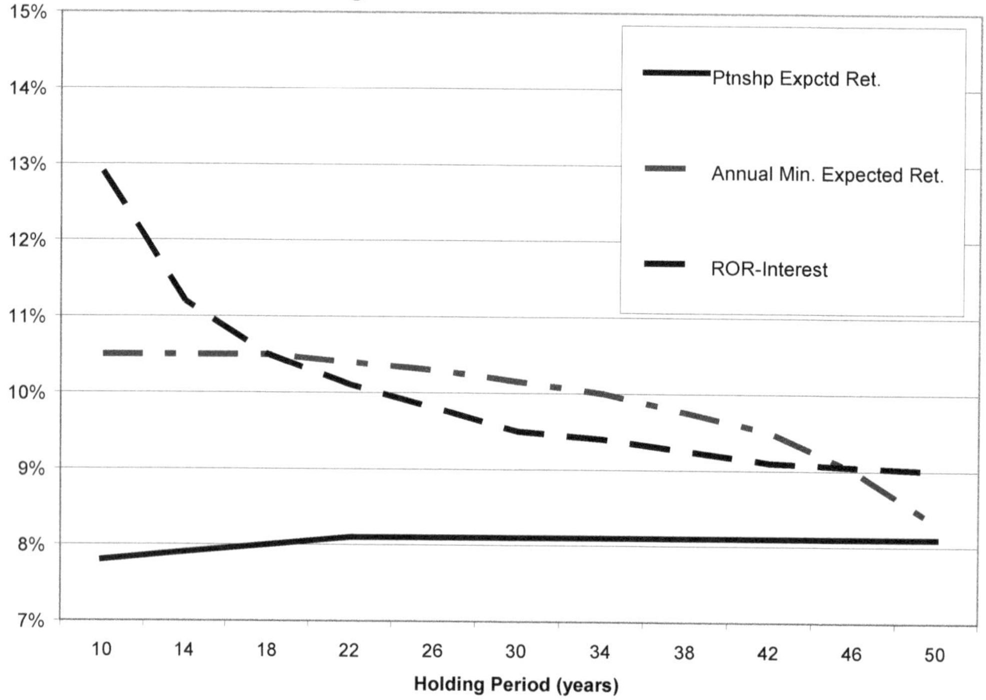

Figue 2: Minimum RROR

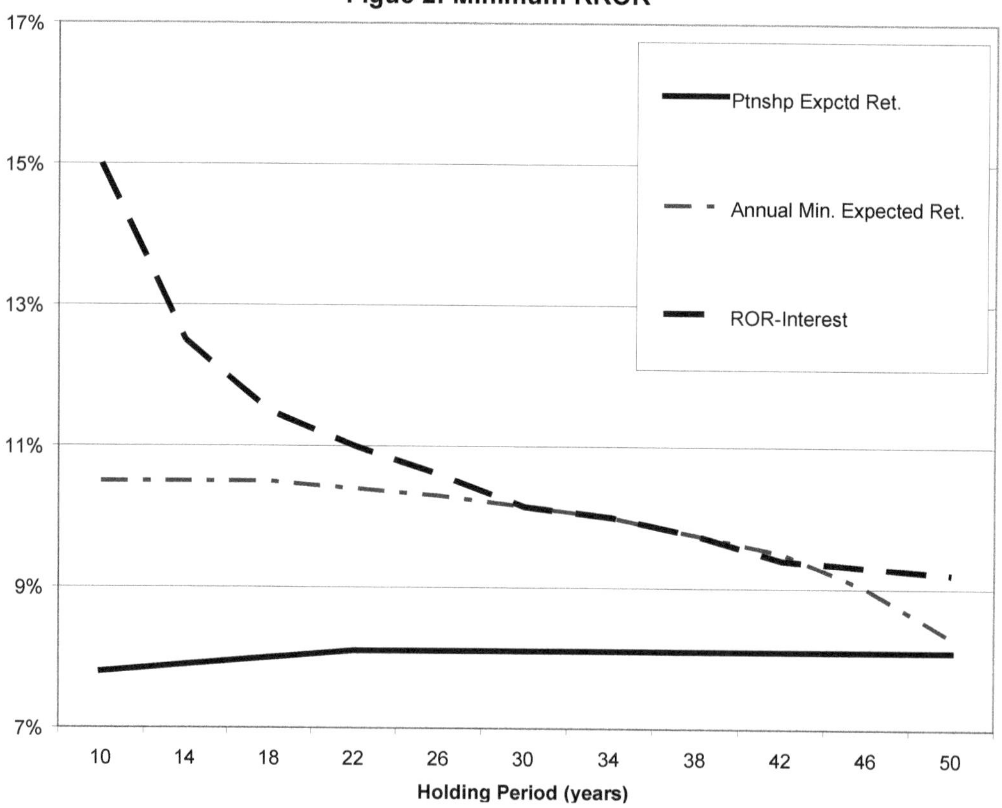

Figure 2 reveals the MIN RROR scenario wherein the implied IRR (concave line) coincides with the MIN RROR (dotted line). The indicated fair market value of the MIN RROR case is a price of $525.

As shown in Table 5, the minimum acceptable price by the seller is $525 whereas the maximum price paid by the buyer is $630. These prices represent the bid-ask spread found in all negotiated market transactions. The buyer and the seller almost never get exactly what they want—an accommodation is usually reached somewhere in the middle of the spread between the two.

Table 5
Two Asset Class Scenario Indicated Discounts at Minimum ROR and Maximum ROR

NAV (100%)		$10,000,000
Pro-Rata NAV	**10.00%**	$1,000,000
Minimum Price		$525
Total Discount from NAV		47.50%
Maximum Price		$630
Total Discount from NAV		37.00%
Indicated Value		$578
Total Discount from NAV		42.25%

With a minimum price (bid) of $525 and a maximum price (ask) of $630, a price spread of $105 is seen. This spread is about ten percent of the NAV of the PIC and about 17 percent of the asking price. In the context of an actively marketed security in the public marketplace, this spread would be abnormally wide. However, since the investment at issue here is an illiquid investment in a very long-term vehicle, we contend the spread is not unreasonably large and is entirely consistent with such investments as indicated by the research on bid-ask spreads.

Kryzanowski and Li, echoing what we cited from Amihud and Mendelson, state, "Although brokerage commissions are material, the bid-ask spread represents the major part of trade costs. Theory suggests that investors who expect to hold a security longer (shorter) will own stocks with larger (smaller) bid-ask spreads. If this is true, then stocks with higher (lower) bid-ask spreads should have longer (shorter) average holding periods."[22]

To put the magnitude of the bid-ask spread in context, we refer to Longstaff, "The illiquidity induced changes in the optimal portfolios has major effects on asset prices. We show that assets with identical cash flow distributions, that would otherwise have the same value, can differ by as much as 25 percent in their prices when one is liquid and the other is not. Thus, the model can produce large discounts for illiquidity similar in magnitude to those documented in many empirical studies."[23]

Conclusion

Assuming the mid-point of the range is the most probable settlement price of the hypothetical transaction, a price (fair market value) of $578 is indicated. If the buyer pays $578 for his ten percent interest in the Partnership in year one, by the end of the Partnership, his ROR will be 9.2 percent, or an ROR of 110 basis points more than the 8.1 percent achieved by the Partnership. While this may strike the reader as a very low ROR for an investment in such an entity, it must be borne in mind that this price equates to a discount from Net Asset Value of 42.25 percent.

Of course, we know the Partnership might liquidate at some point before its natural termination in year fifty. The highest expected ROR for the buyer of the interest would be 13.9 percent in year ten. While this is a good return, it is hardly a bonanza. We think the consistent reasonableness of the expected returns provided by the use of NICE, shows the robustness of the model and provides convincing evidence of its reliability as a valuation methodology for pass-through entities.

---

1. William H. Frazier, "Quantitative Analysis of the Fair Market Value of an Interest in a Family Limited Partnership," *Valuation Strategies*, January/February 2005, 5-17, 45-46. Here, we are describing the applied mechanics we have developed to the basic premise expressed in the original article.
2. Z. Christopher Mercer, Quantifying Marketability Discounts: Developing and Supporting Marketability Discounts in the Appraisal of Closely Held Business Interests (Memphis: Peabody Publishing, LP, 1997).
3. The use of the QMDM was recently rejected for this reason in *Temple v. United States*, 2006 U.S. Dist. LEXIS 16171 (March ten, 2006); "[the] holding period assumptions are enough, in the absence of a holding period requirement in the Ladera Agreement, to concern the Court with the reliability of that aspect of [the appraiser's] calculations."
4. Aswath Damodaran, "Marketability and Value: Measuring the Illiquidity Discount," Stern School of Business, July 2005, 50.
5. Shannon P. Pratt, *Valuing a Business: The Analysis and Appraisal of Closely Held Companies* Fourth Edition, ed. Shannon P. Pratt, Robert F. Reilly, Robert P. Schweihs, (McGraw – Hill, 2000) 40.
6. Yakov Amihud and Haim Mendelson, "Asset Pricing and the Bid-Ask Spread", *Journal of Financial Economics,* v 17 (1986), 223-250.
7. Francis.A. Longstaff, "How Much Can Marketability Effect Security Values?" *Journal of Finance*, v 50, 1767-1774.
8. Steven A. Sharpe, "How Does the Market Interpret Analysts' Long-term Growth Forecasts?" Federal Reserve Board, Finance and Economics Discussion Series Paper 2002-7 *http://www.federalreserve.gov/pubs/feds/2002/200207/200207abs.html*
9. In *Temple v. United States*, 2006 U.S. Dist. LEXIS 16171 (March ten, 2006), an appraiser is criticized for assuming the holding period of the investment is equal to the stated 50-year term of the partnership. "The Court finds that it is inappropriate to assume a particular holding period for the hypothetical buyer."
10. David F. Swensen, Pioneering Portfolio Management: An Unconventional Approach to Institutional Investment, (The Free Press, 2000).©
11. The exact same thing may be said about restricted stock. While it is restricted from trading in the public marketplace, it, too, can be sold in a private placement.
12. Karan Bhanot, "What Causes Mean Reversion in Corporate Bond Index Spreads? The Impact of Survival," *Journal of Banking and Finance,* v. 29, Issue 6, June 2005, 1385-1403
13. "Estimating the Real Rate of Return on Stocks Over the Long Term", Papers by John Y. Campbell, Peter A. Diamond, John B. Shoven, Presented to the Social Security Advisory Board, August 2001, *http://www.ssab.gov/estimated%20rate%20of%20return.pdf.*

14. Akiko Fujimoto and Masahiro Watanabe, "Time-Varying Liquidity Risk and the Cross Section of Stock Returns." (February 2006). EFA 2005 Moscow Meetings Available at SSRN: *http://ssrn.com/abstract=676369.*

15. See Note 3 above.

16. For another view of this topic see our article "Pure Blockage" which can be downloaded from the BVR website.

17. See Note 8 above.

18. See Note 1 above.

19. Roger Grabowski, "Equity Risk Premium: What is the Current Evidence?" *Business Valuation Review,* Fall 2005.

20. Burton G. Malkiel, "Returns From Investing in Equity Mutual Funds 1971 to 1991," *The Journal of Finance,* Vol. 1, No. 2, June 1995.

21. Gary E. Porter and Jack W. Trifts, "Performance Persistence of Experienced Mutual Fund Managers," *Financial Services Review,* Vol. 18, 415-430.

22. Lawrence Kryzanowski and Bin Li, "What Determines the Holding Period of an Investor?" *Canadian Investment Review,* Fall 2000.

23. Francis A. Longstaff, "Asset Pricing in Markets With Illiquid Assets," (January 2005) AFA 2006 Boston Meetings Paper. http://ssrn.com/abstract=687298.

Chapter 9

Good News, Bad News for FLPs and LLCs – Opportunities and Challenges for All!

By Owen Fiore, JD, CPA

For nearly a dozen years, the IRS and taxpayers, their attorneys and appraisers, have been sparring over the validity and use of Family Limited Partnerships (FLPs) and Limited Liability Companies (LLCs), both as pass-through entities for income tax purposes and as vehicles to save gift and estate taxes through so-called "valuation discounts." Numerous courts have issued decisions related to these entities and their composite interests, and while the cases give no clear directions on their funding, formation, and appraisal, some clear success factors have emerged. Further, the recent and heavily redacted IRS Appeals Guidelines identify the critical issues involved in these cases, including the estate tax pitfalls that FLPs and LLCs can potentially face in the provisions of IRC Sec. 2036(a), and the appropriate valuation methodology to apply to their interests.

During the past year, since the most recent publication of *BVR's Guide to Business Valuation Issues in Estate and Gift Tax* (2007), a number of FLP/LLC court decisions have covered several important areas, including: 1) the application of Sec. 2036(a) and availability of its exception for a "bona fide sale for full and adequate consideration"; 2) the use of "fixed dollar value" formula gifts and estate transfers to support appraisals for a taxpayer's valuations; and 3) developments in appropriate methodologies for valuing FLP/LLC interests. This article summarizes these recent developments and outlines the various factors that will maximize FLP/LLC opportunities for taxpayers and their advisors in family wealth planning.

The 2036(a) Estate Tax Trap and How to Avoid It

Several court decisions provide guidance for taxpayers, their tax counsel and appraisers—including two notable IRS victories. In *Estate of Bigelow v. Commissioner* (Sept. 2007), the Ninth Circuit Court of Appeals denied the taxpayer's 37% estate tax discount related to a poorly designed and improperly executed FLP. The court affirmed the Tax Court's finding of an implied agreement for Mrs. Bigelow, the founder and general partner, to enjoy FLP income and benefits beyond her pro rata share. Additional "bad facts" in the case included: 1) Mrs. Bigelow remained personally liable on the mortgage encumbering the real estate that was the FLP's primary asset; 2) the FLP failed to observe partnership formalities; 3) the formation and funding of the FLP left Mrs. Bigelow impoverished, but for receiving partnership distributions beyond her pro rata share; and 4) the FLP did not shield her from creditors. Finally, the court found that the FLP served no clear business (non-tax) purpose—and these cumulative factors ultimately led to a bad outcome for the taxpayer estate.

In an opinion authored by Judge David Laro, the Tax Court set an even higher bar for FLP/LLC success in *Estate of Rector v. Commissioner* (Jan. 2008). Once again, the critical factor in this case was the decedent's funding the FLP with most of her wealth, leaving insufficient liquid assets for her income and support. Just as in *Bigelow*, the FLP failed to observe partnership formalities and made numerous distributions to the decedent without equalizing distributions to the other partners, who were family members. The FLP failed to qualify for the "bona fide sale" exception to the application of 2036(a), because the court could not find a "significant non-tax business purpose." Judge Laro raised the hurdle higher by holding that that gift-giving is a testamentary purpose and by itself did not qualify as significant business purpose (but compare the *Mirowski* case below). In essence, *Rector* is the latest among the series of cases that have declined to apply the Sec. 2036(a)(1) exception when the FLP/LLC has no substantial business "reality," but is designed primarily to reduce or eliminate estate tax while providing continuing economic benefits to the transferor-decedent. Tax attorneys and business appraisers must be aware of these "operational reality" issues, and wherever possible, add value to their clients by avoiding the "bad facts" that lead to FLP challenges by the IRS and taxpayer defeats in court. Notably, in cases where an FLP/LLC fails to escape the reach of Sec. 2036(a), the court doesn't need to consider the valuation of the underlying interests, and the work of appraisers is lost.

Recently, an estate succeeded in qualifying for the "bona fide sale" exception to Sec. 2036(a), which meant that the court could consider the underlying appraisals to obtain proper valuation discounts for the entity interests. In *Estate of Mirowski v. Commissioner* (March 2008), Judge Chiechi delivered a welcome boost to business appraisers who try to determine appropriate discounts for fractional interests in FLPs and LLCs. The case also involved several "good facts" that impressed the court, including the Mirowski family history, its strong family values and intentions—especially those of the widowed mother and decedent, Anna Mirowski, who wanted to keep the family together by creating a common investment fund for the future.

Specifically, with the help of her advisors, Mrs. Morowski set up the LLC in August 2001, funded it a few days later, and gifted her three daughters' trusts an aggregate of 48% in limited partner interests in September 2001. Four days after transferring assets to the LLC, Mrs. Mirowski died quite suddenly from diabetes. From these facts, Judge Chiechi found that: 1) at no time before her death did Mrs. Mirowski, her family, or her physicians expect her to succumb so quickly; 2) the testimony of her daughters clearly indicated they were to collectively manage the family assets; 3) the bulk of the assets were pooled, to allow for continued investment opportunities; and 4) each of the daughters (or their trusts) shared the assets equally. Together, these findings created a real and significant non-tax business purpose for the Mirowski LLC, sufficient to meet the "bona fide sale" exception in Sec. 2036(a)(1).

Mirowski follows a short line of cases, including *Estate of Stone v. Commissioner* (2003), in which the Tax Court has found that Sec. 2036(a) does not apply due to availability of the "bona fide sale" exception. To support a similar finding, there must be evidence of a strong, non-tax purpose for the FLP or LLC, pro rata capital contributions by the partners (or members) and recognition of their capital interests.

McCord and *Christiansen*: 'Fixed Dollar Value' Formula Clauses

As a protective backstop for the valuation of FLP/LLC interests, the underlying transfer documents should state that the entity transfers comprise a number of shares or units that equals X dollars, "as finally determined for gift (or estate) tax purposes." This approach invokes a clear and understandable adjustment clause rather than any elimination of the transfer.

In *McCord v. Commissioner* (2003), the Tax Court rejected such a fixed-formula clause in a gift tax situation—but in 2006, the Fifth Circuit issued a stinging reversal, finding that the transfers had an "ascertainable value," despite their expression in dollars instead of percentage interests. Following this decision, in *Estate of Christiansen v. Commissioner* (Jan. 2008), the IRS challenged a formula clause in a charitable transfer as a "condition subsequent" and "against public policy." However, the Tax Court found there was no valid public policy argument favoring the IRS and accepted the concept, at least in the charitable gift context. Clearly, appraisers should find that a fixed-dollar formula clause will bolster their valuations, despite continuing uncertainty in the general area of FLP/LLC acceptance and affirmation by the courts.

Astleford and *Holman* – Instructive Gift Tax Decisions.

Two recent gift tax cases did not invoke Sec. 2036(a), but involved legal and valuation issues that deserve careful review by tax advisors and appraisers.

First, *Astleford v. Commissioner* (2008) considered a real estate investment partnership and its various gifts of partnership interests. Among the FLP assets was a 50% interest in the taxpayer's real estate venture, thus presenting the Tax Court with the issue of "layered' or tiered discounts. The court, in an opinion by Judge Swift, upheld the legal basis for the layered discounts; that is, it accepted the general concept that lack of control and lack of marketability discounts could apply at both the "parent" (partnership) level and also the "subsidiary" or holding company level. But in terms of the actual discounts, the Tax Court exercised its broad discretion, as trier of fact, to "mix and match" (or disregard altogether) the valuation methods, data, and determinations by the experts for both the taxpayer and the government. Accordingly, appraisers and attorneys must be cognizant of this judicial approach, and in the appropriate case, they may want to develop alternative valuation methodologies, assumptions of value, and conclusions. Their analysis should include the specific and reasonable basis for all methods and determinations. Ultimately, the *Astleford* court accepted substantial discounts for the FLP interests at stake, and the taxpayer was well-served by its counsel and appraisal experts. The court also did not appear troubled by the timing of the FLP formation, the transfer of assets and apportionment of interests—which were virtually simultaneous.

Compare *Holman v. Commissioner* (May 2008), in which the Tax Court considered an FLP that was formed and then funded six days later with Dell Computer stock as its sole asset. The IRS argued that such a short time between assignment of partnership interests and asset transfer should qualify as a "step transaction," or a single transaction resulting in an indirect gift of the stock. The court disagreed, and though it declined to draw a "bright line" concerning the passage of time sufficient to except a transfer from the step transaction doctrine, it ruled that in this case, six days was sufficient. In valuing the FLP interests, the court also ignored certain transfer restrictions (per IRC Sec. 2703(a)), which did not serve a valid business purpose. But it permitted substantial discounts, relying on the IRS's appraiser as the more credible and "thoughtful" of the parties' experts. Appraisers and attorneys could debate the court's analysis of the experts and their determination of marketability discounts; after reviewing the complete record, the trial transcript and exhibits—including the valuation reports, their determinations and data—reasonable authorities could differ regarding the relative strength of the respective experts. However, when a Tax Court judge states that he "lacked confidence" in the taxpayer's expert, that is likely to end the debate.

Lastly, the IRS's *Appeals Coordinated Issue Settlement Guidelines: Discounts for Family Limited Partnerships* (October 2006) points out that each valuation stands on its own and is specific to the facts and circumstances of that case. This particularity remains both the challenge and the opportunity for business appraisers and tax advisors to provide true value-added services for their clients while maintaining independence, credibility, and adherence to professional standards.

FLP/LLC: Summary of Success Factors

Based upon these cases, business appraisers, tax attorneys and financial advisors should heed the following "success factors" when utilizing FLPs or LLCs as wealth-management devices, including the discounted valuation of their interests:

- Design an effective plan with non-tax purposes. At the outset, and to avoid conflicts of interest, consider retaining independent legal counsel for the respective family members, and, above all, develop realistic and well-supported non-tax business purposes for the FLP or LLC.

- Avoid senior impoverishment. If the entity truly has a non-tax purpose, then its assets need not include the senior person(s)' personal residence or other funds needed for ongoing support. This has been a critical issue in a number of cases, including *Bigelow* and *Rector*.

- Transfer assets with related liabilities. This was also an issue in *Bigelow*; i.e., that the transferor should not retain liabilities and transfer only assets, especially if this requires entity distributions to pay the debt.

- Consider non-transferor general partner. Despite the common desire by FLP founders to stay in control, they may want to reconsider retaining complete management responsibilities. Comments in *Rector* suggest that to avoid application of IRC Sec. 2036(a), the transferor must relinquish "absolutely, unequivocally, irrevocably and without reservation" all title to and use/enjoyment of the transferred assets.

- Maintain proper capital accounts. Management of the FLP must observe formal partnership accounting, including proportional credits or charges for contributions and distributions. This is a hallmark requirement for availability of the "bona fide sale" exception to use of 2036(a) by the IRS.

- Follow entity formalities and agreements. Most of the "bad facts" that defeated taxpayers over the past dozen years included the entity's failure to follow the partnership or LLC agreements and be operated independently of its owners.

- Avoid non-pro rata distributions. This is another key factor for success, which will help preserve the entity for tax purposes.

- Consider changing business or investment plan. While not essential, having management develop a new business plan or change the make-up of investments may support the entity's "operational reality."

- Show a multi-generational management purpose. If the entity's objective includes wealth preservation, management, and education for the family's younger generations, make sure to properly document this purpose and plan.

Some combination of these success factors should help insure the continued viability of family limited partnerships and related entities as vehicles for wealth planning and preservation. Retaining the "operational reality" of these entities will allow appraisers to opine successfully on the transfer tax value, including discounts, of FLP or LLC entity equity interests upon sale, gift or at death.

Section 2

Conference & Teleconference Transcripts & Presentations

Valuation Issues in Estate & Gift Tax

Moderator: Blake Lyman
Speakers: Linda Trugman, Jay Fishman, Chris Treharne

Blake Lyman: Hello and welcome to *Valuation Issues in Estate & Gift Tax*. My name is Blake Lyman, Professional Program Manager at BVR.

As we're frequently reminded at this time of year, the Internal Revenue Code can change and with some speed. Via politics, case law, accounting principles, or the response to creative circumvention, these changes can affect the business valuation process in unseen ways, particularly with the inclusion of appraiser penalties.

Today, BVR welcomes three experts on this subject: Linda Trugman, Jay Fishman, and Chris Treharne.

Linda Trugman is Vice President of Trugman Valuation Associates, Inc. Her business valuation experience includes a wide variety of assignments including closely-held businesses, professional practices, and thinly traded public companies. Her litigation support services have been rendered for a variety of purposes including, but not limited to family law matters, business damages, estate and gift tax matters, and breach of contract.

Jay Fishman, FASA, is Managing Director of Financial Research Associates, and has been actively involved in the appraisal profession since 1974. He specializes in the valuation of business enterprises and their intangible assets. He has co-authored several books including *Standards of Value: Theory and Application* and the highly acclaimed *Guide to Business Valuation* both with Shannon Pratt. He was appointed to the Internal Revenue Service Advisory Committee in 2008.

Chris Treharne is the founder of Gibraltar Business Appraisals, Inc. Prior to founding Gibraltar, Chris was the vice president of a regional business valuation firm. Having prepared numerous presentations and authored papers on S corporation valuation issues, Chris is nationally recognized as an expert on the topic. At the request of the Honorable David Laro, the U.S. Tax Court, and Dr. Shannon Pratt, he co-authored a chapter on the topic in their book, *Business Valuation and Taxes: Procedure, Law, & Perspective.*

It's always a pleasure to welcome these three to our teleconferences and you can read much more about them on their webpage for today's teleconference.

But before we get going, I'd like to remind you of the details of our teleconference. Your attendance today is eligible for two CPE credits. In order to receive those credits, you must complete a brief survey on today's teleconference at the conclusion of our presentation. A link to our survey is included with your registration email which included instructions on how to dial in today. A link is also available on the reading page for today's teleconference.

This survey will be active for five business days and will require you to fill in three four-digit CPE codes. Simply write down the codes as they are read and fill them in when asked in the survey.

I'll read the CPE codes three times during today's conference – one hour through the presentation, at the conclusion of the presentation, and right now. The three four-digit CPE codes for today's conference are 3642, 4109, and 8832. Once again, that's 3642, 4109, and 8832. If you are logged into our Beacon Live Web Platform, you will see those numbers appearing on your screen now.

We'll be taking questions during the session by email only. Please send questions to *tc-questions@bvresources.com*. That's *tc-questions@bvresources.com*. That email address is on the bottom of each of our presentation slides today, so please send in your questions for our esteemed panelists.

And with that, we welcome Linda Trugman, Jay Fishman, and Chris Treharne. Jay?

Jay Fishman: Thanks, Blake, and thanks to BV Resources for putting this together and thanks for Linda and Chris for inviting me.

Just a quick disclaimer, I'm not a tax lawyer and I'm not teaching anyone tax law, but for the last – I don't know – ten years or so, I've been working on appraisal issues at Capitol Hill and with various government organizations and that's given me, I think, some perspective on what's happening.

If we can put the first slide up – I borrowed this from Bob Dylan in saying, "The times they are a-changing," because what's happening is for the last – I don't know – seven or eight years, there's been a lot of dissatisfaction with appraisals being used for tax-related matters. It started many years ago with people giving non-commercially patented technology to universities in taking large deductions and the Treasury Department and the Joint Committee on Tax.

The Joint Committee on Tax is a combination of staff from the House Ways and Means instead of banking and they're the ones that kind of formulate initial tax policy. They've shown a lot of dissatisfaction with the quality of the appraisers and the quality of the appraisals that they've been getting. So with this administration in these economic times in a way to look for more revenue, they decided to put the focus to a large extent on appraisers and those appraisers doing tax-related appraisals.

Linda, Chris, and I are BV appraisers but I can tell you that this applies to all disciplines.

In fact, one of the hot buttons right now is the so called façade easements where people buy a building and allocate a certain amount of money to a façade for historical, for other preservation purposes, and those valuations have been under particular scrutiny as well.

So if the times are a-changing, there's a cold wind blowing and it's going to get chilly for all of us and I think that we have to be careful and understand the rules and responsibilities when we take on valuations for tax-related purposes.

So if we look at the next slide, there are three major pieces of legislation that prompted all of these and I did spend a lot of time on this but I'm not going to tie them all back because as somebody said to me yesterday, it's kind of like a jigsaw puzzle. The most important one is the middle one, the Pension Protection Act of 2006 (PPA of 2006), but it was amended by one of them. These really form the basis of my comments today.

The way it usually works is that Congress will issue a tax bill and then it'll leave it up to the Internal Revenue Service to do regulations and rules on how they're going to implement the tax bills.

So with these three pieces of legislation, we have two sections that everyone should be kind of aware of and that is Section 6694, which is for tax preparers, and then the big one that we're going to talk about today is 6695A, which deals with valuation misstatements.

The PPA was really done for charitable contribution purposes and for people who are looking to substantiate reporting deductions. It applies to appraisals done after August 2006 and there are three thresholds. The ones we need to be concerned about are the ones that are in excess of $5,000 and the ones that are in excess of $500,000. If an appraisal is in excess of $500, there's a form called 8283 that the appraiser, him or herself has to sign acknowledging that this is correct and that they wouldn't participate in any valuation errors. If it's over $500,000, one has to attach the appraisal in order to get the deduction.

This led to a whole series of definitions that the Internal Revenue Service went to and some of them, we were very happy about – what makes a qualified appraisal and what makes a qualified appraiser – because under the new statutes, it is only those appraisals done by qualified appraisers resulting in qualified appraisals that will allow the deduction. So this had the IRS looking for a long time as to what a qualified appraisal is.

There are a lot of definitions but the one that people should be most interested in is, "A qualified appraisal is an appraisal that complies with generally accepted appraisal standards." Now that's a term that we use generically, and if you belong to a professional society, you say it's those standards.

The IRS needed some universal standard to look through and a universal standard that just doesn't apply to business valuation but applies to all disciplines.

So as it currently stands in the temporary regulations, reports done in accordance with generally accepted appraisal standards are those reports that conform with the substance and principles of the Uniform Standards of Professional Appraisal Practice, known as USPAP.

I want to point out again that USPAP has a personal property section, a BV section and, of course, it has a real property section. I think that was probably one of the appeals that the Service had and that it cut across lots of disciplines.

What is a qualified appraiser? There are lots of definitions. Again, the one that we probably note most familiar with is in the temporary regulations, which says, "A qualified appraiser is one that has a designation from a recognized professional appraisal organization on the basis of demonstrating competency."

There are other qualifications too. You don't necessarily need the appraiser in all aspects, in other kinds of disciplines. There may be other kinds of people without designations who may be considered qualified appraisers.

Where it stands at the present time is these regulations have come out – there was an appeal process and people commented on it – and we understand right now that the regulations are over at the Treasury Department awaiting the Treasury Department's approval.

So that's where we are with the issue of "qualified appraiser," "qualified appraisal."

The implementation of the tax preparer penalty, which is Section 6694, that's another controversial issue. I had testified a year and a half ago about whether appraisers are, in fact, tax preparers. There are certain criteria that have to be met. One of the biggest ones is that you have to believe that what you're doing results in a substantial portion of the tax paid by the taxpayer.

I don't know about your practice, but in my practice, we'll do an appraisal. Maybe that's enough to let us know that it's substantial because our fees aren't insubstantial. But we'll do the appraisal. We'll be probably hired by the tax attorney. They'll file the 706. We'll hear nothing. We may hear nothing forever. We may hear that there was a tax examination. We may hear that there was a tax examination and that we should go to a meeting. But often, these things get resolved without the appraiser being involved at all.

So that was one of the issues I had asked about, whether an appraiser would be considered a non-signing tax preparer. My view was it was not because of the reasons that I've just said.

Unfortunately, I didn't win that argument and the IRS has come out with a regulation that indicates that appraisers are considered non-signing tax preparers and, therefore, fall under the penalty and provisions of IRS Section Code 6694.

I'm going to leave that there right now. They did say that not only could you fall under 6694, but if there's a valuation misstatement for not just charitable contributions but for estate and gift tax purposes, you also would fall under 6695A which calls for penalties upon substantial and gross valuation misstatements.

So one of the issues was, here we are, an appraiser can be penalized under both sections.

The IRS did say in their clarification, they gave us that they will not stack. So if there's a 6694 issue, it won't be compounded with a 6695A issue. So I think you should know that and take some comfort.

Let's go to the next slide. I've said this before, "Congress passes laws that explain its intent in broad terms and implementation," and it's the implementation where the rules of the road are kind of defined.

So if we look on the next slide, we'll talk about 6695A. As I said, the penalties will not be stacked.

6694 contains some words that we're all going to have to become familiar with, and they're very well known in the Tax Code but they really haven't been applied as it deals with appraisals, and that is whether the appraisal has proved to be the "realistic possibility" of the correct value, the "substantial authority" of the correct value or "more likely than not" the correct value.

For tax preparers, they fall under the "substantial authority" and "more likely than" not portions.

A general loose interpretation means that as you go up the range of these words, you find yourself having to establish the probabilities of 33 percent, 50 percent, or more than 50 percent.

As I said, that's interesting if you have a tax issue like a tax shelter where you can produce facts and you can produce tax authorities. How that's going to be applied to appraisers is a really interesting issue.

Let's go to the next slide. Now we're kind of at the heart of the issue. When you sign that Form 8283, you pledge that you will be bound by 6695A, which says that you will be subject to penalty for a gross or substantial valuation misstatement.

How is that defined? It's defined as follows:

As applied to non-cash charitable contributions, a substantial valuation misstatement exists when the claimed value of the property is 150 percent or more of the amount determined to be the correct value. A gross valuation misstatement occurs when the claimed value is 200 percent or more of the correct value.

For estate and gift tax purposes, a substantial valuation misstatement exists when the claimed value of the property is 65 percent or less of the amount determined to be the correct value. A gross valuation misstatement exists when the claimed value is 40 percent or less of the amount determined to be correct.

So of course, the most important issue is who gets to determine what the word "correct value" means and at what point, and I'm going to revisit that in a second.

Then the second issue is probably more important. The penalties are severe but not particularly onerous. The amount of penalty imposed is either the lesser of the greater of 10 percent of the amount of the underpayment or $1,000 or 125 percent of the gross income received by the person for the preparation of the appraisal.

The issue, I think, is not so much the monetary penalties. The issue that's more important is what does this do to our credibility as appraisers and, therefore, our livelihood.

In August 2010, the IRS Office of Small Business/Self-Employed – that's the division under which these issues are addressed – issued an implementation procedure which was called "penalty for valuation misstatements attributable to incorrect appraisals." In those, it extended the "qualified appraiser," "qualified appraisal" issue now, not just the charitable contributions, but it really applies now to all tax-related valuation issues.

It calls for a procedure that the IRS will use now in pursuing one of these assessment penalties.

The first thing to know is these penalties can be assessed by a tax examiner, an estate and gift tax lawyer, or some other type of tax compliance officer at any point during the assignment.

The second is that there's a separate case that will be set up during the tax examination.

So there's a tax examination, and from that, the examiner, the appellate, or the estate tax lawyer gathers information to determine whether or not a valuation misstatement has occurred and whether or not there will be a penalty assessed to an appraiser or whether they will contemplate a penalty assessed to an appraiser.

Another one will be that the review of the appraiser's report on the tax return will not be done in front of the taxpayer – that's wonderful – and there's a whole list of other things.

The examiner can list what they call a field specialist. The IRS has certain subject matter specialists – there are three or four different categories – and they're called field specialists. The one that we probably most deal with are engineers and they really deal with the valuation issues. If the examiner has a problem, they can call upon a field specialist to help with the examination and determination as to whether there's a penalty or not.

There's a safe harbor built in here. The safe harbor indicates that if the appraiser can determine that "more likely than not", can convince the IRS that "more likely than not" their valuation was the correct valuation, then they can find themselves relieved of any penalty issues.

However, as I said before, what does that exactly mean? As we all know, taxpayers can come in front of examiners with a host of valuation issues, a host of other tax issues, and they can come to a resolution, and oftentimes, they may end up by adjusting the value as a way to solve the tax examination.

Does that constitute a valuation misstatement? I think the worst example that I can think of is the *McCord* case in which it went all the way to the Tax Court and which they found for the government and then was reversed.

The questions that have to be answered are: At what point is the valuation misstatement determined? What determines what the correct or proper value is? What does "more likely than not" mean? No one really knows and that's a really big problem.

Two weeks ago, at the request of most of the appraisal organizations, the IRS held hearings on February 18, 2010 with the OSP (Office of Servicewide Penalties) – they are the people that are responsible for implementing these procedures. All the large organizations – the American Bar Association, Tom Hilton for the AICPA, a gal from NACVA, Howard Lewis from IBA, and me who was there on behalf of the American Society of Appraisers – offered testimony about these issues.

There are a couple of problems. The first problem is the percentage tests, the 150 and 200 or the 40 and 65. There's no differentiation between asset categories. So if you're looking at a financial derivative, the certainty as to what the correct value is could be large even in best circumstances. That would apply to the same test as you would a single family home.

One of the arguments we've had with the Service is that this should be a little more flexible and allow larger tolerances.

Having said that, you have this escape or safe harbor if you can prove your value was "more likely than not" the correct value.

The problem with that issue is what does "more likely than not" mean in the context of a valuation. You can't just get the facts and find authority.

In valuations, I don't know what your experience is, but my experience is that, generally speaking, the valuation approaches are applied properly, the methods are applied properly, but the difference always often results from the variables. Somebody has a different discount rate. Somebody has a different discount for lack of marketability.

The question is: What is the appropriate quantum? I'm not sure and they're not sure what "more likely than not" means.

The third and really important issue is the so called "soft letter" or "appointment letter." If a case is opened and it's opened at the group level, this is the first time. The appraiser then gets a letter. It's a letter form 4477. They call it an "appointment letter." The Office of Professional Responsibility (OPR) calls it a "soft letter." It informs the appraiser that a valuation misstatement penalty case has been opened against him or her and invites them to come and discuss the appraisal issue with the appropriate party, whether it's the examiner, the appellate, or the estate and gift tax lawyer. The IRS views this as really an accommodation to the appraiser for the first time to give the appraiser the chance to kind of explain.

This is an example of unintended consequences. Here, you get a 4477 letter. Do you have to notify your carrier? If you're a state certified general real estate appraiser, do you have to notify the Real Estate Appraisal Board? Or if you're someone like me who testifies in court and someone asks me, "Have you ever been cited for disciplinary reasons or any other reasons for valuation misstatements?" You have to say, "Yes, I got a letter from the IRS."

Now people may not understand that that's the beginning of the process, not the end of the process.

So as an appraiser, you end up having the stigma of getting this letter without any real ability to defend yourself as to what it was before its issue.

One of the things all the organizations argued about was that instead of sending this letter, they ought to do what they do with the tax preparers, which is call the appraiser in and have a discussion first and allow that to happen. That way, there's nothing in writing if you're asked if there was a possible valuation misstatement letter. This would be a "pre" kind of interview before they actually decide to open the case.

Whether or not we've got traction on that, I'm not sure, but I can tell you that this is a really big concern for everyone in the appraisal profession.

So where we stand now is that the Office of Servicewide Penalties, in fact, took into account all these statements at the hearing and we're waiting to hear back as to what at least their temporary regulations will be in terms of the implementation of the process.

Now if what I've said to all of you scares the dickens out of you, it should and that's the intent. This is a real, real difficult time for appraisers doing tax-related appraisals.

Appraisals are difficult to do at first but now we're operating in a world in which there are no real rules that we can use to kind of protect ourselves.

The other issue that appraisers always talk about is that there's a complaint that these penalties are all one-sided. That is, the IRS expert or the IRS examiner who may take an outrageous position is not subject to these penalties. So the IRS, in essence, is the judge, the jury, the prosecutor, and that kind of due process doesn't seem to be fair. But they're the government, so you have to work within those parameters. I will say that they have tried to listen to us and perhaps we'll be fortunate enough to convince that at least from a procedural point of view, they need to take a look at this.

Let me end by just talking about one more thing. You will recall that I said that in doing one of these examinations, they can look at a field specialist; they can bring a field specialist in.

Well, one of the things that folks in the appraisal community have worked with in terms of the Service is having their specialists be trained properly, is having dialogues with them, and up until two years ago, they had something called a Valuation Policy Council that people were invited to to have exchanges with the field specialists so that at least we can all agree that we're working from the same body of knowledge.

Let me end by saying this, the IRS folks really believe that these regulations are necessary to get the bad actors out of the appraisal profession. I don't think there's any disagreement that those people who are performing poor appraisals, who are advocates, who are making up things certainly should be taken to task for them. What they tell you confidentially is, "We're really trying to just get the bad actors out, those who make up comps, those who make up facts."

But nonetheless, these rules and regulations are on the books, and if they're on the books, there may be a change in attitude at the Service and they can be used in a broader way.

So rest assured that the leaders of our profession are looking at these issues and there's a constant dialogue with the Service.

I think I'll stop here. Thank you for indulging me for so long and I'll hand it back to Linda.

Linda Trugman: Jay, this question hasn't come from a listener but I've got a question. I'm very often asked by people, primarily CPAs, about the issue of independence in valuations being submitted to the Internal Revenue Service and whether or not the IRS is looking at all at appraisals that are done by the same firm that does either the 706 or the 709 or does the underlying tax and accounting work for the particular client. I'm just wondering if you have heard anything from the IRS if they are looking at an issue like that or whether or not they are taking a harder look at those types of situations.

Jay Fishman: Well, my first reaction is that in those situations, they should go out and get an independent appraisal and use firms like ours. But to seriously answer your question, I've not heard that as a big complaint, and they're just getting the ball rolling. They don't tell us how many cases there are.

By the way, again to scare you, but this happens to be fact, if they find there's a pattern of these misstatements, then you can be turned over to the Office of Professional Responsibility of the Internal Revenue Service for possible disbarment. Now that may mean you just can't do IRS work but that implication isn't great.

So Linda, I've not heard of particular examples of, "Look, it's the accounting firm doing the valuation." I think right now they're really at the tip of the iceberg and the examples they keep throwing out are the ones that I mentioned – you made up the comps, you made up a fact, that building really isn't there. It's those kinds of things to start with.

By the way, I'm not sure that a lot of this is business valuation related. It may be more other discipline related, particularly this façade easement issue I know they're looking at very importantly.

Chris Treharne: The big one out here in the West has also been a controversial issue.

Jay Fishman: That's right – Denver is a hub for that issue.

Linda Trugman: Okay, one of the listeners asked a question, "Can you give out the website where we can download the testimony before the committee?" Jay, do you know, does the Internal Revenue Service post this or is this just a question of the organizations who are testifying posted on their various websites?

Jay Fishman: I think the answer is I don't know about the IRS. If you want to check, you just *irs.gov*. This will get you to the IRS website and you can enter this.

I have noted that the various organizations – NACVA, ASA, IBA, AICPA – have posted it. In my example, you can go to ASA's website. You don't have to be a member and you can download a PDF copy of my testimony. I know, because I did it, you can do the same thing with NACVA.

I don't know if the IRS has it all in one place. It should be publicly available. But I know the professional societies have posted it as have the American Bar Association, which was another one of the people who testified.

Linda Trugman: For the listeners on this call who were provided with the website for the readings for this conference, the ASA letter, ASA testimony that Jay submitted is included in there as is the bar associations. As far as the other organizations, as Jay said, you should probably check back with them.

We also had another question asking about equal interest in property. The question was, "Is there a defense against unity of interest theory?" I know that Chris and I are not sure exactly what the listener is asking about. Jay, do you have any sense as to what that might mean?

Jay Fishman: My first answer would be you ought to ask Gary Trugman. After all, he wrote the book. But I think it has to do with how title is taken on real property, whether it's taken by tenants in common and can you divide that up. But I'm really not familiar with it.

Chris Treharne: The definition of it is the "equal interest in property held by joint tenants" but I don't understand the relevance of that to –

Jay Fishman: I think they want to take a discount.

Linda Trugman: If the listener could resubmit the question possibly –

Chris Treharne: Some clarification.

Linda Trugman: With a little bit more detail, yeah, and clarification, we'll try and answer it for you.

One comment that I just want to make to the listeners is that the three of us are not attorneys, which I know Jay has already mentioned. Although I'm a CPA, the three of us are not tax practitioners, we all solely work in the valuation and litigation support arena. So some of the questions, if they're too tax or legal oriented, we're not going to be able to answer them because we just don't work in those arenas.

A question came through, "If you receive a letter from the IRS saying that the return in question has been accepted, does that mean the return is no longer subject to an audit?"

My understanding is that you have to get a closing letter on an estate. I don't know about a gift tax return.

If there are any CPAs out there who know the answer to that question and want to submit it to BV Resources, I'll be happy to read it to the group.

But Jay and Chris, do you know anything different than I do?

Chris Treharne: I do not know.

Jay Fishman: No. Someone asked this, the issue in Denver is the historic or façade easements, and, in fact, *The Denver Post* had an article about the Internal Revenue Service and some of their state certified general appraisers. So that's the issue.

Linda Trugman: Okay. We have what appears to be more of a general valuation question but here's the scenario. The subject company is a privately held company with no likelihood of going public. The interest to be valued is a 100 percent interest. The multiple was derived from 15 transactions obtained from Pratt's Stats®. All the transactions related to private entities and were for a 100 percent interest. The assignment is to arrive at a level of value controlled, non-marketable.

Question number one: "Assuming no adjustments were made to the reported numbers, what would be the derived level of value?"

I've got a suggestion for that answer, but Jay or Chris, do you want to –

Chris Treharne: I value it as controlled, non-marketable.

Jay Fishman: Yeah.

Chris Treharne: But certainly that's an area that is controversial in our profession. Is the questioner asking if we should then apply a lack of marketability discount to that? My answer to that would be I typically do not, which is a very clear I have occasionally but very seldom do I do it, and if I do, it's a very small discount.

Jay Fishman: This whole issue about discounts for lack of marketability for controlling interests troubles me. I'm in Chris' camp on this one. Most of the time no, but never say never – if it's an oddball business, then maybe.

I think people lose sight of this – under any circumstances, whether you own a controlling interest in a public company or you own a controlling interest in a private company, you do not get your money in three days. In fact, one could argue it's harder to sell a public company than it is a private company because you have to go through a number of SEC and to do hurdles.

Then the second thing – and Mike Belofsky [sp] wrote an article about this many years ago – the lack of marketability in the private market may be more of a reflection of an information effect than it may be pure marketability, and that is that public companies are more organized, they're used to reporting better, their books are in better shape (unless, of course, you're an oil company in Texas called Enron). So I think there's that issue.

So we don't typically do it on a pro forma basis.

It looks like if your comps are private, then that would be my starting point.

Chris Treharne: I would add to that, Jay, too, that if there is a marketability discount and you're relying strictly on transactions from Pratt's Stats®, there's a marketability discount embedded in those transaction multiples.

Jay Fishman: Correct.

Chris Treharne: The other perspective that I often take – and again, this is not a universal answer because I'm like Jay, this is my typical answer but certainly not always the case – if the standard of value is fair market value, the hypothetical investor has the obligation to maximize his or her value over that interim holding period between the day he or she makes the decision to sell and the day that transaction actually closes.

If, during that period, he or she is maximizing his or her value, then the present value of those interim cash flows is the same value as the transaction date. So there's no effective illiquidity associated with that.

That's a hypothetical answer but that's what fair market value is too.

Linda Trugman: Well, the second part of that question – and I think this is where the listener was going – was, "If you make normalization adjustments to the cash flow, what would be your derived level of value?"

My personal take on this question is that you would not apply the multiples to an unadjusted cash flow stream because the multiples are controlled and you should be applying those multiples to a control cash flow stream.

If you applied the multiples to an unadjusted cash flow stream, then my take on that is that you've got a bit of fruit salad there because you're mixing minority and control issues there.

That's got nothing to do with marketable, non-marketable. That's strictly got to do with control and lack of control.

Chris Treharne: Jim Hitchner's most recent – maybe it wasn't most recent – maybe it was October 2009 – *Financial Valuation and Litigation Expert* talks about some of the issues associated with using private databases.

Personally, I think they're a good sanity check. Occasionally, they're a good use for determining value but I use them more as a sanity check. Part of the reason is – what are historical earnings? Are those pro forma earnings that some business broker has put together or are they actual earnings?

Now Pratt's Stats® we have a little more confidence. They may be actual earnings, but bottom line is we end up relying on the broker or whoever is reporting that information to provide it to us, and we don't really know whether that historical metric of economic value – earnings or cash flow or whatever it is – has been adjusted or not to market the business.

Jay Fishman: I was going to say, first of all, welcome to *Valuation Issues in Estate & Gift Tax*. But Linda, I would say one caveat to what you're saying is you have assumed that the comparables were adjusted as well.

Chris Treharne: Yes.

Linda Trugman: True, true. Well, I don't know that I assume that the comparables are adjusted as well. I think I'm just assuming that the multiple, because it was a control transaction, is a control multiple and, therefore, should be applied to a control cash flow stream, which just goes to show that we can all interpret these things a little bit differently.

We are going to get away from the penalty situation a little bit. I know that there have been a couple of questions that have come in that ironically are on some topics that we're hoping that we will cover in the next 55 minutes.

Chris Treharne: Linda, may I interrupt for a second?

Linda Trugman: Sure.

Chris Treharne: It just occurred to me that we forgot – and this also makes a good segue from Jay's segment of the presentation to ours – I've come up with a great question that is the segue. State taxes were appealed on the first of this year, so why are we having this session?

Linda Trugman: Because we all believe that they're going to come back.

Chris Treharne: Exactly.

Jay Fishman: But they're not examining this year's anyway.

Linda Trugman: Yeah –

Chris Treharne: Yeah, yeah.

Linda Trugman: And that is true too.

Chris Treharne: But if you look in your handouts, you will also see – actually, I don't know, Blake, how you posted it, whether it was in the original email format or not – from some organizations back in D.C. with whom I've been working, the S Corporation Association and Venn Strategies, they gave me an interesting perspective on where we stand as of Tuesday of this week. The most likely possibility seems like it's going to be to reinstate the estate tax and it's going to be reinstated at the pre-repeal levels, so $3.5 million exemption and 45 percent rate. There may be an allowance for two senators, Lincoln and Kyl's amendment to reduce the rate to 35 percent and raise the exclusion to $5 million. However, if they do that, they have to offset the lost revenues associated with that proposed change.

Some of the interesting proposals for those offsets – one of them is to allow taxpayers to prepay the tax, which they would do at a lower tax rate, so there would be an incentive for taxpayers to do it, and it's government funny money manipulation. In doing that, they get the benefit of having tax receipts even though their net receipts long term will be less than they would be if they had no prepayment benefit. The government accounts for it as a current receipt that offsets lost revenues.

There's also a proposal that there will be some imposition of a toll or a tax on the creation of family foundations.

Then also in the Obama budget, Obama has proposed repealing discounts for lack of control and lack of marketability, which is not anything new. That's happened before.

So that's just a quick transition, Linda, and why don't we move on to the rest of the program as we have a plan then?

Linda Trugman: Just FYI, we're referring to FLPs (family limited partnerships) as a generic entity. A lot of comments about FLPs are also appropriate to LLCs (limited liability companies) and, in some cases, to corporation holding companies.

We have all done a lot of work and answered a lot of questions from people and came to the conclusion that there are a lot of valuation experts out there that seem to get certain issues confused and don't totally understand what we're doing when we're doing valuations for estate and gift tax purposes.

So I'm going to toss this over to Chris to explain just some of the basic concepts that, as appraisers, we really need to keep in mind before we actually sit down and put pencil to paper to do valuations for these purposes.

Chris Treharne: Thanks, Linda. It surprises me that I get phone calls and emails, and when I teach for ASA and IBA, I get questions from my students with respect to this first bullet on this slide that we need to keep in mind that gift taxes and estate taxes are transfer taxes. It's the ownership interest that is transferred that's being taxed, not the ownership status of the transferor pre-gift or the transfer status of the transferee post-gift.

So if you've got a controlling shareholder that's transferring a minority interest to a family member, value it as a minority interest even if the transferor still owns a controlling interest after the transfer.

Similarly, if transferring a minority interest from an elder generation to a younger generation now puts that younger generation into a control position, the transfer is a minority interest even though it puts the younger generation in a control position.

We have to remember that these are hypothetical transfers. These are transfers between hypothetical buyers and sellers. Fair market value is very clear on that. In fact, in our little practice management tip in our reports, we actually define the proper noun "Investor" as a hypothetical buyer *and* (not "or" but *and*) a hypothetical seller.

Revenue Ruling 93-12 was the result of a number of repeated failures including *Estate of Bright* on the part of the Service to effectively try to promote the family attribution argument which 93-12 now overrides and is consistent with a number of Tax Court decisions.

Here's also another little practice management tip that sounds like it may be even inconsistent with the comments I just made. The situation here is you've got an ownership interest that has two classes of securities. Maybe it's voting and non-voting stock. Maybe it's a general partnership interest and a limited partnership interest. Now this applies to estate taxes only, okay? It's not gift taxes. A gift tax falls back to the first bullet. It's the ownership interest transferred. On estate taxes, if a decedent has control of the company *and* the economic value of a non-controlling interest – so in that case, maybe non-voting stock – an appraiser must aggregate and value both ownership interest at the control level of value.

Let me be real clear, this is not for every situation where a decedent owns voting and non-voting stock or general partnership and limited partnership interest. Yes, one of those classes of securities does have superior rights over the other. But if you do not have control over the economic value of that non-controlling ownership interest, you do not have to aggregate it.

Specific example, a controlling owner makes a decision that he wants to pay out dividends as a sole general partner who has that right under the partnership agreement. Clearly, the limited partner is going to benefit from that. So if he owns a 60 percent limited partnership interest and only 1 percent general partnership interest, he's going to benefit very much from that ability to control, owning the class of securities with superior rights and being able to control the economic value of the class of securities with inferior rights.

Next slide, Blake,

This is a topic that is important to me having focused a lot of my energy over the last 20 years on S corporation issues. I think it's important for us, as a profession, to recognize that in spite of five adverse Tax Court opinions, my experience has been the challenges of tax-affecting S corporation income are rare.

If you do not tax-affect S corporation income, it's my opinion, assuming a 40 percent tax rate, that you immediately overstate the value of the ownership interest by 67 percent. That has huge tax implications for the taxpayer.

I know a lot of people out there are saying, "But there are five Tax Court rulings in favor of it." That's not enough – it really isn't enough. I can go through reasons that are beyond the scope of this presentation and I won't do it, why that isn't enough. Feel free to call me or email me and I'll be happy to tell you what those reasons are.

My personal experience, having been in a highly visible position since, I believe, 1993 on this particular issue when I first proposed the Treharne Model, I have been challenged once. That was only in the last 12 months for not tax-affecting. Ultimately, the case was settled very close to my value. It was within $300,000 of my value. So they eventually capitulated on the S corporation tax-affecting issue.

Also, I know another prominent appraiser in this profession who's done follow-on work for the *Gross* family, the *Gross* family being the original case that provided the adverse basis for not tax-affecting. He's done numerous follow-on valuations, tax-affecting S corporation income using his model and has never been challenged.

So I think it's important for appraisers to understand that and proceed with what they believe is the best economic outcome or the best economic opinion based on their knowledge.

Look at Nancy Fannon's book that has all four models in it plus her simplified model – a lot of good information out there.

Do also be aware, to tie into Jay's earlier presentation, that if you have a 40 percent tax rate, you can very easily be in a substantial valuation misstatement immediately, and if you use the models that are out there, that helps moderate some of that difference and maybe pull you out of that category of a substantial misstatement.

I have not let that deter me from tax-affecting S corporation income in using my model to do so.

Linda Trugman: Before you move on to discounts, we've got a bunch of questions that I think maybe some people are going to want answered.

Chris Treharne: Okay.

Linda Trugman: "There was a mention that the new rules (the penalty rules) are still under review. Does that mean that these penalties are not applicable yet?"

Jay Fishman: No, it doesn't. The new rules aren't final, so we're operating under the interim rules, but no, they are, in fact, operative now.

Linda Trugman: "Can you repeat what the penalties are?"

Jay Fishman: Sure. The amount of a penalty with respect to an appraisal misstatement shall be equal to the lesser of – I know it's confusing – the greater of (a) 10 percent of the amount of the underpayment attributable to the misstatement or (b) $1,000 or 125 percent of the gross income received by the person for the preparation of the appraisal.

Linda Trugman: Then the last question is, "You mentioned that Form 8283 needs to be completed for charitable gifts. Is the same form required for estate tax?"

I believe that's only associated with income tax returns, isn't it?

Jay Fishman: Yeah, well, 8283 is for non-cash charitable contributions. I do not believe there is a similar form for 706.

Linda Trugman: We've received several emails about the closing letter, and I was right, there's a closing letter for 706 but not for 709 and somebody actually sent me a redacted closing letter and that seems to be what stops the whole process basically.

As far as 709, you have a statute of limitations on 709. So I believe once the three-year statute of limitations is gone, you're okay.

But again, if you are not a tax preparer or if you are not a CPA or somebody who is dealing with taxes all the time, I would strongly suggest that you go somebody who actually specializes in that area and get the proper information.

The next question, "Is the sale of a minority interest in a family controlled entity subject to 6695A?"

Jay Fishman: Well, if the sale was based on the appraisal and they're challenging it as non-arm's length, I would think yes, but again, I'm not a tax expert – I'm not a tax lawyer.

Linda Trugman: My understanding is 6695A is it's a valuation misstatement, so if the valuation was done and the IRS says that it's not right and the range of differences in values makes it subject to a penalty, then it's subject to a penalty. I don't remember seeing any exceptions. It strictly has to do with valuation, right?

Jay Fishman: I think – I'm not sure – but I would think not.

Linda Trugman: Blake, do you want to give those codes again?

Blake Lyman: Yeah, thanks, Linda, I'll interrupt here and read our CPE codes again for today's conference. Those codes are 3642, 4109, and 8832. Once again, that's 3642, 4109, and 8832.

Linda Trugman: No problem, Blake.

"How is the Service treating the S corporation premium for 100 percent controlling issue? On this issue, does the Service treat a controlling interest any different from the minority interest?"

Chris Treharne: I don't know, but I will tell you that I have come to the conclusion after a number of discussions with my colleague, Nancy Fannon, that we should be using the S corporation models on controlling interests as well as minority interests.

In fact, if you want to muddle your brains up for the day, there are a number of studies out there that show that private transactions in C corporation businesses, there's no significant difference between C corporations and S corporations at the control level based on studies, IBA database, Pratt's Stats®, and BIZCOMPS®, I believe.

Here's the conundrum – I don't think that S corporations emulate C corporations, I think C corporations emulate S corporations, and that's why there's no difference in value.

More specifically, under the fair market value standard, the controlling shareholder again has the obligation to maximize his or her value. He or she is going to pay as much compensation as he or she can to do avoid a double taxation of company income within the IRS reasonable compensation limitations and thereby emulate an S corporation paying out excess distributions.

Jay Fishman: Linda, there's a question about where you find the 4477 letter, and it's the memorandum for all examiners, estate and gift tax attorneys, and appellate that I reference in our materials, and there's a form letter in there that has the form or the penalty letter. It's 6-2009 and it's the package. So if you get a hold of the package with the August 18, 2009 memo in it, it's connected to that.

It says, "We are proposing a penalty under Internal Revenue Code Section 6695A, Substantial and Gross Valuation Misstatements Attributable to Incorrect Appraisals. This penalty is based on our review of the appraisal(s) relating to a federal tax matter that you prepared on behalf of the taxpayer(s) named above. We have scheduled a meeting to give you an opportunity to discuss the facts or legal arguments you or your representative may present to the Service in considering the appropriateness of the penalty."

That's a soft letter. You're going to knock me out with it. I hope I don't ever get one.

Linda Trugman: That makes three of us, I would say.

Chris Treharne: Yep.

Jay Fishman: Hopefully, they'll change the procedure.

Linda Trugman: I didn't ask this before, and I haven't seen anybody else ask it – am I correct that pretty much all of the organizations that were represented at that IRS meeting on August 18, 2009 pretty much took the same positions –

Jay Fishman: Yes.

Linda Trugman: With respect to most of this? So there's consensus in the profession about all of this –

Jay Fishman: Yes.

Linda Trugman: Of the penalties and the 4477 letter and all that?

Jay Fishman: Correct, I think that's a fair statement.

Linda Trugman: All right, next question, "Is there any empirical method for estimating control discounts that is generally accepted or recommended by the IRS?"

I've never heard of anything.

Chris Treharne: I'm unaware of any other than just doing the research you need to do.

Linda Trugman: I think towards that question, where we can, a lot of us try and do it, at least on an operating company, through the cash flow, and then we don't have to worry about control premiums or lack of control discounts.

Chris Treharne: I think that's an important point to make, Linda, that maybe we gloss over. In our shop, we differentiate between valuing a holding company and an operating company. When we're valuing a holding company, we often use lack of control discounts to value minority interests because that's how the market data is presented. However, when we're valuing an operating company, we very seldom use lack of control discounts, and instead, adjust the minority interest income and/or cash flow streams to reflect the cash flow available to the minority owner and that gives us a direct to minority interest valuation. There's a lack of control discount required in that latter method.

Jay Fishman: This gives me an opportunity to comment on some articles I read suggesting that merger arbitrage be the best proxy – everything is a proxy these days – for discounts for lack of marketability. Merger arbitrage is when a company is trading at 7and then there's an announcement that it's being sold at 9. Over time, it's supposed to approach that 9.

I do not believe that it is good proxy. I think the difference between those kinds of imperfections, by and large, is due diligence risks. They're not liquidity risks.

Chris Treharne: I think a follow-on to that, Jay, too is one study was done on one year's data in the Mergerstat® database probably 10, 15 years ago now that showed that 40 percent of the companies acquired in that year of data subsequently were resold at a loss, which mean they were purchased for too much.

Jay Fishman: In finance, it's called the buyer's curse.

Chris Treharne: They spend a lot of money to show that that happens regularly.

Jay Fishman: Someone asked about IRS recognition of SSVS (Statement on Standards for Valuation Services) and USPAP. It's clear to me the IRS is not going to recognize anything as *the* standard. In fact, when Howard Lewis was the program manager, they created their own set of standards. I believe that SSVS conforms to the substance and principles of USPAP. So I think that's about as general as they're going to get.

Linda Trugman: There's another question that just came in, "Could you please comment on what S corporation models are the most appropriate to use? Is there any consensus on the use of the SEAM (S Corporation Economic Adjustment Model) model?"

I think we have to table that one.

Chris Treharne: That's a program in itself. They're all good.

Linda Trugman: Besides that, I think what you have to do is you've got to investigate all of them and know the strengths and weaknesses of all of them and make a determination in your own firm as to which one you feel you can best use and support. You've got to be able to explain what you're doing. They all work but they all have nuances as well. So you just have to make a determination.

You've got the author of one of the models on the phone so how are any of us going to turn around and say, "Oh, no, his isn't better – this one's better?" It's not a better or worse. They're all legitimate models and you have to understand all of them and figure out which one you're going to use.

Chris Treharne: All of them are fundamentally sound. All of them have some nuances to them. I will tell you in our practice, we, of course, routinely use the Treharne Model, but we have also used the Treharne Model in combination with SEAM, and that's no put-down on Mercer's model or Grabowski's model. They're equally valid. They all have a lot of commonality to them and it's just really the method of implementation, the procedures you use, and your ability to be able to defend that in a coherent manner should it get challenged.

Linda Trugman: I had asked the question about the control discounts. I think we've answered this but, "If a 30 percent interest is gifted to a person who already owns a 30 percent interest, would it be correct to apply a control premium, a control discount, or neither?"

I think that goes back to Chris' explanation of the fact that this is a transfer tax of the hypothetical buyer and seller and you should be valuing it as a 30 percent interest.

There may be swing values somewhere along the lines depending upon what the rest of the ownership looks like, so that might cause a difference in what you do.

Chris Treharne: Sure. If the 30 percent is all voting stock, it would be valued as a controlling interest if there is no other voting stock. There are a lot of "if" and "it depends" issues, but generally speaking, recalling that gift and estate taxes are transfer taxes between a hypothetical buyer and a hypothetical seller, one would value the 30 percent interest typically as a non-controlling ownership interest with consideration given to lack of control and lack of marketability discounts.

Linda Trugman: We've got a follow-up on the "unity of interest" theory.

"The 'unity of interest' theory of an estate tax valuation holds that all interest in an entity includable in the *Gross* estate must be added together and valued as a unitary holding. For example, in connection with a family limited partnership where a decedent owns a controlling voting interest in the FLP, as well as LP interest lacking control, the two interests must be aggregated as a unitary controlling interest. In the FLP, the result is to eliminate any minority interest discount for the LP interest. Is there a defense to this?"

I don't think there is. There's actually case law on that particular subject and I don't know the citation right off hand.

It's different in a gift, but in an estate, if there's a controlling voting interest and then a non-voting interest, they're supposed to be combined as one big control interest. That's my understanding.

Chris Treharne: For estate tax purposes only, yes.

Jay Fishman: It's the *Estate of Curry*.

Chris Treharne: Actually, *Ahmanson Foundation v. United States* was where it was originally addressed, and then *Estate of Curry* affirmed it. That's a Tax Court decision instead of U.S. District Court, and it accepted the U.S. District Court's opinion in *Ahmanson Foundation*. It's actually not in the body of the text of *Curry*. It's in a footnote. It's footnote number 8 or footnote number 13 in *Curry*. So don't look for it in the body of the text because it's not there – it's in a footnote.

Thank you, Jay, you're right.

Linda Trugman: Okay, another S corporation question is, "Real estate holding company has always been an S corporation. Owner died owning 100 percent of the stock. Real estate lots inside the S corporation have appreciated greatly so you have built-in gains. Anyone buying the stock of the S corporation will now get a stepped-up basis in the lots. Can you take valuation adjustment for the built-in gains tax?"

Chris Treharne: The answer to that is the answer that we're faced with on every valuation assignment. You have to look at every assignment, and if you think there's an economic basis for your conclusion, then go with it.

Sorry to be so vague but that's it – I don't think there's enough facts there to really give a conclusive opinion.

Linda Trugman: Yeah, and I think that a lot of us wrestle with, when we're dealing with pass-through entities that have big built-in gains, exactly how we handle them. So I think Chris is right – it's a valuation by valuation issue.

Blake, if you'll move on to the next slide, I think that there's probably a lot of interest in this issue.

Jay and I participated in Judge Laro's tax conference in October 2009 out in San Diego and Chris was there. There are clearly a lot of issues having to do with discounts for lack of marketability and Judge Laro seems to want us, the valuation community as a whole, to come up with one specific way that we're all going to agree to apply discounts for lack of marketability so that there's less judgment in it and the Tax Courts don't really have to deal with this issue anymore. I think the consensus at the end of the day back in October 2009 was, "Nope, that's not going to happen." So we thought we would kind of throw it out there and just talk a little bit about discounts for lack of marketability.

Chris, do you want to get started?

Chris Treharne: Yes, look at the slide that's up here. I want you, just as an overview, to note that there is a relationship between the two red-letter portions of the text.

I've been concerned in a number of Tax Court rulings that I've read that said that the Court was going to rely on the most recent studies, which happen to be the 2000 Columbia Financial Advisors' studies, which have since been supplanted, so don't let me get off this slide, Linda, without giving Trugman Valuation Associates a plug.

The 2000 Columbia Financial Advisors' restricted stock study came with a 13 percent marketability discount.

We have to keep in mind here and we have to take responsibility for this, that we have failed the Tax Court in that we have failed to properly educate the Tax Court.

Here's an attempt at education more specifically. The Columbia Financial Advisors' result of 13 percent DLOM (discount for lack of marketability) represents transactions with a one-year holding period under Rule 144A. They say, "Well, these are the most recent studies that have been done so we'll rely on those rather than these really high discounts that were from the original restricted stock study, Revenue Ruling 77-287, which is, depending on who you want to talk to, 33 percent for small companies."

The various other restricted stock studies that have average discounts from 33 to 35 percent net range, well, those discounts, the Tax Court said, are no longer relevant because they're old. I disagree and I think it's important for us to make this argument in our reports.

Actually, a little side bar here too, for those of who aren't familiar with gift and estate tax appraisals, recognize that your report is your direct testimony in Tax Court. If you do not make a point in your report that is favorable to your client, your client's attorney cannot bring that point up in court except on cross-examination, which means that the IRS has to bring it up, and clearly, if it's in your client's favor, the IRS is not going to bring it up. So your report is your direct testimony in Tax Court.

Make sure your reports are complete and have all the information in them that they need. This is a specific recommendation from me that you need to have this discussion with regard to the most recent DLOM study from Columbia Financial. That's a one-year holding period.

All of the other studies are two-year holding periods. Some of the two-year studies, under Rule 144A, in fact, have also much a bigger market, so much greater demand than under Rule 144, which is what the original restricted stock studies are based upon.

Original restricted stock discounts are at 33, 35 percent range. Once they increase the number of eligible investors, qualified institutional investors, the discounts decrease to the numbers you see here in the table – 27.7, 26.7, 21, 21.

Columbia Financial Advisors reflects a one-year holding period. So if you compound their 13 percent to two years, you get a 24.3 percent average discount, which is very consistent with the other two-year holding period studies.

Again, I think if you make the point in your report that yes, the Columbia Financial Advisors study is relevant, but we have to adjust it and recognize that it's got a one-year holding period where the other studies have two-year holding periods, and, in the case of the original Rule 144, a much smaller marketplace because the number of qualified institutional investors was increased when Rule 144 became Rule 144A.

My opinion is all of these restricted stock studies are consistent and we should be making a point in our reports of informing the Tax Court the reliance on the most recent Columbia Financial Advisors' study is not at all inconsistent with the prior restricted stock studies.

If you think your minority interest isn't going to be liquid within two years, you ought to be looking at least at 26, 27 percent – 33, 35 percent discounts to begin making your adjustments if you're using a *Mandelbaum* analysis.

Just to be clear, if those of you who are not familiar with *Mandelbaum*, that is a Tax Court decision, Judge Laro, I believe, 1996. If you're not familiar with it, you're doing gift and estate tax work and you're using marketability discounts, I strongly recommend that you find that ruling and study it.

With that, Linda, let me take a little deviation here. Your firm just completed a study on marketability discounts, a more current study, and it was published in the most recent issue of *Business Valuation Review*, which just came out last week. So why don't you give us a little oversight of that and what the conclusion was that your firm came up with?

Linda Trugman: I really wasn't part of that. We've got an analyst in our office who primarily handled that, but I do know the study was done after the holding period was changed to six months, and, of course, it was during the period of time where the market was going a little bit crazy. Our average discount came out to be 18.1 percent. Primarily, what we found drove the discount was market volatility.

It's interesting because when we did our presentation last year, we were all asked to use different models and different methods. One of the things that I did that's not on this slide but worth bringing up is I was asked to come up with discounts for lack of marketability using the Valuation Advisors Pre-IPO database and the FMV Opinions' Discount for Lack of Marketability Restricted Stock Study. What I found is that there was a not great deal of correlation in the underlying data and the discounts that you came up with, and we found that to be very similar. I think that's the reason why the Tax Courts are having such a problem with this whole benchmarking, that there's not a lot of relationship in the data and that a lot of these companies that issue restricted stock don't even have earnings. So how do we make them comparable to our subject company? That's why I believe they're looking for us to quantify things a little bit more.

What we've started doing in our shop, even on estate and gift tax valuations at this point, is we're starting to look at various stock option models and we're benchmarking but we are trying to support it with some type of an option pricing model.

Jay Fishman: Can I ask a question or two here?

Chris Treharne: Absolutely.

Linda Trugman: Absolutely.

Jay Fishman: It's about estate and gift tax valuation. My friend, Joe Vinzo [sp], has raised two, I thought, pretty interesting points. The first point he made was when the three of us had a discussion about Pratt's Stats® and the multiples, whether they're control, whether they have marketability, whether they don't have marketability. We came to somewhat different answers. Now some of that was a function of us not knowing the facts. But his point is that's the nature of business valuation as well. I'm older than both of you combined probably and we have more of a body of knowledge now than we've ever had, but to say that's there a unified body of knowledge and say, "This is the way it is," I think is problematic. So when the IRS has to determine what's the proper value, that's a real daunting task.

The second point he makes, just to summarize it, is it a level playing field? That is, is my counterpart, either the field specialist or the appraiser or the tax examiner, are we working off that same body of knowledge?

One of the areas that we fear is abusive is that this whole 6695A – and my friend, Chuck Rettig, could talk about this more than I – could be used as leverage in a negotiation, and that's really problematic. If that happens, you should report to the supervisor, and that's very interesting academically, but if you're sitting there in the trench and somebody does that, you have to do what you think is in your best interest and your client's best interest to be ethical.

The other thing I found is that some of the field specialists are not trained in the areas that they're supposed to be trained in, and there's a tax examination that went on in the West Coast where the field specialist was a BV person and they were opining as to a real estate issue.

A couple of the things that I've talked to the IRS about is renewing this Valuation Policy Council and having more outreach with the professional appraisal community so that we can all work on the same body of knowledge and then the disagreements can be narrowed into those judgments. The disagreements may be narrowed but not the quantum of the disagreements.

The other thing I've suggested is some kind of peer review. If these cases are as egregious as they say they are, then if somebody sends me an appraisal, I don't need to know the name. It can be redacted. They can send the facts and we can talk about them. Then I want them out of the business as well.

Those are two suggestions that I've had discussions about where I think it might mitigate the problems a little bit, a kind of peer review board or something like that, so that it takes at least some degree of a judge, jury, and prosecutor out of the process.

So those are two things I saw that came up that I thought were pretty good points.

Chris Treharne: Yeah, I agree with what Jay has said and I'd just like to more emphatically say at this time that I think we're looking for a silver bullet on this marketability discount issue, in particular, and it's certainly, I think, a general issue with the uncertainty of business valuation. But we're looking for a silver bullet for the DLOM that I don't think exists.

Jay Fishman: That's what came out in our San Diego conference pretty much.

Chris Treharne: Yeah, we have to continue to do the best we can, come up with a supportable conclusion, but I don't know of a silver bullet.

Linda Trugman: Is anybody using LEAPS (Long-Term Equity Anticipation Securities)?

Chris Treharne: Am I? No, there is an ASA webinar coming up this month or next month. I've been reading about LEAPS. I want to incorporate them into our analysis. I want to incorporate the Longstaff Look-Back Put Option.

We currently use a *Mandelbaum* analysis, a ten-point *Mandelbaum* subjective adjustment procedure.

We then also use, which is another bullet point on the slide that's up, the QMDM (Quantifying Marketability Discount Model) to support our subjective *Mandelbaum* analysis. We use the QMDM a little different than Chris Mercer and his group in that we use it to overcome what I consider the objections in the Tax Court cases where it's appeared. We use an Extreme Analysis on the variables that affect the choice of a marketability discount and then we come up with a minimum number.

Jay Fishman: You use it to set the limits.

Chris Treharne: Yeah, exactly. We feel like if we come up with these extreme numbers out of the five variables that are used in QMDM and it gives us a minimum of a four-year holding period, and we don't have any expectation that that interest is going to be sold within four years or could be liquidated within four years, we feel comfortable with our *Mandelbaum* subjective conclusion. That's the way I intend to use LEAPS, the Longstaff Look-Back Put Option, and any other I use. I think that's the only way we can do it today. There's no magic bullet.

Linda Trugman: Yeah, I agree. I think that just saying the average studies have been 25 to 40 percent and, therefore, we're using 35 percent is not enough.

Chris Treharne: Or worse yet, that the case law says. We're not attorneys.

Linda Trugman: Yeah, right.

Chris Treharne: Don't cite case law. We're not attorneys.

Linda Trugman: It's just like the S corporation issue. I think the best advice we can give to the listeners on the call is you've got to learn what there is to know about as many of these different models as possible and put them in place to test them. But make sure that you understand them before you start putting them in your report. I think that's the biggest problem. If you're just going to run a bunch of mathematical models and throw them all into a report and say, "therefore," you're not helping yourself. But I do think that that's where we're going to have to go with it.

I know I saw in *BVWire* last week that Mercer Capital used QMDM in a case – and there are a number of these cases out there, I think – where the Service believed that legally, they were going to have these transactions go away. The family limited partnership was going to all get thrown back into the estate. So they never questioned the discount. So when it came time for the case, the discount didn't get challenged.

I don't know, though, folks, when you see those kinds of things, that you can automatically say, "Well, they were able to use QMDM and they got away with the 50 percent discount. Therefore, the courts have now accepted QMDM." I'm not saying that they haven't but I don't think that that's a blatant acceptance of the model. If they don't question the discount and they don't talk about the discount, then I don't think that that's just their way of saying, "We were okay with it." I think it's really that the Service didn't argue it in the particular case where it came up.

Chris Treharne: Linda, why don't we move on? I want to throw out just one more comment and let's move on to the next slide here.

In addition to the Trugman study, there's Management Planning, Inc. Their winter 2009 newsletter perspectives indicated that they completed a study from 2000 to 2007, isolated 1,600 transactions. The average discount for those 1,600 transactions was 14.6 percent. So again, this is a one-year holding period. This is not a six-month holding period or two-year holding period.

For the roughly 100 companies whose privately placed stock was registered – if it's registered, that's one obstacle that's already been overcome to marketability – the average discount was 9.5 percent. We'd expect it to be lower than the average.

For the roughly 200 companies whose stock was unregistered, the average discount, however, was 18.7 percent, which is consistent with the Trugman study.

The bottom line is, I think, again, if you do a good job of explaining the one-year studies versus the two-year studies versus a more limited marketplace, you can easily justify starting at 33 to 35 percent as your benchmark for your *Mandelbaum* analysis.

Blake, do you want to move on?

Linda Trugman: I'm sure everybody in every marketplace that's represented on this phone call is dealing with the attorneys who are looking for "cheap." They only want a "discount letter." They only want a "calculation." They want "short and sweet" and "cheap." I don't even know that they're looking for "qualified appraisals" anymore. I don't know that they're looking for "supportable conclusions of value." They're looking for "cheap." So we thought we would throw a slide in there to talk about whether or not "calculations" and "discount letters" meet adequate disclosure and whether or not you're serving yourself as well as your client well by doing that type of work.

Jay Fishman: All I know is if you do a letter and the client relies upon it and there's tax examination, they're going to use it to back up their discount. That's subject to these penalties.

Chris Treharne: I think appraisers are putting themselves in jeopardy if they do "letter appraisals" or "discount letters" or "calculations." They don't comply with Revenue Ruling 59-60. They don't comply with USPAP. They don't comply with BV standards. I think you're putting yourself in personal jeopardy.

Linda Trugman: We've got about five minutes or so left so I thought maybe we could try and get through a couple more of the questions that have come in.

"I've seen rules that require a qualified appraisal for charitable gifts. Are qualified appraisals also required for estate and gift taxes?"

Chris Treharne: I think Jay said that is the case, correct, Jay?

Jay Fishman: No, it's not the case. The PPA rules apply only to charitable contributions.

Chris Treharne: I thought you said the SSVS extended to gift and estate.

Jay Fishman: They extended the penalties to estate and gift. Again, I'm not a tax lawyer. That was another thing, that 6695A is extended to income tax, estate and gift tax. The rule that it has to be a qualified appraiser doing a qualified appraisal I do not believe has been extended to it. I don't think that's relevant anyway. If you're going to be subject to these penalties, then it seems to me that you want to be doing a qualified appraisal.

Chris Treharne: As a practice management issue, follow Jay's recommendation. There's no other choice.

Linda Trugman: I don't know why you wouldn't want to be a qualified appraiser doing a qualified appraisal. Essentially, what that means is that you're trained and you're following standards and you know what you're doing. I would think that that's at least a head start to heading off some of these penalties. There's never a guarantee. But if you're not qualified to do this work, you probably shouldn't be doing it.

Jay Fishman: I would submit that in order to prove that it's "more likely than not" the correct value, the starting point should be an appraisal that subscribes to somebody's standards. They're all pretty much the same anyway. I think that would be the step in the right direction.

Linda Trugman: "Is there a requirement to include an appraisal declaration in an appraisal report stating, 'appraiser understands an appraisal for tax purposes may be subject to a penalty?'"

Jay Fishman: I do not believe that there's such a certification for anything other than non-cash charitable contributions. I believe Form 8283 only applies to that.

Chris Treharne: Even though your statement is correct, Jay, we do in our reports, and I don't recall where I heard that, whether it was in an ASA conference or something, that we should include it even though the form does apply to just charitable gifts. I do it just to cover my backside, just as a practice management issue.

Linda Trugman: That's interesting. We don't do that.

I think we answered this, "Is the valuation of a minority interest in a family controlled entity for purposes of a sale subject to 6695A?" That one, we talked about already.

The one topic that we didn't get to that we might want to – Blake, if you can move on – is the "fact or fiction" question.

Chris Treharne: Good one, yes.

Linda Trugman: Probably we have all heard that the Internal Revenue Service will not allow discounts above 30 percent. I've heard 25 percent at times. There are all kinds of rumors out there about what the Service will and won't allow.

Frankly, when it comes to holding companies, I think we all know that what Treasury or whoever is in charge wants to do is just disallow discounts on those types of entities because it would raise tax dollars for them.

I think it's more an issue of if it's more than 25 percent, you can expect an argument. I don't think that they've come out and said something like that.

So I went through some Tax Court cases. Most of them are Tax Court memos. A couple of them are District cases. We've got three slides of cases, cases that have clearly allowed discounts of more than 30 percent.

I am not suggesting, and I think we probably made this pretty clear, that you should not be relying on Tax Court cases. The facts and circumstances of every case are different. But I think if you go back and you read some of these cases and see why certain things were accepted and why certain things were not accepted, it may help give you some ideas of how to support your discounts in your report.

For example, on the second slide, if you look at the very top one, the *Miller* case, "overall discount of 35 percent – not disputed," that's exactly what I was referring to when I was talking about the QMDM a few minutes ago.

If the Service does not raise the issue of discounts because they're convinced that they're going to be able to do away with the family limited partnership under Code Section 2036 or something like that, it does not mean that they're accepting the 35 percent discount. It just means that it was raised as an issue.

I don't know what kinds of experiences you've been having, Chris and Jay, with IRS reports and discounts.

Chris Treharne: I have had very favorable experiences. I have taken some very severe discounts, 72 percent on a 38 percent common stock interest settled at 69 percent. I have had closing letters at 67 percent and 65 percent, settlements at 67, 65 percent.

Linda Trugman: It's facts and circumstances driven.

Chris Treharne: Absolutely.

Jay Fishman: 1-800-call Treharne.

Chris Treharne: My staff is listening in the other room and they know that I'm pretty anal so our reports are pretty detailed and substantial.

We do a lot of farm and ranch work, entities that own farm and ranch property. The minority interest in those, we had one that was worth $12 million net asset value, the 38 percent common stock interest. Its best year would have generated $200,000 in net income.

I think this is what won the settlement for us, is the argument we use, that a minority investor would be better off investing in short-term Treasury bills. It would have less risk and a higher rate of return – not even Treasury bonds – Treasury bills.

Linda Trugman: On that note, I think we have pretty much run out of time. I do know that we did not get to all of the questions, and so we will try and get back to BV Resources with answers to those, and they will post them up on the website that had all of the reading materials. Of course, you can always continue to send questions and we will try and do what we can to answer whatever we can.

We thank you all for coming.

Blake?

Blake Lyman: Well, thank you, Linda, and thank you, Jay, and thank you, Chris. If you do have any further questions for the panel today, please send them to us via email at *tc-questions@bvresources.com*. That's *tc-questions@bvesources.com*. We'll go ahead and collect answers from our panelists and post them to our reading page, as Linda mentioned. We'll also send out an email notification as soon as those are available.

As a reminder, to receive your CPE credits for today's teleconference, you must complete and submit our brief survey at the conclusion of the teleconference. A link to that survey is provided in your dial-in instructions email and on the reading page for today's teleconference.

Please allow five business days for those CPE surveys to be processed, at which point we will distribute CPE certificates via email.

Once again, today's three four-digit CPE codes are 3642, 4109, and 8832. Once again, that's 3642, 4109, and 8832.

Transcripts and recordings of this and all teleconferences are available via our On-Demand Packs. You can find more information on teleconference On-Demand Packs at *bvresources.com/training* where you can also find more information on future BVR teleconferences, webinars, and live events.

If you have any questions related to the content or format of this teleconference, please email BVR at *tc-questions@bvresources.com*. That's *tc-questions@bvresesources.com*.

Thank you. You may now disconnect.

Valuation Issues in Estate & Gift Tax

BVR
What It's Worth

Business Valuation Resources, LLC
(888) 287-8258 or (503) 291-7963
www.BVResources.com

Linda Trugman
CPA/ABV, MCBA, ASA, MBA | Trugman Valuation Associates, Inc.
Jay Fishman
FASA | Financial Research Associates
Chris D. Treharne
ASA, MCBA, BVAL | Gibraltar Business Appraisals, Inc.

Send questions to:
TC-Questions@BVResources.com

Disclaimers

- IRS Circular 230 Notice: To ensure compliance with requirements imposed by the IRS, we inform you that any U.S. tax advice contained in this communication (or in any attachment) is not intended or written to be used, and cannot be used, for the purpose of (i) avoiding penalties under the Internal Revenue Code or (ii) promoting, marketing, or recommending to another party any transaction or matter addressed in this communication (or in any attachment).

- While today's panel may discuss factors that reflect legal positions, they are business appraisers and not lawyers. Attendees to today's conference and those viewing the archived materials produced today should rely on legal advice from qualified attorneys.

- Comments made in this presentation are intended for general use and may not apply to a specific valuation assignment.

Send questions to: TC-Questions@BVResources.com

2

Valuation Issues in Estate & Gift Tax

Overview

- The Times They Are A-Changing

Send questions to: TC-Questions@BVResources.com

3

Valuation Issues in Estate & Gift Tax

Statutory Authority

- American Jobs Creation Act of 2004 (AJCA of 2004)
- Pension Protection Act of 2006 (PPA of 2006)
- Small Business and Work Opportunity Tax Act of 2007 (SBWOTA of 2007)

Send questions to: TC-Questions@BVResources.com

4

Valuation Issues in Estate & Gift Tax

Requirements

- IRS to redefine the term "Qualified Appraiser" and "Qualified Appraisal"
- Implement Tax Preparer Penalty Provisions under IRC Section 6694
- Implement Penalty Provisions under IRC Section 6695A for substantial and Gross Valuation Misstatements

Send questions to: TC-Questions@BVResources.com 5

Valuation Issues in Estate & Gift Tax

•CONGRESS PASSES LAWS THAT EXPLAIN ITS INTENT IN BROAD TERMS SO IMPLENTATION IS DONE BY RULES AND REGUALTIONS PROMULGATED BY TREASURY AND INTERNAL REVENUE SERVICE

Send questions to: TC-Questions@BVResources.com 6

Valuation Issues in Estate & Gift Tax

Regulations

- **Proposed Final Regulations for Charitable Contribution Deductions (August 7, 2008)**
  - Sets thresholds information necessary to substantiate deductions for non-cash charitable contributions
  - Provides definitions of "Qualified Appraisal" and "Qualified Appraiser"

Send questions to: TC-Questions@BVResources.com 7

Valuation Issues in Estate & Gift Tax

Regulations (con't)

- **Final Regulations Implementing Amendments to Tax Preparer Penalties under Section 6694 and 6695A of the IRC (December 2008)**
  - Appraisers are Non Signing Tax Preparers
  - Penalties Will Not Be Stacked
  - Penalties
  - Definitions of "Realistic Possibility", "Substantial Authority", and "More Likely than Not"

Send questions to: TC-Questions@BVResources.com 8

Valuation Issues in Estate & Gift Tax

Regulations (con't)

- **Code Section 6695A and SBSE Memorandum 04-0809-015 "Penalty for Valuation Misstatements Attributable to Incorrect Appraisals"**
  - Imposition of Penalty, Amount of Penalty, and Exceptions or Safe Harbors
  - Penalty Assessment Procedure
    - Separate and distinct case
    - Develop facts and circumstances
    - Penalties not proposed in the presence of the taxpayer
    - Penalty not proposed until related tax examination is complete at the group level
  - Use of Field Specialists

Send questions to: TC-Questions@BVResources.com 9

Valuation Issues in Estate & Gift Tax

Controversies

- Use of percentage tests for all assets
- How is "correct" or "proper" value determined, and by whom?
- What does "more likely than not" mean in a valuation context?
- Issuance of the so called "appointment" or "soft letter" 4477 prior to having the appraiser explain their reasoning and associated intended or unintended consequences
- The *McCord* factor
- Use of the rule as leverage

Send questions to: TC-Questions@BVResources.com 10

Valuation Issues in Estate & Gift Tax

General Comment

- During today's presentation references may be made to family limited partnerships (FLPs). Those comments may also apply to LLCs, and possibly corporations.

Send questions to: TC-Questions@BVResources.com

11

Valuation Issues in Estate & Gift Tax

Points to remember in Gift Tax vs. Estate Tax

- Gift and Estate taxes are transfer taxes
  - Valuation should only consider the *transferred* ownership interest, *not* the total pre- or post-ownership interests of the transferor or transferee
- Issues *specific to estate taxes*:
  - If an ownership interest has control of the company *and* the economic value of the noncontrolling interest, an appraiser must aggregate and value both ownership interests at the control level of value
- Fair Market Value (FMV) considerations:
  - Remember that FMV is defined as a transaction between a *hypothetical* buyer *and* (not "or") seller. In the case of a transfer between family members, the relationship between the parties should not be considered (Rev. Rul. 93-12, *Estate of Bright*)

Send questions to: TC-Questions@BVResources.com

12

Valuation Issues in Estate & Gift Tax

S-Corp Tax Affecting

- In spite of five adverse Tax Court opinions, challenges of tax affecting S corp income are rare
- If challenged:
  - Tax affecting S-corp income may put the appraiser into a substantial misstatement category unless some of the recommended adjustments between S and C corps are made
    - (e.g. dividend tax and income tax adjustments, plus basis build-up, if appropriate)
  - Of course, challenges to other parts of the appraisal (e.g. DLOM) might push an appraiser over the substantial valuation misstatement threshold even if the recommended S corp adjustments are made

Send questions to: TC-Questions@BVResources.com 13

 Valuation Issues in Estate & Gift Tax

Discounts for Lack of Marketability

- Contrary to recent Tax Court rulings, the 2000 Columbia Financial restricted stock study's 13% DLOM (1-year holding period, 1997-1998 data) reflects the impact of holding periods on DLOMs, not fundamental changes in magnitude of the discounts
- SEC Rule 144A restricted stock DLOM studies (two-year holding period):
  - Columbia Financial (1997-1998 data) 2-year *compounded DLOM* 24.3%
  - MPI (1980-1995 data) 27.7%
  - Columbia Financial (1990-1995 data from MPI study, above) 26.7%
  - Hall & Pollack (1991-1992 data) 21%
  - Johnson (1991-1995 data) 21%
- Recognizing the smaller pool of qualified institutional investors associated with Rule 144 (versus Rule 144A), it's not difficult to make a leap to the 33%-35% benchmark (derived from Rev. Rul. 77-287 and the original Rule 144 restricted stock studies) many appraisers use for a *Mandelbaum* analysis.
- Are the now dated pre-IPO DLOM studies still useful benchmarks?
- What quantitative tools are being used, if any, to justify a *Mandelbaum* analysis DLOM?
- In spite of its Tax Court criticisms, is the QMDM a useful tool?

Send questions to: TC-Questions@BVResources.com 14

 Valuation Issues in Estate & Gift Tax

Discount Letters and Qualified Appraisals

- Are "discount letters" "qualified appraisals"?
  - Do they comply with Revenue Ruling 59-60, USPAP or BV standards?
- Are calculations qualified appraisals, and do they meet the Adequate Disclosure Regulations?
- Importance of complying with the Adequate Disclosure Regulations

Send questions to: TC-Questions@BVResources.com 15

Valuation Issues in Estate & Gift Tax

The IRS and Discounts

- The Internal Revenue Service will not allow discounts above 30%:

- Fact or Fiction?

Send questions to: TC-Questions@BVResources.com 16

Valuation Issues in Estate & Gift Tax

Valuation Discounts

- *Astleford* (TCM 2008-128): Tiered real estate
  - Court allowed an absorption discount on 1,187 acres
  - 30 percent discount on 50 percent interest in GP
  - FLP interest
    - DLOC – 16 and 17.5 percent
    - DLOM – 22 percent
- *Holman* (130 T.C. No. 12): Dell stock
  - DLOC – 11.32, 14.34 and 4.63 percent
  - DLOM – 12.5 percent
- *Gross* (TCM 2008-221 – not the S corp case): Marketable securities
  - 35 percent overall discount – not disputed

Send questions to: TC-Questions@BVResources.com 17

 Valuation Issues in Estate & Gift Tax

Valuation Discounts

- *Miller* (TCM 2009-119): Marketable securities
  - Overall discount of 35 percent – not disputed
- *Keller* (Civil Action No. V-02-62): Bonds
  - 47.51 percent
- *Murphy* (Case No. 07-CV-1013): Interest in various entities
  - LP interest – 41 percent
    - Restricted stock/blockage discount – 5, 10.6, 1.3 percent
    - DLOC – 12.5 percent
    - DLOM – 32.5 percent
  - GP interest –DLOC – 20 percent
  - Minority interest in GP interest
    - DLOC – 11.1 percent
    - DLOM – 32.5 percent

Send questions to: TC-Questions@BVResources.com 18

 Valuation Issues in Estate & Gift Tax

Valuation Discounts

From Litchfield v. Commissioner – T.C. Memo 2009-21
Asset holding company (S corp.)

	Estate's Expert	IRS's Expert	Judge's Ruling
LRC			
Built-in Gains Taxes	17.4%	2.0%	17.4%
Lack of Control	14.8%	10.0%	14.8%
Lack of Marketability	36.0%	18.0%	25.0%
LRS			
Built-in Gains Taxes	23.6%	8.0%	23.6%
Lack of Control	11.9%	5.0%	11.9%
Lack of Marketability	29.7%	10.0%	20.0%

Send questions to: TC-Questions@BVResources.com

19

BVR Valuation Issues in Estate & Gift Tax

Additional considerations, time permitting

- Real estate limited partnerships (RELPs):
  - What discounts are appropriate for RELPs?
  - When should REITs be used to value real estate FLPs versus actual RELP transaction data?
  - Recognizing that the RELP data is disappearing, how can it be used?
  - Is using Partnership Profiles Annual Discount Study appropriate for a valuation date many months after the guideline RELP transaction dates?
  - Do RELP discounts include DLOM?
- Should cash, or a portion of it, be discounted when using a P/NAV method for a FLP owning marketable securities or cash?
  - What methodologies should be employed in determining an appropriate discount?

Send questions to: TC-Questions@BVResources.com

20

BVR Valuation Issues in Estate & Gift Tax

Additional considerations, time permitting

- Utilizing FLPs in Estate Planning (Section 2036)
  - Some Tax Court rulings have disallowed FLP transfers because they are not bona fide sales, yet FLPs are still an effective estate planning tool when properly employed
  - Key indicators which may exclude an FLP from being considered a bona fide sale:
    - Commingling personal and entity assets
      - Taxpayer dependence on partnership assets for living expenses
      - Taxpayer treating FLP property (house) as if personally owned
    - Improper sequencing of formation, capitalization, and subsequent transfers of partnership interests
    - Improper transfer of property to an FLP upon formation
    - Disproportionate distribution of partnership assets to owners
    - Implied agreements among partners

Send questions to: TC-Questions@BVResources.com 21

Valuation Issues in Estate & Gift Tax

Practice management considerations

- Leave lawyering to the lawyers:
  - An expert's job is to inform the judge or jury of his/her BV (not legal) opinions
  - Assist the client's attorney (who is not your attorney) with preparation, but don't offer legal opinions

- Marketing opportunity: *Estate of Williams* says that business appraisers may be qualified to value tenant-in-common real estate interests ("poor man's FLP"). These may be valued as LP interests (per Pratt).

- Oil & gas partnership interests: If using a P/NAV method, be sure to recognize that the guideline partnership's NAV is based on the present value of proven reserves (not total reserves) discounted at a 10% discount rate

Send questions to: TC-Questions@BVResources.com 22

Valuation Issues in Estate & Gift Tax

Valuation Issues in Estate & Gift Tax
UNITED STATES
BVR
What It's Worth
Business Valuation Resources, LLC
(888) 287-8258 or (503) 291-7963
www.BVResources.com
Linda Trugman
CPA/ABV, MCBA, ASA, MBA | Trugman Valuation Associates, Inc.
Jay Fishman
FASA | Financial Research Associates
Chris D. Treharne
ASA, MCBA, BVAL | Gibraltar Business Appraisals, Inc.
BVR
© 2010, Business Valuation Resources, LLC
Send questions to:
TC-Questions@BVResources.com

Shielding Your FLPs and FLLCs Against IRS Attack

Moderator: George Hawkins
Speakers: Spencer Jeffries, Bruce Johnson, and Stephanie Loomis-Price

Excerpts from Business Valuation Resources' June 1, 2005 telephone conference transcript. The entire telephone conference transcript can be found online.

G. Hawkins: First of all, my first question to you would be, in what areas has the IRS successfully challenged partnerships in the last couple of years?

S. Loomis-Price: In about the last five years or so, in addition to the split-the-baby on valuation issues that we've seen consistently from the courts, most recently, the IRS has had some limited success attacking partnerships under Section 2036 of the Internal Revenue Code, which is a part of the Chapter 14 enactment that you were referencing earlier. Section 2036 is what estate planners call a "string statute." In essence, if you transfer assets to a partnership or to an LLC, but keep certain kinds of strings attached, the Internal Revenue Code states that the transferred assets are included in your estate when you die even though you've given them away. So simply put, if I transfer Exxon stock to a partnership and exchange for an 80% partnership interest on the condition that I get to receive the dividends declared by Exxon over time, under Section 2036, the Exxon stock, rather than the 80% partnership interest that I own at my desk, is included in my estate.

G. Hawkins: You've given a gift that's not really a gift.

S. Loomis-Price: Or you've made a transfer, right.

G. Hawkins: Right.

S. Loomis-Price: In this case, when you're transferring to a partnership, it's not a gift—it's actually a sale because you're transferring assets in exchange for a partnership interest. But yes, under the Internal Revenue Code, you've made a transfer that is basically ignored for estate tax purposes.

And typically though, the strings that the IRS is pointing to are more subtle than the example I've given where I've said, "I'm just going to keep the income based on the asset that I'm transferring." For instance, the IRS likes to look at things like if I transfer $20 million in Exxon stock, a $500,000 vacation home and some jet skis to a partnership in exchange for that same 80% interest in the partnership, but after formation, I continue to use the vacation home and the jet skis as if I still own them, the IRS is likely to argue that all of the assets that I contributed to the partnership, including the Exxon stock, even though I haven't touched it in any way, come back into my estate under Section 2036. And the rationale that they use is that there's an implied agreement at the inception, at the formation of the partnership, that I would continue to have the right to use the assets that I was about to contribute to the partnership even though I no longer own them. And it's in these bad facts cases, such as in my example, where the IRS has had recent success in disregarding partnerships.

G. Hawkins: And thus, basically, the *Strangi* case is a good example of that, isn't it?

S. Loomis-Price: *Strangi* is a good one—*Reichardt, Schauerhamer, Harper, Thompson*—the list has gotten fairly long all in the last five, or five-and-a-half years.

G. Hawkins: Well, when you advise a client in forming a partnership, what kind of things can be done to avoid the implications of Section 2036?

S. Loomis-Price: Well, there's a rather long list, and much ofthis comes from having read the 10 or 14 or so cases and kind of pulling together the facts that the courts are pointing to. The very first thing is to remember that preparation for the transfer tax audit or dispute begins at the estate planning level. It's very important to consider what you write, in an e-mail, in a memo to the file regarding reasons for partnership formation, in time records for attorneys and accountants, in letters back and forth with appraisers. You need to keep in mind that your ultimate audience may be an IRS agent, a judge or even a jury depending on the jurisdiction that you end up in.

You should evaluate the potential assets that you would contribute to the partnership, and the first step in that is to consider whether you have, if you are the client, sufficient assets to form a partnership. And I typically would not recommend forming a partnership without $5 to $7 million to put into the partnership. And along with that is the requirement that there be sufficient assets outside of the partnership to maintain your standard of living.

I would make sure that you put no personal use assets into the partnership. By personal use assets, I'm referring back to that vacation home and those jet skis, because unless you're willing to pay rent to the partnership to reimburse it for your use of its assets, then you probably shouldn't put it in the partnership to begin with.

G. Hawkins: Stephanie, a minute ago, you mentioned that you thought clients ought to put in at least $5 to $7 million in assets into a partnership, and before we got on the phone here earlier, you were explaining some of the rationale for why that was the case.

S. Loomis-Price: Sometimes what we see is that families with $1 or $2 or $3 million that want to enter into this agreement to form a partnership because they know that it has great benefits, lots of which are non-tax reasons, but also for the tax reasons, often are not prepared for the administrative expense that comes along with a partnership. For instance, the first thing that I recommend is hiring a really good partnership accountant, and sometimes your long-time family accountant is not one who has a handle on the partnership issues that will need to be addressed over time.

You would also need to be willing to pay attorney's fees over time as things change, as interests are transferred. And those expenses can add up quickly, and typically, the smaller partnerships are ones where those expenses are more balked at than accepted as a matter of course.

You also need to consider whether the family is ready for an audit. We have been told that particularly, in every estate tax return including a limited partnership interest, the return will be audited. So that's something that each family who's considering creating a partnership needs to know up front and needs to consider whether they're willing to hold their feet tothe fire when it comes to dealing with the IRS.

G. Hawkins: So in other words, really, if someone is not willing to spend the time and all the professional fees to do it right, they run the risk that they're going to disregard some key things in the management and operation and the legalities of taking care of the ongoing partnership that are going to create valuation problems.

S. Loomis-Price: That's exactly right. There are numerous other steps that you can take, both in formation and then in maintenance as well, so.

G. Hawkins: What should partnership owners avoid in how they operate the partnership to minimize some of the risk of IRS attack?

S. Loomis-Price: One of the first things that we like to see is that on formation, having had the partners discuss partnership terms, so taking a look at the management structure and figuring out who's going to be in charge, how they're going to handle things, considering whether to change the investment policy from the policy that was held by the major contributing partner prior to formation and afterwards so that we can at least have an argument to avoid the circuitous recycling of value classification that's used by the Tax Court in *Harper* and others.

To the extent possible, or not contained in the partnership agreement, to then document those discussions and decisions related to the management structure, related to compensation to be paid to managers, related to the investment policy, to expected distributions, transfer restrictions on partnership interest, and terms of the partnership. In other words, give us as much meat as possible to work with in arguing that this is a bona fide sale for full and adequate consideration, which gets us out of the 2036 purview because it's a congressionally written exception, because having that negotiation, that back and forth that's negotiated and documented, helps us prove to the IRS that this is, in fact, an arm's length transaction.

G. Hawkins: Separate and apart from what is in the minutes of the partnership or in the documentation regarding how it's managed and all the issues that you just raised, is it helpful for us as business appraisers to note that in the report?

S. Loomis-Price: Most certainly. If you are able, through your due diligence, to talk with the general partners or the limited partners of the partnership, and determine that, in fact, there appears to have been some give and take, or that each of the partners was represented by separate counsel, for instance, like we had in the *Stone* case, although that's kind of an ideal world, if you do have that, I think it does promote the bona fide sale part of 2036, and it's something that appraisers should at least document to the extent that they have access to that information.

*****

G. Hawkins: How do privileges impact valuation issues related to partnerships? And what do you mean by privileges?

S. Loomis-Price: There are various legal privileges that enable attorneys, for the most part, to keep confidential information that has been provided by a client. For instance, there's the attorney/client privilege. This privilege protects all communications from clients to attorneys. It is the IRS's position that it does not do the converse. It does not protect an attorney's communications to the client unless that communication would reveal the client's initial communication to the attorney. So that's something to keep in mind. That issue has not been addressed. The *Frederick* case in the 7th Circuit has given us some guidance as to when litigation begins, which governs the work-product doctrine. A lot of attorneys will tell you, "Well, this is attorney/client privileged and it's work-product covered, but the work-product doctrine, which covers my thoughts as an attorney, as opposed to the client's communication, only begins once anticipation of litigation has begun." And according to *Frederick* in the 7th Circuit, when the audit letter is received is when the attorney work-product coverage begins.

There's also the tax practitioner's privilege, which is a fairly new privilege under the Internal Revenue Code, Section 7525, which covers any communication that, if had with an attorney, would have been privileged, but if had with a tax practitioner. It has some interesting limitations, however. It's only in non-criminal matters before the IRS or a federal court brought by, or against the U.S. And it does not cover communications involved in tax return preparations. So my advice there would be—if you are a tax practitioner and you are working with a client and both giving them, or communicating with them on things that might otherwise be covered by the attorney/client privilege and you are also preparing a tax return, to segregate your files so that the tax return file is separate and apart and it's much easier to cover with the tax practitioner's privilege those communications that are not related specifically to the tax return preparation.

G. Hawkins: Well, let me raise something I see quite a bit as a business appraiser. A lot of business appraisers get this initial reaction from an attorney. We'll get a call from an attorney that says, "We're thinking about forming an LLC or an FLP, and we want to send you the operating agreement, we're trying to maximize discounts. We want you to tell us what changes we can make in the operating agreement to maximize discounts." And I've tended to avoid that, and really out of perception, even though I'm going to be totally unbiased in my appraisal, I'm concerned about the perception that I'm participating in the process of developing the operating agreement and how that's going to look after the fact to someone who sees any communication about that as if I somehow collaborated to generate discounts. How would that, under what you've just discussed, some of the privilege rules, in a litigation case, how would that affect how a Tax Court judge might view the appraiser's role or not view it? Or would or would it not taint it?

S. Loomis-Price: I think depending on how the matter progresses, that could taint things significantly. I myself have never run into that situation. I've never either asked an appraiser to be in on the formation, nor have I heard of or dealt with a case where that has happened. But at the planning level, we, the law firm, will often engage the appraiser rather than having the tax payer do so to protect the attorney/client privilege, because under a case in the 2nd Circuit called *Kovel*, we can engage an appraiser to assist us in providing legal advice to our clients, and the appraiser is being hired then by the attorney to help the attorney provide legal advice. However, once an appraiser is designated as an expert witness, all privilege protections as to that appraiser are stripped, and anything written to the appraiser, even prior to his or her designation as an expert, is discoverable by the IRS. Theoretically, anything that's said to the appraiser is discoverable as well. It's just much harder to establish exactly what was said. So I would counsel appraisers not to get involved at the formation level in terms of looking at an agreement and suggesting way to maximize discounts.

*****

G. Hawkins: What are the key issues that you think are important when valuing a non-controlling interest in real estate.

S. Jeffries: Well, there are several, and one of which Stephanie's already mentioned. The first issue is, is it truly a non-controlling interest? I'm not an appraiser, but I spent a huge amount of time talking to appraisers, and I talk with appraisers that are at the upper tier level, you know, like you and Bruce, and I also talk to MAIs who are getting into this the very first time, so it really runs the gamut. And too often, when I speak to them, or when we have this discussion on the kind data they're looking for, and I ask them if it's truly a non-controlling interest, they are not quite sure. That is a real issue and also an issue of whether or not that the person who owns the non-controlling interest also owns some sort of general partner or other controlling interest in the entity. They own them both at the same time, which has been talked about already, which is an issue. And when I say is it truly a non-controlling interest, it really means four things and it's quite simple. They can't control the distribution of earnings, they cannot control the reinvestment of earnings, they cannot sell or determine when the underlying assets would be sold, and they really just can't control or otherwise manage the activities of the entity. And there should be governing documents that establish that it is truly a non-controlling interest. I think, George, you said that, you know, the IRS will be the ultimate, probably the ultimate audience of this and there needs to be documents that establish that it is truly a non-controlling interest in every respect, and that that holder of that non-controlling does not also own the controlling interest. And this is an issue simply because of all the people I talk to, many of them are not quite sure, and then they call me back two or three weeks later and they're still trying to find the documents and they have more questions.

There's another issue that's out there that's come up recently in conversations I've had, and I don't know how this is handled—perhaps one of you do. But sometimes the holder of the non-controlling interest, they cannot control the entity, but they do have some blocking power. Maybe it's a 50/50 interest or maybe they own 25 or somewhere between 25 and 50%, for instance. And they do have some ability—they cannot unilaterally cause anything to happen, but they can at least block the other partner's ability to do something. And that's another issue out there especially when they're trying to apply our data in valuing a non-controlling interest.

But, those are the key issues, establishing whether or not it is truly a non-controlling interest in making sure that the governing documents of the entity, whether it's an FLP or an LLC or whatever it is, making sure that those governing documents do indeed establish clearly that what they are valuing is a noncontrolling interest.

*****

G. Hawkins: When an appraiser uses the Partnership Profiles data that your firm creates when they're valuing a limited partner interest or an LLC, what are some of the considerations that they should use in using that pricing data and what kind of pitfalls can they try to avoid?

S. Jeffries: Well, they need to—the primary factors that the real world uses—you know, Revenue Ruling 59-60 says basically, "Go out into the real world and find out how something like this might trade." And there's four factors that buyers of these truly non-controlling interest use when they value, or when they value and price these interests. One is the historical performance of the entity with respect to cash flow, distributions, and so forth.

Probably the most important factor is whether or not the entity pays regular operating distributions. If it pays regular operating distributions, it will be priced in a way that is dramatically different from, for instance, an undeveloped land partnership that is not supposed to pay any operating distributions or any distributions at all for years and years. But the key factor really is whether or not, historically, it has paid operating distributions. I do know that, in many cases, people call me and they're setting up a deal and that's hard to know because there is no historical performance, but I believe there at least needs to be some kind of conversations with management as to whether or not they expect it to pay operating distributions or not, and that is a huge issue.

Another issue out there is whether or not the entity has debt on it. Whether there's debt, and then the amount of debt has a major impact on how the thing is going to be priced, how it would be priced in the real world. Obviously, if you've got a real estate entity that owns its real estate on an all-cash basis with no debt and it pumps out operating distributions on a frequent basis, that's going to be at the lower end of the discount spectrum. If it has so much debt on it that it's struggling under the debt just to make ends meet at the end of the months, it will definitely be at the higher end of the discount spectrum. So distributions and debt matter the most.

Probably the fourth factor out there would be the operating timeframe of the entity until it is liquidated. This seems to be especially true for entities that are not expected to pay any distributions and how long it is expected to be in operation before it's liquidated. I know this is a very difficult one especially when you're dealing with FLPs, but that is definitely worth having a discussion with management about in documenting it.

A couple of comments I'll make as far as how the real world is pricing these things under Revenue Ruling 59-60—is often people will get hung up on what type of a property it is, whether it is apartments or shopping centers or office buildings or hotels. The best I could tell from having followed this market since the early 1990s is it doesn't seem to make that much difference between different types of income-producing properties because those are going to be valued at the property value. Whether or not hotels are in vogue or not, that's going to be a factor that's going to be a determination that's made at the property level. And of course, my data does not get into the property level—it gets into—to an interest in the entity that owns the property, and of course, it has to be a non-controlling interest.

But, I wouldn't get hung up on the property types that much. It's whether or not it pays distributions and whether or not it has debt on it. It's really, it's really quite, quite simple. And of course, if it's undeveloped land, all bets are off and that will be valued in a different way.

G. Hawkins: Couldn't the type of property, though, and the quality of the property affect the attractiveness of the interest or lack thereof? For example, if one of your traded secondary partnerships that I'm using to value my private limited partnership that I'm valuing, if your traded one that I'm relying on has Class A office space and I'm with mostly national credit quality tenants with very low risk of default, and even though that is captured in the appraisal of that underlying property, and I'm valuing a family limited partnership that has a Class C office space, small office building that's older, not as attractive, has non-credit quality local tenants that tend to default and turn over a lot, that puts my income more at risk or my ability to pay distributions, and it has probably less long-term capital gain upside potential, won't that affect the value of my limited partnership interest, the differences and the quality of the properties, for example?

S. Jeffries: Yeah. I think it will. I understand, George, exactly what you're saying. But I've never been able to quantify that difference. Of course, I do believe that most of that difference will be taken into account at the property level. For instance, say you take a high-end hotel or just a regular Days Inn or something, the high-end hotel is going to be valued at maybe a seven percent CAP at the property level, while the

Days Inn may be more of a 10 or 12 or something like that. So that definitely will be taken into account. But I don't know how I don't know how to quantify that when you get down to the valuing the noncontrolling interest in those entities. But I understand exactly what you're saying. But, like I said, I think that most of that will be taken into account at the property level.

G. Hawkins: That makes sense. Perhaps you could share with our listeners sort of a brief understanding of the secondary limited partnership market and what it is and its implications for business appraisers.

S. Jeffries: Okay. There are literally hundreds of publicly registered limited partnerships and REITs that have been formed over the years that are publicly registered. That means they make all their filings with the Securities and Exchange Commission and so forth, but they are not publicly traded, nor were they meant to be publicly traded. And what has happened over the years, and this really started in the late 80s, and we began tracking this market in the early 90s, is there evolved the secondary market where, when people get to the point where they want to sell this interest. There are different firms out there right now, there's about eight to ten independent companies that match up buyers and sellers of these non-traded interests. Most of these interests are in real estate entities, whether it's limited partnerships or REITs, and of course, like I said, there are non-traded REITs in partnerships. A lesser—I mean I'm talking 90% are in real estate—equipment is much less, equipment partnerships can be anything from computers to aircraft. Some partnerships own cable television systems. Some own oil and gas properties. There are also some venture capital funds out there. But these interests do trade out there in the secondary market, and like I said, it sort of began in the late 1980s and it still exists today. All of the trading firms that trade these entities are NASD registered. They are NASD broker dealers. That means that they are subject to all the NASD rules, including the best execution rules, which means they are duty bound to get multiple bids for the units and then sell the units to the highest bidder, and they're subject to NASD audits and so forth.

All of the firms out there have some type of auction process. Probably the most well known is American Partnership Board, and you can go to their website, it's *apboard.com*, and you can literally once you've registered and set up an account with them, you can bid on these units that come up—it's an eBay like bidding.

But there are multiple bidders for basically all of the interest that trade in the secondary market. They are, primarily, they are limited partnerships, but there is some trading in non-listed REITs that have come out in recent years, but really that's probably only 20% of the total. We began tracking this market in the 1990s and what I mean by that is, we collect prices from the secondary market firms and we publish them every 60 days. We put them all in Excel Spreadsheet, it spits them all out with partnership or REIT name, high and low trading prices, number of units traded, number of transactions, weighted average trading price, the distribution yield based on that price we report at asset values, and so forth—we reported thousands of trades over that time. Recently, I figured up volume in this market that we followed since about 1994, and it's probably $1.3 to $1.5 billion dollars. The market used to be much more active than it is now. Right now it's probably about a $60 million dollar a year market out there.

*****

G. Hawkins: This is going to be for both you, Spencer, and also for Bruce, because I know both of you worked on this book where you kind of coined this approach, which really deals with how is the rate of an investment more important than the end resulting discount that falls out of the equation more important when you value a family limited partnership? In other words, when we look at the discount to net asset value, for example, is that really the result of something else or is it a cause or an effect?

B. Johnson: That's really the essence of probably what we're talking about here today, you know, when we're valuing family limited partnership interest. We have a client who's interested in what the discount is, and the attorney who wants to represent the client and is interested in what the discount is, and of course, the IRS who's interested in what the discount is because they're looking at what the tax impact is going to be. But as appraisers, it's hard not to, but we have to keep from being so focused on the discount that we get caught up in some of these other issues, and the discount for lack of marketability, the double-counting that we're talking about, is one of those issues. And I'm sure Spencer will add to this, but, when these investors are buying and trading these interests, it only takes about seven to ten days for one of these interests to sell. It may take 60 days for the transaction to complete.

But these guys are buying these interests based on rates of return. They forecast the distributions and when they think it'll liquidate and get the internal rate of return or discount that to present value, and they're demanding somewhere around a 20% rate of return based on liquidation horizon and debt and other risk factors.

S. Jeffries: The real issue in pricing or valuing really any investment is the rate of return that is being sought by the buyer. You know, investors in the real world, which, and I watch pricing in the real world for these non-controlling partnership interests, they determine how much they will pay for an investment based upon a rate of return that reflects what they believe to be the risk and potential benefits—potential return of that investment. And I believe that the discounts are the means, or one of the means, by which they get to a particular rate of return. I think the discount is easy to see, but really the discount is reflecting a particular rate of return that they are looking at. I guess, in other words, if I can say this more clearly, a discount really reflects a rate of return that the buyer is seeking—the discount is more of a means to an end rather than the end. And I think that often, in the conversations I have with appraisers, is they're getting into the issue of discounts, but they're kind of missing the boat because I believe the discounts simply reflect a rate of return.

And as a matter of fact, I was on a panel in New York City last week with one of the buyers—one of the major buyers of these non-controlling, non-traded interests that trade out in the secondary market, and they talked about rates of return and so forth and what they are looking for. And, of course, their big issue is not only in establishing a rate of return, but also factoring into that they bought this thing and they cannot control the liquidation of it, or any aspect of it. And also they bought something that is somewhat thinly traded and may be difficult to market especially if they buy a large amount of it.

I do believe that, the FLP book gets into this issue of how to do valuations under the income approach using rate of return data, and I believe that, if at all possible, someone should consider doing a valuation under both the market approach, which gets into the issue of discounts, and also under the income approach, which takes a different look at it looks at it from the standpoint of rates of return.

B. Johnson: Well, just going back to when George and Spencer were talking about the discount for lack of marketability and whether that's double-discounting if you use the PPI data to get to one stage and then if you apply a discount for lack of marketability. I know we'll talk about this more in depth later, but really it's just getting away from the discount mentality and looking at, you know, if an investor—a third party investor was going to buy this interest, what kind of rate of return would they demand to offset the risks that they were exposed to. I mean there are alternative investments out there. They could buy stocks, REITs, bonds—all different types of investments and they would expect some kind of rate of return—so what kind—how much higher rate of return would they demand for buying this privately-held, non-controlling interest in an FLP? And when you use that theory to determine what your lack of marketability discount is, then not only do you come up with something reasonable, it's also supportable, and that's what we found when dealing with questions from the IRS or in Tax Court.

Frankly, in the *Estate of Church*, the IRS was just asking me question after question about discounts and, they can always find somebody that'll argue discounts with you, whether it's 15% or 40% or whatever. But when you get it back to rate of return, which is how investors buy and sell securities—financial securities—then you can actually talk with some relevance about whether the value you'd come up with is reasonable. In that *Estate of Church* case, the IRS was arguing a zero discount, and I had what looked like an astronomical discount of 57% on the interest, but actually my rate of return on investing it was a little over 15%, and their rate of return with a zero discount was six percent, and back in 1999, you could buy a long-term government bond for six percent—a risk-free government bond. So their argument that a zero discount didn't make any sense. Who would buy this privately-held, noncontrolling interest for a return that you could get if you just turned around and bought a risk-free government bond?

*****

G. Hawkins: We have an email that came in yesterday from one of the listeners who says, "I've used the FLP income approach suggested in the Johnson and Jeffries text, your book, for FLP holding only raw land, as I believe their approach to be less subjective. However, the IRS economists reviewing the file in my case alleged the approach resulted in the use of an income approach, which they claimed was not suitable. I arrived at a combined 45% discount on a gift made in 2001 and the IRS economists arrived at 15%. The client preferred not to litigate, and we recently settled at a combined discount of 30%, which I consider very low for this partnership, which held only raw land, but it avoided litigation expense. What would the authors in this case, the two authors who are here with us, respond to an agent—what would you say who argued that their method resulted in an asset method inappropriately used with an income method?"

B. Johnson: Well that frequently comes up because the IRS obviously wants to focus on the discount, and that's the way these FLP interests have been valued for years. But when you look at if this wasn't an FLP interest that owned raw land, if it was a trucking company, you wouldn't be necessarily focusing on the discount. You'd be talking about what would the discount rate be, and what would this or that be, what the growth rate, some of those factors that ultimately impact the discount.

G. Hawkins: You'd be looking at what the cash flows were worth.

B. Johnson: Absolutely. And so when I get into these situations, yeah, I'm very up front. I don't have anything to hide. I want to talk to them about, "Well, you know, if you in—ended this at a 15% discount, what kind of return would you be?" What's the liquidation horizon? You know, is that 15% reasonable and how did they get it? Versus, I assume that Mr. Brophy, if he used the income approach, he was doing a forecast of a liquidation of the raw land at some point in the future. And so even in a five or ten-year horizon, which is usually pretty quick, you usually end up with a rate of return of 15%, you'll still end up in the 40% discount range on undeveloped land. So it all comes back to shifting the discussion toward rate of return and what's reasonable for an investor. It may not be what they want to hear or what they want to accept, but then again, we're valuing these based on third party transactions, not on what the IRS will accept or won't accept.

G. Hawkins: So what in effect you're saying, you're bringing it back to a common sense analysis. You're basically shifting from some ambiguous discount that really has no relation to anything to actually shifting the focus to how would somebody, when you're explaining to the agent, what would you want as a rate of return on this. And then if the rate of return is below, for example, in your example earlier, below a risk-free rate, that wouldn't make any sense given the risk.

B. Johnson: Yes, that's correct. The example I give a lot of times is when I go to Wal-Mart, if I see a lawn mower there for sale for $150 and it says 50% off discount, I don't know if that 50% discount really means anything. I need to go to Sears or Target or another store and find out if the options and everything that I'm getting with that lawnmower is comparable to prices at other stores. And so if you've compared your partnership interest to other interests out there, other alternative investments from a rate of return perspective as well as from a market approach perspective, then you have some concrete objective evidence to show that what you've done is reasonable.

G. Hawkins: Why is the cost approach, this discount to net asset value kind of approach that we talked about, not held up well in court when valuing FLP interest? And if you could explain what you mean by the cost approach here.

B. Johnson: From the cost approach, I guess my partner, Jim Park, coined these words, "Slapping on discounts." But the cost approach is basically taking the net asset value of the partnership, which is defined as taking the market value of the assets minus the liabilities, and then applying discounts for lack of control and lack of marketability. And generally, most people justify those using either lack of control discount studies, and then for the marketability, they're using IPO restricted stock studies.

G. Hawkins: So for example, they might take a *Mergerstat Control Premium Study*™, take the reverse of it, and come up with what they're calling, or implying as a minority—implied market minority discount, and using that to get to the minority portion of the discount.

B. Johnson: That's correct. And, it's important to read those studies and understand them, because what happens is when you get in court, the Tax Court is going to look at that and look at the underlying data in those studies. I mean if you look at most restricted stock studies, I've done one of them out there, the underlying companies that that's based on don't have anything to do with a raw land limited partnership. And so to take the average from a restricted stock study and then compare it to the FLP you're valuing, this doesn't make any sense, and that's what happens when you get into court is they just haven't found that data to be comparable.

G. Hawkins: And you read my mind on another question. I want to jump ahead on that, and when you develop a discount for lack of marketability in an FLP that holds marketable securities. The IRS and the Tax Court has really questioned the validity of restricted stock studies that really relate to operating businesses, not things that hold easily understood marketable securities. How then would you develop a marketability discount where you've got an FLP, for example, that holds marketable securities like stocks and bonds or whatever?

B. Johnson: Well, first of all, I wouldn't use the studies. I think they're important. I put them in the appendix of our reports to show that in arm's length transactions, between third parties, discounts do occur for lack of control and lack of marketability. And by reading each one of the studies individually, I think everybody should have copies of those studies and understand them. You can see why those discounts occur, because somebody's not willing to pay the same amount as net asset value when they don't possess the same amounts of control or marketability as somebody that controls that asset or that interest. But for developing a discount for lack of marketability, whether it's for a real estate FLP or a business or a marketable securities FLP, what we do is base it on the rate of return. We'll use the income and the market approach to calculate a noncontrolling marketable value, basically, the value less the discount for lack of control, if you want to look at it that way. And then from there, we have to decide, "Okay, if this was marketable, this would be the value, but it's not marketable, how much more of an increased rate of return would I require to invest in this?" So you have to discount that amount, that level of value a certain amount to increase the rate of return and what's reasonable.

G. Hawkins: Are you building in a holding period like Chris Mercer's Quantitative Discount for Lack of Marketability Method?

B. Johnson: No, usually I take into account liquidation horizon in the discount for lack of control in the income approach. When I'm using an income approach, I forecast earnings, and if there's an expected liquidation or a possible liquidation, then I'll use say a five or ten-year liquidation horizon as one of my two or three scenarios in the income approach. So by the time that I've gotten to marketability, what I'm really looking at is, I can't really sell this interest, and if something goes wrong with it and I want to sell it, how much more rate of return would I want to hold it longer? It's more of a horizon risk adjustment than it is worrying about liquidation, because I don't control liquidation anyway.

G. Hawkins: Bruce, if we could jump to the situation where you have a family limited partnership that's got a mix of different asset classes. For example, it's got marketable securities in terms of, let's just say it's equities, publicly traded equities, and then it's got raw land and it's got an income-producing shopping center, for example. It's my understanding, in some of the speeches that Internal Revenue Service folks have given on the subject, that they expect, and I hate to get back to the term "discounts", but they expect to see the discounts developed both for minority interest and for lack of marketability based on each individual asset class. In other words, they expect the valuation to be bifurcated where you come up with a discount applicable to each asset in the pool of total assets where it's going to be weighted and you end up with an overall minority discount and a lack of marketability discount. And I think if I jump ahead with you, I think I would guess that your analysis is going to be developing a rate of return for each asset class. Is that correct?

B. Johnson: Yes. Under the income approach, what we've done since the mid-90s is use a weighted average return. If I own an interest in FLP, and it owns several different asset classes, I'm going to develop a weighted average discount rate and then forecast the return of each one of the assets, total that, and discount, and then take the present value of that. But from a market approach standpoint, I'm going to do the same thing except I'm going to be looking at taking the net asset value of each one of the equities, the bonds and the real estate, and dividing those out, and then looking at alternative investments. If I wanted to recreate that composition of assets, I could go out and buy closed-in funds and real estate limited partnerships and buy that same mix. I wouldn't be able to find a fund or a company that's exactly like that, but what we do is divide out the assets and then apply price to net asset value ratios to the equities that are comparable to closed-in funds that hold equities and then get a price to net asset value for real estate limited partnerships that is comparable to the type of real estate held in that FLP.

McCord Reversal and its Effect on Valuation

Moderator: Steve Akers
Speakers: William Frazier and John Porter

Excerpts from *Business Valuation Resources'* October 18, 2006 telephone conference transcript. The entire telephone conference transcript and presentation can be found online.

J. Porter: The McCords filed a gift tax return reporting the value of the gift, and the value was based upon the values determined in the Assignment Agreement or the values stated in the Assignment Agreement. Roughly $6.9 million was subject to gift tax and that was the interest transferred to the non-charity donees. And everything else qualified for the charitable deduction.

S. Akers: So John, I just want to make clear that that's what we're talking about then with a defined value clause, that what is transferred to the family members is actually defined by formula and is designed so that, in effect, you would cap what the potential gift tax exposure would be.

J. Porter: That's right. To state it simply, the fair market value—they transferred all 82% of their limited partnership interests. The first $6.9 million worth of units of that 82% went to noncharity donees and everything else went to charity, and that was basically our position.

S. Akers: So in that case, the goal would be that the gift would be $6.9 million, or the dollar amounts, whatever they were, and that would be it. And it really wouldn't matter what the appraisals were. That would just vary the percentage interest that passed.

J. Porter: The gift, subject to gift tax, to the non-charity donees would be $6.9 million. There's also obviously a gift to the charity, which qualifies for the charitable deduction, which is everything above that amount. You're exactly right.

Another feature of this transaction was the non-charity donees agreed to be liable for any gift tax—for all gift tax. It's basically your standard net gift transaction. But they also agreed to be liable in the event that Mr. or Mrs. McCord or both of them died within three years of making the gift for any estate tax that was due under 2035 if Mr. and Mrs. McCord died within three years of making the transfer. We computed that amount basically using the Internal Revenue Service's (IRS) actuarial tables and the then existing estate tax rates, and that further reduced the amount of taxable gift for purposes of calculating the gift tax headed by Mr. and Mrs. McCord.

The IRS audited the McCords' 1996 gift tax return, and in the Notice of Deficiency after audit, the Service asserted a number of positions. First, they said, "Basically, we're going to apply a step transaction or substance-over-form theory with respect to this series of transactions. And we're basically going to say that at the end of the day, what the charities received was roughly $500,000, the price at which their interest was purchased back in June of 1996, literally six months after the transfer."

The Service also argued that, in essence, what the donees received—the non-charity donees received was 82% of the units in the Partnership less the cash, and that instead of the value applied using Will Frazier's appraisal, the value should be, in essence, twice that amount. And the Service, at that time, did not have a valuation report.

The Notice of the Deficiency was issued without taking into account the net gift, and so as you can imagine, the deficiency was fairly large. I think it was in excess of $4 million.

And our position was fairly simple, and that is, we had three arguments. One was that the Assignment Agreement governed the nature of the interest transferred. Going back to fundamental principles of transfer tax law, we know that state law property rights govern. And once you determine the nature of the property rights transferred under state law, then you apply the hypothetical willing buyer/willing seller test to determine the value of those state law property rights for gift tax purposes. And so our position was—under Texas law and the terms of the Assignment Agreement, what the non-charity donees received were units in the Partnership having a fair market value of approximately $6.9 million. Everything else went to charity, and therefore, qualified for the charitable deduction. And that should be the end of it. The Assignment Agreement governed the transaction.

We also argued that the best evidence of value is an arm's length transaction between unrelated parties at or near the valuation date. And in our view, our Confirmation Agreement was very good evidence of value because ultimately, the charities and the sons, relying on Will's appraisal, determined the interest in the Partnership that each was entitled to receive. And if the government was going to ignore the Assignment Agreement, we said, "Okay, well, then respect the valuation analysis that these independent parties, who were represented by independent counsel, placed on the interest in the Partnership when deciding how to allocate those interests among themselves."

And then the third argument we had, which was also a very good one, which is, Will's valuation analysis was sound, and therefore, no change should be made.

Needless to say, the Service didn't buy our arguments. And also, the Service was arguing that the Assignment Agreement was void against public policy based on the *Procter* and *Ward* decisions.

We got to the Tax Court and we tried the case in 2001—May of 2001. Our trial judge was Judge Foley. And the government hired an appraiser who determined that the valuation discounts—the discounts for lack of marketability (I believe his position was) should be 7.23%, and the discount for lack of control should be roughly 8 to 10%, is my recollection. And Will testified in support of his appraisal which had discounts of approximately 46%.

The government stipulated that it had the burden of proof, that we met the various prerequisites under Section 7491, to the shift the burden of proof to the government. But importantly, we had stipulated, because the facts supported it as I said earlier, that there was no prearranged deal with the charity as to the value of their interest or the percentage interest in the Partnership that each charity was entitled to receive under the Assignment Agreement.

W. Frazier: I was wondering maybe you could just take a minute for the audience and explain why the burden shifted, and why it shifts and why it doesn't shift.

J. Porter: Well, under Section 7491, which came into play as part of the Taxpayer Bill of Rights in 1998, Taxpayer Bill of Rights II, there's a provision which allows taxpayers in certain circumstances to shift the burden of proof to the government in tax cases. And there a number of prerequisites you have to meet, some substantiation requirements, but the most important requirement is that you have to have reasonably cooperated with the request for information from the IRS, both at the audit level and in litigation, and you have to come forth with credible evidence supporting your tax position. And the government stipulated that we had, in fact, done that in this case. And so the burden of proof, the Service agreed, had shifted to them.

We tried the case before Judge Foley, and literally, we did our briefing. The Court asked for a couple of additional briefs on some issues of law. And roughly, two years after trial—we didn't hear anything for a long time—and two years after trial, the Tax Court issued its opinion. Interestingly, it was an opinion which Judge Foley, our trial judge, was in the dissent, along with Judge Chiechi.

But the Majority opinion basically took a little different tact than either the government was arguing or than we had faced in having to do our briefing. What the Majority concluded was that the Assignment Agreement itself was not self-effectuating, that to look to determine the percentage interest in the Partnership that each donee received, you had to look to the Confirmation Agreement. And recall, that was an agreement that was entered into by the donees, not the donor. It was entered into by the donees two months after the transfer. And looking at the Assignment Agreement, what the Majority concluded was that the non-charity donees received 77 of the 82% interest transferred by Mr. and Mrs. McCord, and that the charities received the other 5%.

And then the Court engaged in roughly about a 60-page valuation analysis that essentially, at the end of the day, split the difference between Will's valuation analysis and the government's expert's valuation analysis, and then determined basically that additional gift tax was owed.

With respect to our—and the government challenged the component of the net gift transfer that related to the donees' agreement to be liable for any additional estate tax paid if Mr. and Mrs. McCord died within three years of death. Basically, their argument was that that was too speculative to be taken into account in valuing the gift.

Our argument is it's a contingent liability which effects value, and contingent liabilities are valued all the time in connection with transfer tax issues or in connection with valuation. And it was easy to value the contingent liability simply using the government's actuarial tables. But the Court disagreed with our position—the Majority disagreed with our position.

As I said, Judge Foley was in the minority—I say in the minority—Judge Foley wrote a dissenting opinion which was joined by Judge Chiechi which basically said that state law property rights govern and that what Mr. and Mrs. McCord transferred was interest in the Partnership having $6.9 million worth of value to the non-charity donees, and that the government had not met its burden of proof to prove anything otherwise.

There was another dissent issued by Judge Laro, joined by several other judges, which took the position that the charitable deduction that was ultimately allowed by the Court (or the Majority opinion), which was slightly greater than what was taken on the return, should not be allowed basically because at the end of the day, what the charities received was cash in the Partnership of about half a million dollars.

S. Akers: Tax Court reasoning, that this will come in later with our discussion of how we plan these, that part of their reasoning was that the clause was not "self-effectuating," that it took this subsequent agreement of the parties to determine what interest passed. And they suggested that the answer might have been different if the clause had been drafted in a way to say that, "You determined this formula based on values as finally determined for Federal gift tax purposes."

J. Porter: The taxpayers appealed, and during the pendency of the appeal, Mr. McCord passed away. The arguments we made in the Fifth Circuit were virtually the same as we made at the Tax Court level. And in addition, we challenged the Majority's valuation analysis. The oral arguments were held literally in May of 2004.

And in August of 2006, two years later, the Fifth Circuit issued its opinion, basically, reversing on every issue of the Tax Court's decision. I say every issue. It reversed the Tax Court's decision on the defined value clause and it reversed the Tax Court's decision on the net gift issue. It didn't need to reach the valuation issue per se that we had raised because the Court basically found that the value was determined based upon the values assigned to the non-charity donees in the Assignment Agreement.

What's interesting about the Court's analysis is they focus—and this at page 20 of the opinion—I think is really the key language in the opinion—what the Fifth Circuit said was that the Majority's opinion constituted legal error because it relied upon the post-gift Confirmation Agreement to determine basically the value of the interest transferred, the nature of the property transferred. Because as you recall, what the Majority did was look to the Confirmation Agreement to determine the percentage interest in the Partnership that each of the donees received. And what the Court said is that—and the language that I love in the opinion—"It's clear beyond cavil that the Majority should have stopped with the Assignment Agreement's plain wording." In other words, the plain wording of the Assignment Agreement said that what was transferred to the noncharity donees were units in the Partnership having a fair market value of $6.9 million. And the Fifth Circuit said, "By not relying on that language, by not stopping with this Assignment Agreement, and instead, continuing on to the post-gift Confirmation Agreement's intra-donee concurrence on the equivalency of dollars to percentage interest in the Partnership, the Majority violated the firmly-established maxim that a gift is valued as of the date it is complete. And the flip side of that maxim is that subsequent occurrences are off limits."

This ties back to some of the questions that were asked in some of our arguments at Oral Argument in the Fifth Circuit because ultimately, one of our primary positions was—what Mr. and Mrs. McCord intended to do by executing this Assignment Agreement was to specifically define the value of the units being transferred to the non-charity donees. And therefore, the idea was that they would cap their gift tax exposure. In other words, all they wanted to transfer to their sons and the GST Trust were units in the Partnership having a fair market value of $6.9 million.

And the fact that the Service says that two months after this transfer, that the charities—and this is, of course, the Service's position, essentially—that the charities made a bad bargain with the sons and the GST Trust because the Service says that they didn't get enough units, because the Service says the value of the units was greater than what was stated in Will's report. The fact that the Service said that the charities made a bad bargain shouldn't affect the gift tax that Mr. and Mrs. McCord owe as a result of transferring those interests.

And so what the Fifth Circuit said is you look at the Assignment Agreement and the dollar value formula contained in that to determine the value of the units transferred by Mr. and Mrs. McCord to the non-charity donees, and that the Majority's failure to do so was clear legal error.

With respect to the 2035 net gift issue, the Fifth Circuit agreed with our position that there's nothing speculative about the fact that if either Mr. or Mrs. McCord were to die within three years of following the gift, that the non-charity donees would have the obligation to pay the additional estate tax that could result from the inclusion of the gift tax paid under 2035. The only question is—how do you compute that contingent liability? And the Court said that, "Basically, the manner in which we did it in connection with filing the gift tax return—that is, reliance on the IRS's actuarial tables—was a reasonable method of estimating the effect of that contingent liability on the value of the interest transferred."

As I said, the opinion came out on August 22. The Service had until two weeks ago Friday, to file a petition for rehearing either before this panel of three judges or a petition for rehearing en banc where the Service would request the entire Court to consider the opinion, or reconsider the opinion. The Service let those days come and go and no petition for rehearing was filed, and so the case has now gone back or going back to the Tax Court. This Fifth Circuit opinion reversed and essentially ordered the Court to enter judgment for the petitioners consistent with the opinion. And therefore, basically, the ultimate determination will be that there was no deficiency owed by the taxpayers in connection with the transaction.

The Service does have a right, if it chooses to, to appeal the case to the United States Supreme Court, but I think the chances of that are really remote. This does not involve a split in the circuits and it also does not involve a constitutional question.

Now one of the issues that the Service has argued with respect—or did argue at the trial court level, but which really dropped out of the body of their briefing, was that the defined value clause was void as against public policy. It should be ignored, relying on the Fourth Circuit's decision in *Procter* and the Tax Court's decision in *Ward* and *McClendon* and a number of other cases. Those cases involve clauses which, because of some adjustment, either at the audit level or after litigation by the IRS to the value of the interest transferred, there's an adjustment in either the purchase price if the transaction was a sale, or if it's a gift, units go back to the donor. It really affects the nature of the interest transferred.

The Service, in its briefing before the Fifth Circuit, requested that basically if the Court was going to go in our direction with respect to our state law property rights argument regarding the Assignment Agreement, that the case be remanded back to the Tax Court for consideration of the *Procter/Ward* analysis.

And what the Fifth Circuit said—and this was the subject of some of the Oral Argument as well—is the Fifth Circuit said, "Respondent has not briefed that issue"—or said, "The government has not briefed that issue and has therefore waived it." And so some are saying that *McCord* is distinguishable because the Fifth Circuit chose not to address the *Procter/Ward* analysis.

My take on it is a little different. I think if this Court had determined that this Assignment Agreement was void against public policy, there's no doubt in my mind that these judges would have addressed that issue. And it's also—there's some interesting language in the opinion where the Court is addressing this waiver argument, where they say, "Not surprisingly, the government did not urge the public policy argument on appeal, and instead, focused on trying to support—devoting its efforts on appeal solely to supporting the methodology and holdings of the Majority." And so when the Court says, "Not surprisingly, the government didn't raise this argument," what that says to me is the Court's view is that they didn't raise the argument because they knew ultimately, you know, that the argument didn't have merit with respect to this particular agreement. Because this defined value agreement that the McCords used was not a value adjustment clause that was at issue in *Procter* and *Ward*, but it was truly a defined value clause specifying the dollar value of the units being transferred. And there's no condition subsequent, like you saw in *Procter* and in *Ward*, that would change the nature of the interest transferred.

I hear that distinction made by a number of people including folks from the Service. But the bottom line is if you look at the language that the Fifth Circuit used in its *McCord* opinion, I think it's very clear that the Fifth Circuit didn't believe the public policy argument held any weight.

*****

S. Akers: Very interesting valuation issues were raised in the case and gone through in great detail in the Tax Court opinion, and Will, you were right there in the middle of that. Give us some background of what went on in the appraisal process in the valuation discussion with the Tax Court.

W. Frazier: Okay, one thing I've learned from this is when you're in a program with two other attorneys, make sure you don't go last. But no, all that very complicated analysis and overview is important because it's very important to understand what was happening here. And I might say for the appraisers out there, because of the *McCord* case, you're likely to see more of these defined value types of transfers in the future, and while it really doesn't affect how you do your value, it is important to understand the mechanism of the transfer. For example, one of the criticisms I got from the Tax Court when we did our appraisal was, "Well, you know, the transfer was for 41% interest, or blocks (as they called it), and you valued a 1%." Well, you know, if the transfer was actually a fixed dollar amount, how could we do a percentage interest because that doesn't come until after we've determined the value? And that's why the 1 percent—it was valued on a 1% unit basis, and then it was basically arithmetic after that.

Another important point is that what we valued and I think what the Tax Court agreed with that we valued was an assignee interest in the partnership, not a limited partnership interest. Therefore, issues like voting rights don't come into play.

But one thing I do want to say about the valuation aspect of the case is that I have heard some say that the *McCord* case is a very complicated and important legal case and has a lot to do with defined value clauses. But it doesn't shed much light on the valuation issue with respect to family partnerships and other types of pass-through entities.

But, you know, the major valuation flaw that it seems to me in reading the opinion, from my layman's standpoint, that the Fifth Circuit was trying to make was that, you know, the major flaw was the dispute between the Assignment Agreement and the Confirmation Agreement and the fact that they occurred at two different points in time, and you really can't jump back and forth between time periods in doing the valuation, which is what the Tax Court did. So that was clearly the most egregious error that the Tax Court made.

However, the language of the Fifth Circuit is, I think, supported from a valuation standpoint in a broader context too. And I'll bring you—for example, this is wording out of the case from the Fifth Circuit. It says, "The Majority first proceeds independently to appraise the donated property, eventually reaching a value precisely halfway between those of the experts. As we hereafter hold, as a matter of law, that the methodology employed by the Majority in determining the taxable and non-taxable values of the various donations constitutes legal error. The results of the Majority's independent appraisal of the donated interest in McCord Interests, Ltd., LLP (MIL) and their values for gift tax purposes become irrelevant for the amount of gift taxes owed by the taxpayers." Then it also says, "The values ascribed by the Majority being derived by its use of its own imaginative but flawed methodology may not be used in any way in the calculation of the taxpayers' gift tax liability."

What I think can be extrapolated from that—it's not a bright line but it's a very strong argument that can be made—is that one may not rely on the *McCord* case for valuation methodology in any way. Now I know there will be some that will dispute that. They'll say that the *McCord* case was reversed on other grounds, but to me, the language is fairly clear that value methodology—any nuance you take from the valuation methodology in the *McCord* case is if you attempt to do that, you're on very thin ice.

And I think the *McCord* case is made for some very bad valuation judgments and has influenced some later cases, I think heavily and I think to the detriment of the valuation profession. For example, a recent case, the *Kelley* case, was a family limited partnership (FLP) case, and the Court really didn't rely heavily on either expert, but instead, chose to rely on its own methodology, which they're entitled to do, but they relied most heavily on the *McCord* case in determining its marketability discount. I think, in the future, that probably shouldn't happen. Also, in the *Kelley* case, they relied on the *Lappo* case, but in the *Lappo* case, they also relied heavily on the *McCord* case. So I think there was sort of a domino effect that occurred because of *McCord*, and hopefully, we'll get a chance to revisit some of those valuation, I think, errors that came into being as a result of the *McCord* case. I'm not saying that the Fifth Circuit endorsed one appraiser over the other. They clearly did not. It's just that what they did do was knock out the effects of the Tax Court's, or the Majority's, valuation methodology and also the government's expert.

What the Fifth Circuit said with regards to the work that Dr. Bajaj did in the case was that they basically gave it no weight. They said that the Tax Court rejected the Bajaj opinion, although they did his study (but his opinion), and the Fifth Circuit rejected the Tax Court's appraisal. The Fifth Circuit held that the Tax Court's rejection of the Bajaj opinion was not erroneous. It says that—quoting the case—"given the Majority's non-erroneous rejection of the Commissioner's expert's values." So again, that doesn't say anything about whether the methodology was good or bad. It's just that it's like it never happened.

J. Porter: You know, Will, along those lines, assuming we didn't have the Assignment Agreement's defined value clause, if we look to a case like the recent *Kohler* case, where burden of proof really was an issue that the Court looked at as opposed to what it's done in some other cases, where it really says, "We're not deciding this case on burden of proof." But in *Kohler*, you had the taxpayer's expert testify and then you had the government's expert testify, and the Tax Court rejected the government's expert and said, "Basically, the government has not carried its burden of proof." Had we applied those same principles in the *McCord* case, ignoring the Assignment Agreement, it seems to me like your report would have carried the day because the government's expert had a bunch of holes poked in his report. And the Tax Court, you know, clearly, as the Fifth Circuit pointed out, properly rejected his valuation analysis. So clearly, you know, how the underlying court applies the burden of proof can have a significant impact.

W. Frazier: Without doubt. You know, if the government doesn't reach its burden of proof, then I guess the valuation argument that they put on is sort of moot.

J. Porter: That's the fundamental question. And it's hard to compare cases like *Kohler* where burden of proof was a real issue to some of the other cases, including *McCords'* Majority analysis when it got into the valuation analysis and basically said, "On this issue, burden of proof is not a real important point and we're going to decide the case based on a preponderance of the evidence."

W. Frazier: One other point that came up—and this was a real, kind of surprise for me—it had to do with just the terminology for valuation. We were criticized by the Court for not using—we obviously used the fair market value standard for tax and that's really all I was familiar with—but we were criticized for not using the phrase, "fair market value as finally determined for tax purposes." And frankly, I was unaware of that as a valuation standard with regard to taxes. Thankfully, two of the dissenting judges, Judge Foley and Judge Chiechi, both said that, "There's no material difference between fair market value determined under Federal gift tax valuation principles and fair market value as finally determined for Federal gift tax purposes." You know, they mean the same thing and that was sort of a red herring, and I think the Fifth Circuit agreed with that.

J. Porter: I think the language in the Tax Court's opinion dealing with "as finally determined for tax purposes" didn't deal with the standard of value that you applied, but it dealt with the language in the Defined Value Agreement because the language was $6.9 million of units, and basically—and I'm paraphrasing it—were transferred to the non-charity donees. And what the Majority said was, "Had the Assignment Agreement used the language 'as finally determined for gift taxes purposes,' we might have ruled differently." Thereby, looking at a clause, you know, the "as finally determined" language is something that you see throughout the Treasury regulations, in the charitable deduction area, the marital deduction area, the 2702 regulations for Grantor Retained Annuity Trusts (GRAT), and also in a lot of the government's pronouncements on these issues. And so I think that's where it was as opposed to telling you, "You needed to use a different standard of value in preparing your report."

But as we'll talk in a minute, the use of the "as finally determined for gift tax or estate tax purposes" can have very real state law implications and transfer tax implications because the *McCord* Defined Value Agreement specifically defined the dollar value of the transfer to the noncharity donees $6.9 million. "As finally determined for Federal estate tax purposes" language basically leaves that determination up to either the IRS, if the taxpayer settles with them on the valuation issue, or to a finder of fact, whether it's your tax court judge or a jury in a district court trial.

*****

W. Frazier: There are a couple of things that I think because of the overturn of the *McCord* case with respect to the Bajaj method that I think maybe can be revisited now. And for one thing, for the last three years since the *McCord* Tax Court case came out, I've been silent on this because our case was under appeal and it would have been inappropriate for me to make public comment about it. But I think those strictures have been lifted and I think, you know, I have some things I might like to say on the methodology because I continue to see it used. And when I speak of the methodology, I mean to the extent that the Bajaj study is being used and it is actually a very good study, a very thorough study. But some of the conclusions drawn from it, I think, are incorrect. I probably don't have enough time to go into them but I would just basically say the Court's extrapolation of the 20% lack of marketability discount from the study itself is flawed and it can't be supported for a couple of reasons. One is that the study includes registered shares, and when we're valuing closely held stock or partnership interest that are closely held that have no ability to be registered, the extent to which the registered shares impacts the study makes it flawed. And so to that extent, the registered part of the study needs to be excluded.

And secondly, what the *McCord* Court thought they had in the way they used the study is not what they really wound up with. It's a real complicated statistical analysis. So basically, what the Court was after was two things. Number one, they wanted a study that included sizeable blocks or percentage size since what was transferred was a 40% interest. Although, I think that was an irrelevant point. But their main point was that the securities held in the McCord Partnership weren't that risky, and to compare them directly with restricted stock studies, which, for the most part, were comprised of small cap or micro cap, very volatile public companies was a mismatch. And, you know, there is some truth to that. Although, I think that is countered to a large extent by the holding period of the Partnership as opposed to the holding period of the restricted stocks.

But nevertheless, what the Tax Court used from the Bajaj study did not encompass the very characteristics they wanted to. And if you have the underlying data, you can see that that's not the case. So I think that's an issue that can be revisited.

Secondly, in determining the minority interest discount where a partnership or a pass-through entity holds real estate assets, the use of Real Estate Investment Trusts (REITs) to determine the minority interest discount, I think, are improper. The main reason being what happened in *McCord*, the discount from net asset value of the REITs was only 2%, and that's because the REITs, for the most part, are income-generating securities. They generate a very high current yield to the holders of the REIT securities, and I think that's, for the most part, why people buy REITs, and probably the real estate aspect is probably secondary. And for that reason, since they are generating a very high current yield, they tend to trade close to net asset value, as opposed to our partnership, which was distributing no cash from its real estate assets. As a matter of fact, they were leveraged assets and didn't have the ability to distribute cash to the partners. And I think that was a very, very extreme difference between the two. Nevertheless, the Court didn't see it that way.

But interestingly enough, the discount for minority interest on the real estate assets in the Partnership was 20%. The reason was they used the Wruck study which came up with a discount for marketability of 18%, and they added that 18% to the 2% and came up with a 20% minority interest discount, which is a clear case of mixing apples and oranges. This is a discount for minority interest, not marketability. And, you know, so to the extent that is used—and I think that analysis was used again in the *Peracchio* case, and that is certainly wrong, and that is something that needs to be revisited as well.

So again, to kind of sum up, to make the assumption that the *McCord* case, from the Fifth Circuit, doesn't add anything to the valuation argument, if you will, from the standpoint of family limited partnerships, I think is untrue. I think what it does is it opens the door for us to revisit a lot of issues that we thought were more or less lost during that three-year period while the *McCord* case was being appealed. Now that the appeal has come down, I think some of these issues will be revisited, and then hopefully, we'll get some either additional court cases or additional appellate decisions that will turn things around for us, at least I certainly hope so.

*****

S. Akers: Let's start talking now about planning implications from the *McCord* case. What do we do for the future going forward in light of the Fifth Circuit case? We've talked about the appraisal issues in the sense that even using defined value clauses or dollar value clauses does not mean that appraisals are not important. In fact, quite the contrary—they are just as important as ever because in this case, for example, the appraisal directly was used by the parties to come to an agreement of what percentage interest passed to the various parties in implementing the dollar value approach.

Similarly, if the clause that is used is one that gears the formula to values, "as finally determined for Federal gift tax purposes," and so whatever gift tax value you come up with in the gift tax audit is then going to determine the percentage interest that passed to the various parties. Well, then we all know that a very important part of the gift tax audit will be the appraisals by the parties. So this, in no way, minimizes at all the importance of appraisals in the process. It is just designed to try to put a cap around the amount of the gift tax that would be implicit in a particular transaction.

Will defined value clauses be used more in light of the *McCord* case? Differences of opinion on that for people that live in Texas like Will, John, and I, and that live in the Fifth Circuit, states governed by the Fifth Circuit Court of Appeals. I think that planners in those states feel a significant amount of comfort coming out of the *McCord* case.

Well, two caveats—one is this concept that the *McCord* case did not just clearly recognize a defined value clause. But I just don't think, personally, that that's the right analysis of the *McCord* case, and I think it did acknowledge that what this value clause was doing was transferring a dollar amount, and the Court did not have a problem with that.

The second caveat that we have to place on this case is that it specifically said that it was not addressing the public policy issues because those issues were not formally presented to the Court by the IRS. I agree with John that as you read this case, I just can't but reach the conclusion that this three-judge panel, if it had considered the public policy grounds, would have ruled that there were no public policy concerns. This case gave absolutely no hint of any kind of a smell problem. In the Tax Court case, there were some of the opinions where the judges did have a smell test problem with this approach and felt that it was abusive of the system. The IRS argument is that, "This is abusive of the system because"—one of the arguments coming out of the *Procter* case is that, "No matter what we do in the gift tax audit, we can't come up with anymore gift taxes, and so therefore, it ought to just be against public policy to use this kind of a clause." There was absolutely no hint in this case of any kind of a smell problem.

And indeed, there was a discussion in the case pointing out to the olfaction, that Judge Foley had referred to, that some of the judges were concerned with the olfaction of the case. And the Fifth Circuit pointed out that really what he was saying that that was a collegially correct term for a smell test. And this Fifth Circuit panel just had no problem—did not even give a hint of a smell test problem. If they had had any concern that there was an abuse going on here, that would have been at least hinted that somewhere in the case and hinted out that, "On another day when we can consider the public policy issues, these are issues there." There was just none of that.

Even so, IRS agents, I have no doubt, are still going to find these abusive. Now I hear reports that in some cases, they don't. But I do know in other situations, that IRS agents have told me that they view these clauses as just highly abusive in the sense that they just undo whatever the agent does on the audit.

To some degree, even so, so what, a high-dollar transaction is going to generate a lot of scrutiny by the IRS agent in any event. Are you really doing anything that hurts yourself if you throw in the additional argument of having a defined value clause?

So my guess is that at least in the Fifth Circuit Court of Appeals, we are going to see planners using defined value clauses more often, and I think even outside the Fifth Circuit in light of the fact that there is now a circuit court of appeals case. Now albeit, the Fifth Circuit is viewed as a taxpayer's circuit. But even so, we now have a circuit-level court of appeals case that did not have a smell problem with a defined value clause, and I think in light of that, that planners are going to be more inclined to use those clauses than they were in the past.

John, I might get your input on this issue of—should I use this clause? From a litigator's perspective, would you rather have a case where there was a gift transfer that used a defined value approach or do you think that that creates a smell problem around it and you'd rather litigate it without that clause?

J. Porter: I like having the clause in there because it gives me something else to argue. You recall that we had three arguments in *McCord*. One was that the defined value clause worked and it set the value of the interest transferred to the non-charity donees. Of course, in *McCord*, we have the Confirmation Agreement. We argued that those arm's length negotiations provided the best evidence of value. And then our third argument was that our valuation analysis was sound. In most typical transfer tax audits where maybe mom or dad has transferred a 50% interest in the partnership, typically, the only argument you have is argument number three, that the valuation analysis is sound. And so what this technique does is it gives me, as a litigator, additional arguments to assert against the Service. And quite frankly, I think, particularly in the Fifth Circuit, they're fairly strong arguments. But one of the things to note is that the Fifth Circuit's Assignment Agreement analysis wasn't just based on Fifth Circuit case law. It relied on a Supreme Court case, *Ithaca Trust*, and it also quoted some cases from different circuits, which basically—like *Propstra* out of the Ninth Circuit and *McMorris* out of the—I think it's out of the Tenth Circuit—which basically say, "Post-transfer valuation events should not be taken into account for purposes of determining the interest transferred." So I like it. I think it gives additional ammunition in the litigation. But, you know, I will say this—it very well could, at the examination level, raise issues that might not otherwise be present when somebody's looking at your transfer tax return.

*****

S. Akers: Another question a lot of people are asking about—should the clause now be designed with the *McCord* approach of basing the formula on a willing buyer/willing seller test or should you base the formula of what percentage interest passed to the various parties based on values "as finally determined for Federal gift tax purposes?"

Using the *McCord* approach, a willing buyer/willing seller test approach—an advantage of that is that you don't have the mechanical problem of having to wait, when in the *McCord* case, turned out 10 years to see what percentage interest was transferred.

Part of the design in the *McCord* case, John, as I understand it, is that having this Confirmation Agreement actually helps support the value, that you have parties at arm's length with each other.

In determining what percentage interest was passing. Perhaps it would be somewhat of a lesson of red flag abuse from an agent's point of view in that the agent doesn't see specifically the formulas based on values "as finally determined for Federal gift tax purposes." Whatever I come up with in the gift tax audit is directly going to affect the percentage interest that passes. So perhaps it wouldn't be as much of a perceived abuse situation by the agents and less of a *Procter* problem because of that.

It is important that the Fifth Circuit specifically approved the willing buyer/ willing seller standard. Now that's not to say that it would not have approved the formula with a formula basing what percentage interest passed "as finally determined for Federal gift tax purposes," but what is specifically approved was that willing buyer/willing seller approach.

I do think it's just critical, if you're using that approach, that you don't have any kind of a "winkwink" understanding among the various parties of what ultimately is going to pass of the percentage interest as they apply the dollar value transfer. And the Fifth Circuit emphasized, various different times, that there was not any kind of implied understanding among the parties as to what percentage interest was going to pass under this clause.

Some disadvantages of using that approach as opposed to the "as finally determined for Federal gift tax purposes"—in effect, if you use this willing buyer/willing seller approach and you don't have the ability just to tie your formula to the value "as finally determined for Federal gift tax purposes," then you're, in effect, having the parties decide what is passing under that willing buyer/willing seller test. Well, the effect of that is you put all the gift risk on the parties. And so, for example, if the surviving spouse is receiving the excess value over what passes under the dollar value transferred to the children, then if there's an incorrect valuation in that subsequent agreement of what percentage interest passed between the children and the spouse, the spouse has the gift tax problem. So in effect, you've just transferred this gift tax risk from the original donor to the parties who are entering into that agreement. Now we don't have that concern if it's a charity involved. A charity is not going to be making a gift. Now we may get attorney general involvement. I understand there now may even be an intermediate sanctions problem, and that one way of avoiding that would be for the charity to get its own independent appraisal. But we don't have a pure gift tax risk per se like we might with other parties.

So kind of the bottom line of where I would come down on that is that if you're using a charity as receiving the excess transfer that is not transferred under the dollar amount, the willing buyer/willing seller approach, rather than using "as finally determined for Federal gift tax purposes," may very well be a good approach. On the other hand, if you're not using a charity or a political party as receiving that excess, it may well be that you'd want to use the "as finally determined for Federal gift tax purposes" so that you don't put all that gift risk on the party to that second transaction.

So just some general comments—with all of this, there's no right or wrong—you're going to hear different, very well-respected planners doing it different ways, but those are some of the issues as I see them.

Fighting Legal Pitfalls with Family Limited Partnerships: A Practical Guide for Forming, Operating, and Defending FLPs

Moderator: Stephanie Loomis-Price
Speakers: Paige Ben-Yaacov, Garry Marshall

Excerpts from Business Valuation Resources' February 22, 2007 telephone conference transcript. The entire telephone conference transcript and presentation can be found online.

S. Loomis-Price: The first step in forming, operating, and defending a family limited partnership is to step back and actually consider whether it's appropriate to form the partnership at the outset. I'm currently on slide five, and here we talk about, "*Keeping Your Potential Future Audience in Mind*." Your preparation for the transfer tax audit begins really at the estate planning level. You should consider what you write in emails particularly because people tend to get rather casual in emails, in memos to the file regarding reasons for formation of the partnership, in letters to the client explaining the partnership and the advantages and disadvantages of those of the partnership, in time records for attorneys and accountants, et cetera.

You should keep in mind that the IRS [Internal Revenue Service], a judge, or even a jury may eventually review those documents that are written during the planning stages. And we are starting to see more and more that the IRS is requesting both in audit and in formal discovery for electronic email as well.

You should consider and document all substantive non-transfer tax reasons that fit the situation and avoid a template laundry list. It's not surprising that the IRS might be skeptical of witness testimony at trial five or 10 years after formation as to the reasons for forming the partnership, but they tend to take contemporaneous documents saying the same things as gospel. So it's really important to get those written reasons written into the file.

P. Ben-Yaacov: In addition, you need to consider whether the clients are ready for a partnership. Think about the sophistication of your clients. Just one kind of anecdotal thing that I have here—I have some clients where I explain to them about pro rata distributions beforehand. They seem to get it. They understand that if they have a 10 percent interest in the partnership, they get 10 percent of distributions that come out. And then six months down the road, I find out that the distributions weren't made pro rata. They had every intention. They didn't do it on purpose. Somehow the math just didn't work out even when they consulted with an accountant.

And the clients, you also need to consider whether they're willing to comply with the partnership agreement's terms. They need to understand that assets contributed to the partnership are no longer theirs. They're not available for their use. They are partnership assets.

And of course, the clients' willingness to pay professional fees over time.

G. Marshall: And Paige, I think this issue of professional fees is really important. The client has to realize that they're going to have to spend money to hire good experts. Everything that's done up front really sets the stage and impacts your ability to defend these things down the road. Trying to be cheap on the front end will oftentimes cost you much more on the back end.

P. Ben-Yaacov: I think that's an excellent point. The clients also need to think about what assets they have available to put into the partnership. When thinking about these assets, make sure that they don't want to put risky assets into a partnership with other valuable assets. And I think that can be best explained by an example. Let's say your potential partners have a ranch or something like that that they want to put into a partnership. What if they have people coming down to the ranch or they lease out—they have a hunting lease on it? There's the possibility that somebody could be injured on the ranch, and that person is going to look to the partnership to reimburse them for any injury they have, any kind of recovery they're looking to the partnership. So the partnership should have insurance to cover that situation. But if the recovery exceeds the insurance, that potential plaintiff is going to be looking to the partnership's other assets. So you never want to put something that can throw off liability, like a ranch or something else, into a partnership with cash, stocks and bonds that can be available to satisfy a liability.

The second and third bullet points here on this slide—no retirement plans, no IRAs [Individual Retirement Accounts], no stock in S Corporations—there's tax reasons why those assets just don't work in a partnership.

And the last bullet point—if you want to contribute stock in a closely held corporation to a partnership, you need to think about Section 2036(b) of the Internal Revenue Code. As I'm sure most of you are aware, that section says that if you try to give away stock in a closely held entity, and you retain the right to vote the stock, it's as if you never gave it away, and it's included back in your estate for estate tax purposes when you pass away. So if somebody puts stock into a partnership that retains the right to vote that stock, you're going to have those issues. Consider whether the partnership should have the right to vote the stock or if you should have some alternative arrangement, or if you want the partnership to have the right to vote the stock, consider what members of the partnership management will exercise that right.

S. Loomis-Price: We're moving to slide eight, still evaluating the potential assets that should be contributed to the partnership. And I would recommend that you refrain from contributing personal use assets to a partnership unless the partners and others are willing to provide rent to the partnership for using those assets. And what we mean by that, for instance, would be a beach house or the jet skis, or the ranch and the hunting lease that Paige was talking about a moment ago, unless the partners are really truly willing to treat this as a business asset. It shouldn't be contributed to the business to start out with.

Partners should retain enough assets outside of the partnership to support their lifestyle. And you might consider doing a cash flow analysis to make sure that, in fact, there's sufficient cash outside of the partnership—and by cash, I mean by more general usable assets—outside of the partnership to maintain the lifestyle.

G. Marshall: And if assets that are hard to value are contributed to the partnership—and these may include real estate or interest in other private entities—they could be private equity fund interests, hedge fund interests—they need to be appraised in order to calculate the initial ownership percentages in the partnership upon contribution. You also have to consider transfer restrictions on these assets and obtain the appropriate consents where necessary.

P. Ben-Yaacov: And if real estate or other non-liquid assets are going to be contributed to the partnership, in addition to any appraisal issues, you need to consider—as Garry just mentioned, you also need to think about how the partnership is going to get enough cash to maintain those assets, think about property taxes, other taxes, insurance, maintenance.

Likewise, if you have assets that are subject to debt, whether it's margin debt, mortgages, other kinds of debt, you have to consider income tax issues. If you take the mortgage example, think about your client has property subject to a mortgage that the client wants to contribute to the partnership. Well, after that property goes into the partnership, who's going to be making the mortgage payments? The partner who contributed the property and who hopefully previously was making the payments should not continue making those payments. That property is now partnership property, so the partnership should take on the obligation of making the payments. If the partner were to continue making the payments, the IRS may try to make hay out of this in the 2036 concept, retaining those bad strings that caused the assets to be included back in your estate. And also, every time the partner makes a payment on the mortgage, that increases the value of the property that is now in the partnership. So the partner is doing something to increase the value of the partnership property and the partner needs to receive compensation for that, whether in terms of having their partnership interest increased or in some other adjustment to the partnership. And that's something that needs to be documented. The other partners of the partnership need to consent. And honestly, I mean it can be a real administrative hassle.

So on the flip side, if the partner isn't going to be making the mortgage payments anymore, think about—does the partnership have enough cash to make the payments? And if the partnership does, the partner who contributed the property may have income to report on their income tax return because the partnership has relieved that partner from an obligation. If the partner wants to avoid that, the partnership agreement needs to have language about how that partner is still on the hook for the mortgage if the partnership misses a payment.

And then the last bullet point on this slide 9—you also need to think about investment company rules. The general rule is that when properties are contributed to a partnership, there's no income tax gain. But there is an exception to that. In the investment company rules, if the contribution of the properties results in diversification for the partners, then you could be triggering gain.

G. Marshall: And Paige, along this line of discussion, what Stephanie was talking about just a second ago, I had a recent example, a client example, where an FLP was formed and an office building was the primary asset of the partnership. But one of the partners was occupying the building and a lease had not been formalized yet, and we strongly encouraged the client to formalize the agreement preferably on reasonable market-based terms before we proceeded and completed our appraisal.

P. Ben-Yaacov: Yeah, definitely. That's a good point.

S. Loomis-Price: Once you figured out which assets you think you're going to contribute to the partnership, it's important to also consider who your potential partners might be. You should consider the health of the partners. For instance, in the *Stone* case, we saw the court consider the fact that Mr. and Mrs. Stone, the elderly clients there, were in good health at the time that the partnership was formed, and that was a factor in holding that that partnership should be upheld, and the assets were not included back in the Stone's estate under Section 2036. And on the contrary, in *Strangi*, what we saw the court consider was the fact that the elderly client there was, in fact, in very bad health, and so that was a factor in the court's determination that Section 2036 applied.

You should also consider having each of the partners make meaningful contributions to the partnership, but there are cases where we've had meaningful contributions where the courts still did not uphold the meaningful contributions as a factor.

You should also be aware of anti-diversification rules, which Paige mentioned briefly a moment ago.

P. Ben-Yaacov: And I had mentioned how that might tie in, but one of the ways to get around the anti-diversification rules is to have one partner contribute the majority of the assets and the other partner contribute de minimus assets, which is an exception to the anti-diversification rules. But then you have this issue with not all partners having meaningful contributions.

S. Loomis-Price: You should also engage and consult with advisors who have extensive experience in this area. It's important to avoid kit partnerships. We've seen a few cases where those partnerships were basically just knocked out of the water in part because there wasn't the tailoring and the full thought going into creating the entity.

Any attorney or accountant who will be involved with the partnership should be consulted sooner rather than later because the sooner they're involved, the sooner they can make sure that all the Is are dotted and all the Ts are crossed.

*****

P. Ben-Yaacov: When the partners are forming the partnership, they need to discuss all of the partnership terms to consider. When you're thinking about the management structure, talk about who's going to run the partnership. If one of the stated non-tax reasons for forming the partnership is to involve the family and educate them about the family assets and the family's investment philosophy, involve them in the management. Make them perhaps co-managing partners or something like that that make your management structure reflect the non-tax reasons that you stated for forming the partnership. Think about what the managers are going to receive in terms of compensation.

Think about what the partnership's investment policy will be. In dealing with the IRS, it can be helpful if the partnership's investment strategy is not the same as the one that the individuals had before the partnership was created. And of course, that makes sense because prior to formation, the individuals had certain needs that their investment philosophy was focused on. After formation, you've got a partnership. The partnership needs to be managed in light of what's best for all of the partnerships. Sometimes, however, it can be okay if the partnership just happens to have the same investment philosophy that the partners had beforehand if it makes sense for all the partners after formation. You might think about the *Schutt* case. But what's important is to sit down and discuss it and to have a meeting with the partners so they can figure out which way they want to go.

Also talk about expected distributions, whether the transfer of partnership interests will be restricted, how long the partnership is going to last. There's no right or wrong answer. Just make sure that everyone is on the same page.

S. Loomis-Price: And in an ideal world, you would have separate counsel for all participants. What we're finding is that the courts are looking to how many attorneys were involved in relation to how many partners are involved in considering whether the creation of the partnership meets the bona fide sale for full and adequate consideration exception to Section 2036.

On a more practical level, having different attorneys involved really goes to keeping everyone involved, making sure that the agreement is fully negotiated, and that the partnership agreement is actually read and understood by the partners.

G. Marshall: Stephanie, it seems to me that some of these "bad facts" cases recently have noted the lack of active negotiations on the part of each of the partners. I assume that's a real important aspect of this.

S. Loomis-Price: The more active negotiation we can point to, the better off we are both in audit and in court. And so in that regard, you might hear people say, "We don't want to see drafts of partnership agreements in the file." From a litigation perspective, I can tell you to the extent that there are drafts and it shows that there are changes that were requested by one party versus another, that really helps me establish that this, in fact, was a bona fide sale, that it was negotiated—this isn't just a family deal.

You should also ensure that schedules to the partnership agreement are complete. The partnership agreement should accurately set forth assets contributed to the partnership and the resulting ownership's interest in the partnership. And in fact, some states are now requiring that there be a complete list attached to the partnership agreement showing the assets contributed, their values at the time of formation, and the resulting partnership interest.

P. Ben-Yaacov: And not only should the partnership schedules show the assets that were contributed to the partnership, you need to take all those extra steps to make sure that the assets really are transferred, and all the transfer work is done. I like to have fees and other transfer documents prepared prior to the formation date. That helps to ensure that transfer of the title really happens. I like to have the parties sign the transfer documents at the same time as the partnership agreement and the other formation documents.

It's amazing kind of what you see when you actually prepare the transfer documents. I usually refer to any transferability restrictions. It helps me to see what consents we need to obtain. There may be an unrelated third party who has to sign off on the transfer of the assets to the partnership.

And then also, you need to make sure, of course, that the partners own the assets to be contributed to the partnership before the partnership is created.

S. Loomis-Price: One of the things that the IRS likes to point to is kind of the more nitty-gritty in terms of details with formation of a partnership such as whether or not the partners filed for an employer identification number fairly soon after creation of the partnership. It seems rather common sense, but it's the type of thing that can fall through the cracks. And unfortunately, it's also the type of thing that the courts and the IRS are pointing to to show that this wasn't respected as a separate entity.

P. Ben-Yaacov: And once you have that employer identification number, you can go ahead and create the partnership bank accounts and the brokerage accounts, follow up with the client or the accountant, whoever is handling those things shortly after the partnership is formed to make sure that everything has been done.

S. Loomis-Price: Almost immediately, a good partnership accountant should be engaged. Accounting issues, what we're finding more and more, can make or break a court's view of whether to respect the existence of the partnership.

Things you might take into account when determining who you should choose as your accountant would be their understanding of the fact that initial ownership interest should not change in the absence of additional capital contributions, redemptions, and sales; knowledge of and familiarity with Section 754 elections; an understanding of protective claims; and perhaps extensive experience with audit procedures.

P. Ben-Yaacov: One good rule of thumb when thinking about a good partnership accountant—if the client doesn't already have an accountant engaged, you might, when interviewing accountants, ask them how much of their practice relates to partnership accounting, how many partnership returns they prepared, that kind of thing.

In forming the partnership, you also need to make sure that the partners receive interest in the partnership and proportioned to the fair market value of the assets that each of them contributed to the partnership. And the fair market value of the assets that each contributed to the partnership needs to be reflected in each partner's capital account. And I know that in the business world, this isn't always the model that people use. One partner may be contributing the experience and the know-how—another partner is contributing the assets. So their contributions—their partnership interests don't reflect the fair market value of what the property they contributed to the partnership. But it's hard to follow that kind of model in a family situation because you have the gift-on-formation argument that we've seen in some of the cases. There are also Section 2701 issues that you run into. It's a very complicated area of the law. It's really best just to avoid it by forming pro rata partnerships with each partner getting a partnership interest that reflects the fair market value of the assets they contributed.

S. Loomis-Price: And next, this is another issue that we see the IRS kind of picking on and looking at in determining whether or not people are treating partnerships as separate business entities. Consider amortizing partnership set-up fees. That's something that you would see if you were setting up a partnership with Exxon or with Texaco, but it is something that tends to fall through the cracks on a family limited partnership.

P. Ben-Yaacov: Sometimes, as Garry mentioned earlier, assets that are hard to value will be contributed to the partnership and you might not know the value of the assets being contributed on the date the partnership actually is formed. So you might find out the values later. And when that happens, you just need to come back and amend the partnership agreement effective as of the date of formation to say, "We thought the values were X. It turns out they're Y. As a result, the partnership interests are so forth." And we also like to see language in the partnership agreement itself that reflects that the parties intend to do this.

S. Loomis-Price: And again, from a litigation standpoint, be prepared to produce documents in your file to the IRS if necessary. The best evidence of formation rationale often comes from the correspondence prepared in connection with the estate planning transaction to start out with, and it's best to keep your potential audience in mind. Of course, many of those documents may be attorney-client privilege and that privilege can be asserted. However, what we found is that the assertion of a privilege may lead to negative inferences by the IRS.

Next, we turn to maintenance of the partnership on slide 23. Consider filing tax returns for each year in existence. Even if you form the partnership on the 20th of December, you might consider going ahead even though it is an administrative hassle, filing an income tax return for that partial stub year. Again, it's one of the things that the Service points to in saying, "Well, you've treated this rather informally because if you had been Mobil, you would have filed a tax return for those 10 days even though there wasn't much activity."

And someone recently asked me, "Is it really worth paying $500, $1,000, $5,000 to file a tax return for a small portion of the year?" And my answer in return was, "Is it really worth losing the validity of the partnership over a $5,000 accounting bill?" If the answer is yes, you might have to go back to the very first slide, which was consider whether you want to form a partnership in the first place.

You should check with relevant state authorities to determine whether annual or bi-annual registration statements are required. What we're finding with the IRS is that almost immediately upon filing a petition, whether in the tax court or other fora, the IRS is checking with the relevant secretary of state to determine whether the partnership is in good standing.

P. Ben-Yaacov: In addition to complying with any tax returns that need to be filed and other reports, make sure that the partners are complying with the terms of the partnership agreement.

Look to see whether they're having periodic meetings, if required. Look to see whether there are annual statements that are required, annual distributions, payments on preferred interest, that kind of thing. If there are periodic meetings required, make sure those are held. Even if they're not, it makes sense to think that the partners will get together informally or talk about things. And they might want to consider taking minutes at those meetings because a lot of times, there'll be talk about what investment philosophy the partnership should have or what distributions the partnership will make. And it's funny how after you have the meeting or get off the call, memories fade. So consider taking minutes but also be careful about what is written and that goes back to what Stephanie said in the beginning about keeping your potential future audience in mind. Any of these minutes may become later bedtime reading material for the IRS, and so make sure there's nothing in there that you wouldn't want to share.

And to help your clients comply with the terms of the partnership agreement and do all these things they're supposed to be doing, you might consider providing a summary memo to them. You might think about periodically reviewing their records as if you were the IRS. And if your client is willing, think about holding an annual meeting with them so you can go over a checklist to make sure they're doing everything they're supposed to do.

*****

G. Marshall: Paige, what are your thoughts on making annual exclusion gifts with partnership units? I've seen, in some cases, clients do this without an appraisal, where they may have an appraisal that's a few years old and they simply apply the same discounts to the updated net asset value.

P. Ben-Yaacov: I'm glad you brought this up because this is actually one of the questions we've received by email. And we've received a couple of others that we may go back to at the end of the presentation, but we're kind of further along.

But on the annual exclusion question, I have seen clients do that, and my concern when they don't get an appraisal is that they don't have any protection on future gift tax liability. If you have an annual exclusion gift, of course, you don't have to document it on a gift tax return. But eventually, if your client passes away and there's an estate tax return filed, the IRS may start digging, they might see that at one point the client had an interest in the partnership, and they might ask, "How did that client get rid of all their partnership interest?" So then you have to go back to all these prior transfers, which should have been properly documented, and hopefully, there is something there in the file that indicates how the client determined that the value was under the annual exclusion limit. But there's absolutely no protection on it. It could be 20 years later and the IRS has the benefit of hindsight, which they're not supposed to use, but with the benefit of hindsight, you can see how the assets in the partnership might have appreciated. And they might claim that the transfers were greater than the annual exclusion limit and that a gift tax return should have been filed then—was not filed then. A gift tax was due and not paid, and you have to think about interest, and all that kind of stuff.

So I really would prefer to see clients get a good appraisal every time they make a transfer of a partnership interest regardless of whether it's intended to be an annual exclusion gift or not. And then that will give them—and then if they also report it on a gift tax return, that will give them the protection of a three-year statute of limitations. The IRS has three years to look at it. If they don't, they can't come back later and argue that the value was higher than we thought.

The problem is that the clients just don't want to pay the transaction cost for a smaller gift. They don't want to hire an appraiser to value a gift for an annual exclusion amount.

So I kind of would prefer to actually see the client, if it meets with their goals, just make a bigger taxable gift to make the transaction cost worth it.

G. Marshall: Let's go to page 36 of the materials. At death, you need to review the partnership agreement to determine the character of the interest that's passing, whether it's a general partnership interest or a LP interest or an assignee. And there are some special valuation rules that come into play under chapter 14 with respect to say a general partnership interest that, per the terms of the agreement, may automatically convert upon death or a transfer. And in that case, these special rules have to be applied in terms of the valuation.

Paige, can you talk about that for just a moment?

P. Ben-Yaacov: Sure, as you mentioned, you're referring to chapter 14, and if your partnership agreement was put in place after the date of those rules, which I think was 1990—it's been awhile since I looked at it—then if your general partner interest, for example, converts to a limited partnership interest upon the general partner's death or if there's a lapse of voting rights or liquidation rights, you have a lapse. And basically, you have to value the interest as it existed prior to the general partner's death. And sometimes that may not cause a problem, but think about if the interest is passing to a spouse and you're trying to get the marital deduction, what's interesting is that for valuation purposes, on the federal estate tax return, you have to show a higher value, but what's passing to the spouse is actually limited partnership interests with a lesser value, and I have real concerns about marital deduction issues.

G. Marshall: And what happens if the estate remains a general partner but loses managing partner status? Does that also constitute a lapse?

P. Ben-Yaacov: I think that's an excellent question. I've never fully researched it, but I think there's an argument that that is not a lapse because if you think about it, think about a big corporation like Exxon or something. There's somebody who is the president of Exxon, and that's kind of akin to the managing partner of a partnership in a way. It's who has responsibility for running the partnership. But when the managing partner of Exxon passes away, nobody expects that his heirs get to step in and be the manager and that's not a lapse or anything. And I know that we're in a different situation and that's not a closely held partnership or anything like that. But I think analogies can be drawn and I think there's a very good argument that the loss of managing partner status is not a lapse, but full disclosure, I haven't fully researched it.

G. Marshall: Well, I guess a related issue here now that we're talking about chapter 14, an example that I have of a client I worked with, it was an old partnership pre-1990, had a provision that upon death, the other partners could buy the deceased partner's interest at essentially a capital account balance, which was a lot lower than the fair market value. And the issue that we ran into there was in the previous death that occurred with a partner, that provision had not been invoked, and so we could not rely exclusively on that. We did give it considerable weight, but we thought it would be disingenuous to just say that even though economically, it would make sense, that they would exercise that right and pay a value that's below fair market value because it hadn't been done in the past. There was a bad precedent with that.

P. Ben-Yaacov: Yeah, and there's case law too on whether those kinds of buy/sell agreements can be used in setting value or whether they provide weight. And then once you get past 1990 and you have chapter 14, there are specific requirements that have to be met in order to consider those types of buy/sell arrangements.

S. Loomis-Price: Also, at death, it is important to go ahead and look at the partnership agreement to see whether the executor steps into the partnership's shoes of the decedent's partner because sometimes we have seen that provision in various partnership agreements.

You should consider maintaining the partnership interest in the hands of the executor rather than distributing it to any beneficiary who may be entitled to it during the estate administration until a closing letter is received from the IRS. We've had difficulty in various matters where the partnership interest was distributed fairly shortly after death and certainly before the IRS became involved. And the complexity involved afterwards just made it quite clear that it's a lot easier if that partnership interest is still in the hands of the executor as opposed to in the hands of the beneficiary.

Once a closing letter is received, you should document the transfer from the estate to the beneficiary and that should be executed by both the executor and the beneficiary.

Next, we turn to transfers by redemption, and this is one of the more sticky areas simply because of the complexity of the mechanics of a redemption to start out with. And I have had numerous matters in which trying to explain why a redemption does not affect the value of a remaining partner's interest has gotten more and more difficult depending upon on who I'm working with with the IRS.

You should review the partnership agreement to ensure that the partnership is not prohibited from redeeming the interest. Document the redemption to be executed by both partnership management and the transferring partner. And ensure that the books and records of the partnership reflect the decrease to the transferring partner's interest and the corresponding proportionate increase to all the remaining partner's interest.

*****

S. Loomis-Price: My next question is from Jarrod Taylor in West Virginia, and his question is, "Would you recommend the patriarch with the significant assets use his annual exclusion to gift assets to his children whom would then use that gift as their capital contribution in the formation of the partnership?"

And I'm going to take the first stab at this and I'm going to ask Paige for her thoughts as well. But I will say that, for instance, in the *Stone* case, we had not only gifts of cash by the parents, but also gifts of real estate, and these were prior to the formation of the partnerships. And then each of the individual children used those assets—and perhaps others and perhaps not—to fund the partnerships that were set up for each of them. And the court pointed to the fact that formal deeds were filed. They were filed in the county records. Those children had those assets. They owned them outright before the formation of the partnerships.

And I've since seen this issue in other matters where the timing was not quite so clear, and the Service has pointed to that as not quite meeting the standard of *Stone*.

So the clearest thing that I can say is I don't have a problem with this, but I do think that it's important to make sure that there is a time period that elapses between the gift to the child and the child's contribution to the partnership. And I would also say that if that child is a minor, you might want to have a third party involved, whether it's an independent third party or a separate family member entirely, who is serving as the guardian, if you will, although it doesn't have to be that formal a relationship, but someone who is actually making the decision on behalf of the child.

P. Ben-Yaacov: I think those are good points. I like having a family limited partnership, it implies involvement by the family, and that's one of the very good non-tax reasons to involve family members, to teach them about the management of assets. And if the children don't have assets on their own, then yeah, that makes sense for the patriarch to give them annual exclusion gifts before the contribution to the partnership, and then have those children contribute the assets to the partnership as their capital contributions. As Stephanie pointed out, you need to make sure that the timing on that is clear. But I do like that idea very much.

And also, if you're giving annual exclusion gifts to the children—$12,000 is a lot to me—I wouldn't mind if somebody handed me $12,000, but it's not a lot to play with in terms of being able to diversify and invest in different things. So I think it makes sense for the children to contribute that into a bigger pot of money and have more investment options, which is another great non-tax reason for the formation of the partnership.

Sometimes what I see happen is that over the course of years, a patriarch will have created a present interest trust or a Crummey trust for children, and so there's this trust that has a small amount of assets in it. And the question comes up, "Can the trustee of that trust contribute the assets to the partnership?" And I think that there are a lot of good reasons for doing that to facilitate the management of those assets and so forth. But when a trustee gets involved in that area, the trustee has to be careful because of its fiduciary obligations to the child. What the trustee is doing is contributing assets with a value of X to a partnership and receiving back a partnership interest with a value, something less than X. So kind of the flip side of what Stephanie was saying to involve a guardian on behalf of the child or someone kind of looking out for the child's interest. If a trustee does this on behalf of the child, the trustee should involve the child in the decision if they're old enough to meaningfully participate.

And also, I mean the trustee is changing the nature of the assets. If it's a present interest trust, at age 21, the child has the ability to take those assets out of the trust. I mean the trust should terminate unless it's extended. And that would be the child's decision. So now the child, instead of receiving assets that they can go do whatever they want with at age 21, might be getting a limited partnership interest in a partnership.

So while I like the idea both of having children contribute individually to a partnership and trustees of trusts for children contribute, there are special issues for trustees to consider.

Hot Issues on FLPs/LLCs: Reality, Recognition, and Valuation

Moderator: Shannon Pratt
Speakers: Owen Fiore, George Hawkins, and Curtis Kimball

Excerpts from Business Valuation Resources' October 21, 2003 telephone conference transcript. The entire telephone conference transcript can be found online.

S. Pratt: To start out the panel, I'll ask this question, directed to Owen. I've often heard you use the phrase, Owen, "the partnership between attorney and appraiser" and, more recently, "the valuation spectrum." Briefly, what do you mean by these expressions and how do they relate to the timing that the attorney should bring the appraiser into the case?

O. Fiore: As an estate planner and tax litigator, what I've found over the years is that the tax attorney or CPA and other advisor must work in a very close, cooperative manner with appraisers. That means that the appraiser is independent, and the attorney respects that. What it relates to is the fact that the appraisal process, when dealing with pass-through entities like our subject today, FLPs and LLCs, involves looking at the enterprise, or as the case may be, the NAV value of the entity, and then dealing with the specific interest that is being valued, whether that's a partnership interest, an LLC interest, an assignee interest, or whatever it may be. That's really what that relates to. Now, in the valuation spectrum, as we'll see later when we talk about 2036(a) and some of the issues involved, we'll find that the attorney cannot walk away from the client when they sign the documents. The attorney or CPA, as the case may be, must really assist the client in operating the entity. The timing of the appraiser being involved is—in my view is that the appraiser can be an extremely helpful professional early on at the time of planning, at the time of compliance, namely the gift or the estate tax return, and certainly in appeals, and eventually, if necessary, in Tax Court.

S. Pratt: Well, the first rule for using a pass-through entity as an effective estate planning tool, is it's got to be recognized as a valid entity. Now, in *Hackl*, the partners were deemed to have future interests, which are not recognized as valid gifts. Curt, could you please define "future interest"? And then, Owen and George, could you please chime in on the implications of that?

C. Kimball: Well, as used in the *Hackl* case, §2503 discusses the issue of annual gift exclusions. You're now allowed to utilize $11,000 to any one individual transferee of annual gifting. In that particular case, the future interest is—it's actually a legal term, so I'm sure Owen will have some comments on that. It includes issues like reversions, remainders, and other interests, whether they're vested or contingent in that matter. In essence, it's anything that will be a future received obligation that is not going to be received in the immediate future. It is something that is not directly tied to a security such as a bond or another kind of security that has the delayed payout. It really more relates to other types of ownership interests that don't have an immediate payout.

S. Pratt: To not qualify as gifts under the IRS regulations. In other words, "future interest," you're telling us, Curt, is something that the participant gets no benefit from immediately.

C. Kimball: Right. It's the possession or enjoyment at some future date in time that's the critical issue. In fact, you could have a valid entity that issues this, but in this case you might have an issue of when the benefits are received.

O. Fiore: One of the pleasurable cases that I was able to be involved in in 1991 was *Estate of Cristofani,* which dealt with contingent remainder interests. Those contingent remainder interests were determined by the full Tax Court in the *Cristofani* case to be present interest. The problem in the *Hackl* case, which involved a tree farm that had some four or five years to go before there would be any merchantable timber—the problem in that case was that the partnership agreement was drafted in such a way so that Mr. Hackl, one of the two donors with his wife, was named the lifetime manager. Ostensibly, the agreement said that you could not transfer anything. So the regulations under the gift tax regulations say that they have a present interest. You must have a present, substantial, economic interest and benefit to enjoy either income or principal. My view is that, first, many people use annual exclusions in other ways, so they don't worry about annual exclusions, even though they're $11,000 per donor/per donee. But, by the same token, if you're going to expect to have these exclusions—like, in *Hackl,* there were like 88 per year type of thing. Then you have to draft the agreement rather carefully and craftily so that it meets the qualification.

My view on legal issues, to be very honest with you folks and your attendees, is that my view is that on legal issues the appraiser, yes indeed, can be a great help without having the downside of malpractice exposure by relating tax advisors and CPAs to the issues that the appraiser sees in making sure that the appraiser gets the right legal assumptions up front so that the appraiser can use the legal assumptions properly in the appraisal report and go on with his or her analysis of the appraisal methodology and the conclusions of value.

C. Kimball: Do you provide appraisers with a written set of legal assumptions, or do you merely discuss them, or is there some myth of written and oral discussion on those issues?

O. Fiore: The answer to that is there's a mix, but in a recent case we've just settled with Judge Paige Marvel this last Monday—we had a case scheduled for trial. What we did was the original—this was a general partnership case with a 42% interest in the decedent's estate. The first appraisal valued it as a general partnership interest. You can imagine that the IRS appraiser, who did the same thing, came up with 42%. You've got the right to dissolve and all that sort of stuff. We basically, for our trial report, valued it as an assignee interest, and it went from 0 to 25% discount, which is less than the 32% that the 706 showed, but the client was extremely happy. You can provide them a written analysis that was attached, now listen to this, attached to the appraisal report of the legal assumption memo provided by counsel for the taxpayer.

G. Hawkins: I think several things to try to avoid *Hackl* problems attorneys basically have chosen kind of one of three paths or all three of them. One is they try to assure some sort of income distributions from the entity to say that there is some current economic benefit. Another would be that they assure that they don't have any restrictions on the gifted interest that make it impossible for a donee to sell the interest. The third, which is the most common that we've seen after *Hackl,* was having some kind of put right, where the holder of the interest has the right to put it back to the entity and have the value determined in some way. That's problematic. That's one where I could see where an appraiser could help the attorney before they draft it, because sometimes attorneys—the way they define the put right is based on net asset value, which certainly defeats the ability possibly to get discounts if somebody can put it back at net asset value. So we've seen some horror situations where people have already put in language like that and had done gifts and had this put right that really is self-defeating.

O. Fiore: I think that what this shows is that the business valuation appraiser has a real contribution that can be made to assist the attorney in drafting the agreement if you get in early enough. That's part of Shannon's question. How do we get the appraiser involved? My belief is that the appraiser should be involved at least as a consultant early on.

*****

S. Pratt: Now, a series of cases ran afoul of §2036(a) because the donor retained "enjoyment of the property" after it was allegedly donated to the partnership. Most of these cases involved activity after the formation of the partnership.

For example, Ms. Schauerhamer, who was your client, Owen, put partnership money into her own personal bank account, which was a no-no. That got the partnership disqualified. There were other cases where the donors took out monies or there were monies taken out by the donors disproportionately to the other partners. One recent case said—the *Kimbell* case said that the provisions of the partnership agreement itself were enough to disqualify under §2036. Now, is the IRS likely to use that tactic in the future, and how could retaining the appraiser avoid this problem?

O. Fiore: This is a very broad and difficult question, and I have to go back just a little bit for our listeners because 2036(a) is intended—when you look at my NYU material, you'll see that. I've actually recently updated for the California State Bar annual tax meeting.

I think the issue of 2036(a)—first we have to step back and emphasize that that is an estate tax issue. We know, and later on we'll probably get a chance, Shannon, with your good questioning, to talk about *Lappo* and *Peracchio*. Last month, you had an excellent discussion with John Porter and others on the *Lappo* case, and *Peracchio* came up afterward. Those cases both point out that for income and gift tax purposes, family limited partnerships and LLCs are alive and well. When you get to 2036(a), 2036(a) was constructed to make sure that incomplete or testamentary transfer type gifts did not eliminate estate tax being applied to those gifts. Therefore, it's a very broad section. It's almost like in the income tax area—the difference between gross income, assignment of income, and deductions. It's a very broad section. People have not focused on that until the last few years. In my case, the *Schauerhamer* case, was the first of those cases in 1997. Then you had *Reichert* and *Thompson* and *Harper*, and then you have *Strangi I* and *II*.

So one of the things to think about 2036(a) is to remember that FLPs, as Judge Cohen even said in *Strangi I,* are alive and well, and the IRS cannot use suspicions on estate planning motives to kill off an FLP if the Is are dotted and the Ts are crossed. Now, when you get to 2036(a), however, you've got two sections, not just one. You've got 2036(a)(1) that all the cases before *Kimbell* and *Strangi II*, *Strangi II* being the second decision of the Tax Court in May of this year—you've got all the cases dealing with 2036(a)(1). The issue there has been: was there an implied agreement that mama or dad or whoever was the donor would keep control of everything and enjoyment, retained enjoyment, until date of death? That's a very broad standard. It's an implied agreement with or without a contractually enforceable situation. Then, 2036(a)(2), which is the new issue that the IRS is so excited about, that says that if the donor retains the right to designate the enjoyment by someone else with other people, with or without other people being involved, that basically is the same problem in that everything comes back at the estate. That one is really up in the air. Now the *Kimbell* case, you refer to the case where the partnership agreement was enough to disqualify. The *Kimbell* case was an extremely poorly drafted partnership agreement, with all due respect to whoever drafted it, and that is it relieved mama as general partner from any fiduciary obligation whatsoever in the written document. I don't think any lawyer that's listening in, or any of your friends, the appraisers that are here, would write an agreement like that. I think that *Kimbell* is distinguishable, even though it is on appeal. Yet that doesn't answer the 2036(a)(2) problem. In the—one last comment, which I think is significant, is in the *Byrum* case, Chief Justice Powell, who wrote the decision for the U.S. Supreme Court, made a clear statement. He said, "This court...," now this is back in '72, and this is the big bruha about whether *Byrum* applies to family partnerships. He said, "This court has never held that merely having management rights is enough to bring in 2036(a)(2)." Now, sadly, Judge Cohen ignored that. But remember, Judge Cohen's opinion in *Strangi II*, this last May 20, was a one-judge decision. It does not have precedent value of any significance. It likely, according to Norm Lofgren, the attorney for the taxpayer, once the decision documents are entered, it likely will be appealed to the Fifth Circuit, thankfully.

G. Hawkins: You said that the agreement waived the fiduciary obligation of the GP. But didn't alsothe agreement give Mrs. Kimbell the power to remove the GP and make herself the GP?

O. Fiore: You're absolutely right. It was so broadly written. It's almost like a *Hackl* type of thing, where, I really believe, unnecessarily, the senior person, who probably doesn't know anything about the agreement anyway, assuming they read it, the senior person has all of these rights that they don't really need. Frankly, in the *Lappo* and the *Peracchio* cases, the gift tax cases, both of those senior people gave away virtually everything, and yet as of the date that I understand that this thing occurred, they were still general partners. So, when I was at the Notre Dame Tax and Estate Planning Institute, I met the lawyer for *Lappo*. I, from the podium said, "Let's go out and give away that general partnership interest." Why do you want to be general partner and subject yourself to 2036(a)(1) or (2) when you've already given away everything to the kids?

*****

S. Pratt: Turning to another subject, any security, but especially interests in pass-through entities, can be described as a "bundle of rights." Please describe what rights the appraiser should consider, the sources of information about what the rights are, and how those rights impact value. I'm going to ask you, Curt, to comment first on this question. This will probably be the longest answer of the session. Then I'm going to ask George and Owen to add to it.

C. Kimball: Well, that is a very broad question, since what we need to look at as a foundational issue is, of course, as Owen said in our working closely with the attorneys who are part of this case, is to look at the legal bundle of rights, which typically are embodied in the partnership agreement. If it's an LLC, it's embodied in the operating agreement and the other agreements. There may be side agreements also with respect to any of these interests. It really is important to understand from a business standpoint what the issues are that are laid out, because a number of these limited partnerships and LLCs are designed like a tailor-made suit to the facts and circumstances of each group of individuals who are involved in the wealth management of the assets that are within those asset management entities. So, that's the first source. Of course, how those rights impact value goes to two broad categories of what we call adjustments for the relative lack of control and adjustments for the relative lack of marketability of the specific interest that's being transferred, sold or otherwise—

S. Pratt: Right. And, Curt, I'd like to inject an emphasis here that when you're discussing the minority interest or discount or the lack of control discount or the lack of marketability discount, you should emphasize what those rights and limitations are. Few appraisals do that.

G. Hawkins: That's the real problem with so many FLP and LLC valuations. Appraisers just assume blindly that what they're valuing is a minority interest that lacks control. Then they assume to go ahead and take real estate limited partnerships that are publicly traded or closed-end funds and try to develop discounts. But what they should first do before they even start doing the valuation is to carefully read the agreement and understand what the rights and the lack of rights are of the GP and the LP or the manager and the members and understand what those say, because you can have a minority interest that has control that may be a limited partnership interest but may be able to control the entity. Conversely, you can have the GP interest that may not have much control at all.

O. Fiore: One of the things that is very important is to understand where the appraiser needs to have the input of counsel because, of course, it is not helpful to the appraiser to be making legal judgments. That is not to say that lawyers can make good legal judgments. It's just to say that we need to get the information from the lawyer in terms of legal assumptions as to how things work. One of the things that I've found very helpful in FLP cases, because IRS generally, and their favorite appraisers, who will remain nameless, but we all know their names—one of the things that is very helpful is to recognize that the hypothetical willing buyer or willing seller standard applies to the interest gifted or at death. The other ownership interests, all the real people, when that came up in the *Simplot* case, where Judge Jacobs was reversed by the Ninth Circuit, he determined, with the help of the IRS appraiser, that there should be a 3% premium for control. Unfortunately, he based it, because the Ninth Circuit reversed it, on the value of the whole company, which was sort of nuts. But he said that somebody would pay a premium for a seat at the table. It's sort of interesting. If there were three or four Simplots sitting at the table, and the Fiores showed up with this hypothetical interest, guess who would go get the coffee? So the whole point is that you have to look at the reality. Another interesting case is the 1997 case, Tax Court Memo No. 1997-53, Judge Swift dealt with a bank holding company in New York State, and Martin Hanan for the IRS [of] Business Valuation Services, said there should be a 35% premium for a 27% interest because the hypothetical buyer would use that as a lever to get control. Judge Swift clearly said—

S. Pratt: As I recall, Judge Swift clearly—

O. Fiore: He knocked them off.

S. Pratt: He knocked off the IRS on that one.

O. Fiore: The reason for that is our hypothetical willing buyer and willing seller standard, which takes into account all of these interesting bundle of rights, still has to recognize that there are real people as the other owners of that entity.

S. Pratt: Owen, earlier you used the term "an assignee interest." That certainly relates to this bundle of rights. Now, how does an assignee interest differ from a normal limited partnership interest?

O. Fiore: Well, this has been—the cases that refer to this that are cited in my materials, such as *McLendon* in the Fifth Circuit, *Adams* in the Fifth Circuit, and we had this recent case, as I mentioned, before Judge Marvel, and we dealt with the assignee interest. What is an assignee interest? Well, one of the things that Stacy Eastland, who is John Porter's partner some years ago and now with Goldman Sachs, one of the things that Stacy has always pointed out is that you cannot make someone my partner. Let's say that the group of us on the phone, not counting the attendees, are all partners. Well, generally speaking, you can't make somebody else your partner. The difference between a corporation and a partnership is the personal nature of the partnership relationship. Therefore, generally speaking, for general partnerships and also limited partnerships—you've got to look at each state's statute. That's why the lawyers have to be involved. Generally speaking, the transfer, the hypothetical willing buyer and willing seller transfer, is of an assignee interest. In this case, we basically converted or changed the first appraisal by the same appraisal firm—it's a good firm in Los Angeles, friends of ours—we changed their first assumption that it was a general partnership interest. We said, no it's not a general partnership interest; it's an assignee interest. Therefore, the discount went from 32 to 36% for trial. The IRS guy came in and appraised a general partnership interest and said 15. We quickly changed the burden of proof because the IRS had said zero, and that's under the *Mitchell, Simplot* and *Morrissey* cases. All of a sudden, the IRS was faced, and the national office recognized, with the whole shift in the burden of proof, and we settled at 25 for marketable securities partnership. So that shows how the appraiser and the lawyer working together can really come up with an excellent result, because, after all, when you get into the Tax Court trial and you have the Tax Court judge being the appraiser because he or she is the trier of fact, all bets are off, as we know from some of the cases. So I think that the appraiser needs to be involved early on.

S. Pratt: And my understanding is that an assignee interest has none of the benefits of a limited partnership interest other than to receive distributions.

O. Fiore: No votes, just the economic right to get distributions, but no votes. That's key, particularly in a general partnership.

C. Kimball: Shannon, this is Curt. Would you say, all other things being held equal, then, that an assignee interest of a limited partnership is worth probably something less than the value of the corresponding limited partnership?

S. Pratt: Absolutely, because that relates to the bundle of rights. The assignee doesn't have as many rights as the limited partner.

O. Fiore: It may not make much difference if it's a 2% or 20%, even, LP interest. Whether it's an LP interest or a nonvoting "economic interest," because that's sort of like those studies that talk about voting and nonvoting stock in the public marketplace. Where it becomes of interest, like was involved in the *Jones* case, which is a very interesting case that's cited in my materials and that we may talk about later—in the *Jones* case, amazingly, Mr. Jones made a gift of an 83% LP interest to his son in one partnership and four 16% interests to his daughters in a second partnership. A couple of good things about *Jones.* The Tax Court said clearly that you do not aggregate gifts. Sixteen% was separate. But, when they looked at the 83%, the lawyer, like I've done in cases, including *Schauerhamer*, any port in the storm, said, "oh, that's an assignee interest." They said, "Well that's fine, Mr. Lawyer." The Tax Court said, unfortunately, the appraiser valued a partnership interest. Your assignment documents were the partnership interest. The books recorded a partnership interest. So it's a little late to say it was an assignee interest.

*****

S. Pratt: In an estate where the estate holds both a general and a limited partnership interest, must the limited interest be aggregated with the general interest, thus reducing or even eliminating the applicable discounts?

G. Hawkins: Yes. We've actually had to deal with this a number of times, and it's one of the more frustrating situations because the whole plan in gifting is to avoid any ending up and having to make that decision of somebody dying with a GP interest in the LP interest. I've asked a number of attorneys this question about whether you can or can't. Probably 90% have told me the same answer. The answer I always get, and I've looked at the cases—you may be familiar, Owen, with something that says differently. If you do, I'm glad to hear it. The *Ahmanson* case, and then also, basically, the *Estate of Bernard Curry*. In *Ahmanson,* the court basically said—somebody died owning voting and nonvoting stock. They basically said that you had to look at it as if it were a package as opposed to being two discrete, separate groups of shares, one voting and one nonvoting. Basically, in *Ahmanson,* they said basically that the principle that the discount cannot attach to the nonvoting shares when they're considered part of a package with sufficient voting shares to give control. They said they were, in effect, aggregated. The analogy here to somebody dying with the sole GP interest in a number of LP interests is the same thing. The issue, though, that's been raised to me, where I've had the 10% of attorneys that have argued against that is they have maintained that a GP has the fiduciary obligation that somebody holding shares does not. I'm interested in what Owen has to say about that or any other position that might deal with whether you could discount the LP interest in that circumstance.

O. Fiore: I think one of the interesting things that this shows is that we would have worked out something, whether it's putting the GP interest in an entity and giving away interest in it or something, to avoid that question having to be answered. That's why appraisers have to get in early. In the *Ahmanson* case, basically what they were doing is the voting stock was going to an individual, and the nonvoting to charity. They basically shifted tremendous increased value to the voting, saying that they were tied in. Ahmanson was the home savings and loan family complex down in California. I think—I know the IRS position is clearly that you aggregate the two. Aggregation is an interesting point. I would say that the 10% of the lawyers that have talked to you,

George, that say you don't have to aggregate, at least that's an argument. The problem is it's not an argument that's going to get you anywhere until you get to trial. In a way, there's only one place—I should mention this—there's only one place where FLPs and LLCs have a benefit from nonaggregation. That's the case that we all are happy about, the *Mellinger* case in 1999.

The real key was that you do not aggregate QTIP interest with survivor trust interest. The IRS was frustrated as heck about that. That's one of the ways to—when you have husband and wife with real estate or husband and wife and one dies and the QTIP trust in the survivor's trust sets up a family partnership or LLC after the first death, because that way they get to double stuff up in basis, at least in community property states, and then you structure that whole program so you have an aggregation in the gross estate. But for valuation purposes, amazingly, and the IRS has conceded this, amazingly you have nonaggregation. I tried to push that to general power of appointment trusts in the *Fontana* case. I was unsuccessful, but we ended up getting a million-dollar refund in that case. I think the whole idea is that we can really, we meaning the appraisal community, can really help the attorneys to help them think about these things about what it is that's going to be transferred. I'm concerned about whether a general or limited are going to be different. The only thing I would raise is that I would try to argue the assignee interest so that it doesn't make any difference if they're aggregated. If you have a general that's an assignee interest and a limited that's an assignee interest, who the heck cares as to whether it's general or limited if there's no right to vote. That's a argumentative position.

*****

S. Pratt: The next question is, What are "restrictive management agreements," and what are their implications for valuation?

G. Hawkins: First, everybody ought to get a copy of a particular article that was written on this, which was in *Trusts & Estates* in May 2003 by David Handler and David Sennett. It's a very good article and explains it in more detail. Basically, a restrictive management agreement is attempting to bring the benefits of an FLP without having an FLP for marketable securities. Basically, a bank or bank trust department—somebody sets up an account with a bank trust department as an investment manager, and they sign a restrictive management agreement, which gives that entity or the manager the exclusive right to control the assets invested, usually for a fixed time period, typically for about five years. The theory under that is that the manager can use that time period to have total discretion over the investments and make long-term investment decisions where they're not having to deal with people that want to get in and get out and so on and make better investment performance decisions that are going to benefit everybody. At least, that's the theory. I think in some ways it's the bank trust department that benefits because the client can't leave. That's the theory behind it. The valuation implication is that if you gift an interest in that—we're going to talk about that in a minute. I think Owen is going to talk probably about what is the ownership interest there. The theory is that that's like a restricted stock, where you don't have the ability to sell it and you have lack of liquidity for that five-year period and that you might be able to look at it either using some sort of put option as the right to quantify, the fact that you've got to buy portfolio insurance for the fact that you can't get out of this restrictive management agreement for that five-year period, or some type of collar cost of a put in the call to see what the implications of hedging your position in that would be, or looking at restricted stock discount studies as a way of measuring that discount and other ways of doing it. But it's an attempt basically to create sort of the same restrictions that an FLP would have, except here you really can't get out of it at all. The real question, though, is what do you own? Owen, I'd like to turn that over to you.

O. Fiore: Let me add another reference for folks. The first one is the May article, which really caught my attention because I've been a member of the advisory board for *Trusts & Estates* magazine for some time. It said: "Avoid FLPs". I called David Handler and David Sennett of the Wachovia Bank. They co-authored this article. It was really a good article. I thought it had some deficiencies, but of course that's what lawyers are there for. I called David Handler, and he said, "I didn't pick that headline. I wasn't saying avoid FLPs. I was saying that the RMA, the restrictive management account," which is originally designed by Roy Adams when he was at Kirkland Ellis, and now he's with another firm so he's retitled it but it's the same deal—he said, "I didn't say that." What happened was in the August issue of *Trusts & Estates*—you should also refer to the August issue. It says: "FLPs vs. RMAs". Now, obviously, we can set aside—

S. Pratt: RMAs being restrictive management agreements.

O. Fiore: Yes. Restrictive management agreements, which are a two-party transaction between the owner of the securities and the investment manager. Now, by the way, if you think that some financial planner can do this, you can't do this. The reason is that §206(2) of the Investment Advisors Act of 1940 makes it unlawful for an investment advisor to basically do anything that is irrevocable in terms of his investment advice. It's restricted, and that's a no-action letter of SEC, July 19, 1984, under Robert D. Brown Investment Counsel Incorporated. What this really means is a bank and trust department. Frankly, since in my estate planning mode I represent clients, and I'm thinking, as I think I mentioned earlier about 1999, I would no more advise my client to let a bank or bank trust department have a five-year anything than the man in the moon, certainly not in 1999. Now, they're just struggling to get back. I just wouldn't do that. Plus the fact that—Danny Markstein, who's a wonderful lawyer friend of mine with ACTEC, the American College of Trust and Estate Counsel in Birmingham, Alabama, had just done a paper that he's presenting next week in Charleston at the ACTEC fall meeting on how do RMAs work and are they significant. I'll just mention that. The point is some lawyers believe that you cannot have an irrevocable agency agreement. There is something called an agency coupled with an interest. I've got in front of me—I'm sitting here right now in New York about to go to the NYU Tax Institute. I'mlooking at three appraisal reports, including by a large firm and two small investment firms, on RMAs. One says 37% for a three year RMA; 47% for a five-year. Another one says 10%. The one in the middle, the large firm, which is the only one that's got significant number of pages, says 35%. Not one of those appraisers deals with the legal issues of what is an RMA, and I'm extremely concerned. My positive comment would be, because of 2036(a)(2) and this management stuff and the *Byrum* case and all that stuff, I would maybe be quite interested in combining an RMA with an FLP; not picking either or but combining them so you have the kids be owners with the FLP. But, instead of the senior person, mom and dad, being the manager, have them sign up the RMA so that then Judge Cohen won't say it's all back in their estate.

*****

S. Pratt: What are some of the most common errors of appraisers in evaluating FLP interests?

C. Kimball: I guess I'll go first. The first thing is to get your starting points right. The net asset value of all the assets and liabilities in the portfolio of assets and liabilities held by the entity is very important. You'll see a number of these court cases where there were glitches in terms of that that tended to erode some of the confidence of the court in the expert. It's a good idea to get your story straight regarding the underlying net asset values first. I think that the other areas that come up is looking at the history and the outlook for the management of the specific entity and the cash flows—the cash, incomes, and expenses of the entity, both its history and outlook for that because we can see sometimes where in taking discounts, we may end up with an unusually large or unusually small yield on the entity. Also look at the distribution policies of the entity. That issue becomes, I think, very important to look at. Then, of course, the adjustments for the relative lack of control and the adjustments for the relative lack of marketability. Courts are very demanding these days about the basis for your opinion for these things and what you've chosen with respect to your guideline entities for your valuation and the basis of empirical studies or theoretical constructs for adjustments for marketability. It's important to nail down all of the sets of assumptions you've used and go into some detail about how those things link directly to the actual subject entity interest that you're valuing. It's very important.

O. Fiore: I want to refer to *Lappo*, which is in the materials sent to participants, and *Peracchio*. In *Lappo*, here's a quote that exactly supports what you say in referring to the taxpayer's appraiser: "It seems most likely that the upward adjustments are to some extent" —oh, this is horrible— "plugged numbers used to justify his [the taxpayer's appraiser] ultimate very round minority interest discount figures of 30 and 35%." Then, in the *Peracchio* case dealing with the government's appraiser and his marketability discount, where he said that the marketability discount is somewhere between 5 and 25%, and he used 15. The Tax Court judge, and in this case was Halpern, said, "That's the midpoint. I'm going to treat the top point," and I don't agree that this is right, but "I'm going to treat the top point as a government concession on the marketability discount." So I think you're absolutely right on. It's so important. I remember, John Porter in Shannon's program last month pointed this out. It's so important to look at the specifics and really deal with those specifics and not treat it as a "standard" if there is such a thing sort of deal.

G. Hawkins: I'd like to amplify what Owen just said. Basically, the number one problem we see with every FLP where it's flawed is that the appraiser didn't start and look at the rights of the interest being valued in the first place. They just made the standard assumption that it was a typical LP interest or typical membership interest, and they didn't bother to read the agreement to really understand that in context of the state law and case law to understand what the implications were. You've got to start with that framework. Then, even worse, even if they did, they don't articulate it in the report. How on earth is the IRS examiner looking at it going to understand the decisions that you've made as an appraiser are right if they can't read an articulate description of why that's the case in the report. Also, if you don't do that, I would argue that you haven't met the IRS' adequate disclosure guidelines for doing it, so the statute of limitations arguably might not start running.

O. Fiore: I think that's very important because most people, if you think about it, and *Lappo* and *Peracchio* are good examples of it, if they could get the valuation discount, that's sort of frosting on the cake. The real key is that 100% of the postgift, or in the case of *Peracchio,* postsale appreciation, is free of transfer tax, except if 2036(a) applies, which we talked about some. It's very important to think about that and to start to run the statute of limitations. My view is that if I had my druthers and were advising the client on something, I would hate to have them name the partnership The Fiore Family Limited Partnership. We want them to name it the State Street Trust Partnership or something. I would like them also to buy a bunch of publicly syndicated partnerships at the same time and put all that stuff on the return. Then, it's up to the Service to ask the right questions. Why make it easy for them to pull the return in Cincinnati?

C. Kimball: Just remember that adequate disclosure rules do apply mostly to gift taxes, although I've seen that issue raised in the estate tax context about the adequacy of the report.

O. Fiore: Of course they apply to nongifts, except for compensatory gifts. That means that—in *Peracchio*, it was very interesting that all in one day there was a huge gift of LP interest, there was a huge installment sale, which I suspect from the opinion was a straight installment sale and no skin and no installment sale to defective grantor trust, and therefore that installment sale all on the same day—it's interesting—was treated—you could only conclude from the opinion—as two separate transactions. Frankly, I would suggest that you would separate those by a few days or a few months. I was a little surprised that there was no issue raised by that in the gift tax case.

*****

S. Pratt: How can you make your appraisal more bulletproof?

G. Hawkins: Well, I think there's some other things too. First of all, you don't develop minority discounts using Mergerstat Control Premium data and then taking the reverse of that in assuming it's a minority discount.

S. Pratt: I've said that many times.

G. Hawkins: We see it over and over again, though. Another one is the failure to really properly compare the FLP or LLP that you're valuing with truly similar comparables. I mean, a great example. You have an FLP that's got five bank stocks, but then you go find a closed-end fund that's of general equity securities that are widely diversified. What you really ought to find is a closedend firm that holds bank stocks or financial stocks. Or, suppose you're valuing an FLP with apartment projects, and the appraiser goes and uses Partnership Profiles data on average discounts for real estate limited partnerships in general and applies that. That's like saying you can value a local telephone company using the P/E ratio for the Wilshire 5000 stock index. You have to find something that's reasonably similar.

S. Pratt: This raises a related question that came in from Mark Hand. Is there a better data for lack of control discount level for FLP other than the closed-end mutual fund studies? I don't consider those to be good comparables, since they are professionally managed, diversified, and marketable.

G. Hawkins: Those are real things that could be considerations that he could use when he's valuing his FLP. For example, if you have an FLP that's got five stocks that each one holds 20% of the total net asset value, and it's managed by a nonprofessional investor, as compared to the closed-end fund that's got a manager with a long track record and a widely diversified portfolio of 150 different stocks, no one holding a big percentage, then that—granted, it's not a perfect comparable, and it may be the best universe that we have to look to. I think the argument there is if you've got that situation, then there's arguably a greater discount that ought to be applied to his FLP because you don't have professional management and you do have concentrations of assets in one or several stocks.

C. Kimball: In the *McCord* case, the court is willing to listen to those kind of arguments to share the distinctions between the subject entity interest and the guideline securities that you're utilizing, but you have to make a very strong argument for that, and you have to be consistent. Where it isn't consistent, the court will be less receptive to those arguments.

G. Hawkins: It's equally true in real estate FLPs also. If you think about a typical publicly traded partnership, it's going to probably have—the real estate partnership is probably going to have investment-grade quality types of properties, and most of the tenants are going to be national credit quality types of tenants that are real strong tenants that you can rely on for the income stream that they produce. But, when you're valuing your typical FLP, more often than not the real estate is probably going to be noninvestment grade, and the tenants are going to probably be a mix of credit quality and what are called local noncredit quality tenants. The property may not have as much capital gain potential and other things that both increase its risk and also reduce its potential for appreciation. Those are real factors.

*****

S. Pratt: Could the panel please comment on the built-in gains discount and FLPs, if any? What recent case law is there? Can you or can you not take a capital gains discount in the pass-through entity?

O. Fiore: That's great, and that's a good issue to sort of end the first part of our discussion with—the general discussion. We all know about the *Davis* case.

That is a very important case. We also know about the *Dunn* case where the Tax Court was extremely criticized, as was the IRS, for not allowing a dollar-for-dollar discount on built-in gains. But, now we're talking about pass-through entities. I'm not going to get into the sub-S area, because that's a whole different area. Don't take any of this as applying to sub-S because there's some special problems there. But, in the FLP and LLC, the issue is that on the death of one of the several partners of an FLP or an LLC treated as a partnership, you have a valuation of that interest. From the standpoint of the partnership being a separate entity from the underlying assets, you have a situation where there's no stepped-up basis unless there had previously been a 754 election filed, which is binding on all future transfers. Let's assume that's not the case. In this case, therefore, the question is, is there likely to be or is it important that it's even likely or not likely that there's a 754 election, which would mean you've stepped up the inside basis of the partnership assets as to the interest of the estate, let's say.

The problem that we have is we've got the *Jones* case and 116 Tax Court and regular Tax Court decision 121. Then there was the 2001. Now, the *Jones* case, which we referred to before on other issues, the judge said, these are all family members; therefore, they're obviously going to elect 754.That totally violates the hypothetical willing buyer and willing seller standard. There's no assumption that a hypothetical buyer is going to get the benefit of the stepped-up basis because of the 754 election, which is a partnership election. My view is that that issue is still an open issue. Yet, after the *Jones* case, there's been no case that I'm aware of where they have considered that issue. My view would be that if you're using net asset value in the entity, which of course is a precondition for using this issue, then the built-in gains issue should be important. Further, there is the principle of substituting investment. I mean if you've got 10 buildings in the FLP, and the estate has a 20% interest going to this hypothetical buyer, the hypothetical buyer could get full stepped up basis for its purchase price if he doesn't discount it by just buying a similar building. So why the heck would he not discount buying a partnership interest where he does not know whether the partnership, even though later on they may do it, is going to elect 754? Further, there's an excellent Ninth Circuit case on this. That's the case of *McClatchy*, the Ninth Circuit case that dealt with the investment letter restrictions that were agreed to be 15% at the date of death of Mr. McClatchy, who had founder's stock. When Mr. McClatchy died, it was clear that the executors of his estate, 25 days later when they got letters testamentary, would not be affiliates, and therefore the restrictions would lapse. The Ninth Circuit panel, two to one, said you get the 15% discount, we reverse the Tax Court.

C. Kimball: I would add a couple of things. I think that the taxpayer's attorney in the *Estate of Dailey* case did get the IRS' expert to admit that the built-in unrealized capital gains on underlying assets in the absence of a 754 election should be a consideration in establishing the discount. I don't know whether the court actually took any judicial notice of that. I think that was involved in the *Dailey* decision. Furthermore, as Owen said, if you had Microsoft stock, I can go out and buy Microsoft stock on the open market and get my basis in that; whereas, if I bought a limited partnership interest with highly appreciated Microsoft stock, I would be in an entirely different tax position. I think if you talked to investors in syndicated real estate limited partnerships, in that market you'll find that those investors do indicate that a 754 election, a step up in basis, is a significant consideration for them when they think about what their investments are.

O. Fiore: I remember back a few years ago, before the *Davis* case was decided. We had a case of 100%-owned C corporation that had real estate that was actually under water. They had refinanced it, and their debt exceeded the basis, so they really needed a 50% discount rather than a lesser discount to take into account the built-in gains issue. We went right up to the courthouse step in the *Kett* case, and we got our 40% discount. The client said, "What chance do we have to get 50?" I said, "Well, do you want to settle it, or do you want to pay us a couple of hundred thousand dollars more?" They said, "No, we'll settle at 40; that's great." I think people who are buyers really understand this. I've got a good friend of mine, Mike Friedlander down in Los Angeles, who has really evaluated this. In the real estate marketplace, he's got evidence that shows that real estate buyers, if they were to buy a partnership interest with this built-in gains issue, and they couldn't assure themselves of a 754 step up, they would discount it. I mean why wouldn't they? It's against their economic interest not to discount it. Then you go over to the hypothetical seller. My view of the hypothetical seller that IRS always touts is that the hypothetical seller must take into account the economic reality. I'm not bothered by that hypothetical seller problem.

G. Hawkins: The only thing I would add about *Jones* is there were two entities involved there, one where the interest had control. The court reasoned that they could force the 754 election because it would be in their best interest to do so. That's why they didn't allow the built-in gain. But, the throwaway one was the other entity where the Jones estate had a minority interest that didn't have control. They went ahead, even though the minority interest could enforce the 754 election, they really kind of reasoned away that one, the ability to take any built-in gains discount because they said the administrative costs wouldn't be burdensome. But what they really never discussed was the fact that the interest couldn't cause the 754 election to occur. That's where I really think it's off the mark. I'm wondering, if that same situation or case were heard and that issue was pursued persuasively if the court wouldn't have determined differently.

IRS New Rules: Pension Protection Act and Beyond

Moderator: Blake Lyman
Speakers: Spencer Robert Cimasi, William Forsberg, Michael Gregory, Howard Lewis.

Blake Lyman: Welcome to *IRS New Rules: Pension Protection Act and Beyond*, a BVR teleconference featuring Robert Cimasi, William Forsberg, Michael Gregory, and Howard Lewis. My name is Blake Lyman, Professional Program Manager for BVR.

Before we begin I would like to lead you through the details of our teleconference. For your attendance to this 100-minute presentation, you will be eligible for 2.0 CPE or 1.5 CLE credits. In order to receive those credits, you must complete a brief survey on today's teleconference at the conclusion of our presentation.

A link to our survey is included with your registration email which included instructions on how to dial in today. A link is also available on the reading page for today's teleconference. The survey will be active for five business days and will require you to fill in three CPE/CLE codes. Those will be read throughout our presentation. Simply write down the codes as they are read and fill them in when asked in the survey. Surveys without these codes cannot be processed for credit.

We will be taking questions during the session by email only. Send questions to *tc-questions@bvresources.com*.

The Pension Protection Act should be well known by all appraisers practicing for the IRS. Since its passage in 2006 it has been updated through IRS guidelines, rules, and notices. While changes in legislation have increased appraisal opportunities, they have also significantly increased penalties to practitioners.

Joining us today to discuss appraiser penalties and other IRS rules, are Robert Cimasi, William Forsberg, Michael Gregory, and Howard Lewis.

Robert Cimasi is President of Health Capital Consultants, a nationally recognized healthcare financial and economic consulting firm. With over 25 years of experience in serving clients in over 49 states, his professional focus is on the financial and economic aspects of healthcare service sector entities. In 2006, Mr. Cimasi was honored with a prestigious Shannon Pratt Award in Business Valuation conferred by the Institute of Business Appraisers.

William Forsberg, an attorney in Indianapolis, focuses his practice on estate planning, taxation, and corporate law. He is a frequent national lecturer who has published several articles on tax and estate planning, and has been quoted in such national publications as the *Wall Street Journal*.

Michael Gregory is a Territory Manager with the Internal Revenue Service with a responsibility for valuation specialists covering 14 states. As an engineer and valuation specialist with the IRS, Mike has prepared, reviewed, and testified on various topics, and has written technical articles on valuation and expert witness topics. He has managed technical teams addressing litigation vehicles on valuation issues.

Howard Lewis is the Executive Director of the Institute of Business Appraisers. Formerly the IRS National Program Manager for Engineering and Valuation Program, Howard has dedicated his career to elevating appraiser professional responsibility through the development of standards, ethics codes, and strengthened government oversight. Howard implemented technical subcommittees to administer over appraiser penalties under sections 6701 and 6695A of the Internal Revenue Code.

You can read much more about Robert, William, Michael, and Howard on our website for this teleconference. It is a pleasure to have them all join us today. And with that, we turn it over to Robert Cimasi.

Robert Cimasi: Thank you all for joining us. We have a very prestigious panel here today and I am pleased to serve as the moderator for that. I would like to point out that all of you should be logged in right now and have a PowerPoint presentation in front of you. We are going to start with a brief timeline of events. This is a milestone chronology of some of the key things that have happened here over the last four or five years that speak to this topic and thought it might be of interest to do this to try to put this in context.

Then we are going to break this up into several different sections including the background of the Pension Protection Act which Howard Lewis is going to chat about. Bill Forsberg is going to discuss legal aspects of the code from the perspective of an attorney. He will talk about what some of the code definitions are and how that applies. Mike Gregory is then going to take over and take us up to date as to exactly what are the pitfalls for appraisers before the Service and how these are being applied by the Service, the process that the IRS is using to review appraisals and assess penalties. And he will discuss in brief how we can avoid that sort of exposure and liability as appraisers.

Bill Forsberg is then going to come back and talk a little bit about this concept of the uneven playing field in terms of the distinction between valuation experts on behalf of the Service and the same experts that may be working on behalf of the taxpayer. We are then asking Howard Lewis to come back and talk about some of the opportunities that this presents to valuation firms out there.

Then we will be taking questions throughout. We hope that you will email those in. We will have a general panel discussion about the topic to conclude.

Starting with the timeline, you can see going all the way back to the latter part of 2004 with the American Job Creation Act, this created penalties for those practicing before the IRS. There is mentioned Chief Counsel Advice which was issued in section 6701 that added penalties for appraisers. Then going forward with the Pension Protection Act of 2006, when that was signed in August of that year, that actually applied certain penalties that hadn't been seen before that point.

There has been clarification since then as well as there has been a significant clarification through section 6701 in terms of providing those penalties. Circular 230 established certain transitional standards and actually spoke to the issues of who is a qualified appraiser and exactly how do we define a qualified appraisal. These are topics we are going to be discussing throughout but I think it is useful to see how these have progressed.

I suspect, and that will be a topic that will be talked about today, that this is not the last of this progression and that we will see this will continue to evolve as time goes forward. Having said that, I think that what we are going to do now is have Howard Lewis step in and talk a little bit about the milestone chronology of how this has come about with the Service over this period of time. Howard?

Howard Lewis: Thank you very much, Bob and the rest of my fellow panelists. Welcome to those joining this session today. The timeline that Bob referred to is really an excellent tool. I might suggest that when you have a little bit more time than we had on the screen that you take a look at some more of the components and elements a little bit more carefully.

The timeline started in 2004. My own timeline, personal involvement in these issues of appraiser professional responsibility and work quality actually began in 1976 when I came on board with the Internal Revenue Service. It accelerated greatly in the mid to late 1980s and ultimately in the year 2000 when I became the National Program Manager for the Engineering and Valuation Program.

I can be held accountable and responsible for elevating the importance of the issue of appraiser professional responsibility and penalties, and identifying the problems that the Service experienced over the years with administering over its responsibilities in this area, and in arguing for, advocating for, and ultimately participating in the development of these solutions and the approaches in new statutes and announcements, and ultimately regulations that of course continue to be promulgated and executed and implemented.

I would like to tell you why I took such a personal role in this activity. The background I think is, if not interesting, at least it is important and relevant. Let me start by saying that the best majority of appraisal that the Service receives in connection with a tax filing matter are excellent and acceptable – the vast majority. However, there are so many that are received, in fact, one measure of the number of even non-cash charitable contributions that require valuation, amounts to the millions per year.

The vast number of appraisals that the Service has to deal with over the years, and that number tends to increase over the years, results in the reality that although the majority of appraisals submitted are fully acceptable, qualified, and accepted, there still remains a large number that are not acceptable, that indicate a lack of qualifications, and that are not accepted. That produces a great deal of effort on the part of Internal Revenue Service appraisers and other staff and team members to deal with its administrative responsibilities.

I was personally involved in that for many years. The fact that there are literally thousands of identifiable, unacceptable appraisals, and very seriously unacceptable appraisals, was very clear to me as a bag-carrying appraiser, and ultimately as a manager, and finally as the individual responsible for the last eight and a half years up through August, of solving some of these.

The problems measured in terms, as I said, of numbers of appraisals and dollars that were involved, and harm to the government and the Treasury, was really enormous, many, many billions of dollars per year.

That provoked me to seek solutions.

Fast forwarding, we are going to hear what some of those solutions turned out to be: The Pension Protection Act, the Notice Implementing, the initial temporary rules and ultimately regulations, and subsequent sections of the code such as 6695A that has brought a lot of attention to this issue.

Bob, if you could go back to the previous slide, I am going to cover that now and begin to cover some of these issues. Fast forwarding, we face today an unprecedented environment: the meltdown of our financial system, the obvious lack of professional responsibility on the part of many in financial industry segments that we are all observing, we are all paying for, and we are all affected by.

It raises issues such as ethics and standards that are not unlike the issues that affect appraisers. I have dealt with these for years. In connection with Internal Revenue Service matters, the ultimate consequence for an unacceptable appraisal should be significant and serious. That involves potential penalties and even disbarment of appraisers from practice before the Internal Revenue Service.

Bill and Mike are going to talk about many of these things later. It raises issues such as quality. It suggests the increasing importance and critical importance of review and quality assurance of our work. It makes the issue of accreditations and credentials and credibility more important than ever. And it provides us as well in our profession for an opportunity to help shape the future.

We are self-regulated, at least up to now. We do have responsibilities and I pose here some questions that I believe we must ask ourselves. What are our responsibilities as business appraisers and members of the financial community in this esteemed and fascinating profession of ours in terms of assuring the public and our customers and clients and reviewers that we are doing an adequate job? That our opinions can be relied on?

Have we let partisanship get in the way of progress? Has any of that provoked a reaction on the part of the Service to impose penalties and ultimately some fairly serious ones under 6695A for which there is much less flexibility and opportunity for debate and discussion? To what extent is that going to cause very serious problems for our profession and our professionals? Have we missed an important opportunity? Are we continuing to be inactive? What are the risks of such inaction and will we ultimately contribute to our profession and society in dealing with some of these very important issues?

I will get back to some of these things later in terms of standards unification and some other proposals. There are business opportunities as well. We can take the opportunity and in fact take advantage of the situation that poses many problems but that we can turn that into, in my view, an economic advantage that we as individuals in our firms and representatives, can use.

We need to mean what we say. Is there are a role of government? I will pose some questions to Mike later in the panel as to how the Internal Revenue Service can contribute to professionals' ability to deal more effectively with these issues. Have we been asking those questions and who should anybody trust now?

I gave a little bit of the history. Circular 230 has been the guideline for professional responsibility for a number of professionals including appraisers for a very long time. Appraisers fit in that document and those regulations, but there was a problem.

The problem was that the way the statutes were enacted originally required a finding on the part of the service that an appraiser whose work was unacceptable and deemed to be unacceptable, must have been shown to have aided and abetted in the willful, intentional understatement of tax. That standard was not applied to any other professionals, covered by Circular 230, not the actuaries, not the accountants, not the attorneys, and not the enrolled agents.

It caused a serious problem of tax administration in that appraiser poor work, unacceptable work, could not be dealt with and addressed through the professional responsibility process unless they were in effect committing fraud, because that is the equivalent of what the standard of aiding and abetting really represented.

The outcome of the inability of the Service to deal acceptably and responsibly with the appraiser irresponsibility was ultimately the Pension Protection Act of 2006 and subsequently IRC section 6695A dealing with valuation misstatements and understatements. Although there is an exception that Bill and Mike will talk more about, it is not a good situation.

Is this what we really asked for? This is what we are now confronted with and we will now continue with the presentation and talk more about the details, the specifics, and the problems, and even some solutions.

Let me suggest in my last minute that we need, and I will amplify this later, more disclosure from the Internal Revenue Service. Mike Gregory will tell you the number of penalties that have been asserted and some information about the nature of the issues that they involve, but in my opinion we need more information. We need more information about the problems that the Service sees and in more detail, solutions that they suggest could help, penalties that they do assert so that we can, as professionals, assure that we are not trapped by those practices, and also best practices that work.

I think in order to make that happen, in part, and one important part, is that the Service must be willing to restore, expand, and continue the partnerships with the appraisal societies and other stakeholders that did make such a positive impact over the years 2000 to 2008, and current administration must be encouraged and motivated to enable that to happen. Thank you very much.

Robert Cimasi: Thank you, Howard. I wonder if we might ask Bill Forsberg from Minneapolis, an attorney that by the way is Vice Chair of a committee for the American Bar Association, to talk to us a little bit about the actual legal aspects of the codes that are involved. Bill?

William Forsberg: Thanks, Bob, and thanks, Howard, for that great presentation, kind of background on what I am going to be talking about which are some of the mechanics of the new law. This is the new law that came about as a result of the Pension Protection Act of 2006. This law is a specific statutory code section 6695A dealing with penalties for preparers.

I am going to walk through the code section. I am going to talk a little bit about what some of the terms mean and then give some examples of how the penalty is applied, the mechanics and the mathematics of it, so everybody knows and has a sense of how it is applied. Then I am going to talk a little bit about how I really got involved in this.

As Bob suggested, that was through an ABA committee. When the 6695A came out, the IRS allowed comments to be submitted. The committee, that I was the chair of, put a task force together. We came up with some comments that we submitted to the IRS on 6695A. I think we brought out a number of interesting points that give us some pause for concern about how this might be enacted.

This is a statute that requires the penalty to be imposed. There is no discretion, at least the way I read it, that the IRS can have with regard to whether or not a penalty is imposed. It is a straight mathematical calculation.

Let's walk into 6695A and look at what it means. Again, 6695A came as a result of the Pension Protection Act. It imposes new penalties on appraisers for substantial or gross valuation misstatements. Those are terms that are actually borrowed from code section 6662 dealing with penalties on taxpayers, but the same terms would apply for penalties for appraisers.

What is a substantial and gross valuation misstatement and what is the penalty? The penalty is if a person, and again, this is right out of the code, it says "person" – it doesn't say "appraiser" – it says "person." I will talk a little bit about that concern.

If a person prepares an appraisal of the value of property and such person knows, or reasonably should have known, that the appraisal would be used in connection with a return or a claim for refund, and the claimed value of the property on a return or claim for refund which is based on such appraisal results in a substantial valuation misstatement under chapter 1 (that's the income tax code), or a gross valuation misstatement with respect to such property, then such person shall pay a penalty. That amount is determined under subsection (b).

Let's go to subsection (b). I will just tell you what the penalty is and then I'll come back with some examples. The amount of the penalty is kind of a convoluted language, but basically, it is equal to an amount which is the lesser of two things. One is the greater of 10 percent of the underpayment attributable to the misstatement or $1,000, or 125 percent of the gross income received by the person described who prepared the appraisal. That is 125 percent of the appraisal fee.

Basically it is one of two prongs. It is the amount of the tax or the appraisal fee, whichever is lesser. Then there is the diminimus amount of $1,000. We will talk a little bit about the exception. The exception is that no penalty will be imposed if the person establishes to the satisfaction of the Secretary that the value established in the appraisal is more likely than not the proper appraisal.

So what do some of those terms mean? A substantial valuation misstatement – again, this can apply in two contexts. In the income tax context or the estate and gift tax context. Obviously, on the income tax side, the valuation misstatement would be considered to be too high. The way they define substantial valuation misstatement occurs when under the income tax laws if the claimed value of the property on the return is 150 percent or more of the value that is determined to be correct.

If the ultimate value determined to be correct is $100 and the amount that is claimed on the return is $150, then you run into a problem with a substantial valuation misstatement.

A higher level of misstatement is a gross valuation misstatement. That is where the claimed value of the property is 200 percent or more of the value that is determined. That is where you claim on an income tax return, let's say a charitable deduction for some property is $200 and the actual correct value finally determined by the Service is determined to be $100.

That is on the income tax side. The flip side is true on the estate tax side. Obviously on the estate tax side the lower the value, the lower the tax. So on a gross valuation misstatement, it occurs if the claimed value is 40 percent or less of the value ultimately determined. And a substantial valuation occurs when the claimed value is 65 percent or less of the value ultimately determined to be claimed.

You really have to know what the ultimate determination of value is and what is claimed. You compare those. You apply those to the mathematical numbers that are contained within the code here. Then you determine what that amount is and whether or not there has been a valuation misstatement. Then the penalty is applied to that.

Let's just walk through a couple of examples. Here you have Bill; he charges $20,000 for an appraisal. The appraiser values the property at $3 million, resulting in an income tax benefit to the taxpayer of about $900,000 putting them in the 30 percent bracket. But the correct value, or the value that is finally determined to be correct, is $1.6 million and that results in an income tax benefit of only about $480,000.

The penalty applies because the claimed value of $3 million is more than 150 percent of the correct value of $1.6 million. The penalty against Bill is $25,000 which is 125 percent of his fee because this is less than 10 percent of the underpayment. The underpayment is 10 percent of $420,000 or $42,000. That is a situation where you have a pretty substantial appraisal number and there is a pretty substantial valuation problem. The amount of penalty is capped at 125 percent of the appraiser's fee.

Example 2 is where Bill charges $40,000 for the appraisal. The appraisal values the property again at $3 million resulting in tax benefit of $900,000. The correct value is $1.6 million and the benefit is $480,000. The penalty applies because the claimed value of $3 million is more than 150 percent of the correct value.

The penalty against Bill, though, is $42,000 which is 10 percent of the underpayment of $420,000 because that amount is less than 125 percent of the fee which is $50,000.

Let's go to Example 3. This is a smaller appraisal number. Bill charges only a small amount for the appraisal of $1,500. The appraisal values the property at $15,000 resulting in an income tax benefit of $4,500, again a 30 percent bracket. The correct value is $7,500 resulting in an income tax benefit of only $2,250.

The penalty applies because the claimed value of $15,000 is more than 150 percent of the correct value of $7,500. The penalty against Bill is $1,000 because this amount is greater than 10 percent of the tax understatement of $2,250 or $225 and less than 125 percent of the fee.

Depending upon the fee, depending upon the underpayment, and depending upon the amount that is charged for the appraisal, you have to know these factors when you determine and calculate the amount of the penalty.

Those are just the mechanics of 6695A. When the American Bar Association put together this task force, we were asked to look at 6695A and we were asked to do that primarily in the context that we were concerned about valuation issues dealing with estate and gift tax. That is the area that I practice in. But we were also concerned about appraiser's penalties generally because of the nature of this particular code section.

We came up with nine different comments that we made to the IRS. Some of these comments have already been addressed by subsequent notices that the IRS has put out. One is whether or not 6695A in fact applies to estate and gift tax valuation. It was not clear from the language of the code section whether it applied. We understand based on legislative history that the main concern, at least one of the main concerns, raised were the income tax issues and appraisals that were being made. But subsequent notices have clarified that this Code Section 6695A in fact does apply to both income tax and estate and gift tax.

One of the questions we had was, "What does that language in 6695A that says 'any person'?" We think that this applies to appraisers, but what is an appraiser? For example, is a person representative of an estate who is not an appraiser, who is an individual, who is not preparing an appraisal but simply reports the value of an item on an estate tax return – does that constitute an appraisal for purposes of this particular code section?

Really, the question became, "What do they mean by person? Is that a corporation? Is that an individual? Is that an appraiser? Is that anybody who works with the appraiser? Is that anybody who has any relationship with the appraiser or provides information to the appraiser or provides data to the appraiser? What is the demarcation line for purposes of when a person is deemed to be an appraiser for purposes of preparing an appraisal in Code Section 6695A?"

Also, what does it mean to prepare an appraisal? Again, that issue relates to what point in time is somebody deemed to be preparing an appraisal? If an appraiser is preparing the appraisal or an individual is identifying something on a return that has value, what people who brought information forward to that person who is reporting it, at what point in time are they involved in the appraisal process such that they might be subject to 6695A?

The next comment that we made was, "Does it apply to the individual appraiser or to the appraisal firm or anybody in the firm or just the managing partner of the firm? Is it an individual penalty or does it apply to the firm as a whole?"

I think this was a concern that we had. The comments that we suggested was that it only applied to the firm and/or the signing partner or the managing partner, the one who was ultimately responsible for signing off on the appraisal report. I think there had been some subsequent notices indicating that in fact the appraisal firm would be subject to this penalty as well.

One of the biggest issues that we had with 6695A dealt with the issue in comment number 6 dealing with, "To what extent will 6695A come to bear on an appraiser's relying on expert opinions about the nature of the property's interest in the appraisal?"

What I mean by that is, if for example, an appraiser gets a legal opinion from a lawyer saying that the interest to be valued is an assignee's interest in a partnership versus a limited partnership interest or a general partnership interest, and the appraiser values that interest based on that legal opinion, and the IRS determines later that the interest to be valued is in fact not an assignee's interest but some other interest that maybe has in general a higher value, will that appraiser be subject to 6695A because remember that 6695A is straight mathematical mechanical calculation of penalty.

That was an issue we raised also. Related to that was an issue dealing with, "What if you have multiple appraisers? What if you have a discounted appraisal of a family limited partnership and underlying asset in the partnership might be real estate? What if you get an underlying real estate appraisal and you get a discounted appraisal that FLP interests? Which appraiser is going to be reliable if the entire appraisal is deemed to be incorrect by the Service? Will they share that responsibility?"

Will the Service look at the individual appraisals separately to determine and impose penalty or will they just impose it on both appraisers based on their relative contribution? It is really unclear as to exactly how that penalty would be imposed and who would be responsible for that penalty.

Does it constitute false precision? Again, this is issue is really whether, because we have straight mathematical calculations of penalty, there is no wiggle room. The issue is that different property interests have different tolerances for appraisal purposes.

For example, if you have real estate which might have a narrower tolerance or range of values, that is going to be subject to the same 6695A penalties as maybe a hard to value asset maybe like an assignee's interest in a family limited partnership or a closely held business interest or some other interest that is not quite as narrow a tolerance in terms of value.

But the penalty applies equally to both of those interests. There is no wiggle room; there is no exception to this penalty. There is no good faith exception to the penalty in a straight mathematical calculation.

One other issue is, "When is this penalty going to be imposed?" As far as we know, there is no statute of limitation on this penalty. The penalty can be imposed independently of any penalty that might be imposed against the taxpayer. It can be imposed at any time during the course of the administration of the tax that is being reviewed by the Service as the taxpayer and it could be a very, very long period of time before this penalty is imposed.

One of the issues is whether or not the ultimate resolution that the taxpayer has with the Service is somehow binding on the appraiser or is it going to be an independent determination of value. All those questions were raised in that comment.

The next comment was that, "Do the Code Section 6695A penalty provisions apply equally to appraisers relied on by the government in tax controversy matters?" This is kind of the uneven playing field that I will touch on a little later.

The code section doesn't apply to the government's appraisers; it only applies to the taxpayers' appraisers who prepare a return based on the code section as identified. It does not apply at all to government appraisers. It only applies to the taxpayers' appraisers.

Finally, we will talk about this, too, is the exception. The exception to this penalty is not like the old exception which was a good faith exception. There was some discretion in the Service in their ability to either apply the penalty or not apply the penalty. This penalty provision is not discretionary. If you look at the literal language of 6695A, it says "shall apply." It is not discretionary. It doesn't say "may" or "the secretary or the IRS has discretion." It is a mandatory penalty and it will apply.

The exception is somewhat hollow. Basically, the exception is that you have to determine, you have to convince the Service that in fact and demonstrate this exception to the government's inspection that they are in fact wrong.

How can one really do that after the Service has already determined that you in fact have a bad appraisal or your appraisal is off? How are you supposed to convince the Service to fall within that exception if there has already been a determination that the value is incorrect?

So the exception seems a bit hollow and it doesn't seem to provide any basis for the taxpayer to really alleviate themselves from this penalty provision.

Those are the comments that we made relative to 6695A. Now Michael Gregory is going to talk a little bit about the penalties and the IRS and the history of what has been going on and give us some update on what penalties have been imposed under not only 6695A but other code sections.

Robert Cimasi: Bill, thank you very much. I would like to thank you for following up with the legal aspects of this after Howard's background. Before we ask Mike Gregory to actually get into some of the pitfalls of the Pension Protection Act and how the IRS is actually applying these assessment penalties, I think we are going to take a quick break so Blake Lyman can give us the first of our CPE/CLE codes to let everyone know. I think he will tell you that you have to write these down so you can get your CPE credit.

Blake Lyman: Thank you, Bob. The first CPE/CLE code is 8675. As a reminder, please send questions to *tc-questions@bvresources.com*. Thank you, Bob.

Robert Cimasi: Thank you very much. Now we are going to ask Mike Gregory to step in and discuss with us some of the applications of the PP provisions to the process and to how those of us who do appraisal work go about the valuation process. Then he will talk a little bit about how we may avoid exposure in liability. Mike?

Michael Gregory: Thank you very much, Bob. I appreciate your introduction and I am very happy to be here with Howard Lewis and Bill Forsberg in this discussion here today. I want to first note that the comments I am presenting here are my own personal opinions and they may not reflect the position of the IRS. I do that because we are in an education venue here and I think it is important to have dialogue back and forth with respect to these types of issues.

Let's take a look at the professional responsibility we have as appraisers and as valuers and how that is applied relative to this particular code section, and look at the penalties we are applying here within the IRS. I am going to talk a little bit about the history. Howard has done that already, so I am going to do this relatively quickly. I am going to talk about some of the key points from the Pension Protection Act. Again, William has done a very good job of presenting some examples on that, so I am not going to reiterate this.

I am going to share with you what the information is that I have today. It is actually pretty dated. It goes back to May of 2008, but I will share with you the numbers of what it looks like in terms of penalties.

First of all, I am going to take a look at valuation issues. Let's look at the Internal Revenue Code. If you just pull up the Internal Revenue Code and we did a quick edit on that, you will find that there are over 243 sections of the code that have something to do with valuation. When you come back and look at the number of returns each year, we are talking about 15 million tax returns that the taxpayers file that have something to do with valuation-related issues.

Therefore, this is an area that is very prevalent and it is an area that we have to address. We are addressing this of course under the standard of fair market value.

The Director of the Office of Professional Responsibility is Michael Chesman. He made a comment here and you can read that on the screen. The gist of the comment is take a good look at the work you are being asked to provide a service and decide whether you want to provide that service given the potential risk of what might be involved with respect to this someday going to litigation or someday being under audit by the IRS. He is saying that sometimes the best decision might be to walk away from that job or walk away from an employer if they are putting you in a position where you may be at risk.

What is the real purpose of us working these types of issues and partnering with you and discussing these types of things? It is because we really want to strengthen partnerships. We want to see a tax system that operates with a high degree of integrity and we want to increase voluntary compliance. We think if we have standards that are clear and we target this at folks who are not complying with the law, then that will help in terms of the enforcement of the law and appropriate tax payment by various parties.

We are trying to prepare a system that is going to be fair and diligent and effective relative to all the parties associated with a given tax return.

In terms of the history, Howard did a great job of going over the background. He was the Engineering Program Manager from the year 2000 through 2008, so he gave you some very good background there. The chart that was put together by Bob Cimasi that we had at the beginning ran through some history relative to the legislation.

We are not trying to outreach in various presentations by making these types of presentations and letting you know what has happened to date and where we are. We have three broad code sections that we had been working with prior to the Pension Protection Act of 2006. Code 6700 related to promoters.

Code 6701 was already discussed and Howard indicated some of the shortcomings we had with applying aiding and abetting penalties. And there were cases where we worked with, and we are still working with, what were called abusive tax avoidance transactions. The acronym is ATAT. You might be applying an injunction against a given promotion on the part of a promoter relative to some tax issues. But our intention and the application of penalties is to be fair and consistent in terms of the administration of these penalties.

Code 6701 had a $10,000 penalty which related to a corporate tax liability and $1,000 if related to a person. Again, there was the heavy hammer potentially being presented to the Office of Professional Responsibility and losing the ability to practice before the IRS which would have a significant impact on any practice in other venues as well, or an injunction against a tax promoter from the Department of Justice.

This leads us into when a penalty is proposed. We look at current penalty investigation process. Today, if a valuer for the IRS completes their work and there is a conclusion relative to a case, we make a recommendation to what is called the Lead Development Center, the LDC, which is located in our Small Business Self Employed Business Unit. They are located in Laguna Nigel, California.

They would review through the recommendation for the penalty and they would authorize a separate investigation relative to the application of a penalty on a case. At that point it might be assigned, or would be assigned to the Abusive Tax Avoidance Transaction group or the ATAT group that looks at tax shelters and other penalties like this.

There would be a team formed. They would have an ATAT agent who would have the valuator or the valuer associated with this. We would also bring on board other appropriate parties such as counsel and technical advisors and Internal Revenue Service.

The questionable appraiser conduct would be reviewed. What would we really be looking for? We are looking for examples such as facts that don't exist. The appraiser made up the information. Purposefully excluding a valuation approach that precludes credible results. Let's say we had a going concern and it was valued as a liquidated entity. Ignoring strong market evidence – just picking out a few comparables that are clearly outside the spectrum of reasonableness and only applying that as the information that was available.

Another one is presenting false information, lying with respect to the facts, or including assumptions as to future events that are implausible. Let's say the building of a Mall America in a rural area in North Dakota as an example. Assuming forms of ownership that don't exist and intentional disregard for professional standards, and we give a considerable weight to that with the standards of folks who are certified in the various societies.

Then, is there any participation by an appraiser that might result in a value determination that intended to reduce the tax without objective and credible evidence to support that appraisal?

The enactment date is August 17, 2006. There is an exception there for easements. We have already had some discussion around the application of the penalty. Code 6695A removed the threshold restriction. It relaxes the knowledge standard. It also improved the definition of qualified appraisal and qualified appraiser. I won't go into that in these discussions. If something comes up in the questions and answers, then that can go into that arena.

But basically, it now came forward with a new definition. In the amount of the penalty and how it was determined, that was presented by Bill, so I will skip right past this slide.

Then it says there is an exception. As Bill said, this is a hollow exception relative to the penalty. The hollow exception in my mind is that if you can convince the valuer and the IRS who came up with their value that their value is more likely than not to be incorrect, the penalty would not apply.

I look at that as if I have done the work, or here in the IRS, if one of our employees has, and we say that we think the value is $100 and the taxpayer says the value is $150, if we can convince that individual that his value of $100 is more likely to be wrong, then the penalty wouldn't apply.

In my own personal opinion, I look at that as a hollow exception as well.

A qualified appraiser can be an individual. Looking at the appraisers' designations, are they recognized as an appraiser? Do they meet the minimum education requirements? Do they perform appraisals regularly? Do they meet other requirements?

A qualified appraisal is an appraisal of property. The property has to be determined what that means, legal definitions and applications of those in different forms. It has to be conducted by the qualified appraiser in accordance with what the normal standards might be.

Through May 2008 we had 146 penalties that were asserted against six different appraisers. We made recommendations to the Office of Professional Responsibility regarding six different appraisers. The types of appraisers that were referred were conservation easements, facades and open space, abuse of Schedule A deductions (you can think of contributions there), the estate and gift tax valuations and pension funds valuations with limitations.

Looking at the inventory, there were a total of 100 referrals. Twenty-five were approved; 10 were recommended, but were not yet approved by that lead development center; 35 were recommended for suspension, still being developed factually; just under 10 were discontinued; and we surveyed or it was determined an investigation wasn't warranted in 10 cases of approximately the first 100 that were referred.

If you want to get additional information on this, not on the comments specifically, but on the number of penalties applied, but to get additional references relative to penalties in the IRS and what we are working on currently, here is a website you can go to and take a look at. The AICPA also has information available.

Robert Cimasi: Mike, thanks very much. I think that is a terrific presentation on this. I would like to ask Bill Forsberg now if he could jump back in. We don't have any slides on this particular aspect of it, but I would like to, if we could Bill, go back for a couple of minutes and talk to us about this concept of the uneven playing field.

My understanding is, from what we've read and from what you, Howard, and Mike presented, that if I happen to be working for the Service and I come up with an opinion of value that is found to be 150 percent off from what is finally decided upon to be – and I am using this word as a euphemism – the correct "value," that there isn't any penalty that would apply to me because I am employed by the Service.

But at the same time, if I happen to be employed by the taxpayer and it is ultimately determined that I am 150 percent off in terms of my value, I am then subject to all these penalties up to and including being barred from practicing before the Service again. I wondered if you might discuss that and the impact that has in terms of the taxpayer and those of us who are doing the appraisal work.

William Forsberg: I would be happy to do that. Thanks Bob. When I talk about the uneven playing field, I point to a number of aspects about the new code section that suggests it is somewhat quite onerous on the appraiser for a number of reasons.

First of all, I mentioned that there is no statute of limitation on this penalty. Typically, a taxpayer will file a tax return and there is a three year statute of limitations on the ability of the Service to go back and actually audit the return and impose a penalty absent fraud.

There is no statute of limitation with regard to this penalty that I am aware of. At any time in the process whether the appraisal process takes a year or six years, the Service could impose a penalty. The other part is that it is a mechanical, mathematical calculation. There is no wiggle room here. There is no ability of the IRS to use its discretion which I think is a valuable thing to determine whether in a particular fact situation a penalty shouldn't be imposed even if it is outside the mathematical boundaries.

There might be factual situations where a penalty wouldn't be appropriate maybe because the nature of the property interest that was being valued was just very difficult to value. The tolerance levels were wide and they just happened to fall outside the mathematical penalty calculations of 6695A. But here, there is no discretion. It is a straight mathematical calculation.

The wording of the code section says "shall apply." It is not discretionary. Again, it does not apply to the government's appraisers. That is the uneven playing field that we have been talking about. Does that somewhat have a chilling affect on the taxpayers' appraisal in terms of their appraisal?

The other one is the exception is hollow. Mike has talked about that. It really is no exception in my view. If you have to convince the Service that after the termination of a misstatement has already been determined that they are somehow wrong in their determination.

The other issue is really what happens when a taxpayer settles with the Service during the course of an examination. Is that settlement binding on the appraiser for purposes of penalty? Maybe the taxpayer wanted to settle and pay the tax and be done with it. That resulted in a finally determined appraisal number much higher than maybe the appraiser would have been able to convince the Service if the appraiser was involved in the process.

What if that appraiser who did the appraisal, and that was the appraisal that was used for purposes of reporting, wasn't the appraiser who was representing the taxpayer going forward in terms of the determination of actual final determined value.

Robert Cimasi: That was one of the questions that one of our participants posed. I would like to a break and I will direct this question to you. One of our participants sent the following email, "Suppose the taxpayer and the IRS make a deal to substantially lower the value on an item which was appraised in exchange for a no change or higher value in some other entity or piece of property. To what extent would there be liability on the appraiser in a process in which he or she has no participation?"

William Forsberg: My understanding is that if that were the case, there was a settlement made by the taxpayer that even though that settlement was made that wouldn't necessarily be binding relative to 6695A for the purposes of that appraiser. I suspect the appraiser would have an independent ability to challenge that higher value that was settled with the Service with the taxpayer so that the penalty wouldn't be imposed.

But I don't know that is necessarily clear.

Robert Cimasi: Let me ask you, if I could, let's take an opportunity here to ask Mike and Howard to jump in on this point. Mike Gregory, what is your view as to if in fact the IRS and the taxpayer, without the knowledge of the appraiser, were to reach settlement on one piece of property or one appraisal, is part of an overall settlement with many whatever pieces of property? Would there be a penalty that would be applied to the appraiser in which he had no participation?

Michael Gregory: Clearly, this is a very good example that will likely have to make its way through this penalty screening process. My personal opinion would be we are taking a look at what would be the fair market value of that asset. If this was a matter of negotiation that took place with respect to that given asset, then I don't think that would be the determination for fair market value.

I think that if indeed a fair market value was determined and then that fair market value was determined to be in excess of the percentages we talked about earlier in the application, then I think there would be a recommendation back here to the Lead Development Center. That penalty group would have to screen this relative to what all the facts are.

What you can start doing with this example is putting in and hypothesizing a series of different facts. Those different facts will lead you in different directions. Our intention is to try to apply the penalty when it should be applied into the appropriate value on that penalty.

I would say, without additional information with respect to the facts, I would think that the penalty would be applied just on the face of this simplistic example. Howard, do you have any comments?

Howard Lewis: My comment is that I agree with what you said, Mike. In the very early creation and developmental stages of this, this was one of the very specific examples that we gave to counsel and to Treasury as we knew they were beginning to consider these languages. I do agree with you, Mike. I think if this is reasonably interpreted it would fall within the exception in my opinion, and this is not a rare occurrence. It is something that I think will occur probably quite frequently.

William Forsberg: I think one clarification that I would like to make is I think the penalty applies the valuation misstatement of a particular piece of property, not as to the entire value of all property that is being reviewed by the Service. Each individual property has to be reviewed. If there is a settlement by the taxpayer exchanging values for one value, I think as Mike and Howard has said, I think the Service would probably allow the appraiser to defend his appraisal of the one property that was used as a negotiation for settlement.

A determination would be somewhat independent of the settlement that is made by the taxpayer.

Robert Cimasi: Bill, those are excellent comments. Just to get back to the question that our participant posed, in the event that we had a taxpayer, I will try to give some specific hypothetical here. If a taxpayer had three pieces of property that were subject to estate or gift tax, and property one, which was the smaller of the properties, the appraiser comes up with a number. The IRS appraiser comes up with a different number that is far more than 150 percent off.

The other two properties are much larger and have a lot more exposure for the taxpayer. During the course of the discussions between the taxpayer's legal counsel, and the Service, probably not the valuation end of the Service, I would suspect, they would say, "Well, we will reach a settlement on this. If you will agree that the fair market value that you were going to base the tax on for the smaller of the properties is $2 million, then if you agree to that, then we will settle out in a way that will be accessible to the taxpayer and the Service on the two big pieces of property."

This may or may not be anything that has to do with the reality of fair market value of the smaller property. In that event the Service and the taxpayer have now agreed that the fair market value for that smaller value for tax purposes is that dollar amount. If there is that settlement or agreement, does that become the "correct" value that you talked about in your presentation earlier?

William Forsberg: I don't think the settlement amount is the correct value. It is really an interpretation of what the statute says. I think the correct amount would be probably an independent determination made by the Service relative to the appraiser's appraisal and that negotiation, not necessarily what the taxpayer settled, especially if there was some horse trading going on.

I think the correct value would be based on the Service's independent review of the fair market value of that particular piece of property.

Robert Cimasi: Is the Service required to go back to their valuation side in that case and have their valuation side comment as to what the "correct" end value is? Mike?

Michael Gregory: Let me go back to the question and what Bill just said there. In our comment here once again, I think the purpose of the Lead Development Center is to come in and look at the application of the penalty relative to fair market value. You have used the term settled with the IRS relative to the differences here.

That jargon actually means something within the Internal Revenue Service. When we work a case on examination, we can work to resolve issues. If we have a case which is un-agreed and it goes to the Appeals Division of the IRS or proceeds into litigation, we are now involved with the term of settlement or settling the case.

When you are involved with settling the case with folks at appeals and the folks in counsel or the Department of Justice, if we are going to district court or U.S. Court of Claims, they are now using the term in terms of settlement because of the hazards of litigation, although this is a factual issue in terms of fair market value.

It is becoming more complex depending on a number of different avenues here. I think the real key though, so we don't lose focus on this, and picking up on your example, and also with what Bill has just said, is if this were to be referred to Lead Development Center, the question would be on the small parcel, what is the fair market value? Then with respect to that small parcel, what was the value presented by the appraiser?

When we were done answering that question, it appeared the penalty was applicable, then I think they would launch it for an investigation of the penalty. Now you would have counsel involved, potentially technical advisors, the valuers involved, and also an ATAT agent who is looking to apply that penalty consistently with respect to other taxpayers in similar veins.

I don't believe the settlement decision for that particular property, on that smaller property, would be the determining value.

William Forsberg: Can I make one more comment?

Mike, you made a distinction between what sounded like a resolution at the agent level versus a settlement at the appeals level.

Michael Gregory: Yes.

William Forsberg: Do you think it would be more likely that a resolution would have more weight in terms of the penalty resolution, their determination whether or not a penalty might be imposed versus a settlement which really sounds like there is more horse trading going on and this is really to avoid litigation?

Michael Gregory: I think at the factual level with the Revenue agent, it now comes down to for an estate or gift tax arena, the Revenue agent is really what is called an estate tax attorney. If we are dealing in something in small business self employed or governmental entities or wage or investment or large or midsize business division, those are revenue agents.

When that factual determination is made, there is also discussion with the manager on that case and now it comes down to how that determination was made for that guide. The manager may come back in and say, "I am using my managerial authority. This is diminimus in nature," or, "Given that this wasn't fully factually developed."

There are a number of things that can enter into how that report is written that would have an impact in terms of, "Was that fair market value in the determination of the agency?" I would suggest that probably in that case it would not be written that this was fair market value; it would be written that this was a determination made by the manager on that case given the facts associated with the case.

It has somewhat to do with how that might be written. Do you have any other comments there Howard that you want to add?

Howard Lewis: No, Mike, I think you have all covered it very well. Once again, I will just reiterate that in the development of all of this language, these potential situations were rather easily identifiable. We did identify them. We shared them with the attorneys who were involved with this.

The other thing that I think is really relevant is that there is no one, Mike can assure everybody of this, there is no one in the Service, appraisal or any other segment of the organization that wishes to, or would even easily permit anyone to be penalized if we thought that it was inappropriate, certainly based on some kind of agreement that was made outside the realm of fact.

Robert Cimasi: Thank you very much. We have a quick housekeeping duty to handle here. Blake, I am going to ask you if you will step back in and give the second of the CPE codes to the group.

Blake Lyman: Thank you Bob. The second CPE/CLE code is 3091. As a reminder, please send questions to *tc-questions@bvresources.com.*

Robert Cimasi: We have another question here for Bill Forsberg. In finishing up on your section here, you mentioned the term "chilling effect" on the taxpayer and tax appraiser earlier when it comes to this concept of the uneven playing field. Could you address what is meant by that and how that might really actually play out in terms of the process?

William Forsberg: I think we have talked a little bit about that before Bob. When this first came out, at least I got wind of the fact that some appraisal firms, even some bigger appraisal firms, were simply worried about this penalty and chose not to do any tax appraisals that related to some sort of tax, whether it is gift or estate tax or income tax.

In and of itself, these appraisal firms have decided not to do appraisals because of the penalty and were choosing to get out of the business. That in of itself has a chilling effect. I suspect, too, that to the extent that an appraiser has more heightened liability for penalties, and we will talk a little bit about Circular 230 because I think that is the big exposure that the appraiser has.

They may be less likely to give a more aggressive appraisal, whatever that term means. Maybe that was one of the reasons for 6695A is to kind of try and go after some of these appraisers who were providing appraisals that were way off the mark. I have to believe in every context that an appraiser will think twice about doing an appraisal and will be apprised of 6695A and the Circular 230 disqualification rules that are now applicable up to a greater extent than they were before so that they may in fact be less aggressive in their appraisal.

That was kind of the chilling effect that I kind of sensed might happen. I don't know if that is played out in terms of actuality, but I suspect it might.

Robert Cimasi: In conversations that I have participated in at conferences in the past, a question was raised as to why this legislation would have passed in a way that if the real concern was to weed out bad appraisals or bad appraisers, why that wouldn't apply to the same appraiser but in particular who he is employed by? Why wouldn't it apply to the appraiser if he was employed by the IRS if we are going to talk about bias and try to weed out bias and incompetent appraisals?

What distinction would the legislature have had here to have passed this as to make it a differentiation between who the actual employer was?

William Forsberg: I would have to agree with you. I don't know why it wouldn't be good public policy to have it apply to both the taxpayer's appraiser and the Service's appraiser.

Robert Cimasi: Howard, is that something that you could comment on?

Howard Lewis: Only to the extent that clearly the penalties were designed and written to cover certain types of misstatements and understatements. If there were to be an error of such a magnitude submitted by an appraiser engaged by the Service, it would most likely go in the opposite direction and it wouldn't fit the statute anyways.

That was not an intention, but I think it is a fact. This would probably require at least some type of technical correction or maybe even a new statute altogether.

I think the reality is that the perceived problem was rather clear. The problem was that the Service was receiving a large enough number of unacceptable appraisals by or from taxpayers that constituted the problem that needed to be addressed.

Robert Cimasi: Thank you. And Howard, while we have you, if we might ask you to discuss some of the opportunities that this proposes for valuation firms and appraisers that are doing this type of work going forward, and how we can benefit from this as a profession.

Howard Lewis: Okay, Bob, thank you very much. I think that in every troubling situation one can certainly look for potential opportunities. I strongly believe that there are opportunities here for practice development. I would like to outline some of my thoughts in that regard.

When I refer to these issues, I am going to refer to firms of a certain size and that would likely be four or five or six or more appraisers. If we are dealing with a sole practitioner, then some of these issues might apply. All definitely do not. A smaller size firm I would suggest could take advantage.

Also, some of the issues that I would like to talk about, but the larger size firms which I would define as being a firm that has five or six or more appraisers, and there are many firms that have dozens, scores, or even hundreds of appraisers and professionals. I think there is a significant opportunity here that can demonstrate and result in an economic advantage.

Do appraisers have a bad name? Sometimes we do. In the 1980s, real estate appraisers had a pretty bad name. In the current financial meltdown environment, to some extent appraisers, and to a much larger extent, financial professionals of many other kinds, have a bad name. It is not good that we have a bad name and we need to take every step and make every effort to prevent that happening. If it does happen, we need to address it.

Not all valuation firms have, and not all valuation firms deserve the same reputation. I spent over 30 years reviewing work of valuation firms, appraisal firms, and taxpayers of enormous variety. Those who did their own appraisal work to those who hired the largest most prestigious firms whether in the appraisal profession or on Wall Street or otherwise.

These firms do not all have, nor do they deserve the same reputation. Not all valuation firms deserve the reputation they have in my view. Some have a reputation that is greater than perhaps they might deserve and probably the converse is probably true as well.

There is an overall enigma. There is a problem that I just want to take a moment to address. That is, and is effected, by results from the IRS examination process of valuation issues. Here is the problem. As I mentioned at the beginning of my first segment, the vast majority of appraisals, the vast majority of business appraisals that are prepared, that are executed, that are used, that are submitted and reviewed by the Internal Revenue Service, are fully acceptable. The vast majority is accepted and there is a minority, but it is a large number that are problematical.

The fact is that the IRS process is such that it is designed to filter and screen and result in as many of those bad appraisals hitting the desks of IRS' appraisers and audit teams as possible. The process works pretty well in that the appraisal staff sees ordinarily and spends the vast majority of its time on truly unacceptable appraisals. The problem is that unless the appraisers are very careful, unless management is very careful to continually point this out, as I did at every opportunity, Service appraisers could fall into the unwitting trap and situation of thinking that the vast majority of appraisals are horrible because that is typically what they see.

We all have a role to play in that to make sure that all of the professionals including the Service's appraisers understand that while they may see eight out of ten appraisals that they deal with as being seriously problematical or flawed, that does not mean that eight out of ten appraisals that are prepared by professionals are flawed in any degree and certainly to the degree that filters of the IRS work very effectively to process.

What are the indicia of a credible valuation firm? I would suggest the following. I have a few slides here that will suggest areas of focus that valuation firms of a variety of different sizes can and I believe should specifically address and focus on to assure itself and themselves that they have taken all the appropriate steps to insure the highest level of quality and professional responsibility, and then advertise the market that they have done so.

Then prospective clients, prospects, and customers, will know that the firm has taken affirmative steps, specific steps, to single themselves out as being exceptional.

Indicia – a credible valuation firm should have an appropriate recruiting selection and education process in place for its appraisers. Many do; many do not. Many may not have addressed such a process very carefully recently. A credible valuation firm adheres to a set of ethics and standards rules and makes it very clear to the public what those rules are and what the consequences are of not adhering to those rules.

A credible valuation firm has an appropriate peer review and quality review process in place. More and more, in current times, this particular element of practice becomes most significant. A firm must be confident that the work being produced by the firm is peer reviewed, is acceptable, and that there is a formal process for doing so.

IBA recently introduced a major revision of its course in *Business Appraisal Review*, and is focusing significantly and energetically on providing such opportunities to the professional community. And the credible valuation firm has taken appropriate action on referrals of information pertaining to violations of these issues regarding its staff.

Regarding recruiting, selection and education, firms should document the minimum knowledge, skill, and ability requirements, have a core training curriculum, and a continuing education curriculum that addresses the growing needs and individual needs of its appraisal staff and appraisers.

Firms should have an optimal design combination of accredited and non-accredited staff members that the firm has evaluated and can demonstrate is adequate for the services it provides.

What about the core training curriculum? One size does not fit all. A firm's training curriculum must distinguish between the appropriate and different levels of employee knowledge, skill, and ability. It must be periodically, regularly, and continually evaluated for sufficiency and for its accomplishment.

It should include an appropriate mix of internal training and external training elements. It must include appropriate testing features. It is not enough to sit folks in a classroom; it is vital that they be tested on the knowledge that they have gained and the skills that they have acquired. It should include a very structured and documented on-the-job training process.

As good as the training curricula are from IBA and each and all of the appraisal organizations, they only go so far. On-the-job training is a responsibility of management of the local firm.

As for continuing education, the firm should provide an appropriate amount and frequency of regular such CPE. It must include technical issues that again are appropriate for the level of needs for individual staff members. And very importantly, must, and I think we fall down in this area, include periodic and regular ethics and standards content and focus.

Those ethics and standards rules must be those that are generally accepted in the profession. They must be the subject of regular focus by firm management. It is not enough to say that our firm adheres to USPAP. It is required that ethics and standard rules be the subject of regular education, documentation, and review.

And the firm must have a process for addressing questions that arise and enabling staff to elevate and resolve issues of concern.

I talked about the great importance of peer review and quality review. The process must be documented and staff must be informed. It must be regularly monitored and evaluated and perhaps by an independent organization that is equipped to do so, and to lend assistance to the firm to assure that it is in place.

It must be designed to provide quality assurance and control information to management. It is not enough to do the reviews; it is required to follow up on the reviews in a systematic process and it should be utilized to address not only quality concerns, but also identify best practices because the result of peer review will not only be correction actions, but also the identification, as I say, of best practices.

That information should be shared widely and effectively. I believe that a firm that addresses these issues of review, standards, ethics, focus, education and training, can set itself apart from the typical firm in the marketplace, can assure the public that it has done so, can market itself accordingly, and can find the economic advantages that result.

Robert Cimasi: Howard, thank you very much. That is a terrific presentation of the things that we need to look at and the opportunities that present themselves for firms that can operate within this new sort of regulatory scrutiny environment from the service of our work product.

Before we go into taking some questions and get into some discussion here, Blake, I think this might be an appropriate time for you to break in and give us the last of your CPE codes, if you would please.

Blake Lyman: Thank you, Bob. The final CPE/CLE code is 4853. Please send questions to *tc-questions@bvresources.com*. Thank you.

Robert Cimasi: Blake, thanks. I would like to take a couple of questions that we have had sent to us already. I hope there will be more coming. Then we are going to leave a few minutes here for some final comments from each of our panel participants today.

One question that was asked was, "In light of previous tax court cases that have been reversed against the Service, if a penalty is imposed on the taxpayer's expert in a case is reversed, is the penalty then also reversed?"

How would that work from your perspective? Let's start with Bill Forsberg. Bill, how would that work because we all know that there are those instances where cases have been appealed and reversed in the tax court against the IRS? How would that work if a penalty has already been assessed against the appraiser in one of those cases?

William Forsberg: I think the answer may not be a great answer, but I think that is unclear. I think my understanding is that the appraiser penalty would be in that determination of whether there is a penalty would be based on a final determination of fair market value independent on what any kind of court decision might be or whether there is a reversal in a court decision. I think those penalties will be independently determined.

Robert Cimasi: Is there an opportunity for an appeal in a case like that?

William Forsberg: That is one question that I had. Maybe the best procedural person to ask would be Mike. If a case is referred to the Lead Development Center for penalty, there is a review and an authorization for investigation and there is a recommendation and determination made. What are the appeal rights of someone from a final determination of LDC in terms of a penalty?

Michael Gregory: I don't actually know the full level of procedures, but I do know that once a determination has been made through the Lead Development Center, it is now referred to the Office of Professional Responsibility. The Office of Professional Responsibility is going to bring in the individual and the firm in question and the facts that are on the case. In fact, there will be a determination made by the Office of Professional Responsibility.

There is also an appeals process with the Office of Professional Responsibility on the determination. I am not knowledgeable with respect to the administrative components associated with it, but conceptually that is what would take place in the Office of Professional Responsibility.

William Forsberg: Maybe we should talk a little bit about that. I think that is a very good point. One of the things that the Pension Protection Act did was that it really eliminated the requirement that a civil penalty under 6701A, that is the aiding and abetting penalty, be imposed before there is a referral to OPR (Office of Professional Responsibility).

I think now that penalty requirement is no longer there. There can be an independent referral to OPR without that penalty being imposed. My understanding, at least generally, of the procedural requirements for OPR is that obviously the appraiser is given notice and an opportunity for a hearing, then there is a proceeding before an administrative law judge.

A complaint is filed against the appraiser and the hearing is before the administrative law judge. Then that can be appealed to a delegate of the secretary of the treasury which would be the IRS office of the chief counsel for determination of a final decision.

If that final decision is against the appraiser, then the appraiser could be disqualified for five years. That disqualification would provide that the appraiser is barred from presenting evidence or testimony before the IRS or the Treasury Department in any administrative proceeding and their appeals have not probative value or effect in any proceeding.

This would also include even testimony or evidence relating to appraisals completed prior to the offense. The OPR referral and the disqualification, the appraiser is probably more onerous than the appraiser of appraisal penalty under 6695A. I think that is what the appraisers are most concerned about.

This would be basically putting the appraiser out of business. If that is the route that has to take place, I think the appraiser would be more concerned about that process probably than the actual monetary penalty that might be imposed.

Robert Cimasi: Bill, just to clarify – if Joe Jones, the appraiser, has five matters before the Service for five different clients, sometimes as we all know this takes a matter of years to work its way through the process. In the fifth matter, the most recent matter, Joe Jones is found to have run afoul of the requirements that we talked about today, and is therefore barred from his work being presented before the Service, then if I understand your comment correctly, then the previous four appraisals that he has done that are before the Service that haven't been finally accepted are also now subject to being disregarded.

So those taxpayers at that point would have to go out and get a new appraiser. Is that what I am understand you are saying?

William Forsberg: That is my understanding. To the extent that that appraiser has been disqualified, any prior evidence or appraisals that he has completed prior to the disqualification will not have any probative effect. That taxpayer would be required to go out and get a new appraisal.

Robert Cimasi: So in effect that would be a death sentence for the appraiser or the appraisal firm. Obviously there would be all sorts of litigation and malpractices from clients against that appraiser if that were to happen even if those prior appraisals were pristine and of no objection.

Mike or Howard, could you comment on that?

Michael Gregory: I think that would be a correct interpretation with what Bill just presented here. That would be my best guess.

Robert Cimasi: That's great. Another question that was just raised here and I would like to throw it out for discussion is just to clarify this appeal process. How can an appraiser defend himself if he is dragged into this? In the case of a federal court where there is a *Daubert* or *Kumho* challenge, if the case is settled, the appraiser has no standing, as case law has held this over a number of years, to go in and defend himself in the event that a judge disqualifies him in a case that settles.

There is no standing. The appraiser has no place to go. There is nothing for him to do. If I understand correctly, in this case though, that even if the IRS and the taxpayer were to reach agreement on a particular matter that was before the Service, and it results in a disqualification of the appraisal, the appraiser is going to have an opportunity of due process to be able to defend his work product and to reverse the disqualification.

Is that a correct surmise?

Michael Gregory: Yes, and I think a real key point here is that the application of the penalty is actually a separate case, separate and distinct from the taxpayers case. Just keep that in mind. Remember, in my presentation there was a referral from one of our valuers back to the Lead Development Center. They accepted that particular case for an application of a penalty regardless of whatever else may be going on with that tax return with whoever it was who was being audited.

Now the penalty is being applied against this appraiser and appraisal firm relative to the valuation work that was done. As a result of the application of that penalty, a recommendation was made to the Office of Professional Responsibility. It is at that point the appraiser is informed that this investigation has taken place and the appraiser is now being asked to come forward and respond back to an allegation in the application of the penalty.

Robert Cimasi: Thank you, Mike. We have a new question that just arrived. The question is, "Have the presenters seen valuation firms offer in their retainer engagement letters in order to proactively address the liability for any appraiser penalty? Do the presenters see the penalty as indemnifiable items? In other words, can the appraisers push the liability for any penalty on to their clients?"

I will throw that out for comment here. What have we seen in terms of valuation firms altering their engagement letters in engagement agreements?

William Forsberg: I have seen or heard from appraisal firms attempts to do that, but if that would come across my desk I would definitely not go with that appraiser. I would throw it out. I don't think that is an appropriate contract for the taxpayer to be indemnified for any penalties. This is not something that the taxpayer should have to bear. I would negotiate the contract without those provisions.

Robert Cimasi: Howard, have you picked up anything through the institute of any of the member firms that have discussed this or heard anything about this?

Howard Lewis: No, it strikes me as really completely untenable. I would agree with Bill. I wouldn't expect that any user of services would agree to engage such an appraiser under those terms.

Robert Cimasi: Mike, have you picked up on any of this? Have you heard anything about the engagement agreements being changed?

Michael Gregory: I have not.

Robert Cimasi: I can add that what I have seen is language that is being added and accepted by the taxpayers legal counsel that requires the taxpayer and the legal counsel to keep the appraiser in the loop, to notify the appraiser given the fact there is going to be a settlement amount that would call into question the opinion of value that the appraiser has issued on behalf of the taxpayer.

I have seen that language that essentially says they have an obligation to notify the appraiser so that the appraiser gets advanced knowledge that there is some problem going on. The fear that I think that addresses is that appraisers are being kept in the dark and not knowing that the taxpayer has in fact decided to cut a deal with the Service that would then call the appraiser's good faith valuation number into question.

I have seen that language, as a matter of fact, in a case we are involved in with another firm, just here a couple of months ago. I think that in that case it was accepted by legal counsel. Bill Forsberg, what is your view on that in terms of if there was that kind of language in terms of the taxpayer being advised to keep the appraiser informed if in fact a settlement had been reached at a different number than the appraisal came in?

William Forsberg: The taxpayer is hiring the appraiser for purposes of preparing the appraisal and providing services. I just don't know if I would want that kind of provision requiring the taxpayer to do something. If he didn't do it, he would be in breach. I have some concerns about that.

Robert Cimasi: You can understand though that the appraiser might want to know that information, right?

William Forsberg: Yes, I understand the appraiser would want to know that and be informed, but I don't know that I would make it a requirement or obligation of the taxpayer to inform them. I don't know if there is an independent way that the appraiser could find out about it.

It is a real problem. On the one hand you want to make sure that the taxpayer who is entering into a contract isn't going to be overly burdened. Again, you want to make sure that the appraiser isn't out of the loop.

Robert Cimasi: Thank you very much. We have sort of extended beyond our period of time here, so I am going to go around and ask each of our presenters if they have a final comment to make. Let's start with Howard Lewis. Howard, do you have any final concluding comments?

Howard Lewis: Thank you. I must say that I enjoyed this opportunity. I think that this information is extremely important and I am glad that those who did choose to call in had this opportunity. I think that there is plenty more that will be coming. We all must be up to date with developments in this regard. I do hope that the Service will take every opportunity to communicate some of the things that I mentioned in my presentation that will help professionals understand their responsibilities better.

I also hope that the Service will communicate changes and impacts of this process as they begin to occur.

Robert Cimasi: Howard, thank you very much for the work that the Institute of Business Appraisers is doing in terms of getting this out to its members.

Mike Gregory, do you have any concluding comments?

Michael Gregory: Thank you very much for the opportunity to be here today. Relative to several of the comments that were made, I do share in the concerns of the elements of false precision, no statute of limitations, and the more likely than not standard. This is the only penalty that I am aware of that we are involved with within the Engineering and Valuation Program that does not have the caveat to allow the Treasury Secretary to determine when to impose the penalty rather than strictly an application based on the percentage of the determination.

I would hope that if a technical correction were to go forward, that would be an element to allow for management to intervene and make a determination within the Engineering and Valuation Program should the statute come up for consideration.

I think overall the intent on the part of congress in implementing this law was again, to give the authority to the Treasury Department to apply the law in an appropriate fashion in an area that is deemed as being abusive in the application by some appraisers. I think in actual application, we have to be very careful in terms of how we do apply this in the consideration.

Although when we apply penalties, we are always trying to be reasonable with respect to the taxpayer, I am concerned that there could be applications when we within the IRS in the valuation field may not want to apply the penalty, that our hands may be tied based on the shell provision of the law. That is a concern that I have as an implementer of the policy, not a determiner of the policy.

Thank you.

Robert Cimasi: Mike, thank you very much. Bill Forsberg?

William Forsberg: I would echo what Mike said. I think this 6695A needs a technical correction. I would like to see discretion in the IRS to impose a penalty or not impose a penalty. I think I would be more comfortable with that than a straight statute that said "shall impose."

Also, I think there should be a good faith exception. I think the exception that is there is hollow. There has to be a number of factual situations where you would probably fall within the penalty environment of 6695A, but the facts and circumstances suggest that there has been a good faith attempt to comply with the laws. There should be an exception for that similar to what there was before.

Robert Cimasi: Thank you, Bill Forsberg. I want to say that I think it is very impressive that we are able to get the cooperation of Mike Gregory and the Internal Revenue Service to participate on this program and several other programs that we have done like this. I hope that will continue going forward to carry on in a tradition that Howard Lewis started many years ago to try to have this outreach to stakeholders so that between the Service and the appraisal profession.

I have to also add that Bill Forsberg, the work that you have done with your colleagues at the American Bar Association in many ways is looking out for the interest of the appraisal profession and raising extremely important issues, for instance, the issue of the uneven playing field and the fairness of the legislation, and the intricacies of very complex applications of several different codes to what we do day in and day out.

I want to thank everyone and Business Valuation Resources for allowing this program. I concur that I think that six months down the line we should perhaps take another look at this because things will probably change. I want to thank all of our participants for your participation today. I believe you know how to get a hold of all of us if you have any follow-up questions.

Thanks very much Blake. And, thank you participants and panelists for being a part of this program today.

William Forsberg: Thank you, Bob.

Michael Gregory: Thank you, Bob.

Blake Lyman: This concludes today's presentation *IRS Appraiser Penalties: Pension Protection Act and Beyond* co-presented with the Institute of Business Appraisers. BVR would like to thank Robert Cimasi, William Forsberg, Michael Gregory, and Howard Lewis for their expertise, the IBA for their partnership, and all of our listeners for attending.

As a reminder, to receive CPE and CLE credit, listeners must complete and submit a brief survey on this teleconference. A link to this survey is provided in your registration email. The survey will be active for five business days and must be completed before we can process certificates.

If you have any questions related to the content or format of this teleconference, please email BVR at *tc-questions@bvresources.com*. Thank you. You may now disconnect.

IRS Appraiser Penalties:
Pension Protection Act and Beyond
BVR
What It's Worth
Business Valuation Resources, LLC
(888) 287-8258 or (503) 291-7963
www.BVResources.com
Robert James Cimasi
MHA, ASA, CBA, AVA, CM&AA | Health Capital Consultants, LLC
William S. Forsberg
Esq. | Leonard Street and Deinard
Michael A. Gregory
ASA, AVA, MBA, PE | Internal Revenue Service
Howard A. Lewis
AVA, ABAR | Institute of Business Appraisers
BVR
© 2009, Business Valuation Resources, LLC
Send questions to:
TC-Questions@BVResources.com

New Rules: Pension Protection Act (PPA) and Beyond
BVR
What It's Worth
Business Valuation Resources, LLC
(888) 287-8258 or (503) 291-7963
www.BVResources.com
Howard A. Lewis
Executive Director
Institute of Business Appraisers
BVR
© 2009, Business Valuation Resources, LLC
Send questions to:
TC-Questions@BVResources.com

Unprecedented Environment

- Professional responsibility
- Ethics
- Standards
- Penalties
- Quality
- Peer review
- Accreditations
- Help shape the future

Send questions to: TC-Questions@BVResources.com

4

IRS Appraiser Penalties: Pension Protection Act and Beyond

We are self regulated

- What are our responsibilities?
- Are we doing an adequate job?
- Have we let partisanship get in the way of progress?
- Are we missing an important opportunity?
- What are the risks of inaction?
- Will we contribute to our profession and society?

Send questions to: TC-Questions@BVResources.com 5

BVR IRS Appraiser Penalties: Pension Protection Act and Beyond

Why so many standards?

- What are we really committed to?
- Do we really mean what we say?
- What will it take to get to the next level?
- What is the role of government?
- Are we asking the right questions?
- Who do you trust now?

Send questions to: TC-Questions@BVResources.com 6

BVR IRS Appraiser Penalties: Pension Protection Act and Beyond

Appraiser Professional Responsibility and the IRS

- A little history
- Treasury Circular 230 – IRS Office of Professional Responsibility
- Howard A. Lewis – National Program Manager, 2000-2008
- Practitioners and Circular 230
- Where did appraisers fit?
- Was there a problem?

Send questions to: TC-Questions@BVResources.com 7

IRS Appraiser Penalties: Pension Protection Act and Beyond

IRC section 6701 – Aiding and Abetting

- What does that mean?
- Why a different standard for appraisers?
- What were the consequences of this?
- What was proposed?
- What was the outcome?
  - Pension Protection Act of 2006

Send questions to: TC-Questions@BVResources.com 8

IRS Appraiser Penalties: Pension Protection Act and Beyond

Is This What We Asked For?

- IRC section 6695A
  - Substantial valuation misstatement
  - Substantial E&G understatement
  - Gross valuation misstatement
- Exception
  - "More likely than not"
- Office of Professional Responsibility
  - Discipline actions

Send questions to: TC-Questions@BVResources.com 9

IRS Appraiser Penalties: Pension Protection Act and Beyond

What Might we Need?

- More disclosure from the IRS
  - Problems they see
  - Solutions that help
  - Penalties they assert
  - Best practices that work
- Restore, expand and continue the partnerships with the appraisal societies and other stakeholders that made a positive impact from 2000 – 2008

Send questions to: TC-Questions@BVResources.com 10

IRS Appraiser Penalties: Pension Protection Act and Beyond

New Appraiser Penalties Code Section 6695A

BVR
What It's Worth

Business Valuation Resources, LLC
(888) 287-8258 or (503) 291-7963
www.BVResources.com

William S. Forsberg
Leonard, Street and Deinard
Minneapolis, MN

Send questions to:
TC-Questions@BVResources.com

New Appraiser Penalties Code Section 6695A

- Pension Protection Act-Code Section 6695A:
  - The Pension Protection Act of 2006[1] imposes new penalties on appraisers under Code Sec. 6695A for substantial or gross valuation misstatements.
    [1] The Pension Protection Act of 2006, Pub. L. No. 109-280, 120 Stat. 780 (2006) (the "PPA").

Send questions to: TC-Questions@BVResources.com

12

IRS Appraiser Penalties:
Pension Protection Act and Beyond

New Appraiser Penalties
Code Section 6695A

- Code Section 6695A:
  - *§ 6695A. **Substantial and gross valuation misstatements attributable to incorrect appraisals.***
  - ***(a) Imposition of penalty.*** *If (1) a person prepares an appraisal of the value of property and such person knows, or reasonably should have known, that the appraisal would be used in connection with a return or a claim for refund, and (2) the claimed value of the property on a return or claim for refund which is based on such appraisal results in a substantial valuation misstatement under chapter 1 (within the meaning of section 6662(e)), or a gross valuation misstatement (within the meaning of section 6662(h)), with respect to such property, then such person shall pay a penalty in the amount determined under subsection (b)*

Send questions to: TC-Questions@BVResources.com

13

IRS Appraiser Penalties: Pension Protection Act and Beyond

New Appraiser Penalties
Code Section 6695A

- Code Section 6695A: (Cont.)
  - ***(b) Amount of penalty.*** *The amount of the penalty imposed under subsection (a) on any person with respect to an appraisal shall be equal to the lesser of (1) the greater of (A) 10 percent of the amount of the underpayment (as defined in section 6664(a)) attributable to the misstatement described in subsection (a)(2) , or (B) $1,000, or (2) 125 percent of the gross income received by the person described in subsection (a)(1) from the preparation of the appraisal.*
  - ***(c) Exception.*** *No penalty shall be imposed under subsection (a) if the person establishes to the satisfaction of the Secretary that the value established in the appraisal was more likely than not the proper value.*

Send questions to: TC-Questions@BVResources.com

14

IRS Appraiser Penalties: Pension Protection Act and Beyond

New Appraiser Penalties
Code Section 6695A

Example 1. Bill charges $20,000 for the appraisal. The appraisal values the property at $3 million, resulting in an income tax benefit from the deduction of $900,000. The correct value is $1,600,000, resulting in an income tax benefit from the deduction of $480,000. The penalty applies because the claimed value of $3 million is more than 150% of the correct value of $1,600,000 (i.e., $2,400,000). The penalty against Bill is $25,000 (125% of the $20,000 fee), because this is less than 10% of the tax underpayment (10% of $420,000, or $42,000).

Send questions to: TC-Questions@BVResources.com

15

IRS Appraiser Penalties:
Pension Protection Act and Beyond

New Appraiser Penalties
Code Section 6695A

Example 2. Bill charges $40,000 for the appraisal. The appraisal values the property at $3 million, resulting in an income tax benefit from the deduction of $900,000. The correct value is $1,600,000, resulting in an income tax benefit from the deduction of $480,000. The penalty applies because the claimed value of $3 million is more than 150% of the correct value of $1,600,000 (i.e., $2,400,000). The penalty against Bill is $42,000 (10% of the tax understatement of $420,000), because this amount is less than 125% of the $40,000 fee (i.e. $50,000).

Send questions to: TC-Questions@BVResources.com

16

IRS Appraiser Penalties:
Pension Protection Act and Beyond

New Appraiser Penalties
Code Section 6695A

Example 3. Bill charges $1,500 for an appraisal. The appraisal values the property at $15,000, resulting in an income tax benefit of $4,500. The correct value is $7,500, resulting in an income tax benefit of $2,250. The penalty applies because the claimed value of $15,000 is more than 150% of the correct value of $7,500 (i.e. $11,250). The penalty against Bill is $1,000, because this amount is (1) greater than 10% of the tax understatement of $2,250 (i.e. $225), and (2) less than 125% of the $1,500 fee (i.e., $1,875).

Send questions to: TC-Questions@BVResources.com

17

IRS Appraiser Penalties: Pension Protection Act and Beyond

New Appraiser Penalties
Code Section 6695A

- The Task Force-Comments to the IRS
  - *The American Bar Association ("ABA") Section of Real Property, Probate and Trust Law ("RPPT") submitted comments to the Internal Revenue Service on February 14, 2007 on the issues surrounding new Code Section 6695A. The ABA RPPT task force was headed William S. Forsberg, Esq. of Leonard, Street and Deinard, Minneapolis, Minnesota, and by Hugh F. Drake, Esq. of Brown, Hay & Stephens, LLP, Springfield, Illinois.*

Send questions to: TC-Questions@BVResources.com

18

IRS Appraiser Penalties: Pension Protection Act and Beyond

New Appraiser Penalties
Code Section 6695A

- The Comments to the IRS

1. Will Code Sec. 6695A apply to estate and gift tax valuations or solely to income tax valuations?
2. What is the reach and scope of the "any person" language of Code Sec. 6695A?
3. What constitutes the preparation of an "appraisal" under Code Sec. 6695A?
4. Will Code Sec. 6695A apply only to individual appraisers in a firm, the appraisal firm as a whole, or both?
5. To what extent will Code Sec. 6695A come to bear on appraisers relying upon expert opinions about the nature of the property interest to be appraised?

Send questions to: TC-Questions@BVResources.com

19

IRS Appraiser Penalties: Pension Protection Act and Beyond

New Appraiser Penalties
Code Section 6695A

- The Comments to the IRS (Cont.)

6. Does the penalty calculation constitute false precision, particularly where different assets have dramatically different valuation variances?
7. Would penalties imposed by Code Sec. 6695A be imposed only after final resolution of a tax controversy case?
8. Do the Code Sec. 6695A penalty provisions apply equally to the appraisers relied upon by the government in tax controversy matters?
9. How can the exception to Code Sec. 6695A be implemented when the determination of whether a valuation was more likely than not a proper value is made after (emphasis added) the Service has already determined a penalty should be imposed?

Send questions to: TC-Questions@BVResources.com

20

IRS Appraiser Penalties: Pension Protection Act and Beyond

Penalties and the IRS

BVR
What It's Worth

Business Valuation Resources, LLC
(888) 287-8258 or (503) 291-7963
www.BVResources.com

Michael A. Gregory
ASA, AVA, MBA, PE
Internal Revenue Service

March 18, 2009

Send questions to:
TC-Questions@BVResources.com

The Latest Developments in Appraiser Professional Responsibility

- The comments and views presented by Michael Gregory may not reflect the position or policy of the IRS. The opinions offered are those of Michael Gregory

Send questions to: TC-Questions@BVResources.com

22

IRS Appraiser Penalties:
Pension Protection Act and Beyond

Professional Responsibility in Federal Tax Matters

- Introduction
- Pension Protection Act of 2006 Key Points
- Penalty investigations update

Send questions to: TC-Questions@BVResources.com 23

IRS Appraiser Penalties: Pension Protection Act and Beyond

Introduction

- Disputes over valuation fill our dockets, and for good reason. Approximately 243 sections of the Code require fair market value estimates in order to assess tax liability, and 15 million tax returns are filed each year on which taxpayers report an event involving a valuation-related issue. It is no mystery, therefore, why valuation cases are ubiquitous.

Send questions to: TC-Questions@BVResources.com 24

IRS Appraiser Penalties: Pension Protection Act and Beyond

Introduction

- **As a corporate employee if you believe that you have witnessed high level misconduct, and you cannot, despite your best efforts, stop the misconduct – your only remaining course is to leave the company and disassociate your self from the company.**
  - OPR Director – Michael Chesman at October 10 IRS financial services industry conference in New York sponsored by the Tax Executives Institute

Send questions to: TC-Questions@BVResources.com 25

IRS Appraiser Penalties: Pension Protection Act and Beyond

Introduction - Practitioner Oversight

- Strengthen partnerships - integrity and compliance
- Clear, robust, current and meaningful standards of conduct
- Vigorous, targeted and effective system of oversight
- Fair, diligent and effective system of sanctions

Send questions to: TC-Questions@BVResources.com 26

IRS Appraiser Penalties: Pension Protection Act and Beyond

History

- increased public awareness
- legislation
- outreach to the appraisal community
- conducting penalty investigations
- nominal success

Send questions to: TC-Questions@BVResources.com 27

IRS Appraiser Penalties: Pension Protection Act and Beyond

The Law from 1985 to PPA '06

- IRC § 6700 - Promoters
- IRC § 6701 – Aiding and Abetting
- IRC § 7408 – Injunctions
- Engineering program goal –
  - Fair and consistent administration of these sections

Send questions to: TC-Questions@BVResources.com 28

IRS Appraiser Penalties: Pension Protection Act and Beyond

The Law 1985 – Present
Penalty & Sanction Basics

- Penalty – IRC § 6701
  - $10,000 – Document related to a corporate tax liability
  - $1,000 – Document related to tax liability of any other person
- Sanctions
  - OPR – Disqualification
  - DOJ - Injunctions

Send questions to: TC-Questions@BVResources.com 29

IRS Appraiser Penalties: Pension Protection Act and Beyond

The Law 1985 – Present
Penalty Investigation Process

- Referrals to Lead Development Center (LDC) in SBSE
  - Review and authorize investigation
  - Assignment to Abusive Tax Avoidance Transaction group
  - Team formation
    - ATAT agent and Valuator
    - Area Counsel, Technical Advisors

Send questions to: TC-Questions@BVResources.com 30

IRS Appraiser Penalties: Pension Protection Act and Beyond

The Law 1985 – 2007
What You Really Want to Know!

- Questionable Appraiser Conduct
  - Assuming facts that do not exist
  - Purposefully excluding a valuation approach that produces credible results
  - Ignoring strong market evidence
  - Presenting false information
  - Including assumptions as to future events that are implausible

Send questions to: TC-Questions@BVResources.com 31

IRS Appraiser Penalties: Pension Protection Act and Beyond

The Law 1985 – 2006
What You Really Want to Know!

- Questionable Appraiser Conduct
  - Assuming forms of ownership that do not exist
  - Intentional disregard of professional standards of appraisal practice
  - Any participation by an appraiser that results in a value determination intended to reduce tax without objective and credible evidence to support the appraisal

Send questions to: TC-Questions@BVResources.com 32

IRS Appraiser Penalties: Pension Protection Act and Beyond

Pension Protection Act of 2006
PL 109-280 (H.R. 4)

- Enactment Date – August 17, 2006 (Exception for easements)
- **New Civil Penalty - §6695A - Appraisers**
- Removes "Threshold Restriction
- Relaxes the Knowledge Standard

Send questions to: TC-Questions@BVResources.com 33

IRS Appraiser Penalties: Pension Protection Act and Beyond

Pension Protection Act of 2006
PL 109-280 (H.R. 4)

- Improved Definitions
  - Qualified Appraisal
  - Qualified Appraiser

Send questions to: TC-Questions@BVResources.com 34

IRS Appraiser Penalties: Pension Protection Act and Beyond

PL 109-280 – New Civil Penalty Computation of 6695A Penalty

- The amount of the penalty is equal to the lesser of--
  - (1) The greater of--
    - (A) 10 percent of the amount of the underpayment attributable to the misstatement, or
    - (B) $1,000, or
  - (2) 125 percent of the gross income received by the appraiser from the preparation of the appraisal.

Send questions to: TC-Questions@BVResources.com 35

IRS Appraiser Penalties: Pension Protection Act and Beyond

PL 109-280 Exception to 6695A Penalty

- If the appraiser
  - establishes to the satisfaction of the Secretary
  - that the value established in the appraisal was
  - more likely than not the proper value.

Send questions to: TC-Questions@BVResources.com 36

IRS Appraiser Penalties: Pension Protection Act and Beyond

PL 109-280
Definitions of Qualified Appraiser and Appraisal

- Qualified appraiser – an individual
  - Appraisal designation
  - Recognized professional appraiser organization
  - Or, minimum education/experience requirements
  - Regularly performs appraisers for compensation
  - Meets other requirements

Send questions to: TC-Questions@BVResources.com

37

IRS Appraiser Penalties: Pension Protection Act and Beyond

PL 109-280
Definitions of Qualified Appraiser and Appraisal

- Qualified appraisal
  - an appraisal of property
  - conducted by a qualified appraiser
  - in accordance with generally accepted appraisal standards and pertinent regulations.

Send questions to: TC-Questions@BVResources.com

38

IRS Appraiser Penalties: Pension Protection Act and Beyond

Status of Penalty Investigations

- 146 penalties asserted against six appraisers
- OPR Referrals – 6 appraisers
- Types of referrals
  - Conservation easements – facades and open space
  - Abusive schedule A deductions
  - E&G valuations
  - Pension fund valuations - limitations

Send questions to: TC-Questions@BVResources.com 39

IRS Appraiser Penalties: Pension Protection Act and Beyond

Status of Penalty Investigations

- Total Referrals - ~ 100
  - Approved – ~25
  - Recommended (Not yet approved) – ~10
  - Suspended (Insufficient information – still being developed factually) – ~ 35
  - Discontinued (Developed – no action necessary) – Under 10
  - Surveyed (Investigations not warranted) – Under 10

Send questions to: TC-Questions@BVResources.com 40

IRS Appraiser Penalties: Pension Protection Act and Beyond

References

- IRS Practitioner Website
  - http://www.irs.gov/taxpros/index.html
- AICPA

Send questions to: TC-Questions@BVResources.com 41

IRS Appraiser Penalties: Pension Protection Act and Beyond

New Rules: Pension Protection Act (PPA) and Beyond [continued]

BVR
What It's Worth

Business Valuation Resources, LLC
(888) 287-8258 or (503) 291-7963
www.BVResources.com

Howard A. Lewis
Executive Director
Institute of Business Appraisers

Send questions to: TC-Questions@BVResources.com

Business Development Opportunities?

- Looking for the economic advantage
- Do appraisers have a "bad name?"
- Not all valuation firms have or deserve the same reputation
- Not all valuation firms deserve the reputation they have
- The enigma of the IRS examination process of valuation issues

Send questions to: TC-Questions@BVResources.com 43

IRS Appraiser Penalties: Pension Protection Act and Beyond

Indicia of the Credible Valuation Firm

- Has an appropriate recruiting, selection and education process in place for its appraisers
- Adheres to a set of ethics and standards rules
- Has an appropriate peer review/quality review process in place
- Has taken appropriate action on any and all referrals of information pertaining to ethics, standards, professional responsibility and competency issues regarding its staff

Send questions to: TC-Questions@BVResources.com 44

IRS Appraiser Penalties: Pension Protection Act and Beyond

Recruiting, Selection and Education

- A documented minimum set of knowledge, skill and ability requirements
- A core training curriculum
- A continuing education curriculum
- A combination of "accredited" and "non-accredited" staff members that the firm has evaluated and can demonstrate is adequate for the services provided by the firm

Send questions to: TC-Questions@BVResources.com

45

IRS Appraiser Penalties: Pension Protection Act and Beyond

Core Training Curriculum

- Distinguishes between appropriate levels of employee KS&A
- Is periodically evaluated for sufficiency and accomplishment
- Includes an appropriate mix of "in-house" and external training elements
- Includes appropriate "testing" features
- Includes a documented "on-the-job training" process

Send questions to: TC-Questions@BVResources.com

46

IRS Appraiser Penalties: Pension Protection Act and Beyond

Continuing Education Curriculum

- Provides for an appropriate amount and frequency of regular CPE
- Includes technical issues appropriate for the level of KS&A for individual staff
- Includes periodic ethics and standards content

Send questions to: TC-Questions@BVResources.com

47

IRS Appraiser Penalties: Pension Protection Act and Beyond

Ethics and Standards Rules

- Are generally accepted in the profession
- Are the subject of regular focus by firm management
- Include a process for addressing questions that arise and enables staff to elevate and resolve issues of concern

Send questions to: TC-Questions@BVResources.com

48

IRS Appraiser Penalties: Pension Protection Act and Beyond

Peer Review / Quality Review

- Is documented and informed to staff
- Is regularly monitored and evaluated
- Is designed to provide quality assurance and control information to management
- Is utilized to address quality concerns and best practices

Send questions to: TC-Questions@BVResources.com

49

BVR

IRS Appraiser Penalties: Pension Protection Act and Beyond

IRS Appraiser Penalties: Pension Protection Act and Beyond

Questions & Discussion

BVR
What It's Worth

Business Valuation Resources, LLC
(888) 287-8258 or (503) 291-7963
www.BVResources.com

Robert Cimasi
MHA, ASA, CBA, AVA, CM&AA | Health Capital Consultants, LLC

William Forsberg
Esq. | Leonard Street and Deinard

Michael Gregory
ASA, AVA, MBA, PE | Internal Revenue Service

Howard Lewis
MS, AVA | Institute of Business Appraisers

BVR

Send questions to: TC-Questions@BVResources.com

Section 3
Court Case Abstracts

Abstract Summary Table

Case Name	Date	Court	State / Jurisdiction	Judge	Comments	Page
Abraham, Estate of, v. Comm'r (I)	02/18/04	United States Tax Court	Specialty Federal	Ruwe	The Tax Court determined that IRC sec. 2036 should apply to recapture the value of the assets transferred to three family limited partnerships. The First Circuit affirmed all aspects of the Tax Court determination as unfavorable to the estate.	3-301
Abraham, Estate of, v. Comm'r (II)	05/25/05	United States Court of Appeals	1st Circuit Federal	Lynch		3-330
Adams v. United States (I)	03/17/99	United States District Court	Northern District of Texas	Fitzwater	The District Court concluded that valuation discounts for marketability, minority interest, uncertain rights and undesirable mix of assets were inappropriate because an assignee had a right to received its pro rata share of the partnership's net asset value. The Fifth Circuit remanded the case back to the District Court stating that the District Court must consider evidence by both parties.	3-105
Adams v. United States (II)	05/07/00	United States Court of Appeals	5th Circuit Federal	Fitzwater		3-156
Adams v. United States (III)	08/27/01	United States District Court	Texas	Fitzwater		3-210
Adams, Estate of, v. Comm'r	03/28/02	United States Tax Court	Specialty Federal	Colvin	The Tax Court considered the valuation of a controlling block of stock in a S corporation.	3-235
Alan Baer Revocable Trust v. U.S., Inc.	3/18/09	United States District Court	Nebraska	Bataillon	United States District Court Cites Noble in Considering Subsequent Events	3-423
Amlie, Estate of, v. Comm'r	04/17/06	United States Tax Court	Specialty Federal	Gale	The Tax Court determined that a buy-sell agreement satisfied sec. 2703 and the Lauder test such that it fixed the value of a minority interest in closely held bank stock for estate tax purposes.	3-360
Anderson, W.G. v. United States	12/28/05	United States District Court	Western District of Louisiana	Hicks	The issues concerned DLOM, market approach valuation of interests, starting value, and choice of comparables.	3-349
Armstrong, Estate of, v. United States (I)	02/24/00	United States District Court	Western District of Virginia	Crigler	The District Court denied the estate a valuation reduction for estate taxes and attendant costs paid by the estate after the gifts had been included in the decedent's gross estate because the gifts were included in the decedent's gross estate. The Appellate Court affirmed that a donee seeking to invoke the net gift doctrine must demonstrate that payment of the gift taxes was a condition of the gift at the time of the transfer, and that the obligation was not contingent, speculative, or illusory.	3-146
Armstrong, Estate of, v. United States (II)	01/15/02	United States Court of Appeals	4th Circuit Federal	Motz		3-228
Astleford v. Comm'r	05/05/08	United States Tax Court	Specialty Federal	Swift	The Tax Court decided on a case involving family limited partnerships and "layered" real estate holding entities. The Court considered the comparable data from sales of publicly-traded REITS to sales of registered RELPS and accepted a sizeable combined discount for DLOM and control for a 50% general partnership interest; and a fairly substantial discount for the "tiered" ownership interests in the RELP.	3-411

Case Name	Date	Court	State / Jurisdiction	Judge	Comments	Page
Atkinson, Estate of, v. Comm'r	10/16/02	United States Court of Appeals	11th Circuit Federal	Per Curiam	The Court of Appeals determined that an estate may not make a charitable deduction for an amount passing from a charitable remainder annuity trust (CRAT) to the charity when the CRAT regulations are not followed from formation through termination.	3-264
Auker, Estate of, v. Comm'r	05/19/98	United States Tax Court	Specialty Federal	Laro	The Tax Court handed down a five-point test for use when considering a market absorption discount.	3-83
Bailey, Estate of, v. Comm'r	06/17/02	United States Tax Court	Specialty Federal	Thornton	The Tax Court considered the valuation of two 25 percent interests in a corporation that owned and operated motels.	3-250
Baird, Estate of, v. Comm'r (I)	09/28/01	United States Tax Court	Specialty Federal	Gerber	Relying primarily on one of the estate's three experts, a buyer-seller of fractional interests who considered twelve factors in the determination of the discount, the court concluded that the record and the expert's reports supported a fractional interest discount of 60%.	3-218
Baird, Estate of, v. Comm'r (II)	07/11/05	United States Court of Appeals	5th Circuit Federal	Jolly	The Fifth Circuit reversed and remanded on the issue of costs. It found that before the IRS issued the notices of deficiency, the taxpayers had provided enough information to the IRS to alert it to the fact that the in-kind partition described in the forester's report was not viable. The court also concluded that the IRS's estimate of the costs of a hypothetical in-kind partition was speculative and unsupported.	3-335
Barge v. Comm'r	04/23/97	United States Tax Court	Specialty Federal	Halpern	The Tax Court used a classic DCF model to determine the value of an undivided interest in timberland.	3-59
Barnes v. Comm'r	11/17/98	United States Tax Court	Specialty Federal	Colvin	The Tax Court valued gifts of less than a one% interest in two closely held regional telephone companies.	3-96
Barudin, Estate of, v. Comm'r	08/26/96	United States Tax Court	Specialty Federal	Swift	IRS expert cited unnamed market studies indicating 25.8% to 45% marketability discount range.	3-50
Berry, Estate of, v. Comm'r	04/24/07	United States Tax Court	Specialty Federal	Flaherty	The Tax Court found the FLP served no legitimate business purpose, and affirmed the state's denial of estate tax discounts.	3-387
Bigelow, Estate of, v. Comm'r (I)	03/30/05	United States Tax Court	Specialty Federal	Colvin	The Tax Court applied sec. 2036(a) to recapture the value of real property transferred by a decedent to a family limited partnership.	3-327
Bigelow, Estate of, v. Comm'r (II)	09/14/07	Court of Appeals	9th Circuit Federal	Gould	The Ninth Circuit failed to accept the "per se" rule and determined that the criteria for the "bona fide sale" exception are interrelated with the inquiry into the family limited partnership's "legitimate" (non-tax) business purpose.	3-397

Case Name	Date	Court	State / Jurisdiction	Judge	Comments	Page
Black, Estate of, v. Comm'r	12/14/09	United States Tax Court	Federal Circuit	Halpern	At issue was whether contributions of stock to an FLP constituted bona fide transfers for adequate consideration, sufficient to value the FLP interests at fair market value (with discounts) for estate tax purposes.	3-425
Blount, Estate of, v. Comm'r (I)	05/12/04	United States Tax Court	Specialty Federal	Gale	The Tax Court rejected the estate's position that a buy-sell agreement fixed the value of the stock for estate tax purposes because the agreement was not similar to comparable agreements entered into by parties at arms'-length and because the decedent could unilaterally alter the agreement in life.	3-305
Blount, Estate of, v. Comm'r (II)	10/31/05	United States Court of Appeals	11th Circuit Federal	Birch	The Eleventh Circuit affirmed the Tax Court's decision that the buy-sell agreement could not set the value of BCC for estate tax purposes, but reversed on the inclusion of the insurance proceeds as nonoperating assets.	3-343
Bommer Revocable Trust v. Comm'r	08/20/97	United States Tax Court	Specialty Federal	Ruwe	The Tax Court concluded that a buy/sell agreement was not controlling for estate tax purposes.	3-63
Bongard, Estate of, v. Comm'r	03/15/05	United States Tax Court	Specialty Federal	Goeke	The Tax Court issued a two prong analysis for determining whether the bona fide sale for adequate and full consideration exception to sec. 2036 is satisfied.	3-326
Bonner, Estate of, v. United States	06/04/96	United States Court of Appeals	5th Circuit Federal	Per Curiam	The Fifth Circuit reversed the Tax Court and found that fractional interest discounts should be applied.	3-44
Borgatello, Estate of, v. Comm'r	08/18/00	United States Tax Court	Specialty Federal	Wells	The Tax Court valued a real estate holding company using the net asset value method.	3-161
Bosca, Estate of, v. Comm'r	07/08/98	United States Tax Court	Specialty Federal	Whalen	The Tax Court rejected petitioner's argument that no value was transferred when the decendent exchanged voting common stock for nonvoting common stock in a closely-held corporation.	3-89
Branson, Estate of, v. Comm'r (I)	07/13/99	United States Tax Court	Specialty Federal	Parr	The Tax Court determined that the estate underreported the value of the stock for estate tax purposes, but permitted the heir to offset the overpaid capital gains taxes against the estate tax owed.	3-119
Branson, Estate of, v. Comm'r (II)	09/05/01	United States Court of Appeals	9th Circuit Federal	Sneed	The Court of Appeals determined that an estate was entitled to recoup capital gains taxes paid by the heir in connection with the sale of the estate's stock.	3-214
Brocato, Estate of, v. Comm'r	12/29/99	United States Tax Court	Specialty Federal	Vasquez	The parties determined the size of the blockage discount by reference to the average time on the market, and used the discounted cash-flow method to account for the additional time on the market.	3-139

Case Name	Date	Court	State / Jurisdiction	Judge	Comments	Page
Brookshire, Estate of, v. Comm'r	10/08/98	United States Tax Court	Specialty Federal	Swift	The Tax Court accepted the undiscounted value proposed by the estate's first expert which was computed using three valuation methods—the guideline company method, the discounted cash flow method, and the capitalization of earnings method.	3-95
Cartwright, Estate of, v. Comm'r (I)	06/20/96	United States Tax Court	Specialty Federal	Colvin	The Tax Court decision turned on the Court's interpretation of the shareholder agreement and past transactions with withdrawing	3-45
Cartwright, Estate of, v. Comm'r (II)	07/12/99	United States Court of Appeals	9th Circuit Federal	Silverman	members of the firm. The Appellate Court affirmed the use of the 1973 buy-sell agreement to value the stock but reversed that valuation for the inclusion of advanced client costs and works in progress as assets of the practice.	3-117
Casey, Estate of, v. Comm'r	03/27/96	United States Tax Court	Specialty Federal	Gerber	The Tax Court declined to apply a discount for lack of control to a fractional interest in a liquidating trust, whose beneficiaries had relinquished control of the assets to the trustee; thus, creating a unity of ownership.	3-43
Cavallaro v. United States	04/01/02	United States Court of Appeals	1st Circuit Federal	Lynch	The Court of Appeals considered whether an accountant's communications regarding transfer tax and merger issues were privileged communications.	3-239
Church v. United States (I)	01/18/00	United States District Court	Texas	Garcia	Court rejected the IRS' position that a gift tax was due on the formation of an FLP two days prior to the decendent's death. The partnership was formed for bona fide business purposes.	3-143
Church v. United States (II)	07/18/01	United States Court of Appeals	5th Circuit Federal	Per Curiam		3-208
Cidulka, Estate of, v. Comm'r	03/25/96	United States Tax Court	Specialty Federal	Scott	The Tax Court valued the company using the an income capitalization method where the income multiplier was determined by reference to comparable transactions.	3-41
Cloutier, Estate of, v. Comm'r	02/13/96	United States Tax Court	Specialty Federal	Laro	The Tax Court failed to appy a marketability discount and found fault with the estate's appraiser for failing to consider a control premium, for writing a brief report, and for looking solely at the willing seller to the detriment of the willing buyer.	3-34
Cook, Estate of, v. Comm'r (I)	07/09/01	United States Tax Court	Specialty Federal	Gerber	Partnership formed solely for the purposes of holding cash and the right to future lottery payments. Valued according to annuity tables without marketability discount.	3-205
Cook, Estate of, v. Comm'r (II)	11/13/03	United States Court of Appeals	5th Circuit Federal	Duhe	The Court of Appeals considered whether deviation from the annuity tables in Sec. 7520 was warranted in the valuation of a lottery prize.	3-296

Case Name	Date	Court	State / Jurisdiction	Judge	Comments	Page
Costanza, Estate of, v. Comm'r	02/19/03	United States Court of Appeals	9th Circuit Federal	Gilman	The Court of Appeals determined that an intrafamily transaction involving a self-canceling installment note (SCIN) was a bona fide transaction within the meaning of IRC sec. 2001(b).	3-270
Cullison, Estate of, v. Comm'r	06/17/98	United States Tax Court	Specialty Federal	Parr	The Tax Court determined that the taxpayer's accountant provided them with faulty advise and improperly valued an annuity by failing to use the interest rate required by the treasury regs.	3-84
D'Ambrosio, Estate of, v. Comm'r	11/26/96	United States Court of Appeals	3rd Circuit Federal	Nygaard	The Third Circuit reversed the Tax Court and concluded that the decedent received adequate consideration under IRC sec. 2036 when she exchanged her stock for an annuity.	3-54
Dailey, Estate of, v. Comm'r (I)	10/03/01	United States Tax Court	Specialty Federal	Foley	This case involves both gift and estate tax matters, because the decedent dies shortly after gifting 45% and 15% interests, retaining a 40% interest in the estate.	3-220
Dailey, Estate of, v. Comm'r (II)	12/09/02	United States Tax Court	Specialty Federal	Foley	In a later proceeding, the taxpayer was not awarded costs related to the issue of discounts, even though the tax-payer won on that issue, because the IRS was substantially justified in maintaining its position and has a reasonable basis in law and fact.	3-265
Dallas v. Comm'r	09/28/06	United States Tax Court	Specialty Federal	Colvin	The Tax Court agreed with the IRS' position that the inter-family transfers were "bargain gifts." Also determined that S corporations should not be tax-affected.	3-378
Davenport v. United States	10/18/05	United States District Court	Southern District of Texas	Froeschner	The District Court excluded an expert's valuation because it failed to take into account the fact that the donor of the gifted stock did not have clear title to that stock because the stock was the subject of estate tax litigation from the donor's grantor.	3-342
Davis v. United States (I)	12/19/05	United States District Court	New Hampshire	McAuliffe	Court assesses whether fair market value of non-marketable an-nuity varies from present value of IRC annuity tables. The District	3-346
Davis v. United States (II)	06/13/07	United States District Court	New Hampshire	McAuliffe	Court held that the value determined under the annuity tables was the proper value of the lottery payments.	3-392
Davis, Estate of, v. Comm'r	06/30/98	United States Tax Court	Specialty Federal	Chiechi	The Tax Court criticized IRS expert for not considering all restricted stock and pre-IPO studies.	3-87
Deputy, Estate of, v. Comm'r	06/13/03	United States Tax Court	Specialty Federal	Gerber	The Tax Court based its discounts on a unique combined discount matrix designed to "replicate an investor's decision process."	3-278
Desmond, Estate of, v. Comm'r	03/10/99	United States Tax Court	Specialty Federal	Vasquez	The Tax Court valued a controlling interest in a paint and coatings manufacturing company using the discounted future cash flow and market comparables approaches.	3-103

Case Name	Date	Court	State / Jurisdiction	Judge	Comments	Page
DiSanto, Estate of, v. Comm'r	12/27/99	United States Tax Court	Specialty Federal	Colvin	The Tax Court determined that a post-valuation date redemption between the decedent's children and the company as well as the company's subsequent bankruptcy was not probative.	3-136
Disbrow, Estate of, v. Comm'r	02/28/06	United States Tax Court	Specialty Federal	Laro	The Tax Court determined that sec. 2036(a) applied to recapture of the value of a residence transferred to a general partnership and leased to the decedent.	3-354
Dockery v. Comm'r	03/19/98	United States Tax Court	Specialty Federal	Colvin	The Tax Court rejected both trial experts and adopted the valuation report filed with the gift tax returns.	3-77
Dunn, Estate of, v. Comm'r (I)	01/12/00	United States Tax Court	Specialty Federal	Gale	The Tax Court considered the valuation of a majority interest in a heavy equipment rental company. The IRS argued that due to the large disparity between the asset and earnings valuations that the asset value should be used and the earnings value should be disregarded, but the Tax Court rejected this argument because the company was an operating company properly valued under the earnings approach.	3-140
Dunn, Estate of, v. Comm'r (II)	08/01/02	United States Court of Appeals	5th Circuit Federal	Wiener	The Court of Appeals reversed the Tax Court decision by ruling that 100% of the built-in capital gains tax should be recognized when determining the fair market value of a corporation under the asset approach, but should not be considered when determining the fair market value of stock under an earnings approach.	3-254
Eddy, Estate of, v. Comm'r	08/16/00	United States Tax Court	Specialty Federal	Parr	The Tax Court refused to permit the estate to use the alternate valuation date because the estate's tax return was filed beyond the time prescribed by law.	3-160
Eisenberg v. Comm'r (I)	10/27/97	United States Tax Court	Specialty Federal	Hamblen	The Tax Court refused to permit the taxpayer to apply a discount for built-in capital gains tax because the parties stipulated that a liquidation of the company was not foreseeable.	3-68
Eisenberg v. Comm'r (II)	08/18/98	United States Court of Appeals	2nd Circuit Federal	Carman	The Court of Appeals reversed the Tax Court decision and concluded that a discount for built-in capital gains could be applied when valuing gifts of stock for the gift tax.	3-90
Erickson, Estate of, v. Comm'r	04/30/07	United States Tax Court	Specialty Federal	Kroupa	The Tax Court held that the bona fide sale exception did not apply and the assets transferred to the FLP should be included in the value of the decedent's gross estate under § 2036.	3-388
Ferguson, Estate of, v. Comm'r	04/07/99	United States Court of Appeals	9th Circuit Federal	Choy	The Court of Appeals affirmed the Tax Court's finding that the donated stock had ripened into a right to receive the amount offered for the stock in the tender offer.	3-111

Case Name	Date	Court	State / Jurisdiction	Judge	Comments	Page
Fleming, Estate of, v. Comm'r	10/27/97	United States Tax Court	Specialty Federal	Chiechi	In valuing the business, the Tax Court considered pre-valuation date sales when applying a premium to the company's trade note receivables, and it applied both marketability and minority interest discounts.	3-69
Fontana, Estate of. v. Comm'r	03/28/02	United States Tax Court	Specialty Federal	Foley	The Tax Court determined that at the time of death the decedent "had control and power of disposition over the property" and upheld the IRS's determination that the stock should be aggregated.	3-238
Foote, Estate of, v Comm'r	02/05/99	United States Tax Court	Specialty Federal	Jacobs	The Tax Court permitted a blockage discount of 3.3% on the decedent's 2.2% interest in a NYSE stock.	3-100
Forbes, Estate of, v. Comm'r	03/23/01	United States Tax Court	Specialty Federal	Thornton	The Tax Court rejected the IRS's calculation of the discount, which was determined based on comparable sales, because the sales were distant in both locale and time from the valuation date.	3-184
Ford, Estate of, v. Comm'r	12/08/93	United States Tax Court	Specialty Federal	Chiechi	The Tax Court rejected the estate's expert because he valued the holding companies using weighted combination of earnings and asset approaches.	3-26
Freeman, Estate of, v. Comm'r	08/13/96	United States Tax Court	Specialty Federal	Halpern	The Tax Court disregarded the estate's expert because he failed to explain his valuation approaches or supply information regarding his selection of comparable companies.	3-49
Furman v. Comm'r	04/30/98	United States Tax Court	Specialty Federal	Beghe	The Tax Court accepted a valuation of the company using the EBIDTA multiple method including discounts for key person, marketability and minority interests.	3-78
Gavin, Estate of, v. United States	05/08/97	United States Court of Appeals	8th Circuit Federal	Magill	The Eighth Circuit reversed the District Court and permitted an IRC. Sec. 2032A election.	3-61
Gilford, Estate of, v. Comm'r	01/12/87	United States Tax Court	Specialty Federal	Hamblen	The value of publicly-traded stock was determined by reference to the average daily trading price, adjusted for blockage and its restricted status.	3-23
Gimbel, Estate of, v. Comm'r	12/19/06	United States Tax Court	Specialty Federal	Swift	The valuation of a large block of restricted public shares with the Tax Court concluding the appropriate methodologies, marketability discounts, and consideration of post-valuation events.	3-384

Case Name	Date	Court	State / Jurisdiction	Judge	Comments	Page
Gloeckner, Estate of, v. Comm'r (I)	03/25/96	United States Tax Court	Specialty Federal	Halpern	The Tax Court determined that a redemption agreement did not control the fair value market of the decedent's stock for estate tax purposes.	3-42
Gloeckner, Estate of, v. Comm'r (II)	08/18/98	United States Court of Appeals	2nd Circuit Federal	Cardamone	The Court of Appeals reversed the Tax Court decision by concluding that the kin did not benefit from the agreement and that the relationship was a business relationship, not a kinship relationship.	3-91
Glover, Estate of, v. Comm'r	08/02/02	United States Tax Court	Specialty Federal	Jacobs	In considering the value of a malpractice claim, the Court deviated from its normal position and used a post-valuation date settlement, as stipulated by the parties, as the starting point for the claim valuation.	3-256
Godley, Estate of, v. Comm'r (I)	08/04/00	United States Tax Court	Specialty Federal	Gale	The Tax Court valued five 50% partnership interests, which were all subject to buy-sell agreements. The buy-sell agreements were disregarded for valuation purposes because they were found to be testamentary devices. The Tax Court applied a marketability discount, but not a minority discount.	3-157
Godley, Estate of, v. Comm'r (II)	04/15/02	United States Court of Appeals	4th Circuit Federal	Wilkinson	The Court of Appeals held that the Tax Court did not err in refusing to apply a minority discount to the decedent's 50% interests.	3-242
Gray, Estate of, v. Comm'r	02/05/97	United States Tax Court	Specialty Federal	Colvin	In reaching a decision, the Tax Court listed a twelve-question analysis to determine whether a transfer was a dividend or a loan.	3-57
Green, Estate of, v. Comm'r	12/29/03	United States Tax Court	Specialty Federal	Thornton	The Tax Court considered the valuation of a minority interest in a closely held commercial bank with the block being valued using the discounted net income, public company guideline, and comparable transaction approaches.	3-297
Gribauskas, Estate of, v. Comm'r	08/26/03	United States Court of Appeals	2nd Circuit Federal	Van Graffeiland	The Court of Appeals reversed the Tax Court's valuation of lottery payments finding that deviation from the annuity tables was warranted under the facts of this case and concluded that a lack of marketability discount was appropriate.	3-287
Gross v. Comm'r (I)	07/29/99	United States Tax Court	Specialty Federal	Halpern	The Tax Court determined whether it was appropriate to tax affect earnings in determining the share value using the discounted cash flow method.	3-122
Gross v. Comm'r (II)	11/19/01	United States Court of Appeals	6th Circuit Federal	Cohn	The majority of the Court of Appeals decided that tax affecting was not appropriate in this case.	3-222

Case Name	Date	Court	State / Jurisdiction	Judge	Comments	Page
Hackl v. Comm'r (I)	03/17/02	United States Tax Court	Specialty Federal	Nims	The Tax Court determined that the annual gift tax exclusion was inapplicable because the gifts were gifts of future interests.	3-234
Hackl v. Comm'r (II)	07/11/03	United States Court of Appeals	7th Circuit Federal	Evans	The Court of Appeals affirmed the Tax Court decision, holding that the restrictions on transfer in the operating agreement meant that the gifted shares were "essentially without immediate value to the donees."	3-285
Harper, Estate of, v. Comm'r (I)	06/30/00	United States Tax Court	Specialty Federal	Wells	The Tax Court determined that a limited partnership's liquidation restrictions were not more stringent than the applicable state law.	3-155
Harper, Estate of, v. Comm'r (II)	05/15/02	United States Tax Court	Specialty Federal	Nims	The Tax Court found that the commingling of funds, history of disproportionate distributions and testamentary intent in the FLP's formation supported the inclusion of the assets in the decedent's estate.	3-244
Heck, Estate of, v. Comm'r	02/05/02	United States Tax Court	Specialty Federal	Halpern	The Tax Court rejected a valuation using the public guideline company approach based on two comparables in similar lines of business because this was too few comparables to make a valid comparison.	3-230
Heckerman v. Commissioner	7/27/09	United States District Court	Washington	Coughenour	IRS Challenges Family LLC As Indirect Gift, Including 58% Marketability Discount	3-428
Helis, Succession of, v. United States (I)	07/03/01	United States Court of Federal Claims	Federal Claims	Bruggink	The Court of Federal Claims rejected the minority discount because the IRS applied it to only the real property assets of the partnership rather than all the partnership's assets, and because the IRS found more control than warranted in a 50% interest.	3-198
Helis, Succession of, v. United States (II)	01/08/03	United States Court of Federal Claims	Federal Claims	Bruggink	The Federal Court of Claims determined that interest paid to the IRS under sec. 6166 and deducted by the estate under sec. 2503, but later refunded, should be added back when making the final estate accounting.	3-266
Hendrickson, Estate of, v. Comm'r	08/23/99	United States Tax Court	Specialty Federal	Beghe	The Tax Court rejected a valuation performed using the DCF method because it concluded that the CAPM was not appropriate for valuing small closely held companies. It additionally took issue with the calculation of Beta and the application of a small stock capitalization premium.	3-125
Hess v. Comm'r	08/20/03	United States Tax Court	Specialty Federal	Ruwe	The Tax Court did not rely on any one valuation put forward by the experts in arriving at its valuation conclusion.	3-285
Hewitt v. Comm'r	10/29/97	United States Tax Court	Specialty Federal	Tannenwald, Jr.	The Tax Court concluded that a taxpayer who donated stock to a charitable organization was not entitled to a deduction greater than their basis in the stock.	3-71

Case Name	Date	Court	State / Jurisdiction	Judge	Comments	Page
Hillgren, Estate of, v. Comm'r	03/03/04	United States Tax Court	Specialty Federal	Cohen	Factors considered by the Tax Court included the commingling of personal and business funds, negotiation over the FLP agreement, post-death adjustments to the FLPS books, among others.	3-302
Hjersted, Norman B, Estate of, In the Matter of (I)	06/02/06	Court of Appeals	Kansas	Sundby	Concerns the application of discounts to an FLP that one spouse creates to disinherit the other. The Court of Appeals held that discounts for lack of marketability and control did not apply to a family limited partnership.	3-367
Hjersted, Norman B, Estate of, In the Matter of (II)	02/01/08	Supreme Court	Kansas	N/A	On remand, the Trial Court should consider whether the wife's situation was comparable to a minority shareholder and entitled to an undiscounted value, the Supreme Court said.	3-406
Hoffman, Estate of, v. Comm'r	05/09/01	United States Tax Court	Specialty Federal	Ruwe	The Tax Court considered the valuation of promissory notes, a minority interest in a family partnership holding real estate, and a minority interest in a real estate development S corporation.	3-191
Holman v. Comm'r	05/27/08	United States Tax Court	Specialty Federal	Halpern	The Tax Court determined 1) whether the transfer of assets constituted a direct or indirect gift; 2) whether the limited partnership should be treated (and valued) analogous to a trust; and 3) what discounts for lack of control and marketability apply to the gifts.	3-417
Hoover, Estate of, v. Comm'r	11/01/95	United States Court of Appeals	10th Circuit Federal	N/A	The Court of Appeals confirmed that the concept of fair market value includes a discount for lack of marketability and control for purposes of Section 2032A.	3-31
Huber v. Comm'r	05/09/06	United States Tax Court	Specialty Federal	Goeke	The Tax Court determined that the value of closely held stock was established by the price used in recent transaction of that stock for gift tax purposes where that price was established by an appraisal obtained by the subject company for its internal purposes.	3-363
Hughes, Estate of, v. Comm'r	12/27/05	United States Tax Court	Specialty Federal	Colvin	The Tax Court determined that the amount paid on a demand note after the death of the decedent was not deductible under sec. 2053 as a claim against the estate because the transaction was not bona fide nor completed at arm's-length.	3-348
Jameson, Estate of, v. Comm'r (I)	02/09/99	United States Tax Court	Specialty Federal	Gale	The Tax Court concluded that the net asset approach was the appropriate valuation method and included a discount for the built-in capital gains tax on the underlying timber property.	3-101
Jameson, Estate of, v. Comm'r (II)	09/18/01	United States Court of Appeals	5th Circuit Federal	Jones	The Court of Appeals reversed the Tax Court decision ruling that the court improperly particularized the hypothetical buyer as a strategic buyer of decedent stock.	3-215

Case Name	Date	Court	State / Jurisdiction	Judge	Comments	Page
Janda v. Comm'r	02/02/01	United States Tax Court	Specialty Federal	Vasquez	The Tax Court criticized both restricted stock studies and QMDM as used in this case. Experts also applied a 10% minority discount.	3-175
Janis v. Comm'r	08/21/06	United States Court of Appeals	9th Circuit Federal	McKeown	The Ninth Circuit affirmed the Tax Court's determination of the fair market value of an inherited art collection for partnership basis purposes, inclusive of a blockage discount.	3-373
Jelke, Estate of, v. Comm'r (I)	05/31/05	United States Tax Court	Specialty Federal	Gerber	The Tax Court calculated the built-in capital gains tax discount by reference to a time-value of money analysis, which considered the turnover rate of the company's stock portfolio.	3-332
Jelke, Estate of, v. Comm'r (II)	11/15/07	Court of Appeals	United States	Hill	The Court of Appeals approved a "dollar-for-dollar" reduction for the entire built-in capital gains tax liability of a minority interest in a closely held corporation, overruling the Tax Court's prior allowance of only a partial discount.	3-399
Jones, Estate of, v. Comm'r	03/06/01	United States Tax Court	Specialty Federal	Cohen	The Tax Court determined the value of limited partnerships in two FLPs using the net asset value method less discounts for secondary market, lack of marketability, and built-in capital gains.	3-179
Jorgensen, Estate of, v. Commissioner	3/26/09	United States Tax Court	Federal	Haines	Terrible FLP facts preclude analysis of discounts.	3-430
Jung, Estate of, v. Comm'r	11/10/93	United States Tax Court	Specialty Federal	Chabot	The Tax Court valued a medical textiles manufacturing company using the discounted cash flow method.	3-24
Kahn, Estate of, v. Comm'r	11/17/05	United States Tax Court	Specialty Federal	Goeke	The Tax Court concluded that a discount was not applicable to individual retirement accounts (IRAs) to account for the built-in gains that would be taxable to estate or beneficiaries upon their distribution.	3-345
Kaufman, Estate of, v. Comm'r (I)	04/06/99	United States Tax Court	Specialty Federal	Laro	The Tax Court rejected both experts for a variety of reasons including failure to adequately describe comparable companies, failure to address the aspects of control held by the block when determining the marketability discount, and failure to consider the net asset value of the business.	3-109
Kaufman, Estate of, v. Comm'r (II)	03/15/01	United States Court of Appeals	9th Circuit Federal	Noonan	The Ninth Circuit reversed the Tax Court decision by concluding that the Tax Court erred when it failed to value the estate's minority stockholding by reference to two sales of minority blocks occurring shortly after the valuation date.	3-182
Keller v. United States	09/30/05	United States District Court	Southern District of Texas	Rainey	The District Court denied the government's motion for summary judgment on the issue of the applicability of sec. 2036 to look through a FLP.	3-339

Case Name	Date	Court	State / Jurisdiction	Judge	Comments	Page
Keller v. United States	8/20/09	United States District Court	Texas	Rainey	Another taxpayer win: court accepts 47.5% Discount for formed (but not funded) FLP.	3-433
Kelley, Estate of, v. Comm'r	10/11/05	United States Tax Court	Specialty Federal	Vasquez	The Tax Court determined the appropriate lack of marketability and minority interest discounts to apply to an interest in a family limited liability partnership holding cash and certificates of deposit.	3-340
Kerr v. Comm'r (I)	12/23/99	United States Tax Court	Specialty Federal	Jacobs	The Tax Court determined that the restrictions in FLP agreements could not be removed by family partners. The Court of Appeals affirmed that discounts were appropriate.	3-132
Kerr v. Comm'r (II)	06/10/02	United States Court of Appeals	5th Circuit Federal	Duhe		3-247
Kimbell v. Comm'r (I)	01/15/03	United States Tax Court	Specialty Federal	Buchmeyer	The Tax Court accepted the IRS's argument that the transaction was not a bona fide sale for full and adequate consideration because the parties were related. The Court of Appeals vacated this holding and remanded the case to determine whether decendent's interest was that of an assignee or limited partner.	3-267
Kimbell v. Comm'r (II)	05/20/04	United States Court of Appeals	5th Circuit Federal	Davis		3-308
Klauss, Estate of, v. Comm'r	06/27/00	United States Tax Court	Specialty Federal	Colvin	The Tax Court rejected a valuation that used the CAPM and a build-up model that included a small-stock premium.	3-152
Knight v. Comm'r	11/30/00	United States Tax Court	Specialty Federal	Colvin	The Tax Court rejected taxpayer's expert because his testimony was not objective.	3-170
Koblick v. Comm'r	04/03/06	United States Tax Court	Specialty Federal	Goeke	The Tax Court determined the fair market value of a minority interest in a company was donated to a charitable organization, as part of a plan by all shareholders of the company to donate all the stock to the nonprofit organization.	3-358
Kohler v. Comm'r	07/25/06	United States Tax Court	Specialty Federal	Kroupa	A "textbook case" on how to value a large, closely-held corporation, complete with discussion of dividend method and appropriate discounts.	3-369
Kohlsaat, Estate of, v. Comm'r	05/07/97	United States Tax Court	Specialty Federal	Swift	The Tax Court ruled that the transfer of property qualified for 16 annual gift tax exclusions.	3-60
Korby, Estate of, v. Comm'r (I)	05/10/05	United States Tax Court	Specialty Federal	Goeke	The Tax Court determined the value of assets contributed to a FLP was includable in the decedent's gross estate. Court of Appeals confirmed, noting that the IRS had always maintained that they both retained an interest in the FLP assets.	3-328
Korby, Estate of, v. Comm'r (II)	12/08/06	United States Court of Appeals	8th Circuit Federal	Bye		3-383
Kosman v. Comm'r	03/11/96	United States Tax Court	Specialty Federal	Colvin	The Tax Court was forced to reach a conclusion based on weak evidence.	3-38

Case Name	Date	Court	State / Jurisdiction	Judge	Comments	Page
Krapf v. United States	03/19/96	United States Court of Federal Claims	Federal Claims	Smith	The Court of Federal Claims determined that the transactions were relevant only when (1) there had been no material change in the company between the valuation date and the transaction date, or (2) if the subsequent information was foreseeable on the valuation date.	3-40
Langer v. Comm'r	10/30/06	United States Tax Court	Specialty Federal	Haines	The Tax Court provided insight on the appropriate valuation date and five factors in considering relevant sales comparables.	3-380
Lappo v. Comm'r	09/03/03	United States Tax Court	Specialty Federal	Thornton	The Tax Court relied primiarly on the Bajaj private placement study in arriving at its conclusion regarding the marketabilty discount, while looking at closed end fund data for its minority interest discount.	3-288
Lehmann, Estate of, v. Comm'r	08/26/97	United States Tax Court	Specialty Federal	Hamblen	The Tax Court determined that the IRS expert lacked supporting evidence in his analysis.	3-65
Leichter, Estate of, v. Comm'r	03/06/03	United States Tax Court	Specialty Federal	Gerber	The Tax Court found flaws including the application of seemly duplicitous discounts, brevity and conclusory nature of the report, and the use of companies in the market approach that were not comparable.	3-271
Litchfield, Estate of, v. Comm'r	1/29/09	United States Tax Court	Federal	Swift	New tax court decision on discounts and embedded taxes hinges on experts.	3-435
Lockett, Estate of, v. Comm'r	02/09/98	United States Tax Court	Specialty Federal	N/A	The Tax Court denied the estate a charitable deduction for property with historic significance held in trust, because the decedent did not possess a charitable intent to transfer the property on the date of her death.	3-73
Lundquist v. United States	02/23/99	United States District Court	Eastern District of New York	Kahn	The District Court found that sec. 483 characterzies a payment as principal or interest without affecting the valuation of the gift.	3-102
Maggos, Estate of, v. Comm'r (I)	09/23/97	United States Tax Court	Specialty Federal	Laro	The Tax Court rejected taxpayer's motion for summary judgment on gift tax liability resulting from a redemption of a majority interest in a corporation's stock. After recalculating both experts' valuations, the	3-66
Maggos, Estate of, v. Comm'r (II)	04/11/00	United States Tax Court	Specialty Federal	Ruwe	Tax Court found that the valuation resulted in the same fair market value.	3-150

Case Name	Date	Court	State / Jurisdiction	Judge	Comments	Page
	01/24/96	United States Tax Court	Specialty Federal	Ruwe	The Tax Court clarified the definition of 'Fair Market Value' when it warned that the hypothetical sale should not be separated from the actual facts that would affect the value of the subject company's stock.	3-33
Magnin, Estate of, v. Comm'r (II)	07/13/99	United States Court of Appeals	9th Circuit Federal	Schroeder	The Court of Appeals reversed the Tax Court and determined that 'adequate and full consideration' under IRC Sec. 2036 for the transfer of a remainder interest is the actuarial value of the remainder interest.	3-120
Magnin, Estate of, v. Comm'r (III)	02/12/01	United States Tax Court	Specialty Federal	Ruwe	The Tax Court rejected the estate's expert because he used the wrong standard of value and found fault with the IRS's expert because the companies used in the market approach were not comparable to the subject company.	3-177
Malkin, Estate of, v. Comm'r	9/16/09	United States Tax Court	Federal	Halpern	'Sham" funding plus pledging FLP assets for personal debt adds up to taxpayer loss.	3-440
Mandelbaum v. Comm'r	06/12/95	United States Tax Court	Specialty Federal	Laro	The Tax Court listed nine non-exclusive factors to be considered when determining the size of a discount for lack of marketability or illiquidity.	3-28
Manship, Estate of, v. United States	04/13/06	United States District Court	Eastern District of Louisiana	Noland	The District Court determined that documents produced by an appraiser were not covered by the work product or attorney-client privilege because any claim to the privileges had been waived.	3-359
Marmaduke, Estate of, v. Comm'r	10/14/99	United States Tax Court	Specialty Federal	Swift	The Court Tax concluded that the illiquidity discount should be greater than that indicated in the ESOP appraisal because the block of stock was fourteen times larger than the largest block of stock redeemed by the ESOP.	3-129
McClatchy, Estate of, v. Comm'r (I)	04/03/96	United States Tax Court	Specialty Federal	Nims	The Tax Court ruled that unregistered and restricted Class B stock in a publicly-held corporation should be valued without the limitations imposed on it under SEC Rule 144.	3-44
McClatchy, Estate of, v. Comm'r (II)	06/26/98	United States Court of Appeals	9th Circuit Federal	Tashima	The Ninth Circuit reversed the Tax Court's decision denying the estate a discount for SEC Rule 144 restrictions.	3-85
McCord v. Comm'r (I)	05/14/03	United States Tax Court	Specialty Federal	Vasquez	The Tax Court rejected pre-IPO studies and restricted stock analyses, but also concluded that appropriate discounts could not be inferred entirely from illiquidity costs from private placements.	3-274
McCord v. Comm'r (II)	08/22/06	United States Court of Appeals	5th Circuit Federal	Weiner	The Court of Appeals reversed the Tax Court's valuation of gifts because the lower court relied on a post-valuation date event in computing value.	3-374

Case Name	Date	Court	State / Jurisdiction	Judge	Comments	Page
McCormick, Estate of, v. Comm'r	08/07/95	United States Tax Court	Specialty Federal	Gerber	The Tax Court valued interests in a real estate partnership and accepted a valuation using the asset approach, plus various discounts.	3-29
McFarland, Estate of, v. Comm'r	09/19/96	United States Tax Court	Specialty Federal	Laro	The Tax Court rejects motion to value partnership only on going concern premise.	3-51
McLendon, Estate of, v. Comm'r (I)	12/28/95	United States Court of Appeals	5th Circuit Federal	Jones	The Court of Appeals concluded that the Tax Court erred when it valued interests in a partnership as partnership interests rather than assignee interests.	3-33
McLendon, Estate of, v. Comm'r (II)	03/09/98	United States Court of Appeals	5th Circuit Federal	Jolly	The Fifth Circuit reversed and rendered a decision for the estate on its use of the annuity tables pursuant to Rev. Rul. 80-80 when determining the amount of the annuity.	3-75
McMorris, Estate of, v. Comm'r	03/20/01	United States Court of Appeals	10th Circuit Federal	Briscoe	The Court of Appeals ruled that claims against an estate, being deductible under IRC Sec. 2053 (a)(3), should be valued as of the date of death.	3-183
Mellinger, Estate of, v. Comm'r	01/26/99	United States Tax Court	Specialty Federal	Cohen	The Tax Court declined to aggregate publicly traded stock includible in the decedent's gross estate under IRC sec. 2044 and 2033.	3-98
Melton, Estate of, v. United States	12/04/95	United States District Court	Western District of Texas	Primomo	In deciding to apply the minority discount, the magistrate determined that a shareholder with a 50% of the stock can block action by other shareholders but is unable to control the corporation.	3-32
Miller, Estate of, v. Comm'r Internal Revenue	3/27/09	United States Tax Court	Federal	Goeke	New FLP case: taxpayer's first asset transfer merits discount, but not second	3-442
Mirowski v. Comm'r	03/26/08	United States Tax Court	Specialty Federal	Chiechi	The Tax Court found Section 2036(a) not to be applicable due to availability of the "bona fide sale" exception.	3-408
Mitchell, Estate of, v. Comm'r (I)	10/09/97	United States Tax Court	Specialty Federal	Jacobs	The Tax Court applies discounts for key person and pending litigation.	3-67
Mitchell, Estate of, v. Comm'r (II)	05/02/01	United States Court of Appeals	9th Circuit Federal	Wardlaw	The Court of Appeals reversed the Tax Court's decision and remanded it for the Tax Court to shift the burden of proof to the Commissioner and to provide sufficient explanation on how they reached their valuation conclusion.	3-188
Mitchell, Estate of, v. Comm'r (III)	04/09/02	United States Tax Court	Specialty Federal	Jacobs	In calculating the appropriate minority discount, the Tax Court increased the discount size by 6% for increased the lack of marketability inherent in a minority block of stock, but declined to add a marketability discount.	3-240
Mueller, Estate of, v. Comm'r	11/05/96	United States Tax Court	Specialty Federal	Ruwe	The Tax Court rejected the estate's claim for equitable recoupment of taxes paid based on a valuation of the estate's stock.	3-53
Murphy v. U.S.	10/2/09	United States District Court	Arkansas	Barnes	Major victory for taxpayer & appraiser in classic FLP case	3-444

Case Name	Date	Court	State / Jurisdiction	Judge	Comments	Page
Negron v. United States	06/04/07	United States District Court	Northern District of Ohio	Aldrich	In this case involving a lottery winner, the District Court found that the annuity tables produced an unrealistic and unreasonable result in valuing the annuity.	3-391
Noble, Estate of, v. Comm'r	01/06/05	United States Tax Court	Specialty Federal	Laro	The Tax Court valued the interest at its post-death sale price, adjusted for 3% inflation, stating that there had not been any material change in circumstances between decendent's death and the date the shares were sold after decendent's death.	3-322
Nowell, Estate of, v. Comm'r	01/26/99	United States Tax Court	Specialty Federal	Cohen	The Tax Court concluded that that estate should not aggregate the limited partnership units in which the decedent had a right to receive income for life with partnership units the decedent placed in trust.	3-99
O'Neal, Estate of, v. United States (I)	07/26/01	United States Court of Appeals	11th Circuit Federal	Hill	The Court of Appeals determined that a claim against an estate, which is deductible under IRC sec. 2053(a), should be valued on the date of death.	3-209
O'Neal, Estate of, v. United States (II)	07/31/02	United States District Court	Northern District of Alabama	Johnson	The District Court, on remand from the Court of Appeals, considered the date-of-death value of claims made against the decedent's estate as a result of transferee gift tax and generation-skipping transfer tax liabilities.	3-253
Okerlund v. United States (I)	08/23/02	United States Court of Federal Claims	Specialty Federal	Wilson	Both experts used the public guideline company and discounted cash flow method to value the minority blocks of stock.	3-258
Okerlund v. United States (II)	04/09/04	United States Court of Appeals	Federal	Gakarsa	The Court of Appeals determined that the use of post-valuation date information may be considered when valuing a company on the valuation date, but only to the extent that profile of the company on the valuation date and on the ex post date are similar.	3-303
Peracchio v. Comm'r	09/25/03	United States Tax Court	Specialty Federal	Halpern	The Tax Court was displeased with both experts' analyses, criticizing one for relying on past cases to determine the discount and the other for relying on overall average discounts from the studies.	3-291
Pierre v. Comm'r	8/24/09	United States Tax Court	Federal Circuit	Wells	Tax court split 9-to-6 on preserving family LLC for gift vs. income tax purposes	3-448
Polack v. Comm'r (I)	06/10/02	United States Tax Court	Specialty Federal	Marvel	The Tax Court determined that the IRS correctly relied on the testimony of an unrelated shareholder in making its income projections and in its treatment of the corporate assets.	3-248
Polack v. Comm'r (II)	05/03/04	United States Court of Appeals	8th Circuit Federal	Loken	The Court of Appeals affirmed the Tax Court's decision not to consider the post-valuation date operations of the company in determining the value of closely held stock on the earlier valuation date.	3-304

Case Name	Date	Court	State / Jurisdiction	Judge	Comments	Page
Rabenhorst v. Comm'r	02/29/96	United States Tax Court	Specialty Federal	Wright	The Tax Court considered a pre-valuation date redemption and an appraisal performed using the public company guideline method.	3-37
Rakow v. Comm'r	05/27/99	United States Tax Court	Specialty Federal	Gale	The Tax Court accepted the valuation using the discounted future cash flow method over objections by the IRS and applied a minority interest discount.	3-115
Rauenhorst v. Comm'r	10/07/02	United States Tax Court	Specialty Federal	Ruwe	The Tax Court considered whether the anticipatory assignment of income doctrine should be applied to recharacterize the transfer of warrants to four charitable organizations.	3-263
Rector v. Comm'r	12/13/07	Court of Appeals	United States	Laro	The Tax Court adopted a "step transaction" approach, finding that decedent's transfer of assets to the FLP and her subsequent gifts of the limited partner interests were part of a "single plan" to minimize her Federal estate tax without entailing a significant nontax business purpose or a genuine pooling of assets.	3-402
Reichardt, Estate of, v. Comm'r	03/01/00	United States Tax Court	Specialty Federal	Colvin	The Tax Court determined that the estate must include the value of partial interests in real property in its gross estate under IRC sec. 2036.	3-147
Renier, Estate of, v. Comm'r	09/25/00	United States Tax Court	Specialty Federal	Gale	The Tax Court valued the business using the capitalization of equity method and rejected the IRS' capitalization rate which was computed using WACC.	3-165
Robertson v. United States	01/13/06	United States District Court	Northern District of Texas	Kaplan	Court favors reliance on academic research and empirical data as opposed to purely subjective factors (vulnerable to adjustment) to affirm IRS discount.	3-352
Rodgers, Estate of, v. Comm'r	04/20/99	United States Tax Court	Specialty Federal	Chiechi	The Tax Court calculated the value of a real estate operating company's properties and included an absorption discount.	3-112
Rosen, Estate of, v. Comm'r	06/01/06	United States Tax Court	Specialty Federal	Laro	The U.S. Tax Court applied a multifactor analysis to determine whether the objective facts indicated whether an FLP had a legitimate and substantial nontax purpose.	3-364
Scanlan, Estate of, v. Comm'r	07/24/96	United States Tax Court	Specialty Federal	Laro	IRS expert applied only a 4% discount to redemption sale price to account for minority status and other factors.	3-49
Schauerhamer, Estate of, v. Comm'r	05/28/97	United States Tax Court	Specialty Federal	Foley	The Tax Court concluded that three FLPs should be disregarded, and the value of their assets included in the value of the decedent's gross estate under IRC sec. 2036.	3-62

Case Name	Date	Court	State / Jurisdiction	Judge	Comments	Page
Schott v. Comm'r (I)	05/09/01	United States Tax Court	Specialty Federal	Cohen	The Tax Court concluded that grantor retained annuity trusts (GRATs) from the plaintiffs should be valued as single life annuities rather than dual life annuities.	3-194
Schott v. Comm'r (II)	02/18/03	United States Court of Appeals	9th Circuit Federal	Noonan	The Court of Appeals reversed the Tax Court and concluded that GRATs established for the life of the grantor and the life of the grantor's spouse could be valued as a dual-life annuity under sec. 7520.	3-269
Schusterman v. United States	08/22/95	United States Court of Appeals	10th Circuit Federal	Baldock	The Court of Appeals determined that the safe harbor interest rates of IRC sec. 483 were inapplicable for purposes of valuing a note for the gift	3-31
Schutt, Estate of, v. Comm'r	05/26/05	United States Tax Court	Specialty Federal	Wherry	The Tax Court rejected all the experts, finding that they made assumptions regarding the companies without explaining their base for those assumptions.	3-331
Schwan, Estate of, v. Comm'r	07/13/01	United States Tax Court	Specialty Federal	Nims	The Tax Court determined that a redemption agreement had no impact on the underlying assets' value prior to death and therefore was a testamentary device to be disregarded.	3-207
Senda v. Comm'r (I)	07/12/04	United States Tax Court	Specialty Federal	Cohen	The Tax Court determined that the limited partnership form should be disregarded for gift tax purposes when the contribution of property occurred on the same day as gifts of limited partnership units from the contributor to his children and where the partnership formalities were not respected by the contributor/general partner.	3-311
Senda v. Comm'r (II)	01/06/06	United States Court of Appeals	8th Circuit Federal	Benton, Jr.	The Court of Appeals determined that a transfer of publicly stock to a FLP made close in time to a gift of FLP interests was an indirect gift of the pro rata share of the public stock for gift tax purposes where the petitioner could not conclusively show that which event occurred first.	3-351
Shackleford v. United States (I)	07/29/98	United States District Court	Eastern District of California	Karlton	The District Court considered whether unreceived lottery payments should be valued as a commercial annuity or as a private annuity, including deviations from the annuity tables for lack of marketabilty.	3-90
Shackleford v. United States (II)	08/28/01	United States Court of Appeals	9th Circuit Federal	Thomas		3-212
Shepherd v. Comm'r (I)	10/26/00	United States Tax Court	Specialty Federal	Thornton	The Tax Court held transfers to FLP were indirect gifts of real estate.	3-168
Shepherd v. Comm'r (II)	02/28/02	United States Court of Appeals	11th Circuit Federal	Hull	The Court of Appeals affirmed the Tax Court's characterization of transfer of real property to an existing partnership as an indirect gift to the other partners which enhanced the value of their interests.	3-232

Case Name	Date	Court	State / Jurisdiction	Judge	Comments	Page
Simplot, Estate of, v. Comm'r (I)	03/22/99	United States Tax Court	Specialty Federal	Jacobs	In this complex case, the Tax Court valued a large, closely held, agri-business company using, in part, a discounted cash flow method and another market approach. The Ninth Circuit reversed the Tax Court's ruling and ordered entry of judgment in favor of the estate on remand because "the Tax Court erroneously attributed a premium to minority voting stock."	3-106
Simplot, Estate of, v. Comm'r (II)	05/14/01	United States Court of Appeals	9th Circuit Federal	Noonan		3-195
Smith (Estate of Crosby) v. United States	02/14/96	United States District Court	Mississippi	Russell	The District Court accepted the larger yield of a promissory note based on testimony for the estate's expert who considered factors including lack of marketability and lack of indenture/covenant.	3-35
Smith, Estate of Helen J., v. Comm'r	11/05/99	United States Tax Court	Specialty Federal	Gale	Tax Court accepted taxpayer's expert who relied on Management Planning, Inc. study.	3-131
Smith, John David v. United States	11/15/04	United States Court of Appeals	5th Circuit Federal	King	The Court of Appeals concluded that retirement accounts should not be discounted for potential future income taxes.	3-317
Smith, Sidney E. Jr., v. United States (I)	06/30/04	United States District Court	Western District of Pennsylvania	Baxter	A magistrate for the District Court determined on summary judgment that Sec. 2703(a) applied to disregard restrictions on the transfer of FLP interest contained in the FLP agreement.	3-310
Smith, Sidney E. Jr., v. United States (II)	07/22/05	United States District Court	Western District of Pennsylvania	Baxter		3-338
Snyder, Estate of, v. United States	08/20/99	United States Court of Federal Claims	Federal Claims	Turner	The Court of Federal Claims permitted the estate to deduct a environmental liability settlement over the objection of the IRS.	3-124
Speer v. Comm'r	07/16/96	United States Tax Court	Specialty Federal	Ruwe	The IRS argued that the payments should be taxed as a constructive dividend and as a gift, while the petitioners stated that the agreement was at arm's length and on fair and reasonable terms.	3-46
Stinson, Estate of, v. United States (I)	10/02/98	United States District Court	Northern District of Indiana	Miller, Jr.	The District Court found that forgiveness of corporate debt was not a gift of a present interest to the corporation's shareholder, and, therefore, the annual gift tax exclusion could not be claimed by the donor. The Seventh Circuit affirmed the District Court's finding.	3-94
Stinson, Estate of, v. United States (II)	05/26/00	United States Court of Appeals	7th Circuit Federal	Evans		3-151
Stone v. United States (I)	05/25/07	United States District Court	Northern District of California	Henderson	The District Court determined whether an undivided minority interest in a collection of paintings should be valued inclusive of a fractional interest discount. Having failed to receive persuasive evidence, the Court permitted the estate to take a 5% discount for its 50% interest in the art collection.	3-389
Stone v. United States (II)	08/10/07	United States District Court	Northern District of California	Henderson		3-393

Case Name	Date	Court	State / Jurisdiction	Judge	Comments	Page
Stone, Estate of, v. Comm'r	11/07/03	United States Tax Court	Specialty Federal	Chiechi	The Tax Court determined that the value of property transferred to five FLPs should not be included in the decedent's gross estate under sec. 2036(a)(1) because the decedent received FLP interest proportionate to the fair market value of the assets he transferred.	3-294
Strangi, Estate of, v. Comm'r (I)	11/30/00	United States Tax Court	Specialty Federal	Cohen	A divided Tax Court rejected the IRS's attempts to recapture the value of assets transferred to a FLP for transfer tax purposes. The Court of Appeals remanded the Tax Court's finding that the IRS's claim that the FLP's assets should be included in the decedent's estate under sec. 2306 (a), but affirmed the Tax Court on all other issues. On remand, the Tax Court found that section 2306 applied because there was no arm's-length transfer, and there was a mere "recycling" of value. Fifth Circuit affirmed the Tax Court's decision on remand.	3-172
Strangi, Estate of, v. Comm'r (II)	06/17/02	United States Court of Appeals	5th Circuit Federal	Clement		3-252
Strangi, Estate of, v. Comm'r (III)	05/20/03	United States Tax Court	Specialty Federal	Cohen		3-277
Strangi, Estate of, v. Comm'r (IV)	07/15/05	United States Court of Appeals	5th Circuit Federal	Jolly		3-336
Temple v. United States	03/10/06	United States District Court	Eastern District of Texas, Lufkin Division	Heartfield	The District Court rejected a marketability discount computed using the QMDM because the expert failed to adequately explain her assumption with respect to the required holding period input.	3-355
Thompson, Betty W. v. Comm'r	10/17/96	United States Tax Court	Specialty Federal	Dean	The court denied the petition for cost recovery on the basis that the taxpayer failed to show she had paid or incurred any fee or cost.	3-53
Thompson, Estate of Josephine, v. Comm'r (I)	07/26/04	United States Tax Court	Specialty Federal	Swift	The Tax Court disagreed with the estate's valuation of a 20% interest in a century-old, closely held company and labeled the experts as inexperienced and revalued the company itself. The Second Circuit affirmed the Tax Court's valuation, but added $68 million in non-operating assets to the company's capitalized income.	3-312
Thompson, Estate of Josephine, v. Comm'r (II)	08/23/07	Court of Appeals	United States	Jacobs		3-395
Thompson, Estate of Theodore, v. Comm'r (I)	09/26/02	United States Tax Court	Specialty Federal	Jacobs	The Tax Court determined that the value of the assets the decedent transferred to two FLPs were includable in the gross estate under IRC sec. 2036 (a). The Court of Appeals for the Third Circuit affirmed.	3-260
Thompson, Estate of Theodore, v. Comm'r (II)	09/01/04	United States Court of Appeals	3rd Circuit Federal	Scirica		3-315
Trenchard, Estate of, v. Comm'r	05/30/95	United States Tax Court	Specialty Federal	Laro	The Tax Court valued the gift as the difference between the value of the contributed property and the value of the preferred stock received.	3-28

Case Name	Date	Court	State / Jurisdiction	Judge	Comments	Page
Trompeter, Estate of, v. Comm'r (I)	01/27/98	United States Tax Court	Specialty Federal	Laro	The Tax Court concluded that the redemption of the decendent's preferred stock did not fix the value for estate tax purposes because it was too far removed from the valuation date; however, it was relevant to the determination of value on the valuation date. The Ninth Circuit reversed the Tax Court's valuation of closely held, preferred stock, but affirmed the Tax Court's finding that the stock would be redeemed pursuant to its terms. The Tax Court, on remand from the Ninth Circuit, reconsidered and explained its present value methodology and discount rate applied when determining the fair market value of preferred stock.	3-72
Trompeter, Estate of, v. Comm'r (II)	01/30/02	United States Court of Appeals	9th Circuit Federal	McKeown		3-229
Trompeter, Estate of, v. Comm'r (III)	02/04/04	United States Tax Court	Specialty Federal	Laro		3-300
Trotter, Estate of, v. Comm'r	09/21/01	United States Tax Court	Specialty Federal	Nims	The Tax Court, agreeing with the IRS, included the value of a condominium in the gross estate under IRC sec. 2036(a).	3-217
True, Estate of, v. Comm'r (I)	07/06/01	United States Tax Court	Specialty Federal	Beghe	The Tax Court concluded the buy-sell agreements were not controlling because they failed the fourth prong of the Lauder test—the agreements amounted to a testamentary device. The Court of Appeals affirmed the Tax Court's decision.	3-199
True, Estate of, v. Comm'r (II)	12/02/04	United States Court of Appeals	10th Circuit Federal	Seymour		3-318
Van Zelst v. Comm'r	11/15/96	United States Court of Appeals	7th Circuit Federal	Easterbrok	The Court of Appeals rejected the donor's charitable deduction for the value of property and mineral rights in Alaska.	3-54
Vinikoor v. Comm'r	04/27/98	United States Tax Court	Specialty Federal	N/A	The Tax Court determined that a transfer of stock was a gift rather than a loan even though the parties executed a note.	3-78
Wall v. Comm'r	03/27/01	United States Tax Court	Specialty Federal	Beghe	The Tax Court criticized both experts on other aspects of their opinions, and adopts the IRS notice of deficiency value.	3-185
Weinberg, Estate of, v. Comm'r	02/15/00	United States Tax Court	Specialty Federal	Whalen	The Tax Court criticized taxpayer's expert's use of a single comparable and IRS expert's use of QMDM.	3-144
Welch, Estate of, v. Comm'r (I)	05/06/98	United States Tax Court	Specialty Federal	Laro	The Tax Court disallowed a discount for built-in capital gains taxes on appreciated real property, which was under the threat of condemnation on the valuation date. The Court of Appeals reversed the Tax Court decision by ruling thatthat the availability of a section 1033 election does not prohibit the application of a capital gains tax deduction, but is a factor to be considered under the willing buyer-willing seller standard.	3-81
Welch, Estate of, v. Comm'r (II)	03/01/00	United States Court of Appeals	6th Circuit Federal	Holschuh		3-148
Williams, Estate of, v. Comm'r	02/12/98	United States Tax Court	Specialty Federal	Colvin	The Tax Court determined the per-acre value of fee ownership of undeveloped timberland and farmland.	3-73

Case Name	Date	Court	State / Jurisdiction	Judge	Comments	Page
Wright, Estate of, v. Comm'r	01/29/97	United States Tax Court	Specialty Federal	Swift	The Tax Court valued the largest minority block of a bank holding company and considered the fact that the stock was thinly-traded OTC and had a waiting list of investors.	3-56
Young, Estate of, v. Comm'r	05/11/98	United States Tax Court	Specialty Federal	Wright	The Tax Court denied an estate a fractional interest discount on property the decedent and his wife, both resident aliens, owned as joint tenants with the right of survivorship.	3-82

Estate of Gilford v. Commissioner

Citation: 88 T.C. No. 4
Court: United States Tax Court
State/Jurisdiction: Specialty Federal
Date of Decision: January 12, 1987
Judge: Hamblen

In the *Estate of Saul R. Gilford v. CIR*, 88 T.C. No. 4, the United States Tax Court considered the valuation of restricted stock. The decedent was the president and chairman of Gilford Instrument Laboratories, Inc., a publicly traded company. Gilford "designed, manufactured, and sold scientific instruments for use in the fields of science, medicine, and industry." After a drop in net earnings, the board of directors held a planning meeting in October 1979. The directors, including the decedent, discussed the possibility of Gilford being vulnerable to take-over attempts. They noted that in planning for such an event, "Any talk concerning a merger was purely hypothetical and of a defensive posture." The decedent died on November 17, 1979. The directors held a meeting on November 27, 1979 to fill the decedent's positions and to discuss the future growth of the company. There was no discussion of a sale or merger possibilities. Subsequent meeting's minutes did not reveal any discussion of a sale or merger. On May 30, 1980, the board of directors "agreed to merge Gilford with Corning Glass if certain conditions were met." On October 10, 1980, the merger was approved.

On the date of his death, the decedent was the largest shareholder, owning 381,150 shares (representing 23 percent). However, the stock was restricted pursuant to SEC Rule 144 because the decedent was an affiliate of the company. An expert was hired to value the decedent's shares. To establish the fair market value, the expert examined the "three characteristics of decedent's stock: (1) its market price at the date of death; (2) the size of the block of stock; and (3) the restricted nature of the stock."

Because the date of death was a Saturday, the expert averaged the market prices of the previous Friday's and following Monday's stock price to arrive at an average of $11.31 per share. The expert next considered the size of the block and its restricted status. He determined that the large block would warrant a blockage discount because the market could not absorb the decedent's stock at the average trading price. Therefore, he added 2% for blockage to his lack of marketability discount. He next considered the restrictions imposed on the stock under SEC Rule 144. He "utilized the four factors of Rev. Rul. 77-287, 1977-2 C.B., 319, 320, to evaluate the market value of the restricted Gilford stock." The four factors are: "the size of the issuing company measured by its sales", "the size and pattern of its earnings", "the trading market", and any "resale agreement provisions." After examining these factors and the restricted stock studies, the expert concluded a 33% discount for these factors would be appropriate. To the average market value, he applied a 35% lack of marketability discount which rendered the per share value to $7.35. The IRS disagreed. It concluded that a sale or merger "was foreseeable" on the date of death. Therefore, it valued the stock at the $24 per share received in the 1980 merger. Both parties addressed the Tax Court.

The IRS argued that the merger in October 1980 was probative of the fair market value of the stock on the valuation date. The Tax Court stated that under Fed.R.Evid. 401, the merger, which occurred less than one year after the decedent's death, was admissible as "relevant evidence." However, the Tax Court rejected the IRS's position that the merger price set the fair market value because the merger was not foreseeable on the decedent's date of death.

The Tax Court next examined the estates per share figure. The Tax Court agreed with most of the estate's expert's valuation. It found that the expert had properly concluded the $11.31 market value by averaging the market price over two days. It agreed with a 33% discount for restricted stock, which the expert supported within "the procedures outlined in Rev. Rul., 1977-2 C.B. 319." The court also noted that his discount corresponded to the results of the SEC Institutional Investor Survey, which the Rev. Rul. 77-287 relied. However, it rejected the expert's 2% blockage discount because "[the expert] does not give convincing reasons why a blockage discount should apply, and he does not give a definitive blockage discount percentage, preferring to factor it into the total discount." Therefore, the Tax Court ruled the appropriate fair market value of the Gilford restricted stock was $7.58 per share.

This abstract originally appeared in *Valuation Case Digest*, authored by John J. Stockdale, Jr.

Estate of Jung v. Commissioner

Citation: 101 T.C. 412
Court: United States Tax Court
State/Jurisdiction: Specialty Federal
Date of Decision: November 10, 1993
Judge: Chabot

In the *Estate of Mildred Herschede Jung v. CIR*, 101 T.C. 412 (1993), the United States Tax Court valued decedent's stock. On the date of decedent's death, October 9, 1984, the decedent owned 20.74% of the outstanding shares in Jung Corp, representing 20.83 of the voting stock. Jung Corp. and its wholly owned subsidiaries manufactured medical grade elastic textiles, wheelchairs, and wooden crutches. Jung Corp. received many purchase offers during its history, but none were considered. Two years after the decedent's death, the assets of Jung Corp. were sold, and the corporation was liquidated and dissolved. The sale price was $175 per share. The estate's tax return reflected the value of the decedent's interest on the date of her death. An independent appraiser determined the value. "He valued Jung Corp. by (1) calculating its return on equity and its return on capital employed, and (2) using a price/earnings multiple based on market comparables and applying the multiple to Jung Corp.'s weighted earnings for 1980 through 1984." He then applied a 30% minority and lack of marketability discount. He concluded that the decedent's stock had a fair market value of $2.7 million. The IRS disagreed, and the case proceeded to the Tax Court.

The Tax Court examined the parties' valuations. The estate's first expert was the appraiser who prepared the appraisal attached to the tax returns. His testimony did not materially change from his initial appraisal. The estate's second expert used the market comparable approach, a discounted cash-flow approach and a capitalization of earnings approach. He averaged his findings and concluded that the decedent's interest had a fair market value of $2,950,500 after applying a 35% discount for lack of marketability. The discount was determined after considering private placement of stock between 1979 and 1984. The estate's third expert, a professional appraiser from a national accounting firm, divided the subsidiaries into three groups: elastic textile operations; healthcare products; and non-operating assets. He used the market comparable approach and the discounted cash-flow method to value the first two groups. The last group was valued at book value. He applied a 35% lack of marketability discount to the total, based on stock studies and a 25% minority interest discount based on the SEC Institutional Investor Survey. He valued the decedent's interest at $3,372,000.

The IRS's two experts prepared a joint report, using the discounted cash-flow method and market comparable approach. They did not give significant weight to their market comparable approach valuation because, "they had difficulty in developing a reliable sample of comparable firms." They applied a 20% minority and 25% lack of marketability discount. The experts concluded Jung Corp. had a value of $8,903,766.

The IRS argued that the 1986 sale and liquidation of Jung Corp. should be considered in determining the company's value. The estate argued that the transaction was, "irrelevant because the sales and liquidation were unforeseeable at the valuation date." The Tax Court determined that on the valuation date, a sale of the corporation was not foreseeable, and thus, the sale did not affect the fair market value of the corporation on the valuation date. However, it found the sale may be used as evidence of the value of the corporation on the valuation date. It stated, "When viewed in this light – as evidence of value rather than as something that affects value – later-occurring events are no more to be ignored than earlier-occurring events."

The Tax Court found that the estate's third expert and the IRS correctly used the post-valuation date sale and liquidation in support of their discounted cash-flow method valuations. It noted the most accurate method for valuation was the discounted cash-flow method used by those experts. Based on those valuations, the Tax Court concluded that the decedent's interest had an undiscounted value between $6.7 and $7 million.

Next, the Tax Court discussed the applicability of the discounts. Both parties agreed that discounts were applicable, but disagreed as to the amount of the discounts. The Tax Court concluded that, "We agree with [the estate] as to the marketability discount and with [the IRS] as to the minority discount." It concluded that a 35% lack of marketability discount and no minority interest discount were appropriate. It found that minority considerations had been considered in the experts discounted cash-flow method analyses, because the discounted cash-flow method provides a minority valuation, where the capital asset pricing model (CAPM) is used.

This abstract originally appeared in *Valuation Case Digest*, authored by John J. Stockdale, Jr.

Estate of Ford v. Commissioner

Citation: T.C. Memo. 1993-580
Court: United States Tax Court
State/Jurisdiction: Specialty Federal
Date of Decision: December 8, 1993
Judge: Chiechi

In the *Estate of Ray A. Ford v. CIR*, T.C. Memo 1993-580, the United States Tax Court examined the valuation of five, family owned, closely held companies. The decedent's main company, Ford Storage & Moving Co., was a transfer and storage business. Three other companies owned property and warehouses that were leased to Ford Storage. The last business, Ford Bros. Van & Storage Co., leased moving equipment to Ford Storage. The decedent controlled Ford Storage and one other company and held minority interests in the rest. The IRS rejected the estate's valuation of the companies. Both parties presented the Tax Court with expert testimony.

The estate's expert was a finance professor, who was not a full time appraiser and did not belong to any appraisal associations. He noted that Ford Storage acted as the operating company, while the other four companies were holding companies. He stated that operating companies were usually valued using the earnings approach, and holding companies were valued using the net asset value method. However, the expert used the same weighted valuation method (75% for multiple of earnings and 25% for book value) for the five companies. He applied a 33% lack of marketability discount to the value of each company. He also applied a 7% minority interest discount to the real estate holding companies.

The Tax Court rejected this expert's opinion, noting "that defects in the methodology used by [the estate's] expert render it incapable of yielding persuasive determinations of fair market value for the stock at issue." The defects included (1) a disregard of the well-established valuation principle that holding companies should be valued using the net asset value method; (2) failure to separate the non-operating assets from the operating assets of Ford Storage, a blended company; (3) failure to explain his reasoning behind his weighted average valuation formula; (4) failure to explain his choice of multiples applied in his earnings approach; (5) failure to explain why the book value of the assets was appropriate when appraisals of the properties were available. The Tax Court noted, "We conclude that the fair market value of the assets, rather than unadjusted book values, would have been considered more important by a hypothetical willing buyer and willing seller in arriving at the fair market value of the stock at issue on the valuation date." The Tax Court also rejected the expert's use of discounts because he did not explain how he arrived at his conclusions. It stated, "[the expert] affords us no grounds upon which to decide whether a hypothetical willing buyer and willing seller would have applied discounts of the magnitude he employed..."

The IRS's expert also found that Ford Storage was the operating company, and the other four businesses acted as holding companies. She valued them separately, first examining the holding companies. She determined the fair market value of the companies was the fair market value of their assets. She did not apply discounts to the companies controlled outright or whose aggregated stockholdings represented control of the company (block sale assumption). To the other companies, she applied a 20% minority interest discount and a 10% lack of marketability discount. The court rejected the position that a lack of marketability discount was inappropriate to a controlling interest and applied a 10% discount to all the companies. It next considered whether stockholdings of the controlled companies should be aggregated with stock in the same corporation owned outright by the decedent. The IRS's expert asserted, "stock in each of the Ford companies would be sold as a block so as to maximize the value of that stock (block sale assumption)." While the Tax Court accepted the IRS's asset based valuation, it rejected the block sale assumption. The assumption did not consider the willing buyer because the block sale assumption would allow the willing seller to maximize the combined value of decedent's stockholdings. The IRS alternatively argued that if discounts were necessary, a 20% minority interest discount and a 10% lack of marketability discount would be appropriate.

Finally the IRS's expert valued Ford Storage. She concluded that Ford Storage actually was a blended operating/holding company. The expert accordingly divided its valuation to reflect the fair market value of the operating assets and non-operating assets. The non-operating assets were valued at their net asset value. The operating assets were valued by using "the asset value method [including goodwill calculated using the excess earnings approach], the discounted cash flow method, and the market comparable method [including a 35% control premium]." The effects of lack of marketability were considered in the valuation of the operation assets. The expert then added the value of the non-operating assets to the value of the operating assets determined under each method. She determined that the market comparable method was the least persuasive because there were few companies sufficiently comparable to Ford Storage. After considering the results determined using the net asset value and discounted cash flow methods, she valued the decedent's interest at $894,720. The expert concluded there was no need for a minority interest discount, because the decedent held a majority of the stock in Ford Storage and that no further lack of marketability discount was applicable since it had been considered in the valuation of the operating assets. The court agreed with regard to the minority discount, but applied a 10% discount for lack of marketability to the valuation of the no operating assets. The Tax Court accepted the IRS's valuation with adjustments.

This abstract originally appeared in *Valuation Case Digest*, authored by John J. Stockdale, Jr.

Estate of Trenchard v. Commissioner

Citation: T.C. Memo. 1995-121
Court: United States Tax Court
State/Jurisdiction: Specialty Federal
Date of Decision: May 30, 1995
Judge: Laro

In *Estate of Helen* M *Trenchard v. CIR,* T.C. Memo 1995-121, the Tax Court considered a situation in which an older married couple formed a corporation with their child and grandchildren. The question was whether a gift had been made to the child and grandchildren upon the formation. The couple contributed most of the farm property and received preferred stock and debentures in return. The other stockholders contributed a lesser amount of assets, most of which they had received through gifts from the older generation. In return, they received all of the common stock of the corporation and certain other securities

The court concluded that gifts had been made, determined the amount of the gifts through appraisal, and upheld penalties for failure to file timely returns. The Court first concluded that gifts had been made. It's analysis was based on a consideration of the nature of the farm property donated compared to the relatively poor investment characteristics of the securities received by the older couple. It also considered the historical pattern of gifts made to the younger generation and the fact that the family patriarch was almost solely responsible for all phases of the operation.

After determining that gifts had been made, the court determined the amount of the gifts by determining the difference in value of the property contributed to the corporation less the value of the securities received. The valuation of the farm property was based almost entirely on the taxpayer's expert witness. The court determined the value of the securities received after considering elements of expert appraisal presented by both sides.

This abstract originally appeared in *Valuation Case Digest*, authored by John J. Stockdale, Jr.

Mandelbaum v. Commissioner

Citation: T.C. Memo 1995-255, 1995 Tax Ct. Memo LEXIS 256
Court: United States Tax Court
State/Jurisdiction: Specialty Federal
Date of Decision: June 12, 1995
Judge: Laro

The parties stipulated to freely-traded minority interest values, so the only issue was the discount for lack of marketability. Paul Mallarkey (BDO Seidman) testified for the IRS. He cited three restricted stock studies, and concluded a 30% discount for lack of marketability.

Roger Grabowski (Price Waterhouse) cited seven restricted stock studies and three of the private transaction prior to IPO studies by Baird & Co. and Willamette Management Associates, as well as a number of specific company factors (e.g., restrictions on sale), and concluded a 70% discount for lack of marketability on some valuation dates and 75% on others. The opinion does not indicate that either expert cited empirical evidence about factors associated with individual discounts being higher or lower than the studies' averages.

Judge Laro used the studies cited by Grabowski as a starting point (35% average discount for restricted stock studies and 45% average discount for private transactions prior to IPO's). He listed 9 factors that might cause the marketability discount for a given instance to be higher or lower than the benchmark averages, concluding that, on balance, the facts and circumstances in the particular case led to a lower discount for lack of marketability than the benchmark averages. The factors cited were:

- Financial statement analysis
- Dividend policy
- Nature of the company, its history, its position in the industry, and its economic outlook
- Management
- Amount of control in the transferred shares
- Restrictions on transferability
- Holding period for the stock
- Company's redemption policy
- Costs associated with public offering

Estate of McCormick v. Commissioner

Citation: T.C. Memo. 1995-371
Court: United States Tax Court
State/Jurisdiction: Specialty Federal
Date of Decision: August 7, 1995
Judge: Gerber

In the *Estate of Lucile Marie McCormick v. CIR,* T.C. Memo 1995-371, the Tax Court predetermined the value of interests in two general partnerships that were holding real estate. In reaching it's decision, the Court reemphasized its position on certain factors it considered important in the case.

The purpose of the partnerships was to hold real estate related investments. All parties involved valued these partnerships by using an asset-based approach. That is, the value of assets less liabilities less discounts for minority and marketability. An income approach was not used by either party nor considered by the Court. A market approach was also not used directly. However, market data was given extensive consideration in the determination of minority and marketability discounts. In this case, experts for both parties emphasized the asset-based approach and the Court based its decision on this approach. This approach is also presented as the primary approach in Rev. Rul 59-60. It is interesting to note, however, that some evidence from the real world seems to indicate that investors put at least as much emphasis on income return as asset value in asset holding companies. A way to bridge the gap between these two approaches is consider the income return as one factor in the amount of discount to be applied. The income return factor is also important for operating companies and should be added to the list of factors in the *Mandelbaum* case.

The taxpayer's expert was the son of the taxpayer and was a real estate broker but not a qualified appraiser. He was not approved as an expert by the Court. On the other hand, the IRS expert was a qualified appraiser and the Court embraced virtually all of his opinions as to asset values. The taxpayer also put forward a CPA as an expert with regard to property under development. The CPA valued this property using a discounted cash flow method in which virtually all of the assumptions were made by the taxpayer. The Court gave this work no credence. On the other hand, the IRS expert seemed to support all of his work in detail and the Court accepted virtually all of his work.

The Court's opinion in this matter makes it clear that an expert should be: 1) unrelated and independent of the taxpayer (2) specifically qualified and certified to value the type of property under consideration (3) able to support conclusions independently from the sole opinions of the taxpayer (4) able to provide detailed support for opinions. The Court rejected a 10% reduction for selling expenses from the selling price based on comparables because the value was based on comparable sales and buyers would consider such costs in their purchase decisions.

The Court conceded that buyers considered the impact of taxes in their purchase decisions but refused to allow a separate additional deduction for certain built-in taxes because the taxpayer had not shown that these tax consequences were less favorable for the subjects than for comparables. The Court agreed that provisions of applicable state law which favored minority interests in partnerships in relation to such interests in corporations were factors to be considered in determining the amount of minority discounts. The court refused to aggregate the various interests that had been gifted to different parties and at different times for the purpose of determining the value. In the case of the minority interest discount, both experts presented evidence concerning the price of publicly-held companies holding real estate compared to the value of the real estate held and presented analyses to support their positions. In the case of the marketability discount, both experts presented information concerning the selling price of public stock in comparison to private transactions and with a varying degree of analyses to support their particular positions. After considering all factors, the Court allowed discounts for minority interest of 18% to 32% for the various interests at different valuation dates. In addition, it allowed an additional marketability discount for each entity that varied from 20% to 22%. The amount of the discounts allowed by the Court was between the amounts testified to by the experts. The amount of detail and support provided by the experts in this case seemed to be of equal value in the Court's mind.

This abstract originally appeared in *Valuation Case Digest*, authored by John J. Stockdale, Jr.

Schusterman v. United States

Citation: 63 F.3d 986, 1995 U.S. App. LEXIS 23926
Court: United States Court of Appeals
State/Jurisdiction: 10th Circuit Federal
Date of Decision: August 22, 1995
Judge: Baldock

Taxpayer transferred assets in return for a promissory note bearing interest at the then current "safe harbor" interest rate, which was below the prevailing market rate. The issue is whether or not the difference between the value of the note discounted at the prevailing market rate and the value of the assets transferred constituted a gift, or whether the taxpayer was entitled to rely on the safe harbor rate as a discount rate to determine whether a taxable gift was made.

Two prior cases in other circuits had reached opposite conclusions on the same issue. The Tenth Circuit ruled in favor of the IRS. The Court concluded "Taxpayers made a gift to the trusts consisting of the difference between the value of the stock and the present discounted value of the promissory notes. The IRS was entitled to tax this amount as a gift under 2501(a)(1)."

> In sum, we hold that although the promissory notes bore interest at the 483 safe harbor rate, the IRS was entitled under 2512 to determine the discounted present value of the notes using the prevailing market interest rate.

Estate of Hoover v. Commissioner

Citation: 76 AFTR2d Par. 95-5602
Court: United States Court of Appeals
State/Jurisdiction: 10th Circuit Federal
Date of Decision: November 1, 1995

In the *Estate of Hoover v. CIR*, 76 AFTR2d Par. 95-5602 (10th Cir. 1995), the U.S. Tenth Circuit Court of Appeals considered the value of a family limited partnership holding a cattle ranch. It confirmed that the concept of fair market value includes a discount for lack of marketability and control for purposes of Section 2032A. The Tenth Circuit Court rejected the Tax Court's reasoning that fair market value assumes an alternative definition under Sec. 2032A due to the ruling in the *Maddox* case, 93 T.C. 288; the appellate court stated that "the concept of fair market value is not in itself altered by [Section 2032A]."

The appellate court found that fair market value involves a determination of all the relevant factors, including a minority discount. Moreover, the court found that without such adjustments, the fair market value could not be established. It clarified that the sec. 2032A maximum $750,000 special use reduction is to be applied only after determining the fair market value. The IRS issued Action on Decision, CC-1998-006, in which it acquiesced to the Tenth Circuit's decision in this case.

This abstract originally appeared in *Valuation Case Digest*, authored by John J. Stockdale, Jr.

Estate of Melton v. United States

Citation: 77 AFTR2d Par. 96-612 (WD TX 1995)
Court: United States District Court
State/Jurisdiction: Western District of Texas
Date of Decision: December 4, 1995
Judge: Primomo

In the *Estate of Melton* (77 AFTR2d Par. 96-612), a U.S. magistrate recommended to the U.S. District Court the inclusion of a 10% minority discount in addition to a 25% marketability discount on a 50% interest in a closely-held company for estate tax purposes. The IRS contested the application of the minority discount because a marketability discount had been allowed. The magistrate noted that a minority discount is conceptually different from a marketability discount and that the application of a marketability discount does not preclude the application of a minority discount. The magistrate stated "the minority discount for tax purposes is given based on lack of control. A shareholder with 50% of the stock can block action by other shareholders but does not have sufficient interest to control corporate affairs."

This abstract originally appeared in *Valuation Case Digest*, authored by John J. Stockdale, Jr.

Estate of McLendon v. Commissioner (I)

Citation: 77 AFTR2d Par. 96-398
Court: United States Court of Appeals
State/Jurisdiction: 5th Circuit Federal
Date of Decision: December 28, 1995
Judge: Jones

The U. S. Court of Appeals for the Fifth Circuit reversed and remanded the Tax Court's decision in the *Estate of McLendon*, 77 AFTR2d Par. 96-398 (5th Cir. December 28, 1995). The appellate court found that partnership interests had been valued, but that "assignee interests in partnership interests" should have been valued.

An agreement, signed by related parties five months prior to the decedent's death, provided for the transfer of assignee interests in family owned partnerships in exchange for a retained life interest in the partnerships. These retained life interests would be valued as annuities using the actuarial tables of Reg. Section 25.2512-5(t) and not as partnership interests. Under the facts of the case, Mr. McLendon's death was ruled not imminent at the date of the transaction.

It was further ruled that "... the character of a transfer will not be interpreted specially for estate tax purposes because of its interfamily nature...The principle of treating ownership interests in closely held companies according to objective criteria is generally relevant. The objective criteria here are specified by Texas law governing transfers of partnership interests." The appellate court remanded the case to the Tax Court for a re-evaluation of the property according to the correct application of actuarial tables.

This abstract originally appeared in *Valuation Case Digest*, authored by John J. Stockdale, Jr.

Estate of Magnin v. Commissioner (I)

Citation: T.C. Memo. 1996-25
Court: United States Tax Court
State/Jurisdiction: Specialty Federal
Date of Decision: January 24, 1996
Judge: Ruwe

In the *Estate of Cyril I. Magnin v. CIR*, T.C. Memo. 1996-25, the Tax Court clarified how fair market value is to be applied as a standard. The Estate Tax Regulations, Section 20.2031-1(b) define fair market value as "the price at which the property would change hands between a willing buyer and a willing seller, neither being under the compulsion to buy or to sell and both having reasonable knowledge of relevant facts." The court further stated that the standard of value is objective, noting the use of a "purely hypothetical willing buyer and seller" and citing the *Propstra,*

680 F.2d 1248,1251-1252; *Estate of Newhouse,* 94 T.C. 193, 218; and the *Estate of Mueller,* T.C. Memo. 1992-218, cases. However, the court warned that this hypothetical sale should not be separated from the actual facts that would affect the value of the stock of the subject company.

This abstract originally appeared in *Valuation Case Digest*, authored by John J. Stockdale, Jr.

Estate of Cloutier v. Commissioner

Citation: T.C. Memo. 1996-49, 1996 Tax Ct. Memo LEXIS 58
Court: United States Tax Court
State/Jurisdiction: Specialty Federal
Date of Decision: February 13, 1996
Judge: Laro

The *Estate of Joseph Cloutier* held 100% of the stock of Corporation for General Trade (CGT) at the time of Mr. Cloutier's death. CGT's primary asset was a television station. Other assets included rental real estate. The parties stipulated to the value of 100% of CGT's stock "without regard to any marketability discount or control premium that might otherwise apply." The only issue in this case was whether a discount for lack of marketability applies to the stipulated value and, if so, the amount of the discount.

In making the appraisals that led to the stipulated value, "all of the appraisers relied primarily upon transactional and financial data compiled by Paul Kagan Associates, Inc., and none of the appraisers determined CGT's value by reference to the price of stock that was listed on a public exchange."

Jim Alerding testified for the estate that a 25% discount should be applied. He reached his conclusion, mainly by attempting to apply the factors recently set forth in the *Mandelbaum* case.

Judge Laro noted that Mr. Alerding "relied on studies of property that were not comparable to the subject property in order to form a 'benchmark' on which to base his conclusion concerning the amount of a marketability discount."

Judge Laro stated, "Although a marketability discount may apply in some cases where 100% of the stock of an unlisted corporation is held by one shareholder, a discount for lack of marketability is inapplicable when the value of the unlisted stock is not determined by reference to the price of listed stock...." He concluded, "Because the stipulated value has not been shown to be representative of CGT's 'freely traded value,' no discount for marketability is allowable."

Smith (Estate of Crosby) v. United States

Citation: 923 F. Supp. 896
Court: United States District Court
State/Jurisdiction: Mississippi
Date of Decision: February 14, 1996
Judge: Russell

The issue was the value of a note in the estate as of April 28, 1988. The estate tax return showed a value of $3,348,500 for the decedent's undivided two-thirds interest in the note, based on a valuation report by Chris Mercer of Mercer Capital Management, Inc.

Taxpayer pays and files claim

The IRS mailed notice of deficiency in January 1992, valuing the interest at $4,400,000. The estate paid $410,838 tax on the deficiency, plus interest, for a total payment of $714,195.70, and contemporaneously filed a Claim for Refund.

The IRS retained Scott Hakala of Business Valuation Services, who issued a report dated June 20, 1995, valuing the undivided two-thirds interest in the note at $4,300,000.

Does undivided interest impact value?

Prior to trial, it was discovered that the original note had been reissued as two exchange notes in 1981, so the estate actually held 100% of a note in the amount of two-thirds of the original note. Mercer issued an addendum to his report dated July 27, 1995, revaluing the interest upward to $3,553,222 (reducing the negative impact of lack of marketability since it was not an undivided interest). Hakala testified that the discovery of the exchange promissory note had no impact on his valuation.

The note was originally issued by St. Regis Paper Co. in 1977, payable over a period of 20 years in equal annual principal payments of $515,600. Each principal payment received a payment of 6% simple interest from the inception of the note to the date of payment, resulting in each payment becoming progressively larger due to the increasing amount of interest. Both the original and replacement notes were unsecured, consisting of a single page, lacking any indenture or protective covenants that would be required by the public market or an institutional financing source.

St. Regis was merged into Champion International Corporation, a Fortune 500 company, who assumed responsibility for the note in 1985. Payments were made timely by St. Regis and subsequently by Champion.

Both appraisers discount cash flows

Both Mercer and Hakala used the approach of discounting the note's cash flows to a present value. They both used yields on publicly traded debt of Champion as a starting point in developing their discount rates.

They were in substantial disagreement as to how much adjustment was necessary to compensate for the differences between the estate's promissory note and Champion's publicly traded debt. Mercer added 5.5% to Champion's public debt yield, justified as follows:

Marketability	0.5%
Lack of Indenture/Covenants	1.0%
Lack of formal acknowledgment by Champion	1.0%
Subordination to all better documented debt of Champion	1.0%
Uncertainty regarding the legal entity bearing liability	1.0%
Unusual payment schedule	0.5%
Lack of divisibility	0.5%
Total adjustments	5.5%

Mercer had difficulty getting a response from Champion as to the status of the note at the time of his original valuation. He finally got a one-page letter acknowledging the note, but with few details. Hakala made no independent effort to contact Champion, but obtained information through a deposition of Gerald Hoot, a Champion representative, three months after filing his report. It was only through this deposition that it was learned that replacement notes had been issued for the undivided interest.

Lack of information a problem

Mercer testified that the difficulty in obtaining information and the various deficiencies in the note precluded most of the normal buyers from the market for it, including financial institutions, mutual funds, insurance companies, pension funds, and all but the largest individual investors. The court notes that "Hakala, while acknowledging the numerous deficiencies in the estate's promissory note, refused to allow any more than a 0.5% addition to his interest rate."

The court reviewed and acknowledged the validity of the factors cited by Mercer and concluded, "The evaluation of Hakala is not consistent with the facts of this case and did not take such factors into account. The Court therefore adopts the opinion of Mercer and places a value on the estates promissory note at $3,553,222.00."

Rabenhorst v. Commissioner

Citation: T.C. Memo 1996-92, 1996 Tax Ct. Memo LEXIS 91
Court: United States Tax Court
State/Jurisdiction: Specialty Federal
Date of Decision: February 29, 1996
Judge: Wright

The issue is the fair market value of minority shares of a privately held life insurance company.

Taxpayer made gifts of stock in December 1988 based on an appraisal at $385 per share as of June 10, 1988, by Jerry Willis, a former insurance examiner and industry consultant.

Second appraisal 5% lower

In response to IRS initiation of an examination of the gift tax return, taxpayer hired David Chaffe to conduct a second appraisal. Chaffe appraised the stock at $176.13 per share, and the IRS determined the value at $445 per share.

The court stated: "Neither side has convinced us that its computation of the per-share stock price accurately reflects the true value, but petitioners (taxpayer) have advanced the more convincing argument." This despite the Court's following criticisms:

> Troubled by the brevity of Chaffe's report.
>
> Does not provide a discussion of the computation or model used.
>
> He considered a variety of factors, but he does not elaborate to any significant degree as to what effect such consideration had on any particular variable involved in his computations.
>
> Considered the stock value of several publicly traded insurance corporations, but he failed to provide any explanation of how such share values influenced his calculations.

Court questions expert's appraisal skills

The IRS used the Willis methodology, but updated it to year-end 1988 figures. The Court stated, "Although we agree with the respondent that it makes more sense to value a gift of stock made in December 1988 using financial data as of December 31, 1988, rather than December 31, 1987, we question whether the computation respondent used ... was appropriate."

> Willis testified that he was unfamiliar with the use of minority discount factors ... and had never before valued a minority block of shares ... coupled and viewed in conjunction with his unfamiliarity with relevant revenue rulings and Treasury regulations, we are inclined to question his appraisal skills.

Court considers 5-year old redemptions

In reaching its conclusion of value, the Court also gave some weight to stock redemptions, even though they were five years earlier and involved family members.

The Court concluded that the value of the stock was $296 per share, with no details as to how it arrive at that figure.

Kosman v. Commissioner

Citation: T.C. Memo 1996-112, 1996 Tax Ct. Memo LEXIS 107
Court: United States Tax Court
State/Jurisdiction: Specialty Federal
Date of Decision: March 11, 1996
Judge: Colvin

The issue in this case is the value of minority shares of Kosman, Inc., a family holding company owning shares of stock of small banks. Other owners of the bank stocks are a variety of family members (beyond just those in the subject holding company) and bank employees.

The court pointed out that "Petitioner (taxpayer) has the burden of proving that respondent's (IRS) determinations in the notice of deficiency are erroneous ... Respondent has the burden of proving the increased deficiency asserted in the amended answer."

The gift tax return was based on an appraisal by Grant Thornton, an accounting firm. The experts at trial, not named in the opinion, were Gary Wahlgren of Wahlgren & Mace, Inc. for the taxpayer, and Robert J. Strachota and William Herber of the Shenehon Company for the IRS.

Experts' valuations of underlying holdings

In order to deal with the holding company stock valuation, the court first dealt with the issue of the values of the bank stocks.

The respective experts' opinions and the court holding on the value of the shares of Kosman's largest bank stock holding was as follows (000 omitted):

Date	Taxpayer's Expert	IRS's Expert	Court Holding
September 30, 1986	$2,810	$4,644	$3,278
March 31, 1987	$2,991	$4,644	$3,530

Both experts used a guideline company market method, and the IRS expert also used a discounted income method, with a discount rate of 14%, "because that rate is used to value a Standard & Poor's small capitalized company."

The taxpayer's expert used 60% of book value because the bank was slightly stronger financially than the best comparable, which sold at 57% of book value. (All of the taxpayer's experts comparable banks were in the same state.)

IRS evidence doesn't support conclusion

The IRS expert used all out-of-state bank comparables. The court stated, "Respondent's experts did not adequately address whether economic conditions in those bank markets and in northwestern Nebraska were similar." They said that the subject bank was worth less than the 86% of book value at which one of the comparables traded, yet valued it at 125% book value.

The court concluded that the subject should be at 70% of book value, in spite of past transactions at 90% to 115% of book value. The court said, "The shareholders received higher prices for their shares because of their association with the corporation." With respect to the income approach, the court said, "We do not believe that a 14% discount rate recognizes the economic outlook for Scottsbluff National Bank."

Discounts at holding company level

Since both parties experts used a 10% minority interest discount, the court accepted that figure. To support the 25% discount for lack of marketability for the holding company stock, taxpayers expert cited the 1971 S.E.C. restricted stock study and a 1994 *Wall Street Journal* article about discounts on stock sold to foreign investors under regulation S.

The IRS expert cited the FMV Opinions study, which they alleged showed discounts of 10% to 20% for stocks of banks such as those in the holding company. They believed an additional 10% at the holding company level was sufficient in addition to the 9% DLOM already applied to the bank stock at the underlying asset level.

Taxpayers expert "did not ... explain why he chose a 10% discount for nonvoting shares. The IRS expert based is 4% nonvoting discount on the Lease, McConnel and Mikkleson study published in the *Journal of Financial Economics* in April 1983.

Normally, the above series of discounts is taken sequentially (multiplicatively), that is, with each discount applied to the value resulting after the previous discount. Readers who examine the numbers will see that, in this case, the court, without explanation, applied the discounts at the holding company level additively. The final values for the voting shares are exactly 25% less than the pre-discount values, and the final values for the nonvoting shares are exactly 29% less than the pre-discount values.

Krapf v. United States

Citation: 77 AFTR2d Par. 96-643
Court: United States Court of Federal Claims
State/Jurisdiction: Federal Claims
Date of Decision: March 19, 1996
Judge: Smith

The *Krapf* case (77 AFTR2d Par. 96-643) was remanded back to the Federal Claims Court for a valuation of a 1976 charitable contribution of a minority interest in a closely-held company. There were a number of pre- and post-gift transactions. The court was directed to determine the probative value of these transactions using only standard tests of relevancy.

The court originally considered the relevancy of these transactions using a more restrictive test. That is, the transactions would only be relevant if (1) there was no material change in the conditions of the company since the valuation date, or (2) the subsequent information could have been foreseen at the valuation date.

Pre-gift transactions were considered to be irrelevant to the value because they were between interested parties. However, these transactions were considered by the court to be indicative of the fact that the company was a going concern. Post-gift transactions were not considered to be reliable because the company's condition was fluctuating after the valuation date.

The court used a net asset value method, going concern basis but without intangibles to value the company and applied a 33% minority discount to arrive at the per share value.

This abstract originally appeared in *Valuation Case Digest*, authored by John J. Stockdale, Jr.

Estate of Cidulka v. Commissioner

Citation: T. C. Memo 1996-149, 1996 Tax Ct. Memo LEXIS 157
Court: United States Tax Court
State/Jurisdiction: Specialty Federal
Date of Decision: March 25, 1996
Judge: Scott

The major issue was the value of stock in an outdoor advertising sign company (SOAI) that was redeemed by the company on January 25, 1982. The IRS contends the redemption price undervalued the stock, resulting in a gift to the remaining stockholders.

The first issue was whether the stock redeemed should be valued on a minority or a control basis. The amount of stock actually redeemed was 49% of the outstanding stock, after gifts of 3% of the stock on the same day as the redemption.

The Court ruled, "We conclude from the facts in this case that the 40 shares given...to his son and his son's family on January 25, 1982, and the redemption of the remaining shares...was one transaction. It was planned as one transaction...both occurred on the same day...the only reason that it was done as two, separate transactions was to avoid gift taxes...we considered a majority interest in the stock of SOAI to be the interest to be valued."

The income capitalization method, utilizing operating income, was recognized by both taxpayer's and IRS experts, but there was a major difference in the proper amount of income to be capitalized. The main adjustment by taxpayer's expert was for excess salaries.

One of the IRS experts did no actual analysis of the subject company expense structure, but concluded that operating income should be 34% of revenues "*based on a study of other companies*" (emphasis supplied). The IRS expert "stated that depreciation should not properly be considered as an operating expense, and that the rent paid by SOAI was paid to members of the Cidulka family and, therefore, was suspect." He also concluded that "there were other questionable items."

The Court concluded: "It is clear that petitioner's expert and respondent's expert each in effect made a judgment determination as to the operating income of SOAI. We conclude that from that this record an accurate operating income for 1981 cannot be determined."

Ruppert, an MAI, testified for the IRS that outdoor sign companies sold on a multiple of gross revenue basis, and produced a table of gross multipliers in sales he knew of. All were asset sales.

In January 1986 (four years later), SOAI sold its assets to its major competitor for what amounted to 2.89 times gross revenues.

The Court stated, "In our view, the sale by SOAI in January 1986 of all its assets has relevance in determining an appropriate multiplier to determine the fair market value of SOAI's assets on January 25, 1982."

"Based on this record, we conclude that the best valuation we are able to make of the stock of SOAI at January 25, 1982, is on the basis of the 1981 net sales multiplied by a proper multiplier and adjusted to the value of the stock by reducing this amount for liabilities and other necessary items. We, therefore hold that an asset sale of SOAI on January 25, 1982, should be at a multiplier of 2.5 applied to SOAI's net sales for the year 1981. The fair market value of the SOAI stock can be ascertained from this figure by making the adjustments made by respondents witness, Mr. Loe."

Estate of Gloeckner v. Commissioner (I)

Citation: T.C. Memo 1996-148, 1996 Tax Ct. Memo LEXIS 158
Court: United States Tax Court
State/Jurisdiction: Specialty Federal
Date of Decision: March 25, 1996
Judge: Halpern

The issue is the value of a controlling interest in the stock of a wholesale horticultural company as of the decedent's estate's alternate valuation date, January 21, 1991.

The executors timely filed Form 706, valuing the shares at $2,298,161.25, the amount paid for the shares under a redemption agreement entered into in 1987, based on an appraisal by KPMG Peat Marwick. The IRS notice of deficiency valued the shares at $6,000,000. At trial the IRS conceded that the value was, at most, $4,580,000.

The Court quoted criteria established in prior cases as to whether a redemption agreement can fix the value of stock for Federal estate tax purposes:

- Price must be fixed and determinable under the agreement
- Agreement must be binding on the parties both during life and after death
- Agreement must have been entered into for a bona fide business reason and must not be a substitute for a testamentary disposition (not a device to pass the decedent's shares to the natural objects of his bounty for less than full and adequate consideration)

The Court also noted, "In *Estate of Lauder*..., we looked to whether the price to be paid for the decedent's stock under the agreement reflected adequate and full consideration in money or money's worth as of the date the agreement was executed."

The Court stated further, "The burden is on the executors to prove that the price to be paid for the decedent's shares under the 1987 redemption agreement reflected adequate and full consideration in money and moneys worth when the agreement was executed. Rule 142 (a). The executors have failed to carry that burden. The price terms in the 1987 redemption agreement were determined pursuant to the 1987 appraisal. The 1987 appraisal was the subject of a motion in limine by respondent to exclude that document from evidence because of the executors failure to comply with Rule 143 (f), which concerns itself with expert witness reports. Respondents motion was granted, and the 1987 appraisal was not received in evidence as an expert witness report."

The Court agreed that the agreement was binding, that the price was fixed and that the agreement served a bona fide business purpose. But *there was no evidence in the record to show that the price at the time of the agreement represented full and adequate consideration.*

This left the Court with little to rely on other than the testimony of the IRS expert, Henry Sherman. The Court said, "We...find Shermans opinion to be helpful.... We do not, however, completely agree with Sherman because we find some weaknesses in his analysis...

- did not make an on-site inspection...
- did not interview the company's management...
- could find no comparable companies
- did not adequately consider the effect of competition...
- did not take into consideration the 1988 sale...we do not believe that the 1988 sale should have been disregarded."

With no further explanation the Court concluded a value of $4,000,000.

Estate of Casey v. Commissioner

Citation: T.C. Memo 1996-156, 1996 Tax Ct. Memo LEXIS 166
Court: United States Tax Court
State/Jurisdiction: Specialty Federal
Date of Decision: March 27, 1996
Judge: Gerber

The issue is the value of a 5% interest in a liquidating trust. The only dispute is the appropriate discount from NAV.

Taxpayer discounted 30% for minority and 30% for marketability, which, when applied sequentially, aggregated 51%, which taxpayer rounded to 50%. IRS discounted 9.2%, reflecting the time value of money until the estimated date of receiving proceeds.

The Court ruled against any minority discount, on the basis that all participants willingly turned over control to a trustee to facilitate liquidation, so control should not be an issue. Regarding marketability, the Court reasoned that the trust was not a "going concern," that liquidation proceeds were foreseeable, although with some uncertainties, and concluded a 15% discount for lack of marketability.

Estate of McClatchy v. Commissioner (I)

Citation: 106 T.C. 206, 106 T.C. No. 9, 1996 U.S. Tax Ct. LEXIS 9
Court: United States Tax Court
State/Jurisdiction: Specialty Federal
Date of Decision: April 3, 1996
Judge: Nims

The sole issue in this case was whether a discount for restricted stock was appropriate when the restrictions that applied to the public stock during the decedent's lifetime became inapplicable by reason of the decedent's death.

The Court noted, "The Federal securities law restrictions ... were not self-imposed or voluntarily made, and did not result from an agreement or arrangement by decedent."

Citing *Ahmanson*, (674 F. 2d 761, 9th Cir. 1981) the Court concluded "it is undisputed that value is to be determined at the moment of death ... We think 'the interest that passes' in the case before us is the value of the shares unencumbered by securities act restrictions."

Estate of Bonner v. United States

Citation: 77 AFTR2d Par. 96-868
Court: United States Court of Appeals
State/Jurisdiction: 5th Circuit Federal
Date of Decision: June 4, 1996
Judge: Per Curiam

In the *Estate of Louis F. Bonner, Sr.* (77 AFTR2d Par. 96-868), the Fifth Circuit Court of Appeals reversed a District Court's summary judgment and valuation of undivided fractional interests in two real properties and a boat. At the time of his death, Mr. Bonner held directly fractional interests in the properties and the boat. He was also the beneficiary of a QTIP trust established by his wife's will. This trust held the remaining fractional interests in the subject properties, which were taxable to Mr. Bonner's estate.

The court rejected the argument that the fractional interests held directly merged with those held by the trust. It emphasized that the estate tax is assessed on the interest that passes and not on the interest held by the decedent or by the legatee after death. It also stated that the estate should be required to pay taxes only on those assets the decedent directs and controls. In this case Mr. Bonner's "... estate did not have control over the trust assets such that it could act as a hypothetical seller negotiating with willing buyers free of the handicaps associated with fractional undivided interests. The valuation of the assets should reflect the reality."

The Appellate Court determined that two fractional interests who aggregated 100% were not merged and it reversed the district court and remanded the case back for a proper valuation of the estate's interests in the properties, including a fractional interest discount.

This abstract originally appeared in *Valuation Case Digest*, authored by John J. Stockdale, Jr.

Estate of Cartwright v. Commissioner (I)

Citation: T.C. Memo 1996-286, 1996 Tax Ct. Memo LEXIS 299
Court: United States Tax Court
State/Jurisdiction: Specialty Federal
Date of Decision: June 20, 1996
Judge: Colvin

Decedent owned 71.43% of the stock of a law firm (CSB) which specialized in personal injury law, with earnings based on contingent fees. At decedent's death, the firm paid the estate $5,062,029, which was the entire amount of the proceeds of a life insurance policy taken out by the law firm. The issue in the case is how much of that amount was payment for decedent's stock in the firm, and how much was payment for services rendered by decedent prior to his death, and thus subject to income tax.

Taxpayer's expert, Alan W. Johnson estimated that all of the company's stock was worth $5,200,000 and that decedent's 71.43% was worth $3,714,000. IRS' expert, Herbert T. Spiro, estimated the decedent's 71.43% interest was worth $907,594. Ultimately, however, the decision in the case turned not particularly on the classic battle of experts but rather on the Court's interpretation of the shareholder agreement and past transactions with withdrawing members of the firm.

The Court said it did not think a hypothetical willing buyer would pay anything close to Johnson's value for the stock, citing several reasons:

- CSB did not pay dividends
- Decedent could not sell his stock without the other shareholders' consent

- Ownership of the stock did not entitle the holder to any CSB earnings
- There was no relationship between stock ownership in CSB and compensation
- The nature of CSB's personal injury practice was uncertain

The record does not support a finding that the stock was worth 10 times as much as was paid for another shareholder's stock a year earlier, or 20 times an amount paid to another shareholder prior to that.

The Court concluded that the value of the stock was $1,105,762, based on its interpretation of the shareholder agreement, plus a 15% control premium testified to by Mr. Spiro, plus a $62,029 "concession" granted by the IRS for "premium adjustments and interest."

The court ruled that the balance of the payment to the estate was made because decedent performed services for CSB, such as bringing cases to CSB.

An interesting note was the court's reaction to taxpayer's argument that Spiro's report was inadmissible because it included his legal opinion about the meaning of the shareholder agreement. The Court stated, "Petitioner is sounding a false alarm. We do not consider Spiro's legal opinions in deciding this case... However, it is appropriate that Spiro disclose the assumptions he made about the rights of CSB and decedent under the 1973 agreement and the 1988 amendment. Knowing his assumptions helps us to evaluate his conclusions. We agree with his assumptions and believe he used the proper analysis to value CSB stock.

Speer v. Commissioner

Citation: T.C.Memo 1996-323, 1996 Tax Ct. Memo LEXIS 339
Court: United States Tax Court
State/Jurisdiction: Specialty Federal
Date of Decision: July 16, 1996
Judge: Ruwe

The ultimate issue in this case is whether taxable gifts or constructive dividend income were received by the son of the controlling shareholder of Home Shopping Network (HSN), through Pioneer Data Processing (Pioneer), of which the son was (or is) sole owner.

Starting in 1981, a company called Home Shopping Channels, Inc. (HSC), started selling merchandise through televised programs in the Tampa Bay area. HSC contracted with Pioneer to develop customized software (referred to in the case as "Local Software") for customer maintenance, order taking and inventory control.

In 1985, HSC turned down a proposal to go national, but entered into a License Agreement among HSC, HSN and Pioneer (which owned the "Local Software") wherein HSN would pay HSC 2% of its gross profits, of which 1% would be remitted to Pioneer for its computer programs, licenses and tapes. HSC would continue its activity in Tampa, and HSN would expand to the rest of the nation.

Pioneer then worked with Burroughs to develop "National Software," based on the original "Local Software," expanded to meet HSN's greater needs.

HSN pays Pioneer directly

In 1986, HSC merged into HSN, and HSN subsequently paid the 1% payment under the License Agreement directly to Pioneer. Payments to Pioneer were:

Calendar Year	Amount
1985	$56,011.30
1986	$700,645.57
1987	$2,434,457.52
1988	$2,453,928.21
1989	$2,637,191.00
1990	$3,136,668.00
1991	$3,639,988.00
1992	$3,441,262.00

In 1993, the father sold his stock in HSN to Liberty Media Corporation. Litigation followed regarding the licensing agreement, and ultimately Pioneer received $4,500,000 to terminate the agreement.

IRS says License Agreement a sham

The IRS argued that the License Agreement was a sham to distribute profits of HSN to the son of HSN's controlling stockholder, and the payments should be taxed as a constructive dividend and as a gift. Petitioners argued that the agreement was arm's length and on fair and reasonable terms.

The Court concluded that the father did not control HSC at the time of the Agreement, and it was entered into on an arm's length basis. The Court stated, "We must assess the reasonableness of the License Agreement at the time it was entered into without benefit of hindsight."

Both parties presented expert testimony as to the value of the Local Software as of the date of the License Agreement. The taxpayer's expert also valued the License Agreement. The Service didn't independently value the Agreement—rather they relied upon the actual license payments as their evidence of value.

IRS at $58,394; taxpayer $2,900,000

Douglas F. Benn and Udo W. Pooch, using a model called VALPRO (developed by Mr. Benn), testified for the IRS that Local Software had a value of $58,394.

Petitioner's expert, Robert F. Reilly of Willamette Management Associates, used several models and reached an overall valuation of Local Software of $2,900,000. He then compared this value to the value of the License Agreement. Using a discounted cash flow model, he concluded that the value of the License Agreement when entered into was $2,600,000.

Is deal reasonable at arm's length?

The Court stated, "We need not determine the precise value of the software. We need only compare the value of Local Software with the reasonably anticipated value of the future license payments in order to determine whether the terms of the agreement are reasonable when judged by the standards of an arm's-length transaction."

The court noted:

> (1) HSN needed a software program;
>
> (2) HSN needed such software quickly;
>
> (3) HSC and Pioneer . . . had a tested, working, and successful program . . .;
>
> (4) Local Software could be used to develop the supplemental National Software; and
>
> (5) the success of HSN's new business endeavor was highly speculative . . .
>
> Under the circumstances, we think that HSN's agreement to pay 1% of its gross income for the software was reasonable. It is immaterial that HSN's success may have gone beyond the parties' wildest expectations . . .
>
> We hold that Mr. Speer did not receive constructive dividend income . . . as a result of payments made by HSN to Pioneer pursuant to the License Agreement. It follows that petitioners did not make gifts . . . in amounts equal to these license payments to their son . . .

Estate of Scanlan v. Commissioner

Citation: T.C. Memo 1996-331, 72 T.C.M. (CCH) 160
Court: United States Tax Court
State/Jurisdiction: Specialty Federal
Date of Decision: July 24, 1996
Judge: Laro

The estate, through expert witness David Chaffe, of Chaffe & Associates, Inc., argued for a combined discount of 35% on a valuation that included comparable company analysis. The issues of interest in this case were the appropriate valuation and discounts to apply to a minority (5.76 percent) position in the voting stock of a closely held telecommunications company.

The IRS valuation was premised on a redemption sale of shares that occurred two years after the decedent's death. The IRS applied a 4% combined discount to reflect "his minority interest in the company, a minor increase in earnings and the deflation of the dollar between the date of his death and the date of the redemption agreement."

The court allowed a 30% combined discount applied to a valuation starting with the redemption price two years after decedent's death. In addition to the minority and marketability discounts, the court adjusted the price "to account for the passage of time, as well as the change in setting." Although it allowed a 30% combined discount, the court indicated, it was "unable to determine the discounts with specificity."

Estate of Freeman v. Commissioner

Citation: T.C.Memo 1996-372, 1996 Tax Ct. Memo LEXIS 391
Court: United States Tax Court
State/Jurisdiction: Specialty Federal
Date of Decision: August 13, 1996
Judge: Halpern

The Tax Court determined the value of unlisted shares and an option in a corporation engaged in the semiconductor industry. Both sides presented expert testimony as to the value of the shares; however, the court found the taxpayer's expert unreliable and accepted the IRS' valuation of the corporation in full.

The court for a number of reasons disregarded the taxpayer's expert's testimony. Foremost among them was his failure to adequately explain his approaches to valuation. He valued the corporation using the capitalization of earnings, capitalization of revenues and return on equity methods. However, in his expert report he failed to supply any comparable company data or to discuss the capitalization rates he used any further than to say they were "appropriate" and link them with

Dow Jones Industrial Averages. In an earlier report, appended to the gift tax return, he did discuss comparable company data, but no explanation is given as to why the data was withheld from his expert report. In contrast the IRS' expert provided detailed information about both his income and market approaches.

The taxpayer's expert was further disregarded because he ignored data discussing any growth the company had in earnings and revenues and its potential for future growth. In contrast, the IRS' expert noted that the corporation's growth was "meteoric." The corporation was expected to exceed 43% growth in sales compared to a 25% industry average. Of the eight companies, the IRS' expert compared to the company, only one exceeded this growth.

The final point on which the court took the taxpayer's expert to task was the amount of discount for minority interests and lack of marketability. The taxpayer's expert applied a 20% discount for minority and 25% for illiquidity. The court dismissed this expert's application of a minority discount because he arrived at market value for a single share of the corporation's stock, and then multiplied that by the number of shares. The court stated, "We assume that in valuing a single share of stock, the market would recognize the minority position of the share, and that no further minority discount would (nor could) be demanded."

The court accepted the IRS' expert's 10% marketability discount because a ready market for the corporation's stock was emerging rapidly at the valuation date. The corporation had discussed initiating an IPO prior to decedent's demise, and in fact, did successfully complete an IPO eight months later. Moreover, venture capital investors had purchased much of the corporation's preferred stock. The court stated, "We assume that venture capital investors invest with the hope, if not the expectation, that a public offering will not be too far off."

This abstract originally appeared in *Valuation Case Digest*, authored by John J. Stockdale, Jr.

Estate of Barudin v. Commissioner

Citation: T.C.Memo 1996-395, 1996 Tax Ct. Memo LEXIS 403
Court: United States Tax Court
State/Jurisdiction: Specialty Federal
Date of Decision: August 26, 1996
Judge: Swift

The issue is the value of one general partnership unit (out of 95) in FC Partners as of decedent's date of death, December 31, 1989. FC Partners' only significant assets were two commercial office buildings in Manhattan.

The partnership units could not be sold or transferred without consent of a majority of the partnership units. One individual owned or controlled a majority of the units.

For recent years preceding the valuation date, the partnership paid cash distributions of $40,000 per partnership unit. There had also been one extra distribution at the time of a refinancing.

Petitioner's Federal estate tax returns included a date of death value of $280,000. The record does not reflect how the value was calculated. On audit, respondent (the IRS) determined a value of $721,960. Prior to trial, petitioner revised the date of death value to $200,000, and respondent asserted a value of $596,000.

In arriving at a combined minority and marketability discount of 67.5%, petitioners expert relied heavily on the price of one prior sale of a fractional interest in a partnership unit relative to the then-current underlying asset value.

Respondent's expert relied on various market studies that indicated a discount of approximately 19% for minority interest. However, he concluded 15% because he thought an owner could effectively participate in management.

Respondent's expert relied on various market studies which indicated appropriate discounts for lack of marketability between 25.8% and 45%. However, he concluded that the marketability discount should be only 15% because of good management, regular cash distributions and quality tenants.

On the minority interest discount, the Court concluded 19%. The Court said, "respondent's expert erroneously assumes that an owner of each general partnership unit could participate meaningfully in management." The Court added, "Although, under New York State law, any general partner . . . arguably had the legal authority to dissolve the partnership, . . . we believe that such authority would have little impact on Mr. Silvers effective control."

On the marketability discount, the Court concluded 26% (the low end of the range of studies submitted by respondent). The Court noted good management and "a history of significant cash distributions," but also no public market, and that transfer would be subject to the controlling owners approval.

Estate of McFarland v. Commissioner

Citation: T.C.Memo 1996-424, 1996 Tax Ct. Memo LEXIS 443
Court: United States Tax Court
State/Jurisdiction: Specialty Federal
Date of Decision: September 19, 1996
Judge: Laro

In this case the Personal Representative of the deceased asked the court for partial summary judgment by asserting "the Court *must* use a going concern methodology to value a 20% partnership interest."

The partnership, which began as a turpentine and timber business, had been in the decedent's family since at least 1934. Subsequently, the stock had been passed down through the family a number of times and in 1991, the decedent owning a 20% interest, died.

Instead of valuing decedent's interest on a going concern basis, the Service valued the partnership by reference to comparable land and timber sales and added 20% of this value to 20% of the fair market value of the other assets of the partnership. After applying a 10% minority discount and another 15% discount for lack of marketability, the Service listed the fair market value of decedent's interest at $1,147,177.

On the Estate Tax Return, the Personal Representative reported the fair market value of decedent's interest to be $533,895 and, subsequent to audit, reduced the value to $179,615.

The Personal Representative relied upon a prior case in which the partnership agreement provided that "The death of a partner shall not cause the dissolution or termination of this partnership." According to the Tax Court, the language in the prior case compelled the court to value the business on a going concern basis.

While the Tax Court agreed that the facts of the relied upon case and the case at bar were somewhat similar, it found that the language in McFarland's will stating "My said executrix and trustee is hereby given full authority and power * * * to continue and carry on any business in which I am engaged at the time of my death, including the continuation of any partnership in which I may be interested at the time of my death..." allowed, but did not require, the trustee to continue the partnership in the event of decedent's death.

The Tax Court concluded by stating, "We do not believe that we would be properly discharging our duty if we were to set forth at this point one (and only one) method of valuation that must be used to determine the fair market value of Decedent's partnership interest. Cases of valuation require us to determine the price that a hypothetical willing buyer would pay a hypothetical willing seller, both persons having reasonable knowledge of all relevant facts and neither person being under any compulsion to buy or sell. It would be inappropriate for us at this juncture to limit our consideration to one method in order to determine this price. ... accordingly, we will deny petitioner's motion for partial summary judgment."

Thompson, Betty W. v. Commissioner

Citation: T.C. Memo 1996-468, 1996 Tax Ct. Memo LEXIS 482
Court: United States Tax Court
State/Jurisdiction: Specialty Federal
Date of Decision: October 17, 1996
Judge: Dean

The taxpayer's motion for administrative cost recovery was the basis of this case. In an earlier proceeding, the IRS and the taxpayer had stipulated to the $124 per-share valuation contained in the expert witness report of Z. Christopher Mercer, ASA, of Mercer Capital Management, for the taxpayer.

Although the basis of the valuation was not disclosed, the taxpayer's former valuation of $113.52 per share, as computed by James M. Grant, CPA, was similar. Grant's valuation was based upon an average of a capitalized earnings value and book value, reflecting a 35% discount for lack of marketability and the transfer of a minority interest.

The IRS had determined a value of $240, based upon a comparable company, and reflecting a 20% lack of marketability discount. The court denied the petition for cost recovery on the basis that the taxpayer failed to show she had paid or incurred any fee or cost in the matter. Although not reported in the court's decision, the discount awarded was 30% as stated in the Mercer report.

Estate of Mueller v. Commissioner

Citation: 107 T.C. No. 13
Court: United States Tax Court
State/Jurisdiction: Specialty Federal
Date of Decision: November 5, 1996
Judge: Ruwe

In the *Estate of Bessie I. Mueller v. CIR*, 107 T.C. No. 13, the Tax Court considered the application of equitable recoupment when it found that the estate was not liable for any additional tax. The estate originally assigned a $1,505 per share date-of death value to the stock of the Mueller Co. 67 days later, the estate sold some shares for $2,150 per share and reported the gain. The IRS concluded that the stock had a date-of-death value of $2,150 per share and notified the estate of a deficiency as well as a $1,152,649 unrelated tax credit. In *Mueller I*, T.C. Memo. 1992-284, the Tax Court ruled that the date-of-death value of the stock was $1,700 per share. This resulted in an increase of $957,099 in estate tax and an overpayment in capital gains tax resulting from the sale of stock of $265,999, which was time-barred. The estate amended its claim, entitling it to equitable recoupment of the overpaid tax. In *Mueller II*, 101 T.C. 551, the court found that the estate was not liable for any additional tax, but rather was entitled to a refund due to the difference between the increase in estate tax and the tax credit.

This case results from the estate's contention that it is entitled to equitable recoupment of the capital gains overpayment because the capital gains tax and the estate tax revolve around one related transaction - the valuation of the stock. The IRS contends that this is an offensive use of a defensive doctrine. "A party litigating a tax claim in a timely proceeding may, in that proceeding, seek recoupment of a related, and inconsistent, but now time-barred tax claim relating to the same transaction." *United States v. Dalm*, 494 U.S. 596 (1990). The Tax Court ruled that the estate was not entitled to equitable recoupment of the capital gains tax because there was not an addition to tax, and, in fact, the estate received a refund due to the unrelated tax credit. The court, therefore, viewed the main event as the overall taxation of the estate, and did not express an opinion whether the claim met any other criteria for equitable recoupment. However, a number of dissenting opinions were issued.

The dissenting judges found the majority's opinion to present the government with a windfall by treating the overall taxation of the estate as the main event for purposes of equitable recoupment. The dissenting judges found that the equitable recoupment claim should be allowed, provided the claim met all the material requirements, "so long as it did not exceed the additional tax due as a result of the increased valuation of the shares; i.e. recoupment should be applied to correct the error on a transactional basis, not just on the basis of whether some amount is finally determined to be owed to the party who received the windfall. As there is no issue as to the entitlement of the credit, the "main action" in the instant case is not the entire liability of the estate for tax, but rather the additional estate tax claimed with respect to the shares."

This abstract originally appeared in *Valuation Case Digest*, authored by John J. Stockdale, Jr.

Van Zelst v. Commissioner

Citation: No. 96-1833
Court: United States Court of Appeals
State/Jurisdiction: 7th Circuit Federal
Date of Decision: November 15, 1996
Judge: Easterbrok

In *Theodore W. Van Zelst, et al. v. Commissioner*, No. 96-1833 (7th Cir. 1996), the U.S. Court of Appeals for the Seventh Circuit considered the value of property in Alaska donated to the National Park Service. The donor purchased the property including mineral rights from his employer for $30,000 in 1983. He donated the land in 1985, claiming a $2.75 million charitable donation. This value was supported by expert witnesses, who based this figure on a prospective use combining a luxury resort with a working mine on this property.

His first expert opined that the property could produce 100 tons of 5% copper ore per day for five months of the year. The expert determined the present value of the operation in 1985 was $650,000. The remaining $2.1 million was another expert's valuation of the resort use. The plaintiff argued that this "...would have been uniquely attractive because the tourists could have visited a working mine." However, the court noted that "these days the back-country devotees who make pilgrimages to Alaska are more likely to be repulsed" by than attracted to the destruction of wilderness. The court also received the IRS' expert testimony which found the "valuation was fantasy" and that the property had restricted access, high slope, and a location which did not receive direct sunlight. It further heard testimony from another expert regarding the value of mining operations in 1985. This expert found that the proposed mine would have a negative cash flow in 1985 due to the low price of copper.

The court affirmed the $38,000 value ($28,000 for the property and $10,000 for the potential to mine) because (1) there were no other resorts or producing copper mines in the area, (2) price of copper was $.67 per pound and falling in 1985, (3) four previous corporations did not make the mine profitable, (4) the mining claim had lain fallow for 46 years, and (5) there was no other bid for the property in 1983.

This abstract originally appeared in *Valuation Case Digest*, authored by John J. Stockdale, Jr.

Estate of D'Ambrosio v. Commissioner

Citation: No. 95-7643 (3rd Cir. 1998)
Court: United States Court of Appeals
State/Jurisdiction: 3rd Circuit Federal
Date of Decision: November 26, 1996
Judge: Nygaard

In the *Estate of Rose D'Ambrosio v. CIR*, No. 95-7643 (November 26, 1996), the United States Court of Appeals for the Third Circuit considered whether a remainder interest in stock should be included in the gross estate at its full, fee simple value. The decedent owned 50% of the preferred stock in Vaparo, Inc. When she was 80 years old, the decedent transferred her stock to Vaparo in exchange for an annuity of $296,039 per year. Furthermore, she retained her income interest in the stock. The parties stipulated that the remainder interest was equal to the value of the annuity. The decedent died two years later, after only receiving $592,078 in annuity payments and $23,500 in dividends. The estate did not include any interest in Vaparo in its calculation of the gross estate. The IRS issued a deficiency and required that the estate submit the "full fee simple value of the Vaparo shares... less the amount of annuity payments decedent received during her life."

The estate argued before the Tax Court that the decedent had received adequate consideration for the transfer. In making its decision, the court considered the case law, including *Estate of Gregory v. Commissioner*, 39 T.C. 1012 (1963) and *Gradow v. United States*, 11 Cl. Ct. 808 (1987), *aff'd*, 897 F.2d 516 (Fed Cir. 1990). The Tax Court stated, "Decedent did not receive adequate and full consideration under section 2036(a) for her 470 shares of Vaparo preferred stock, we hold that her gross estate includes the date of death value of that stock, less the value of the annuity." The estate appealed.

On appeal, the Third Circuit found the cases the Tax Court cited were "either inapposite or unpersuasive..." The court in *Gregory* found the estate received much less than the value it transferred. The Third Circuit noted, "the holding in *Gregory* does not extend to the issue now before us: whether, when a remainder is sold for its stipulated fair market value, the consideration received is inadequate because it is less than the fee simple value of the property." The *Gradow* case is similar to the *Gregory* case. In *Gradow* the court paid special attention to the language of section 2036. It noted the language imparted "that 'property' refers to the fee simple interest and that adequate consideration must be measured against that value." The Third Circuit noted that where 'property' is mentioned, the section also says the value should include "the extent of any interest therein". It determined that the use of the word 'interest' is subject to the same definition as 'property'.

The Third Circuit concluded that the Tax Court erred when it relied on these cases. It found that the decedent received full consideration for the value of the remainder interest and that her transfer was not done to avoid tax consequences. It reversed and remanded the Tax Court's decision. One of the Third Circuit's judges dissented. He noted, because "the Tax Court's opinion is supported by well-established case law and the plain language of the Internal Revenue Code, [it] should be affirmed."

This abstract originally appeared in *Valuation Case Digest*, authored by John J. Stockdale, Jr.

Estate of Wright v. Commissioner

Citation: T.C. Memo 1997-53, 1997 Tax Ct. Memo LEXIS 50
Court: United States Tax Court
State/Jurisdiction: Specialty Federal
Date of Decision: January 29, 1997
Judge: Swift

At issue is the value of Clyde Wright's 201,408 shares of common stock of the Wilber Corp., which owns 100% of the common stock of Wilber National Bank. At the time of his death, Wright owned 23.8% of the 847,524 outstanding shares. Experts for both sides based their valuations on the approximately 10,000 shares of Wilber Corp. traded each year on the over-the-counter market. No blocks over 500 shares were ever traded, and the average sales price was $50 per share in October 1990.

Taxpayer applies blockage discount

Petitioner's first expert, Harold Wade Schuessler, of Alex Sheshunoff & Co., valued Wilber Corp. at $7,653,504, or $38 per share, utilizing both a comparable sales and a discounted cash flow approach using a 12% rate of return. Petitioner's second expert, Robert Clore, of Cowen & Company, focused on the significant size of the block of stock and, given the limited type and number of investors that would be capable of purchasing the block, applied a blockage discount.

Both experts concluded that, as of the valuation date of October 20, 1990, the value of the shares owned by Mr. Wright at the time of death was $38 per share.

IRS expert applies control premium

The expert for the IRS, David Fuller, of Business Valuation Services, Inc., relied primarily on a market-transaction approach, and determined that on October 20, 1990, the stock was worth $67.34 per share, reflecting the initial $50 per share value plus a control premium. Fuller concluded that the petitioner's expert's valuations of Wilber Corp. were unreasonably low and inconsistent with Wilber Corp.'s strong financial position. He also relied heavily on a hypothetical scenario in which a single group of investors might purchase decedents entire block of stock, and further use this block to force other minority shareholders to sell their shares to the purchasers to acquire at least 51% of Wilber Corp. Finally, Fuller concluded that because the market for Wilber Corp. was thin, (not for lack of buyers, but for lack of willing sellers), no blockage discount should apply.

Scenario found unlikely

The court found the testimony and valuations of the petitioner to be more credible. In addressing the hypothetical scenario where investors would purchase decedent's entire block, plus an additional 27.2% of the shares, the court found it unlikely, and unsupported by the facts. The court noted that the hypothetical sale effectively ignores the requirement in Wilber's articles requiring a 66 2/3% super majority for decisions regarding the merger, consolidation, dissolution or sale of all or substantially all of the assets of the bank. The court used as a starting point the petitioner's expert's $38 value. Accounting for the banks excellent financial condition and the thinly traded shares, the court adjusted the $38 per share upward, and concluded that the value per share was $45.

Estate of Gray v. Commissioner

Citation: T.C. Memo. 1997-67
Court: United States Tax Court
State/Jurisdiction: Specialty Federal
Date of Decision: February 5, 1997
Judge: Colvin

In the *Estate of Jewell E. Gray v. CIR*, T.C. Memo. 1997-67, the Tax Court considered, among other issues, whether transfers made by Beth W. Corp., a personal holding company, to its president and primary shareholder were loans deductible from the estate under Sec. 2053(a). The IRS and the estate stipulated that the undiscounted value of Beth of W. Corp. (assuming that the transfers were not loans) equaled the net asset value of its holdings. The court also considered whether the stipulated value should be further reduced for a built-in capital gains tax liability arising from the sale of 56 acres to a trust, and by a 40% discount for marketability.

1. Related Party Transfer

Beth W. Corp. transferred $1.7 million to decedent for which she executed a number of promissory notes. Only $103,000 had been paid back on the date of death, and many of the notes were past due. Beth W. Corp. filed a claim against the estate for the amount past due, declared the loan an asset on its balance sheet, but had not made any demands for payment from decedent or her estate. The court weighed the relevant factors enumerated in previous cases in determining whether the transfers were dividends or loans:

- (1) Does the shareholder control the company?
- (2) Is the company restricted in the amount it can lend the shareholder?
- (3) Has the company had substantial earnings and paid a large amount of dividends?
- (4) Is the shareholder able to repay the amount transferred?
- (5) Does the corporation seek repayment?
- (6) Is there evidence of indebtedness?
- (7) Is there a fixed repayment schedule?
- (8) Is the transfer secured?
- (9) Is there a written loan agreement?
- (10) Do the parties treat the transactions as loans in their records?
- (11) Has the borrower made repayments?
- (12) Does the borrower intend to repay the amount transferred?

In concluding that the transfers were dividends, the court gave lesser weight to written evidence and greater weight to the parties' behavior. It considered important the failure to repay, lack of effort to collect, absence of a repayment schedule, lack of adequate collateral or a loan agreement, and lack of objective evidence of intent to repay.

2. Built-in Capital Gains Tax

The court further considered whether the stock should be discounted for the tax liability due on built-in capital gains tax from the sale of 56 acres of land to an irrevocable trust. On the date of death, the trust had possession of the property but had not found a buyer and the note was past due. The trusts had paid the interest due on the note, but still had not found a buyer by the time of trial nor had the corporation foreclosed on the property. The court determined that it was speculative if, when and for how much the trust would sell the property. Therefore, the court disallowed the deduction of this potential liability.

3. Marketability Discount

The court lastly considered applying a marketability discount to the stipulated value of the stock. The estate's expert testified that a 40% discount was appropriate based on an analysis similar to that used in *Mandelbaum v. Commissioner*, T.C. Memo 1995-255. affd. 91 F.3d 124 (3rd Cir. 1996). The court dismissed this analysis for lack of showing that Beth W. Corp. was similar from the standpoint of marketability. The IRS contended that no discount was appropriate because a marketability discount could not be applied to a controlling interest. It further contended that this discount should not be applied because the stock was valued by reference to its net asset value, not the as freely traded value. The court disagreed with the IRS on both counts, and applied a discount of 15%.

This abstract originally appeared in *Valuation Case Digest*, authored by John J. Stockdale, Jr.

Barge v. Commissioner

Citation: T.C. Memo 1997-188, 1997 Tax Ct. Memo LEXIS 221
Court: United States Tax Court
State/Jurisdiction: Specialty Federal
Date of Decision: April 23, 1997
Judge: Halpern

At issue is the fair market value of a 25% undivided interest in timberland owned by Barge, which was the subject of gifts made by Barge in 1987.

Petitioner (taxpayer) argued that the fair market value of the 25% interest in the timberland was $4,750,000, and Respondent (IRS) argued the fair market value was at least $8,413,050. Both parties stipulated that, as of the date of the 1987 gifts, the fair market value of the entire interest was $40 million. The court heard expert testimony from two experts for Petitioner, and one for Respondent.

Petitioner's expert, Richard H. Pinkowski, Jr., a registered forester, considered an income capitalization approach. He advocated using a 14% capitalization rate to account for the investment risks of the property. However, the Court found Pinkowski's testimony unpersuasive, citing his limited experience with that type of analysis, and because of the fact that he merely applied an income capitalization model he obtained from a journal article. Furthermore, he projected future income based only on past income from one year, 1987.

Respondent's expert, Earl Flowers, also a registered forester, relied exclusively on a market comparison approach. However, on brief, Respondent concedes that the value of the 25% interest should be determined by considering the present value of the benefit to be received on partition.

The Court relied on testimony from Petitioner's other expert, Thomas J. Ebner, a forest consultant, with respect to prospective cash flows. Ebner calculated that an average cash flow applicable to a 25% interest was $341,000 per year. He also noted that, because the partners only received 86% of that cash flow, a hypothetical purchaser of the interest would only receive $293,000 per year. Ebner concluded that an investor would capitalize the estimated $293,000 cash flow at 10%. He did not consider the potential for partitioning.

The Court considered the potential partitioning of the property, using a 10% capitalization rate, a partition period of four years, a future income stream of $293,000 per year, a $41 million total value at the end of four years, and estimated partition costs of $662,500 allocated evenly over four years. Considering the above, the Court determined the fair market value of the 1987 gift to be $7,404,649, as shown in the accompanying table.

Court's Valuation of 25% undivided interest in timberland

Year	Income	Costs	Payment	Total	Value
1	$293,000	$165,625	0	$127,375	$115,795
2	$293,000	$165,625	0	$127,375	$105,268
3	$293,000	$165,625	0	$127,375	$95,699
4	$293,000	$165,625	$10,250,000	$10,377,375	$7,087,887
					$7,404,649

Estate of Kohlsaat v. Commissioner

Citation: T.C. Memo 1997-212, 1997 Tax Ct. Memo LEXIS 247
Court: United States Tax Court
State/Jurisdiction: Specialty Federal
Date of Decision: May 7, 1997
Judge: Swift

At issue is whether or not the transfer of property in an irrevocable trust is eligible under section 2503(b) for the annual $10,000 gift exclusion with respect to each of 16 contingent beneficiaries of the trust.

While auditing the petitioner's Federal estate tax return, respondent denied the gift exclusions on grounds that the contingent beneficiaries did not hold open interests in the trust. IRS argued that the substance-over-form doctrine should apply to deny the gift tax exclusions.

The court found that the transfer of the property did in fact qualify for 16 annual gift tax exclusions under section 2503(b).

Estate of Gavin v. United States

Citation: No. 96-3462 (8th Cir. 1997)
Court: United States Court of Appeals
State/Jurisdiction: 8th Circuit Federal
Date of Decision: May 8, 1997
Judge: Magill

In the *Estate of Verdon Gavin,* No.96-3462, May 8, 1997, the U.S. Court of Appeals for the Eighth Circuit considered the estate's IRC sec. 2032A election where a qualified heir received a 1/7th interest in and farmed the land. This heir had the right under the March 1990 through 1991 lease to pay the estate either 50% of the livestock and crop proceeds or $10,000 per year as rent; thereafter, it was the estate's option. The decedent groomed the qualified heir to take over the farm and granted him the option to buy the farm for $1,000 per acre in his will. This heir further had the right according to the will to have one year to secure financing after making his intent to purchase known. The IRS determined that the six remaining heirs were disqualified from the benefits of sec. 2032A because they were "mere landlords collecting a fixed rent" from the qualified heir when this heir opted to pay rent instead of cropshare. The District Court granted summary judgment to the IRS and this appeal followed.

The Appellate Court determined that the six remaining heir did not removed themselves from the family farming business but were dependent upon its production. The court enumerated the factors that it found to be important in defining continued qualified use: 1) the identity of the farmer. Here a qualified heir; 2) the non-farming heirs accepting financial risk of family farming. Here in the 1990-1991 lease agreement, the remaining heirs' share of the production proceeds were capped at $10,000, and they may have received less or nothing at all had the year been poor for farming; 3) The non-farming heirs' dependency upon production. In the lease years beginning in March 1991 and thereafter the non-farming heirs would receive at least $10,000 in rent or 50/50 cropshare; therefore, they were dependent upon the production of the farming heir in order to receive more than $10,000; 4) The will locked the non-farming heirs into holding the property until the farming heir decided to purchase it, and his decision to do so was dependent upon the revenue he could receive from farming.

The court found that the combination of the these factors show that the heirs did not seek to abuse sec. 2032A, but chose to allow the farming heir to run the farm until he could purchase the remaining heirs' interests. "Once he bought out the other heirs, ...[farming heir] became the sole qualified heir, and because he continued to actively farm... [The land] has been continuously put to a qualified used by a qualified heir."

This abstract originally appeared in *Valuation Case Digest*, authored by John J. Stockdale, Jr.

Estate of Schauerhamer v. Commissioner

Citation: T.C. Memo 1997-242, 1997 Tax Ct. Memo LEXIS 276
Court: United States Tax Court
State/Jurisdiction: Specialty Federal
Date of Decision: May 28, 1997
Judge: Foley

The decedent, Dorothy Schauerhamer, established three partnerships to which she gifted assets, primarily commercial real estate. She then gifted interests in the partnerships to a long list of family members.

On the estate tax return, the amounts gifted were excluded, but the remaining values of the partnership interests were included at a discounted value. The Tax Court decision states, "The amounts included were based on advice from competent tax professionals and a property appraisal company."

Decedent violates partnership agreement

The partnership agreements required that all income from the partnership be deposited in partnership accounts. However, decedent deposited income from the partnership assets into her personal checking account.

The court ruled, "Where a decedent's relationship to transferred assets remains the same after as it was before the transfer, section 2036(a)(1) requires that the value of the assets be included in the decedent's gross estate."

Business Valuation Update™ has been advised by the estate's counsel that a motion for reconsideration was filed June 26th with the Court and the IRS has been ordered to file its objections by July 30th.

Good faith averts Sec.6662 penalty

On the Code Section 6662 penalty issue, the court stated, "We conclude that petitioner acted reasonably and in good faith in relying on the advice of tax professionals and property appraisers. As a result, petitioner is not liable for the accuracy-related penalty for negligence."

Bommer Revocable Trust v. Commissioner

Citation: T.C. Memo 1997-380, 1997 Tax Ct. Memo LEXIS 457
Court: United States Tax Court
State/Jurisdiction: Specialty Federal
Date of Decision: August 20, 1997
Judge: Ruwe

The issue is the effect, if any, of a buy-sell agreement on the value of shares of CamVic Corp. that are includable in the estate of Cameron W. Bommer (decedent).

In 1975, CamVic and its shareholders executed a Buy-Sell Agreement requiring any stockholder wishing to sell to offer the stock back to the company and/or to other shareholders at $11,333.30 per share. Terms were 10% down, with the balance in ten equal annual installments at 5% per annual interest.

The buy-sell price was based on a computation by the parties' attorney. Neither the parties nor the attorney obtained a professional business valuation of the stock nor appraisals of the assets owned by the company.

The agreement could be altered by the written consent of the holder(s) of at least 75% of the issued and outstanding shares. At the time of the agreement, decedent held a beneficial interest through the CWB revocable trust in 86% of the outstanding CamVic stock, and had retained the right to vote those shares. His wife, Marcella, owned 1.9%.

In 1981, CamVic and its shareholders revised the Buy-Sell Agreement. The only significant revision was to provide that the written consent of the holder(s) of at least seven eighths (87.5%) would be required to alter the provisions of the agreement. The revised agreement did not change the price, and the parties did not negotiate regarding the price.

The court stated that the attorney's contemporaneous handwritten notes regarding the revision recorded the following: "Addendum @ para 13 changed 75% control to 7/8 rather than .75 purpose is to set estate tax value ... we want $11k/sh value @ death."

Decedent died in 1990. Petitioner reported a value of $11,333.30 per share for 117.7568 shares on the estate tax return. Following decedent's death stock was transferred from the estate to the Company and to other stockholders at the Buy-Sell Agreement price of $11,333.30 per share. The Company paid cash and the other stockholders purchased on the agreement's payment terms.

In its notices of deficiency, the IRS determined the fair market value of CamVic stock includable in decedent's gross estate to be $75,278.22 per share, increasing the gross estate by $7,529,951.

The Court started its opinion by listing requirements for making a buy-sell agreement price controlling for Federal estate tax:

- The price must be fixed or determinable
- The agreement must be binding on the parties both during life and after death
- The agreement must have been entered into for a bona fide business reason
- It must not be a substitute for testamentary disposition

The Court quoted Internal Revenue Code Estate Tax Regs. Section 20.2031-2(h), "such price will be disregarded in determining the value of the securities unless it is determined under the circumstances of the particular case that the agreement represents a bona fide business arrangement and not a device to pass the decedents shares to the natural objects of his bounty for less than full and adequate consideration in money or money's worth."

The Court concluded that "petitioners have not met their burden of proving that the price per share set forth in the Buy-Sell Agreement or the Revised Agreement reflected adequate and full consideration for decedents interest in CamVics stock ... further proceedings will be necessary to determine the actual fair market value of CamVic stock at the time of decedents death."

The Court agreed with the IRS that the original agreement was not binding during life. The Court also noted that decedent could have changed the terms under the Revised Agreement with the consent of his wife (1.9% owner), and if she predeceased him he would have the requisite shares. The Court concluded, "We view the Revised Agreement as an attempt to remedy an estate tax problem ..."

Taxpayer advanced the argument in defense of the "binding during lifetime" position that decedent would have breached his fiduciary duty to the other CamVic shareholders if he had unilaterally altered the provisions of the agreement to his advantage and the minority shareholders detriment. The Court said," Petitioners argument is unpersuasive, as it is certainly not a breach of any fiduciary duty for a majority shareholder to sell his stock at the highest price possible." (emphasis supplied.)

With respect to the agreements price, the Court made the following observations:

> the purchase price ... was fixed ... not subject to any reevaluation ... We find it unrealistic to assume that decedent ... would have negotiated a fixed price ... if he had been bargaining with unrelated parties ...
>
> the generous payment terms ... are a further indication of their testamentary nature ...

> an inference of the testamentary device can be drawn from the manner in which the parties selected the $11,333.30 price ... Decedent was an experienced businessman, yet he failed to obtain a professional appraisal ...

Estate of Lehmann v. Commissioner

Citation: T.C. Memo 1997-392, 1997 Tax Ct. Memo LEXIS 471
Court: United States Tax Court
State/Jurisdiction: Specialty Federal
Date of Decision: August 26, 1997
Judge: Hamblen

At date of death, decedent owned a 1% general partnership interest and a 23.9650903% limited partnership interest in LKB Associates, a limited partnership organized under the laws of the District of Columbia. The principal asset of the partnership was a leased fee interest on ground on which the lessee maintained a 99-room hotel.

Taxpayer at $399,000; IRS at $808,000

Taxpayer showed decedent's interest on the estate tax return at $399,000, based on a valuation by P. Richard Zitelman of the Zitelman Group. The IRS initially determined the fair market value was $1,070,000. At trial, the IRS claimed a value of $808,000 based on a report and testimony of Richard L. Parli, a certified general real property appraiser.

The parties agree that decedent's interest shoud be valued as a limited partnership interest. The IRS expert used the "fractional discount method," whereas taxpayer's expert used the discounted cash flow (DCF) method.

IRS expert lacks supporting evidence

The court stated, "Parli failed to explain adequately how he derived the individual discounts ... (he) summarily concluded that each individual discount is 'typical' without providing any evidence, e.g., comparables of market data ... we conclude that Zitelman's methodology provides the most reliable basis for valuing the decedent's interest."

However, the court declared:

> We have found weaknesses in Zitelman's analysis ... Some of Zitelman's assumptions are unreasonable ... Zitelman's report lacks a wholly objective analysis of the willing buyer/willing seller standard ... We find incredible the proposition that any partner ... would be willing to sell ... for such a low amount as to generate an internal rate of return of 15% to 22% ... Ignoring the views of a willing seller

is contrary to the well-established rule ... Zitelman's calculations are also inaccurate." (Among the inaccuracies was using year-end discounting when the lease required monthly payments.)

Weaknesses in mind, court modifies analysis

The court concluded, "With the weaknesses discussed above in mind, by modifying Zitelmans analysis ... we conclude that the value ... was $699,853."

Estate of Maggos v. Commissioner (I)

Citation: T.C. Memo. 1997-431
Court: United States Tax Court
State/Jurisdiction: Specialty Federal
Date of Decision: September 23, 1997
Judge: Laro

In the *Estate of Mary D. Maggos v. CIR*, T.C. Memo. 1997-431, the Tax Court considered whether to grant the estate summary judgment against the IRS on their claim of underpaid gift tax. Maggos owned 56.7% of a Pepsi bottling company in Illinois. As part of her estate plan, she transferred her stock in exchange for a $3 million promissory note to her son, who operated the company. Upon her death, the note was to be transferred to him under her will. The purchase price was not determined through an arm's length negotiation nor was an appraisal of the company requested. Two years after the redemption, her son sold the company for $22 million. The IRS claims that Maggos did not receive adequate consideration for her stock and thus made a gift. Maggos counters that she was fraudulently induced to sell her stock for less than its full value, or, in the alternative, that the sale was a bona fide arm's-length transaction that was simply a bad bargain for her. The estate further claims that she did not make a gift because she lacked donative intent.

The Tax Court determined that this issue was not ripe for summary judgment, because a question of fact remained. Although Maggos filed two suits in district court regarding the alleged fraudulently induced sale, the court found that the filing of suits was not enough to convince it that she was defrauded. Especially when factors indicating a donative intent were ascertained. The court found four factors, which indicated donative intent: "Ms. Maggos sold her shares to [the company] without an independent appraisal of [the company's] value, and she bequeathed the promissory note to her son. The value of the note was substantially less than the value of her stock, and the price for her stock was not set through arm's-length negotiations." Thus, the court dismissed the estate's claim for summary judgment and ordered conclusions regarding donative intent to be made at trial.

This abstract originally appeared in *Valuation Case Digest*, authored by John J. Stockdale, Jr.

Estate of Mitchell v. Commissioner (I)

Citation: T.C. Memo. 1997-461, 1997 Tax Ct. Memo LEXIS 546
Court: United States Tax Court
State/Jurisdiction: Specialty Federal
Date of Decision: October 9, 1997
Judge: Jacobs

The issue is the fair market value of 1,226 shares of Paul Mitchell Systems common stock, constituting 49.04% of the shares outstanding, as of April 26, 1989, the date of Paul Mitchell's death.

No comment on expert reports

The valuation for the estate tax return was prepared by KPMG. At trial, expert witnesses for the taxpayer were George B. Weiksner of C.S. First Boston and Kenneth W. McGraw of Patrikof & Co. Valuation expert for the IRS was Martin D. Hanan of Business Valuation Services. Because there was a compensation dispute which affected the income approach numbers, the IRS also called E. James Brennan III of Brennan, Thomsen Associates, Inc. as a compensation expert.

Although the Court's opinion describes each expert's methodology, it offers little guidance for appraisers because there is not a single word about what the Court liked or disliked about any of the experts' reports or testimony. Instead, the Court started with an alleged (although disputed) offer for the entire company and proceeded to work out its decision from there. The positions of the various parties and experts and the Court's conclusion are shown in the accompanying box.

'Moment of death' rule important

The "moment of death" concept of valuation for estate tax purposes is important, because it requires that the focus be on the *property transferred*. This means, in this case, without the services of Paul Mitchell. Since the Court considered him a very key person, the alleged offers to buy contemplated his continuing service, and there was a marked lack of depth of management, the Court determined a 10% discount from the company's enterprise stock value.

While the Court applied the key person discount at the enterprise level, it applied a $1.5 million discount for the uncertainties of pending compensation litigation at the 49.04% minority interest level.

Eisenberg v. Commissioner (I)

Citation: T.C. Memo 1997-483, 1997 Tax Ct. Memo LEXIS 567
Court: United States Tax Court
State/Jurisdiction: Specialty Federal
Date of Decision: October 27, 1997
Judge: Hamblen

Respondent alleges deficiencies in Petitioner's Federal gift taxes owed for the years 1991, 1992 and 1993. Before the Court are cross-motions for summary judgment on the sole issue of whether the Petitioner, when valuing her privately-held stock, may account for the full amount of the built-in gain on the corporation's only asset.

From inception, Petitioner held all issued and outstanding common stock of the corporation, comprising 1,000 shares. During the time period in question, the company was a subchapter C Corporation for tax purposes. The only asset other than cash was a building in Brooklyn, New York, and the corporation received income from the rent payments generated.

Both parties agreed that the net asset value method is appropriate for the valuation of the corporation's stock. The parties were also in agreement as to the fair market value of the subject property, and the valuation of the shares on Petitioner's federal gift tax returns. Furthermore, both sides agreed on the gains the corporation would have realized if the property had been disposed of in a taxable disposition. However, the parties diverge on whether, in arriving at the corporation's net asset value, adjustments should be made to reflect costs that would, potentially, be incurred if its assets were liquidated.

Petitioner argued that a willing purchaser of the stock would have discounted the otherwise applicable fair market value as a result of the tax liability inherent in the property. Conversely, respondent argues that petitioner is not entitled to reduce the fair market value of the stock to account for potential capital gains taxes since no sale or liquidation occurred.

The Court agreed with the respondent that a discount for capital gains taxes does not apply in this case. The Court stated that, "This Court has repeatedly held that no reduction in the value of closely-held stock to reflect potential capital gains is warranted where the evidence fails to establish that a liquidation of the corporation or sale of the corporation's assets is likely... Moreover, we also held that a discount to asset values for the 'lost use of money is inappropriate because it fails to recognize that the underlying assets will themselves appreciate, most likely, at a rate similar to that applied as a discount."

Citing *Ward*, *Andrews* and *Cruikshank*, the Court further stated, "...taxpayers may not obtain a valuation discount for estate and gift tax purposes based on an event that may not transpire." Hence, "when liquidation is only speculative, the valuation of assets should not take these costs into account because it is unlikely they will ever be incurred."

The Court concluded by granting respondents motion for summary judgment and denying petitioners motion for summary judgment, with a decision entered for respondent.

Estate of Fleming v. Commissioner

Citation: T.C. Memo 1997-484, 1997 Tax Ct. Memo LEXIS 566
Court: United States Tax Court
State/Jurisdiction: Specialty Federal
Date of Decision: October 27, 1997
Judge: Chiechi

The issue is the value of a 50% stock interest in a small consumer loan company with a book value of $2,168,839.

Both experts (Richard Bernstein of Bernstein, Phalon & Conklin for the taxpayer, and Monty Harrell, and economist employed by the IRS), relied exclusively on the market approach, each starting with both a guideline company method and a transaction method.

Court comments on credentials

The Court noted that Bernstein is a member of the American Society of Appraisers (ASA) and Harrell, although not a member of ASA, has taken ASA business valuation courses. The Court added "We evaluate opinions of experts in light of the demonstrated qualifications of each expert and all other evidence in the record."

Judge Chiechi further added, "The persuasiveness of any expert's opinion depends largely upon the disclosed facts on which it is based."

Guideline company data inadequate

Bernstein selected three publicly traded guideline companies engaged in consumer lending.

However, according to the Court, "Mr. Bernstein did not explain in his report or adequately explain at trial why the three guideline companies ... were comparable ... and why he selected only three ... (also), Mr. Bernstein did not adequately explain, and has not convinced us, that his determination of the market multiples for the guideline companies that he selected are proper ... For these reasons, we are not persuaded that the results that Mr. Bernstein reached under his modified market multiple method are reliable, and we shall not give any weight to these results."

Estate of Fleming positions and conclusion
Estate tax return $1,000,000
Amended return $726,000
IRS Notice of Deficiency $1,257,460
Taxpayer witness at trial $604,777
IRS witness at trial $1,110,000
Court's conclusion $875,000

After he prepared his report and before trial, Mr. Harrell discovered deficiencies in the data ... on which he relied in applying the market multiple method, leading him to abandon that method at trial.

Guideline method good if data OK

The Court observed, "we agree with both experts that ... the combined use of the market multiple method and the transaction method would produce a better indication of value than the use of only the transaction method.

However, as discussed above, ... we are left with a deficient record from which to determine the effect of the market multiple method ... Nonetheless, we shall determine the fair market value ... by applying our better judgment to a record that we find to be inadequate in that and other respects ... "

This left the Court with a starting point of $1,200,814. for the 50% interest, based on factors on which both experts agreed in the transaction approach. All the comparative transactions except one were 100% interests.

Minority/marketability should be distinct

Bernstein opined to a combined 35% discount for minority and lack of marketability. Harrell opined to only a 10% minority discount, and no discount for lack of marketability.

The Court stated, "*Discounts for a minority interest and for lack of marketability are conceptually distinct* (emphasis added) ... Mr. Bernstein did not specify how much of the 35-percent combined discount that he applied was attributable to the fact that decedent did not own a controlling stock interest ... On brief, petitioner, who has the burden of proof, does not insist that a minority discount in excess of 10% be applied in this case."

Both minority and DLOM for 50% stock

On the issue of marketability, the IRS contended there should be no discount because the comparative transactions were in stock for which there was no ready market.

The Court stated, however, "we find that there was even less of a ready market for decedent's 50% stock interest (than those for which the purchasers acquired 100%)—consequently, we conclude that, in addition to a minority discount, some amount of lack of marketability discount should be applied ..."

The Court concluded, "Based on the record before us, and using our best judgment, we find that the fair market value ... was $875,000."

Hewitt v. Commissioner

Citation: 109 T.C. No. 12
Court: United States Tax Court
State/Jurisdiction: Specialty Federal
Date of Decision: October 29, 1997
Judge: Tannenwald, Jr.

In *John T. and Linda L. Hewitt v. CIR*, 109 T.C. No. 12, the Tax Court held that the Hewitts were not entitled to a deduction for their charitable donation of stock greater than their basis in the stock even though the claimed basis was based on the fair market value of the stock. The Hewitts were shareholders in a corporation that provided tax preparation services in three states. The company was closely held but traded either through the company or through a securities company. Both parties stipulated it was not a public company at the time of the donation.

The Hewitts gifted shares to a charitable organization in 1990 and in 1991. They determined the fair market value of the stock by averaging the 317 company trades that occurred between 1990 and 1991. They did not have the stock appraised nor did they attach an appraisal summary to the tax return. Furthermore, the return did not identify the stock that was gifted or the number of shares gifted. It only reflected the cost and the claimed value of the stock. The IRS disallowed the deduction in excess of the basis because it lacked a qualified appraisal. The Hewitts brought this action claiming they substantially complied with the statute and regulation or that there was a market for the stock.

The Tax Court ruled that they had not substantially complied with section 1.170A—13, Income Tax Regs. Which requires gifts in excess of $5,000 *to be appraised*. It also determined that the Hewitts' alternative argument was without merit. The fact that the stock was traded through the company and through a securities dealer did not make the stock "publicly traded" and, thus, exempt from the appraisal requirements. See sec. 155(a)(2)(A).

This abstract originally appeared in *Valuation Case Digest*, authored by John J. Stockdale, Jr.

Estate of Trompeter v. Commissioner (I)

Citation: T.C. Memo 1998-35, 1998 Tax Ct. Memo LEXIS 36
Court: United States Tax Court
State/Jurisdiction: Specialty Federal
Date of Decision: January 27, 1998
Judge: Laro

Although there are other assets at issue in this case, our review is limited to the value of 1,533.482 shares of a certain class of Sterling Holding Co. preferred stock as of the alternate estate valuation date, September 18, 1992.

The estate reported a value of $10 per share, a total of $15,335, on decedent's Federal estate tax return, based on a valuation by Patricia L. Bates, of the accounting firm of Frankel, Lodgen, Lacker, Golditch & Sardie. This was in spite of the fact that Ms. Bates had valued the stock a month earlier at $462,000, net of a 70% discount for minority and lack of dividend payments.

The IRS contends that the value is $1,947, 845 on the basis that the stock was redeemed for that amount on January 17, 1994 (about 16 months after the valuation date). The IRS did not call a witness at trial.

Taxpayer called Herbert T. Spiro, a professor until 1988 and currently a consultant on economic feasibility and financial analysis. He utilized 10 public preferred stocks in the high "D" and low "C" ratings, since Sterling had not been paying dividends. Based on these preferreds, He calculated the freely traded value of the Sterling preferred at 15% of par value, or $150 per share. He then reduced that value by 20% to reflect lack of marketability. This resulted in a total value of $184,018 (1533.482 shares x $120= $184,018).

Judge Laro said, "The Sterling preferred stock was a better grade than a "C" or "D" rated security." He discussed Sterling's financial status, and noted that one of Spiro's comparables, TWA, had filed for bankruptcy, and another's financial condition resembled that of TWA.

Using contractual redemption amounts and a discount rate of 4% from the contractual redemption dates, Judge Laro valued the stock at $2,708,536. Since "the estate has not persuaded us that the actual fair market value was less than respondent's determination," Judge Laro sustained the IRS valuation of $1,947,845. Judge Laro also upheld the fraud penalty.

Estate of Lockett v. Commissioner

Citation: T.C. Memo 1998-50
Court: United States Tax Court
State/Jurisdiction: Specialty Federal
Date of Decision: February 9, 1998

In the *Estate of Edna Pearce Lockett v. CIR*, T.C. Memo. 1998-50, the Tax Court considered whether the estate could claim a charitable deduction for the donation of property with historic significance. Decedent owned 1,160 acres in Florida, known as Fort Basinger, which included an Indian burial mound, her home (Zachary Taylor's base during the Seminole Indian Wars) and other structures. In accordance with her will, her assets were "pour[ed] over" into a trust following probate. The trust was directed in its agreement to "...set aside [decedent's home] by the trustees as a historical site. The designation of the site and management shall be in the discretion of the trustees." The estate did not contain enough liquid assets to pay the estate transfer tax; thus, the trustees entered into a part sale/ part gift arrangement with the Water District. The trust donated the portion with historical significance and sold the remainder under the promise that decedent's home would be preserved as a historic site. The estate claimed the donation as a charitable deduction under IRC section 2055(a). The IRS disallowed the deduction because decedent's intent to transfer Fort Basinger to a charitable organization was not ascertainable at the time of her death.

The Tax Court noted "[a] recurring problem is whether the decedent directed the transfer to a qualifying organization or whether the estate fiduciary made the transfer in the exercise of his discretion; only in the former case is a deduction generally allowed." The court determined from the language of the trust agreement that decedent did not possess a charitable intent to transfer the property to a qualified organization, and that the trustees had wide discretion in disposing of the property. Thus, the court disallowed the charitable deduction because "...the value of the transfer to a charitable entity was neither 'presently ascertainable' at the date of decedent's death, nor was the possibility that the property would not be transferred to a qualifying organization so remote as to be negligible."

This abstract originally appeared in *Valuation Case Digest*, authored by John J. Stockdale, Jr.

Estate of Williams v. Commissioner

Citation: T.C. Memo 1998-59, 1998 Tax Ct. Memo LEXIS 61
Court: United States Tax Court
State/Jurisdiction: Specialty Federal
Date of Decision: February 12, 1998
Judge: Colvin

The Tax Court decision in the case of *Estate of Ellie B. Williams*, adds to the body of law on the valuation of undivided real estate interests.

Ellie and her husband owned about 8,700 acres of undeveloped timberland and farmland in Florida. They had no children. After her husband died in 1962, Ellie's niece's husband, Robert Driggers, began helping her with the management of the property. They had a close personal relationship, according to the court, similar to a mother and son.

In 1980 and again in 1983, Ellie transferred to Robert an undivided one-half interest in some of the real estate. Ellie died in 1992.

The issue before the court was the value of the real estate interests transferred during Ellie's lifetime, and of the undivided one-half interest in 843 acres of land that she owned at the time of her death.

The court analyzed the testimony of two real estate valuation experts, and determined the per-acre value of fee ownership of the parcels in question. Judge Colvin then addressed the issue of whether a discount should be allowed for the fractional interests.

Expert applies combined discount

Three experts gave testimony relevant to the discount issue on behalf of the Estate. Dr. Donald C. Wiggins, a business appraiser, applied a combined discount of 44% (30% for lack of control, followed by 20% for lack of marketability) to the pro rata value of the one-half interest. Frank Scruby, a Florida real estate attorney, estimated the cost of partitioning the property.

Donald M. Pitts, a Florida banker, testified that banks will not make loans to the owner of a fractional interest in real property without the consent of the other co-owner.

IRS provides no experts

The IRS presented no expert testimony on the discount issue. It conceded that a 5% discount, but no more, would be proper. The IRS's real estate appraiser admitted on cross-examination that an undivided one-half interest in real property has a limited market and that a fractional interest may be discounted, although he did not quantify the amount of the discount.

IRS argues discount limited to partition costs

The IRS apparently did argue that the discount should be limited to partition costs. Scruby, the Estate's expert, had estimated the partition costs at less than 5% of the property's value. The IRS cited this testimony in support of its 5% discount.

On this record, Judge Colvin agreed with the Estate's expert and applied a discount of 44% to arrive at the value of the gifts and of the interest held by the decedent at her death.

The opinion rejects the IRS's argument that the discount should be limited to the estimate of partition costs, because, according to the court, that position "does not give adequate weight to otherreasons for discounting a fractional interest in real property, such as lack of control and the historic difficulty of selling an undivided fractional interest in real property..."

Estate of McLendon v. Commissioner (II)

Citation: 135 F.3d 1017, 1998 U.S. App. LEXIS 4105
Court: United States Court of Appeals
State/Jurisdiction: 5th Circuit Federal
Date of Decision: March 9, 1998
Judge: Jolly

Because the facts were not in dispute, the only question before the Court of Appeals was whether or not Gordon B. McLendon was sufficiently close to death on March 5, 1986, to require him to depart from the actuarial tables published by the Commissioner of Internal Revenue in valuing a remainder interest and related annuity.

After a long struggle with esophageal cancer, McLendon received great news from his oncologist that, "By clinical and laboratory objective criteria, the present condition of your illness must be characterized as 'complete remission.' It is therefore necessary for me as a physician, to advise you of the risk that the disease might recur, but to state frankly and without hesitation that the possibility that your disease has been permanently eradicated is definite and significant and in my professional opinion, should form the basis for your planning for the future."

Transactions relied on revenue ruling

Given his improved situation, McLendon entered into a private annuity transaction with his son and the newly established McLendon family trust on March 5, 1986. The transaction transferred remainder interests in McLendon's partnership holdings to his son and the Trust in exchange for $250,000 and an annuity paid to McLendon for life. In valuing the remainder interests and annuity, McLendon referred to the Commissioner's actuarial tables (Revenue Ruling 80-80) for calculating life expectancy. Based on this figure, McLendon determined that the remainder interests had a value of $5,881,695, and that the annuity would need to be $865,332 to match.

Two months later, the cancer recurred, and Gordon McLendon died on September 14, 1986. The estate tax return relied on a presumption that McLendon received full and adequate consideration for the assets transferred in the annuity transaction. The Commissioner disagreed, and challenged both the use of the actuarial tables and certain aspects of the valuation of the partnership interests, and declared an estate tax deficiency of several million dollars.

Court 'not obliged to follow revenue ruling'

On September 30, 1993, the Tax Court issued its first opinion in the case and agreed with the Commissioner, holding that use of the actuarial tables was improper because McLendon's life expectancy was reasonably predicable at the time of the transaction. In an unpublished opinion, the Court of Appeals reversed the Tax Court on the valuation questions, but remanded for clarification the applicability of Revenue Ruling 80-80. In its second opinion, the Tax Court stated that although neither party had argued a position inconsistent with Revenue Ruling 80-80, the court "had felt not obliged to follow the ruling."

Tax court fighting a losing battle

On its second appeal, the Appeals Court noted that:

> As the prior panel foresaw, the remainder of this case turns on the applicability of Revenue Ruling 80-80... We note at the outset that the Tax Court has long been fighting a losing battle with the various courts of appeals over the proper deference to which revenue rulings are due. Whereas every circuit recognizes some form of deference, the Tax Court stands firm in its own position that revenue rulings are nothing more than the legal contentions of a frequent litigant, undeserving of any more or less consideration than the conclusory statements in a party's brief. Although the Supreme Court has not spoken definitively on the subject, its recent jurisprudence tends to support the view that the courts owe revenue rulings a bit more deference than the Tax Court would have us believe... and in the absence of a definitive statement from on high, the Tax Court continues to ignore them in toto.

Commissioner held to published rulings

The Appeals Court cited *Silco*, stating that the case stands for the proposition that the Commissioner will be held to his published rulings in areas where the law is unclear, and may not depart from them in individual cases. Furthermore, under *Silco*, the Commissioner may not retroactively abrogate rulings in an unclear area with respect to any taxpayer who has relied on it.

Reversed and rendered

Applying *Silco,* the court stated that McLendon went to great lengths to comply with the law, and that, "The Commissioner ignored the clear language of his own ruling in declaring deficiencies, and it is precisely this kind of tactic that *Silco* declares to be intolerable." The court concluded that when the Commissioner has specifically approved a valuation methodology, like the actuarial tables in Revenue Ruling 80-80, "[The Commissioner] will not be heard to fault a taxpayer for taking advantage of the tax minimization opportunities inherent therein... The Tax Court's manifest failure to apply the ruling was clearly wrong." Reversed and rendered for the estate.

Dockery v. Commissioner

Citation: T.C. Memo 1998-114, 1998 Tax Ct. Memo LEXIS 114
Court: United States Tax Court
State/Jurisdiction: Specialty Federal
Date of Decision: March 19, 1998
Judge: Colvin

At issue is the value of petitioner's closely held stock in Crossroads Company, a reinsurance company domiciled in the Cayman Islands, that he gifted to his children on January 1, 1992, and January 1, 1993. Based on a June 1992 appraisal by KPMG Peat Marwick, petitioner reported on his gift tax returns that the fair market value of Crossroads' stock was $303 per share. Respondent determined that the fair market value of Crossroads' stock was $704 per share on January 1, 1992, and $1,010 per share on January 1, 1993.

Petitioner hired Thomas L. Gallagher, a property and casualty actuary with Tillinghast-Towers Perrin, to appraise Crossroads' common stock. Gallagher projected future earnings from policies in effect on the gift dates by reviewing the policies' past results and analyzing Crossroads' loss reserves. He projected that Crossroads premiums would grow by 5% per year for the next five years, the loss ratio would be 160% for the first year and would decrease over the next four years, and that the underwriting expenses would be 12.5% of earned premium for all five years.

Gallagher discounted the earnings by 20%, and estimated that the fair market value of Crossroads stock was $0 on January 1, 1992, and $331 per share on January 1, 1993.

Respondent did not call an expert to testify. Raymond T. Wise is an IRS estate and gift tax attorney, who used two methods in calculating the value of Crossroads stock. Wise adjusted the balance sheet, subtracted his adjusted liabilities from total assets, and determined that the book value of the stock was $1,241 per share on January 1, 1992, and $1,580 per share on January 1, 1993. He also multiplied Crossroads average pretax income by a P/E multiple of 5X, and weighted the P/E method by 60%, and the book value method by 40%, and applied a 35% discount for lack of marketability. Wise concluded that the stock was worth $704 per share as of January 1, 1992, and $1,010 as of January 1, 1993.

The court rejected both Gallaghers and Wises valuations, and instead accepted KPMG Peat Marwicks original valuation. The original appraisal was based on discounted value of the future dividend stream available to a U.S. owner of Crossroads stock. KPMG Peat Marwick used a discount rate based on the then-current market hurdle rate (the actual rate was not available) for investments of comparable risk. KPMG Peat Marwick estimated that Crossroads stock was worth $505 per share, and applied a combined 40% minority and marketability discount, concluding that the fair market value of the common stock was $303 per share for both gift dates. The court held that the fair market value was in fact $303 per share.

Vinikoor v. Commissioner

Citation: T.C. Memo 1998-152
Court: United States Tax Court
State/Jurisdiction: Specialty Federal
Date of Decision: April 27, 1998

In *Greg Vinikoor v. CIR*, T.C. Memo. 1998-152, the Tax Court considered whether a transfer of stock was a gift or a loan. In 1987, Mrs. Vinikoor's grandfather transferred 7,000 shares of stock to the Vinikoors. The parties executed a promissory note, which identified the transfer as a loan. In 1990, the Vinikoor's disposed of the stock. On their tax return, they claimed a stepped-up basis in the stock for capital gains tax purposes. The IRS disagreed. It claimed that the transfer was a gift, and the Vinikoors' basis was the same as their grandfather's basis: Ten cents ($.10) a share instead of the stock's fair market value in 1987.

The Tax Court noted that whether a transfer between related parties is a bona fide debt is a question of fact. The court provided a list of factors it uses to determine whether the debt is bona fide. The court asks whether "(1) there was a promissory note or other evidence of indebtedness, (2) interest was charged, (3) there was security or collateral, (4) there was a fixed maturity date, (5) a demand for repayment was made, (6) any actual repayment was made, (7) the transferee had the ability to repay, (8) any records maintained by the transferor and/or the transferee reflected the transaction as a loan, and (9) the manner in which the transaction was reported for Federal tax purposes is consistent with a loan." The court found that while a promissory note was executed, the parties did not otherwise treat the transfer as a loan. The transfer did not have a maturity date, the debt did not bear interest, and no repayment or demand for repayment was made. Thus, the court determined that the Vinikoors' were not entitled to a stepped-up basis in the transferred stock.

This abstract originally appeared in *Valuation Case Digest*, authored by John J. Stockdale, Jr.

Furman v. Commissioner

Citation: T.C. Memo 1998-157, 1998 Tax Ct. Memo LEXIS 158
Court: United States Tax Court
State/Jurisdiction: Specialty Federal
Date of Decision: April 30, 1998
Judge: Beghe

Before the Tax Court, for purposes of determining the taxable gifts of Royal G. Furman, and the taxable gifts and taxable estate of Maude G. Furman, is the determination of the fair market value of shares in Furman's Inc. (FIC), a closely held company. Specifically, the court must determine whether the shares of common stock exchanged for preferred stock of FIC was $300,000 as petitioners contend, or $540,540, as respondent contends, or some other amount. Also at issue, for purposes of computing Maude's taxable estate, the court must determine if the fair market value of the shares of FIC she transferred to Robert G. Furman in 1980, was $62,016, as petitioner contends, or $147,600 as respondent contends, or some other amount.

FIC is a Florida C corporation, founded for the purpose of operating a Burger King restaurant franchise. At the trial date, FIC operated 27 Burger King restaurants along the west coast of Florida. Royal died on June 29, 1990, and Maude died on June 12, 1992. Robert Furman, as personal representative executed and filed the required estate tax returns.

The IRS relied on the expert report of Hugh Jackson Shelton. In his report, Shelton represented that he possessed certain qualifications and credentials to perform business valuations, which he did not in fact have. His report also suggested that he was a member of the American Society of Appraisers (ASA), an organization to which he never belonged.

WACC methodology deemed questionable

Shelton used a capitalized earnings method to value the FIC stock at the time of the 1980 gifts. He used the CAPM with a beta of 1 to arrive at a cost of equity of 18.44%. Shelton reasoned that Burger King would be no more or less volatile than the industry as a whole, but provided no other justification for his beta. Shelton proceeded to compute the WACC, to arrive at his capitalization rate. The court noted that, "Mr. Shelton computed WACC in a manner that did not conform to the accepted method... First, Shelton modified the WACC formula by weighting FIC's debt and equity based on book value, rather than market value, to arrive at a WACC of 11%. Considering that the parties have stipulated risk-free rates of 11.86% and 14.4% in 1980 and 1981, respectively, it is obvious that Mr. Shelton's result is incorrect." Furthermore the court, "...was puzzled why Mr. Shelton would want to apply a marginal tax rate to compute an after tax figure, only to then attempt to convert it back to a pretax figure."

Shelton capitalized earnings before interest, depreciation and taxes (EBDIT), to arrive at firm value, to which he then applied a combined discount of 17% to reflect minority interest, marketability, and a "control premium discount." Regarding the control premium discount, Shelton theorized that a swing vote potential existed. Shelton concluded that FIC's stock was $22,522 per share.

Court rejects expert's valuation 'in toto'

Regarding Shelton's valuation, the court stated, "With the exception of his assessment of the prospects for economic growth on the west coast of Florida, we reject, in toto, Mr. Shelton's analysis and conclusions." The court then turned its attention to the estate, who relied on the expert report of Mr. Francis Burns and Mr. Brian Oliver, both with IPC Group, LLC (IPC).

IPC valued the FIC shares using both a capitalized income method and an EBITDA multiple. In its income approach, IPC used net cash flow to equity, and applied the CAPM using data from

Ibbotson Associates. IPC applied a 35% marketability discount, and a 30% minority discount to the value of the shares. However, the estate relied on IPC's second valuation method, the multiple of EBITDA.

Experts apply 5X EBITDA multiple

IPC determined the EBITDA of FIC for the fiscal years 1979-1981. IPC further determined that a multiple of 4-6 times EBITDA was a commonly used valuation guideline that should be applied in this case. Ultimately IPC applied a multiple of 5.0 for both 1980 and 1981. Equity value per share was determined to be $20,842 in February 1980, and $26,245 in August 1981. To those values, IPC applied a 30% minority discount, 35% marketability discount, and a 10% key person discount, for a total discount of 59.05%. IPC determined fair market value per share to be $8,535 in February 1980, and $10,747 in August 1981.

Regarding IPC's findings, the court stated, "We accept IPC's valuation under the EBITDA multiple approach as the most accurate measurement of value available, but we do not accept the percentages of minority interest and marketability discounts that were applied. We also reject IPC's use of a multiple of 5.0 as unreasonable in light of FIC's growth potential and the prevailing economic conditions... Because we think that IPC has not properly taken into account FIC's potential for growth, we find 6.0 times EBITDA to be the proper multiple to be employed in the valuation of the FIC stock."

Court applies 40% combined discount

The court stated that a 40% combined minority and marketability discount was most appropriate, and agreed with IPC's application of a 10% key person discount. The court also did not believe any control premium was warranted, because "...we are required to value the shares as if they were transferred to a hypothetical buyer and are not permitted to take into account the circumstances of the actual transferee in valuing the shares." The court concluded that for purposes of computing the taxable gifts of Royal and the taxable gifts and estate of Maude, the fair market value of 24 shares of FIC common stock by each decedent in 1981 for preferred stock of FIC was $424,552, and the fair market value of the six shares transferred to Robert was $82,859.

Estate of Welch v. Commissioner (I)

Citation: T.C. Memo 1998-167, 1998 Tax Ct. Memo LEXIS 165
Court: United States Tax Court
State/Jurisdiction: Specialty Federal
Date of Decision: May 6, 1998
Judge: Laro

At issue is whether the estate of Welch is entitled to discount the value of stock for built-in capital gains taxes, causing a deficiency of $59,987 in federal estate taxes. Welch was a minority shareholder in two closely held companies, Electric Services, Inc. (ESI) and Industrial Sales Co., Inc. (ISC).

Mercer Capital uses NAV method

The estate engaged Mercer Capital, who used the net asset value method to value ESI at $670,000, and ISC at $1,809,000, as of the date of death. In arriving at the values, Mercer Capital excluded real properties from its calculations because it believed that the properties were targeted for sale to the city of Nashville. Additionally, Mercer Capital did not apply any discount for built-in capital gains.

In determining the value of the shares for estate tax purposes, the estate combined the Mercer Capital valuation with the real properties, and made adjustments.

Gains avoided by both companies

On March 4, 1994, coexecutor Newton acquired all of the voting and nonvoting shares of both companies. The purchase price for the nonvoting shares of ESI and ISC was $1,021 and $1,276 per share, respectively. The remainder of the purchase price was allocated equally between ESI's and ISC's voting stock. Newton further indicated that both companies would purchase real property to relocate the businesses once their respective properties were lost to the Metropolitan Government of Nashville and Davidson County due to condemnation proceedings. Additionally, both ESI and ISC elected on their 1994 corporate tax returns not to recognize gains realized from the compulsory or involuntary conversion of property under IRC section 1033(a)(2).

Turning to the value of the stock the court stated, "In determining the value of unlisted stocks, actual arm's length sales of such stock in the normal course of business within a reasonable time before or after the valuation date are ordinarily the best criteria of market value. In the absence of arm's length sales, the value of closely held stock must be determined indirectly by weighing the corporation's net worth, prospective earning power, dividend paying capacity, and other relevant factors."

The estate argued that a willing seller and willing buyer would discount the value of the stock to reflect built-in capital gains. Conversely, respondent argues that the estate had not established that a liquidation was eminent, that the discount was not warranted where only real estate, not the companies, were subject to condemnation, and that the discount in not warranted where both companies could, and did, avoid the recognition of gains under section 1033(a)(2).

Realized gains too speculative

Citing *Eisenberg,* the court found that the potential for capital gains tax recognition was too speculative to warrant a discount, and that the estate failed to show that it was likely that either of the companies would pay built-in gains taxes upon sale. Finally, the court stated that "A section 1033 election was available to the estate on the applicable valuation date. The estate presented no evidence that on or near the valuation date either corporation considered recognizing the built-in capital gain and foregoing the election under section 1033." As a result, the court upheld the respondent's deficiency determination.

Estate of Young v. Commissioner

Citation: 110 T.C. 297, 1998 U.S. Tax Ct. LEXIS 24
Court: United States Tax Court
State/Jurisdiction: Specialty Federal
Date of Decision: May 11, 1998
Judge: Wright

Respondent determined an estate tax deficiency of $154,545. At the time of death, decedent and wife owned five real properties as joint tenants. The first of three issues before the court was whether or not the properties were joint tenancy or community property. The court held that the property was joint tenancy, because when a husband and wife take property by deed as joint tenants, the presumption of community property is rebutted, and that the two types of interests are mutually exclusive.

The second issue was whether a discount for lack of marketability was applicable to the property. The court stated that, "The fractional interest discount, as applied in section 2033, is based on the notion that the interest is worth less than its proportionate share, due in part the problems of concurrent ownership. These problems are created by the unity of interest and unity of possession. However, at the moment of death, the co-ownership is severed, thus alleviating the problems associated with co-ownership. We conclude that the Young property is not entitled to a fractional interest discount."

The court concluded by rejecting any discount for lack of marketability, and holding petitioner liable for additional taxes associated with late filing.

Estate of Auker v. Commissioner

Citation: T.C. Memo. 1998-185
Court: United States Tax Court
State/Jurisdiction: Specialty Federal
Date of Decision: May 19, 1998
Judge: Laro

In the *Estate of Eldon L. Auker v. CIR*, T.C. Memo. 1998-185, the Tax Court considered whether a market absorption discount could be applied to all decedent's real property. The decedent held, in trust, real property outright and through various corporate entities. Most of the estate's property was located in Genesee County, Michigan. Certified real property appraisers appraised the real property. They valued most of the properties using the sales comparison method. However, the decedent held three apartment complexes, which were valued using the income capitalization approach because there were no comparable sales. A certified business appraiser valued the business entities. He determined the businesses' values by reference to the appraised real property values, including applicable discount. He applied a combined marketability and lack of control discount between 35% and 40% to each minority interest. The estate also engaged a CPA firm that concluded a 15% market absorption discount should apply to all the estate's real property. Thus, the estate reduced the appraised values of the real property and business interests proportionately for the market absorption discount, and reported the adjusted values on its estate tax return. The Service disallowed the application of a market absorption discount, and the case proceeded to trial before the Tax Court.

At trial, both parties presented expert witness testimony regarding the appropriateness of a market absorption discount. The estate's first expert was an economist. The court disregarded this expert's testimony regarding the real estate market in Genesee County as duplicative because the appraisers in determining their fair market values considered it.

The estate's second expert, a certified business appraiser and CPA, used a four-factor test to determine whether a market absorption discount was appropriate. The factors were (1) the depth of the market, (2) the size of the subject properties vis-^vis the total property in the market in terms of the actual number of properties being sold and the level of the market, (3) the time required to sell the properties, and (4) the market trend as it related to the size of blockage discounts. He concluded that a discount was appropriate. He determined that a 20% discount was appropriate based on the median discount taken in nine resolution trust company sales. The Tax Court disregarded this expert because it found him to be biased. "We decline to accept the opinion of a man whose only appearance in this case seems to be as a spokesman for the interests of his clients and the estate." It further found that his opinion was based on incorrect assumptions including that an across-the-board discount could be applied to each parcel and that "any market absorption discount for the subject property could be tied directly to the RTC's disposition of real estate held by insolvent S&L's."

The IRS's expert was a real estate appraiser with substantial experience in Genesee County. This expert opined that the apartment complexes could be sold to an institutional investor, such as a

REIT, or a buyer from outside the county within four to six months. He concluded that no discount should apply. The court also did not agree with this expert. It found that while a buyer may come from outside of Genesee County, a market absorption discount might still apply.

The court applied its own five-point test to determine the applicability and size of a market absorption discount. The first point examined the assets to be valued and characterized the assets by type because "[t]he mere fact that many parcels of real estate are marketed contemporaneously does not mean that a discount for market absorption applies to any or all parcels." The second point determined the value of the assets. The third point compared the number of assets in each category to the number of assets of that type traded in the market over a reasonable time. The fourth point determined the amount of additional time required to sell the assets that could not be sold in a reasonable time. The last point discounts the assets not sold in a reasonable time.

Applying this test, the court concluded that only the apartment complexes could qualify for a market absorption discount. In doing so, the court refused to look through the corporate entities and discount the real property held there. It found that "the entities were viable going concerns on the applicable valuation date, and neither a sale nor a liquidation of the entity-owned real estate was contemplated at that time, we conclude that the entity-owned real estate is ineligible for a market absorption discount." The court further determined that the real estate market at the valuation date could not have handled the introduction of the three apartments. The court found that six months was a reasonable time to market and that it would take 42 months to dispose of all three apartments. It used the weighted average of apartments' capitalization rates to determined the time-value of money and discounted the average value of the apartments to present value. Thus, it concluded that a market absorption discount of 6.189% should apply to the apartments only.

This abstract originally appeared in *Valuation Case Digest*, authored by John J. Stockdale, Jr.

Estate of Cullison v. Commissioner

Citation: T.C. Memo. 1998-216
Court: United States Tax Court
State/Jurisdiction: Specialty Federal
Date of Decision: June 17, 1998
Judge: Parr

In the *Estate of Suzanne W. Cullison v. CIR*, T.C. Memo. 1998-216, the Tax Court determined whether the value of a private annuity received in exchange for real property equaled the value of that property, resulting in no estate tax. The decedent held four parcels of Arizona farmland. She wanted to transfer the property to her grandchildren, but also wanted the property to be offered to the remaining grandchildren, if one wished to sell the property. To that end, the decedent and her grandchildren entered into a private annuity agreement wherein they purchased the property for an annuity of equal value. The property was not used as collateral for the annuity. Thereafter, the property was contributed to a family partnership and the grandchildren given partnership interests.

The decedent's accountant, a CPA, was engaged to determine the annual payments for her private annuity valued at $1,865,500, the aggregate value of the property. He concluded that the decedent had 8.9 years of life remaining, and that 9% interest (a rate slightly higher than that for Arizona land contract sales) was appropriate. He consulted a loan amortization table and concluded that the annual amount due on a 9-year, $1,865,500, 9% loan was $311,165.

The IRS audited the decedent's estate and concluded that she made an indirect gift to her grandchildren. The IRS determined that the value of the annuity was less than the value of the property, resulting in a gift. The court concluded that the value of the property was $1,865,500. It also agreed with the IRS that the annuity had a value of $1,360,724, and that the excess was a gift to her grandchildren. The court determined that this was due primarily to faulty tax advice. The court found that the decedent's accountant did not reasonably value the annuity. This accountant applied an interest rate below that required by the gift and estate tax regs. In effect at the time. Moreover, the rate was unreasonable in light of the fact that the payments were not secured by the property. Furthermore, this expert did not follow the proper procedures in effect at the time of the transaction. Thus, the court upheld the determination that decedent did not receive adequate and full consideration because the value of the land exceeded the value of the annuity.

This abstract originally appeared in *Valuation Case Digest*, authored by John J. Stockdale, Jr.

Estate of McClatchy v. Commissioner (II)

Citation: 147 F.3d 1089, 1998 U.S. App. LEXIS 13576
Court: United States Court of Appeals
State/Jurisdiction: 9th Circuit Federal
Date of Decision: June 26, 1998
Judge: Tashima

The issue before the Court of Appeals was whether Charles K. McClatchy's stock holdings should be valued with the federal securities law restrictions which had been in place before his death or without the restrictions once they were transferred to his estate. The case is an interesting twist on the "moment of death" concept of value.

Affiliate status restricts stock's transferability

McClatchy was Chief Executive Officer of McClatchy Newspapers, Inc. at the time of his death in 1989. He owned over 2 million shares of Class B stock in the company. His stock was subject to federal securities law restrictions on the sale or distribution of his shares because of his status as an affiliate of the corporation. The restrictions limited the marketability of the stock . It was agreed that the shares were valued at $12. 375 per share before his death, subject to the restrictions, reflecting 20% discount for lack of marketability from the freely tradable price of $15.56 at the date of his death.

The estate filed an estate tax return reporting the value of the stocks to be $12.375 per share. The Commissioner issued a notice of deficiency, valuing the stocks without the restrictions, and assessing a deficiency of $5,784,910 plus a penalty of $1,156,982.

IRS concedes 15% blockage discount

The estate protested the decision and the IRS conceded that a blockage discount of 15% should be used in valuing the stocks and that no penalties were due. Although this left only 5 percentage points difference between the IRS' 15% "blockage" discount settlement offer and the 20% DLOM claimed by the estate, the estate went forward with the appeal.

The Commissioner argued that McClatchy's death is one of those rare instances that alter the value of the property, because, once the stocks were transferred to his estate the restrictions "evaporated".

The Appellate Court distinguished this case from others where the value changed at the moment of death with the following explanation:

> In the instant case, death alone did not effect the transformation in the stock's value. The value of the stock was transformed only because the estate was a non-affiliate...

The affiliate or non-affiliate status of an estate depends on the status of the executor or other person who serves in any similar capacity. The personal representatives for the estate were not issued letters testamentary until 25 days after McClatchy's death. The restrictions therefore did not evaporate at the moment of death.

The Court of Appeals thus REVERSED, finding the value to reflect the 20% discount for lack of marketability due to affiliate status.

Estate of Davis v. Commissioner

Citation: 110 T.C. 530, 110 T.C. No. 35, 1998 U.S. Tax Ct. LEXIS 35
Court: United States Tax Court
State/Jurisdiction: Specialty Federal
Date of Decision: June 30, 1998
Judge: Chiechi

The issue in this case was the value of each of two 25-share blocks (out of 97 shares outstanding) of ADDI&C, gifted on November 21, 1992. ADDI&C was a C-Corporation, primarily a holding company, whose primary asset was more than 1 million shares of Winn-Dixie stock with a very low cost basis.

The valuation revolved around three primary areas of dispute:

- Trapped in capital gains: whether or not there should be a discount from net asset value for this factor, and, if so, how much
- Blockage: whether or not there should be a discount from Winn Dixie's NYSE price for this factor, and, if so, how much.
- Discount for lack of marketability: how much.

The experts for the taxpayer were Alex Howard of Howard Frazier Barker Elliott, Inc. and Shannon Pratt of Willamette Management Associates. The expert for the IRS was John Thomson, of Klaris, Thomson & Schroeder, Inc.

Perhaps the most important statement in the Court's opinion is the following:

> We reject respondent's position that, as a matter of law, no discount or adjustment attributable to ADDI & C's built-in capital gains tax is allowable in the instant case.

The following are brief excerpts from the Court's elaboration on this critical point:

> Although Dr. Pratt recognized in his expert report that as of the valuation date it would have been possible for ADDI&C to convert to an S corporation, he did not consider conversion to S corporation status to be likely ... such an assumption would have impermissibly limited the hypothetical willing buyer of each of the two blocks of stock at issue to certain individuals and entities who were permitted as of the valuation date to be shareholders of an S corporation, see sec. 136(b)(1)(B) and (C), thereby improperly excluding as a hypothetical willing buyer of each such block, for example, a C corporation...

> ... we agree that as of the valuation date it was unlikely that ADDI&C would have converted to an S corporation. Based on the record before us, we reject respondents unwarranted assumptions that ADDI&C could have avoided all of ADDI&Cs built-in capital gains tax by having it elect S corporation status and by not permitting it to sell any of its assets for 10 years thereafter, and the record does not establish that there was any other way as of the valuation date by which ADDI&C could have avoided all of such tax.
>
> We are convinced on the record in this case, and we find, that, even though no liquidation of ADDI&C or sale of its assets was planned or contemplated on the valuation date, a hypothetical willing seller and a hypothetical willing buyer would not have agreed on that date on a price for each of the blocks of stock in question that took no account of ADDI&Cs built-in capital gains tax. We are also persuaded on that record, and we find, that such a willing seller and such a willing buyer of each of the two blocks of ADDI&C stock at issue would have agreed on a price on the valuation date at which each such block would have changed hands that was less than the price that they would have agreed upon if there had been no ADDI&Cs built-in capital gains taxes of that date.

The Court rejected taxpayers position that the full amount of the trapped-in capital gains tax should be deducted in arriving at the underlying net asset value, noting that no liquidation of the Winn Dixie stock was contemplated. Instead, the Court adopted the position of reflecting the capital gains tax by adding 15 percentage points to what the discount for lack of marketability otherwise would be without consideration of the capital gains issue. This was approximately consistent with the positions of both Mr. Thomson and Dr. Pratt.

On the issue of a discount from Winn Dixies NYSE price for blockage, Mr. Howard and Dr. Pratt included such a discount and Mr. Thompson did not. The Court recognized that it probably would have taken 5 to 6 months to sell the block without depressing the price under the SEC rule 144 dribble-out method. Nevertheless, without further discussion, the Court stated, "Petitioner has the burden of establishing that a blockage and /or SEC rule 144 discount should be applied ... we find that petitioner has failed to satisfy that burden."

On the issue of marketability, both Mr. Howard and Dr. Pratt testified to a discount of 35% (apart form the capital gains issue), and Mr. Thompson testified to 23%.

Mr. Howard relied on a number of restricted stock studies (private placements of restricted public stocks) and the Baird & Co. pre-IPO discount studies (private transactions in stock before an initial public offering ultimately took place). Dr. Pratt relied on the same studies plus three others: one additional restricted stock study; the Willamette Management Associates' pre-IPO discount studies; and transactions in publicly registered limited partnerships that, like ADDI&C, were not making distributions to partners. Mr. Thompson relied on some, but not all, of the restricted stock studies considered by Mr. Howard and/or Dr. Pratt, but did not consider the pre-IPO studies.

In leaning toward the higher end of the marketability discount range, the Court stated that "we found those (Mr. Howards and Dr. Pratts) reports and the additional testimony of Dr. Pratt at trial to be quite helpful in ascertaining the lack-of-marketability discount that we shall apply in this case ... Mr. Thomson should have considered the ... data reflected in those pre-IPO studies because they, together with the restricted stock studies, would have provided a more accurate base range and starting point for determining the appropriate lack-of- marketability discount ..."

Estate of Bosca v. Commissioner

Citation: T.C. Memo 1998-251, 1998 Tax Ct. Memo LEXIS 252
Court: United States Tax Court
State/Jurisdiction: Specialty Federal
Date of Decision: July 8, 1998
Judge: Whalen

The issue for decision in these consolidated cases is the value of the gifts that the decedent made to his two sons, by means of a 1990 transaction in which he and his wife exchanged voting common stock in his closely held corporation for nonvoting common stock, with the result that his two sons ended up owning all of the voting stock of the corporation.

In the 1990 transaction, decedent recapitalized his corporation, effectively surrendering his 50% share of voting common stock for an equal amount of nonvoting common stock. The corporation canceled the voting stock it received in the transaction and thus gave 100% voting rights to decedent's two sons.

The Tax Court rejected petitioner's argument that no value was transferred to the corporation or his sons in the transaction.

The issue became whether the stock that was transferred to the company should have been valued as a single block of 50% or as two blocks of 25%.

Respondent argued that the stock exchanged should be treated as a single block and valued accordingly. The Tax Court disagreed, however, noting that such an approach violates the principle that separate gifts should be valued separately. The indirect gift of the voting rights was decided as two gifts: one to each of his sons.

According to stipulation by the parties, had the stocks been valued as a single block, a 25.62% premium would have been added to the value of the nonvoting common stock for an aggregate tax liability of $970,830. Instead, the stocks were treated as two separate blocks of 25% and a premium of 2.72% was applied to the value of the nonvoting common stock for a tax liability of $103,040.

Estate of Shackleford v. United States (I)

Citation: 82 AFTR2d Par. 98-5133 (ED CA 1998)
Court: United States District Court
State/Jurisdiction: Eastern District of California
Date of Decision: July 29, 1998
Judge: Karlton

In the *Estate of Thomas J. Shackleford v. U.S.A., et al.*, 82 AFTR2d Par. 98-5133 (July 29, 1998), the U.S. District Court, Eastern District of California, considered, on summary judgment, the proper method to determine the value of unreceived lottery payments. The decedent won $10 million in the California State Lottery. The lottery payments were nontransferable. The decedent elected to receive his prize in twenty equal payments, but died after receiving only three. The estate argued that the remaining payments should be valued as a commercial annuity. It also argued, in the alternative, that a deviation from the annuity tables was required if the payments were to be valued as a private annuity because the payments were unmarketable. The estate presented testimony that the value of the future payments was $2.4 million. The IRS argued that the payments should be valued as a private annuity and valued at $4 million by reference to the annuity tables in effect on the date of death. The IRS moved for summary judgment.

The District Court ruled that unreceived lottery payments must be valued as a private annuity. It concluded that the payments could not be valued as a commercial annuity, because they were not issued by "a company regularly engaged in the sale of commercial annuities." However, the court refused to grant summary judgment regarding the value of the lottery payments. It determined the estate presented a disputed factual issue by showing that a more realistic valuation method may be available.

This abstract originally appeared in *Valuation Case Digest*, authored by John J. Stockdale, Jr.

Eisenberg v. Commissioner (II)

Citation: 155 F.3d 50, 1998 U.S. App. LEXIS 20109
Court: United States Court of Appeals
State/Jurisdiction: 2nd Circuit Federal
Date of Decision: August 18, 1998
Judge: Carman

This decision reverses the U.S. Tax Court decision, which disallowed a discount from net asset value reflecting potential capital gains taxes for a C corporation with a piece of commercial real estate as its major asset. It remands the case to the Tax Court to determine the gift tax liability taking into consideration the potential built-in capital gains tax liability, even though "no liquidation, sale or distribution of the corporation was planned."

The Court stated:

> In the past, the denial of a reduction for potential capital gains tax liability was based, in part, on the possibility that the taxes could be avoided by liquidating the corporation. These tax-favorable options ended with the Tax Reform Act of 1986 (TRA)
>
> Now that the TRA has effectively closed the option to avoid capital gains tax at the corporate level, reliance on these cases in the post-TRA environment should, in our view, no longer continue.

The Court cited favorably *Estate of Davis v. Commissioner*. In *Davis*, the court rejected as universally cumbersome and confining the IRS contention that the corporation could have avoided capital gains taxes by converting to S corporation status, and holding the assets for ten years, and said that a discount for the potential capital gains tax should be recognized.

The Second Circuit went on to elaborate:

> Our concern is not whether or when the donees will sell, distribute or liquidate the property at issue, but what a hypothetical buyer would take into account in computing fair market value of the stock.
>
> The issue is not what a hypothetical willing buyer plans to do with the property, but what considerations affect the fair market value of the property he considers buying. While prior to the TRA any buyer of a corporation's stock could avoid potential built-in capital gains tax, there is simply no evidence to dispute the fact that a hypothetical willing buyer today would likely pay less for the shares of a corporation because of the buyer's inability to eliminate the contingent tax liability.

The Second Circuit concluded by vacating the Tax Court decision granting the IRS motion for summary judgment and remanding the case to the Tax Court to determine the gift tax liability consistent with this opinion.

Estate of Gloeckner v. Commissioner (II)

Citation: 152 F.3d 208, 1998 U.S. App. LEXIS 20114
Court: United States Court of Appeals
State/Jurisdiction: 2nd Circuit Federal
Date of Decision: August 18, 1998
Judge: Cardamone

The only issue in this case is whether the price in a stock redemption agreement entered into between the decedent and the corporation is determinative for estate tax purposes.

Interpretation of Treasury Reg. 20.2031-2(h)

The key issue is the interpretation of Treasury Regulation 20.2031-2(h). Under this regulation, which calls for a case by case evaluation, four requirements have evolved for a redemption price to be binding for estate tax purposes:

1. Price of the stock must be fixed or determinable by a formula within the agreement.

2. Estate must be obligated to sell the stock at a fixed price upon the shareholder's death.

3. In the event the decedent shareholder chose to sell his shares during his lifetime, he must have been obligated to sell them at the price fixed by the agreement, and not by any price he otherwise might have chosen.

4. Agreement must represent a bona fide business arrangement and not a device to pass the decedent's shares to the natural objects (next of kin) of his estate for less than an adequate and full consideration.

The Commissioner does not dispute that the agreement meets the first three requirements. The argument is that Gloeckner drafted the agreement as a testamentary (will) device to transfer the stock to the natural objects of his estate without paying full consideration.

There are two issues that must be assessed to determine if the agreement meets the fourth requirement:

- The agreement must be a bona fide business agreement.

- The agreement must not be a means of transferring Gloeckner's estate to his natural objects in order to avoid being subjected to normal estate tax laws.

Comprehensive valuation sets redemption price

The company retained KPMG Benchmark to determine the value of the stock as of June 30, 1987. KPMG produced a comprehensive written analysis, valuing the stock at $440 per share. On July 10, 1987, Gloeckner signed a redemption agreement requiring the corporation to redeem enough shares from his estate at $440 to pay the estate taxes.

Gloeckner also gifted some shares to Joseph Simone, an unrelated company officer in his mid-30s, whom Gloeckner wanted to own and manage the company after his death. He also willed to Simone any shares remaining in his estate after the redemption.

Estate files at redemption price

Gloeckner died three years later. The estate tax return listed the value of Gloeckner's stock at $2,298,161.25-which was equal to the redemption price and the amount paid by the company to buy all his shares. Despite decedent's intent to spare his kin the burden of paying any estate tax, the proceeds from the stock redemption were insufficient to cover the amount due, so the estate paid tax and administrative expenses of about $1 million. In assessing a tax deficiency, the Commissioner placed a value of $6,000,000 on the shares.

There was no dispute that the redemption agreement was a bona fide business arrangement. The Court of Appeals stated "This test is sufficiently satisfied when the purpose of a restrictive agreement is to maintain current managerial control-whether by family or outsiders."

Tax Court claims 'testamentary device'

In ruling against petitioners at trial, the Tax Court found that Gloeckner's redemption agreement served a testamentary purpose, and that the estate had failed to show that the agreement reflected full and adequate consideration when it was executed.

(Each party was to have submitted expert reports by Jan. 20, 1995. On Jan. 27, petitioners told the court in writing that they would use the 1987 KPMG Benchmark report. The Tax Court granted Commissioner's motion in limine to exclude the KPMG report because it was not timely filed, even though the Commissioner had received the report during discovery.)

The Tax Court criticized certain aspects of the Commissioner's expert report and valued decedent's stock at $4 million, resulting in a reduced tax deficiency at $561,077.79.

Did a 'natural object' benefit?

The Court of Appeals stated, "the first question to ask is whether a natural object of decedent's family benefits from the conveyance in the restrictive agreement." The Court of Appeals concluded that Gloeckner's kin did not benefit from the agreement and that the relationship with Simone was a business relationship, not a kinship relationship. The Tax Court's order is reversed, with instructions to vacate the deficiency.

Estate of Stinson v. United States (I)

Citation: 82 AFTR2d Par. 98-5469 (ND IN 1998)
Court: United States District Court
State/Jurisdiction: Northern District of Indiana
Date of Decision: October 2, 1998
Judge: Miller, Jr.

In *Lavonna J. Stinson Estate v. United States*, 82 AFTR2d Par. 98-5469 (October 2, 1998), the U.S. District Court for the Northern District of Indiana considered whether IRC Sec. 2503 applied to gifts to corporations. In 1981, Lavonna Stinson sold 267 acres to Stinson's Inc. for $398,700. The purchase price was payable in monthly installments over twenty years. Stinson's Inc. was a closely-held company owned by five of the decedent's progeny. Between 1982 and 1985, the decedent forgave a total of $147,000 due on the property sale, in annual amounts not exceeding $50,000. The decedent did not report the gifts to the IRS. The IRS audited her estate tax return and discovered the gifts to the corporation. It brought this action to recover the gift tax due on the $147,000 gifted to the corporation.

At trial, the Stinson estate argued that no gift tax was due. It reasoned that a gift to the corporation was an indirect gift to the shareholders of a present increase in the value of their shares. It concluded that since the annual gifts were less than $50,000, and Stinson's Inc. had only five shareholders, and the $10,000 per donee annual applied; then, no tax was due. The IRS argued that gifts to a corporation are not present interests but gifts of future interests in property to the shareholders. The estate disagreed. It reasoned that "a gift to the corporation is an indirect gift to the shareholders (by affecting stock value) that does not depend on any future event or contingency for its ownership or enjoyment; the gift is the present increase in the market value of the stock, which each stockholder is free to enjoy at any time by simply selling his or her stock." The district court agreed with the IRS and awarded them summary judgment. It noted that Rev.Rul. 71-441 addressed gifts to corporations. Therein, "The IRS explained ... that although a gift to a corporation is a gift to its shareholders, ... the shareholders have no present or immediate right to use, possess, or enjoy the donated property or the income from that property."

This abstract originally appeared in *Valuation Case Digest*, authored by John J. Stockdale, Jr.

Estate of Brookshire v. Commissioner

Citation: T.C. Memo 1998-365, 1998 Tax Ct. Memo LEXIS 370
Court: United States Tax Court
State/Jurisdiction: Specialty Federal
Date of Decision: October 8, 1998
Judge: Swift

Ann Brookshire owned 219,710 shares of common stock in Brookshire Grocery Co., representing 9.79% of the total shares outstanding, at the time of her death on Nov. 20, 1993. Of those, 112,884 shares were *not* subject to a stock purchase agreement. Petitioner and respondent agreed to a value of $58.75 per share for such shares.

The disagreement centers on the 106,825 shares subject to the agreement, for which the buy/sell "formula price" was $73.43 per share at the time of decedent's death. The court concluded-without dispute-that, for federal estate purposes, the formula price set forth in the buy/sell and stock purchase agreements does not control the value of the stock.

Decedent's estate filed a timely return, also valuing the stock subject to the agreement at $58.75 per share. Respondent filed a notice of deficiency based on $73.43 per share for the buy/sell agreement stock, a difference of $1,568,191.

A few weeks before trial, respondent's expert, Ron Lint, formerly with Weaver & Tidwell, submitted a report opining to a value of $89.14 per share, further increasing the difference over the estate filing.

Brookshire Grocery Co. was founded in the 1920s and, at the time of decedent's death, owned 96 retail grocery stores located in rural communities in the South. Brookshire additionally owned two food and merchandise distribution centers that supplied approximately 80% of the products sold in Brookshire stores; two bakery plants; a milk processing plant; and a photo processing center.

Brookshire was experiencing increased competition from Wal-Mart Super Centers. The competition was resulting from 20- 40% drops in sales for Brookshire and Wal-mart had plans to open more stores in the future that would be in direct competition with Brookshire.

Petitioner hired two experts to value the Decedent's stock. The first expert was Charles Wilhoite of Willamette Management Associates. Wilhoite utilized three different methods to arrive at a value of $6,302,734, or $59 per share. In arriving at this amount he used the guideline company method, the discounted cash flow method, the capitalization of dividends method, and then applied a 45% discount for lack of marketability.

Petitioner's second expert, Robert Conklin of Berstein Phalon Conklin, valued the stock at $5,237,679, or $49.03 per share. In arriving at this figure he utilized the guideline public company method, the discounted cash flow method, the transaction method, and then applied a 40% discount for lack of marketability.

Respondents expert utilized the guideline public company method, the discounted cash flow method, the capitalization of dividends method, and then applied a 34% discount for lack of marketability.

Respondents expert used three companies as comparables that had significant sales other than retail grocery and were not comparable to Brookshire. He failed to take into consideration the increased competition from Wal-Mart and the Court determined that, because of this, the values that he arrived at were overstated.

The court determined that the petitioners first expert properly analyzed the facts and circumstances surrounding Brookshire. The earnings multiples that he used adjusted for the increased competition from Wal-Mart and the decrease in Brookshires net income. The Court concluded that the appropriate discount to use to reflect the lack of marketability was 40% and assigned a value of $6,895,618 to the stocks, or $64.55 per share.

Barnes v. Commissioner

Citation: T.C. Memo. 1998-413
Court: United States Tax Court
State/Jurisdiction: Specialty Federal
Date of Decision: November 17, 1998
Judge: Colvin

In *Louise B. Barnes, et al. v. CIR*, T.C. Memo. 1998-413, the Tax Court considered the value of stock in two regional telephone companies for gift tax purposes. The Barnes family controlled Rock Hill Telephone Co. and its subsidiary, Home Telephone Company. Rock Hill was controlled by a voting trust holding 52% of the common stock. Rock Hill also had non-voting stock. The Barnes family had taken certain precautions so Rock Hill would remain family-owned and controlled, including the implementation of the voting trust and the purchase of insurance to pay death taxes. The Home Telephone Company was also controlled by the Barnes family and had only one type of stock. Both corporations operated in rural South Carolina, and had a policy of declaring conservative annual dividends. In 1992, small gifts of stock, representing less than 1% ownership interests, in both companies were given to family members. The stock of both corporations was appraised. Home was valued at $230 per share while Rock Hill's non-voting stock was appraised at $220 per share. The IRS disagreed with the valuations of the stocks and the case proceeded to trial. At trial, both parties presented expert witnesses as to the value of the stocks.

The taxpayers' expert valued both companies using an income and market comparable approach. He used ten guideline companies and compared them with Rock Hill and Home by various price-to-earnings, price-to-cash-flow multiples and by dividend yield. He concluded that using the actual dividends provided the best evidence of value. He adjusted his capitalization rate to include a 5.1% small stock risk premium. He applied a 45% discount for lack of marketability to Rock Hill and a 40% discount for lack of marketability to Home. He further applied a non-voting stock discount of 3.66% to Rock Hill. He determined that the fair market value of each was $220 and $230 per share respectively.

The IRS' expert valued the companies using the market and discount future cash flow approaches. The court did not permit the discounted cash flow analysis to be admitted into evidence at trial because "key data ... was not available at trial for petitioners to cross-examine." Thus, the court only considered his market analysis. He used seven comparable companies to arrive at his pre-discounted value. He applied a 5% non-voting stock discount to the pre-discounted value of Rock Hill. He further applied a 25% discount for lack of marketability to both companies. He determined that the fair market value of Rock Hill was $351 per share and Home was $375 per share.

The Tax Court determined that the taxpayers' expert provided the best evidence at trial. It accepted his appraisal almost entirely. It concluded that his reliance upon a market comparison of actual dividends was the most accurate basis because "[a] prospective minority shareholder of Home or Rock Hill stock would almost exclusively consider dividend yield rather than discounted cash-flow or income capitalization to estimate the value of stock in either of these companies because of the likelihood that he or she could only recoup his or her investment through dividends." It declined, however, to accept his application of a small stock risk premium. The court concluded that the companies were "financially sound and that investments in [the companies] were much less risky than in other comparably sized companies since the business of [the companies] is highly regulated." It also found that his assessment of a 3.66% discount for non-voting stock to be more appropriate than the IRS' 5%. It found that 3.66% was the average discount taken for non-voting stock in a study of 43 public companies with both voting and nonvoting stocks.

The court also approved of the taxpayers application of a 40% and 45% discount for lack of marketability. Both experts used restricted stock and IPO studies in determining the size of the discounts. The IRS took issue with the taxpayers' reliance on the IPO and restricted stock studies. It argued that the companies in the studies were not comparable to the subject companies in terms of marketability, size, profitability, etc. The court rejected this argument, noting that the IRS' expert failed to account for those points in his analysis. The court then reasoned that a larger discount was appropriate because (1) the family intended to remain in control of the companies, (2) the family had a history of maintaining control of the company, (3) the family had taken steps to insure that the company would remain under family control for future generations through the implementation of voting trust, the purchase of insurance and by bringing younger generations into the business, (4) the stocks were not listed on a public exchange or sold over-the-counter, and (5) the stock transferred had no aspects of control.

In rejecting the IRS' expert, the Tax Court noted that he failed to account for the difficulties in reselling a 1% interest in a closely-held company as well as its history of small dividends. The court also noted that, unlike the taxpayers' expert, this expert did not visit the businesses' locations nor did he talk with its management.

This abstract originally appeared in *Valuation Case Digest*, authored by John J. Stockdale, Jr.

Estate of Mellinger v. Commissioner

Citation: 112 T.C. 26, 112 T.C. No. 4, 1999 U.S. Tax Ct. LEXIS 4
Court: United States Tax Court
State/Jurisdiction: Specialty Federal
Date of Decision: January 26, 1999
Judge: Cohen

Decedent, the widow of Frederick N. Mellinger, held Frederick's of Hollywood stock in three capacities:

- As income beneficiary of a QTIP irrevocable marital trust established by her predeceased husband under IRC § 2056(b)(7);

- As beneficiary of a revocable trust that she established herself; and

- 50 shares outright.

Stock not aggregated for valuation

The first issue in this case is whether the stock in the irrevocable marital trust should be aggregated with the stock in the revocable trust and the stock owned outright for purposes of ascertaining the fair market value of the stock passing from decedent's estate.

Citing *Bonner v. United States*, 84 F.3d 196, 198 (5th Cir. 1996), the Tax Court found that the decedent's stock should not be aggregated. The reasoning gleaned from Bonner was that:

> The assets, although taxed as if they passed through Bonner's estate, in fact were controlled at every step by Mrs. Bonner.

25% blockage discount applied to fair market value of publicly traded stock

The second issue is the fair market value of decedent's blocks of stock, and whether a blockage discount should be applied in determining the value of decedent's stock:

> A blockage discount may be applied when the block of stock to be valued is so large that it cannot be liquidated in a reasonable time without depressing the market. Sec. 20.2031-2(e), Estate Tax Regs. The concept of blockage is essentially one of timing.

Both parties presented expert testimony to establish the blockage discount. After thoroughly reviewing the testimony and qualifications of the three experts, the court concluded that the appropriate blockage discount (also referred to as a marketability discount) should be 25%.

Estate of Nowell v. Commissioner

Citation: T.C. Memo. 1999-15
Court: United States Tax Court
State/Jurisdiction: Specialty Federal
Date of Decision: January 26, 1999
Judge: Cohen

In the *Estate of Ethel S. Nowell v. CIR*, T.C. Memo. 1999-15, the Tax Court considered whether partnership units in which the decedent held the right to receive income for life should be aggregated with partnership units decedent placed in trust for estate tax purposes. The decedent had limited partnership units placed in a revocable trust of which she was the income beneficiary for life. She also received income from additional limited partnership units because she was the beneficiary of a QTIP trust formed by her late husband. His estate claimed a marital deduction in the partnership's underlying assets. Her estate included the value of the partnership units it held under IRC sec. 2038 and the QTIP trust's partnership units under IRC sec. 2044 in the gross estate. It valued the units held by each trust separately, and included combined discounts from net assets value for marketability and lack of control ranging from 50% to 65%. On audit, the IRS disallowed the proposed discounts. It claimed that all the partnership units passing through the decedent's estate should aggregate.

The Tax Court disagreed with the IRS. It reasoned that an "analysis of section 2044 and the accompanying regulations there under does not indicate that Congress intended that property interests includible under section 2044 should be merged or aggregated with interests in the same property included in the estate pursuant to section 2038 for purposes of determining Federal estate tax value." Accordingly, the Tax Court concluded that the limited partnership units held by the decedent and the QTIP trust should be valued separately even though the value of both blocks were included in the decedent's gross estate.

The court also considered whether the units passing at death were partnership interests or assignee interests. The court noted that the estate tax is assessed on the value of the property transferred upon one's death, not the value held by either the decedent or her legatee. It further noted that state law defines the property transferred upon death. Here, the limited partnership was organized under Arizona law. The Tax Court consulted the state law and determined that an assignment of a limited partnership interest provides the assignee with the right to receive the assignor's distribution, but not the right to exercise the powers of a partner, unless the partnership agreement provides otherwise. The court then turned to the language of the partnership agreement and concluded that power over the limited partnership units could only be assigned with the consent of the general partner. The court concluded that "determination of whether ... [the assignees] will be treated as limited partners... can be made only by taking into consideration whether the remaining general partners will consent to their admission as limited partners, subjective factors that cannot be taken into consideration under the objective standard of the hypothetical seller/buyer analysis." Thus, the court concluded that the limited partnership interests must be valued as assignee interests.

This abstract originally appeared in *Valuation Case Digest*, authored by John J. Stockdale, Jr.

Estate of Foote v. Commissioner

Citation: T.C. Memo 1999-37, 1999 Tax Ct. Memo LEXIS 37
Court: United States Tax Court
State/Jurisdiction: Specialty Federal
Date of Decision: February 5, 1999
Judge: Jacobs

The issue in this estate tax matter is the appropriate blockage discount, if any, to apply in valuing decedent's shares of Applied Power stock. The parties agreed to the fair market value of the stock apart from blockage, but differed greatly in their positions regarding the blockage discount.

A blockage discount is appropriate where a block of stock could not have been sold on the valuation date (or within a reasonable period thereafter) without affecting market price.

Estate's expert relies in part on reported blockage discount cases

The estate offered the report and testimony of Robert E. Kleeman, Jr., CPA, of Clifton Gunderson, LLC, in support of its claim that a 22.5% blockage discount should be applied. Kleeman reviewed information about Applied Power that was available before the decedent's death, including the trading prices and volumes of Applied Power stock on the NYSE and the relative size of decedent's block compared to the total outstanding stock of Applied Power.

Kleeman also reviewed 18 reported Tax Court cases that involved determination of a blockage discount and were factually similar. Using the discounts awarded in those cases, Kleeman calculated a blockage discount of 22.5% to be applied to decedent's block of Applied Power stock.

IRS expert considers many factors

The IRS offered the report and testimony of Robert L. Davis, CFA, of Southwest Securities, Inc., in support of its claim that a 3.3% blockage discount was appropriate. Davis considered at least 16 factors in reaching this conclusion, including:

- Decedent's shares were only 2.2% of the total shares outstanding
- Decedents block was equal to the number of Applied Power shares traded during a 29-day period
- The trading "float" of the stock
- Dividend-paying record of company
- Current outlook for company
- The percentage of institutional ownership of stock
- Effect of trading more than 50,000 shares of stock on eight separate trading days.

Court adopts IRS experts opinion

The court concluded that Davis' report was more reliable than Kleeman's because Davis properly considered all the relevant factors. The court adopted Davis' opinion in toto.

Estate of Jameson v. Commissioner (I)

Citation: T.C. Memo 1999-43, 1999 Tax Ct. Memo LEXIS 42
Court: United States Tax Court
State/Jurisdiction: Specialty Federal
Date of Decision: February 9, 1999
Judge: Gale

The primary issue in this estate tax matter was the fair market value of decedent's 98% stock interest in Johnco, Inc., a holding company with timberland as its principal asset.

Four significant 'findings' regarding methods and discounts

The court made the following significant findings:

- The asset method is "most reasonable in a case like this one, where the corporation functions as a holding, rather than an operating, company and earnings are relatively low in comparison to the fair market value of the underlying assets."

- Where a timber company must recognize built-in capital gains under IRC § 1231, because of its IRC § 631(a) election, each time it cuts and sells timber, valuation of the company must take this built-in capital gains into account.

- A 3% marketability discount is appropriate in this case because 97% of the assets of the corporation are highly marketable and only 3% of the assets are unmarketable.

- The existence of a 2% minority shareholder does not support a "nuisance discount" because a hypothetical buyer of the 98% interest would overlook this factor in light of the desirability of the timberland owned by the company.

Lundquist v. United States

Citation: 83 AFTR2d Par. 99-568 (ND NY 1999)
Court: United States District Court
State/Jurisdiction: Eastern District of New York
Date of Decision: February 23, 1999
Judge: Kahn

In *Henry E. Lundquist v. United States of America*, 83 AFTR2d Par. 99-568 (February 23, 1999), the U.S. District Court for the Northern District of New York considered whether the safe harbor interest rate, IRC sec. 483, applied to gift tax valuations. In 1979, the decedent sold 6,894 shares of publicly traded stock to a trust for the benefit of her lineal heirs for $1,006,524 or $146 per share. The purchase price was payable quarterly over twenty years and carried 6% interest. The IRS determined that the sale was completed for less than fair market value. It valued the stock by determining the median price the stock traded on the date of the gift. It concluded that the fair market value of the stock was $147.9375 per share. It also determined that the interest rate carried by the note was below the 8.8% market rate. Thus, the IRS concluded that a taxable gift had been made. The estate paid the tax and filed this refund suit.

Before the District Court, the estate moved for summary judgment, arguing that the IRC sec. 483 safe harbor interest rate applied to gift tax valuations. It claimed that "just as the government may not apply a higher interest rate than the safe harbor rate for purposes of determining income tax, they similarly may not use a rate higher than the safe harbor rate to determine the present value of the installment payments for gift tax purposes." Following the Tenth Circuit's decision in *Schusterman v. United States*, 63 F.3d 986, 990 (10th Cir. 1995), the court rejected the estate's claim. It noted that "At issue in valuation for gift tax purposes is whether the present [value] of the whole payment is equal to the value of the equivalent portion of the consideration." The court determined that IRC sec. 483 only characterizes the payment as principal or interest, but "[t]he character of payment does not affect its value for gift tax purposes." Thus, the court granted the IRS summary judgment, denying the estate a refund.

This abstract originally appeared in *Valuation Case Digest*, authored by John J. Stockdale, Jr.

Estate of Desmond v. Commissioner

Citation: T.C. Memo 1999-76, 1999 Tax Ct. Memo LEXIS 84
Court: United States Tax Court
State/Jurisdiction: Specialty Federal
Date of Decision: March 10, 1999
Judge: Vasquez

The Tax Court considered the application of a discount for potential environmental liabilities and a control premium. On the June 17, 1992 date of death, the decedent held 136,000 of 166,000 (81.93%) shares in a paint and coatings manufacturing company. The company is a hazardous waste producer and its environmental liabilities, which were potentially large, were unknown on the valuation date.

The estate's expert valued the business using the net asset value, the discounted future cash flow, and the market comparable approach. He valued the business at $12.1 million under the net asset value approach. However, he did not consider the potential environmental liabilities when he deducted the company's liabilities from its gross asset value. He then valued the business at $8.1 million using the discounted future cash flow method. In doing so, he utilized a 19% discount rate. He lastly concluded the company was worth $10.4 million under the market comparable approach. He used two public paint and coating manufacturers as comparables. He applied a 30% discount to their market multiples to account for the difference in total sales, total assets, and total market capitalization between the public companies and the subject company. To the marketable minority value, he applied a 25% control premium. The expert then weighted the value determined under each approach equally and found that the as-if-freely-traded value of the business was $10.2 million on the valuation date.

He then determined that a 25% marketability discount should be applied to that value. He considered the following factors in determining whether to apply a discount and its size: (1) the availability of public market; (2) the company's recent financial performance; (3) the future outlook for the company and industry; (4) the company's distribution policy; (5) the restrictions on the transferability of the stock; (6) the expected holding period of the stock; (7) the cost or expectation of a public offering; (8) the number of existing shareholders; (9) the size of the interest and the control inherent in the interest; and (10) the potential environmental liabilities. He concluded that the fair market value of the stock was $46.07 per share on the alternative valuation date. The estate reported this value on its tax return.

The IRS disagreed with the size of the estate's marketability discount. Its expert's report was limited to the application and size of a marketability discount to the subject company. He was instructed to assume that the unadjusted value of the company, including environmental liabilities, was $10.2 million. The expert determined that a marketability discount was appropriate but only within the range of zero to five percent.

The case proceeded to trial before the Tax Court. The court began by calculating the unadjusted value of the company. It rejected the net asset value determined by the estate as "vague and generally unhelpful." (The court's opinion does not indicate why it reached this conclusion). It valued the business by using the estate's two other approaches, weighting them equally. The parties disagreed as to the amount of the marketability discount and control premium applied under the valuation approaches.

The IRS argued that a discount for potential environmental liabilities should not be applied to the values determined under the market and income approaches because the liabilities were considered when the comparable companies were selected. The Tax Court agreed regarding market approach. It found that "paint and finishing companies trade at lower multiples as a result of the potential environmental liabilities associates with the industry." However, it found that a discount for the environmental liabilities was appropriate under the discounted cash flow method. The discount rate was determined using the capital asset pricing model (CAPM). In doing so, the estate's expert relied on the betas (a measure of a company's market volatility) of eight public companies. The court did not receive any evidence, which indicated, "The Betas of the eight comparable paint companies were higher than normal due to potential environmental liabilities faced by these companies."

The court then considered the size of a marketability discount. It concluded that a marketability discount of 30% was appropriate. 10% of that discount was attributable to the potential environmental liabilities. In determining the discount size, the court considered the following factors: (1) There was no public market for the stock; (2) the profit margins were lower than the industry average; (3) the stock was subject to a restrictive share agreement; (4) a public offering of the stock was unlikely in the future; (5) the size of the interest is so large that it may be hard to find potential buyers in the future who could finance such a purchase; and (6) it had large potential environmental liabilities. Thus, the court applied a 30% discount for marketability to the unadjusted value determined by the income approach and applied a 20% discount for marketability to the market approach's unadjusted value.

Lastly, the court considered the application of a control premium. The parties agreed that the estate's interest was a controlling interest. However, the estate's expert only applied a control premium when determining the value under the market method. The court found that the control premium should be applied under both the income and market approaches. It found that "the income method assumed the continuation of [the company's] present policies and did not account for a change in control. This method therefore produced an unadjusted value based on a minority interest." The court then applied a 25% control premium in determining the value under the income approach. After considering the discounts and adjusting for them, the tax court concluded the decedent's interest was worth $6.6 million.

Adams v. United States (I)

Citation: 83 AFTR2d Par. 99-691 (ND TX 1999)
Court: United States District Court
State/Jurisdiction: Northern District of Texas
Date of Decision: March 17, 1999
Judge: Fitzwater

In *Patricia M. Adams, et al. v. United States of America*, 83 AFTR2d Par. 99-691 (March 17, 1999), the U.S. District Court for the Northern District of Texas considered the fair market value of an estate's 25% assignee interest in a dissolved partnership. The partnership was established by the decedent and her siblings to hold family owned assets including "ranch land, marketable securities, and oil and gas royalty and working interests." The estate reported the fair market value of decedent's 25% assignee interest as $7,480,975.43, including discounts for lack of control and lack of marketability, as well as portfolio discounts and a discount for uncertain rights and potential litigation. The IRS disagreed with the application of the discounts and adjusted the value upward to $7.6 million. The estate paid the additional tax and brought this refund suit. The parties stipulated that the net asset value of the dissolved partnership was $33,081,400. The only issue before the court pertained to the application of valuation discounts. The district court concluded that under Texas law, "a hypothetical buyer is legally entitled to receive Mendenhall's 25% share of Taylor Properties' net asset value" which was worth $8,270,350 on the June 23, 1992 date of death. It then turned to the proposed valuation decrements.

The District Court first considered the application of a minority/lack of control discount. It concluded that a "willing buyer would not decrease his offer merely because he could not actively participate or direct the partners' actions in liquidating or valuing the assets. The partners would be under a strict fiduciary duty to the assignee while performing these tasks. ... Any lack of control of the assignee is adequately offset by this fiduciary duty."

The court then considered the application of a portfolio discount. This valuation decrement accounts for the unattractive mix of assets held by an invest company. The court rejected the application of this discount. It concluded that the hypothetical buyer of the assignee interest was not purchasing an interest in an investment company, but purchasing the right to receive 25% of the investment company's net asset value.

The court also considered the application of a lack of marketability discount. The court again declined to apply the proposed discount. It reasoned that any defects in the underlying assets had already been considered in the determination of the fair market value of the underlying assets.

The court also declined to apply a discount for any uncertain rights or potential litigation associated with the assignee interest. The court found that Texas law and the partnership agreement clearly explained the rights of and the fiduciary duties owed to the assignee. Thus, "the court finds that there is not a palpable potential for litigation."

The court lastly considered reducing the net asset value for potential selling costs. The court concluded, "Because the net asset value would include a charge to repay the cost of selling the partnership's assets, a buyer would decrease his offering price accordingly." The court then determined that a 5.4% discount was appropriate to compensate for the selling costs. After reducing the amount of the selling costs, the court concluded that the 25% assignee interest was worth $7.82 million. Since the value of the interest as calculated by the court is greater than the value stipulated to by the parties, the court denied the estate the refund.

This abstract originally appeared in *Valuation Case Digest*, authored by John J. Stockdale, Jr.

Estate of Simplot v. Commissioner (I)

Citation: 112 T.C. 130, 112 T.C. No. 13, 1999 U.S. Tax Ct. LEXIS 15
Court: United States Tax Court
State/Jurisdiction: Specialty Federal
Date of Decision: March 22, 1999
Judge: Jacobs

If you had the opportunity and capacity to invest $3.9 million in a minority interest in a business that was reasonably likely to sell or merge—you might. But, you might not if your $3.9 million investment in this minority interest would result in a loss of about $3.8 million-or almost your entire investment-if the sale actually occurred. That's what a hypothetical willing buyer would be faced with based on the court's conclusion in *Estate of Richard R. Simplot v. Commissioner*, 112 T.C. No. 13, 1999 WL 152610, filed March 22, 1999.

And that's not the only interesting aspect to this case. The experts had widely disparate conclusions. The appraisers for the IRS advanced what I believe to be flawed logic, which the court accepted.

Richard R. Simplot died on June 24, 1993. His estate held, among other assets, a 23.55% minority interest of the voting class and a 2.79% minority interest of the nonvoting class of the common stock of J.R. Simplot Company.

The estate return was filed based on an appraisal by Morgan Stanley & Co., which failed to deduct treasury shares in the per-share calculation. Prior to trial, this error was corrected. The IRS determined a deficiency of $17.6 million in estate tax and assessed $7.1 million in penalties.

The company had sales of $1.8 billion and reported net income of $37.8 million for its fiscal year ending Aug. 31, 1993. The company, with diversified operations, was one of the two largest potato processors in the world, and was the major supplier of frozen french fried potatoes to McDonald's Corporation.

In addition to its operations, it owned 5.3 million shares of common stock of Micron Technology, Inc., a publicly traded manufacturer and marketer of semiconductor memory components and personal computers. With a mean price on the date of death of $34.63 per share, the market value of the Micron stock was $182.1 million. The basis in the Micron shares was not disclosed but by inference was about $13 million, suggesting an imbedded capital gain of some $169 million.

The voting shares were owned by the decedent and his three siblings. The largest block of Class A voting stock was a 29.4% block, and the other two were 23.6% like blocks owned by the estate. The capital structure, based on a prior recapitalization, reflected one share of voting stock per 1,848 shares of nonvoting stock, which the court noted as unusual.

Four major issues relating to valuation

There were four major valuation issues in this case.

(1) What is the marketable minority interest value of the company?

(2) What premium, if any, is applicable to a minority interest of the Class A voting stock?

(3) What are the appropriate marketability discounts applicable to the Class A voting and the Class B nonvoting shares?

(4) What is the appropriate consideration of the imbedded tax liability pertaining to the Micron Technology stock held by J.R. Simplot company?

Marketable minority value

Paul Much developed his valuation at the marketable minority interest level through a combination of the guideline company method on a total invested capital basis applied to major components of the company, and a debt-free discounted cash flow method applied similarly to the two major groups of the business. Herbert Spiro used a debt-free net cash flow method and a guideline company (net equity) method. The primary difference in conclusions related to Much's use of a seasonally high debt figure in his calculation.

The court made adjustments to Much's debt figure and reconciled his result with Spiro's, using $720 million as the value of the companys equity on an operating basis.

Court accepts capital gain deduction

Both Much and Spiro treated the Micron stock as a non-operating asset and deducted the estimated cost of a secondary offering of the stock in their appraisals. Both appraisers deducted the full amount of the imbedded capital gain tax on the Micron stock. Much then applied a 6%

minority interest discount. The court accepted the reduction of value for imbedded gains, but did not agree with Much's minority interest discount.

The court concluded that the fair market value of the Company's equity on a marketable minority interest basis was Spiro's $830 million figure ($720 million operating value plus $110 million for Micron stock).

Without discussion, the court accepted the advice of both appraisers that the full amount of the imbedded capital gains tax liability was an appropriate deduction from value in this case!

Voting premium for Class A stock

Much examined 14 transactions involving the sale, merger or acquisition of public companies with dual classes of stock. In addition, he examined companies with dual classes of shares (voting and nonvoting) trading publicly at the same time. Based on his analysis, he concluded that there should be no premium for the voting characteristics of the subject minority interest of the Class A shares of the company. Much testified that he would not "quibble" with a 5% differential between the two classes on a per share basis. His testimony was supported by that of John Ettelson, who suggested that the typical range of differentials between publicly trading voting and nonvoting shares is on the order of 3% to 7%, possibly somewhat higher.

Spiro analyzed available (unnamed) studies and suggested using an aggregate voting premium, which spread 10% of the value of the enterprise ($83 million) across the 76.445 Class A voting shares (1/20th of 1%) pro rata. Gilbert Matthews' testimony supported the concept of a similarly "aggregate" premium. Matthews suggested a range of aggregate premiums from 3% to 7%.

Courts determination of minority values

The court basically dismissed Much's analysis regarding the voting class differential and valued the Class A and Class B blocks held by the estate and used a modification of the Spiro/Matthews' analysis.

The court began with Spiro's $830 million marketable minority value of the company, or $5,871 per share (which represented about 170% of book value and a price/earnings multiple of about 22x). Referring to Matthews, the court applied a 3% aggregate voting premium. The effect of spreading this 3% of entity value aggregate premium ($24.9 million) across only 76.445 shares yielded, after a 35% marketability discount, a value for the Class A shares of $215,539 per share (which is about 62x book value and represents a price/earnings multiple of some 806x the net earnings of the company).

Spiro valued the Class B nonvoting shares at $3,523 per share, while Much reached a conclusion of $2,964 per share. The Court's methodology yielded a conclusion of $3,417 per share. The difference in the valuations of the Class B nonvoting shares is far more consistent with what is normally seen between appraisers than the Class A voting differential.

The marketability discount

The experts applied very similar marketability discounts. There was no specific reference to the evidence presented, but all the marketability discounts advanced by the experts were either 35% or 40%. The court agreed with the 35% marketability discount suggested by Spiro and Much for the Class A voting shares and with the 40% marketability discount suggested by Spiro for the Class B shares. This major discount, which is often the source of considerable debate, was resolved by the court almost without comment based on the evidence presented by the experts.

Estate of Kaufman v. Commissioner (I)

Citation: T.C. Memo 1999-119, 1999 Tax Ct. Memo LEXIS 134
Court: United States Tax Court
State/Jurisdiction: Specialty Federal
Date of Decision: April 6, 1999
Judge: Laro

Alice Friedlander Kaufman owned approximately 20% of the stock of Seminole Manufacturing Co. when she died. Her estate filed an estate tax return in which it valued the stock at $29.77 per share. This value was based upon sales of Seminole stock that occurred two months after the valuation date, and upon a Merrill Lynch appraisal as of a date several months before the valuation date.

The IRS determined a tax deficiency based upon its estimate that the fair market value of the stock was $70.79. Petitioners filed a Petition in the Tax Court for a redetermination of their tax. Before trial on the matter, the IRS made certain concessions in its brief and re-estimated that the fair market value of the stock was $56.50.

Prior sales not arm's length transactions

The best indication of fair market value of stock is arm's length sales of other stock of the company on or near the valuation date. In this case, petitioners argued that the two sales that occurred two months after the valuation date, in which 3.25% and 4.67% blocks of stock were sold for $29.77 per share, were the best evidence of value. The court "disagree[d] with petitioners that either sale [was] indicative of the value of the estate's stock."

First, the blocks were not sufficiently similar to the estate's block because they were much smaller.

Second, neither seller was reasonably informed regarding the value of their stock at the time of the sale. Both took the offer made to them by another stockholder because it sounded like a good amount of money. Their testimony revealed "that they were not knowledgeable sellers who aimed to realize the fair market value of their stock."

IRS expert's valuation outdated so not admitted

The IRS presented the expert testimony and valuation report of William K. Fowler, A.M., and employee of the Internal Revenue Service. The court expressed some concern that Fowler might be biased because of his employment relationship with the IRS. The court did not admit the valuation report of Fowler for another reason, however. The valuation date stated in the report was Dec. 8, 1993, which was four months prior to the applicable valuation date. The court found that his report was irrelevant because the valuation date was too far removed.

Taxpayer's experts valuation seriously flawed

The petitioners presented the expert testimony and valuation report of Bret Tack, ASA, of Houlihan Valuation Advisors. The court admitted Tack's report, but then found it to be significantly flawed and unpersuasive. The flaws, which are thoroughly discussed in the Tax Court Memorandum, were that Tack:

- Did not sufficiently explain why the comparative companies he used for his analysis were comparable, and why others that appeared comparable were not used. "A proper valuation report must contain enough data on each similar corporation to allow the Court to make an informed, independent decision as to whether the corporations are sufficiently similar to the subject corporation to perform a proper valuation analysis."

- Did not analyze all three valuation methods. "Valuation experts must thoroughly analyze all applicable methods of valuation, and they may not simply assert without sufficient explanation that they have concluded that a particular method is irrelevant."

- Relied upon faulty assumptions regarding the equivalent value of different share blocks.

- Assumed that there was no market for the estate's stock, when several factors cited by the court indicated that there was a market for the stock.

- Did not address the nature of the two classes of stock issued by the corporation, whether they had cumulative voting rights, or what differences existed between the two classes of stock.

Case determined based on burden of proof

Having failed to admit the report of the IRS expert and then rejecting the report of the petitioners expert as unpersuasive, the Tax Court resolved the case based upon the burden of proof.

[W]e would typically proceed to value the estate's shares on the basis of the record at hand. In the typical case, we find much information and data on the subject corporation, as well as financial studies and data which allow us to compute value and marketability discounts using the *Mandelbaum* and other factors mentioned above. The instant case, however, is atypical. Petitioners, in short, ask us to close our eyes to the inadequate record and adopt without adequate verification Mr. Tack's conclusion and the managerial representations upon which he relied. We decline to do so. Valuation cases require that we determine a value based on the evidence at hand. Whereas we may determine a value with the assistance of experts, if we consider it helpful, we will not accept an experts conclusion when it is unsupported by the record. The record must be built by the parties to include all data that is necessary to determine the value of property in dispute. Valuation experts must perform unbiased and thorough analyses upon which we may rely. Where, as is the case here, the record falls short of the standard which we require, we are left to decide the case against the party who has the burden of proof. Because petitioners bear the burden here, we sustain respondents determination, as modified by concessions in brief. We hold that the fair market value of the estate's stock was $56.50 per share on the applicable valuation date.

Estate of Ferguson v. Commissioner

Citation: 174 F.3d 997 (9th Cir. 1999)
Court: United States Court of Appeals
State/Jurisdiction: 9th Circuit Federal
Date of Decision: April 7, 1999
Judge: Choy

In *Michael Ferguson, et al. v. CIR*, 174 F.3d 997 (9th Cir. 1999), the U.S. Court of Appeals for the Ninth Circuit considered whether the Fergusons could be taxed on the gain in appreciated stock that was transferred to qualified charitable organizations. The Fergusons were officers and directors of AHC, a company that marketed weight loss and dietary supplements and services. The Fergusons collectively held 18% of AHC's stock.

After seeking a merger partner, AHC received a tender offer from DC Acquisitions (DC). DC Acquisitions was a wholly owned subsidiary of CDI. CDI had only one shareholder and director. It offered to purchase AHC for $22.50 per share. (This was a 1084% premium over AHC's tangible book value as of July 22, 1988). Under the terms of the tender offer, if successful, AHC would become a subsidiary of CDI. DC conditioned its tender offer on the receipt of 85% of AHC's outstanding shares in order to effect a short-form merger. However, DC had the option to go forward with the merger if less than 85% of the outstanding shares were received. The Fergusons were offered positions with the new company as well as places on its board of directors, and accepted the proposed positions. Moreover, they were offered the opportunity to exchange their AHC stock for CDI stock. The tender offer began in August of 1988 and closed on September 9, 1988.

During August of 1988, the Fergusons contacted Merrill Lynch and began the process of donating stock to three qualified charitable organizations. The organizations received the stock on September 9, 1988, and tendered it to DC. The Fergusons did not claim any gain on the stock donated to the organizations. The IRS disagreed and found them liable for the gain on the appreciated stock. It relied upon the anticipatory assignment of income doctrine. This doctrine holds that "once a right to receive income has 'ripened' for tax purposes, the taxpayer who earned or otherwise created that right, will be taxed on any gain realized from it, notwithstanding the fact that the taxpayer has transferred the right before actually receiving the income." The case proceeded to trial before the Tax Court.

The Tax Court ruled in favor of the IRS. It concluded that after August 31, 1988, the date when more than 50% of AHC's stock had been tendered to DC, the merger would be successfully completed "and that all AHC stock, even untendered, either already had been converted into cash (via the tender offer) or imminently would be converted into cash (via the merger)." The Fergusons appealed.

On appeal, they argued that the stock had not appreciated into a right to receive cash because (1) AHC's shareholders had not voted to approve the merger by August 31, 1988, and (2) the Fergusons and the charities had not tendered their shares on that date and the tender offer requirements were not met on that date. The court rejected the Ferguson's arguments. It found that while a shareholders' vote approving of the merger is sufficient to show that the stock had ripened, such a vote is not requirement for ripening. It also stated that although the tender offer requirements were not met, DC had received assurances from the Fergusons of their continued involvement in AHC after the merger, and had received enough stock to single-handedly ratify the merger if a long form merger were required. Thus, the Ninth Circuit affirmed the Tax Court's decision, finding the Fergusons liable for the gain on their AHC stock under the anticipatory assignment of income doctrine.

This abstract originally appeared in *Valuation Case Digest*, authored by John J. Stockdale, Jr.

Estate of Rodgers v. Commissioner

Citation: T.C. Memo 1999-129, 1999 Tax Ct. Memo LEXIS 179
Court: United States Tax Court
State/Jurisdiction: Specialty Federal
Date of Decision: April 20, 1999
Judge: Chiechi

The issue in this estate tax matter is the valuation of decedent's 166 2/3 shares of stock representing one-third of the total of Marrero Land, a real estate operating company that engages in "the business of acquiring, developing, managing, improving, maintaining, leasing, and selling real estate." Most of the facts in the case were stipulated, and the Tax Court made factual findings in accordance with the stipulation.

As part of the stipulation of facts, the parties agreed that:

- The aggregate fair market value of Marrero Land's assets, excluding the remaining unimproved real properties, was $50,643,118;
- The aggregate liabilities of Marrero Land as of the valuation date totaled $15,943,694; and
- The aggregate value of the remaining unimproved real properties of Marrero Land, without regard to an absorption discount, was $20,366,470.

The two main issues before the court were:

- Whether an absorption discount should be applied to determine the fair market value of Marrero Land's unimproved real property, before calculating the fair market value of the stock under the net asset approach, and
- Whether a buy-sell agreement should determine the value of decedent's stock.

Small absorption discount appropriate due to market conditions

Petitioner argued that an absorption discount was required to arrive at the fair market value using the net asset method. Respondent argued that "an absorption discount may never be allowed in determining the value of real estate owned by a corporation (or other entity) for estate tax purposes," a matter of law. Respondent relied on *Estate of Andrews v. Commissioner*, 79 T.C. 938 (1982), in support of its argument.

The Tax Court reviewed its findings in *Estate of Andrews*, and found that it did not support respondent's argument. That case was decided on its facts, the most relevant of which was that the possibility of the company liquidating its real estate holdings in the near future was merely speculative. In this case, the Tax Court affirmed the proposition that:

> In determining the fair market value of property includible in decedent's estate, the appropriate inquiry is a factual one: What would a hypothetical willing seller and a hypothetical willing buyer take into account in arriving at a price for the remaining unimproved properties?

To determine whether an absorption discount should be applied in this case, and if so, how much it should be, the Tax Court considered the testimony of the parties' real estate valuation experts, Patrick J. Egan, for petitioner, and Fredrick M. Guice, Sr., for respondent. Egan testified that, based upon his discounted cash flow calculations, and absorption discount of $12,339,871 should be applied. Guice testified that, although the value of the properties was negatively impacted by the relevant market conditions, no absorption discount should be applied.

The Court discussed the valuation reports and testimony of these experts in detail, agreeing with some aspects and criticizing others. Ultimately, the Court determined that an absorption discount of $1.7 million should be applied to the stipulated value of $20,366,470.

Court fails to reach issue of whether buy-sell agreement controls

Pursuant to a buy-sell agreement entered into by the shareholders of the corporation, if a shareholder wished to sell his stock, he had to first offer it to the other shareholders. The price of the stock in any resulting transaction was the book value of the stock. Under a later amendment, transfers of stock following the death of a shareholder were subject to these provisions. The estate argued that the buy-sell agreement price provision should control the fair market value of the stock for estate tax purposes.

Before considering whether the buy-sell agreement should control the maximum value of the stock, the Tax Court thoroughly reviewed the valuation reports and testimony of the business valuation experts: Charles H. Stryker, and David Chaffe III, for petitioner, and Philip W Moore. for respondent. The Court concluded that:

> On the record before us, we are satisfied with the respective valuation analyses of Mr. Stryker and Mr. Chaffe in determining the fair market value of decedent's interest in Marrero Land on the valuation date. However, each of those respective analyses must incorporate our finding as to the aggregate fair market value on that date of the remaining unimproved real properties of Marrero Land. We have incorporated that finding into the respective valuation analyses of Mr. Chaffe and Mr. Stryker, which results in a fair market value on the valuation date of decedent's interest in Marrero Land of $4,611,417 under Mr. Stryker's analysis and $4,000,328 under Mr. Chaffe's analysis. On the instant record, we find that those values set the appropriate range from which we may determine the fair market value of that interest on that date.
>
> Based on our examination of the entire record in this case, and bearing in mind that valuation is necessarily an approximation and a matter of judgment, rather than of mathematics, see *Estate of Davis v. Commissioner*, 110 T.C. at 560, on which the estate has the burden of proof, *see Rule 142(a)*, we find that on the valuation date the fair market value of decedent's interest in Marrero Land is its book value, i.e., $4,316,920.

However, even though the Court found that the value of the stock was book value as provided for in the buy-sell agreement, it expressly declined in footnote 23 to decide whether the buy-sell agreement controlled:

> Because the fair market value of decedent's interest in Marrero Land on the valuation date that we have found does not exceed the book value of that interest (i.e., $4,316,920) determined under amended article VI, we shall not address the estate's alternative position that, because amended article VI controls the fair market value

for estate tax purposes, the maximum fair market value of that interest on that date is its book value.

What is an Absorption Discount?

"The concept of an absorption discount with respect to real estate derives from the concept of a blockage discount with respect to stock. According to the concept of a blockage discount with respect to stock, a block of stock may be so large in relation to the actual sales on the existing market that it could not be liquidated within a reasonable period of time without depressing the market. *See, e.g., Phipps v. Commissioner*, 127 F.2d 214, 216-217 (10th Cir.1942), affg. 43 B.T.A. 1010 (1941); *Page v. Howell*, 116 F.2d 158 (5th Cir.1940); *Estate of Damon v. Commissioner*, 49 T.C. 108, 117 (1967); sec. 20.2031-2(e), Estate Tax Regs. In the case of real estate, the principle of supply and demand may warrant application of an absorption discount. That is because the disposition within a reasonable period of time of similar real properties would result in those properties being in direct competition with each other and other similar real properties in the marketplace. Such an abrupt increase in supply would depress the price for which those properties would sell, assuming that demand were to remain constant."

Rakow v. Commissioner

Citation: T.C. Memo 1999-177, 1999 Tax Ct. Memo LEXIS 214
Court: United States Tax Court
State/Jurisdiction: Specialty Federal
Date of Decision: May 27, 1999
Judge: Gale

In *May T. Rakow v. CIR,* T.C. Memo. 1999177, the Tax Court considered the value of stock Rakow gifted to her progeny. The Rakow family owned all of the stock in a closely held construction company. For the past fifty years, the company engaged in the construction of industrial and commercial buildings, sewer and water treatment plants, as well as underground utilities. In the five years prior to the gift, the company received at least 33% of its revenue from two major clients. The estate valued all the outstanding stock of the company (6,340 shares) on a minority basis as of the October 1, 1992 valuation date. It reported that the stock had a per share value of $354.89 per share. The IRS concluded that the stock was worth $606.65 per share on the valuation date. The case proceeded to trial before the Tax Court. Both parties presented expert valuation testimony to the court.

Rakow's expert valued the stock using two approaches to conclude that the stock was worth $340.93 per share. He first valued the company using the net asset value approach. He received the assets' values (valued on a quick sale basis) from the corporation's CFO. The net asset value was adjusted for depreciation, bad debt and taxes. He did not consider a value for any goodwill in the company under this approach. The tax court rejected this valuation. It concluded that expert relied improperly upon the representations and quick sale values provided by the company's management "rather than on independent appraisals of value in an orderly disposition or as part of a going concern."

Rakow's expert also valued the company using the capitalization of earnings approach. He began by adjusting the corporation's past five years earnings for officers' compensation. He then determined the capitalization rate using three methods: the market comparable method, the build-up method, and based on comparable transactions involving his firm. Using fourteen comparable companies and adjusting their median 1992 P/E ratios for various factors including market and product diversification, future earnings prospects and control among others, he determined that the appropriate P/E ratio was between three and five. Using the build-up method, the expert determined that the appropriate pretax earnings multiple was 3.2. He began his build-up method with the risk-free rate of return on long-term treasury bonds. He then applied a small stock risk premium and a 5% premium for other risks. He also determined a P/E ratio between three and five was appropriate based on his firm's experience with transactions occurring in this industry. He decided upon a P/E ratio of four and concluded that the company was worth $3.1 million on a majority basis. To that value he applied a 30% minority discount. In determining the minority discount size, this expert consulted the *Mergerstat Review* and *Houlihan Lokey Howard & Zukin Control Premium Study*. The tax court rejected the valuation under this approach as well. It concluded that the expert's use of median 1992 P/E ratio was "flawed in that it [did] not focus on the period of time close to the valuation date." The court also criticized the capitalization rate determined under the build-up method. It found the application of a 5% discount for other factors redundant in that many of those factors were accounted for in the small stock risk premium.

The IRS' expert valued the company at $606.65 per share. He averaged the values determined under the market comparable approach and the discounted future cash flow approach less a 23% marketability discount to determine his per share value. He used nine comparable companies and adjusted their earnings ratios for size. He selected the companies based on SIC, products, markets, growth prospects, and risks. To the marketable minority value, he applied a 30% control premium and a 25% marketability discount. The court determined that the adjustments the expert made in an effort to account for the company's size and certain Generally Accepted Accounting Principles used in public company financial reports were somewhat arbitrary. Thus, it found that this method was more prone to error.

The IRS' expert calculated his discounted future cash flow analysis using the company's financial history and future projections. He concluded that a 13% discount rate was appropriate using the weighted average cost of capital. He assumed the capital structure of the company would be 80% equity, based on companies with the same primary SIC (1541/1542 - general commercial contractors).

The IRS argued that this method, "or any method based on a projection of future earnings, is not feasible in the construction industry because of risks inherent in the business, such as poor estimates, delays, litigation over accidents, defects, and nonperformance, and cyclical demand."

The Tax Court disagreed. It found that earnings were an acceptable basis for valuation of this company especially in light of its history of sustained growth. The court did, however, increase the amount of assumed direct costs to bring them in line with the company's and the industry's historical results. It recalculated the value of the company under this method to be $3.8 million. The court then applied a 31% minority interest discount to arrive at a $413.59 per share value. The court calculated the minority discount by considering the inverse control premium for construction companies, based on the testimony from the IRS' expert.

This abstract originally appeared in *Valuation Case Digest*, authored by John J. Stockdale, Jr.

Estate of Cartwright v. Commissioner (II)

Citation: 183 F.3d 1034, 1999 U.S. App. LEXIS 15220
Court: United States Court of Appeals
State/Jurisdiction: 9th Circuit Federal
Date of Decision: July 12, 1999
Judge: Silverman

Robert Cartwright was the majority shareholder, primary rainmaker, and driving force behind the law firm of Cartwright, Slobodin, Bokelman, Borowsky, Wartnick, Moore & Harris, Inc. ("CSB"). When he died, the firm paid his estate the sum of $5,062,029, which the firm had received as proceeds of life insurance on Cartwright, pursuant to a sharholders' agreement.

The firm filed a Form 1099-MISC indicating that $4,080,256 had been paid to Cartwright's estate as "non-employee compensation." On the estate tax return, Cartwright's estate took the position that the entire $5,062,029 was paid to redeem Cartwright's stock in the firm. "The IRS disagreed, finding that $4,080,256 of the $5,062,029 was compensation and that the estate owed $1,142,472 for its tax deficiency."

The estate appealed the notice of deficiency. Two issues were before the Tax Court:

1. "Whether the payment to Cartwright's estate was made solely to redeem Cartwright's stock or whether it was for both Cartwright's stock and his claim to the firm's cases or work in process."

2. The value of Cartwright's stock, including whether the firms work in process and the insurance proceeds should be considered as assets of the firm for purposes of calculating that value.

The answer to the first issue depended upon an interpretation of the shareholders agreement, which provided that the proceeds from Cartwright's life insurance:

> [W]ill be exclusively used to purchase and acquire from the estate and heirs of Robert E. Cartwright all of Mr. Cartwright's stock in the Corporation together with any claim to any cases or work in process that may otherwise be made on behalf of Robert E. Cartwright.

The Tax Court found that pursuant to the "unambiguous" language of this agreement, the proceeds were for both the stock and the work in process. The Court of Appeals affirmed this finding.

The Tax Court valued Cartwright's stock at $1,105,762, and held that the remaining payment to his estate "was taxable as income in respect of a decedent." In valuing the stock, the Tax Court did not consider either the insurance proceeds or the firms work in process as assets of the firm, upon which petitioners expert, Alan Johnson of Johnson-Hershey, made his valuation. It based the valuation on the findings of the IRS expert witness, Herbert Spiro of the American Valuation Group.

Reviewing the valuation for clear error, the Court of Appeals held that the Tax Court had erred in not including the firms work in process as an asset of the firm, "since it would have influenced what a willing buyer would have paid for CSB stock." However, the Court of Appeals agreed with the Tax Court that the insurance proceeds should not have been considered an asset of the firm because it "would not necessarily affect what a willing buyer would pay for the firms stock because it was offset dollar-for-dollar by CSBs obligation to pay out the entirety of the policy benefits to Cartwright's estate."

Accordingly, the Court of Appeals remanded the case for a redetermination of the value of the stock.

Court of Appeals Judge Thomas dissented from the portion of the majority opinion holding that the insurance proceeds were for stock and work in process, stating the following:

> However, a close analysis of the record can only lead to one conclusion: the $5 million paid to Cartwright's estate was compensation solely for his stock in the firm. Under the shareholders agreement, the life insurance proceeds were to be paid to Cartwright's estate for the value of his stock and any claims he had to the firms work in process. At the time of his death, Cartwright had no legal claim to the law firms work in process apart from his shareholder interest. Thus, the entire amount should have been allocated to stock value.

Estate of Branson v. Commissioner (I)

Citation: T.C. Memo 1999-231, 1999 Tax Ct. Memo LEXIS 267
Court: United States Tax Court
State/Jurisdiction: Specialty Federal
Date of Decision: July 13, 1999
Judge: Parr

The primary issue in this estate tax matter is the fair market value of 12,889 shares of Savings Bank of Mendocino County (Savings) stock, and 500 shares of Bank of Willits (Willits) stock, owned by decedent on the date of his death.

Both parties presented expert witness reports and testimony in support of their respective positions, which the Tax Court thoroughly reviewed in its Memorandum Findings of Fact and Opinion. The valuation analyses of the experts with respect to the Savings stock are summarized in Table 1.

TABLE 1: SAVINGS BANK OF MENDOCINO COUNTY VALUATION ANALYSES					
Expert/Court	Method	Per share value	Discount	Per share value	Fair market value
Gasiorowski	Market	$295	55% combined marketability & blockage	$310 weighted average before discount	$170 per share
	Income	$350	55%		
Spiro	Market	$359	20% liquidity*	$295	$293 per share weighted average
	Piece-meal sales	$308	None	$308	
	Income	$331	20% liquidity	$366	
Tax Court	Actual sales 10 months after death	$307	10% blockage	$276	$276

*The court noted that Spiro's liquidity discount was indistinguishable from a marketability discount.

This abstract discusses only the Court's treatment of the Savings stock since the treatment of the Willits stock is very similar.

Court rejects restricted stock and IPO study evidence

The Tax Court accepted certain portions of both expert's analyses, and rejected other portions. Most notably, the Court found that:

> Gasiorowski's [and Spiro's] reliance on the restricted stock studies for the size of the discount factor to be misplaced, since the studies analyzed only restricted stock that had a holding period of 2 years. The Savings shares were not restricted either by law or by agreement. The fact that Savings maintained a waiting list of willing buyers is evidence that the stock's history of low trading volume is due to the shareholder's preference to hold Savings shares for investment, rather than sale.

The Court similarly rejected both experts' reliance on the IPO studies because the market changes evident in those studies did not also exist with respect to the Savings stock.

Assumptions underlying piecemeal sales method faulty

The Court also rejected completely Spiro's use of the piecemeal sales method because many of the assumptions underlying his calculations under this method were faulty. As part of this method, Spiro assumed the seller could obtain a loan of 100% of the stock's value with only the stock pledged as collateral. The Court found that a lender would not make a loan on these terms at the rate opined by Spiro, but that the lending rate would depend upon the creditworthiness of the particular borrower. Accordingly, "Spiro calculated the value of the stock to a particular borrower, not the fair market value of the shares."

Petitioner may deduct expenses of defending position

An additional issue addressed by the court was whether the petitioner could deduct expenses for attorney fees, accountant fees, and appraiser fees incurred in defending its position from the value of the gross estate. The Court found that the answer to this issue depended upon whether "they are allowable by the law of the jurisdiction under which the estate is being administered."

In this case, California law allows the personal representative of the estate to pay these expenses from the estate unless they are incurred solely for the benefit of an individual heir. Since petitioner in this case incurred these expenses to defend against respondent's claim for deficiency, they are deductible from the value of the gross estate.

Estate of Magnin v. Commissioner (II)

Citation: T.C. Memo 1999-231, 1999 Tax Ct. Memo LEXIS 267
Court: United States Court of Appeals
State/Jurisdiction: 9th Circuit Federal
Date of Decision: July 13, 1999
Judge: Schroeder

The Ninth Circuit Court of Appeals considered the proper interpretation of the phrase "adequate and full consideration" in sec. 2036 of the estate tax code. This section pulls back to the decedent's estate the full value of property transferred during the decedent's life for which the decedent retained a life interest unless the decedent received full and adequate consideration by trust or otherwise. Here, the decedent and his father held stock in a chain of clothing stores. The decedent held 33.73% and his father held 28.26%. In 1951, they entered an agreement whereby the decedent would will his stock in trust for the benefit of his children in exchange for a life interest in his father's stock after his father's death. The decedent's father died in 1953. The decedent died in 1988. The IRS determined that the decedent did not receive adequate and full consideration for the transfer of his stock to the trust, and included its full fee-simple value in the decedent's gross estate. The estate disagreed. It claimed that the decedent received adequate and full consideration for the remainder interest he transferred to the trust. The case proceeded to trial before the Tax Court.

The Tax Court determined that the agreement the decedent and his father reached was made at arms-length. However for the purposes of the estate tax, "a finding of an arm's length transaction does not per se establish that the transfer was for 'adequate and full consideration.'" Thus, the court considered the parties' positions. It agreed with the IRS that adequate and full consideration under IRC sec. 2036 "equaled the fee-simple value of the property transferred into the trust." It additionally found that the decedent had not received adequate and full consideration for the property he transferred to the trust even if it were just the remainder interest. The estate appealed.

On appeal, the estate argued that the Tax Court misinterpreted the "adequate and full consideration" clause in IRC sec. 2036. The Ninth Circuit agreed and reversed the Tax Court. It determined that "'adequate and full consideration' is measured against the actuarial value of the remainder interest rather than the fee-simple value of the property transferred to the trust." In reaching this interpretation, the Ninth Circuit relied upon the definition of "adequate and full consideration" under the gift tax, IRC sec. 2512, which defines the consideration as equal to the value of the remainder interest. Furthermore, the Ninth Circuit found that to define the adequate and full consideration as the full fee-simple value of the transferred property would render the exception meaningless since "[n]o rational person would ever purchase a remainder interest for the price of the full fee-simple interest in the same property." The court then remanded the case back to the tax court. It noted that while the tax court found that the value of the remainder interest exceeded the value of the consideration, it failed to set forth its reasoning. The Ninth Circuit stated "the Tax Court should have determined the actual disparity between the values of the transferred remainder and the life estate ... [the decedent] received."

This abstract originally appeared in *Valuation Case Digest*, authored by John J. Stockdale, Jr.

Gross v. Commissioner (I)

Citation: T.C. Memo 1999-254, 1999 Tax Ct. Memo LEXIS 290
Court: United States Tax Court
State/Jurisdiction: Specialty Federal
Date of Decision: July 29, 1999
Judge: Halpern

Petitioners in this case were gifted a total of 373.5 shares of common stock out of 19,680 outstanding shares in G&J Pepsi-Cola Bottlers, Inc. (an S corporation) from their parents, and each filed a Form 709 (United States Gift and Generation Skipping Transfer Tax Return) in a timely manner. Relying upon a business valuation report prepared by David O. McCoy of Business Valuations, Inc., the petitioners reported the value of the stock as $5,680 per share as of July 31, 1992.

Respondent determined gift tax deficiencies, claiming that the value of the stock was $11,738 per share (then subsequently conceded the value to be no more than $10,910). Petitioners sought review by the Tax Court, which found that the value of the stock was $10,910 per share.

Petitioner called two experts, McCoy and Charles Wilhoite of Willamette Management Associates, and respondent called one expert, Mukesh Bajaj of LECG, Inc.

Experts disagree on three issues

There were three areas of disagreement between the parties and experts:

1. Whether it was appropriate to tax affect G&J's earnings in determining the share value using the discounted cash flow method,

2. The lack-of-marketability discount to be applied, and

3. G&J's cost of equity.

The court outlines the valuation conclusions and testimony of the two primary witnesses, McCoy and Bajaj, as well as the testimony of Wilhoite on the "tax affecting" issue.

Expected cash flow need not be tax affected

Petitioners argued that respondent and the court must tax affect G&J's earnings because two internal IRS documents, "A Valuation Guide for Income, Estate, and Gift Taxes" and "An Examination Technique Handbook for Estate Tax Examiners," required this adjustment. After quoting the relevant portions of these documents, the court found that neither required tax affecting as an adjustment in the discounted cash flow analysis of an S corporation.

McCoy applied a 40% corporate income tax rate to "tax affect" G&J's projected earnings. He opined that this adjustment was necessary to address the following concerns:

- The possibility that, if an S corporation distributes less than all of its income, the actual distributions might be insufficient to cover the shareholders' tax obligations,
- The risk that an S corporation might lose its favorable S corporation status, and
- The great disadvantage in raising capital due to the restrictions of ownership necessary to qualify for the S corporation election.

The court rejected each of these concerns:

- Tax affecting G&J's earnings is not an appropriate means of offsetting this possibility. Also, there is no basis for the assumption that insufficient distributions would be made because G&J had always distributed almost all of its income to shareholders.
- Tax affecting G&J's earnings is not appropriate "without facts or circumstances sufficient to establish the likelihood that the election would be lost."
- "This concern is more appropriately addressed in determining an appropriate cost of capital" and does not justify tax affecting G&J's earnings.

Wilhoite also testified in support of tax affecting G&J's earnings, but the court said that it was unclear whether Wilhoite's argument was that the avoided C corporation tax must be adjusted for in the calculations or that the shareholder level tax must be adjusted for, and it did not find his argument persuasive.

Bajaj, on the other hand, applied a 0% corporate income tax rate in conducting his discounted cash flow analysis. He based this rate on the assumption, based on information from management of G&J, that G&J would remain an S corporation and would continue to distribute virtually all of its income to shareholders. The court accepted Bajaj's testimony that no tax affecting was necessary in this case.

Marketability discount applied

McCoy applied a 35% marketability discount based in part on his examination of several studies of closely held and restricted securities, which yielded an average marketability discount of 30%. He coupled this with the fact that G&J stock was subject to restrictions on transferability and a right of first refusal to reach the 35% discount.

Bajaj applied a 25% marketability discount. In reaching this conclusion, he first reviewed a number of restricted stock and pre-IPO studies, but "concluded that the published results were not useful in evaluating discount levels" for a number of reasons:

> Relying more on his own empirical analysis of lack of marketability discounts, and considering such factors as G&J's generous dividend policy and its greater marketability restrictions (i.e., the restrictive transfer agreements), Dr. Bajaj concluded that a conservative estimate of the lack of marketability discount for G&J's shares on the valuation date was 25%.

The court found Bajaj's testimony to be "thorough and more persuasive" and applied a 25% marketability discount as he suggested.

Cost of capital using capital asset pricing model

McCoy used a 19% cost of capital figure in his calculations, which he arrived at in part by using Ibbotson Associates data for small cap and very small cap companies. The court rejected McCoy's cost of capital figure noting the following:

> At trial, Mr. McCoy in fact admitted that G&J did not fall into the Ibbotson definition of a small company. We, therefore, have no confidence in the foundation of Mr. McCoy's analysis on this issue.

Bajaj used a 14.4% weighted average cost of capital, using the capital asset pricing model to reach a 15.5% cost of equity and G&J's actual cost of debt of 8.25%. The court accorded significant weight to Bajaj's testimony, and held that the appropriate cost of capital was 15.5%.

Estate of Snyder v. United States

Citation: 84 AFTR2d Par. 99-5255 (Fed. Cl. 1999)
Court: United States Court of Federal Claims
State/Jurisdiction: Federal Claims
Date of Decision: August 20, 1999
Judge: Turner

In the *Estate of Robert L. Snyder v. United States of America*, 84 AFTR2d Par. 99-5255 (Fed. Cl. 1999), the United States Court of Federal Claims considered a motion for summary judgment regarding the deductibility of a settlement from the gross estate under IRC sec. 2053. The decedent owned a landfill, which he placed in a revocable trust in 1977. The decedent died in 1986. His probate estate consisted of assets worth $6,500. The revocable trust was included in his gross estate since the decedent had control over its assets during his life. In 1988, the Environmental Protection Agency (EPA) declared the landfill a superfund site, and brought suit against the trust for its cleanup. On its tax return, the estate valued the landfill at $1 since the potential liability exceeded the land value by $12 million. The IRS disallowed the deduction for the environmental liability because "it was totally impossible to even estimate Decedent's potential liability at date of death. There is at best only a speculative liability that may or may not materialize over the years." The estate paid the tax due. In August 1997, the superfund site litigation settled. As part of the settlement, the revocable trust had to pay $750,000. The estate then filed this action, seeking to deduct the settlement costs from the gross estate pursuant to IRC sec. 2053 (a)(3) - claims against the estate. The IRS filed a cross motion for summary judgment, arguing that the deduction should be denied because the amount of the settlement exceeded the value of the probate estate.

The Court of Federal Claims denied the Service's motion and granted the estate's motion for summary judgment. The Service grounded their argument denying the estate a deduction on sec. 2053 (c). It argued that the phrase 'property subject to claims' is defined as only property subject to claims in the probate estate for the purposes of this section. The Court of Federal Claims disagreed with this interpretation. It concluded, "the term 'property subject to claims,' as used in section 2053 (c) (2), does not make a distinction between a probate versus a non-probate asset. Rather, it expressly provides that the term 'property subject to claims' means property includable in the gross estate of the decedent which, or the avails of which, would bear the burden of the payment of such deductions in the final adjustment and settlement of the estate...."

This abstract originally appeared in *Valuation Case Digest*, authored by John J. Stockdale, Jr.

Estate of Hendrickson v. Commissioner

Citation: T.C. Memo 1999-278, 1999 Tax Ct. Memo LEXIS 318
Court: United States Tax Court
State/Jurisdiction: Specialty Federal
Date of Decision: August 23, 1999
Judge: Beghe

The issue in this estate tax case was the fair market value of decedent's 1,499 shares of Peoples Trust and Savings Bank of Boonville, Indiana, constituting 49.97% of the 3,000 shares outstanding. Decedent's estate filed a timely Estate Tax Return Form 706, stating the value of 1,486 of the shares to be $2,126 per share.

Respondent sent petitioner a notice of deficiency claiming that the value of the Peoples stock was $5,963.25 per share. This value was based on the appraisal report prepared by David Fuller of Business Valuation Services, Inc., who was respondent's valuation expert at trial. At trial, petitioner's valuation expert, James Magee of Alex Sheshunoff & Co., opined that the fair market value of decedent's shares was $3,000 per share.

The primary issues in this case were the following:

- Treatment of excess assets,
- Selection of comparable companies in the market approach,
- Selection and weighting of market multiples, and
- Discount for lack of marketability.

In addition, although the Court ultimately based its decision on the market approach, it offered some criticisms of Fuller's DCF methodology which should be helpful to other appraisers who use the income approach.

Court separates excess assets

The bank held cash and marketable securities-primarily intermediate term Treasury notes, equal to 22% of assets, compared to 9% or less for peer groups. Fuller separated out cash and securities representing 13% of the total assets and calculated an adjusted operating book value. He separated out the earnings from the excess assets and calculated adjusted operating earnings. He then estimated the company's value on an operating basis and added the value of the excess assets, the latter net of a 10% minority interest discount. The Court accepted that basic methodology.

Magee's comparable 'more exacting'

Both experts valued the company using the guideline company method. The Court made this comment:

> Because value under the guideline method is developed from the market data of similar companies, the selection of appropriate comparable companies is of paramount importance.

In selecting the guideline companies for his analysis, Fuller's primary criterion was geography. All of the companies he chose were significantly larger than Peoples, offered more services than Peoples, and were multi-branch operations.

In contrast, Magee's selection of guideline companies was "significantly more exacting than Fuller's," and the Court relied on his data because "criteria for the selection of comparable companies produced a group of companies that more closely resembled the size and operating characteristics of Peoples than Mr. Fuller's guideline companies."

Magee's first selection criterion was that the guideline companies had to be thrifts comparable in size to Peoples. Further, he divided his guideline companies into two groups, one that reflected minority interests and the other that reflected controlling interests.

> To examine thrift pricing on a control basis, Mr. Magee selected six thrifts (the control group) meeting the following criteria: (1) Thrifts that sold in the Midwest, (2) return on average assets greater than 1%, (3) total assets less than $ 100 million, and (4) transactions that were pending or completed between January 1 and December 31, 1992. In order to examine thrift pricing on a minority basis, Mr. Magee selected 10 thrifts (the minority group)meeting the following criteria: (1) Thrift organizations in the United States,(2) total assets less than $ 150 million, (3) not subject to announced or rumored acquisition, and (4) publicly traded securities as evidenced by listing on a major exchange [or trading market].

Estate has control 'in substance'

The Court noted that there were 29 other shareholders, each of whom owned at least three shares. The Court concluded, "Although the estate shares were numerically a minority interest, they were a controlling interest "in substance." Therefore, the Court focused primarily on Magee's controlling interest transaction guideline companies.

Weight to asset-based multiples

The Court closely scrutinized the multiples used by both experts. Fuller used an average of the price-to-book multiple and the price-to-assets multiple. Magee used an equal weighting of the price-to-earnings multiples and the price-to-book multiples.

Although the Court preferred Magee's data, it ultimately used equal weighting of the price/book and price/assets multiples, because the Court questioned whether the past earnings were representative expectations.

Court criticizes DCF methodology

The Court ultimately gave Fuller's DCF method no weight, but the Court's lengthy criticism of Fuller's DCF methodology is instructive. Fuller used the Capital Asset Pricing Model (CAPM).

The Court criticized Fuller's use of CAPM on three bases:

- **CAPM inadequate because it fails to capture the unsystematic risk.**
  [B]ecause CAPM assumes that an investor holding a diversified portfolio will encounter only systematic risk, the only type of risk for which an investor can be compensated is systematic or market risk, which represents the sensitivity of the future returns from a given asset to the movements of the market as a whole. (citing Brealey & Myers, *Principles of Corporate Finance* 137-138, 143-144 (4th ed. 1991); Pratt et al., *Valuing a Business* 166 (3d ed. 1996).
  Mr. Fuller followed the principles of CAPM and did not make any provision for Peoples' unsystematic risk, based on the assumption that such risk was diversifiable. Yet,

respondent and Mr. Fuller have overlooked the difficulties in diversifying an investment in a block of stock they argued is worth approximately $8.94 million. Construction of a diversified portfolio that will eliminate most unsystematic risk requires from 10 to 20 securities of similar value. See Brealey & Myers, supra at 137-139. Thus, proper diversification of an investment in the Peoples shares owned by petitioner, as valued by respondent, would require a total capital investment of at least $89 million. We do not think the hypothetical buyer should be limited only to a person or entity that has the means to invest $89 million in Peoples and a portfolio of nine other securities.

- **Beta of 1.0 too low. Fuller derived his beta estimate from banks in Value Line, which are much larger, and the Court noted that smaller companies have higher average betas.**
  Beta, a measure of systematic risk, is a function of the relationship between return on an individual security and the return on the market as a whole. See Pratt et al., supra at 166. However, because the betas for small corporations tend to be larger than the betas for larger corporations, it may be difficult to find suitable comparables when valuing a small, closely held corporation . . . there are substantial differences in size and operations between Peoples and the banks on the VL bank list; we do not believe that their betas are representative of the greater business risks faced by Peoples.
  We do not believe that an investment in Peoples, a small, single-location bank, whose earnings were susceptible to impending interest rate mismatches and sluggish local economic conditions, presents the same systematic risk as an investment in an index fund holding shares in 500 of the largest corporations in the United States.

- **Failed to add small stock premium.**
  Although Mr. Fuller cited Ibbotson as his source for equity risk premium, in his initial report he ignored a crucial aspect of the Ibbotson approach to constructing a cost of capital-the small stock premium. In his rebuttal report, Mr. Fuller unsuccessfully tried to persuade us that the small stock premium is not supported by financial theory, characterizing the risk associated with a firm's size as unsystematic risk, for which the market does not compensate. The relationship between firm size and return is well known. It has been found that the greater risk of small stocks is not fully reflected by CAPM, in that actual returns may exceed those expected based on beta. See id. Consequently, when calculating a cost of capital under CAPM on a small stock, it is appropriate to add a small stock premium to the equity risk premium, to reflect the greater risk associated with an investment in a small stock in comparison to the large stocks from which the equity risk premium is calculated. Based on Peoples' size, a mirocapitalization equity size premium of 3.6% should have been added. See Ibbotson at 161. Consequently, even if we accepted Mr. Fuller's beta of 1, which we do not, Peoples' cost of capital should have been at least 18%.

30% DLOM for controlling interest

Fuller applied a 10% discount for lack of marketability, while Magee applied a 30% discount for lack of marketability. Fuller stated that little or no marketability discount was appropriate because decedent's shares were effectively a controlling interest. The Court rejected this argument because it confuses two conceptually distinct adjustments-a discount for lack of marketability and a control premium:

> Although there may be some overlap, because control, or lack of it, is a factor that may affect marketability, even controlling shares in a nonpublic corporation can suffer from lack of marketability, because of the absence of a ready private placement market and the costs of floating a public offering.

The court cited the following factors regarding the marketability of Peoples:

(1) Peoples had few opportunities for growth,

(2) Peoples earnings were subject to significant interest rate risk,

(3) Peoples had no employee stock option plan or history of repurchasing shares, and

(4) There was no readily available public or private market for Peoples shares.

The Court then went on to elaborate with the following:

> While we recognize that elements of control may enhance marketability, we do not think that the estate shares were rendered marketable by virtue of their affective [sic] control... A buyer of the estate shares would either have to sell the block privately, cause Peoples to make a public offering, or seek an acquiror. Any of these three options could take a number of months, and require significant transaction costs for the services of accountants, lawyers, and investment bankers.

The Court approved the 30% discount for lack of marketability for the controlling interest as recommended by Magee. The Court held that the fair market value of decedent's shares was $3,840.76 per share.

Estate of Marmaduke v. Commissioner

Citation: T.C. Memo 1999-342, 1999 Tax Ct. Memo LEXIS 397
Court: United States Tax Court
State/Jurisdiction: Specialty Federal
Date of Decision: October 14, 1999
Judge: Swift

This issue in this estate tax matter was the fair market value on September 7, 1993, of decedent's 366,385 shares of common stock of Hastings Books, Music & Video, Inc. Decedent's holding constituted 22% of the total outstanding shares of the corporation. Another 57% of the stock was owned by other members of the Marmaduke family, 18% was owned by employees of Hastings, and the remaining 3% was owned by a qualified ESOP covering Hastings employees.

In reaching its determination of the value of the stock, the Tax Court had several valuation reports to consider:

> The January 1993 valuation report prepared by A.G. Edwards & Sons, Inc., which included a general value for Hastings' stock as well as a value specific to the stock held by the Hastings ESOP. The A.G. Edwards appraiser applied a smaller discount in valuing the ESOP shares because the ESOP provided for a "put option" that made those shares more liquid.

- The valuation report of Petitioner's first expert, Robert Reilly of Willamette Management Associates.
- The valuation report of Petitioner's second expert, Chris Mercer of Mercer Capital.
- The valuation report of Respondent's expert, Travis Keath of Business Valuation Services.

Sales not indicative of fair market value

The Tax Court and the valuation experts also considered 18 separate sales transactions of Hastings stock that occurred in 1993, all but two of which were for $47 per share. Petitioners first expert rejected these transactions as evidence of fair market value "[d]ue to alleged lack of independent bargaining and negotiations." Petitioner's second expert also rejected these transactions. Respondent's expert, on the other hand, relied on these sales in calculating his transaction method valuation. The Tax Court found that the transactions were not indicative of the fair market value of decedent's holdings.

> The value, however, of decedent's large, minority block of 366,385 shares of stock in Hastings is not controlled by the value of 2000 shares [sold in one of the transactions] nor by the other 1993 transactions involving small blocks of Hastings stock. Respondents expert relies heavily on transactions cumulatively representing less than 1% of Hastings common stock. Decedent's stock, on the other hand, represents some 14 times the total number of shares of stock exchanged during 1993.

30% discount for lack of marketability appropriate given all the circumstances

The Court found that the total equity value of Hastings was $100,000,000, based primarily on the A.G. Edwards valuation report. The only remaining issue was the appropriate discount for lack of marketability.

In reaching its determination that the appropriate discount was 30%, the Court noted that the 15% discount applied by Respondent's expert was "inadequate" because of the size of decedents block of stock. The Court noted that the A.G. Edwards valuation had applied a 20% discount to the ESOP shares "only because of the liquidity available to the Hastings stock held by the ESOP."

Estate of Helen J. Smith v. Commissioner

Citation: T.C. Memo 1999-368, 78 T.C.M. (CCH) 745
Court: United States Tax Court
State/Jurisdiction: Specialty Federal
Date of Decision: November 5, 1999
Judge: Gale

The estate in this case held minority interests in two companies: Jones Farm, Inc. (JFI) (33% of common stock) and First National Bank of Waverly (FNBW) (12% of common stock).

The taxpayer presented two experts, Richard D. Hitt, Jr. of KPMG Peat Marwick and Thomas A. Egan, Jr., ASA, of Management Planning Inc. (MPI). The IRS retained Travis Keath of Business Valuation Services, Inc. and Charles F. Haywood of the University of Kentucky. There were several valuation issues in this case, one of which was the appropriate size of the marketability discounts.

JFI, an Ohio corporation, operated a farm in rural Pike County, Ohio. The parties stipulated an undiscounted net asset value of $1,818 per share, with the appraisers to determine applicable discounts. The court agreed that minority and marketability discounts should be supported and deducted.

Hitt compared restricted securities and pre-IPO stock prices to compute a marketability discount of 45%. He applied this discount to his earnings-based value to reach a per-share value of $243. For his asset-based value, Hitt increased the marketability discount by 5% to account for extra difficulty in selling the farm and for selling costs, resulting in a value of $564 per share.

Egan found a median marketability discount of 29.1% using comprehensive data available from MPI's ongoing study of private placements of restricted stocks. He increased the marketability discount for JFI by 5.9% two reasons. First, unregistered stock sold in private placements can, within two or three years, be sold on the public market, giving it more marketability than JFI's stock. Second, JFI was not held to the same disclosure standards as public companies, making JFI's stock less marketable and the applicable discount higher. Egan concluded that a 35% marketability discount should be deducted from his weighted minority interest value of $675 per share, for a final fair market value of $439 per share.

Keath relied on restricted stock studies, finding an average marketability discount of 30%. After compiling a list of eight characteristics of JFI, he found that the average marketability discount should be increased by 6.8%, resulting in a marketability discount of 36.8%. The application of this marketability discount to Keath's asset-based value produced a value of $1,029 per share.

The court found Egan's report to be very persuasive and well supported by his underlying reasoning. The court concluded, largely on the basis of Egan's report, that a marketability discount of 35% was appropriate and that the fair market value of the decedent's interest in JFI was $439 per share.

Hitt weighted several different methods, applied a marketability discount of 45% using restricted stock studies. Egan used an approach similar to Hitt's but applied a 35% discount for lack of marketability. Haywood used a rather different approach. He estimated the lowest price he thought current shareholders would willingly accept for their stock, and compared this to his prediscounted value. The difference was a 10% discount. In choosing this discount, Haywood considered the shares held by decedent at her death to be a "swing block" of stock, and therefore he thought the marketability discount should be relatively low.

The court criticized Haywood's approach, specifically, using his subjective judgment of the price a willing seller would accept instead of the comparables used by Hitt and Egan. Furthermore, the court disagreed with his conclusion that the decedent's shares were a swing block. After reviewing all the calculations of the experts regarding FNBW's value, the court also agreed that Egan's 35% marketability discount was applicable to determine the fair market value of those shares.

Kerr v. Commissioner (I)

Citation: 113 T.C. 449, 113 T.C. No. 30, 1999 U.S. Tax Ct. LEXIS 58
Court: United States Tax Court
State/Jurisdiction: Specialty Federal
Date of Decision: December 23, 1999
Judge: Jacobs

Baine P. Kerr and Mildred C. Kerr were married in 1942 and had four adult children, all of whom were financially independent.

S. Stacy Eastland, an attorney at Baker & Botts, advised the Kerr's on estate planning matters. In September 1993, Eastland proposed that the Kerr's create two limited partnerships. Eastland further advised them that the partnerships should include a charity as a partner in light of the recent enactment of Section 2704 and to "make sure that traditional valuation rules apply to the partnerships." This would effectively create a situation whereby any "applicable restriction" could not be controlled by the family, which is a requirement under IRC Section 2704(b). Accordingly, the Kerr's decided to assign certain interests to the University of Texas (the University).

The Kerrs' estate plan was accomplished through a complex series of transactions that included the formation of two FLPs (the Kerr Family Limited Partnership (KFLP) and the Kerr Interests Family Partnership (KILP)), and two Grantor-retained annuity trusts (GRATs).

The valuation and gift tax returns

The Kerrs filed Federal gift tax returns for 1994 in which they reported gift tax liabilities attributable to the transfers that they made to the GRAT's trustees and to their children. In an appraisal report attached to the returns, the Kerr's determined the fair market value of the KFLP Class B limited partnership interests that they transferred to the GRAT's trustees by applying a 25% discount for lack of liquidity or marketability to the value of the KILP interests held by KFLP, and a 17.5% minority-interest discount and a 35% discount for lack of liquidity or marketability on the net asset value of KFLP's assets. The Kerr's computed the fair market value of a 44.535% limited partnership interest in KFLP to be $760, 965.

The IRS issued a notice of deficiency to Mr. Kerr determining deficiencies of $698,401 and $10,024 in his Federal gift taxes for 1994 and 1995, respectively. Additionally, the IRS issued a notice of deficiency to Mrs. Kerr determining deficiencies of $698,401 and $10,024 in her Federal gift taxes for 1994 and 1995, respectively. The IRS alleged, among other things, that the Kerr's understated the values of both the KFLP interests that they had transferred to the GRAT's trustees in 1994 and the values of the KILP interests that they had transferred to their children in 1994 and 1995.

The largest portion of the value difference in the KFLP 1994 valuation was attributable to the IRS alleging that part of the restrictions on liquidation set forth in Section 10.01 of the KFLP and KILP partnership agreements constituted "applicable restrictions" within the meaning of Section 2704(b), and that these restrictions should have been disregarded in valuing the limited partnership interests.

The Kerrs filed a motion for partial summary judgment arguing that IRC Section 2704(b) is not applicable for one or all of the following reasons:

- The GRAT's trustees received only assignee interests, as opposed to limited partnership interests,
- The disputed transfers must be valued as assignee interests under sec. 25.2512-1, and
- The restrictions on liquidation set forth in the partnership agreements do not constitute "applicable restrictions" within the meaning of IRC Section 2704(b).

Assignee interest or not?

The Kerrs contended that the partnership interests they transferred to the GRAT's trustees were assignee interests as opposed to limited partnership interests based on a strict interpretation of the KFLP partnership agreement. This was important because under IRC Section 2704(b), if the interests were defined as assignee interests they then, by default, have little if any rights under state law and, accordingly, IRC Section 2704(b) could not be applied to disregard any restrictions. As such, the Kerrs contended and maintained that their children, as KFLP general partners, had to consent to the admission of the GRAT's trustees as limited partners pursuant to Section 3.06 of the partnership agreement.

Unfortunately, since the partnership agreement was not strictly complied with on prior transfers as well as the fact that the references made in all other transfer agreements were to limited partnership interests, the taxpayers lost on this point. The court reasoned the following:

> When KFLP was formed, the Kerr children did not contribute any assets to the partnership. Consistent with the terms of the partnership agreement, the Kerrs were initially the sole general partners of KFLP. Pursuant to Section 4.01 of the partnership agreement, the Kerr's subsequently assigned a portion of their general partnership interests in KFLP to each of their children.
>
> Significantly, under the plain language of section 8.20 of the KFLP partnership agreement, petitioners' inter vivos transfers of general partnership interests to their children, who were permitted assignees within the meaning of section 8.03, should have resulted in the admission of the Kerr children as class B limited partners of KFLP. Petitioners were free, of course, to override section 8.20 of the partnership agreement and admit the Kerr children as general partners of KFLP. Nevertheless, considering the unambiguous terms of section 8.20, it would have been reasonable to expect that petitioners would clearly document the admission of the Kerr children as general partners of KFLP by way of written consents. Given the lack of formality surrounding the admission of the Kerr children as general partners of KFLP, we are left with the impression that petitioners either did not fully appreciate the terms of the KFLP partnership agreement or deemed formal consents to the admission of the Kerr children as general partners to be unnecessary. In either case, petitioners' failure to take any formal steps in regard to the admission of the Kerr children as general partners of KFLP belies petitioners' contention that the Kerr children's formal consent was necessary to admit the GRAT's trustees as limited partners of KFLP.

Applicable restriction or not?

The IRS alleged that Section 10.01 of the KFLP and KILP partnership agreements, which stated that the partnerships shall liquidate upon the earlier of December 31, 2043, or the consent of all the partners, contains restrictions on the liquidation of the partnerships that constitute "applicable restrictions" within the meaning of Section 2704(b). The IRS maintained that these restrictions must be disregarded in valuing the interests the Kerrs transferred to the GRATs trustees and to their children.

The Kerrs contended that Section 2704(b) was not applicable in this case even though the Court concluded that the Kerrs transferred limited partnership interests to the GRATs and to their children. The Kerrs argued that the provisions of Section 10.01 of the partnership agreements do not constitute "applicable restrictions" because of the following:

1. The provisions did not restrict liquidation of the partnerships within the meaning of Section 2704(b)(2)(A), and

2. The Universitys interests in KFLP and KILP demonstrated that the Kerr family did not have the ability to unilaterally lift any restrictions on liquidation within the meaning of Section 2704(b)(2)(B)(ii).

IRC Section 2704(b)(2)(A) broadly defines an applicable restriction:

> [A]ny restriction which effectively limits the ability of the corporation or partnership to liquidate.

However, Section 2704(b)(3)(B) excepts from the definition of an applicable restriction:

> [A]ny restriction on liquidation imposed, or required to be imposed, by any Federal or State law.

In what the Court viewed as an expansion of the exception contained in Section 2704(b)(3)(B), the Secretary promulgated Section 25.2704-2(b), which stated the following:

> An applicable restriction is a limitation on the ability to liquidate the entity (in whole or in part) that is more restrictive than the limitations that would apply under the State law generally applicable to the entity in the absence of the restriction.

Accordingly, the question is really whether the KFLP and KILP partnership agreements imposed greater restrictions on their liquidation than the limitations that generally would apply to the partnerships under state law.

The Texas Revised Limited Partnership Act (TRLPA) Section 8.01 provides for when a Texas limited partnership shall be dissolved. When the Court compared the language of Section 10.01 of the partnership agreements and TRLPA Section 8.01, they concluded that Section 10.01 of the partnership agreements did not contain restrictions on liquidation that constitute applicable restrictions within the meaning of Section 2704(b). This was based upon the fact that Texas law provided for the dissolution and liquidation of a limited partnership pursuant to the occurrence of events specified in the partnership agreement or upon the written consent of all the partners.

As such, the restrictions contained in Section 10.01 of the partnership agreements were no more restrictive than the limitations that generally would apply to the partnerships under Texas law. Consequently, these provisions were excepted from the definition of an applicable restriction pursuant to Section 2704(b)(3)(B) and Section 25.2704-2(b), Gift Tax Regs.

Restrictions should not be disregarded

The Court held the Kerrs transferred limited partnership interests to the GRATs in both form and substance. Pursuant to IRC Section 25.2512-1, the value of the limited partnership interests is equal to the price that a hypothetical willing buyer would pay to a willing seller for the limited partnership interests. The restrictions on liquidation in dispute do not constitute "applicable restrictions" within the meaning of sec. 2704(b) and should not be disregarded.

Estate of DiSanto v. Commissioner

Citation: T.C. Memo 1999-421, 1999 Tax Ct. Memo LEXIS 476
Court: United States Tax Court
State/Jurisdiction: Specialty Federal
Date of Decision: December 27, 1999
Judge: Colvin

The issues in this estate tax matter were as follows:

- The fair market value of Frank DiSanto's (Frank) 186,177 shares (53.5%) of stock in Morganton Dyeing & Finishing Corp. (MD&F) on his date of death, and
- The fair market value of the MD&F stock Grace DiSanto (Grace) was entitled to inherit from Frank's estate (a minority interest) on his date of death.

FMV of Frank's stock

The taxpayers filed a timely estate tax return claiming the fair market value of Frank's MD&F stock was $25.80 per share based upon an appraisal prepared by Deloitte & Touche. The IRS filed a notice of deficiency claiming the stock was worth $52.50 per share.

At trial, petitioners presented the expert valuation report and testimony of Thomas Egan of Management Planning, Inc., who opined that the fair market value of the stock was $23.50 per share. Egan relied solely on the market approach in its valuation, and gave equal weight to MD&F's earnings for a five-year average, five-year weighted average, and latest year. Egan also considered business trends, MD&F's financial position, MD&Fs management situation, and the death of Frank in calculating its fair market value opinion.

Contrary to their expert's report and testimony, petitioners argued at trial and in their post-trial brief that Franks stock was worth only $12.16 per share. They argued that none of the experts took into account the following factors:

- MD&F's water rates were going to increase, which would have resulted in an increased expense of $750,000, twice MD&F's operating income for 1992,
- A lawsuit pending against MD&F by one of its customers,
- Business trends,
- MD&F's financial position,
- MD&F's management situation, and
- The effect of Frank's death.

The court rejected petitioners argument on this issue. First, Egan did consider the last four factors. Second, petitioners offered no evidence to show that the first two factors affected the fair market value of the MD&F stock.

The IRS presented the testimony of Herbert Spiro of American Valuation Group, who did not independently appraise the stock, but critiqued both the Deloitte & Touche and Egans valuations. Spiro criticized Egan's report on the following grounds:

- The conclusions were not adequately justified,
- Egan used only the market approach,
- Some of Egan's comparable companies were not similar to MD&F, and
- Egan incorrectly weighted to MD&Fs earnings figures.

The Tax Court rejected Spiro's criticisms in their entirety, and found that Egan's appraisal was reasonable, credible, cogent, and persuasive evidence that the value claimed in the estate tax return was overstated.

Redemption price not arms length

The IRS further argued that a redemption of Frank's stock by the company at a price of $26.81 per share was evidence of the fair market value of the stock because it was reached in arms-length negotiations.

The court also rejected the redemption price as evidence of fair market value because there were emotional factors involved in reaching that "negotiated" price. Fred DiSanto accepted that price, over the objection of employees and other shareholders, in order to benefit his brothers family and provide continued employment for other family members. The court accepted Egan's opinion, and held that the fair market value of Frank's stock was $23.50 per share.

FMV of Grace's stock

The estate tax return and the Deloitte & Touche valuation it was based upon, valued Grace's stock at $15.53 per share. At trial, the petitioners presented the expert valuation and testimony of Egan regarding the stock inherited by Grace's estate from Frank's estate. Egan valued the stock using the same general principles and assumptions that it used in valuing Frank's stock. According to Egan's valuation, Grace's stock was worth $13 per share on her date of death.

Taxpayers doth protest too much

However, the petitioners argued that the stock was actually worth less than stated in the valuations by Deloitte & Touche and Egan. They argued that the Deloitte & Touche valuation was wrong because the tax return preparer was inexperienced and made errors. The court rejected this argument because there was no evidence in the record to support it.

The petitioners also argued that Egan's valuation was too high, because it did not consider that Grace's estate might never actually own any MD&F stock. The stock had not yet been transferred from Frank's estate, and might not be if it had to be sold to pay administrative expenses of the estate. The court rejected this argument, again because there was no credible evidence in the record to support it.

Finally, the petitioners also presented the expert report and testimony of William H. Frazier of Howard, Frazier, Barker, Elliot, Inc., on the value of Grace's stock. Frazier used a combination of valuation methods, including net asset value, the market approach, the income approach, and the Black-Scholes method. He testified that the fair market value of Grace's stock was $5.88 per share. The court rejected Frazier's valuation because he based it on the assumption that much of the stock would have to be sold to pay administrative expenses of Frank's estate, thereby decreasing the block of stock that would be transferred to Grace.

Estate of Brocato v. Commissioner

Citation: T.C. Memo 1999-424, 1999 Tax Ct. Memo LEXIS 481
Court: United States Tax Court
State/Jurisdiction: Specialty Federal
Date of Decision: December 29, 1999
Judge: Vasquez

The taxpayer was granted a 20% fractional interest discount and an 11% blockage discount with apartment house properties, based on comparable sales and an analysis of market conditions and the economy. In addition to being of significance to property owners, generally, these discounts can influence the entity value of partnerships, corporations, and limited liability companies with partial interest, or a substantial assemblage of properties in a given market area.

The decedent, Eileen Brocato, died in April 1993, owning eight apartment properties in the upscale Marina District of San Francisco, California. This neighborhood achieved unwanted recognition as having been the hardest hit area by the 1989 earthquake. The decedent's properties included seven apartment houses, each with between 12 and 18 units, and one 42-unit building. The underlying values on all real properties, as opined by David Rhoades of David P. Rhoades & Associates, were stipulated to by the parties.

The taxpayer and the IRS litigated two valuation issues:

1. The amount of the blockage discount and which properties to include in the block.

2. The amount of the fractional interest discount.

Blockage discounts are also referred to as "absorption" discounts. While these discounts are most heavily associated with significant blocks of publicly traded stock, Tax Court cases have applied them as well to real property. The blockage discount measures the adverse effect upon fair market value arising from the additional competition that the properties create if offered concurrently on the market.

In *Brocato*, the parties agreed that the decedent's apartment house ownership was sufficiently large that a concurrent offering of the properties would reduce the value, and that this reduction would not be reflected in the appraisal of any one property. The parties disagreed, however, on the definition of the relevant market, the types and locale of buyers within the market, and the method of valuation. Petitioner asserted that a 12.5% discount should be applied to all eight properties, while the IRS argued that a discount of 1.92% should be applied to only seven (excluding the 42-unit property).

The IRS argued, whose expert was Karen Ann Simmons of Karen Ann Simmons & Associates, that the blockage discount is limited to a sale over a time period, applying a discounted cash-flow analysis, and used a 12.5% discount rate. This approach was similar to that used in *Auker v. Comr.*, 75 T.C. Memo. 1998-185. In this case, the Court found the analysis by the IRS' appraiser to be reasonable in this regard, but not as persuasive as the analysis presented by the taxpayer's appraiser.

Paul Talmage of Dana Property Analysis established the marketing period (six months), the size of the market and the rate of absorption, and referenced the San Francisco economy (which was still in a recession at the time of decedent's death), investor pessimism, earthquake concerns, the size of the properties, and the potential pool of investors. Underlying market data from multiple listing services as well as market data published for appraisers and brokers ("Comps Reports") substantiated the market analysis. As a result, the Court applied a test heavily weighted to the sale of the properties within a period of one year rather than protracted over a longer period of time.

Both the blockage and fractional discounts provide lower values than the measurement of the underlying entity value. This decision also reflects an appropriate application of the blockage discount that may have significance to real estate property owners in an extensive array of situations, including the following: subdividers; multiple ownership of single-use properties; and apartment houses or commercial properties, within a given market. It also provides authority for the argument that the scope of the market may be as narrow as a neighborhood under appropriate circumstances.

The IRS did prevail on the issue of excluding the 42-unit property from the blockage discount, recognizing it as being of sufficiently greater value and, therefore, not competitive with the balance of the properties.

The Court granted the full 20% fractional interest discount opined by the taxpayer's expert on three of the decedents properties. Two of those properties were included as well in the blockage discount. Mr. Talmage supported this discount with reference to several sales of partial interests, and distinguished certain sales from others. Both the taxpayers expert and the Court were critical of the partition approach as the measure of the fractional interest discount.

Estate of Dunn v. Commissioner (I)

Citation: T.C. Memo 2000-12, 2000 Tax Ct. Memo LEXIS 13
Court: United States Tax Court
State/Jurisdiction: Specialty Federal
Date of Decision: January 12, 2000
Judge: Gale

The Tax Court considered the fair market value of a controlling interest in a heavy equipment rental company. The decedent held 492,610 shares (62.96-percent) of the company in 1992 on the date of her death, the valuation date. Her husband and her adult son held the remaining shares. The company was located in Texas and leased heavy equipment and operators to refinery and petrochemical businesses. It was the largest heavy equipment rental business in the area due to its superior service and reputation. The heavy equipment rental business is cyclical, and was at its low point on the valuation date. Competition and direct operating costs had increased over the four years prior to the decedent's death, and the corporation had not raised its rental rate in more than ten years. Additionally, the company did not pay dividends between 1987 and the valuation date.

The business was valued for estate tax purposes. The expert used a combination of the asset and earnings approaches. His asset-based approach considered a liquidation of the corporation. He included a 34-percent discount for the built-in capital gains that would be recognized upon a liquidation of the assets. He then valued the business using a capitalization of net income approach. In calculating the net income, he used information from the company's past four and, when available, past five years. He applied a 21.67-percent capitalization rate, which he derived from an Ibbotson Associates' study to the straight average of net income. He weighted the results of both valuations equally and concluded that the stock was worth $3.32 per share on the valuation date. The IRS audited the return and increased the per share value of the estate's stockholding. The parties could not agree upon the value of the business, and the case proceeded to trial. Both parties presented expert witnesses.

The IRS' expert was employed by a big five accounting firm. This expert was not an appraiser; even so, this expert's report was admitted into evidence. She did not perform an independent appraisal of the decedent's stock; this expert performed a critique of the estate's first expert's appraisal. She initially argued that the corporation should not be valued using the earnings approach due to the disparity between values determined under the asset and earnings approaches.

She also argued that the estate's first expert made various errors in calculating his values under both methods. She began by arguing that the estate's expert capitalized the wrong income stream. She claimed that the net cash-flow to equity was the proper income stream. The Service additionally argued that a proper valuation under the earnings approach would have eliminated a 1989 bad debt write-off of $468,000 and would have considered the benefits of an investment tax credit and an alternative minimum tax payment. She also found errors with the estate's asset valuation. She argued that the valuation improperly considered the built-in capital gains due upon a liquidation and failed to consider certain prepaid accounts.

The estate presented its first expert, the appraiser who completed the valuation attached to the tax return. This expert's testimony was not materially different from his appraisal. The estate also presented a second expert witness. This second expert did not perform an independent valuation of the business; rather, he reviewed the first expert's appraisal and critiqued the IRS' expert's report. He concluded that the appropriate earnings base to capitalize was the net income to equity. He further would have capitalized the net cash-flow to equity over a weighted five-years' income. However, this expert believed that the estate's first expert's use of net income produced the correct results because he used a straight average of the past five-years' earnings.

The Tax Court reviewed all the experts' opinions. It rejected the IRS' position that the business should be valued solely by the asset-based approach. It concluded that the subject company was an operating company, which would generally be valued using an earnings-based approach. However, due to the great disparity between the values determined by the asset approach and by the earnings approach, a combination of the two should be used. It weighted the values 65-percent asset-based approach and 35percent earnings-based approach. It concluded that the asset-based approach should be given greater weight because the company was in the low end of its business cycle and had " low profitability, volatility of earnings, high debt, limited customer base, and dependence upon one industry."

The court then turned to the valuations performed under each approach. It began with the asset approach. It concluded that the valuation performed by the estate's first expert gave too much significance to a potential liquidation of the company. The court noted that while the estate had operating control over the company, it lacked a super-majority. Under Texas law a super-majority is required to approve a sale or merger of the company or compel liquidation. See Tex. Bus. Corp. Act Ann. art. 6.03 (West 1991). It further concluded that, based on the remaining two shareholders' testimony, they would have blocked any attempt to liquidate the company. The court then concluded, based on the only valuation in evidence, that the corporation's assets were worth $7.5 million. It then agreed with the IRS that the prepaid accounts should be included in the asset-based valuation because a liquidation of the company's assets would take time and the company would have to operate in the interim, thus consuming the prepaid accounts. It next considered the effect of the built-in capital gains. The court declined to reduce the asset value by the total amount of capital gains using the estate's 34-percent tax rate. It did, however, agree that a hypothetical buyer would consider the amount of the built-in capital gains. Thus, it applied a 5-percent reduction from the assets' value for the potential taxes. It concluded that the company's undiscounted value was $7.92 million under the asset approach.

The court also reviewed the earnings approach valuation. It agreed with the IRS and the estate's second expert that the appropriate earnings base was net cash flow to equity. The court declined to use the party's mix of five-year and four-year averages. It concluded that the most complete information was derived from the four-year history. Thus, it used only information from 1988 through the valuation date. It also agreed with the estate's first expert that the capitalization rate (which was uncontested) should be applied to the straight average because "the weighted average gives too much weight to the lowest point of the [business] cycle."

The court lastly addressed the IRS' arguments. It concluded that, while it is generally correct to eliminate non-recurring items, the bad debt write-off was accounted for in calculating the changes in net working capital when it "incorporated the decrease in accounts receivable that resulted from the bad debt write-off." The court then considered the IRS' embedded tax credits argument. The court found that since the business will continue to be an operating company, liable for the alternative minimum tax, a hypothetical buyer and seller would place no value on the embedded tax credits. Thus, the court determined the undiscounted value of the business to be $1.3 million under the earnings approach. Weighting the results of the two methods 65-35, the Tax Court determined the undiscounted value of the company to be $3.5 million. The court then applied a 15-percent discount for marketability and a 7.5% discount for the lack of super majority (supported by the IRS), and concluded that the decedent's 62.96-percent interest in the company had a fair market value of $2.7 million.

This abstract originally appeared in *Valuation Case Digest*, authored by John J. Stockdale, Jr.

Church v. United States (I)

Citation: 2000 U.S. Dist. LEXIS 714
Court: United States District Court
State/Jurisdiction: Texas
Date of Decision: January 18, 2000
Judge: Garcia

The primary issue in this estate tax refund action was whether Stumberg Ranch Partners, Ltd. was formed for a bona fide business purpose, or was a sham transaction designed to avoid estate and gift taxes.

The Texas limited partnership was formed by the decedent, Elsie Church, and her two children, Marshall Miller and Mary Elsie Newton. Each contributed their undivided interest in the W.R. Stumberg Ranch to the partnership.

In addition, Church contributed approximately $1 million worth of securities to the partnership. Each received an interest in the partnership in proportion to the assets contributed.

Two days after the Partnership Agreement was signed, but before all of the documents related to the new partnership and transfer of the securities to the partnership had been completed, Church died unexpectedly of cardiopulmonary collapse. Prior to that time, Church suffered from breast cancer, but she had received treatment and her cancer was in remission at the time of her death. The court found that Church did not anticipate her death.

The government argued that formation of the partnership was a sham transaction to allow Church to transfer assets to her children before her death, and avoid gift and estate taxes. The court rejected this argument, and found that the partnership was formed for a bona fide business purpose, for several reasons:

- "The failure to complete the paperwork on Friday, October 22, 1993 lends credence to the testimony that the state of Mrs. Church's health and her possible death were not motivating factors in the decision to form the partnership."
- There was substantial evidence that the primary purpose for forming the partnership was to "preserve the family ranching enterprise for themselves and their descendants" by eliminating control over the ranching operations by one or more of the fractional, undivided-interest owners.

- The formation of the partnership eliminated each party's individual right to use and enjoy the ranch property, or to force a partition or sale. This was a significant right to relinquish.
- Church did not retain a unilateral right to alter, amend, revoke, or terminate the partnership agreement.
- Each partner received a partnership interest in direct proportion to the assets contributed. Neither Miller nor Newton received a gratuitous gift of the assets contributed by Church.
- "[T]he Partnership was a bona fide business arrangement, and not a device to transfer property to members of Mrs. Church's family for less than full and adequate consideration in money or money's worth."

On the issue of the value of Church's partnership interest for estate tax purposes, plaintiffs presented the expert valuation testimony of Bruce Johnson. He opined that the value of this interest was $617,591. The court accepted this evidence and found as a fact that the value was $617,591. The court noted that this value:

> [P]resumably could have been challenged given that the valuation of such interests is ultimately a matter of opinion. [However,] the Government chose not to present any valuation evidence of its own. Since the Court must find facts based on the record before it, it accepts Mr. Johnson's uncontradicted estimate.

Estate of Weinberg v. Commissioner

Citation: T.C. Memo 2000-51, 79 T.C.M. (CCH) 1507
Court: United States Tax Court
State/Jurisdiction: Specialty Federal
Date of Decision: February 15, 2000
Judge: Whalen

In this estate tax matter, the Tax Court addressed basic valuation issues dealing with minority interest and marketability discounts in the context of a limited partnership interest.

At the time of her death on Dec. 15, 1992, the decedent controlled a 25.235% limited partnership interest in the Hill House Limited Partnership, which owned and operated an 11-story apartment building in Philadelphia. Partners had rights of first refusal, and the general partner had total discretion over making distributions and consenting to the substitution of limited partners.

The parties agreed that the fair market value of the apartment building was $10,050,000. The points of disagreement included, among other things, the magnitude of the marketability discount for the limited partnership interest.

Both sides agreed that a marketability discount was appropriate. The taxpayer anticipated an argument from the IRS that any such discount should be modest because aspects of marketability supposedly are already present in the public limited partnership market and reflected in the market data.

The taxpayer's expert, Robert M. Siwicki, ASA, focused on that portion of the SEC's restricted stock study dealing with the sale of restricted stock of non-reporting over-the-counter issuers. In terms of size, disclosure requirements, and liquidity, such issuers share similarities with the partnerships that populate the limited partnership market. The SEC data supported a marketability discount of 30%. Siwicki increased that figure by 5% due to the right of first refusal and the "slim prospect of the interest ever being publicly traded," thus arguing for a discount of 35%.

The IRS expert, Dr. Samuel J. Kursh, CBA, adopted the Quantitative Marketability Discount Model (QMDM) for calculating a marketability discount and argued for a discount of 15%, based on assumptions regarding expected growth in value, return requirements of partners, and the holding period.

The Tax Court agreed with Kursh on his selection of 16 comparables over Siwicki's selection of one highly comparable partnership, stating that the use of a single comparable can be "problematic."

The court disagreed with both parties with respect to selection of a marketability discount. The court criticized Kursh's use of the QMDM, "because slight variations in the assumptions used in the model produce dramatic differences in the results." The court criticized Siwicki's marketability discount computation because he "failed adequately to take into account certain characteristics of the subject limited partnership interest that suggest a decrease in the marketability discount. These factors include consistent dividends, the nature of the underlying assets, and a low degree of financial leverage."

The court ultimately determined that discounts of 37% for minority status and 20% for lack of marketability were appropriate in this case. The court's determination represented a combined discount of 50% from net asset value.

Estate of Armstrong v. United States (I)

Citation: 85 AFTR2d par. 2000-561 (WD VA 2000)
Court: United States District Court
State/Jurisdiction: Western District of Virginia
Date of Decision: February 24, 2000
Judge: Crigler

In the *Estate of Frank Armstrong, Jr. v. United States of America*, 85 AFTR2d Par. 2000561 (WD VA February 24, 2000), the U.S. District Court for the Western District for Virginia considered the value of stock gifted to the decedent's children within three years of the decedent's death. In 1991 and 1992 the decedent, then 92 years old and in ill health, transferred stock in his closely held company to his children and grandchildren. They executed a transferee liability agreement, which required the decedent's children to assume liability for any gift tax due on the stock if the stock was valued in excess of $100 per share. The decedent or his grantor trust paid all the gift tax due on the 1991 and 1992 transfers. He died in 1993 and his estate recaptured the value of the gifts. Before a magistrate, his children argued that an amount equal to the taxes and liability assessed on the transfer should reduce the value of the transfers, and that the value of the transfers should be reduced by the amounts equal to the estate taxes and litigation costs expressly or impliedly assumed by the them. The IRS argued that the estate's proposed reductions were speculative on the date of transfer.

The magistrate began by noting that "the value of the gift is the PRESENT value of the gift in the donor's hands at the time of transfer and not either its enhanced or its decreased value after reaching the donee" (emphasis in original). He then rejected the estate's arguments. The magistrate reasoned that the present value of the gifts at the time of their transfer was contingent upon whether the decedent would survive the three-year holding period. He stated, "we have here uncertainty not only over how much tax and litigation costs might be incurred, but whether any would be incurred in the first instance." The magistrate concluded that the proposed reductions were "entirely speculative, so much so that the full value of the stock transferred should not be reduced by the additional contingencies actually arising after the transfer took place."

This abstract originally appeared in *Valuation Case Digest*, authored by John J. Stockdale, Jr.

Estate of Reichardt v. Commissioner

Citation: 114 T.C. 144, 114 T.C. No. 9, 2000 U.S. Tax Ct. LEXIS 8
Court: United States Tax Court
State/Jurisdiction: Specialty Federal
Date of Decision: March 1, 2000
Judge: Colvin

Prior to his death, decedent transferred his life interest in his residence, rental properties and other real properties, and investment accounts to the Reichardt Family Trust and to Reichardt Partners, Ltd., a family limited partnership of which the trust was the only general partner. Sometime thereafter, decedent gifted a 30.4% interest in the partnership to each of his two children.

Upon his death, petitioners filed an estate tax return stating that the decedent's estate held a 36.46% limited partnership interest, with a fair market value of $346,000, and a 1% general partnership interest, with a fair market value of $13,000. Respondent determined a deficiency, claiming that all of the property held by the partnership and trust was includable in decedent's gross estate pursuant to IRC § 2036(a).

The Tax Court found that the property was includable in the decedent's gross estate because "[d]ecedent's relationship to the partnership assets did not change when he conveyed them to the trust and partnership." Decedent retained complete control and management of the assets, and although the petitioners could have exercised some control over the assets, they never did. Nothing changed except legal title to the assets.

In addition, the decedent did not transfer the assets to the trust and partnership for full and adequate consideration in an arm's-length transaction.

Valuation of assets

At trial, petitioners presented the expert report and testimony of James R. Parks and respondent presented the report and testimony of Francis X. Burns regarding the fair market value of the partnership assets. With respect to the real property, Parks relied on the real estate appraisal of Thomas L. Goade, which included a 10% fractional interest discount. Burns did not apply a fractional interest discount. Because Goade was a qualified real estate appraiser and Burns was not, the Court adopted the valued opined by Goade and Parks with respect to the real properties.

Ultimately, the Court concluded that the fair market value of the transferred assets includable in the decedent's gross estate was $1,634,654.

Estate of Welch v. Commissioner (II)

Citation: 2000 U.S. App. LEXIS 3315
Court: United States Court of Appeals
State/Jurisdiction: 10th Circuit Federal
Date of Decision: March 1, 2000
Judge: Holschuh

The issue in this estate tax appeal is whether the petitioners were entitled to apply a discount for a built-in capital gains tax liability on real estate in valuing the stock of the corporation owning the real estate. The real property owned by the corporation was subject to potential condemnation proceedings.

The decedent owned a minority interest in nonvoting stock of the corporation. A minority discount was also applied in valuing the stock, but the IRS did not dispute the applicability or amount of that discount.

The petitioners based the claimed value of the stock in part on the estate tax return on a valuation prepared by Mercer Capital Management, Inc. However, petitioners added to the Mercer valuation the value of the real estate (which Mercer Capital had excluded due to the condemnation proceedings) less the full amount of the potential capital gains tax liability.

Tax Court denied capital gains discount

The Tax Court held that the petitioners were not entitled, as a matter of law, to apply a capital gains discount because of the following reasons:

- The petitioners failed to show that the sale of the real estate or liquidation of the corporation was likely to occur, and
- The corporation had an IRC § 1033 election available that would allow it to avoid the capital gains tax liability.

At trial, the IRS also argued that the discount was not warranted because only real estate, and not the corporation itself, was subject to potential condemnation proceedings.

The Sixth Circuit reversed the Tax Court ruling based upon the Second Circuit's prior decision in *Eisenberg v. Commissioner*, and the IRS acquiescence of that decision. All of the above reasons for rejecting the capital gains discount as a matter of law were rejected in *Eisenberg*. According to that decision, the appropriate consideration for the Tax Court in valuing corporate stock is whether a "hypothetical willing buyer, having reasonable knowledge of the relevant facts, would take some account of the tax consequences of contingent built-in capital gains . . . in making a sound valuation of the property."

Section 1033 does not foreclose discount

The Sixth Circuit specifically addressed the issue of the corporation's potential IRC § 1033 election, stating that the availability of the election does not automatically foreclose the application of a capital gains discount. The Tax Court must consider it as a factor in determining fair market value, just as a hypothetical willing buyer would.

The point is that while a § 1033 election is available, the value of that election and its effect on the value of the stock depends upon all of the circumstances a hypothetical buyer of the stock would consider. The fact that, in the present case, the corporations did exercise the § 1033 election after the valuation date is therefore irrelevant.

IRS offers new argument on appeal

On appeal, the IRS apparently agreed that its arguments before the Tax Court were all rejected by *Eisenberg*. Therefore, "in an effort to salvage a favorable judgment of the Tax Court," the IRS offered a completely new argument on appeal. According to the IRS,

> (1) the estate is clearly not entitled to a reduction for the full amount of the potential capital gains tax, and (2) the estate, which had the burden of proof, did not provide the court with any basis for arriving at a discount of any particular lesser amount.

The Sixth Circuit rejected this argument because the petitioners did present valuation evidence, and that evidence was not challenged by the IRS at trial or questioned by the Tax Court.

Remand for new valuation

The Tax Court rejected the capital gains discount as a matter of law, and did not address the proffered valuation evidence or determine the amount of any capital gains discount. Therefore, the Sixth Circuit remanded the case to the Tax Court for a new hearing to determine the value of the decedent's stock, taking into account the potential capital gains tax liability, § 1033 election, and condemnation proceedings.

On remand, the petitioners, now aware of the required approach to valuation of the stock in light of *Eisenberg*, would need to present expert testimony to satisfy their burden of proof. They may or may not be able to present such testimony, but they should be given the opportunity.

Estate of Maggos v. Commissioner (II)

Citation: T.C. Memo 2000-129, 2000 Tax Ct. Memo LEXIS 154
Court: United States Tax Court
State/Jurisdiction: Specialty Federal
Date of Decision: April 11, 2000
Judge: Ruwe

The issue in this case is whether the decedent's redemption of 567 shares to Pepsi-Cola Alton Bottling, Inc. (PCAB) was indeed a gift to her son, who ran the company. In 1987, PCAB redeemed the shares in the form of a $3 million promissory note. Decedent was represented by "independent and experienced counsel." The price was not negotiated, and the price was determined because decedent's son, Nikita, believed he could support the valuation for gift tax purposes and that is what he could afford.

CAPM and WACC improper

David Fuller of Business Valuation Services (BVS) gave testimony for the IRS and valued the shares at $7,938,000. Fuller analyzed PCAB using a discounted cash flow (DCF), guideline public company, and acquisition analysis. In the DCF analysis, he reported that in 10 years PCAB would be worth 12.5 times net earnings. But the court rejected this analysis, because it believed that a DCF analysis is "suspect when the discount rate is calculated by a weighted average cost of capital (WACC) determination. Such determinations often include a determination of the cost of capital using the 'capital asset pricing model' (CAPM)," and that it didn't believe that "CAPM and WACC are the proper analytical tools to value a small, closely held corporation with little possibility of going public."

Guideline companies too large

Two of the companies BVS selected for the guideline public company were Pepsi-Cola, Inc., and Coca-Cola Co., which the court thought were "so dissimilar in both size and operations to PCAB that [it doubts]the comparisons are meaningful." The other two guideline companies "were also significantly larger, having market capitalizations of $518.3 million and $4.2 billion."

Only a mother would approve

Petitioner's expert, Kenneth McGraw of Corporate Financial Consultants, used a capitalization of cash flows analysis to conclude that the value of the 567 shares was $2,691,120. McGraw found the whole enterprise value to be $6,329,120 and applied a 25% discount for lack of marketability. McGraw chose not to use the guideline public company method, because "there were no public companies comparable enough to use as reliable indicators of value for a small, atypical Pepsi bottler like PCAB."

McGraw found that Nikita's compensation of over $250,000 to be reasonable and made no adjustments to PCABs cash flows in that regard. However, Fuller found that a reasonable compensation would be around $100,000 per year, and the court agreed, stating, "A majority owner of PCAB stock, other than Nikita's mother, would not likely approve of Nikita's salary level." The court found that the value of the shares to be worth $4,900,000 on an aggregated minority basis.

25% DLOM is appropriate

BVS original report concluded that no marketability discount was appropriate. Whereas, McGraw used a 25% discount. Robert Reilly of Willamette Management Associates testified for petitioners that a 30% discount (Reilly used the term "illiquidity discount") was appropriate. The court agreed with petitioner's experts that a lack of marketability discount should be applied because "shares in the company could not be sold with the approval of Pepsi-Cola, Inc," and deemed a 25% discount appropriate.

Battling over control

Reilly testified that the proper control premium was between 34% and 38%. He calculated the average control premium paid in the beverage industry from 1982 to 1986 to be 35.84%. But, Reilly stated in his report that minority shareholders would have to consent to any sale, so the control premium should be turned into a discount because the majority shareholders would have to pay the minority shareholders to obtain consent. The court found this argument to be unpersuasive and applied a 25% control premium.

Therefore, the court concluded that the 567 PCAB shares had a fair market value of $4.9 million, so Nikita received a taxable fight of $1.9 million when decedent redeemed her interest.

Estate of Stinson v. United States (II)

Citation: No. 99-3333 (7th Cir. 2000)
Court: United States Court of Appeals
State/Jurisdiction: 7th Circuit Federal
Date of Decision: May 26, 2000
Judge: Evans

In *Lavonna J. Stinson Estate v. United States of America*, No. 99-3333 (7th Cir. May 26, 2000), the U.S. Court of Appeals for the Seventh Circuit decided whether the forgiveness of corporate debt was subject to the gift tax. Lavonna Stinson sold 267 acres of farmland to Stinson, Inc., a corporation owned by her children and grandchildren. The purchase price was to be paid in installments over 20 years. Between 1982 and 1985, Stinson forgave the corporation $147,000 of principal indebtedness in amounts not greater than $50,000 per year. The decedent did not report the debt forgiveness as gifts, reasoning that they qualified for the $10,000 per donee annual exclusion. After her death, the IRS audited her estate and determined that the debt she forgave was subject to the gift tax.

The IRS argued that the forgiveness of debt is a transfer of property by gift less than 26 U.S.C sec. 2501 (a). "[T]ax applies whether the transfer is direct or indirect ...A transfer by gift from an individual to a corporation is an indirect gift from the individual to the corporation's shareholders for gift tax purposes." 26 C.F.R. sec. 25.2511-1(h)(1). The IRS additionally argued that the forgiveness of corporate debt was a gift of a future interest. The estate argued that any gift up to $10,000 per donee is exempt from tax. The Tax Court agreed with the IRS. It found that the tax code specifies that a gift qualifies for the annual exclusion if it is not a gift of future interest. The estate appealed.

The Seventh Circuit agreed with the Tax Court that the debt forgiven was a gift of future interest, therefore subject to tax. Although the estate argued that the forgiveness of debt increased the corporation's value, the IRS correctly determined that the shareholders would not realize the increased value unless they liquidated or issued dividends. Thus, it was a gift of future interest. The Seventh Circuit cited cases from other jurisdictions that had come to the same conclusion. "[The] sole statutory distinction between present and future interest lies in the question of whether there is postponement of enjoyment of specific rights, powers or privileges which would be forthwith existent if the interest were present."

Howe v. United States, 142 F.2d 310, 312 (7 Cir. 1944). The Seventh Circuit lastly addressed how the gift should be valued. The estate argued that the value of the gifts should be determined by the increase in the shareholders' stock resulting from the forgiveness of debt. Treas. Reg. sec. 25.2511-(2) a) states, "[T]he gift tax is 'an excise upon [the donor's] act of making the transfer [and] is measured by the value of the property passing from the donor..." In this case, the $147,000 of debt forgiven was taxable. The court noted, "The fact that there would be other ways of valuing the gift from the point of view of the donees is not controlling."

This abstract originally appeared in *Valuation Case Digest*, authored by John J. Stockdale, Jr.

Estate of Klauss v. Commissioner

Citation: T.C. Memo 2000-191, 2000 Tax Ct. Memo LEXIS 228
Court: United States Tax Court
State/Jurisdiction: Specialty Federal
Date of Decision: June 27, 2000
Judge: Colvin

This case is important because it supports the use of the small stock premium in developing a discount rate and also the adjustment of market valuation multiples in the guideline public company method.

The issue is the fair market value of 184 out of 460 shares outstanding of Green Light Chemical Co., a home and garden products company, as of Feb. 1, 1993.

Experts were Bruce Johnson of Munroe, Park & Johnson for the taxpayer and David Fuller of Business Valuation Services for the IRS. Both experts used a capitalization of income and a publicly traded guideline company method.

Johnson wrote an article, along with Mike Annin of Ibbotson Associates, analyzing Johnson and Fuller's positions in the case, which we published in the July 1999 issue of *Business Valuation Update*™. The article said that Fuller erred in excluding the small stock premium from the discount rate, because the evidence on which he concluded that the size premium no longer existed was flawed.

Moreover, Annin and Johnson claimed that Fuller was inconsistent by using the 73-year equity risk premium and a much shorter time period to conclude no size premium. Had they used a similar shorter-term equity risk premium, it would have been much higher.

Judge Colvin agreed with this analysis:

> Respondent relies on an article by Bajaj & Hakala, "Valuation for Smaller Capitalization Companies," published in *Financial Valuation: Business and Business Interests*, ch. 12A (Hanan & Sheeler ed. 1998), for the proposition that there is no small-stock premium. We find Johnson's analysis to be more persuasive.
>
> Fuller testified that it is appropriate to use the Ibbotson Associates data from the 1978-92 period rather than from the 1926-92 period because small stocks did not consistently outperform large stocks during the 1980's and 1990's. We give little weight to Fuller's analysis. Fuller appeared to selectively use data that favored his conclusion. He did not consistently use Ibbotson Associates data from the 1978-92 period; he relied on data from the 1978-92 to support his theory that there is no small-stock premium but used an equity risk premium of 7.3% from the 1926-92 data (rather than the equity risk premium of 10.9% from the 1978-92 period). If he had used data consistently, he would have derived a small stock premium of 5.2% and an equity risk premium of 7.3% using the 1926-92 data, rather than a small-stock premium of 2.8% and an equity risk premium of 10.9% using the 1978-92 data.
>
> We conclude that Johnson appropriately applied a small-stock premium in valuing the Green Light stock.

Fuller's 0.7 beta improper

Another issue in the income approach was Johnson's build-up method versus Fuller's CAPM method. Fuller lowered his equity discount rate by multiplying it by a beta of 0.7. Judge Colvin stated the following:

> We disagree with Fuller's use of a 0.7 beta because Green Light was a small, regional company, had customer concentrations, faced litigation and environmental claims, had inadequate insurance, was not publicly traded, and had never paid a dividend. A beta . . . can only be correctly estimated on the basis of the betas of comparable publicly traded companies . . . Fuller stated that he selected the beta based on a review of comparable companies. However, he did not identify these comparable companies or otherwise give any reason for his use of a 0.7 beta. We believe Fuller's use of a 0.7 beta improperly increased his estimate of the value of the Green Light stock.

Judge Colvin also made a somewhat broad statement that "Green Light should not be valued by using the CAPM method because Johnson and Fuller agreed that it had little possibility of going public."

Adjustment to guideline multiples desirable

Both analysts used the same guideline public companies, but Johnson made a downward adjustment to the multiples and Fuller did not. Judge Colvin noted the following:

> Johnson's analysis was more persuasive than Fuller's. Fuller did not adequately consider the differences between Green Light and American Vanguard, the guideline company he considered to be the most comparable . . . He did not adjust the multiples for American Vanguard.

However, the court considered Johnson's adjustment to the multiples to overstate the prospective growth differential, which accounts for the difference between the court's conclusion and Johnson's conclusion.

Court accepts litigation & environmental discounts

Both analysts applied substantial discounts for product liability and environmental claims. Johnson enumerated specific items and discounted by $921,000. Fuller discounted by 10%, which amounted to $1,130,000. The court agreed with Johnson's method, because it "more accurately accounted for the effects."

DLOM 30%

Both experts testified to a 30% discount for lack of marketability, which the court accepted.

Estate of Harper v. Commissioner (I)

Citation: T.C. Memo. 2000-202, 2000 Tax Ct. Memo LEXIS 242
Court: United States Tax Court
State/Jurisdiction: Specialty Federal
Date of Decision: June 30, 2000
Judge: Wells

The issue in this estate tax matter is whether the provisions of the Limited Partnership Agreement for Harper Financial Co., L.P., entered into by the decedent and his two children were "applicable restrictions" for purposes of IRC § 2704.

Under Section 2704, if a restriction on the liquidation of a limited partnership that is contained in the partnership agreement is an "applicable restriction," then it is disregarded in determining the value of the partnership for estate or gift tax purposes. According to Section 25.2704-2(b) of the Gift Tax Regulations, an applicable restriction is defined as:

> An applicable restriction is a limitation on the ability to liquidate the entity (in whole or in part) that is more restrictive than the limitations that would apply under the State law generally applicable to the entity in the absence of the restriction.

The issue came to the Tax Court on the IRS's Motion for Partial Summary Judgment. The parties stipulated to the material facts relevant to this issue. The Tax Court decided, as a matter of law, that the restrictions of the parties' Limited Partnership Agreement were not more restrictive than the liquidation provisions of the California Limited Partnership Act. Accordingly, they should not be disregarded in determining the fair market value of Harper Financial.

Court refuses to reconsider *Kerr*

The court noted that the issue was essentially the same issue that was decided in *Kerr v. Commissioner*, 113 T.C. 449 (1999). The provisions of the limited partnership agreement in that case were very similar to the provisions in this case, and the California partnership law is very similar to the Texas law that was at issue in that case.

> Unable to distinguish the facts or law at issue in *Kerr*, respondent urges this Court to reconsider our opinion in that case. Because the facts of the instant case are indistinguishable from those in issue in *Kerr*, we need not reiterate our analysis undertaken in *Kerr*, which we adopt in this opinion.

Adams v. United States (II)

Citation: No. 99-10497 (5th Cir. 2000)
Court: United States Court of Appeals
State/Jurisdiction: 5th Circuit Federal
Date of Decision: July 5, 2000
Judge: Fitzwater

In *Patricia M. Adams, et al. v. United States of America*, No. 99-10497 (5th Cir. July 5, 2000), the United States Court of Appeals for the Fifth Circuit determined how an assignee interest in a Texas general partnership should be valued for estate tax purposes. The decedent owned a 25% interest in a Texas general partnership. Her estate valued its assignee interest at $7.481 million which included discounts for "lack of control, lack of marketability and poor portfolio diversity". The IRS valued it at $7.604 million, which included a discount for selling costs. The estate paid the deficiency and sought a refund.

Before the District Court, the parties stipulated that the net asset value (NAV) of the assignee interest was $8.270 million. The IRS argued that under Texas partnership law, the fair market value of an assignee interest was its pro rata share of the NAV, discounted by selling costs. The estate included discounts for factors that a hypothetical buyer would consider when purchasing the interest. The District Court concluded that the assignee had the "well-established statutory right" to liquidate or "wind-up" the partnership under Texas law, entitling it to a pro rata share of the partnership's NAV. Thus, the District Court rejected the estate's proposed discounts. The estate appealed.

The Fifth Circuit examined an assignee's rights under the Texas Uniform Partnership Act (TUPA). While an assignee has liquidation rights for cause, the estate did not show cause to demand liquidation. Furthermore, TUPA section 42 states, "When any partner retires or dies, and the business is continued...the partnership may have the *value of his interest* at the date of dissolution ascertained, and shall receive as an ordinary creditor an amount equal *to the value of his interest...*" (Emphasis in original). The court determined that this created an ambiguity and "begged] the question how to value that interest."

Since no other Texas cases addressed the valuation of an assignee partnership interest, the court looked to other jurisdictions for interpretations of the Uniform Partnership Act (UPA). They found that other jurisdictions, including Louisiana and Illinois, held that, "the 'value' owed to a partner's assignee is his pro rata share of the partnership's NAV, *less appropriate discounts*" (emphasis in original). The court found that the UPA's language concerning "the value of his interest" had been viewed as confusing, prompting revision in the Revised Uniform Partnership Act.

The Fifth Circuit stated, "The District Court grounded its holding in the premise that the law establishes to a legal certainty that the assignee of a partner has precisely the same liquidation rights as the assigning partner. We reach the opposite conclusion..." It remanded the case back to the District Court stating, "the District Court must consider evidence from both parties in light of our determination that the liquidation rights of an assignee are *not* clearly established but that, to the contrary, they are unsettled, and must determine the applicability of the various claimed discounts..." (emphasis in original).

This abstract originally appeared in *Valuation Case Digest*, authored by John J. Stockdale, Jr.

Estate of Godley v. Commissioner (I)

Citation: T.C. Memo. 2000-242, 2000 Tax Ct. Memo LEXIS 284
Court: United States Tax Court
State/Jurisdiction: Specialty Federal
Date of Decision: August 4, 2000
Judge: Gale

This case deals with the valuation for estate tax purposes of four Housing and Urban Development (HUD) housing partnerships and one real estate management partnership.

Decedent died on May 11, 1990 owing a 50% general partnership in five partnerships, with his son, Fred Jr., owning the remaining 50%. Four of the partnerships owned HUD housing projects. The fifth partnership, Godley Management Association, was the manager for the housing partnerships. For each of the housing partnerships, Fred Jr. was managing partner, holding the authority for "overall management and control," except that a "major decision" required approval of 75% of the partnership interests.

Option does not control value

On the Federal estate tax return, Decedent's interests in the five partnerships were reported at a fair market value of $10,000 each. The estate argued that an option granted in the partnership agreement to Decedent's son was a bona fide business arrangement and should control the fair market value, or in the alternative, at least depress value.

The Tax Court concluded that the option was not a bona fide business arrangement but a testamentary device and ignored it entirely in determining fair market value, based primarily on conflicting testimony of Fred Jr.

Conflicting testimony

From 1985 through 1994, Fred Jr. was the defendant in an equitable distribution suit brought by his former spouse in which the purchase option was an issue. Fred Jr. testified by deposition and at trial that the options "[were] done for the purpose of circumventing inheritance taxes" and "[were] a gift." In the same proceeding, Decedent also testified that granting the options was a gift. As part of this proceeding, both Fred Jr. and his former spouse retained experts to calculate fair market value. These same experts or their reports were relied upon in the Tax Court dispute.

Court rejects risk of loss argument

The only person testifying for the IRS about the value of the four HUD partnerships was the IRS revenue agent who was called as a fact witness to explain his calculations. The IRS also called as witnesses the two real estate appraisers on whose reports the estate's business valuation expert relied.

The estate utilized two real estate appraisal experts, Tom Keith and David Dvorak, each appraising two of the four HUD properties. Keith's asset valuations were accepted without challenge.

Dvorak's report was challenged in a couple of areas. First, he assumed a 3% vacancy allowance, reduced from the usual 5%. This reduced vacancy rate was due to the HUD guaranty to pay 80% of the contract rent for two months after a tenant vacated. The Tax Court agreed with the IRS that the 1% vacancy rate used by Keith was appropriate.

The Court also disputed the capitalization and discount rate used by Dvorak. He arrived at the income approach value by applying a discount rate to cash flows for the next four years to arrive at a present value. In addition, he capitalized the fifth year cash flow (he termed this the reversionary value), subtracted costs of sale, and then calculated the present value. His total value was the sum of the present value of four years of cash flows plus the reversionary value.

Dvorak used higher than usual discount and capitalization rates in his calculations to account for the risk of being a HUD project. His justification for this was the risk of loss of the HUD subsidies and the above-market income stream resulting from HUD subsidies. The Tax Court did not accept this argument and reduced his discount and capitalization rates, thus raising the values.

Receivables in dispute

Once the real estate values were determined, the next step was to value the partnerships themselves. The taxpayer's business valuation expert, Robert O. Beck III, valued the partnerships using only the net asset approach under the theory that, since rental real estate was the primary asset, the income producing value of the partnerships is captured in the net asset value. The Tax Court agreed with this concept. The Court disagreed, however, with other aspects of the valuation.

The first disputed aspect of the valuation was the treatment of related party receivables. The business appraiser discounted these unsecured receivables to account for the risk of nonpayment. The Court noted that the IRS had allowed the accounts payable of these partnerships to be valued at their full, undiscounted amounts, and disallowed any discount from the face value of the receivables.

Trust funds part of income stream

The second disputed aspect of the partnership valuation was the treatment of the trust funds established and maintained under the financing arrangements of the housing partnerships. The business appraiser assigned no value to these trusts under the theory that these funds were a prerequisite for the HUD subsidies and therefore not available for a purchaser of Decedents interest. The IRS maintained that the trust funds should be included at their full value.

The Tax Court viewed these funds as analogous to working capital and a required part of producing the income stream. The Court believed these were best accounted for by a reduction in the real estate appraisers capitalization rate since the presence of these funds lowered risk.

IRS concedes to DLOM

The final disputed item for the four HUD partnerships was the application of the lack of control and marketability discounts. Beck deducted 15% for lack of control and 25% for lack of marketability. His theory for the lack of control discount for the 50% ownership was the designation of Fred Jr. as managing partner.

The Tax Court opinion discussed the provisions of the partnership agreement, concluding that they did not rise to the level of giving Fred Jr. enough control to cause Decedents interest to be considered a minority.

For the lack of marketability, the IRS conceded on brief that a discount of 15% to 20% was appropriate. The Tax Court concluded that the appraisal expert made a "persuasive case that decedents interests would not be readily marketable In light of all the facts and circumstances and respondents concession, we find that a 20-percent lack of marketability discount is appropriate."

Hypothetical does not merely buy receivables

The last partnership to be valued was GMA, the real estate management company. GMA received a management fee equal to 10% of the HUD housing partnerships rental income. For its valuation argument, the IRS introduced the report of Mitchell Kaye, the expert used in Fred Jr.s spouse in the equitable distribution proceedings. Kaye capitalized income and arrived at a value of $450,000.

Beck argued that this partnership was intrinsically tied to the value of the four housing partnerships. Since the only assets of GMA were its account receivables from the housing partnerships, its fair market value was just the net realizable value of these receivables. The Tax Court disagreed, noting the following:

> We agree with Beck's assertion that the value of GMA was tied to the value of the housing partnerships, but we disagree with his conclusions as to the value of GMA. He failed to recognize that the hypothetical buyer investing in GMA would not merely be buying the accounts receivable on a particular date, but instead would be buying the income stream attributable to 10% of the rental income of each of the four housing partnerships, minus expenses associated with managing the housing partnerships. Thus, we reject Beck's approach altogether.

The Tax Court accepted the $450,000 value arrived at by Kaye, but reduced it by 20% for lack of marketability.

Estate of Eddy v. Commissioner

Citation: 115 T.C. No. 10
Court: United States Tax Court
State/Jurisdiction: Specialty Federal
Date of Decision: August 16, 2000
Judge: Parr

In the *Estate of Edward H. Eddy v. CIR*, 115 T.C. No. 10, the Tax Court considered whether to allow the estate to use the alternate valuation date. The decedent owned 237,352 share of Browning-Ferris Industries, Inc. (BFI). The estate's BFI stockholding represented 0.014% of all BFI's outstanding stock. (Editor note: Using the total outstanding shares on December 31, 1992 as reported in BFI's 10-Q for the first quarter of 1994, the estate actually held only 0.0014% of the outstanding stock.) BFI's stock was publicly traded over the New York Stock Exchange (NYSE). The estate's federal tax return was due on January 13, 1994. The day before the due date, the estate requested a filing extension to July 13, 1994. The estate indicated that it needed the time to establish a correct valuation of the stock. The request was granted.

The estate's brokerage firm informed the estate that their valuation would not be completed on time. The estate then employed a second firm, which completed the valuation on November 29, 1994. This firm "opined that to dispose of the estate's block of shares on the alternate valuation date, October 13, 1993, the estate would have ...to accept 75 cents per share less than that day's mean trading price (the discount for blockage)." This firm did not determine the fair market value of the estate's stock on the decedent's date of death nor did it determine the appropriate blockage discount using the death of death. The estate filed its tax return on January 19, 1996, reflecting the value of the discounted shares on the alternate valuation date.

The IRS accepted the estate's use of the $0.75 per share (approximately 3 percent) blockage discount. However, because the estate's return was filed later than its extension allowed, the IRS concluded that the estate's use of the alternate valuation date was improper. It "determined that the estate must report the fair market value of all the assets as of the date of decedent's death." The estate turned to the Tax Court.

The Tax Court agreed with the IRS, finding that the election to use the alternate valuation date was not available to the estate because of the late filing of its return. It stated, "the election [to use the alternate valuation date] may not be made if the return is filed more than 1 year after the time prescribed by law (including extensions)." The Tax Court also found the estate liable for a failure to file penalty. The Tax Court noted, "we find the fact that the executor was waiting for an opinion of the size of the discount for blockage is not reasonable cause for the failure to file a timely return."

This abstract originally appeared in *Valuation Case Digest*, authored by John J. Stockdale, Jr.

Estate of Borgatello v. Commissioner

Citation: T.C. Memo. 2000-264, 2000 Tax Ct. Memo LEXIS 309
Court: United States Tax Court
State/Jurisdiction: Specialty Federal
Date of Decision: August 18, 2000
Judge: Wells

This issue in this estate tax matter is the fair market value of decedent's 82.76% interest in Valley Improvement Co., Inc. (VIC), a real estate holding company, as of Jan. 12, 1994. The parties stipulated to the value of most of VIC's assets and all of its liabilities. However, they disagreed on the fair market value of VIC's two largest assets, Montecito Village North (MVN) shopping center and Montecito Village South (MVS) shopping center.

The parties also disagreed regarding the appropriate marketability discount to apply to the net asset value of VIC in order to determine the fair market value of decedent's stock in the company.

The Tax Court noted that, in determining the fair market value of real property that the standard is objective, using a purely hypothetical willing buyer and seller who are presumed to be dedicated to achieving maximum economic advantage in any transaction involving the property, which must be achieved in the context of market and economic conditions at the valuation date.

The real estate appraisers, Wayne Holden for the estate and David Marx for the IRS, found both the sales comparison approach and the cost approach to valuing the shopping centers to be insignificant in their analyses. The sales comparison approach was inappropriate because there was a lack of suitable comparables in the local area. Holden did a cost approach analysis, but rejected the result because he found that the estimate of depreciation of older properties, such as the subject properties, is unreliable. Marx did not use the cost approach at all.

Both experts used a discounted cash-flow analysis to value the two shopping centers. The cash flow projections of each appraiser were very similar. Because of the difference in the experts' discount rates, however, their ultimate determinations of fair market value were very different.

Ultimately, the court found that Holden's valuations were too low and Marxs were too high.

Both experts derived their capitalization rate based upon comparable commercial properties.

The capitalization rate is the propertys cash-flow divided by its sales price. The discount rate is ascertained by making adjustments to the capitalization rate, primarily for inflation.

However, Marx limited his comparable properties to those located in the Montecito-Santa Barbara area. Holden, on the other hand, used comparables from 90 miles away in Huntington Beach and Los Angeles.

The court found Holdens use of "widespread, southern California comparables" troublesome, because of the unique character of the Montecito-Santa Barbara commercial real estate market. Accordingly, the court adopted Marxs 9.5% capitalization rate that was based only on local comparables.

Both experts agreed that a 2% adjustment to the capitalization rate was appropriate to account for inflation. However, Marx made a further adjustment for "leasing and selling commissions along with absorption and tenant improvement issues" that reduced the overall adjustment to 1.5%. The court, without further discussion, split the difference and found that "1.75% is a reasonable adjustment to the capitalization rate."

The experts also disagreed regarding the appropriate cash-flow period. Holden used a 7-year period based on general market considerations. Marx, on the other hand, used a 10-year period based on "information from local brokers and national real estate publications." The court found the following:

Although 7 years may be a reasonable cash-flow period in some cases, we are inclined to follow the trends of the Montecito-Santa Barbara real estate market. We find, therefore, that Mr. Marx's estimate of a 10-year cash-flow period is persuasive because it follows more closely Santa Barbaras real estate norms.

Once the court had settled on a fair market value for VICs primary assets, it then set about deciding the fair market value of the decedents 82.76% interest in this real estate holding company. Because there were no arms-length sales of VIC stock, the court turned to the next best valuation method. Citing *Estate of Davis v. Commissioner*, the court found that the net asset value method is the most reasonable method for valuing a non-operating company such as VIC because, in such companies, earnings are relatively low in comparison to the fair market value of the underlying assets.

The net asset value method involves arriving at the companys net asset value (the value of the companys assets less liabilities, where the assets have been adjusted to reflect their fair market value) and then discounting that value to account for various factors that affect its marketability.

For purposes of proving the fair market value of decedents stock, the estate offered the valuation report of James Brockardt, of Management Planning, and the IRS offered the valuation report of Roger Wilde. Both experts used the net asset value method, but differed regarding the appropriate discount to be applied to account for marketability factors. Brockardt applied a 35% discount for lack of marketability, and Wilde applied a 27% discount.

Several factors were included in what the court called the discount for lack of marketability, including a discount for trapped-in capital gains tax. Wilde used a build-up method to calculate his discount, assigning a specific percentage value to each.

Brockardt, on the other hand, did not assign specific values to the factors included in his marketability discount. Rather, he included a general discussion of the factors that he considered in his report. "He bases his total discount on his judgment and consideration of the factors as a whole." The court criticized Brockardt's method because it did not tell the court how much of a discount he assigned to specific factors, most notably the trapped-in capital gains factor.

Accordingly, the court used Wilde's build-up model as a framework to discuss the specific factors and the appropriate discount to be applied to account for each.

The court rejected the first two factors included in Wilde's build-up method calculation. Wilde reduced his overall discount by 5% to account for VICs strong cash-flow and dividend paying capacity. He then increased the overall discount by 5% to account for the general economic conditions in the area of the subject property.

The estate argued that these factors had already been accounted for in determining the fair market value of VICs assets, and the court agreed. The court's reasoning was based in part on the language of Rev. Rul. 59-60, Section 5, dealing with the valuation of stock of a real estate holding company, which states the following:

The market values of the underlying assets give due weight to potential earnings and dividends of the particular items of property underlying the stock.

Holden did not consider these factors in his analysis.

Wilde decreased his overall discount by 2% to account for what he called "management continuity." The estate argued that this factor was also accounted for in the fair market value of the underlying assets. However, the court disagreed.

This factor, the court said, referred to the fact that management of VIC did not require great expertise. Therefore, the company could be transferred to a new owner without the necessity of keeping existing management in place. Ultimately, the court found that this factor was neutral and assigned it no weight.

The largest portion of Wilde's discount, 19%, was attributable to VICs trapped-in capital gains. In his testimony, Brockardt also assigns a specific value, 31.2%, to this factor. The methodology and underlying assumptions of the experts in reaching their discount conclusions was very different. Wilde assumed a 10-year holding period, whereas Brockardt assumed the immediate sale of the assets.

Assuming a 2% growth rate, Mr. Wilde estimates the value of VICs assets to be $22,214,089 for the year 2004. On the basis of such estimated value, Mr. Wilde calculates the built-in gain and applies California's 9.3% capital gains rate and a 34-percent Federal income tax rate to arrive at a future tax in 2004 in the amount of $7,500,008. Applying a discount rate of 8.3% (Long Term AFR + 2% for added risk), Mr. Wilde determines the present value of the future tax to be $3,378,914.

In order to arrive at the discount attributable to the future tax, Mr. Wilde divided $3,378,914 (the present value of the future tax) by $18,223,290 (the total value of VICs real estate and investments) to arrive at a 19-percent (rounded from 18.5 percent) discount.

The court found a major error in Wilde's calculations in that he divided the present value of the future tax by the total value of VICs real estate and investments. Instead, Wilde should have used VICs net asset value in this calculation. Substituting the net asset value for the total value of real estate and investments, the court adjusted Wilde's capital gains discount to 20.5%.

Brockardt did not conduct an "explicit analysis" as Wilde did. Instead, using Holdens fair market values of MVN and MVS, he calculated "the impact of an immediate tax on the net asset value of VIC." For the sake of comparison, the court recalculated Brockardt's capital gains discount using the fair market values of MVN and MVS that it had determined, and found that the effect of an immediate tax would warrant a 32.3 % discount.

The court found that Brockardt's methodology was unrealistic, however, because it did not account for any holding period by a potential purchaser. The court also found that Wilde's 10-year holding period was too long. Therefore, the court looked at the range of discounts opined by the experts, and tried to find a middle ground between the immediate sale and the 10-year holding period. The court concluded that a 24% discount attributable to the trapped-in capital gains was reasonable.

The decedent's stock was subject to a stock purchase agreement which provided that other VIC stockholders must first be given a 15-day option to purchase the stock, and then the corporation must be given a 15-day option to purchase, on the same terms offered to an outside buyer.

Wilde included a discount of 3% in his build-up method to account for this stock restriction. Brockardt did not discuss it, but the estate argued that a large discount should be applied to account for this factor because the stock restriction would most likely result in decedents interest being split into smaller blocks by the other minority stockholders exercise of their rights of first refusal.

The court was not persuaded by the estates argument, and adopted Wilde's 3% discount to account for stock restrictions.

Both experts opined that the net asset value should be discounted to account for transaction costs associated with the ultimate sale of VICs assets. Without any detailed analysis, the court concluded that 6% was appropriate, a middle ground between Wilde's 7% discount and Brockardt's 5.7% discount.

Estate of Renier v. Commissioner

Citation: T.C. Memo. 2000-298, 2000 Tax Ct. Memo LEXIS 350
Court: United States Tax Court
State/Jurisdiction: Specialty Federal
Date of Decision: September 25, 2000
Judge: Gale

The issue in this estate tax matter is the fair market value of decedent James J. Renier's 88.4% interest in the Renier Company, a family-owned electronics retailer in Dubuque, Iowa. The estate claimed a value of $33.02 per share on the estate tax return, based on the valuation report of Jules Steinberg. The IRS served a notice of deficiency claiming the value was $73.89 per share. The estate filed a petition with the U.S. Tax Court for a determination of the fair market value.

At trial, the IRS presented the expert report and testimony of Leonard Sliwoski, of Leonard J. Sliwoski & Associates and the estate presented the expert reports and testimony of Yale Kramer of McGladrey & Pullen and Allan Lannom of Houlihan Valuation Advisors. The Tax Court discussed the reports of the experts in its Memorandum Opinion, and ultimately concluded that the fair market value of the stock was $43.08 per share.

Valuation report disregarded

In his report, Lannom used the market approach (using two sales of privately held companies from the Institute of Business Appraisers Market Data Base) and applied four rules of thumb. He also applied a key-man discount of 10% of Renier's operating assets.

The Tax Court completely disregarded Lannom's valuation report and testimony because of its "summary nature and obvious shortcomings." The Court stated that it was unable to assess the merits of Lannom's valuation conclusions. He did not explain the rules of thumb he used or why they were appropriate; he did not take into account Renier's higher-than-average profitability; he did not justify the earnings and cash-flow figures he employed in his calculations; and he provided no factual background to support his key-man discount.

Income approach most appropriate

Both Sliwoski and Kramer agreed that the income approach was most appropriate for valuing Renier and its operating assets. They also agreed that Renier's nonoperating assets should be excluded and valued separately using the asset approach.

The experts both employed a capitalization of expected future income method, starting with an average of the companys historical reported net income. They also agreed that the reported net income required several "normalizing adjustments." However, the experts disagreed significantly regarding the specific adjustments needed to normalize the net income figures.

The adjustments that the experts disagreed about included the following:

- The amount by which the compensation of certain family-member employees exceeded the reasonable compensation for their positions;
- The amount of excess working capital retained by the company and the estimated interest income that would have been generated as a result;
- The proper method of adjusting for an error in the company's inventory accounting system, which had been corrected on the books with adjustments in 1993 and 1994;
- The proper method of "annualizing" the partial fiscal year used in the data for computing the company's average income;
- Whether to add back the company's interest expense because of the assumed cost of debt used to determine the capitalization rate; and
- The proper method of adjusting for state and federal income taxes.

Reasonable compensation recalculated

One of the primary areas of disagreement was the issue of reasonable compensation. Reasonable compensation is that compensation which would be paid for services in an arms-length transaction. Anything paid above that is excess compensation that must be added back to net income. In determining the excess compensation paid to family-member (or related-party) employees, the Tax Court substituted its own judgment for that of the two experts, because of problems with the experts opinions on this issue.

The Court rejected Kramer's opinion that Renier paid $15,000 per year in excess compensation, for a total excess compensation figure of $86,663. The Court found that Kramer's opinion was "unsupported by any objective criteria." Some of his data and assertions were "no more than a conclusory guess."

The Court accepted Sliwoski's basic methodology, which was based upon a determination of the market replacement cost of the various positions fulfilled by family-member employees. However, he erred with respect to the number of hours that would be required to fulfill the duties of those employees. Therefore, the Court used the market wage and benefit figures that Sliwoski presented, but recalculated the reasonable compensation based upon the number of hours the Court determined, based upon testimony in the record, the employees were required to work to fulfill their duties.

Closely helds and WACC don't mix

The experts also differed in their computation of the proper capitalization rate. Sliwoski opined that a 10% capitalization rate was appropriate, whereas Kramer computed a 22% rate. Sliwoski used a weighted average cost of capital method (WACC), reduced by 6% to account for estimated future growth, to determine the capitalization rate. The weighted average cost of capital is a "blending of the rate of return on equity with the cost of debt incurred in a hypothetical purchase." Citing several prior Tax Court memos, the Court rejected Sliwoski's use of this method as a means of valuing decedents equity interest in a closely held company.

The Court accepted the required rate of return on equity opined by Kramer, which was 24.90%, because it was based upon the correct risk-free rate from 20-year U.S. Treasury bonds. The Court agreed with both experts that this rate of return should be adjusted to account for expected future growth of the company.

The Court found that Sliwoski's 6% growth rate was too high, and Kramer's 3% growth rate was too low. Neither was supported by evidence in the record. Sliwoski's growth rate was not tailored to the company's specific product mix, and Kramer's was based solely on the rate of inflation. The Court ultimately determined that the growth rate should be 4.15% because "the national annual compound growth rate for the items in Renier's product mix, weighted to reflect the percentage of sales of each, was only 4.15% from 1989 through 1993."

Business broker method not justified

Kramer also valued Renier using a market approach method that he called the "business broker method":

> [T]he business broker method postulates that the purchase price of a business equals the market value of the inventory and fixed assets plus a multiple of the sellers discretionary cash-flow, defined as the total cash-flow available to the owner of the business.

The Court rejected Kramer's application of this method because he failed to justify the multiple he applied to the company's discretionary cash flow. He used "his own judgment" rather than providing adequate supporting data. Accordingly, the Court found that "on this record the reliability of the business broker method has not been established."

Shepherd v. Commissioner (I)

Citation: 115 T.C. 376, 115 T.C. No. 30, 2000 U.S. Tax Ct. LEXIS 77
Court: United States Tax Court
State/Jurisdiction: Specialty Federal
Date of Decision: October 26, 2000
Judge: Thornton

The taxpayer owned 50% of a newly formed family partnership and his two sons each owned 25%. The taxpayer transferred to the partnership his fee interest in timberland and stocks in three banks. The Tax Court ruled that these transfers represented separate indirect gifts to his sons of 25% undivided interests in the leased timberland and stocks. Eleven judges signed the majority opinion, five judges signed a concurring opinion, eight judges signed a second concurring opinion, three judges signed an opinion concurring in part and dissenting in part, and one judge signed an additional opinion concurring in part and dissenting in part.

On Aug. 1, 1991, the taxpayer executed a partnership agreement. On the same day, he also executed deeds transferring two separate, undivided 50% interests in leased timberland to the partnership. His two sons did not execute the partnership agreement until Aug. 2,1991. Both the taxpayer and the IRS agree that the partnership came into existence on Aug. 2, 1991, when the sons signed the agreement. On Sept. 5, 1991, the taxpayer transferred bank stock to the partnership.

IRS contests discounts

The taxpayer contended that the gifts to his sons of interests in the land represented two separate gifts of partnership interests and that the gifts of bank stock represented two separate indirect gifts bestowed through enhancements of the previously gifted partnership interests. The taxpayer argued the gifts should be valued giving effect to a 33.5% minority and marketability discount applicable to each son's 25% partnership interest.

Taxpayer made indirect gifts

The IRS did not dispute that the partnership existed or that it was a legitimate partnership. The IRS also agreed that if the gifts of land should be valued giving effect to minority and marketability discounts in recognition of the 25% partnership shares, the appropriate discount would be 33.5%. The IRS contended, however, that the minority and marketability discounts were inapplicable because the gifts should not be measured by reference to the sons' partnership interests. They argued that the taxpayer did not give his sons partnership interests but rather gave them either: (1) indirect gifts of real estate, accomplished by means of a transfer to the partnership, or alternatively, (2) direct gifts of real estate, accomplished before the partnership ever came into existence.

The Court determined the taxpayer did not make direct gifts to his sons, noting, "Petitioner deeded the leased land and bank stock to the partnership. Whatever interests his sons acquired in this property they obtained by virtue of their status as partners in the partnership."

Court disallows DLOM

The Court ruled, however, that the taxpayer had made gifts of indirect interests, thus eliminating the discounts for lack of control and marketability. The Court aggregated the two separate 50% undivided interests transferred to the partnership by the taxpayer "to reflect the economic substance of petitioner's conveyance to the partnership of his entire interest in the leased land." The Court noted that it did not aggregate the separate indirect interests to the sons.

The taxpayer presented three real estate appraisers to support their valuation of the leased timberland. The parties had stipulated to the undiscounted value of the bank stocks. Among the items about which the IRS and taxpayer experts clashed were the discount for the undivided interest, the discount rate to use in calculating the present value of the lease payments, and whether to use pre-tax or after tax lease income in the discounting calculation. The IRS argued that the discount for an undivided interest should be limited to the cost to partition, but this argument was rejected by the Court, which noted that this approach failed to give adequate consideration to other factors such as lack of control in managing and disposing of the property. Ultimately, the court allowed a 15% undivided interest discount.

Knight v. Commissioner

Citation: 115 T.C. 506, 115 T.C. No. 36, 2000 U.S. Tax Ct. LEXIS 88
Court: United States Tax Court
State/Jurisdiction: Specialty Federal
Date of Decision: November 30, 2000
Judge: Colvin

In this case, the Tax Court determined that a Texas family limited partnership could not be ignored for valuation purposes and that § 2704(b) did not apply. The Tax Court ignored the taxpayer's appraisal expert, concluding he was acting as a taxpayer advocate and dismissing the discounts he claimed for portfolio mix, minority interest, and lack of marketability. The Tax Court determined that the discounts for lack of control and marketability should be 15%.

In 1994, the Knight family formed a family limited partnership and a related trust to act as the general partner. They transferred assets totaling $2,081,323 to the partnership, including two personal residences occupied rent-free by their children, municipal bond funds and Treasury notes totaling $1,525,237, and other assets. The partnership kept no records, prepared no annual reports, and had no employees.

Disregard the partnership?

The parties stipulated that the steps taken to create the partnership satisfied all requirements under Texas law. Still, however, the IRS contended that the partnership should be disregarded for gift tax valuation purposes because the partnership lacked economic substance and failed to qualify as a partnership under Federal Law. The taxpayers argued that their rights and legal relationships and those of their children changed significantly when they formed the partnership and made asset transfers. The Court agreed with the taxpayer noting, *"[W]e do not disregard the partnership because we have no reason to conclude from this record that a hypothetical buyer or seller would ignore it."* To the substance over form argument raised by the IRS, the Court replied, *"[W]e believe the form of the transaction here (the creation of the partnership) would be taken into account by a willing buyer; thus the substance and form of the transaction are not at odds for gift tax valuation purposes."*

Gift value limited

The transfer document for the gifts stated that the amount of the gift was "the number of partnership units which equals $300,000 in value." The taxpayers argued that this prevented the IRS from asserting a value in excess of $300,000. The Court disagreed, noting that the taxpayers had offered expert testimony that the gifts were worth only $263,165. The Court concluded, *"We find petitioners' contentions to be at best inconsistent. We treat petitioners' contention and offer of evidence that the gifts were worth less than $300,000 as opening the door to our consideration of respondent's argument that the gifts were worth more than $300,000."*

FMV over fair value

The IRS expert testified about the "fair value" of the partnership interests instead of the fair market value, and the Court did not consider his testimony. The taxpayer expert claimed a portfolio discount of 10% based on a "*report stating that conglomerate public companies tend to sell at a discount of about 10 to 15% from their breakup value.*" The Court noted that the Knight family partnership was not a conglomerate public company and the appraiser gave no convincing reason why the partnership's mix of assets would be unattractive to a buyer. The Court disallowed this discount in full.

The taxpayer expert claimed a 10% minority discount based on the discounts to net asset value for closed end bond funds. The Court noted, "*The 10 funds that [the appraiser] chose are not comparable to the Knight family partnership. We find unconvincing his use of data from noncomparable entities to increase this discount. However, on this record, we believe some discount is appropriate based on an analogy to a closed-end fund.*"

The appraiser claimed a 30% discount for lack of marketability based on initial public offerings of common stock from 1985 to 1993. According to the Court, "*[H]e did not show that the companies...were comparable to the partnership, or explain how he used this data to estimate the discount for lack of marketability.*" The appraiser also listed seven reasons why a discount for lack of marketability applies, but he did not explain how those reasons affect the amount of the discount for lack of marketability.

The Court concluded that the expert "*was acting as an advocate and that his testimony was not objective.*" The Court did believe some discount was appropriate and allowed a combined discount for lack of control and marketability of 15%.

Application of § 2704(b)

The IRS contended that the 50-year term of the partnership and the lack of withdrawal rights for limited partners were applicable restrictions under Internal Revenue Code § 2704(b). The Tax Court disagreed.

Ten judges agreed with this opinion and two concurred in result only. Two judges signed a separate opinion concurring in result. In this concurring opinion the judges said, "*Whether 'the form of the transaction here (the creation of the partnership) would be taken into account by a willing buyer' is not a relevant consideration in determining whether the entity must be respected for transfer tax purposes...The 'willing buyer, willing seller analysis merely establishes the value of a partnership interest, not whether the economic substance doctrine is applicable.*" In a discussion of the economic substance doctrine, the judges concluded, "*If taxpayers, however, are willing to burden their property with binding legal restrictions that, in fact, reduce the value of such property, we cannot disregard such restrictions. To do so would be to disregard economic reality.*"

In a dissenting opinion, Judge Beghe said that the valuation focus should have been on the assets transferred rather than on the partnership interests received. He would have valued the gifts at 100% of the values of the assets transferred to the partnership, less the values of the partnership interests retained by the taxpayers.

Estate of Strangi v. Commissioner (I)

Citation: 115 T.C. 478, 115 T.C. No. 35, 2000 U.S. Tax Ct. LEXIS 89
Court: United States Tax Court
State/Jurisdiction: Specialty Federal
Date of Decision: November 30, 2000
Judge: Cohen

In 1993 and 1994, decedent Albert Strangi was suffering severe medical problems. In 1994, decedent's daughter Rosalie Gulig (who held a power of attorney), attended a Fortress Financial Group estate planning seminar that had as its primary focus the creation of a family limited partnership with a corporate general partner. On Aug. 12, 1994, using the Fortress copyrighted limited partnership and shareholders' agreements, Mrs. Gulig used her power of attorney to form Strangi Family Limited Partnership (SFLP) and Stranco, the corporate general partner of SFLP. Decedent died on Oct. 14, 1994, at age 81. In August 1994, Decedent transferred $9,876,929 of assets to SFLP, 75% of which were cash and securities, in exchange for a 99% limited partnership interest. Stranco owned a 1% general partner interest in SFLP. Decedent owned 47% of Stranco and his four children owned the remaining 53%.

Following the formation of SFLP, various distributions were made by SFLP to decedent's estate and the Strangi children. When distributions were made, corresponding and proportionate distributions were made to Stranco either in cash or in the form of adjusting journal entries. In July 1995, SFLP distributed $3,187,800 to decedent's estate for State and Federal estate and inheritance taxes. In addition, in 1995 and in 1996, SFLP distributed $563,000 to each of the Strangi children. The distributions were characterized as distributions to decedent's estate. In May 1996, SFLP divided its primary Merrill Lynch account into four separate accounts, one in each of the Strangi children's names, giving them control over a proportionate share of the partnership assets. The partnership also extended lines of credit to John Strangi, Albert T. Strangi, and Mrs. Gulig.

The issues before the Tax Court were: (1) Whether SFLP should be disregarded for Federal tax purposes because it lacked business purpose and economic substance; (2) whether the mere existence of SFLP was a restriction on the sale or use of property that should be disregarded pursuant to section §2703(a)(2); (3) whether the transfer of assets to SFLP was a taxable gift; and (4) the fair market value of decedent's interest in SFLP at the date of death.

Business purpose and economic substance

The IRS argued that SFLP should be disregarded in valuing assets under the business purpose and economic substance doctrines. The estate argued that the business purpose and economic substance doctrines do not apply to transfer tax cases but, in any event, SFLP did have economic substance and business purpose. The Tax Court agreed that there were reasons to be skeptical about the non-tax motives for forming SFLP. The opinion provides a scathing analysis of the purported business purpose and the partnership activities with respect to the transactions with decedent's children.

The IRS attempted to argue that the property should be included in the estate under §2036 because decedent retained economic benefits. The IRS motion to apply this theory was denied because it was not timely filed, but the Court did say, "The actual control exercised by Mr. Gulig, combined with the 99-percent limited partnership interest in SFLP and the 47-percent interest in Stranco, suggest the possibility of including the property transferred to the partnership in decedents estate under section 2036."

The Court concluded:

> SFLP was validly formed under State law. The formalities were followed, and the proverbial 'is were dotted and 'ts were crossed. The partnership, as a legal matter, changed the relationships between decedent and his heirs and decedent and actual and potential creditors. Regardless of subjective intentions, the partnership had sufficient substance to be recognized for tax purposes. Its existence would not be disregarded by potential purchasers of decedents assets, and we do not disregard it in this case.

Existence of SFLP as § 2703(a)(2) restriction

The IRS argued that the mere existence of the partnership is a restriction under §2703(a)(2) and its existence should be ignored for valuation purposes. The IRS further argued that the term "property" under §2703(a)(2) refers to the underlying assets in the partnership. The Court concluded, "Unfortunately for respondents position, neither the language of the statute nor the language of the regulation supports respondents interpretation."

Gift at SFLP inception

The IRS alternative argument was that if the partnership was recognized for estate tax purposes, decedent made a gift when he transferred property to the partnership and received a limited partnership interest of lesser value in return. The Court noted:

> Nonetheless, in this case, because we do not believe that decedent gave up control over the assets, his beneficial interest in them exceeded 99%, and his contribution was allocated to his own capital account, the instinctive reaction that there was a gift at

> the inception of the partnership does not lead to a determination of gift tax liability... Realistically, in this case, the disparity between the value of the assets in the hands of decedent and the alleged value of his partnership interest reflects on the credibility of the claimed discount applicable to the partnership interest. It does not reflect a taxable gift.

Valuation of limited partnership interest

Both the IRS and taxpayer's experts determined a 25% lack of marketability discount was appropriate for SFLP. They disagreed, however, on the minority interest discount. The IRS appraiser used 8% while the taxpayer expert used 25%. For Stranco, the IRS expert used a 5% minority interest discount and a 15% marketability discount. The taxpayers expert did not value the interest in Stranco, "because he believed the relationship was irrelevant." The Court adopted the IRS appraiser's valuation and noted the taxpayer's experts "...result is unreasonable and must be rejected." The IRS appraiser selected the lower minority interest discount based on an examination of closed end mutual funds and the Court noted the analysis was "well documented and persuasive."

The estate argued that considering the stock interest in Stranco in valuing the limited partnership interest is incorrect because the shareholder agreement granted the corporation and the other shareholders the right to purchase any selling shareholder's stock. The Court concluded the shareholder agreement was only a factor to be considered and believed the hypothetical seller would market the interests in the family limited partnership and the corporation together and that any transaction would take place only if the two interests were transferred together.

In its conclusion, the Court said:

> In view of our rejection of respondents belated attempt to raise section 2036 and respondents request that we disregard the partnership agreement altogether, we are constrained to accept the evidence concerning discounts applicable to decedents interest in the partnership and in Stranco as of the date of death. We believe that the result of respondent's experts discounts may still be overgenerous to petitioner, but that result is the one that we must reach under the evidence and under the applicable statutes.

In a concurring opinion, two of the 15 judges involved in this opinion disagreed with the application of the economic substance theory, saying, "The Court should conclude that the economic substance doctrine does not apply to disregard a validly formed entity where the issue is the value for Federal gift and estate tax purposes of the interest transferred in that entity."

In dissenting opinions, three judges would disregard the partnership and value the partnership interest at the value of the underlying partnership assets without any discount. And five judges concluded that §2512(b) should be applied, where the excess of the value of the property that decedent transferred to the partnership over the value of the consideration he received is a "deemed gift" subject to the gift tax.

Three of the judges who signed the latter dissenting opinion issued an additional dissenting opinion, suggesting the use of the step transaction doctrine to treat the underlying partnership assets as the property to be valued for estate tax purposes.

Janda v. Commissioner

Citation: T.C. Memo 2001-24, 2001 Tax Ct. Memo LEXIS 34
Court: United States Tax Court
State/Jurisdiction: Specialty Federal
Date of Decision: February 2, 2001
Judge: Vasquez

In November 1992, the Petitioners gifted shares of St. Edward Management Company (the "Company") common stock to their children. Each gift represented approximately 5.3% of the outstanding shares of common stock. St. Edward Management Company owned 94.6% of the common stock of the Bank of St. Edward (the "Bank"), a bank located in a small agricultural community in Nebraska.

In connection with the gift tax return, the Petitioners hired the accounting firm Grant Thornton to perform an appraisal. Grant Thornton determined the fair market value of the stock to be $21.22 per share on a minority, non-marketable basis. In their appraisal, Grant Thornton applied a 10% minority interest discount, and a 20% marketability discount.

Expert prepares valuation report

Philip Schneider & Associates, Inc., was hired by the IRS to perform an appraisal of the Company. The report was completed on Feb. 13, 1998. The expert determined the fair market value of the stock to be approximately $30.50 per share on a minority, non-marketable basis. This amount includes a 20% discount for lack of marketability.

At the Tax Court trial, the Petitioners did not provide testimony by Grant Thornton. The Petitioners' expert witness was Gary Wahlgren. Wahlgren's appraisal report was completed on Feb. 9, 2000 - approximately two years after my report was issued.

Petitioner's expert uses QMDM

Wahlgren determined the fair market value of the stock to be $51.38 per share on a "controlling, marketable" basis. After applying a 10% minority interest discount, Wahlgren determined the fair market value of the stock to be $46.24 per share on a minority, marketable basis.

Using Z. Christopher Mercer's Quantitative Marketability Discount Model (QMDM), Wahlgren determined that a 65.77% marketability discount was appropriate. Therefore, according to Wahlgren, the fair market value of the stock was $15.83 per share on a minority, non-marketable basis.

Experts agree on minority, marketable value

In reviewing Wahlgren's report, the expert noted that the Bank had certain loans that had been previously written off, but management believed that full payment would be received. The existence of these off-balance sheet assets was not disclosed in the information that had been provided to me.

After considering these off-balance sheet assets, the expert agreed with Wahlgren's conclusion that the fair market value of the Company was approximately $46.24 per share on a minority, marketable basis. After applying a 20% marketability discount, the expert concluded that the fair market value of the stock was approximately $37 per share on a minority, non-marketable basis.

Only issue is marketability discount

Because both experts agreed that the fair market value of the Company was $46.24 per share on a minority, marketable basis, there was only one issue for the Tax Court to address. What is an appropriate marketability discount?

The expert relied upon various restricted stock studies and prior Tax Court decisions. The Tax Court criticized these studies as being too general. Because information was not presented regarding marketability discounts for this particular industry, or for companies with the same characteristics as St. Edward Management Company, the Tax Court concluded that my analysis was too subjective.

Business appraisers usually rely on "generalized" studies (restricted stock studies, pre-IPO studies, etc.) in determining an appropriate marketability discount. The Tax Court - as well as business appraisers - would prefer to have more specific data for each appraisal engagement. Unfortunately, more specific data is usually not available.

Mercer developed the QMDM in an attempt to reduce the subjectivity associated with determining marketability discounts. However, it is clear that the Tax Court does not find the QMDM to be a useful tool. In the *Janda* decision, the Tax Court stated: "We find Mr. Wahlgren's application of the QMDM model in the instant case not to be helpful in our determination of the marketability discount." This comment is consistent with the Tax Court ruling in *Estate of Weinberg v. Commissioner,* T.C. Memo 2000-51, 2000 Tax Ct. Memo Lexis 58 (Feb. 15, 2000).

In its rejection of QMDM, the Tax Court stated: "We have grave doubts about the reliability of the QMDM model to produce reasonable discounts, given the generated discount of over 65%." I would offer the following interpretation of this statement. In concluding that a 65.77% marketability discount is unreasonable, the Tax Court must accept that, despite the inherent weaknesses, restricted stock studies provide at least a basic guideline for determining whether a marketability discount is reasonable.

Tax Court concludes 40% combined discount

The Tax Court concluded that a 40% *combined* discount (for lack of control and lack of marketability) was appropriate. Using Wahlgren's conclusion regarding the controlling, marketable value of the Company ($51.38 per share), and applying a 40% combined discount, the Tax Court concluded that the fair market value of the stock was $30.83 per share.

The Tax Court did not provide any justification for the 40% discount. In addition, the Tax Court did not provide a separate minority interest discount and marketability discount. The ruling does indicate, however, that most of the discount relates to concerns over lack of control. The Tax Court stated: "[W]e also believe that most of the concerns regarding lack of marketability relate to the lack of control associated with any transferred block of stock."

In the *Janda* decision, the Tax Court highlighted the problems with using generalized empirical studies to determine marketability discounts. However, the ruling also suggests that restricted stock studies provide a basic guideline for determining whether a marketability discount is reasonable. In addition, the Tax Court rejected (for the second time) the use of QMDM.

Estate of Magnin v. Commissioner (III)

Citation: T.C. Memo. 2001-31, 2001 Tax Ct. Memo LEXIS 41
Court: United States Tax Court
State/Jurisdiction: Specialty Federal
Date of Decision: February 12, 2001
Judge: Ruwe

This case involves a hearing on remand from the Ninth Circuit to provide sufficient analysis of the consideration value of common and preferred stock in two closely held companies transferred and received by Cyril Magnin, the life estate holder. The issue appealed was whether, under Section 2036(a), Cyril received "adequate and full consideration" for the remainder interest he agreed to transfer to his children under the 1951 agreement he made with his father, Joseph Magnin.

Both experts valued the companies using the discounted cash flow and guideline public companies methods. However, their results varied greatly.

IRS valuation

Stephen Stewart of KPMG Peat Marwick LLP, the IRS' expert, valued the common stock by subtracting the preferred stock value from the companies' value as a whole. The preferred stock value was derived from comparing the actual dividend yield to the yield that would be demanded by an investor.

Stewart calculated the value of the consideration received and transferred by Cyril for both companies. He applied the following:

- Guideline public companies method with a 35% discount for lack of marketability, and
- Discounted cash flow method with 20% minority and 35% marketability discounts.

With a $158,000 value of Joseph's stock, Stewart valued the consideration Cyril received by factoring Cyril's age and voting control over the stock to arrive at a $30,500 valuation. He concluded that the remainder interest transferred by Cyril resulted in an overall value of $123,000.

Estate's valuation

Bryan Browning of Valuation Research Corporation, the estate's expert, similarly applied minority and marketability discounts after valuing the companies and subtracting the preferred stocks value. He valued the consideration by combining the shares owned by Joseph and Cyril, which constituted a controlling interest. This required a 40% control premium. Browning then valued Cyril's control value by deducting Joseph's life estate value and Cyril's minority interest. The value of the remainder interest resulted from factoring the percentage of Cyril's ownership interest, the equity values of the companies, and his life interest. Browning valued the overall property transfer value at $42,000.

IRS valuation accepted as least erroneous and more reliable

The court criticized Browning's application of the willing buyer and willing seller standard. He assumed that the hypothetical buyer would be in the same position as Cyril where one could combine previously acquired shares to produce a control premium.

Browning also incorrectly applied a combined minority and marketability discount. The court noted that:

> Discounts for marketability and minority interest are separate and distinct, and this fact must be taken into account when such discounts are applied in order to avoid distorting the valuation. While expert reports and the courts sometimes apply combined discount rates to determine the value of stock, this is a questionable procedure to use if specific rates are determined for each discount and then added together to reach the combined rate. See Pratt, et al., *Valuing a Business: The Analysis and Appraisal of Closely Held Companies,* 314 (3d ed. 1996). In order to ensure accuracy, the minority interest discount should be applied first and then the marketability and liquidity discount should be applied to this figure. Had this been done, the discounts would have yielded a combined discount rate of 51.25%.

Browning's testimony at trial produced further discrepancies regarding the reliability of his valuations. He discounted value from the guideline public companies method for minority interest, although he admitted that most appraisers view the market approach valuation as a minority interest value. According to his testimony, he discounted this valuation to produce a valuation that was more in line with the value he derived from the discounted cash flow method.

The court also noted that Stewart made a "troubling...large mistake" in his original valuation report, which he corrected after trial. He failed to subtract projected capital expenditures.

Although the court ruled that both experts erred in their calculations, the IRS valuation provided a better approximation of the values and was more reliable.

Estate of Jones v. Commissioner

Citation: 116 T.C. 121, 116 T.C. No. 11, 2001 U.S. Tax Ct. LEXIS 11
Court: United States Tax Court
State/Jurisdiction: Specialty Federal
Date of Decision: March 6, 2001
Judge: Cohen

This tax case concerned limited partnership interests gifted to family member partners. Decedent Jones owned surface rights to several large cattle ranches. Jones formed two limited partnerships (JBLP and AVLP) and gave limited partnership interests to his children. The IRS asserted a $4,412,527 deficiency in Jones' 1995 gift tax return upon his death on Dec. 17, 1998.

Transfer upon formation not a gift

The IRS first argued that Jones made taxable gifts upon formation by contributing his property to the partnership. Jones and his children transferred assets to the partnership in exchange for partnership interests. The court found that Jones did not make a gift at formation:

> All of the contributions of property were properly reflected in the capital accounts of decedent, and the value of the other partners' interests was not enhanced by the contributions of decedent.

The court refused to apply IRC § 2704(b), which would disregard the partnership agreement restrictions when valuing the partnership interests that were transferred by gift. The partnership agreement restricted partnership withdrawal, only allowed capital account returns upon termination, and provided a 35-year existence.

The IRS argued that the provisions restrict liquidation and should be disregarded from the valuation. The court found no reason to depart from *Kerr v. Commissioner*, 113 T.C. 449 (1999), which held that the same kinds of restrictions did not limit a partner's ability to liquidate.

The court then determined the nature of the interests transferred by Jones. His estate claimed Jones transferred assignee interests rather than limited partnership interests because the gift recipients did not consent in writing as required by the partnership agreement. Under *Kerr,* he transferred limited partnership interests:

> The evidence shows that decedent intended for the transfers to include limited partnership interests and that the children consented to the transfer of limited partnership interests, having waived the requirement of a writing.

The court noted many particular facts in reaching this finding. The documents were entitled "gifts" and referenced the interests as limited partnership interests, and the 1995 gift tax return referenced "limited partnership interest." The court discussed a number of additional factors.

JBLP valuation

The court agreed with Francis Burns' valuation that applied no discount for lack of control. The JBLP agreement allowed general partner removal by an aggregate 51% interest. Jones transferred 83.08% interest to his son A.C. In effect, he would control management and could compel a sale of partnership property, compel distributions, and force liquidation.

Burns also applied no marketability discount. The court disagreed and applied an 8% marketability discount to "accurately reflect reality" of sale restrictions to third parties:

> Self-imposed limitations on the interest, created with the purpose of minimizing value for transfer tax purposes, are likely to be waived or disregarded when the owner of the interests becomes a hypothetical willing seller, seeking the highest price that the interest will bring from a willing buyer.
>
> The owner of the 83.08% interests has the ability to persuade or coerce other partners into cooperating with the proposed sale. The possibility of litigation over forced liquidation would reduce the amount that a hypothetical buyer would be willing to pay for the interest.

The final JBLP valuation issue concerned the discount for built-in capital gains realized upon liquidation. Capital gains taxes could be avoided by an IRC § 754 election at the time of selling the partnership assets.

Charles Elliot applied a discount for built-in gains because the § 754 election was not certain, based on A.C. Jones' trial testimony. Burns did not apply a built-in capital gains discount.

The court agreed with Burns. The only identifiable situation where a § 754 election would not be made is under heavy administrative burdens: "lots of partners... and a lot of assets." The court found that:

> The buyer and seller of the partnership interest would negotiate with the understanding that an election would be made and the price agreed upon would not reflect a discount for built-in gains.

AVLP valuation

Elliot applied the following discounts to the valuation of the AVLP interest that was transferred:

- Secondary market discount of 45%,
- Discount for lack of marketability of 20%, and
- Discount for built-in capital gains.

Burns, on the other hand, applied:

- Secondary market discount of 38%,
- Discount for lack of marketability of 7.5%, and
- No discount for built-in capital gains.

To determine the secondary market discount ("an overall discount encompassing discounts for both lack of control and marketability for minority interests in syndicated limited partnerships"), the experts used *Partnership Profiles* data. However, the court noted that the experts compared AVLP to differing sets of data. Elliot compared the Jan. 1, 1995 AVLP gift to May/June 1994 data. Burns compared the gift to the May/June 1995 data. The May/June 1995 data would have been available for decedent Jones to survey comparable transactions.

The court found Elliot's valuation "did not survive a sanity check." Ultimately, the court applied:

- Secondary market discount of 40%,
- Discount for lack of marketability of 8%, and,
- No discount for built-in gains (for the same reason one was not applied in JBLP valuation).

Estate of Kaufman v. Commissioner (II)

Citation: 243 F.3d 1145, 2001 U.S. App. LEXIS 3913
Court: United States Court of Appeals
State/Jurisdiction: 9th Circuit Federal
Date of Decision: March 15, 2001
Judge: Noonan

This case is the Ninth Circuit Court of Appeals' decision on appeal of *Kaufman v. Commissioner,* T.C. Memo 1999-119 (1999). The Tax Court had ruled in favor of the IRS, rejecting the estate's valuation expert and evidence of actual sales, and deciding the case under the burden of proof.

Actual sales were arm's length

The Ninth Circuit reversed the Tax Court's ruling and ordered entry of judgment in favor of the estate on remand. The Ninth Circuit found that the evidence of actual sales of Seminole stock near the valuation date "should have been dispositive, viz., the price at which stock owned by the Estate had traded between willing and knowledgeable buyers and sellers."

In essence, the Ninth Circuit found that the actual sales were arm's length transactions that were the best evidence of fair market value. The court noted that the sellers were under no compulsion to sell, that they reasonably relied upon a Merrill Lynch valuation presented by the buyer, and that the evidence of a distant family relationship between the parties did not indicate a lack of arm's length negotiations.

Finally, the court noted that the Tax Court made a factual error that affected its decision. The Tax Court found the actual sales were unrepresentative" because they were much smaller than the estate's block of stock. This finding was based on the incorrect assumption that voting for directors was cumulative, which would allow the holder of the estate's shares to elect a director, thus giving the estate's block a greater value. Under Oklahoma law, however, voting for directors is noncumulative, unless the bylaws of the corporation specify otherwise.

Burden of proof was on IRS

The court also noted that the Tax Court erred in its assignment of the burden of proof in this case. Because the IRS abandoned its notice of deficiency valuation at trial, the Tax Court could not rely on that valuation, and the burden shifted to the IRS to prove a deficiency.

Estate of McMorris v. Commissioner

Citation: No. 99-9031 (10th Cir. 2001)
Court: United States Court of Appeals
State/Jurisdiction: 10th Circuit Federal
Date of Decision: March 20, 2001
Judge: Briscoe

In the *Estate of Evelyn McMorris v. CIR*, No. 99-9031 (March 20, 2001), the Tenth Circuit considered whether post-death events could affect the decedent's tax return. In 1990, the decedent received stock from her husband upon his death. The husband's estate reported that the stock had a fair market value of $1.7 million per share, which became the decedent's basis. In 1991, the company redeemed the stock for $2.2 million per share. Later that year, the decedent died. Her estate paid the federal and state income taxes due attributable to the gain from the stock redemption on her last personal tax return. It also deducted the tax as a claim against the estate under IRC sec. 2053 (a)(3) on its estate tax return.

In 1994, the Commissioner issued a deficiency notice to the decedent's husband's estate. Among the issues was the value of the stock. After the parties settled, the value of the stock was increased, thereby changing the decedent's basis in the stock. Because her basis increased, the taxable gain from the stock redemption "was eliminated and she realized a loss." Thereafter, the IRS disallowed the decedent's use of the section 2053(a)(3) deduction. The estate "took the position that post-death events may not be considered in determining the amount of its deduction for ...[the decedent's] individual income tax liabilities because those liabilities were valid and enforceable claims against the estate at the time of ...[the decedent's] death." The Tax Court ruled in favor of the IRS and the estate appealed.

On appeal, the Tenth Circuit noted that this was an issue of first impression in the circuit. It then considered the leading case on the consideration of post-death events— *Ithaca Trust Co. v. United States*, 279 U.S. 151 (1929). The Supreme Court in *Ithaca Trust* handed down the date-of-death valuation rule: "The estate so far as may be is settled as of the date of the testator's death." The Tenth Circuit noted that while considerations have been made for post-death events since the rule, "we hold that the date-of-death valuation rule announced in *Ithaca Trust* applies to a deduction for a claim against the estate under section 2053 (a)(3)." The court reasoned, "this principle provides a bright line rule which alleviates the uncertainty and delay in estate administration which may result if events occurring months or even years after the decedent's death could be considered in valuing a claim against the estate."

This abstract originally appeared in *Valuation Case Digest*, authored by John J. Stockdale, Jr.

Estate of Forbes v. Commissioner

Citation: T.C. Memo 2001-72, 2001 Tax Ct. Memo LEXIS 94
Court: United States Tax Court
State/Jurisdiction: Specialty Federal
Date of Decision: March 23, 2001
Judge: Thornton

This valuation dispute arose from the undivided real estate interest held by the Forbes QTIP trust. The Forbes established a QTIP trust that included a 42% interest in Malatchie Land Co. (a limited partnership that held the farm real estate) and the assets of Malatchie Farms (a sole proprietorship).

The valuation issue in this appeal concerned the fair market value of 42% and 42.9% undivided interests in two real estate parcels held by the QTIP. By agreement of both parties, the court's remaining issue was what fractional discount should apply.

Expert valuations differ

James Lawton applied a 30% fractional discount to his value of $1,746,795 because of the QTIP's minority interests and because of the restricted pool of potential buyers due to difficulties in securing financing and costs for parcel partitioning. He could not find comparable transactions, but he considered the following:

- Real estate brokers in the same market as the subject property applied fractional interests of 10-30% in partnership liquidations
- Specific characteristics of the property
- Possible intra-family conflicts
- Other factors adversely affecting the marketability of the two undivided interests

Glen Hultquist valued the property at $720,000 by including beneficial interests in the pecan orchards but not the value of the timber. He based this on "the correlated present value of net annual income streams that he projected from hypothetical partitions or forced sales of the subject property under various scenarios."

The court previously disposed of the beneficial interest issues and therefore excluded the values from the QTIP's undivided interest valuation. Hultquist's valuation was 36% less than the undiscounted fair market value of the undivided interests.

The court disagreed with Hultquist:

> We are unconvinced that a discount rate extrapolated from one set of indicated values, under assumptions inapplicable here, would correspond to the discount rate extrapolated from a different set of indicated values if the underlying assumptions were altered.

Hultquist's present value computations are inadequately explained and justified, particularly in regard to the manner in which he derived the projected revenues from his hypothetical partitions or forced sales and the manner in which he derived his chosen 14% equity yield for purposes of his present value computations.

Richard Parks used a comparable sales approach to arrive at an 18% discount. His "comparables" discounts ranged from 25-64% and are as follows:

- A 1989 sale of an office building in Birmingham, Ala.
- A 1961 sale of a 128-acre vacant tract in Jefferson County, Ala.
- A 1981 sale of a 1,600-acre tract known as Bell Plantation (apparently outside of Georgia)

Court upholds estate's discount rate

The court found "no adequate justification" for the 18% discount. Neither party's experts adequately justified their valuation discounts, "a shortcoming that might be attributable in part to a lack of available empirical data." Therefore, the court applied Lawton's 30% valuation discount, which was the same as the federal estate tax return.

Wall v. Commissioner

Citation: T.C. Memo 2001-75, 2001 Tax Ct. Memo LEXIS 97
Court: United States Tax Court
State/Jurisdiction: Specialty Federal
Date of Decision: March 27, 2001
Judge: Beghe

This was a gift tax valuation case in which the sole issue for decision was the fair market value of 9,380 shares of the company's nonvoting common stock, which the majority shareholder gifted into trusts for the benefit of his children. The stock was not listed on an exchange, nor was there any other public market for the stock.

Prior transactions not best evidence of FMV

If there is no market for a company's stock, arm's-length transactions may be the best evidence of fair market value. There were six transactions in the company's stock prior to the gifts. Three of those transactions, however, occurred more than five years before the gifts, and the other three occurred almost two years before. The company's net income declined sharply in the interim period. The court determined, therefore, that the prior transactions were not the best evidence of the fair market value of the stock on the date of the gifts.

Petitioners' expert's reports

In her original report, expert for petitioners, Donna J. Walker, relied almost entirely on the guideline public company method under the market approach to value the stock. Walker gave equal weight to her use of both historical performance measures and forecasted earnings of the company in her guideline public company method. Because this method determines value by reference to the trading prices of minority interests, Walker did not apply a minority discount. She did, however, apply a 40% lack of marketability discount and a 5% nonvoting stock discount.

Walker submitted a revised report in response to respondent's criticism that her original report did not include any income-based determination of value. In the revised report, Walker used the company's historical results to develop what she called "normalized" free cash flow. She then capitalized this amount at a 22.75% capitalization rate (including an equity-risk premium, a small company risk premium, and an additional risk premium for the company's exceptionally small size) less a 5% assumed growth rate to arrive at her total equity value. Walker combined this result with that of the original report to arrive at her final opinion on the value of the stock, which was lower than in her first report.

Respondent's expert's report

Respondent's expert, Gary L. Schroeder, used both a guideline public company method and an income approach to value the stock. His guideline method was very similar to Walker's, except that he only used three companies out of her seven. The other major difference was that Schroeder included in the value the amount of the "media note," a note for an earlier sale of the company's media division assets. Like Walker, Schroeder also applied a 40% marketability discount but concluded that only a 2% nonvoting stock discount was appropriate.

Schroeder's income-based approach differed from Walker's in several respects. First, he again added the value of the media note to the company's predicted future income. Second, he stated that his approach produced a control value and so applied a 17% minority discount to the present value of future income. Third, his determinations of future income and the appropriate discount rate were quite different from Walker's. Finally, he arrived at his appraisal value by assigning the income-based value twice as much weight as the market-based value. The end result was higher than the value stated by the IRS in the statutory notice of deficiency.

Flaws in both experts' market approaches

The Tax Court concluded that Walker's guideline public company method understated the company's value. By failing to include the media note, Walker's method understated the company's earning power. Walker also incorrectly stated management's income projections. Although the court said that this was probably a mere transcription error, it still had the effect of understating management's actual earnings forecasts.

Further, Walker chose the lowest multiples from among the guideline companies due to the company's decline in earnings. This, however, was inconsistent with her conclusions elsewhere in her report regarding the company's comparability to industry norms. Nevertheless, the court found her analysis to be thorough, well explained, and entitled to "some weight."

On the other hand, the court determined that Schroeder's guideline public company method overstated the company's value. Because a minority shareholder could not require liquidation and thus could not realize the media note's full value, the court found that Schroeder should have applied a minority discount to the note's value. Moreover, the court stated that Schroeder should have used more than three guideline companies.

Income approach values entitled to little weight

At the outset, the court recognized the general principle that if the subject company's future income is unpredictable, then income-based approaches will produce inaccurate appraisals of the company's value. As of the date of the gifts, the company's management had predicted only one year of future results, due to the recent fluctuations in net income, the difficulties experienced by its major customer groups, and the unsettled economic conditions.

Because of this difficulty of predicting future revenues, Walker used an average of the company's historical and forecasted results. Citing to *Valuing Small Businesses and Professional Practices*, Pratt, et al., the court cautioned that historical averages or pure extrapolations from those averages are usually inadequate bases for an income approach. An analyst should use such averages only if she can explain why they are a reasonable proxy for future expectations. Thus, the court gave little weight to Walker's value derived from her income approach.

Schroeder's predictions suffered the same flaw in that they were also based to a great extent on the company's average past performance. Additionally, Schroeder did not explain or justify to the court's satisfaction his assumptions about future changes in performance or his choice of discount rates. Thus, the court found that Schroeder's analysis based on his income approach was similarly entitled to little weight.

Court relies on burden of proof

In conclusion, the Tax Court stated that the value of the gifts in the statutory notices of deficiency was presumed to be correct and that petitioners had the burden of proving it incorrect. After weighing all the facts, circumstances, and evidence, the court held that petitioners' expert had understated the value of the stock and thus petitioners had not met their burden.

Estate of Mitchell v. Commissioner (II)

Citation: 250 F.3d 696, 2001 U.S. App. LEXIS 7990
Court: United States Court of Appeals
State/Jurisdiction: 9th Circuit Federal
Date of Decision: May 2, 2001
Judge: Wardlaw

In this ongoing estate tax proceeding, the *Estate of Paul Mitchell* (Estate) appealed the U.S. Tax Court's decision allowing the Commissioner of the IRS to assess an additional $2,404,571 in federal estate taxes. The Estate filed two motions for reconsideration of the Tax Court's valuation of the stock, both of which were denied.

On review, the Estate claimed that the Tax Court erred by: (1) failing to provide a detailed explanation of the methodology used to calculate the fair market value of the stock; (2) miscalculating the value of the stock in a manner inconsistent with its own holding; and (3) failing to shift the burden of proof to the Commissioner.

The Tax Court's valuation

Paul Mitchell (Mitchell), co-founder of the subject company John Paul Mitchell Systems (JPMS), died on April 21, 1989. The Tax Court assigned a $150 million value to the stock based on an offer from another company to acquire JPMS. The court then discounted the company's value by 10% to account for the loss of Mitchell, the key person. From the now $135 million total company value, the Tax Court calculated the value of the Estate's 49.04% share in the company at $66,204,000. Finally, it allowed for a total 35% discount to reflect the combined discounts of lack of marketability and minority interest and a $1.5 million discount to reflect the possibility of a lawsuit.

The Tax Court relied on the testimony of three experts to set the range for discounts. Martin Hanan, a witness for the IRS, testified to a 30% discount for lack of marketability. George Weiksner and Kenneth McGraw, two expert witnesses for the Estate, both testified to a 45% marketability discount. From the testimony of these three experts, the Tax Court concluded that a 30-45% range for a combined minority and marketability discount was established.

Standard for judicial valuation decisions

On appeal, the Estate argued that the Tax Court failed to provide a more detailed explanation of its stock valuation consistent with the guidelines in *Leonard Pipeline Contractors v. Commissioner*, 142 F.3d 1133 (9th Cir. 1998), which was decided between the Estate's first and second motions for reconsideration (and raised by the Estate as a new legal development on its second motion). It also claimed that the Tax Court's decision was internally inconsistent and erroneous. The Ninth Circuit Court of Appeals reviewed the Tax Court's decision *de novo* and concluded that its explanations were insufficient.

In *Leonard Pipeline*, the Tax Court concluded that it was impossible to calculate the values at issue with any "mathematical precision" and instead substituted its own "best judgment." The Ninth Circuit reversed, holding that it was the obligation of the Tax Court "to spell out its reasoning and to do more than enumerate the factors and leap to a figure intermediate between petitioners and the Commissioners. A reasoned decision must give some account of how the judge has reached his conclusion."

Valuation explanation inadequate

The Court of Appeals began its analysis by stating that the Tax Court was comparing "apples and oranges." It noted that the experts relied on by the Tax Court to establish discounts used an estimated publicly traded value of the Estate's minority interest to determine the initial value of the company before applying the discounts. The Tax Court, on the other hand, started with an acquisition value, a $150 million bid by another company, and began discounting from there. The court observed that acquisition value and publicly traded value are different because acquisition prices include a premium for the purchase of the entire company in one transaction. The Tax Court failed to take this into account, which resulted in an inflated tax consequence for the Estate.

Next, the court addressed the marketability discounts applied, commenting that the Tax Court did not explain how it reached a combined marketability discount of 30-45%. The experts testimonies of 30 and 45% discounts were for marketability only, having already accounted for minority interest in their starting values. The Tax Court's $150 million starting value, on the other hand, did not account for minority interest. Moreover, the Tax Court initially misstated the uncontroverted testimony of one of the experts, which actually supported a 61.5% combined discount. The court modified its opinion to correct the testimony, only to deny the Estate's motion for reconsideration. The Ninth Circuit held: "Because the [Tax Court's] range is unsupported by the testimony of any of the experts, singularly or together, it is unclear whether the Tax Court's combined discount actually falls within any particular range that might be supported in the record."

Burden of proof should shift to IRS

The Estate also argued that the Tax Court erred by denying its motion to shift the burden of persuasion, leaving the ultimate burden of proof on the Estate. The Tax Court denied the motion without explanation. The Ninth Circuit reviewed this decision *de novo.*

The court first quoted from *Cohen v. Commissioner,* 255 F.2d 5 (9th Cir. 1959):

> When the Commissioner's determination has been shown to be invalid, the Tax Court must redetermine the deficiency. The presumption as to the correctness of the Commissioner's determination is then out of the case. The Commissioner and not the taxpayer then has the burden of proving whether any deficiency exists and if so the amount. It is not incumbent upon the taxpayer under these circumstances to prove that he owed no tax or the amount of the tax which he did owe.

The Ninth Circuit stated that the IRS's determination of value was shown to be invalid by its own experts. It then reviewed the Tax Court's treatment of the burden of proof throughout the prior proceedings. "The Tax Court treated the [initial] case as one where the burden of proof made no difference; it did not find that one party failed to carry its burden, but proceeded with its own valuation." On the Estate's second motion for reconsideration, the Tax Court erroneously held that the Estate had the burden of proof. Thus, the Ninth Circuit concluded that the Tax Court erred in denying the Estate's motion to shift the burden of persuasion to the Commissioner.

Ninth Circuit's conclusion

The Ninth Circuit expressly stated that it was not reaching the question as to whether the Tax Court correctly valued the Estate, as it was unable to conduct a meaningful review. The court therefore vacated the Tax Court's decision and remanded it for the Tax Court to shift the burden of proof to the Commissioner and to explain its valuation of the stock consistent with the standards established in *Leonard Pipeline.*

A concurring opinion by Circuit Judge Hug further outlined the inconsistency of the Tax Court's decision with respect to the evidence offered in support of the discounts. According to Judge Hug, the testimony of the experts actually yielded a range of 46.2 to 61.5% for a combined minority and marketability discount. The Tax Court's selected combined discount did not fall within that range.

Estate of Hoffman v. Commissioner

Citation: T.C. Memo 2001-109, 2001 Tax Ct. Memo LEXIS 136
Court: United States Tax Court
State/Jurisdiction: Specialty Federal
Date of Decision: May 9, 2001
Judge: Ruwe

Marcia Hoffman's (decedent) estate held a 27.5% interest in Clubside Partnership, which was family owned. Her estate held notes receivable from Clubside. The estate also held a 22.13% interest in WLI, an S corporation that improved, developed, and sold home sites in Florida. The estate and the IRS disputed the value of the two property interests and of the notes receivable.

Notes receivable valuation

Mark L. Mitchell, ASA, valued the promissory notes for the IRS "based on the timing of payments and the rate of return that a holder of the notes would require." He determined the proper return rate by reviewing:

- interest rates of various debt securities;
- corporate bonds of various ratings;
- interest rates for conventional mortgages, 30-year and 1-year Treasury securities, and bank prime loans; and
- venture capital returns.

Assuming the notes would not be paid until the date of maturity, Mitchell applied:

> the 12.5% rate of return to the values he assigned the promissory notes as of the date of maturity, $436,465 and $701,481, respectively. On the basis of a 12.5% rate of return, [Mitchell] concluded that the values of the promissory notes payable to decedent . . . were $56,664 and $91,070, respectively, as of the valuation date.

Mitchell's 12.5% rate of return also incorporated a discount for lack of marketability, although the exact percentage was not specified.

Benjamin Bishop valued the promissory notes for the estate by relying on Moody's, Standard & Poor's, and Fitch rating agencies to find comparable debt securities. He compared the notes to the lowest-ranked securities, which required an approximate 18% rate of return. He applied a 25% lack of marketability discount because "the comparable bonds he used could be sold at any time in the public market while the Clubside notes lacked a public market for sale." This resulted in a total rate of return of 22.5%.

> [Bishop] calculated that the present value of $1 received in 17 years and 4 months; i.e., the length of time between the valuation date and the date of maturity of the promissory notes, was $.039. [He] applied the present value of $.039 to the values as of the date of maturity and concluded that the values of the promissory notes payable to decedent and Hoffman Associates were $17,022 and $27,358, respectively, as of [the valuation date].

The Tax Court criticized Bishop's valuation. His testimony reflected a lack of knowledge concerning the comparable companies used, he failed to properly link them to Clubside, his comparables were "highly speculative, and he lacked knowledge of the line of business that some of the companies were engaged in."

The court agreed with Mitchell's valuation that a 12.5% rate was appropriate and that the values of the notes were $56,664 and $91,070.

Clubside Partnership interest valuation

Mitchell valued the partnership interest in Clubside with a discounted net asset value approach.

> [He] determined the net asset value of the partnership, applied [a 35 percent] lack of marketability and [an 18 percent] minority interest discounts, and then applied this figure to decedent's 27.5% interest.

His calculations resulted in a $338,000 value for the partnership interest.

Bishop valued the partnership interest with a liquidation approach.

> [He] determined the value of decedent's interest by projecting the sale of Clubside's assets over 3 years, subtracting liabilities, applying decedent's percentage ownership interest, and then applying a rate of return he felt a knowledgeable investor would require.

Bishop assumed a "knowledgeable investor" would require a 30% annual return based on these assumptions:

- The interest was an illiquid minority interest in a family partnership that would be difficult to market.
- The only source of cash flow would be from the sale of real property, and no such sales had taken place as of the valuation date.

- The holders of the remaining 72.5% of the partnership were related, would manage the affairs in a responsible manner, and Mr. Hoffman would continue to provide cash to the partnership to pay property taxes.

- The notes and accrued interest thereon would total over $2 million by the year 2012, making a cash return on the partnership equity unlikely.

His calculations produced a $289,913 value for the partnership interest.

The Tax Court accepted Mitchell's valuation. The court criticized Bishop's valuation by noting that the 30% rate of return was based on assumptions, and not supported by the evidence.

Value of WLI stock

Mitchell valued the 770 shares of WLI stock with the capitalized income analysis based on a three-year historical average using three main components:

- The determination of a reasonable level for net profits or net cash flow

- An appropriate cost of capital

- A reasonable rate of growth for the profit stream

He used the Capital Asset Pricing Model (CAPM) to determine the capitalization rate. Mitchell arrived at a 7.5% risk free rate of return based on market yields on 30-year Treasury bonds, a 7.2% market risk premium based on Ibbotson publications, and a 5.3% unsystematic risk premium to account for small company risk.

> [He] estimated a beta of 1.0 because he could not obtain a reliable estimate of beta from comparable publicly traded stock. Mr. Mitchell also relied on data from Ibbotson Associates to determine the additional 5.3% premium for unsystematic risk to account for investment in a small company stock.

From his 20% cost of capital (7.5% + 7.2% + 5.3 percent), he subtracted a 3% growth rate to arrive at a final capitalization rate of 17%. He concluded with a 35% discount for lack of marketability in the final fair market value.

The Tax Court criticized Mitchell's use of CAPM for a small, closely held company and his failure to calculate beta as a "significant shortcoming."

> [Mitchell] has failed to provide the evidence necessary for us to determine whether use of CAPM was appropriate, and whether the figures used in his calculation were reliable.

The court also criticized the use of a 5.3% small stock premium without specific explanation. The court further criticized his handling of intercompany profits, which were inconsistently subtracted in one year and not subtracted in two others.

The court held that the IRS "failed to establish a fair market value above the amount reported on the estate tax return." The court found for the estate on the WLI valuation.

Schott v. Commissioner (I)

Citation: T.C. Memo. 2001-110
Court: United States Tax Court
State/Jurisdiction: Specialty Federal
Date of Decision: May 9, 2001
Judge: Cohen

In *Patricia A. and Stephen C. Schott v. CIR*, T.C. Memo. 2001-110, the Tax Court considered whether a grantor retained annuity trust (GRAT) could be valued as a dual-life annuity. The Schotts each formed a GRAT, which was funded with closely held stock having a fair market value of $5.4 million. The grantor would receive 11.54% of the value of the trust annually for a term of 15 years. If the grantor should die prior to the expiration of the term, then the annuity would be paid to the grantor's spouse for the remainder of the term. The grantor retained the right to revoke the spouse's interest. The Schotts concluded that the annuity interest in each GRAT was a qualified interest under Sec. 2702, and valued the interest as a dual-life annuity. The IRS found that the interests were not qualified interests and valued the interests as single-life annuity interests.

The Tax Court initially noted, "Valuation of a retained interest as a dual-life annuity produces a greater retained value than valuation as a single-life annuity, and correspondingly, reduces the amount of the taxable gift of the remainder." It then considered whether the annuity interests were qualified interests and should be valued as a dual-life annuity. Relying on an earlier ruling, the Tax Court concluded that the interests at issue were not qualified interests because the spousal interest was contingent upon the life of the grantor, and therefore, not fixed and ascertainable on the date of the GRAT's formation. Furthermore, the court noted that the grantor's right to revoke the spousal interest violated Section 25.2702-3(d)(3), gift tax regs. See *Cook v. CIR*, 115 T.C. 15 (2000). Thus, the Tax Court agreed with the IRS that the interests were not qualified annuity interests and should be valued as single-life annuities.

This abstract originally appeared in *Valuation Case Digest*, authored by John J. Stockdale, Jr.

Estate of Simplot v. Commissioner (II)

Citation: 249 F.3d 1191, 2001 U.S. App. LEXIS 9220
Court: United States Court of Appeals
State/Jurisdiction: 9th Circuit Federal
Date of Decision: May 14, 2001
Judge: Noonan

The U.S. Tax Court had ruled in favor of the IRS, rejecting the estate's valuation expert and assigning a 3% premium to the block of Class A voting stock in J.R. Simplot Co. (Simplot). The Ninth Circuit reversed the Tax Court's ruling and ordered entry of judgment in favor of the estate on remand because "the Tax Court erroneously attributed a premium to minority voting stock in the J.R. Simplot Co."

Background on Simplot

Richard R. Simplot (decedent) died on June 24, 1993. His estate held a 23.55% minority interest of the voting class and a 2.79% minority interest of the nonvoting class of the common stock of Simplot. Simplot had reported sales of $1.8 billion, net income of $37.8 million for the fiscal year ending Aug. 31, 1993, and was one of the two largest potato processors in the world.

The company also owned 5.3 million shares and 13% of the common stock of Micron Technology, Inc., a publicly traded manufacturer of semiconductor memory components and personal computers. At the date of death, the market value of the Micron stock was $182.1 million with trapped-in capital gains of $169 million.

At the date of valuation there were 76.445 voting shares (Class A) and 141,288.584 nonvoting shares (Class B) reflecting one share of voting stock per 1,848 shares of nonvoting stock. The voting shares were owned by decedent and his siblings as shown in Table 1.

TABLE 1		
Stockholder	**Number of Shares**	**Percent of Total Shares**
Decendent	18	23.55
Don Simplot	18	23.55
Gay Simplot Otter	18	23.55
Scott Simplot	22.445	29.35
Total	76.445	100

The majority of the nonvoting shares-62.83%-were owned by a trust for the descendants of decedent, Don, Gay, and Scott. The Class A and B shares had equal rights to dividends and to liquidation distributions even though Simplot never paid out dividends. A right of first refusal applied to anyone who wished to sell Class A shares. Any shareholder had to wait 360 days before selling voting shares to an outsider.

The Tax Court decision

In *Estate of Simplot v. Commissioner,* 112 T.C. No.13 (1999), the Tax Court reviewed a valuation of the Simplot stock by the Commissioner of Internal Revenue that resulted in a $801,994 value per share of Class A stock and $3,585 per share of Class B stock. The experts were Herbert Spiro and Gilbert Matthews for the IRS and J. Paul Much and John R. Ettelson for the Estate of Richard R. Simplot (Estate).

There were four issues before the court:

1. The marketable minority interest value of Simplot.

2. Treatment of the trapped-in-capital gains pertaining to Micron stock.

3. The appropriate discount for lack of marketability for both classes of shares.

4. Whether a premium should be applied to the Estate's Class A voting shares.

The Tax Court used inputs from both sides' experts and decided without much discussion on the first three issues as follows:

1. The fair market value of the Simplot stock on a marketable minority interest basis was $830 million, of which $720 represented operating value and $110 non-operating value of Micron stock.

2. The court accepted the advice of both appraisers that the full amount of the trapped-in-capital gains tax liability should be deducted from the Simplot value.

3. The issue of the discount for lack of marketability was decided almost without comment at a 35% marketability discount for the Class A voting shares and 40% marketability discount for the Class B nonvoting shares.

The premium for the voting shares

Regarding the premium for the Class A voting shares, the IRS's experts placed a premium on the voting stock because of the unbalanced ratio of voting to nonvoting shares. The Estate's experts offered empirical evidence that the differential between the two classes should be minimal and that the minority interest in the Class A stock could not provide increased economic benefit to the shareholders.

The court adopted the position of the IRS's experts and assigned a 3% premium to the block of Class A voting shares in Simplot. The premium was based on the whole equity value of the company of $830 million for a total of $ 24.9 million. This decision was based on the Tax Court's observation that a hypothetical buyer of the 18 voting shares "would gain access to the 'inner circle of J.R. Simplot Co. and by having a seat at the Class A shareholders table, over time, the hypothetical buyer potentially could position itself to play a role in the Company."

The court also considered some of the characteristics of the hypothetical buyer as being "well financed, with a long-term investment horizon and no expectations of near-term benefits." The court also noted that in the future the buyer of the 18 shares could become the controlling owner because of the shares being divided among many Simplot descendants.

Ninth Circuit finds three major errors in Tax Court's ruling

The Ninth Circuit noted at the beginning of its analysis that the estate tax is based on the "value of the property in the decedents hands at the time of its transfer by death." The Ninth Circuit determined that the Tax Court committed errors in the following three areas:

- Hypothetical buyer standard
- Calculation of the voting stock premium for the Estate shares
- Insufficient evidence for a control premium

Hypothetical buyer standard

The Ninth Circuit noted that the Tax Court departed from the willing buyer/seller standard by believing that "the hypothetical sale should not be considered in a vacuum isolated from the actual facts that affect value." The Ninth Circuit also found that the Tax Court violated the law by constructing particular possible purchasers. The Court of Appeals further considered that the facts presented as factors influencing the premium calculations were merely speculations and imaginary scenarios as to the purchasers characteristics.

Calculation of voting shares premium

The Tax Court also erred in calculating the control premium pertaining to all the Class A voting shares and then dividing it equally among them. There was no reason to believe that the value attributable to the control of Simplot could be proportionally attributed to a fraction of the total shares. The Ninth Circuit Court noted that "the Tax Court valued an asset not before it - all the Class A stock representing control."

Insufficient evidence for control premium

The Ninth Circuit finally noted that even a controlling block of stock is to be valued at a premium for estate tax purposes only if the Commissioner can show that the buyer will enjoy an increased economic advantage from control. In the Ninth Circuit's opinion, the 18-share minority interest in the Class A voting stock did not offer a clear increased advantage to the shareholders, except for the speculative factors presented by the Tax Court.

The Ninth Circuit finally noted: "In Richard Simplot's hands at the time of transfer his stock was worth what a willing buyer would have paid for the economic benefits presently attached to the stock. By this standard, a minority holding Class A share was worth no more than a Class B share."

The judgment of the Tax Court was accordingly reversed and the case remanded for entry of judgment in favor of the Estate.

Judge Fletcher dissents

Circuit Judge W. Fletcher dissented from this opinion, believing the Tax Court was correct in its decision and valuation of the Class A voting shares.

Judge Fletcher based his dissent on the assumption that any of the Simplot surviving Class A shareholders would probably pay a high premium in order to achieve control. In his opinion, any willing buyer and seller negotiating a price for the 18 shares would be aware of this potential premium. Judge Fletcher finalized his dissent with an "appeal to economic reality."

> Under the majority's view, there is no fair market value whatsoever for the right to vote the 18 A shares. In its view, one A share is worth precisely the same as one B share. The majority therefore concludes that the fair market value of shares representing 23.5% of the voting shares of a company with sales of $1.8 billion and an equity value of $830 million is only $54,450.

Succession of Helis v. United States (I)

Citation: 88 AFTR2d Par. 2001-5085 (Fed. Cl. 2001)
Court: United States Court of Federal Claims
State/Jurisdiction: Federal Claims
Date of Decision: July 3, 2001
Judge: Bruggink

In the *Succession of Betty Felix Helis v. U.S.A.*, 88 AFTR2d Par. 2001-5085 (Fed. Cl. July 3, 2001), the U.S. Court of Federal Claims considered the valuation of a 50% interest in a partnership. The partnership held marketable securities and oil properties. The court found that the partnership's prospects as of the valuation date, April 12, 1980, were not good because pricing control was in effect and the oil properties were old. Both parties presented the court with expert testimony in this refund action.

The court found that the primary issue in this case was the size and applicability of the discounts. The IRS's expert concluded that a 13% minority discount was appropriate. He calculated his discount using Mergerstat Control Premium Studies that indicated a control premium of 44 percent; this converted into a 30% minority discount. He reduced this discount to 13% because he felt that the decedent had more control than the 50% interest represented and because the interest had the ability to liquidate the partnership. This expert further indicated that the minority interest discount should be applied only to the real property assets of the partnership and not to its marketable securities. The estate's expert argued for a 35% minority discount to be applied to the all the partnership's assets.

The experts also applied a lack of marketability discount. The estate's first expert's data indicated a range of 35 to 37%. He reduced that figure and applied a 27.5% discount. The estate's second expert's data indicated a range of 10 to 60%. After considering the improbability of accessing the partnership's assets, this expert concluded that a 50% discount was warranted. The IRS agreed that the floor lack of marketability discount was 35%.

The Court of Federal Claims considered the evidence. It rejected the IRS's expert's valuation. In doing so, it found that he erred in quantifying and applying the minority discount. The court found it appropriate to apply the minority discount to all the partnership's assets, including the partnership's marketable securities. It further disagreed with his quantification of the discount. It found that while the estate held a 50% interest, it did not have control over the partnership. It disagreed with the IRS's expert's "feeling" that the estate held more control than met the eye. It further found the possibility of liquidating the partnership improbable.

The Tax Court then considered the two remaining expert's valuations. It concluded that because both experts had arrived at reasonable valuations, it split the difference between their valuations and ordered that amount to be the value of the estate's interest.

This abstract originally appeared in *Valuation Case Digest*, authored by John J. Stockdale, Jr.

Estate of HA True v. Commissioner (I)

Citation: T.C. Memo 2001-167, 2001 Tax Ct. Memo LEXIS 199
Court: United States Tax Court
State/Jurisdiction: Specialty Federal
Date of Decision: July 6, 2001
Judge: Beghe

This 336-page estate and gift case deals with a $75,935,883 tax deficiency and $30,328,153 in associated penalties asserted by the IRS. The case concerns the value of 1993 gifts made by Henry True Jr. (Dave) and his wife, Jean, the value of Dave's estate at his death on June 4, 1994, and the value of gifts made by Jean in 1994. Petitioners' experts were John H. Lax, ASA, CMA, Arthur

Andersen LLP; Curtis R. Kimball, ASA, CFA, Willamette Management Associates; Robert H. Caldwell, Ph.D., The Scotia Group,Inc.; and Michael S. Hall, CPA, Hall and Hall Mortgage Corp.. Only Lax and Kimball testified on the valuation portion of this case. Respondent's only expert was John B. Gustavson, Gustavson Associates, Inc.

Dave had worked in the oil and gas business since 1938. He and Jean formed True Oil Co. and True Drilling Co. Dave and others founded Belle Fourche Pipeline Co. In 1963, Dave formed Black Hills Oil Marketers Inc. Dave also owned and operated a number of S corporation cattle ranches and a dude ranch (White Stallion, Inc.), another S corporation, which Dave and Jean owned, along with Dave's brother and his brother's wife. The Trues also owned and operated at least 19 other businesses, including a bank holding company, a drilling supply retailer, and an environmental cleanup company.

The trial issues were:

1. Does the book value price specified in the buy-sell agreements control estate and gift tax values of the subject interests in the True Companies (buy-sell agreement issue);

2. If the True family buy-sell agreements do not control values, what are the estate and gift tax values of the subject interests (valuation issue);

3. Did Jean True make gift loans when she transferred interests in the True Companies to her sons in exchange for interest free payments received approximately 90 days after the effective date of the transfers (gift loan issue); and

4. Are the taxpayers liable for valuation understatement penalties? (penalty issue)

Buy-sell agreement issue

There was significant discussion about whether the buy-sell agreements (based on tax book value) should fix the value both for the estate and for the gifts. The analysis focused on the factors in *Estate of Lauder v. Commissioner*, T.C. Memo 1992-736 (1992) (*Lauder II*). There are four parts to this *Lauder II* test. The taxpayers said all four were satisfied, while the IRS claimed only two were.

The four parts of the test are discussed below:

I. Was the offering price fixed and determinable under the agreement? All parties agree this part of the test was passed.

II. Were the agreements binding during life and at death? After analyzing the state law that controlled the buy-sell agreements and past transactions, the court determined that all entities except one passed this part of the test.

III. Were agreements entered into for bona fide business reasons? The purpose of the agreements was to ensure family ownership and control of the True Companies. The taxpayer, the IRS, and the court all agreed that this was a bona fide business reason.

IV. Were agreements substitutes for testamentary dispositions? The IRS argued that Dave True had testamentary objectives in the buy-sell agreements and the court agreed based on the following analysis:

- 1. Testamentary purpose test. Decedent's health when he entered into the agreement. Dave True was in good health when he entered into the agreements, and his subsequent health decline had no bearing on the determination of testamentary purpose.

No negotiation of buy-sell agreement terms

The True children did not have independent legal or accounting advice. The court said that this lack of independent representation among related parties was not dispositive, but it reasonably suggested less than arms-length dealings.

Enforcement of buy-sell provisions

The court said that:

> [T]he family generally complied with the terms of the buy-sell agreements or executed formal waivers when circumstances made it appropriate to deviate from those terms, and concluded this factor did not apply.

Failure to seek significant professional advice in selecting formula price

Dave True consulted only with his accountant about the book value formula price. This accountant stated he had no detailed understanding of valuation methodologies and had no academic or practical experience in valuations. The court said:

> We reject any notion that [the accountant] was qualified to opine on the reasonableness of using the tax book value in the True family buy-sell agreements. [The accountant] was closely associated with the True family; his objectivity was questionable. More importantly, he had no technical training or practical experience in valuing closely held businesses. The record shows no technical basis (in the form of comparables, valuation studies, projections) for [the accountants] assertion that tax book value represented the price at which property would change hands between unrelated parties.

Failure to obtain or rely on appraisals in selecting formula price

For 1973 gifts, Dave True obtained a contemporaneous appraisal of True Oil's oil and gas reserves. This was done primarily for anticipated tax litigation related to the gifts, not for setting up the buy-sell agreement at book value.

Exclusion of significant assets from formula price

The court questioned the reasonableness of omitting the value of proven oil and gas reserves from True Oil's buy-sell pricing formula. Citing *Lauder II*, the court said:

> [W]e cannot passively accept such a formula where, as here, it appears to have been adopted in order to minimize or mask the true value of the stock in question.

No periodic review of formula price

The court was critical that the True Companies buy-sell agreements did not provide a mechanism for periodic review or adjustment to the tax book value formula.

Business arrangements with True children fulfilled Dave True's testamentary intent

According to the court:

> Dave Trues business arrangements with his children fulfilled his testamentary intent, as evidenced by his will and ancillary estate planning documents.
>
> 2. Adequacy of consideration test. This test requires that the formula price (1) be comparable to what persons with adverse interests dealing at arms length would accept and (2) bear a reasonable relationship to fair market value. As the court said,

[T]hese standards must be applied with the heightened scrutiny imposed on intrafamily agreements restricting transfers of closely held businesses.

> 3. Conclusion. The court concluded:
>
> The True family buy-sell agreements do not satisfy the Lauder II test, because they are substitutes for testamentary dispositions. As a result, under Section 2031 and the related regulations, the tax book value buy-sell agreement price does not control estate tax values of interests in the True companies at the issue in the estate tax case.

The court also determined that the buy-sell agreements were not controlling for the gift tax case.

Valuation issue

Once the buy-sell agreements were determined to be testamentary devices, Judge Beghe considered how to value the transferred interests in True Oil, Eighty-Eight Oil, the True Ranches, Belle Fourche, Black Hills Trucking, and White Stallion. The taxpayers had two business valuation experts, both with good valuation credentials. One of these appraisers (first expert) prepared an appraisal for the filing of the estate tax return and the second expert was retained later for the Tax Court trial. The first expert revised his original report for the trial. The IRS utilized asset appraisers but did not present a business valuation expert at trial.

In the interest of brevity and to present this summary in a timely manner, we will discuss some of the key valuation issues without presenting a detailed analysis of each of the companies.

Consideration of buy-sell agreements in marketability adjustments

The second expert considered the existence of the buy-sell agreements in determining both entity values and the discount for lack of marketability. Since the court had determined that the buy-sell agreements were testamentary devices, it did not allow the buy-sell provisions in the agreements, or in some cases the agreements themselves, to be considered in the determination of marketability adjustments.

Adjustment for lack of marketability for controlling interests

The first experts initial report included an adjustment for lack of marketability for control interests. His revised report, however, repudiated these adjustments because the Big 5 CPA firm in which the first expert was a principal determined that "market data did not justify measurable marketability discounts in connection with controlling interests." The second appraiser relied on the restricted stock and pre-IPO studies to determine the discount for lack of marketability for controlling interests, arriving at discounts of 40% and 45%. The IRS adopted the position of the first appraisers revised report with no discount.

The Tax Court disagreed with both appraisers and the IRS and allowed a 20% discount for lack of marketability for a controlling interest.

Use of only the guideline public companies approach

The Tax Court was critical that, for some of the companies, the taxpayers experts used only the guideline public companies approach.

Use of net asset approach for minority interests

The taxpayer argued that the use of the net asset approach is not appropriate for minority interests where those interests have no liquidation rights. The Tax Court disagreed and concluded that the minority interest discount takes this into account.

Swing vote

The IRS argued that many of the minority interests were in fact "swing votes" and should not be subject to any minority interest discounts. The Tax Court rejected this position.

Criticism of use of pre-IPO and restricted stock studies

The Tax Court noted,

> On the other hand, we are troubled by the lack of any clear connection between the [first experts] reports general discussion of restricted stock and pre-IPO studies and the marketability discounts applied to the True Oil subject interests. For instance, there was no showing that the industries represented in the studies had risks and other attributes similar to the oil and gas industry. In fact, one of the pre-IPO studies specifically excluded natural resource companies from the companies being examined.

Despite this criticism the court still allowed a 30% marketability discount in True Oil. The court also noted that the restricted stock studies were more relevant than the pre-IPO studies because the partnership interests were subject to state law transfer restrictions and True Oil was not on the verge of going public.

Minority discount for a general partner

Eighty-Eight Oil was a Wyoming general partnership whose partnership agreement required the partners to jointly manage its affairs. According to the court, "Under Wyoming law, each partner had an equal vote in (among other things) appointing management, setting business policies, making distributions, buying and selling assets, and amending the partnership agreement." Because of these rights, the court allowed only a 10% minority discount for 24.84% and 34.47% ownership interests.

In the case of True Ranches, the court dismissed the premium studies for publicly traded companies used by the taxpayers first expert in determining the minority discount, because a general partner can exert more control than a minority shareholder. The court also dismissed the use of the publicly registered limited partnership studies used by the taxpayers second expert, since these studies dealt with only limited partnership interests, not general partnership interests. The court ultimately decided on a 15% minority interest discount.

Gift loan issue

The court next considered whether Jean made gift loans when she transferred interests in the True Companies to her sons and whether the transfers were subject to similar buy-sell agreements. The court determined that, for federal income tax purposes, Jean sold her stock on June 30, 1994, and her partnership interests on July 1, 1994. The court next considered and held that the deferred payment arrangement may be a below-market loan subject to section 7872, even though no part of the sales price would be treated as interest or OID under sections 483 and 1274. Finally, the court determined that the six-month deferred payment arrangement was a "below-market loan" under section 7872(e)(1)(B) and was a gift loan and not a transaction in the ordinary course of business.

Penalty issue

Finally, the court considered whether the Trues were liable for valuation understatement penalties under sections 6662(a), (g), and (h). The court held that they were liable for the penalties and that the reasonable cause exception didn't apply.

Estate of Cook v. Commissioner (I)

Citation: 2001 T.C. Memo 2001-170, 2001 Tax Ct. Memo LEXIS 202
Court: United States Tax Court
State/Jurisdiction: Specialty Federal
Date of Decision: July 9, 2001
Judge: Gerber

This estate tax case concerns 19 annual installment payments of lottery winnings to a limited partnership in which the decedent held a 2% general partnership interest and a 48% limited partnership interest. The decedent and her sister-in-law informally agreed to jointly purchase lottery tickets and share any winnings. They formed a formal limited partnership after purchasing a winning lottery ticket with a face value of $17 million. The partnership's assets on the valuation date consisted of the future lottery payments and $391,717 in cash.

The IRS determined a deficiency of $873,544 and a penalty of $168,999 in the federal tax on the decedent's estate. The court had to decide whether the right to receive the installments must be valued pursuant to the private annuity tables in the estate tax regulations.

Marketability discount differently applied

The estate reported a $266,269 tax liability. Peter Phalon, expert for the estate, valued the decedent's interests in the partnership at $1,529,749, which were included in the gross estate. Phalon valued the lottery payments at $4,575,000. The IRS determined that:

> the partnership's right to receive the lottery payments had a date of death value of $8,557,850. [The IRS] arrived at this value using the annuity table. [The IRS] then valued decedent's limited partnership interest at $3,222,919, allowing discounts for the lack of a ready market, restrictions contained in the partnership agreement on transfers and admissions of new partners, and the ability of a 50-percent partner to control the partnership.

In response, the estate hired another expert, William H. Frazier, who valued the lottery payments at $6,053,189 and decedent's partnership interest at $2,067,867. The IRS hired its own expert, Francis X. Burns, who valued the lottery payments at $5,762,791 and the decedent's partnership interest at $2,406,413. The experts used various methods, excluding the annuity tables, to value the lottery payments. All of them applied a discount for the inherent lack of marketability of the lottery payments.

Future payments valued by annuity tables

The sole issue for the court was whether the right to the fixed stream of lottery payments should be valued using the annuity tables. The estate argued that the right to receive lottery payments was not an annuity, and even if it were, use of the annuity tables "creates an unreasonable and unrealistic result because the valuation formula in [the regulations] does not take into account the lack of marketability of the lottery payments."

The IRS argued that the right to the payments was an annuity, and that the tables should be used regardless of the marketability of the right. The IRS argued that the "interest in the partnership, not the partnership's right to receive the lottery payments, is the property in which the lack of marketability should be discounted."

The court found that, as in their decision in *Estate of Gribauskas v. Commissioner*, 116 T.C. 142 (March 8, 2001), the fixed stream of lottery payments was a private annuity, subject to minimal risk. The payments were backed by investments in U.S. bonds, which the court found "virtually eliminated" risk of default. "Therefore, use of the tables . . . could hardly create an unreasonable or unrealistic result." The court held that the fair market value of the partnership's right to receive the lottery payments should be determined by the actuarial tables for annuities.

Estate of Schwan v. Commissioner

Citation: T.C. Memo 2001-174, 2001 Tax Ct. Memo LEXIS 207
Court: United States Tax Court
State/Jurisdiction: Specialty Federal
Date of Decision: July 13, 2001
Judge: Nims

The petitioners in this case, decedent's estate and a charitable foundation (the Martin M. Schwan Foundation), challenged the IRS's determination that the estate had a tax deficiency based on a bequest to the foundation, and that the foundation was liable as a transferee.

Until his death on May 9, 1993, Martin M. Schwan was the president and majority shareholder of Schwan's Sales Enterprise (SSE), a company primarily engaged in the production and distribution of frozen foods. Before his death he created an estate plan that included seven trusts and the foundation. Decedent's will devised all his SSE stock at the time of his death to one particular revocable "1992 Trust," which constituted 66.7% of all voting stock and 67.2% of all nonvoting stock.

Agreement provides for redemption of SSE shares

The decedent, the foundation, and the 1992 Trust entered into an agreement providing for future redemption of the 1992 Trust shares (the Redemption Agreement). The 1992 Trust would transfer its shares to the foundation and, on the 10th business day after the due date of decedent's estate tax return, SSE would redeem the shares from the foundation for a purchase price equal to the value as determined for estate tax purposes.

On Aug. 4, 1994, the estate tax return valued the decedent's stock at $869,450,800 and took a charitable deduction for the same amount for the bequest to the foundation. On Aug. 23, 1994, the foundation received cash and a note for the same amount of $869,450,800. At the same time, according to the Redemption Agreement, the remaining SSE minority shareholders (mainly the decedent's children and grandchildren) could redeem both the voting and the nonvoting SSE stock from the foundation for $869,450,800.

In August 1997, the IRS sent a deficiency notice in which it determined the value of the SSE stock was $1,064,591,322, an increase of $195,140,522 over the reported value. The IRS also determined that the fair market value of the SSE shares passing to the foundation for the purposes of charitable deduction was $857,572,432, a decrease of $11,878,368 from the reported value.

Shares at death not subject to redemption agreement

The IRS argued that the Redemption Agreement restricted the foundation interest and led to a lower valuation for purposes of the charitable deduction. The estate argued that the value was the same for both the gross estate and the charitable deduction.

The Redemption Agreement placed no restrictions on decedent's freedom to use or dispose of his interest in SSE; it took effect only upon the transfer to the foundation. Thus, the court found that the shares held at death were not subject to the agreement's restrictions and the instrument therefore had no impact on the stock's value prior to his death. Decedent would have controlled SSE at his death and would have, through his estate plan, passed that control first to the foundation and then to his descendants. The value was divided, not destroyed. The court therefore concluded that the existence of the Redemption Agreement had no effect on the value of decedent's interest in SSE for gross estate purposes.

Church v. United States (II)

Citation: 268 F.3d 1063, 2001 U.S. App. LEXIS 17551
Court: United States Court of Appeals
State/Jurisdiction: 5th Circuit Federal
Date of Decision: July 18, 2001
Judge: Per Curiam

In this estate tax appeal, the Fifth Circuit affirmed the district court's decision in *Church v. United States*, 2000 U.S. Dist. LEXIS 714 (W.D. Tex. 2000) (abstracted in this special report). The only issue for the court was "whether the transfer of the assets was restricted at the time of Church's death."

The Fifth Circuit found that Texas courts hold that "a written partnership agreement constitutes an enforceable contract and governs the rights of the parties."

Regardless of the status of the limited partnership due to the certificate not being filed on that date, the documents that Church had signed imposed restrictions on the assets that necessarily caused their value to be discounted, even if no limited partnership was then formed.

In addition, Texas Revised Civil Statutes state that an entity could operate as a limited partnership before filing a certificate. Tex. Rev. Civ. Stat. Ann. art. 6132a-1§2.01, Source and Comment-Bar Committee (Vernon Supp. 2001).

The court also found that the IRS was apprised of the nature of the refund claim. The estate stated in its refund claim and in its pleadings that it was entitled to a discount for lack of control and marketability without the formation of the limited partnership.

Estate of O'Neal v. United States (I)

Citation: 258 F.3d 1265, 2001 U.S. App. LEXIS 16810
Court: United States Court of Appeals
State/Jurisdiction: 11th Circuit Federal
Date of Decision: July 26, 2001
Judge: Hill

This is an appeal from the United States District Court for the Northern District of Alabama. Appellants sought a refund for estate taxes paid. The issue on appeal was, as of what date should a valid, enforceable claim against an estate be valued?

Facts

The decedent and her husband were minority shareholders in a closely held family corporation, O'Neal Steel, Inc, and gifted all of their stock to their nine heirs. At the time of decedent's death, there was a claim against her estate for transferee gift tax liabilities owed. Nine months after her death, a settlement was reached in the dispute.

Valuation evidence and parties' arguments

The valuation evidence introduced to the court came in the form of the gift tax returns that were filed and the settlement agreement that was reached between the parties. There was no dispute that the estate was entitled to a deduction with respect to claims against it by the nine heirs for reimbursement of their transferee gift tax liability on the decedent's gifts of stock to them.

As to the amount of the deduction, the estate argued that the court should ignore the tax court settlement made by the grandchildren donees nine months after the decedent's death and instead use the $9,407,226 demand amount asserted by the government in its own statutory notices of deficiency.

The IRS argued that the Tax Court settlement of $563,314 was the proper amount of the deduction as it represented the actual amount of taxes ultimately paid.

The district court found in favor of the estate, but reduced the value of the deduction from $9,407,226 to $563,314. The court came to this valuation based upon the Tax Court settlement.

Holding on appeal and rationale

This was an issue of first impression for the Eleventh Circuit, which it framed as follows:

> How do we value this deduction for a claim against the estate? Do we take a valuation snapshot on the day [decedent] died? Or, do we consider events occurring after her death, such as the tax court settlement between the grandchildren donees and the government?

The court noted that, although the estate tax statute is silent on the date for valuing claims against the estate, there are two lines of reasoning the courts follow regarding valuation of the estate when there is an outstanding claim against it, resulting in a split among the circuits.

The first line of reasoning comes from the 1929 Supreme Court decision in *Ithaca Trust Co. v. United States*. The U.S. Supreme Court laid out the general rule that "post-death events must not be considered in valuing the amount of the deduction, as 'the estate so far as may be is settled as of the date of the testator's death.'"

The second line of reasoning comes from a 1929 Eighth Circuit decision in *Jacobs v. Commissioner*. Here, courts take into consideration post-death events as "the claims which Congress intended to be deducted were actual claims, not theoretical ones."

The Eleventh Circuit adopted the U.S. Supreme Court's rationale in *Ithaca* and thus held that the district court erred in considering the post-death Tax Court settlement. However, it also noted that the amount of the deduction was not necessarily the $9,407,226 demand made by the IRS at the date of death. Thus, the court remanded the case to the district court for an evidentiary hearing and a recalculation of the deduction.

Adams v. United States (III)

Citation: 2001 U.S. Dist. LEXIS 13092
Court: United States District Court
State/Jurisdiction: Texas
Date of Decision: August 27, 2001
Judge: Fitzwater

The Mendenhall estate consisted of a 25% assignee interest in Taylor Properties, a dissolved Texas general partnership. The partnership assets included ranch land, securities, mineral royalties, and working interests. The estate valued the 25% interest on the federal estate tax return at $7,480,975.43. The IRS audit valued the interest at $7,604,125.32. The experts in this case were David Fuller (for the IRS) and Robert K. Conklin (for the estate).

This proceeding resulted from the Fifth Circuit's remand of the Mendenhall estate tax refund suit. The trial court refused to apply certain discounts to the partnership interest under the assumption that Texas partnership law gave a partner's assignee the right to force liquidation or to receive its pro rata share of the partnership's net asset value without discounts.

The Fifth Circuit reversed and remanded, concluding that such a liquidation right was "at best unclear and uncertain" under Texas law and that the hypothetical parties to the willing seller/willing buyer transaction would conclude the same. It thus held that the district court was required to determine the value of the decedent's 25% interest in a dissolved Texas partnership, including the various claimed discounts.

The issues on appeal included whether any of the following discounts should apply and, if so, the "quantum" of each:

- Lack of marketability discount
- Lack of control discount
- Portfolio discount

David Fuller valued the estate for the IRS at $7.821 million:

> Assuming the existence of a liquidation right, he arrived at this figure by (1) reducing the partnership's total [net asset value] of $33.081 million by 5.4% to reflect the brokerage expenses associated with liquidation, and (2) multiplying that sum by 25% to compute the partner assignees pro rata share of [net asset value], net of brokerage costs that would be incurred in liquidation. [Footnote omitted.]

Robert K. Conklin applied discounts for lack of control, poor diversification of assets, and lack of marketability in valuing the estate at $3.87 million. He applied a 20% minority interest/lack of control discount, a 10% portfolio discount, and a 35% lack of marketability discount.

The court accepted the Conklin's 20% minority interest discount because he "provided the lone specific analysis of the issues, and his reasoning is consistent with numerous cases that plaintiffs cite ...and is not substantially divergent from the governments own experts figure."

The court accepted Conklin's 10% portfolio discount for poorly diversified assets. The IRS provided no specific alternative valuation. In addition, "the apparent reasonableness of Conklin's opinion" was evidenced by Fullers equivocal testimony on the issue.

The court also accepted Conklin's 35% marketability discount. The court rejected the governments distinction between an ongoing and dissolved partnership as material to the valuation. Furthermore, the court found Conklin's discount on the "conservative end of the median range." Finally, it found that Conklin's assumption about the transferability of an assignee interest was supported by the partnership agreement, which stated that the terms of the agreement were binding on heirs and assignees of partners.

The Fifth Circuit further directed the district court to consider whether a discount for the legal uncertainty surrounding the rights of the assignee should apply. Although the district court recognized that a deduction for legal uncertainty might be warranted, it was not justified on the facts of this case. The court rejected the deduction because it decided the other discounts already took this undesirable characteristic into account. Accordingly, the court held that legal uncertainty was not an additional factor depressing the price.

Shackleford v. United States (II)

Citation: 262 F.3d 1028, 2001 U.S. App. LEXIS 19217
Court: United States Court of Appeals
State/Jurisdiction: 9th Circuit Federal
Date of Decision: August 28, 2001
Judge: Thomas

In 1987, Thomas J. Shackleford bought a California Lottery ticket for $1 and won the jackpot. His prize was the right to receive $508,000 immediately and $508,000 for each of the next 19 years (the "prize"). Unfortunately, he lived to see only three of the 20 payments. In determining Mr. Shackleford's estate tax, the estate had to calculate the value of the remaining 17 payments.

The sole question before the Ninth Circuit was whether, in valuing the prize, the taxpayer could depart from the actuarial tables promulgated by the Treasury. This question was complicated by the fact that for estate tax purposes the tables are "presumptively correct" and the "general rule requires that the tables be used because they provide both certainty and convenience when applied in large numbers of cases."

If the prize was a non-commercial annuity, the statute dictated that the value of the prize be determined by the §7520 tables. Such a determination resulted in a value, less estate expenses, of approximately $4.0 million. The estate, uncertain whether the prize was a non-commercial annuity, filed its return utilizing the tables, paid the estate tax due, and timely filed for a refund. The district court rejected the claim that the prize was not a non-commercial annuity and had a value of "zero."

In determining the value of the prize, the district court considered its characteristics:

1. The prize payments were backed by 17 zero coupon U.S. Treasury bonds, each coming due on the required payment date and equal to $508,000.

2. The U.S. Treasury bonds were owned by The California Lottery Commission.

3. The risk of not receiving payment was similar to the risk of not receiving payment on U.S. Treasury bonds or State of California obligations.

4. The fair market value of the U.S. Treasury bonds backing the prize, as of the date of death, was approximately $4.8 million.

5. California law prohibited any assignment, hypothecation, collateralization or levy of the prize (i.e., the prize had a statutory restriction on marketability).

6. Mr. Shackleford had only the right to receive the prize payments.

The District Court, relying heavily on *O'Reilly v. Commissioner*, determined that departure from the IRS valuation tables was warranted "when use of the tables produces a substantially unrealistic and unreasonable result and when a more reasonable and realistic valuation technique is available."

The District Court then turned its attention to the fair market value of the prize to see:

- (a) whether the tables produced an unrealistic and unreasonable value relative to fair market value, and
- (b) whether the method utilized to value the prize was more reasonable and realistic.

The expert for the taxpayer, Lance Hall of FMV Opinions, Inc. (the author), determined the value of the prize based on an analysis of attempted arm's-length transactions in non-assignable lottery prizes. These transactions were subject to and denied state court approval because of the respective states' statutory non-assignability of the lottery prizes. Based on this analysis, Hall determined a fair market value for the prize of $1.9 million (v. $4.2 million utilizing the tables, and before deduction for estate expenses).

Judge Karlton of the district court determined that the taxpayer had met the "substantial burden of proof," showing both that the tables resulted in a "substantially" unrealistic and unreasonable value, and that a more reasonable and realistic valuation technique was available. However, he adjusted Hall's conclusions for the court costs that would be incurred in attempting an assignment/sale of the prize, and concluded an approximate $2.0 million value for the prize.

The IRS appealed the ruling to the Ninth Circuit. Favoring the IRS were two recent U.S. Tax Court cases, with fact patterns similar to *Shackleford*, in which the court had ruled that the tables must be used to value lottery prizes. One of those cases had dismissed the district court's *Shackleford* decision as an "anomalous position."

In a comical and well-reasoned decision, the Ninth Circuit's Judge Thomas stated that the "the right to transfer is one of the most essential sticks in the bundle of rights," and that "there is little doubt that the statutory restrictions on transfer reduced the fair market value of the right to receive future lottery payments." Judge Thomas also noted that on occasion, when the results would favor the IRS, the IRS argued that departure from the tables was warranted.

In upholding Judge Karlton's decision, the Ninth Circuit enunciated a new standard: "If the taxpayer proves that a more realistic and reasonable valuation method exists that more closely approximates fair market value, courts are free to employ it."

In the author's opinion, the key to the district court's and the Ninth Circuit's decisions to depart from the tables was the ability of the taxpayer's expert to locate arm's-length attempted transactions of lottery prizes. Had a discount for lack of marketability been taken without such data, the author doubts that the courts would have agreed that "a more realistic and reasonable valuation method exists."

Estate of Branson v. Commissioner (II)

Citation: No. 00-70293 (9th Cir. 2001)
Court: United States Court of Appeals
State/Jurisdiction: 9th Circuit Federal
Date of Decision: September 5, 2001
Judge: Sneed

In the *Estate of Frank Branson v. CIR*, No. 00-70293 (9th Cir. September 5, 2001), the U.S. Court of Appeals for the Ninth Circuit considered whether an estate was entitled to equitable recoupment for capital gains taxes paid by the estate's heir in connection with the sale of the estate's stock. The estate owned a minority interest in two closely held banks. The estate had the stock appraised for estate tax purposes. In connection with paying the estate tax, the estate received permission to sell some if its stock. The stock was sold for an amount in excess of that reported on its tax return. The heir reported the gain on her income tax return filed the same year as the estate tax return. The heir used the reported value as her tax basis for reporting the gain under IRC Sec. 1014. The IRS audited the estate tax return and contested the value of the estate's stock. The statute of limitations expired on the income tax matter prior to the matter appearing before the Tax Court.

The Tax Court concluded that the estate had underreported the value of the banks' stock. It predetermined the amount of estate tax due. *See* T.C. Memo. 1999-231. In a separate opinion, the Tax Court concluded that because the revaluation of the banks' stock increased the value of the stock included in the estate, the heir's basis in the stock increased as well. It determined that since the heir's basis increased and since the statute of limitations for the income tax year of the sale had expired, the estate was entitled to equitable recoupment on the overpaid capital gains taxes. Thus, the Tax Court setoff the amount of the overpaid capital gains tax against the amount of the estate tax owed. *See* 113 T.C. No. 2 (1999). The IRS appealed.

On appeal, the IRS argued that the Tax Court did not have the power to apply the doctrine of equitable recoupment. The Ninth Circuit first examined equitable recoupment. It noted that equitable recoupment is a defensive measure against double taxation. In order for a taxpayer to avail itself of this measure it must meet a five prong test: (1) the same transaction or taxable event must be subject to two taxes, (2) the taxes must be inconsistent in that the Tax Code authorizes only a single tax, (3) the tax sought to be recouped must be time barred, (4) there must be an identity of interest between the parties paying the tax, and (5) the court in which the recoupment claim is brought must independently have jurisdiction over the claim. The Ninth Circuit found that the valuation of the banks' stock for estate tax purposes also established the basis for the heir's income tax, and thus satisfied the same transaction requirement of the five-prong test. It further found that the Tax Court had jurisdiction over the estate's tax claim and by extension had the authority to apply the doctrine of equitable recoupment to reduce the increased estate tax due by the time-barred income tax which was overpaid as a result of the increase in the value of the banks' stock. Thus, the Ninth Circuit concluded, "where ... the Tax Court has jurisdiction to redetermine an estate tax deficiency, it may exercise its equitable powers to recoup an income tax overpayment from the same tax year if all the criteria for an equitable recoupment claim are otherwise satisfied." Therefore, the appellate court affirmed the Tax Court's reduction of the estate tax by the amount the heir overpaid her income tax.

This abstract originally appeared in *Valuation Case Digest*, authored by John J. Stockdale, Jr.

Estate of Jameson v. Commissioner (II)

Citation: 267 F.3d 366, 2001 U.S. App. LEXIS 20598
Court: United States Court of Appeals
State/Jurisdiction: 5th Circuit Federal
Date of Decision: September 18, 2001
Judge: Jones

The issue on appeal was whether the Tax Court erred in the valuation of closely held stock and improperly denied a full discount for capital gains liability.

Facts

John Jameson incorporated Johnco, Inc. In 1990, he died and left his shares to his son and his wife, Helen. In September 1991, she died and left her two children equal shares of her estate. A Family Settlement Agreement that divided their mother's estate valued her 80,485 shares of Johnco stock at $4.025 million.

Johnco's primary asset was 5,405 acres of timberland (Timber Property). At trial, the parties stipulated that, at the time of decedent's death, the property was worth $6 million and that Johnco's basis in the property was $217,850.

Valuation evidence

The parties disagreed about how the value of Johnco's interest in the property was affected by the capital gains taxes that the company would incur upon sales of the land. Therefore, both parties presented expert witness testimony on this issue.

Clyde Buck testified for the estate. Buck presented three possible scenarios for a buyer under discount rates that ranged from 20-30%. First, Buck explored the possibilities and consequences of "an immediate 'fire sale' of the Timber Property." Second, he considered the option of "a rapid but controlled sale of Timber Property parcels within twenty-four months." Third, Buck explored the option of maintaining the operation of the Timber Property. Buck reached the conclusion that a buyer of Johnco could "realize the most income through an immediate liquidation." He also stated that, although Johnco was not operating the Timber Property in a wasteful manner, "a buyer would realize the least income by far if it operated the Timber Property as a going concern." Buck then totaled up the taxes that a buyer would incur if they immediately sold the property, and concluded that the Timber Property was worth $4.8 million.

John Lax also testified for the estate. Lax estimated that if a potential buyer financed $5 million to purchase Johnco's property, that Johnco's projected future cash flow would not be enough to cover the debt payments. Lax claimed that "a buyer would demand a return on equity of 17-22% for a risky investment like the Timber Property." Therefore, Lax concluded that a buyer of Johnco would likely "liquidate the Timber Property within a year." He then calculated "the capital gains taxes based on his conclusion," and opined that the Timber Property was worth $4.13 million.

Francis Burns testified for the IRS. Burns argued against any discount due to capital gains "based on an immediate liquidation of the Timber Property by the buyer of Johnco." He testified that it was "counterintuitive" because "it assumed that an entity would purchase Johnco and then immediately turn around and sell what [it] just purchased."

Trial court findings

The Tax Court acknowledged the Family Settlement Agreement, but it refused to adopt the share values that it set because they were reached on the basis of Buck's appraisal. The court decided that Buck's appraisal was "flawed" because it assumed a liquidation of the Timber Property.

On the issue of capital gains tax discounts, the Tax Court refused to apply a discount for capital gains tax liability for the "immediate sale of the Timber Property." Rather, the court concluded that a buyer would likely operate the Timber Property as an ongoing business.

The court designed "a model to estimate the capital gains taxes that Johnco would incur if it operated the Timber Property as a going concern." Neither of the parties had specifically presented evidence on this issue.

The court's model assumed that Johnco would sell 10% of its timber every year and that a 4% rate of inflation would apply. The court:

> estimated that the Timber Property would realize $600,000 in revenues in year one and similar inflation-adjusted revenues in later years. It applied a 20% discount rate, within the range of the taxpayer's expert estimates, and determined that the present value of capital gains taxes Johnco would eventually pay is approximately $873,000. Consequently, Johnco's interest in the Timber Property was worth roughly $5.1 million.

The Tax Court assessed a deficiency against the estate. The estate appealed.

Holdings on appeal and rationale

The Fifth Circuit stated that the Tax Court can use its own calculations in valuing property, but that these "calculations must be tied to the record and to sound and consistent economic principle." It found that the Tax Court erred in its analysis in assessing the value of Johnco stock.

The court of appeals noted that the Tax Court failed when it assumed that a buyer would "most probably... continue to operate it for timber production." Even though the Timber Property may best be suited for timber production, a purchaser "would have to take into account the consequences of the unavoidable, substantial built-in tax liability on the property."

The court further noted inconsistencies in the Tax Court's reasoning when it assumed that a "hypothetical purchaser of Johnco stock would engage in long-range timber production even though the Timber Property's annual rate of return is substantially lower than the investor's required return." The court of appeals called this a "fatal flaw" in the Tax Court's analysis.

The judgment of the Tax Court was vacated and the case was remanded for further proceedings to reconsider the amount of the capital gains discount to the Timber Property, reevaluate the effect of the Family Settlement Agreement, and reconsider the value of the Johnco stock.

Estate of Trotter v. Commissioner

Citation: T.C. Memo. 2001-250
Court: United States Tax Court
State/Jurisdiction: Specialty Federal
Date of Decision: September 21, 2001
Judge: Nims

In the *Estate of Eleanor T.R. Trotter v. CIR*, T.C. Memo. 2001-250, the Tax Court considered whether a condominium transferred by the decedent to a trust should be included in her gross estate under IRC Sec. 2036(a)(1). The decedent and her husband used the condominium, which was titled in the decedent's name only, as their primary residence. In 1993, she transferred the residence to a trust formed for the benefit of her grandchildren. The trustee had the power to withdraw the trust's assets at any time; however, the trust document also permitted the decedent's spouse to live in the condominium for a period of time after the decedent's death. The decedent did not receive any consideration for her transfer of the condominium to the trust. Furthermore, the decedent and her husband lived in the condominium rent-free until her death in 1996. On her estate tax return, the estate did not include the value of the condominium in her gross estate. The IRS concluded that the decedent and the trust had an implied understanding that the decedent would retain exclusive use and enjoyment of the condominium during her life. Therefore, the IRS concluded that the value of the condominium should be included in the value of the decedent's gross estate under IRC Sec. 2036(a)(2).

The Tax Court agreed with the IRS's position. It stated, "courts have been unwilling to decide that no interest was retained within the meaning of section 2036(a)(1) where objective evidence has shown that the decedent's relationship in fact to the property, beyond the transfer of bare legal title, remained largely unchanged." It then considered facts such as the retention of the property by the decedent, the decedent paid no rent to the trust, the trust did not open a bank account, and the trust document considered the occupation of the condominium after the decedent's death by her spouse, as indicative that nothing changed but legal title to the property. Thus, the Tax Court concluded that the decedent retained possession and enjoyment of the property within the meaning of IRC Sec. 2036(a)(2) and that the value of the property should be included in her gross estate.

This abstract originally appeared in *Valuation Case Digest*, authored by John J. Stockdale, Jr.

Estate of Baird v. Commissioner (I)

Citation: T.C. Memo 2001-258, 2001 Tax Ct. Memo LEXIS 292
Court: United States Tax Court
State/Jurisdiction: Specialty Federal
Date of Decision: September 28, 2001
Judge: Gerber

This estates of John and Sarah Baird were consolidated for this proceeding. The only dispute was the value of each decedent's fractional interest in a family trust holding 16 noncontiguous tracts of timberland in Louisiana.

At their respective deaths, John owned a 14/65 (21.5%) interest and Sarah a 17/65 (26.1%) interest in the trust. On their amended returns, both estates claimed 60% fractional discounts. The IRS disallowed the discounts and assessed deficiencies.

The estates and the IRS stipulated to the fair market value of the undivided fee interest on both valuation dates, but they disagreed as to the appropriate fractional interest discounts to be applied.

The IRS agreed that *some* discount was appropriate but claimed that the size of the discounts proposed by the estates was excessive.

At trial, the estates offered three expert witnesses and the IRS presented one. The estates' experts were found to be qualified but the IRS's was not. John A. Young, a real estate appraiser, testified for the estates and prepared a study in which he concluded that fractionalized interest discounts should be at least 50% of the proportionate fee value. His conclusion was based on his analysis of six comparable sales of fractional interests in timberland in Louisiana. He showed that the discounts were substantially larger where buyers purchased a partial interest and did not have control of the fee.

Lewis C. Peters, a forester/real estate appraiser, also testified for the estates. Peters relied on 104 transactions in fractional interests in timberland in Maine and the East Texas/Louisiana area. He did not adjust for differences in control, as did Young, but simply estimated that the average discount attributable to these interests was 55%.

The estates' third expert, James Steele, III, had been in the business of buying and selling rural Louisiana farm and timberland for over 20 years, particularly undivided interests. In his experience, purchases of fractional interests were initially subjected to discounts generally around 60%. When the buyer had acquired sufficient partial interests to hold at least 80%, the discounts suddenly dropped to just over 14%. In his report, Steele concluded that a discount of at least 55% would be appropriate. At trial, however, he testified that the value of the partial interests should be discounted 90% from the fair market value of the full fee interest.

The court found Steele's testimony "helpful and germane" and that his "unique and extensive experience" in the industry made him particularly well qualified on the issue. The court noted the factors Steele considered in arriving at his 55% discount:

- Fair market value of a 100% interest
- Percentage available for sale
- Total number of owners
- "Staying power" of existing owners
- Property location
- Number of tracts
- Number of acres
- Ability to influence management

- Continuity of the tracts
- Access to the property
- Topography
- Mineral value

Steele gave additional reasons for the increase in his discount to 90%, but the court found that most of the reasons were already reflected in his original discount opinion of 55%. Relying primarily on Steele's valuation report, the court concluded that the record and the experts reports supported a fractional interest discount of 60%.

Estate of Dailey v. Commissioner (I)

Citation: T.C. Memo 2001-263, 2001 Tax Ct. Memo LEXIS 299
Court: United States Tax Court
State/Jurisdiction: Specialty Federal
Date of Decision: October 3, 2001
Judge: Foley

The IRS determined that decedent's estate owed amounts for estate tax and gift tax deficiencies. The issue in the Tax Court was the appropriate application of minority and marketability discounts. The experts in this case were Jeff Schumacher of McClure, Schumacher & Associates for the estate and Mukesh Bajaj of LECG, LLC for the IRS.

Facts

Decedent executed an agreement of limited partnership ("Agreement") on Oct. 20, 1992 to form a Family Limited Partnership (FLP). Decedent then took a 1% general and a 98% limited partnership interest while her son received a 1% limited partnership interest. Approximately three weeks later, decedent contributed 400 shares of American Telephone & Telegraph Co. (AT&T) stock; 20,000 shares of Exxon Corp. stock; and 895 shares of Bell South Corp. stock to the FLP. Decedent's son did not contribute any assets to the FLP.

On Dec. 8, 1992, decedent conveyed the following limited partnership interests: 45% to her son, 15% to the son's wife, and 38% to a trust. On that date the FLP owned:

Company	# of shares	Value of shares	Total value
Exxon Corp.	20,000	$60.19	$1,230,750
AT&T	400	$47.94	$19,175
Bell South	895	$49.94	$44,694
		TOTAL	$1,267,619

On March 16, 1995, decedent appointed her son as managing partner of the FLP. Four months later, he replaced her as trustee of the trust and as general partner of the FLP. At that time, decedent's 1% general partnership became a limited partnership interest.

On Jan. 10, 1997, the decedent died. On that date the FLP had:

Company	# of shares	Value of shares	Total value
Exxon Corp.	10,000	$102.88	$1,028,750
American Veterinary Corp.	1,000	$10.88	$10,875
Bell South	7,978	$1.00	$7,978
		TOTAL	$1,047,603

On April 17, 1997, decedent's attorney filed a gift tax return reflecting the gifts of the 45% and 15% limited partnership interests to her son and his wife. On the tax return, decedent reported a 40% discount from net asset value (NAV).

Both the estate and the IRS agreed that the proportionate share of the net asset value of the given and retained interests on December 8, 1992 was $1,267,619 and on January 10, 1997 was $1,047,603. Both parties' experts compared the FLP to closed-end mutual funds, which trade at a discount to NAV. They disagreed however, on the amount of the minority and marketability discounts.

Valuation evidence

The expert for the estate relied on unspecified "published data" and testified that the appropriate discount was an aggregate 40% due to a lack of marketability, control, and liquidity. The expert for the estate also testified that he took into consideration the significant amount of unrealized capital gains relating to the Exxon stock in drawing his conclusions.

The expert for the IRS testified that an aggregate discount of 15.72% should apply on December 8, 1992, and 13.51% on January 10, 1997. He relied in part on an unpublished study that he co-authored and submitted at trial in a revised report. The opinion provides no details on the study. The IRS's expert testified that he did not review the documents to determine whether the FLP had any unrealized capital gains, even though he acknowledged that such gains are "an important source of discounts."

Trial court findings

The Tax Court began by stating that, because the estate had introduced credible evidence, the IRS had the burden of proof. The court was not impressed by either witness, but it stated that the expert for the estate was more convincing and thorough, whereas the IRS's experts testimony was "contradictory, unsupported by the data, and inapplicable to the facts." Thus, the court held for the estate and concluded that a 40% aggregate discount was warranted.

Gross v. Commissioner (II)

Citation: 272 F.3d 333, 2001 U.S App. LEXIS 24803
Court: United States Court of Appeals
State/Jurisdiction: 6th Circuit Federal
Date of Decision: November 19, 2001
Judge: Cohn

Appraisers may soon have to defend their tax affecting in prior S corporation valuations as a result of *Gross*. The case's impact extends into every area of business valuation and is, in our opinion, the most significant business valuation case in the last 20 years.

Facts

G&J Bottling was a large independent Pepsi-Cola bottler in the United States. From 1988 to 1992, the company enjoyed increasing profits and shareholder distributions that were almost 100% of net income. Two separate families, directly and through voting trusts, each owned 50% of the company. The company elected S corporation status in 1982. A 1982 restrictive stock agreement permitted intra-family transfers but prohibited transfers outside the family. The agreement also restricted any transfers that would jeopardize the company's S status. In 1992 five separate gifts of less than 1% interests were made. The taxpayer estimated a value of $5,680 per share. The IRS estimated a value of $10,910 per share.

The dispute

There were two main disagreements in the Tax Court. The first involved the tax affecting of the discounted cash flows of the company used to estimate value by the income approach. The taxpayer's expert tax-affected (i.e., reduced) the company's earnings by an assumed 40% corporate rate, as if the company were a C corporation. This was done even though the company, as an S corporation, did not pay any corporate-level taxes. The IRS's expert did not tax-affect the company's earnings. The second disagreement involved the size of the marketability discount. Because the most significant issue in this case is tax affecting, the marketability discount is not discussed in this abstract.

Arguments for tax affecting

The taxpayer's experts, David O. McCoy and Charles A. Wilhoite, argued that a willing buyer in 1992 would have tax affected the earnings of the corporation for the following reasons:

1. Tax affecting was the generally accepted practice of the business appraisal community in valuing a minority interest in S corporations.

2. S corporations sacrifice growth opportunities and capital appreciation in exchange for current income. Tax affecting is an appropriate adjustment to capture this trade-off.

3. S corporation shareholders are at risk that the corporation might not distribute enough income to cover its shareholder liabilities.

4. The S corporation might lose its "S" status. Tax affecting compensates the investor for this risk.

5. Tax affecting has been approved by the Tax Court in prior decisions.

6. The IRS itself has implicitly endorsed the policy of tax affecting in valuing stock of S corporations, specifically in two internal documents: the *IRS Valuation Guide for Income, Estate and Gift Taxes: Valuation Training for Appeals Officers* and the *IRS Examination Technique Handbook*.

7. The IRS had previously allowed tax affecting of S corporations, including a prior gift tax return of this very taxpayer, filed and accepted four years earlier.

Arguments against tax affecting

The expert for the IRS, Mukesh Bajaj, Ph.D., made the following arguments why the companys earnings should not be tax affected:

1. The company does not currently pay corporate taxes.

2. There is no indication that the company would not continue as an S corporation.

3. The company historically had distributed almost 100% of its net income to shareholders.

4. Because the company receives a benefit (no corporate taxes), this should not be ignored in valuing its stock.

5. The data used to develop the discount rate (Ibbotson) for discounting cash flows is based on public company returns that are after corporate income taxes, but before personal taxes.

Since no corporate income taxes are paid in an S corporation, it is improper to apply this return to the tax-affected earnings of an S corporation.

The Court of Appeals decision

The three-judge panel at the Sixth Circuit Court of Appeals decided that tax affecting was not appropriate in this instance by a two to one vote. Judge Cohn wrote for the majority while Judge Clay wrote the minority opinion on this issue. A summary of the key issues as discussed by both opinions is as follows.

Was tax affecting the accepted method in 1992?

Bajaj stated that he did not know what the accepted practice on tax affecting was in 1992. McCoy stated that tax affecting was the generally accepted practice in 1992. McCoy admitted that there was a growing controversy in 1992 as to the propriety of tax affecting, that the matter was still being debated as of the time of trial, and that if he had to value stock of G&J at the current time, he would need further consideration as to whether he would tax affect.

The majority opinion believes there is no compelling evidence as to what the practice was in 1992. The majority notes the growing dispute as to the validity of tax affecting as of 1992, as well as McCoy's statement that he would give further consideration to tax affecting were he valuing the stock today.

The minority opinion disagrees, noting that although there may have been a growing controversy on tax affecting, this does not mean that it was not the accepted practice in 1992. In fact, McCoy stated in his testimony that it *was* the accepted practice in 1992 and that all the S corporation appraisals he had seen were tax affected. Bajaj did not contradict McCoy's testimony on this point, as he testified that he did not know what the accepted practice was in 1992.

Tax affecting suggested in IRS training manuals

The majority found the fact that the IRS manuals recommend tax affecting irrelevant. The majority notes that each IRS manual has the following disclaimer: "This material was designed specifically by the IRS for training purposes only. Under no circumstances should the contents be used or cited as authority for setting or sustaining a technical position." The majority further stated that "not only do the statements in the IRS manuals fail to affirmatively advocate tax affecting for all S Corporation valuation, both the guide and the handbook provide that [they] are not to be relied upon as binding authority, thus even if Taxpayers relied on these materials, their reliance was not justified."

The minority disagreed, stating that "the principles stated in these materials bear evidentiary weight in support of the notion that a willing buyer and seller would have used the same tax affecting approaches stated therein in valuating shares of G&J stock. Although I do not agree with

Taxpayers contention that the IRS is somehow estopped from now disclaiming tax affecting as a recognized practice, I recognize that these documents reflect a certain acceptance of tax affecting as a valid method of valuation."

Prior tax affected gifts allowed by IRS

The majority argues that "the Commissioner is not precluded from correcting an error. Thus, the fact that tax affecting may have been approved in other cases, and was even approved in prior returns filed by Taxpayers, does not, and should not, preclude a different result in another case, particularly where there is disagreement over whether to tax affect in determining the value of stock in the first place." The majority opinion does not accept the *Bliss* argument made by the taxpayer, stating that *Bliss* is distinguishable because "there was disagreement among the experts as to whether tax affecting was generally accepted."

The minority opinion states: "The notion that willing buyers and sellers would have used tax affecting under the discounted cash flow methodology is further supported by the fact that the IRS had previously approved 1988 taxes paid by Taxpayers based on gifts of G&J stocks valued at a sum determined by tax affecting G&J stock." The minority opinion agreed with the taxpayers reliance on *Bliss* "in which the court held that the Commissioner cannot act retroactively in a particular case where his own regulations are 'broad enough to allow a taxpayers method as one in accordance with generally accepted accounting principles or best accounting practices and one which was consistently followed. [If a taxpayers] method of valuing is substantially in accord with the regulations, great weight must be given to its long record of consistent application of the same method."

Importance of the willing buyer / willing seller standard

The majority states that the standpoint of the willing buyer and willing seller must be considered and implies that tax affecting is a "determination of fair market value based solely on the price-lowering desires of the willing buyer."

The minority opinion comments on this by recognizing that "we are merely determining those factors that hypothetical parties to a sale of G&J stock would have considered as of the gift date. In this regard, I believe that past practices, which the IRS had not deemed to create a deficiency, are demonstrative of the idea that such hypothetical actors would have considered tax affecting G&J stock."

Company may lose its S status

The majority disagrees with the argument that tax affecting is appropriate because the company might lose its S corporation status in the future. The majority bases this belief on the facts at hand, namely the longtime family ownership, the restrictive shareholder agreement that prohibits transfers that would break the S election, and the lack of any indication from the company that the S election was going to be broken.

The minority counters that these restrictive agreements were only for ten-year periods, and the period would expire shortly after the 1992 gifts. Furthermore, the minority opinion notes that there are other ways to break the S election absent a transfer of the shares. Even if the shareholders had no immediate plans to break the S election, this still is no guarantee that it would not be broken at some time in the future.

Ivory tower versus the real world

The majority concludes its opinion with commentary on two of the experts: "Reviewing the conflicting expert's opinions, it appears that Dr. Bajaj's valuation was from an academic perspective, and he clearly took a scholarly approach to the valuation issue. McCoy's valuation, on the other hand, was from the perspective of a business professional, who has performed numerous valuations in his professional career. This distinction is observed not to diminish McCoy's expertise or elevate Dr. Bajaj's, but simply to point out the different ways the experts approached the valuation question to the facts at hand."

Where do we go from here?

While we obviously disagree with the majority's logic, the larger issue we all face is what to do next. In our opinion, the best way to deal with the tax affecting issue is the way we deal with all valuation issues - on a case-by-case basis.

Great facts

To the IRS's credit, it picked a great fact pattern to argue in *Gross*. Some of the many favorable aspects that bolstered the IRS's case are as follows:

1. Company with stable and profitable operations.

2. Consistent annual 100% payout ratio of net income to shareholders.

3. Restrictive agreements that make it difficult to break the S election.

4. No indication from ownership that S election would be broken.

5. Minority interest being valued.

Some of these issues and their impact on the appropriateness of tax affecting are discussed below.

Most likely buyer

A critical issue is the most likely purchaser of the interest being valued. The most likely buyer of a small minority interest is usually an individual. This might support not tax affecting, since the individual buyer may enjoy the same tax-advantaged situation as the other shareholders. If, however, the interest at issue is a controlling interest, the most likely buyer may be a corporation. Then tax affecting may be logically indicated, since a corporate buyer would likely be paying corporate-level taxes and would certainly consider the impact of those taxes on the expected return of the acquired company.

Breaking the S election

It seems logical that shareholders who elect S corporation status would not want to break that election. Restrictive agreements such as in *Gross* may strengthen the argument that the S election probably will not be broken and that tax affecting is not appropriate. However, the fact that existing shareholders *want* to preserve the S election does not *guarantee* that the S election will be preserved. How does the valuator quantify this risk?

Payout ratio

As in *Gross*, an S corporation that pays out nearly 100% of its net income to its shareholders each year weighs in favor of no tax affecting, because a high payout ratio ensures that the shareholders will have enough cash to pay the pro-rata income tax liability "passed through" to them. A situation more favorable for tax affecting is where an S corporation generates positive net income but does not distribute any to its shareholders. Each shareholder would have to find alternative funds to satisfy the pro-rata income tax liability, in effect, experiencing a "negative return" on investment. Or what about the common situation in which an S corporation distributes just enough cash to allow each shareholder to satisfy the pro-rata income tax liability? The shareholders do not have to pay out of pocket, but they are not receiving any "real" return on their investment either. Is tax affecting proper in this instance?

Conclusion

The bombshell of the *Gross* case has just hit and the business valuation world has yet to assess the damage. We believe that using a number of valid approaches strengthens the ultimate valuation result in any case, as it allows the appraiser to examine the preliminary range of values to determine any pattern or logical conclusion of value. The use of a number of different approaches also gives support to the final value should the IRS challenge one of the approaches on the tax affecting issue.

Estate of Armstrong v. United States (II)

Citation: 277 F.3d 490, 2002 U.S. App. LEXIS 636
Court: United States Court of Appeals
State/Jurisdiction: 4th Circuit Federal
Date of Decision: January 15, 2002
Judge: Motz

Decedent held a controlling interest in National Fruit Products, Inc., a privately held corporation. Decedent gave substantial gifts of stock to his four children and paid millions in gift taxes on those gifts. The children signed a "transferee liability agreement," which obligated them to pay any estate or additional gift taxes resulting from undervaluation of the stock. Decedent died less than three years later. The IRS assessed additional gift taxes on the grounds that the stock was undervalued when the original gift taxes were paid. The estate brought this action seeking a refund of both the original and the additional gift taxes.

The estate argued the "net gift doctrine," contending that the children's obligation to pay additional gift taxes as a condition of the gifts had substantially reduced the value of the gifts. The district court found that the children's obligations were contingent and speculative and thus the net gift doctrine did not apply.

The Court of Appeals held that a donee seeking to invoke the net gift doctrine must demonstrate that payment of the gift taxes was a condition of the gift at the time of the transfer, and that the obligation was not contingent, speculative, or illusory.

Reviewing the transferee liability agreement, the court noted that the children only had an obligation to pay additional gift taxes in the event of undervaluation of the transferred property, an event all parties had sought to avoid by careful appraisal of the stock. Because their obligation was premised solely on undervaluation, a probability none of the parties expected to arise, the obligation was "contingent and too speculative to justify application of net gift principles." The Appellate Court affirmed.

Estate of Trompeter v. Commissioner (II)

Citation: 279 F.3d 767, 2002 U.S. App. LEXIS 1252
Court: United States Court of Appeals
State/Jurisdiction: 9th Circuit Federal
Date of Decision: January 30, 2002
Judge: McKeown

One of the main issues before the Tax Court was the value of 1533.48 shares of preferred stock of Sterling Holding Co. owned by the decedent. The stock was subject to a redemption agreement requiring Sterling to repurchase it at a future date.

Issue on appeal

The issue before the Ninth Circuit Court of Appeals was whether the Tax Court sufficiently articulated the reasoning supporting its ruling on the valuation issue. Explicit reasoning is required pursuant to *Leonard Pipeline Contractors v. Commissioner*, 142 F.3d 1133 (9th Cir. 1998). The Ninth Circuit found that the Tax Court did provide sufficient reasoning for some aspects of its valuation conclusion, but not for others. Therefore, the case was remanded to the Tax Court for further proceedings.

First, the Tax Court rejected the valuation of the Herbert Spiro, the estate's trial expert, because of "major shortcomings in the comparability analysis" of his valuation, which was based on comparable publicly traded companies. The Ninth Circuit found that the Tax Court's decision here was well reasoned and its findings not clearly in error.

Second, the Tax Court rejected the IRS position that evidence of the redemption price in January 1994, over a year after the valuation date, was equivalent to fair market value on the valuation date. Again, the Ninth Circuit found the Tax Court's decision on this issue to be well reasoned.

Finally, however, the Tax Court determined the value of the stock based on the redemption agreement formula, and applying a "reasonable discount rate of 4 percent" to determine the present value of the expected future payments under that agreement. Here the Ninth Circuit found that the Tax Court failed to provide sufficient reasoning for its valuation method.

> "[W]e are left without the benefit of reasoning or analysis as to how the four-percent discount figure was chosen. The Tax Court did not specify why it elected to discount the payments at a four-percent rate - and why such a rate was 'reasonable.' The discount figure is significant because it is determinative of whether the Estate has met its burden in challenging the Commissioners fair market value determination."

Estate of Heck v. Commissioner

Citation: T.C. Memo. 2002-34, 2002 Tax Ct. Memo LEXIS 38
Court: United States Tax Court
State/Jurisdiction: Specialty Federal
Date of Decision: February 5, 2002
Judge: Halpern

> This issue in this estate tax matter was the fair market value of decedent's 630 shares (a 39.62% interest) in F. Korbel & Bros., Inc. on February 15, 1995, her date of death. The estate tax return listed the stock at a value of $26,000 per share, and the IRS determined a deficiency claiming that the stock was worth $47,900 per share.

Korbel is a California S corporation that is owned by members of the Heck family, either outright or in trust. Korbel is primarily a producer of premium champagne, though the company also produces some brandy and table wine. The company owns 1,800 acres of landing in Sonoma County, 1,099 acres of which is not used in the business. The unused land had a stipulated value of $2,000 per acre.

Korbel entered into a distribution agreement with Brown-Forman Corp. in 1991, which gave Brown-Forman the exclusive right to distribute Korbel's premium champagne. Pursuant to this agreement, Brown-Forman also had a right of first refusal with respect to any stock offered for sale by a member of the Heck family.

Market approach rejected

Herbert Spiro, expert for the IRS, used both the market approach and the income approach. In his final analysis, he weighted the market approach component at only 30% "due to the lack of perfect comparables." Mukesh Bajaj, expert for the estate, did not use the market approach at all because he found no useful comparables.

After carefully scrutinizing the two comparables used by Spiro, the Tax Court rejected the use of the market approach in this case because it found that the comparables identified by Spiro were too dissimilar from Korbel. With respect to the selection of comparables and the use of the guideline public company method, the court noted:

> As similarity to the company to be valued decreases, the number of required comparables increases in order to minimize the risk that the results will be distorted to attributes unique to each of the guideline companies. In this case, we find that Mondavi and Canandaigua were not sufficiently similar to Korbel to permit the use of a market approach based upon those two companies alone.

TABLE 1			
	Spiro	Bajaj	Tax Court
Total per share value of Korbel stock	$48,100 rounded	$29,694	$32,174
Net operating asset value	$28,266,840 after discounts	$72,041,711 before discounts	$78,091,378 before discounts
Value of non-operating assets	$7,448,000	$5,517,000	$5,517,000
Discount rate (WACC)	16.54%	14.22%	14.22%
Cost of equity capital	16.71% using buildup method	14.70% using capital asset pricing model	14.70% accepted, though neither found to be "better"
Growth rate of sales	4.5% in 1995, 4.0% in 1996, 3.5% in 1997, 3.0% in 1998 and thereafter	2% in 1995 increasing to 4.5% in 1999 and thereafter	4.5% in 1995, 4.0% in 1996, 3.5% in 1997, 3.0% in 1998 and thereafter
Operating margin	13.3% of sales revenues vased on varying averages or different elements	12% of sales revenues based on 5-year simple average	12.3% of sales revenues per Bajaj plus "other income"
Depreciation	4.0% of gross sales based on 2-year average	3.8% of gross sales based on 5-year average	3.8% of gross sales based on 5-year average
Non-inventory working capital	3.5% of sales	5% of sales	5% of sales
Projected average capital expenditures	$4 million annually	Depreciation plus 30% of sales increases - always increasing	$4 million annually
Present value computation	Midyear convention used	Year-end convention used	
Marketability or liquidity discount	15% to stock, 25% to land	25%	25%
Discount due to Brown-Forman right of first refusal	Included in marketability discount	10%	10%
Discount due to S corporation status	10% to stock	n/a	n/a
Minority or lack of control discount	25% to land, 25% to excess cash	n/a	n/a

The Tax Court also found that although Spiro discussed both comparables in his report, he actually utilized only one of them - Mondavi - in reaching his market approach value. The issue then became whether the use of a single guideline company is a permissible application of the market approach. Citing *Estate of Hall v. Commissioner*, 92 T.C. 312 (1989), the court noted that the use of a single comparable has been rejected before.

> In doing so, [the court] observed that '[a]ny one company may have unique individual characteristics that may distort the comparison.' . . . A sample of one tells us little about what is normal for the population in question.

Elements of income approach and discounts

In reviewing the income approach valuations of both experts, the Tax Court found that they disagreed on almost every element of the calculations, "including projected revenues, operating costs, capital expenditures, the rate of return to be incorporated into the discount factor, the nature and amount of nonoperating assets, the amount of long terms debt, and the nature and amount of the discounts." The court accepted portions of each appraiser's analysis, and reached its own value conclusion. The calculations and conclusions of the experts and the court are shown in Table 1, and the court's complete calculations are included as an appendix to the full text of the opinion.

Shepherd v. Commissioner (II)

Citation: 283 F.3d 1258, 2002 U.S. App. LEXIS 3165
Court: United States Court of Appeals
State/Jurisdiction: 11th Circuit Federal
Date of Decision: February 28, 2002
Judge: Hull

J.C. Shepherd formed a family limited partnership (FLP) with his two sons, with each son owning a 25% interest. Shepherd deeded a large tract of timberland to the partnership prior to its formation. At trial, Shepherd argued that gifts to be valued were the two 25% interests in the FLP. The IRS argued that the gifts to be valued were indirect gifts of the timberland. The parties stipulated that, if the gifts were the FLP interests, then a 33.5% combined minority and marketability discount was appropriate.

The full Tax Court heard this matter, and found that Shepherd had transferred indirect gifts of undivided interests in timberland. The Tax Court further found, in valuing the interests, that a 15% fractional interest discount was appropriate.

Holdings and rationale on appeal

The issues on appeal were:

1. whether the Tax Court correctly characterized the gifts subject to taxation as indirect gifts of timberland rather than as interests in the FLP, and

2. whether the 33.5% stipulated combined minority and marketability discount should have been applied to the valuation of the timberland rather than the 15% fractional interest discount.

The Eleventh Circuit held that the Tax Court had valued the correct gifts. Because the FLP was necessarily created (including the son's interests) before the timberland could be transferred to it, 26 C.F.R. § 25,2511-1(h)(1) was clear that the gifts to be valued were indirect gifts of the timberland. "[G]ifts to a partnership, like gifts to a corporation, are deemed to be indirect gifts to the stakeholders 'to the extent of their proportionate interests' in the entity."

The Eleventh Circuit also upheld the Tax Court's application of a 15% fractional interest discount. This figure was based on the testimony of one of Shepherd's experts and took into account "the lack of complete control over the parcel, the risk of disagreement about disposition of the land and the possibility of partition of the land." The Eleventh Circuit rejected Shepherd's argument that the stipulated 33.5% discount should have been applied because the stipulation itself limited that discount to a valuation of an interest in the FLP. In addition, the gifts were to be valued "at the time of transfer" without reference to the partnership interest they later became a part of.

Dissenting

As with the Tax Court disposition of this case (which included a majority opinion, two concurring opinions, and three dissenting opinions), the Eleventh Circuit's disposition was not without controversy. Judge Ryskamp wrote a dissenting opinion, in which he referenced Judge Foley's dissenting opinion in the Tax Court. Ryskamp argued that the transfer of the timberland to the FLP should be considered enhancements to the sons pre-existing FLP interests, and that the gifts to be valued were the FLP interests as enhanced by the value of the timberland.

The dissent also argued that, regardless of the classification of the gifts to be valued, the valuation must take into account the effect of the partnership. Ryskamp states that in this case, the concept of valuing the gifts "at the time of transfer" so as to not take into account the partnership "is not helpful when the nature of the gift is transformed in transit from realty to personalty." He argues that the willing buyer and willing seller would consider the impact of the partnership, and therefore the stipulated 33.5% discount should be applied when valuing the gifts.

Hackl v. Commissioner (I)

Citation: 118 T.C. 279, 118 T.C. No. 14, 2002 U.S. Tax Ct. LEXIS 16
Court: United States Tax Court
State/Jurisdiction: Specialty Federal
Date of Decision: March 17, 2002
Judge: Nims

The taxpayers, Christine and Albert Hackl, formed a limited liability company for purposes of holding and operating tree farming properties. Under the company's operating agreement, the manager, Albert Hackl, had sole discretion in determining whether distributions would be issued to members. Also, members could not sell or transfer their membership units without the consent of the manager.

In 1996, the taxpayers gifted membership units in the LLC to each of their eight children and the spouses of those children. A gift was also made to a trust that was established for the benefit of their grandchildren. The value of the gifts was not an issue in this case. Prior to trial, the taxpayers and the IRS agreed to a stipulation regarding the value of the membership units. The issue in dispute was whether the gifts qualified for the $10,000 annual exclusion.

Under Section 2503(b) of the tax code, the first $10,000 of gifts of present interests in property is excludable from taxable gifts. Gifts of future interests in property do not qualify for this exclusion. Consequently, the disputed issue in *Hackl* was whether the gifts represented present interests or future interests.

In order to qualify as a present interest, the Tax Court indicated that the gift must represent "an unrestricted and noncontingent right to the immediate use, possession, or enjoyment (1) of property or (2) of income from property." Also, the donees must derive substantial economic benefits from these property rights, and the economic benefits must be presently reachable by the donees.

In *Hackl*, the Tax Court determined that the gifts did not qualify as present interests because the operating agreement "foreclosed the ability of the donees presently to access any substantial economic or financial benefit that might be represented by the ownership units." Under the operating agreement, the ability to realize economic benefits was contingent upon a future event - the approval of the manager. A member could not receive distributions or sell their membership units without the prior consent of the manager. This contingency prevented the gifted property from being characterized as a present interest.

Because the gifts did not represent present interests in property, the gifts did not qualify the $10,000 annual exclusion under Section 2503(b). The taxpayers had a resulting tax deficiency—for gifts by each of the taxpayers to children, spouses of children, and grandchildren—of $619,816.

The IRS addressed this same issue in Technical Advice Memorandum (TAM) 9751003. In the February 1998 issue of *Business Valuation Update*™, Philip Schneider and Shawn Fox provided a discussion of TAM 9751003.

In light of the *Hackl* decision, care should be taken to ensure that owners are capable of currently accessing the economic benefits of their ownership interest. If the restrictions on owners are too onerous, gifts may not qualify for the $10,000 annual exclusion.

Estate of Adams v. Commissioner

Citation: T.C. Memo 2002-80, 2002 Tax Ct. Memo LEXIS 84
Court: United States Tax Court
State/Jurisdiction: Specialty Federal
Date of Decision: March 28, 2002
Judge: Colvin

The issue in this estate tax matter is the fair market value of decedent William G. Adams, Jr.'s 178 shares of voting common stock (a 61.59% interest) of Waddell Sluder Adams & Co., Inc. (WSA), an insurance agency that operated as an S corporation.

The IRS offered the expert report and testimony of Herbert T. Spiro in support of its contention that the fair market value of WSA was $1,746,000. The estate offered the expert report and testimony of F. Foster Shriner in support of its contention that the fair market value of WSA was $920,800. The Tax Court ultimately found that the fair market value was $1,161,705.

Spiro used the discounted cash flow method, and Shriner used the income capitalization method, in valuing the WSA stock. Both estimated the discount rate by using the build-up method, starting with a 6.86% risk-free rate based on the 30-year Treasury rate, and then factoring in certain "added risk premiums." The experts' calculations were almost identical - Spiro calculated a 29.14% discount rate and Shriner calculated a 28.17% discount rate. The experts agreed that Shriner's capitalization rate of 20.53%, derived using an estimated growth rate of 6.34%, was appropriate.

One of the major differences between Spiro's and Shriner's valuations, however, was the estimated cash flows to which the capitalization rate was to be applied. The main source of dispute was the treatment of a key employee, Robert B. Gelder, Jr. At the time of decedent's death, Gelder was president of WSA and was extremely important to the company because of the relationships he had maintained with independent insurance agents and with Maryland Casualty Co. (MCC), with whom WSA had a major contract. He "performed all major management functions" but was only slightly involved with underwriting functions. "Gelder had no written employment contract or noncompete agreement with WSA. WSA had no other employee who could replace Gelder in 1995." Gelder's total compensation for 1995 was $548,704.

In determining estimated net cash flows, Spiro used salary estimates of $125,000 annually for Gelder, whereas Shriner used much higher salary estimates.

Spiro projected Gelder's future salary based on the salary of the top 10% of underwriters, even though Gelder spent only 10 or 15% of his time underwriting. Spiro's methodology ignores the fact that Gelder did much more than underwriting.

Shriner used insurance industry data for officers and managers to estimate Gelder's future compensation. That data shows that officers of companies in the insurance industry with assets of $1 million received compensation of 14.6% of gross revenues. Shriner estimated that future compensation of WSA officers would be 14.7% of WSA's gross revenues.

The Tax Court found that Shriner's salary estimates were more reasonable.

Another factual issue that affected the differing valuations of the experts was pending litigation filed by the North Carolina Rate Bureau. The outcome of that litigation could be very costly to WSA, and Gelder would be important to dealing with any adverse outcome.

At the heart of the differences in how the experts dealt with both the importance of Gelder generally and the effect of the pending litigation was the degree to which they investigated the facts. The Tax Court stated:

> We believe that Shriner's approach for estimating the value of WSA stock (before applying a discount for lack of marketability) was more thorough than Spiros. Spiro did not speak with anyone from MCC or investigate the pending litigation. Shriner did those things, and reasonably concluded that it was unlikely that WSA would survive without Gelder.

The court also quoted the following from Spiros report:

> Not having interviewed persons in authority at The Maryland in 1995, it is impossible to determine conclusively whether or not The Maryland would have cancelled or materially modified WSAs personal lines underwriting authority upon the transfer of Mr. Adams interest to another party.

Shriner used the yearend convention for his assumption of when WSA would make payouts to investors. The IRS argued that the midyear convention should have been used. Citing to Pratt, *Cost of Capital*, the court found that:

> There is support for use of the yearend convention on the grounds that payment at the end of the year is better than payment in the middle of the year because payment at the end of the year enables the managers to see how the year has turned out.

Although the evidence included a schedule of how much of Geller's share of the dividends were paid out in what years, this schedule did not indicate when during the year the dividends were paid. Because the IRS failed to present any evidence to support the use of the midyear convention, the court opted in favor of the yearend convention as opined by Shriner.

Shriner increased his capitalization rate to 31.88% to make it a before-corporate-tax rate instead of an after-tax rate. The court found that this increase was improper because an after tax rate should be applied when valuing an S corporation, consistent with the holding in *Gross v. Commissioner*, T.C. Memo 1999-254 (U.S. Tax Ct. 1999), *affd* 272 F.3d 333 (6th Cir. 2001). The court stated:

> We disagree that Shriner's estimates of WSA's prospective net cashflows are before corporate tax because it is appropriate to use a zero corporate tax rate to estimate net cashflow when the stock being valued is stock of an S corporation. [citation omitted] WSA is an S corporation, and its cashflows are subject to a zero corporate tax rate. Thus, Shriner's estimates of WSAs prospective net cashflows are after corporate tax (zero corporate tax rate) and not before corporate tax as the estate contends.
>
> We disagree that Shriner properly converted the capitalization rate because there was no need to do so. The parties agree that Shriners estimated capitalization rate (before he converted it to before corporate tax) is an after corporate tax rate. Thus, as in *Gross*, the tax character of Shriner's estimate of WSA's prospective net cashflows matches that of the unconverted capitalization rate because both are after corporate tax. It follows that Shriner should not have converted the capitalization rate from after corporate tax to before corporate tax because the tax character of both his estimated net cashflows for WSA and unconverted capitalization rates is after corporate tax.

The final valuation issue before the court was the application of a discount for lack of marketability. Both experts applied a discount, and the court agreed that some discount was appropriate.

Shriner testified that a 20% discount was appropriate. He first considered the restricted stock study average discount of 32.89%, and then reduced the average discount considerably because of "his belief that the insurance industry was more stable than the general market."

Spiro testified that a 40 to 45% discount was appropriate. He, too, considered the restricted stock study average discounts, but he also considered pre-IPO study average discounts, which were higher. Spiro considered several factors, including WSA's specialized operations, the size of the block of stock, and elements of control. He also believed that the pending litigation warranted a significant increase in the discount.

The court determined that a 35% discount for lack of marketability was appropriate. The court rejected Shriner's significant reduction from the average because it found that WSA was not as stable as the insurance industry generally. The court rejected Spiro's higher discount, "not because the Rate Bureau litigation should not be considered, but because we believe a 35-percent discount adequately takes into account WSA's vulnerabilities."

Estate of Fontana v. Commissioner

Citation: 118 T.C. 318, 118 T.C. No. 16, 2002 U.S. Tax Ct. LEXIS 17
Court: United States Tax Court
State/Jurisdiction: Specialty Federal
Date of Decision: March 28, 2002
Judge: Foley

The full Tax Court reviewed this federal estate tax matter. The issue was essentially a legal one, but the outcome affected the value to be placed on decedent's stock for estate tax purposes.

Decedent held stock in Fontana Ledyard Co., Inc. He had a 50% interest that he owned outright, and a 44.069% interest in a trust that he held pursuant to a testamentary general power of appointment (GPA). The parties stipulated to the values based upon an average of the valuation reports submitted for trial. The parties agreed that if the stock was aggregated and valued as a 94.069% block, its fair market value was $4,850,000. If the blocks were valued separately, their fair market values were $2,043,500 for the 50% block, and $1,747,500 for the 44.069% block. The difference in value between the blocks valued separately and valued as a single block was $1,059,000.

The estate argued that the two blocks of stock should be valued separately based upon the Tax Court's prior holding in *Estate of Mellinger v. Commissioner*, 112 T.C. 26 (1999). In *Mellinger*, the Tax Court found that the stock the decedent held pursuant to a QTIP trust should not be aggregated with the stock he held outright for valuation purposes. The estate argued that block held in trust pursuant to the GPA was the same and so the blocks should not be aggregated.

The IRS argued that the stock should be aggregated, and that the block to be valued for estate tax purposes was the full 94.069% interest.

The Tax Court held that the stock had to be aggregated for valuation purposes because "pursuant to the GPA, [decedent], at the moment of death (i.e., the critical moment for estate tax valuation purposes), had control and power of disposition over the property." The Tax Court distinguished *Mellinger* on the grounds that the decedent there did not retain control over the ultimate disposition of the stock held in the QTIP trust.

Cavallaro v. United States

Citation: No. 01-2237 (1st Cir. 2002)
Court: United States Court of Appeals
State/Jurisdiction: 1st Circuit Federal
Date of Decision: April 1, 2002
Judge: Lynch

In *William Cavallaro; Patricia Cavallaro v. United States*, No. 01-2237 (1st Cir. April 1, 2002), the U.S. Court of Appeals for the First Circuit considered whether an accountant's communications regarding transfer tax and merger issues were privileged communications. The petitioners owned a tool company. Their sons owned a manufacturing, sales, and service company that supported a glue machine designed by the petitioners' company. In 1994, the petitioners' sons and their company hired Ernst & Young (E&Y) to provide accounting advice regarding transfer tax and merger issues, which included valuations of the company. An engagement letter signed by the sons' company's CFO and an E&Y partner indicated that "[a]ll advice and other services we [E&Y] provide pursuant to this engagement are solely for the benefit of Camelot [the sons' company] ...and not for the benefit of anyone other than the corporation and its shareholders." In December1994, the petitioners, their attorney, E&Y, and the petitioners' sons met to discuss transfer tax and merger issues. The petitioners and their sons eventually agreed to merge the two companies, and sell the resulting entity.

The IRS began investigating the merger. It believed that the petitioners' company was undervalued and the sons' company was overvalued in the merger, which resulted in a disguised gift to the sons in the form of post-merger stock. To that end it subpoenaed all E&Y's records relating to any work performed between 1984 and 1995 for the petitioners, their sons, and their companies. The petitioners sought to quash the subpoena regarding certain documents that contained transfer tax and merger issues. They claimed that the documents were privileged since after the 1994 meeting E&Y began providing services to the petitioners' attorney. The District Court concluded that the documents were not privileged, and the petitioners appealed.

The First Circuit began by noting that, in general, communications between an accountant and a client are not privileged. However, the court noted that the attorney-client privilege may extend to an attorney's agent, such as an accountant. Quoting *United States v. Kovel*, 296 F.2d 918 (2nd Cir. 1961) the First Circuit restated the court's position with regard to privilege and accountants: This logic applies to accountants: "[T]he presence of an accountant, whether hired by the lawyer or by the client, while the client is relating a complicated tax story to the lawyer, ought not destroy the privilege" when "the accountant is necessary, or at least highly useful, for the effective consultation between the client and the lawyer which the privilege is designed to permit." *Id.* at 922. The communication, however, must be made "for the purpose of obtaining legal advice from the lawyer." *Id.* "If what is sought is not legal advice but only accounting service . . . , or if the advice sought is the accountant's rather than the lawyer's, no privilege exists." *Id.; see also United States v. Adlman*, 68 F.3d 1495, 1500 (2d Cir. 1995).

Here, the First Circuit found that no communication was presented between E&Y, the petitioners, their attorney, their sons or their companies that commemorated a change in E&Y's relationship with respect to the petitioners. It found that E&Y had at all times acted as an agent for the petitioners' sons and the sons' company. Further, it rejected the petitioners' argument that E&Y's services were useful to their attorney. The First Circuit noted that an accountant's services must be more than useful to the attorney in order to establish privilege. Thus, the First Circuit declined to quash the subpoena.

This abstract originally appeared in *Valuation Case Digest*, authored by John J. Stockdale, Jr.

Estate of Mitchell v. Commissioner (III)

Citation: T.C. Memo 2002-98, 2002 Tax Ct. Memo Lexis 100
Court: United States Tax Court
State/Jurisdiction: Specialty Federal
Date of Decision: April 9, 2002
Judge: Jacobs

This case is on a remand from the Ninth Circuit Court of Appeals. The Ninth Circuit reversed the prior Tax Court opinion on two grounds. The Tax Court had not properly shifted the burden of proof to the IRS, and it had not provided a sufficiently reasoned explanation of how it reached its valuation conclusion (particularly the application of a 35% combined minority and marketability discount).

Facts

Paul Mitchell and John Paul DeJoria were co-founders of John Paul Mitchell Systems (JPMS), a corporation which marketed hair care products through professional hair salons. When Mitchell died $1,226 JPMC's shares were the part of the estate and a dispute as to their value. Neither Mitchell nor DeJoria had any contract with JPMS regarding their compensation. Minnetonka Corporation on two occasions offered to purchase all of the JPMS stock, and Gillette Co. offered to purchase all of the JPMS stock on one occasion.

Valuation evidence

There were significant differences in experts' opinions. Further, Weiksner valued JPMS 1,226 stock at 20,634,000 to 25,489,000 with a midpoint value of $23,062,000. McGraw valued JPMS 1,226 stock at $29.5 million by using comparative companies analysis. He reached $272 million valuation when applied discounted cash-flow analysis. Hanan's comparable companies analysis valuation showed $81.00 million value of 1, 226 stock. However, he did agree that because of potential disagreement as to the DeJoria's compensation, the value of $1,226 stock could be between $165.3 to $57.7 million.

Holding on remand and rationale

On remand, the Tax Court noted in its opinion that the burden of proof was on the IRS at the outset, but made no mention of how this shift of the burden of proof affected its valuation analysis.

The Tax Court then reviewed the facts and the valuation evidence presented. Finding cause to criticize the valuation opinions of all three experts, the Tax Court stated that:

> We are of the opinion that here the comparable companies and discounted cashflow methods (which are theoretical valuation methods) are not appropriate. We did not use them because (1) there were real-world acquisition offers by Minnetonka and Gillette, and (2) the discounted cashflow and comparable companies analyses, as determined by the estate's experts, produced theoretical values for JPMS that were substantially less than these real-world acquisition offers.

While listed market prices are the benchmark in the case of publicly traded stock, recent arm's-length transactions generally are the best evidence of fair market value in the case of unlisted stock.

The Tax Court further found that the acquisition value it originally started with (i.e., the $150 million Gillette offer) reflected a control, nonmarketable value for the company, and therefore an additional marketability discount was not appropriate. This is why the Tax Court, in its original opinion, had rejected the high combined marketability/minority discounts opined by the experts in favor of a 35% discount.

The Tax Court, reaching the same final valuation conclusion, again applied a 35% discount on remand. The Tax Court found that a 29% discount was appropriate to reflect that the interest had some power, but less than control. This discount was based upon a comparison of the three values opined by Hanan, and the Tax Court explained its reasoning as follows:

> Mr. Hanan's discounted cashflow analysis setting Mr. DeJoria's compensation at $2.5 million, resulting in a value of $227 million, reflects a control value of the enterprise. His analysis setting Mr. DeJoria's compensation at $12 to $17 million, resulting in an enterprise value of $155 million, reflects lack of control. Finally, his analysis setting the compensation at $5 million, resulting in an enterprise value of $218 million, reflects some power but less than control. We think that a comparison of those values demonstrates most accurately the difference between the value of control of the company, the value of shares having some power, and the value of shares lacking any control. A comparison of these values supports a minority discount of 29% for some power but less than control (155/218 = 0.711) and 32% for lack of any control (155/227 = 0.683).

The Tax Court increased this discount by 6% based upon the testimony of McGraw. This additional 6% discount reflected the:

> limited number of prospective purchasers for the stock due to the size of the investment, the minority interest status of the block of stock, and the control exercised by Mr. DeJoria. Mr. McGraw's individual risk reflects lack of marketability specifically related to decedents minority interest.

The Tax Court again applied a 10% key person discount and a $1,500,000 reduction of the 49.04% interest to account for possible litigation. The Tax Court's calculations, which are identical to its original opinion, are shown in Table 1.

TABLE 1: THE TAX COURT'S CALCULATIONS	
Value of JPMS at the moment prior to Mitchell's death	$150,000,000
Less: Discount to reflect the loss of Mitchell to JPMS	($15,000,000)
Value of JPMS at the moment of Mitchell's death	$135,000,000
Percent of trust's interest in JPMS	x 49.04
Value of trust's interest in JPMS before discounts	$66,204,000
Less: Discounts for lack of marketability and minority interest (35%)	($23,171,400)
	$43,032,600
Less: Discount for possibility of lawsuit	($1,500,000)
Value of trust's interest in JPMS after discounts	$41,532,600

Estate of Godley v. Commissioner (II)

Citation: 286 F.3d 210, 2002 U.S. App. LEXIS 6856
Court: United States Court of Appeals
State/Jurisdiction: 4th Circuit Federal
Date of Decision: April 15, 2002
Judge: Wilkinson

Facts

At the time of his death, decedent owned a 50% interest in five general partnerships. The remaining 50% was owned by decedent's son. Four of the partnerships were owned and operated as housing projects under HUD contracts (Housing Partnerships). The fifth partnership, Godley Management Association (GMA), held no real estate or other fixed assets, and served only to manage the operations of the Housing Partnerships.

Decedent's son was the managing partner for the Housing Partnerships, responsible for overall management and taking care of day-to-day operations. He could not, however, make any "major decision" without the approval of 75% of the partnership shares (including buying or selling land or partnership property, securing financing, spending over $2,500, and entering into major contracts). Decedent was still actively involved in the Housing Partnerships.

On decedent's death, his son exercised the options in each partnership agreement to purchase his father's interests for $10,000 each. On the estate tax return, he reported the fair market values as the option prices. The IRS disregarded the option prices, and instead determined the values based on the partnerships' assets and income generated from them. The Service applied a 20% marketability discount but no minority discount, and assessed a deficiency of $247,714.

Valuation evidence

During trial the estate presented expert testimony regarding the value of the partnership interests. The IRS did not present expert testimony but did introduce the report of Mitchell Kaye, a valuation expert who had testified to the value of GMA in an earlier state proceeding.

Trial court findings

The Tax Court determined that the options served a testamentary purpose and therefore disregarded them in valuing decedent's interests. The court modified the valuation methodology of one of the experts and applied a 20% discount for lack of marketability to the Housing Partnerships. It accepted Kaye's report on the value of 100% of GMA. The court did not apply a minority discount to any of the five partnerships. It assessed a deficiency of $247,714 and the estate appealed.

Holding on appeal and rationale

The estate first attempted to argue that the question of whether decedent's fifty% interest represented a lack of control was a question of law. The Sixth Circuit Court of Appeals flatly disagreed: "The question of whether a taxpayer is entitled to a discount is intertwined in the larger question of valuation and valuation determinations are clearly questions of fact."

The Court of Appeals went on to say that, absent some explanation of why control has economic value, no premium or discount is warranted. For several reasons, the court found that "there was little to be gained by having control of these partnerships and little risk in holding a minority interest."

First, the Housing Partnerships were guaranteed a long-term, steady income stream under the HUD contracts, with little risk of losing the HUD contracts. The partnerships collected above-market rents under the contracts, and there was no other use that would increase their profits.

Second, the partnership agreements required the partnerships to annually distribute "net cash flow," so decedent was effectively guaranteed a "reasonable annual distribution of partnership income."

Third, although neither decedent nor his son could alone compel liquidation, the ability to liquidate or sell assets was "of little practical import" given the passive nature of the business and the "almost certain prospect of steady profits."

Finally, the court held that the foregoing reasons applied equally to GMA.

The Sixth Circuit affirmed, holding that the Tax Court did not err in refusing to apply a minority discount to decedent's 50% interests, in light of the "unique nature of the rent-controlled housing business."

Estate of Harper v. Commissioner (II)

Citation: T.C. Memo 2002-121, 2002 Tax Ct. Memo LEXIS 127
Court: United States Tax Court
State/Jurisdiction: Specialty Federal
Date of Decision: May 15, 2002
Judge: Nims

The United States Tax Court considered whether assets transferred to a family limited partnership should be included in the decedent's estate under IRC sec. 2036(a) and examined the value of the assets. The decedent placed various marketable securities, bond funds, brokerage accounts, and a note receivable in a trust. The assets comprised 94% of the decedent's overall estate and had a value between $1.6 and $1.7 million. By 1994, the decedent was in ill health, and he died on February 1, 1995.

In 1994, the decedent's daughter, who was fiscally irresponsible, incurred a judgment in a Hawaii court. In order to secure her inheritance from her creditors, the decedent altered his estate plan, which as written would have permitted his daughter to receive her share of the trust upon his death. He then formed a California limited partnership in June of 1994. The partnership was capitalized with the trust's assets. Upon its formation, the decedent named his son managing general partner, gifting him a .4% general partnership interest. He gifted his daughter a .6% general partnership interest and the trust received a 99% limited partnership interest. The decedent's children were not required to make any contributions to the partnership on its formation. Any act outside of the normal course of business including sale of the partnership's assets, admission of partners, and wind up of the partnership required approval by a majority of interests of the limited partners. Distributions of gains or losses from the partnership were to be made pro rata based on the partners' interests.

In July 1994, the decedent gifted his son a 24% limited partnership interest and his daughter a 36% limited partnership interest. As part of this gift, the partnership reclassified the decedent's remaining 39% limited partnership interest as Class A limited partnership interest which had a guaranteed payment of 4.25% of its capital account balance annually, payable quarterly, in addition to its pro rata distribution of gains or losses.

The trust's assets were transferred to the limited partnership between late July and September 1994. A bank account was not opened for the partnership until September 1994. During the interim, the partnership used the trust's bank account, but no funds were transferred between the two accounts after the formation of the partnership's account.

Distributions from the partnership's account were not made as required by the limited partnership agreement. The decedent received substantially more distributions than required under the agreement, and the distributions were not timed as required by the agreement. After the decedent's death, the executor hired an accountant to prepare the financial books of the partnership and prepare the decedent's gift and estate tax returns.

The IRS issued notices of deficiency to the estate. It believed that the full fair market value of the assets contributed to the limited partnership should be included in the decedent's gross estate under sec. 2036(a) because the decedent continued to enjoy the economic benefit of the assets after their transfer to the partnership. The IRS also contested the estate's valuation of the assets.

The Tax Court first considered the IRS's argument that the partnership should be disregarded and the value of the assets should be included in the decedent's gross estate under sec. 2036(a). The estate conversely argued that this section does not apply because the trust received adequate and full consideration in the form of a 99% limited partnership interest in exchange for the assets it transferred. The Tax Court agreed with the IRS, and disregarded the partnership to reach the transferred assets. It stated, "We focus particularly on the commingling of funds, the history of disproportionate distributions, and the testamentary characteristics of the arrangement in support of our conclusion that there existed an implied agreement that decedent would retain the economic benefit of the assets transferred to ... [the partnership]."

The Tax Court next considered the estate's argument that sec. 2036(a) cannot apply because the trust and the limited partnership entered into a "bona fide sale for an adequate and full consideration." The Court rejected this argument. It noted that the transaction could not be a bona fide sale because a bona fide sale presupposes that the transaction occurred at arm's-length. Here, the decedent stood on both sides of the transaction. The Court stated, "It would be an oxymoron to say that one can engage in an arm's-length transaction with oneself." The Court further noted that little changed in relation to the trust, whether it held the assets outright or through the limited partnership, because no other partner contributed to the partnership. It stated, "There exists nothing but a circuitous 'recycling' of value." The Court continued, "We therefore hold that where a transaction involves only the genre of value 'recycling' ... and does not appear to be motivated primarily by legitimate business concerns, no transfer for consideration within the meaning of section 2036(a) has taken place. Hence, the [bona fide sale] exception provided in that statute is inapplicable."

After concluding that the partnership's assets were includible in the decedent's gross estate under sec. 2036 (a), the Tax Court turned to the valuation issue. Since most of the assets transferred by the trust were readily marketable, there was little disagreement over the value of the bulk of the assets. However, the parties disagreed regarding the value of the note receivable. Both parties presented expert testimony regarding the value of the note.

The note was made in 1991 and originally came due on April 14, 1992. However, it had been renewed annually since the original date of maturity. It had a face value of $450,000 and bore 10%

interest. The interest payments were current at all times. The note was secured by a 45% interest in a $1 million note held by its maker, which in turn was secured by a deed of trust in a mobile home park. The mobile home park was subject to a degree of environmental contamination.

The estate's expert, a business appraiser, valued the note at $300,000 using both an income approach and a market approach. In computing the income approach he applied a 15 present discount rate to reduce the face value to present value. The discount rate was calculated as the interest plus 5%, an amount added to the contract rate in the event of default. In determining his market approach valuation, the expert relied primarily on interviews with the note's maker. Through the interviews, he learned that a 45% interest in the note could be sold for 60 to 70% of its value. Thus, the expert applied that information to the note at issue, and determined that the note could be sold for 65% of its face value.

The Tax Court rejected the estate's expert's valuation. It stated, "[this expert's] ... report was highly conclusory and revealed little about the underlying analysis. As a result, we could neither perform any meaningful evaluation nor ascertain that the conclusions were supported by an appropriate foundation." It specifically took issue with his calculation of the discount rate used in his income approach. It found that the note at issue contained no default provision increasing the interest rate. However, it found that the $1 million note securing the note at issue contained such a provision. It stated that the expert did not explain his reason for applying the provision made with a different debtor far removed in time from the valuation date to the note at issue. The Tax Court also took issue with his market approach valuation. It noted that the expert relied heavily on information obtained from the note's debtor, whom the expert described as an expert in secondary loans. However, the debtor's qualifications were not introduced at trial nor did he testify before the Court. The Court found two errors with this. It stated, "Accordingly, we are asked to accept his [the debtor's] opinions, as reported by ... [the estate's expert], without any opportunity to probe their foundation or any assurances that he was qualified to render them. We also note that his independence for purposes of offering a neutral opinion is not free from doubt." It further noted that the expert did not indicate what sources he utilized in verifying the debtor's opinion. Thus, the Court rejected this expert's conclusions.

The IRS's expert, a real estate appraiser, began by considering the security for both the estate's note and the $1 million note securing the estate's note. He found that both notes were adequately secured. In doing so, he considered the value of the mobile home park, existing liens on the park, and environmental issues. The expert then considered five factors in determining whether the note should be discounted from its face value. "These were: (1) The collateral securing the note; (2) the existence of guaranties relating to the note and its collateral; (3) the interest rate on the note; (4) previously granted extensions of the note's maturity date and the currency of payments; and (5) environmental concerns related to the collateral." He determined that the first two factors favored no discount, the third factor was neutral, and the last two factors favored a discount. Relying on his experience with real property and promissory notes, he concluded that the discount would be within a range of 5 to 15%. He settled on a discount of 10%, which resulted in a value of $405,000 for the note.

The Tax Court agreed with much of the IRS's expert's analysis. However, it disagreed with the expert's finding that the note was personally guaranteed. It found no guaranty document in the record, and remarked that the estate's note's debtor executed the note in his personal capacity. Thereby, making a personal guaranty redundant. It concluded, "In summary then, we conclude that, on the evidence before us, personal guaranties should not be considered as a factor enhancing the value of the ... note." This changed the overall weight of the factors to one in favor of no discount and three in favor of a discount. It then considered the range of discounts provided by the IRS's expert. While finding this information lacking, the Court determined that it had a better foundation than the discount from face value determined by the estate's expert. However, it rejected the expert's proposed 10% discount from face value because the mix of factors he relied on had changed after the Court's analysis. Considering its analysis of the factors, the Court increased the discount to 12% (two-thirds the spread of the given range), and determined that the value of the note was $395,000.

This abstract originally appeared in *Valuation Case Digest*, authored by John J. Stockdale, Jr.

Kerr v. Commissioner (II)

Citation: 292 F.3d 490, 2002 U.S. App. LEXIS 10965
Court: United States Court of Appeals
State/Jurisdiction: 5th Circuit Federal
Date of Decision: June 10, 2002
Judge: Duhe

The issue in this case was whether the restrictions in the partnership agreements were "applicable restrictions" to be disregarded in valuing the transferred interests, thus precluding a marketability discount.

Facts

In 1993, the Kerrs created two family limited partnerships: the Kerr Family Limited Partnership (KFLP) and Kerr Interests, Ltd. (KIL), to make a gift to their children. The Kerrs made capital contributions to KFLP and KIL. In KFLP, the Kerrs and their children were general partners; the Kerrs were also Class A and Class B limited partners. In KIL, KFLP was the general partner; the Kerrs were Class A limited partners; and KFLP, the Kerrs, and their children were Class B limited partners

In December 1994 and December 1995, the Kerrs donated Class B partnership interests in KIL to their children. Also in December 1994, the Kerrs created an irrevocable grantor retained annuity trust (GRAT) to which each grantor transferred assets retaining a right to receive a fixed annuity for a term of years. Each Kerr was the sole trustee of his or her GRAT, and their children and grandchildren were the beneficiaries of the remainder interests via generation-skipping transfer (GST) trusts, called the Kerr Issue GST Trusts.

Valuation evidence

The Kerrs considered the KFLP interests transferred to the GRATs to be only assignee interests, not partnership interests. Accordingly, they applied marketability discounts.

The IRS, on the other hand, contended that the KFLP interests assigned to the GRATs were partnership interests.

Tax court findings

The Tax Court ruled that the interests transferred to the GRATs were partnership interests. Nevertheless, the court held that the partnership agreement restrictions were not "applicable restrictions." Accordingly, the Kerrs were allowed their marketability discounts from the values of the transferred interests.

Holding on appeal and rationale

The court of appeals upheld the tax court decision:

> The three defining features of an "applicable restriction" pertinent to this appeal are that it a) effectively limits the ability of the partnership to liquidate, b) lapses or can be removed by the family after the transfer, and c) is more restrictive than State law.

The court reasoned that those partnership agreements contained restrictions on liquidation of the entire partnership, as well as on the right of a partner to withdraw from the partnership. Additionally, because those restrictions did not meet the removability requirement, they were not "applicable restrictions" to be disregarded in valuing the interests. Therefore, the marketability discounts were appropriate.

Polack v. Commissioner (I)

Citation: T.C. Memo. 2002-145, 2002 Tax Ct. Memo LEXIS 149
Court: United States Tax Court
State/Jurisdiction: Specialty Federal
Date of Decision: June 10, 2002
Judge: Marvel

The issue in this case was the valuation of taxpayer Polack's gift of 1,040,000 shares of Zip Sort, Inc. (ZSI) stock that he gifted to his children on December 31, 1992 (260,000 of his nonvoting stock to each of his four children).

Facts

Polack purchased ZSI on August 1987. ZSI was in the business of printing and preparing bulk mail for clients. In 1990 the U.S. Postal Service instituted the value added refund (VAR) program, in which the Service refunded 9 cents for each piece of presorted bulk mail.

Valuation evidence

Taxpayer's expert, Gerald Gray, concluded that ZSI was worth $2 million, and the gifted 1,040,000 shares were worth 50 cents each. IRS expert Brad Cashion concluded that ZSI was worth $3,800,000, representing $3,630,000 as an operating company and $170,000 in nonoperating assets listed on ZSI's balance sheet. Cashion further concluded that the 1,040,000 shares were worth 90 cents each, although at trial the IRS conceded that the shares were worth 88 cents each.

Tax Court findings

In the absence of arm's-length sales or transfers of stock in ZSI or comparable companies, the court analyzed three differences in the parties' valuations: (1) projected VAR income (VARI); (2) projected annual capital expenditures; and (3) nonoperating assets.

Of these three items, the court stated the first would likely have the most impact on ZSI's value. The IRS projected that ZSI would retain 50% of the gross VARI for each projected year. Polack, on the other hand, projected that ZSI would retain only 21.60% of the projected gross VARI. The Tax Court found that Polack's projection was not based on any evidence or personal knowledge, and was therefore not probative. It also found that the IRS's projection was based on objective and reliable evidence.

Polack also contended that IRS's capital expenditure projections were inconsistent with ZSI's history of expenses, projected level of growth, and projected depreciation. Specifically, he argued that the IRS: (1) improperly reduced ZSI's assets book values during a period of corporate growth; (2) improperly depreciated assets not yet acquired; and (3) failed to recognize that "proper appraisal methodology" would project a growing company's capital expenditures to be relatively equal to its depreciation.

The court rejected all of Polack's foregoing arguments, stating first that he had pointed to no authority that "a decline in a corporation's assets book values is irreconcilable with that corporation's growth." ZSI's growth, it said, was tied more closely to service fees and VARI than to its assets book values. Second, the court found that the IRS never projected that ZSI's accumulated depreciation to exceed the cumulative costs of its assets. Moreover, although the IRS projected annual depreciation to exceed annual capital expenditures in certain years, ZSI's assets book values were "sufficient to accommodate that depreciation." Finally, the court held that Polack ignored the "reality of ZSI's situation" and failed to persuade the court that ZSI's future capital expenditures would match its depreciation.

The final difference in the parties' valuations concerned the $170,000 operating asset. Polack argued that it should be offset by $150,000 because he said the ZSI purchased the asset for him in satisfaction of a debt to a stockholder in this amount. The court dismissed his argument, stating that he did not introduce any evidence, other than his own testimony, to prove that he was the stockholder to whom ZSI owed the $150,000 or that ZSI bought the asset in satisfaction of the debt, in the face of the evidence that the asset was listed on the balance sheet with a $170,000 value.

The court upheld the IRS's valuation of ZSI and concluded that the value of the 1,040,000 shares was 88 cents per share.

Estate of Bailey v. Commissioner

Citation: T.C. Memo. 2002-152
Court: United States Tax Court
State/Jurisdiction: Specialty Federal
Date of Decision: June 17, 2002
Judge: Thornton

In the *Estate of Lewis A. Bailey v. CIR*, T.C. Memo. 2002-152, the Tax Court considered the valuation of a corporation that owned and operated motels for estate tax purposes. The corporation owned a motel in California and one in Arkansas. It had 200 outstanding shares on the decedent's date of death—December 18, 1995. At that time the decedent owned 50 shares outright and he had the right to receive income from a qualified terminable interest property (QTIP) trust that held 50 shares. The QTIP stock was includible in his gross estate, but was not aggregated with the stock he held outright.

The stock was valued using the adjusted net asset method. The motels were valued by qualified real property appraisers in their respective state. In determining the value of each 25% block, the estate applied a 50% combined minority interest, key man and lack of marketability discount. It reported a fair market value of $370,708 per block. The IRS disagreed with that valuation and filed a notice of deficiency, which valued each block at $451,263. In its notice of deficiency, the IRS adopted the estates proposed 50% combined discount.

Sometime after filing its tax return, the estate learned that the decedent held an undivided one-half interest in one of two parcels of real property under the California motel. The corporation owned the remaining one-half interest and the entire second parcel. Before the Tax Court, both parties presented expert testimony regarding the value of the stock. The IRS's expert, who also prepared the valuation for the notice of deficiency, valued the stock based on the adjusted book value of net assets. He relied on the real property appraisals prepared by the estate for the value of the motels. He then applied a 20% minority interest discount and a 27.44% lack of marketability discount (a 41.95% combined discount) to arrive at a fair market value of each 25% block at $415,319.

This expert did not rely on standard marketability studies in determining the size of his lack of marketability discount. The discount was derived using both expected future built-in capital gains liability and stock sale costs. He calculated the present value of the future capital gains liability by assuming a five-year holding period, 7% for selling expenses, 2% annual growth, a 39.06% state and Federal tax rate, and a discount rate of 8%. He then compared the present value of the tax liability with the date-of-death adjusted net asset value of the company to arrive at a 21.44% discount. To that he added 6% for stock sale costs. He indicated that he considered other factors, but did not give those factors any weight because he concluded that the company was a holding company. Thus, he applied a total lack of marketability discount of 27.44%.

The estate's expert, like the IRS's expert, valued the business based on the adjusted book value of net assets. He also relied upon the appraisals of the real property performed in connection with the estate tax return. However, this expert reduced the real property appraiser's valuation of the California property by $193,000 after learning that the decedent held an undivided one-half interest in one of the two parcels the motel sat upon. He then applied a 20% minority interest discount and a 40% lack of marketability discount, for a combined discount of 52%. His lack of marketability discount was based on the restricted stock and IPO studies, which indicated a discount range between 35 and 50%. He concluded that each block had a value of $307,100.

The estate also presented a desk review of the California motel performed by the Arkansas real property appraiser who valued the Arkansas motel for the estate tax return. This appraiser considered the detrimental effect of the decedent's undivided one-half interest in one parcel of real property under the California motel. This expert valued the property as a distress sale because of the clouded title. He concluded that the property was worth $569,000 less than initially appraised.

The Tax Court initially considered how to handle the post-filing discovery of the decedent's undivided fractional interest in the real property. While acknowledging that the fractional interest would decrease the value of the motel and thus the value of the corporation, it would also correspondingly increase the value of the decedent's gross estate. However, the Tax Court rejected the estate's proposed decreases in the value of the corporation. It rejected the discount incorporated by the estate's business appraiser as undocumented. It also rejected the opinion of the real estate appraiser. It determined that valuing the property as a distress sale ran counter to the requirement that property be valued at fair market value. Furthermore, it was skeptical as to how an Arkansas appraiser could know more about the California market than a California real estate appraiser. It lastly commented that even if it were to include a valuation decrement for the clouded title and increase the decedent's gross estate, the estate did not show that the net effect would be to its advantage. Thus, it valued the business as though the decedent's fractional interest did not exist and did not include any amount in the decedent's gross estate for the fractional interest.

The Court then considered the proper application of the discounts. Since both parties agreed that a 20% minority interest discount was applicable, the only issue was the proper size of a lack of marketability discount. The Court rejected both experts' discounts. It found the discount calculated by the estate was not supportable because the restricted stock and IPO studies relied upon assumed a short holding period, and a hypothetical buyer of the corporation would have a long investment horizon. It also rejected the IRS's calculation. It found no basis in the record for the expert's assumptions utilized in his capital gains liability calculation. It further found that the expert did not support his 6% stock sale discount. The Court lastly determined that the expert did not factor in continuity of management when arriving at his discount size even though this expert's own report would support an additional discount for this factor. The Court then determined that the discount as reported on the estate tax return and adopted by the IRS in the notice of deficiency was correct. Therefore, it applied a 50% combined lack of marketability and minority interest discount. Thus, the Tax Court valued each 25% block of stock included in the decedent's estate at $357,738.

This abstract originally appeared in *Valuation Case Digest*, authored by John J. Stockdale, Jr.

Estate of Strangi v. Commissioner (II)

Citation: 293 F.3d 279, 2002 U.S. App. LEXIS 11920
Court: United States Court of Appeals
State/Jurisdiction: 5th Circuit Federal
Date of Decision: June 17, 2002
Judge: Clement

Less than two months before trial, the IRS filed a motion to amend to add a claim that, under section 2036 of the Internal Revenue Code, the estate should include in the gross estate the value of the Strangi Family Limited Partnership's (SFLP) assets transferred from decedent, rather than just his partnership interest. The Tax Court denied the motion to amend because it considered the motion untimely. The Fifth Circuit Court of Appeals reviewed this decision for abuse of discretion.

The Fifth Circuit began by noting the Tax Court's reasoning for denial of the IRS's motion, which was that section 2036 was not an issue because the IRS asserted it "shortly" before trial. The Court of Appeals disagreed with the Tax Court that two months was "shortly" before trial, and it stated that the addition of the claim was unlikely to cause delay or prejudice. Because it found no obvious reason for the denial, the court of appeals found it was an abuse of discretion, reversed that ruling, and remanded for consideration of the 2036 claim.

The Fifth Circuit then reviewed for clear error the question of whether SFLP had a business purpose and economic substance, so that it could not be disregarded for tax purposes. On this issue, it agreed with the Tax Court:

> SFLP's partnership agreement changed the legal relationships between decedent and his heirs and creditors. Potential purchasers of decedent's assets would not disregard the partnership. As the tax court stated, "[r]egardless of subjective intentions, the partnership had sufficient substance to be recognized for tax purposes."

The Fifth Circuit also affirmed the Tax Court on all other issues, including its conclusions: (1) that section 2703 did not apply to the partnership; (2) that decedent's transfer of property to the partnership was not a taxable gift; (3) on discounts and the fair market value of decedents interest in SFLP at his date of death. Regarding the value, however, the court of appeals stated that the Tax Court may revisit this issue after considering the 2036 claim.

Estate of O'Neal v. United States (II)

Citation: No. CV-97-J-2189-S (N.D. Ala. 2002)
Court: United States District Court
State/Jurisdiction: Northern District of Alabama
Date of Decision: July 31, 2002
Judge: Johnson

In the *Estate of Elizabeth Paramore O'Neal v. United States of America*, No. CV-97-J-2189-S N.D. Ala. July 31, 2002), the U.S. District Court, on remand from the U.S. Court of Appeals for the Eleventh Circuit, considered the date-of-death value of claims made against the decedent's estate as a result of transferee gift tax and generation-skipping transfer tax liabilities. In 1987, the decedent and her husband gifted stock in their steel company to their children and grandchildren. On their gift tax returns, they valued the stock under a 1951 buy-sell agreement. The husband died a year later.

After the statute of limitations expired for assessing gift tax, generation-skipping transfer tax and penalties against the decedent and her husband for the 1987 gifts of stock, the IRS claimed the stock was undervalued and sought to recover over $16 million in additional taxes and penalties. It issued notices of deficiency to the decedent's children and grandchildren. The children paid the tax, filed refund claims and filed suits for refund in District Court. The grandchildren filed petitions in Tax Court. During the proceedings, the decedent died.

The estate claimed that it was entitled to a deduction for claims made against it as a result of the children and grandchildren's transferee liability. The Eleventh Circuit found that the estate was entitled to a deduction, but determined the amount should be valued as of the date of the decedent's death and remanded the case to the district court. Before the district court, the estate presented two attorneys as experts, including a retired judge, to testify as to the value of the decedent's children and grandchildren's claims against the estate as of the date-of-death.

Starting with an analysis of the potential transferee tax liability, the retired judge determined that there was a 25% chance for each of four possible outcomes to the transferee tax litigation. He determined the court would: 1) accept the per-share value of the stock as determined by the IRS; 2) accept the per-share value of the stock claimed by the transferees; 3) accept the per-share value of the stock based on a study done by a brokerage firm; or 4) accept a per-share value in between the values determined by the IRS and the transferees. The judge concluded that the expected transferee tax liability, including penalties and interest, was approximately $7.8 million.

Next, he considered whether the children and grandchildren would successfully defend their claims against the estate. He concluded there was 75% chance that they would prevail. He applied that 75% probability to the $7.8 million expected transferee tax liability and determined that the children and grandchildren's claims had a value of $5.8 million as of the date of the decedent's death. The estate's other expert analyzed the potential transferee tax liability by applying three different approaches—the specific approach, the general approach and the blended approach. Under the specific approach, he "examined the methodologies of the appraisers, the comparisons to other companies, the weighting between book value and earnings valuations, and the discounts in order to determine what a court most likely would do in a similar situation." Under the general approach, the expert determined the IRS's success in litigating transfer tax cases involving closely held businesses using a valuation matrix. He concluded that the IRS had a 60% success rate. Based on that rate, he determined the per-share value of the stock that someone who was evaluating the Tax Court case might have arrived at. Using the blended approach, which combined the values determined using the specific and general approaches he concluded the expected transferee tax liability was $9.7 million.

Next, the expert considered whether the children and grandchildren would successfully defend their claims against the estate. He evaluated claim liability law and applied a 20% discount "to account for the hazards of litigation" to the $9.7 million expected tax liability. He concluded that the children and grandchildren's claims had a date-of death rounded value of $7.7 million.

The District Court noted that the methodologies used by both of the estate's experts were "consistent with the way cases are analyzed by lawyers for settlement purposes and for trial and are accepted methods for evaluating cases for settlement and for trial." However, the court found that the former judge's determinations were "more persuasive" due to his experience in resolving cases that were similar to this case. It agreed with his conclusions and found that the date-of-death value of the children and grandchildren's claims was $5.8 million.

This abstract originally appeared in *Valuation Case Digest*, authored by John J. Stockdale, Jr.

Estate of Dunn v. Commissioner (II)

Citation: 301 F.3d 339, 2002 U.S. App. LEXIS 15453
Court: United States Court of Appeals
State/Jurisdiction: 5th Circuit Federal
Date of Decision: August 1, 2002
Judge: Wiener

The U.S. Court of Appeals for the Fifth Circuit considered the Tax Court's valuation of a majority interest in a closely held, heavy machinery retail business. The decedent held a 62.96% interest in the corporation. This interest provided the decedent with operational control over the business, but lacked the supermajority need to effect a liquidation or sale of the business.

The company had been in the business of renting heavy machinery and operators since 1949. As a result of certain economic conditions, the company's earnings had been flat for the four years prior to the valuation date, which eliminated net cash flow available for debt reduction or dividend payment. However, the company held substantial physical assets consisting of equipment, commercial and residential property. Thus, the earnings value and the asset value of the company were widely divergent. As a result, the IRS argued before the Tax Court that the company should be valued solely on the basis of its asset value. In making this argument, the IRS claimed that no discount for built-in capital gains taxes should be recognized in arriving at the asset valuation.

The Tax Court rejected the IRS's argument that company should be solely valued using the asset method. It found that the company was an operating company, which is generally valued using an earnings method. However, because of the great disparity between the earnings and asset valuations, it used a weighted combination (35% earnings value, 65% asset value) to value the company.

The Tax Court also rejected the IRS's argument that the built-in capital gains taxes should not be considered in determining the asset value of the company. The Tax Court found that a willing buyer would consider the built-in capital gains taxes in arriving at the purchase price of the decedent's block. However, it found that since the block could not force liquidation, a liquidation of the company was unlikely. Therefore, it permitted only a discount of 5% of the asset value for built-in capital gains taxes, instead of the 34% tax rate that the company would incur upon the sale of its assets. The estate appealed the Tax Court's decision regarding the consideration of its built-in capital gains tax liability and the weighting of the valuation methods.

On appeal to the Fifth Circuit, the estate argued, "like advertising and transportation costs, commissions, and other unavoidable expenses of disposition of these assets accepted by the Tax Court, the assets' gross value must be reduced by their built-in gains tax liability to reach their net fair market value *for purposes of calculating the asset-based value of the Corporation*." (emphasis in original). The Fifth Circuit agreed. It stated, "We hold as a matter of law that the built-in gains tax liability of this particular business's assets must be considered as a dollar-for-dollar reduction when calculating the *asset*-based value of the Corporation, just as, conversely, built-in gains tax liability would have no place in the calculation of the Corporation's *earnings*-based value." (emphasis in original). Thus, it reversed the Tax Court's decision and rendered the opinion that the full amount of the built-in capital gains taxes should be considered at the effective 34% rate.

In reaching this decision, the Fifth Circuit noted that the Tax Court inappropriately considered the likelihood of liquidation in reaching its decision not to recognize the full amount of the built-in capital gains tax. The Fifth Circuit noted that valuing the corporation under the asset approach, presupposes that the assets will be sold and therefore it is 100% likely that the assets will be liquidated, while an earnings valuation presupposes that the assets of the company will be retained in order to produce the earnings. It concluded, "The likelihood of liquidation has no place in either of the two disparate approaches to valuing this particular operating company. We hasten to add, however, that the *likelihood of liquidation* does play a key role in appraising the Decedent's block of stock, and that role is in the determination of the relative *weights* to be given to those two approaches: The lesser the likelihood of liquidation (or sale of essentially all assets), the greater the *weight* (percentage) that must be assigned to the earnings (cash flow)-based approach and, perforce, the lesser the weight to be assigned to the asset based approach." (Emphasis in original).

The Fifth Circuit then considered the appropriate weight to be applied to the asset and earnings methods. In considering this issue, the court again noted that the Tax Court found that the corporation was an operating company, whose significant physical assets, namely equipment, were used in the production of income, and that it was unlikely that the corporation would be liquidated. It further found important, the Tax Court's rhetorical question: "because Dunn Equipment was an operating the company, the better question is not whether we disregard the earnings-based value, but whether we should disregard the asset-based value." However, it noted that the Tax Court "astonishingly" arrived at a valuation that gave two-thirds of the weight to an asset valuation. The Fifth Circuit then stated, "We view this as a legal, logical, and economic non sequitur, inconsistent with all findings and expressions of the court leading up to its announcement of this step in its methodology." Thus, it reversed and rendered a decision to value the company using an 85:15 earnings-to-asset valuation ratio.

This abstract originally appeared in *Valuation Case Digest*, authored by John J. Stockdale, Jr.

Estate of Glover v. Commissioner

Citation: T.C. Memo. 2002-186
Court: United States Tax Court
State/Jurisdiction: Specialty Federal
Date of Decision: August 2, 2002
Judge: Jacobs

In the *Estate of Frances C. Glover v. CIR*, T. C. Memo. 2002-186, the Tax Court considered the value of a malpractice claim for inclusion in the decedent's gross estate. In the later part of decedent's life, she was paralyzed. Her financial affairs were overseen by an acquaintance who held power of attorney. The acquaintance engaged a law firm to assist her in drafting various documents, including a will and an antenuptial agreement for the decedent. Following the decedent's death in 1991, the decedent's heirs discovered the misappropriation of the decedent's monies by her acquaintance, which was named executor of her estate. Thereafter, will contest actions were brought and the executor was removed. The executor pro tem brought suit against the law firm, who assisted the acquaintance. The executor pro tem and the heirs that discovered the misdeeds agreed that any recovery would be split 40/60 between the estate and the heirs. Sometime thereafter, a Pennsylvania Orphans' Court awarded the estate recovery of $247,500 in attorneys' fees paid to the law firm. Shortly thereafter, nine years after the decedent's death, the law firm, the estate, the executor pro tem and the heirs entered into a settlement agreement whereby all claims against the firm, including the Orphans' Court's order were settled for $750,000. The estate incurred $203,659 in attorneys' fees litigating and settling the estate's claims, leaving a net recovery of $546,341. The IRS and the estate disagreed over the proper value of the claim.

The parties agreed that the appropriate starting point of the valuation of this claim is the amount of the settlement ($750,000). They further agreed that the value of the claim should be reduced by the attorneys' fees incurred by the estate in litigating the claim ($203,659). They lastly agreed that the value of the claim, after allowable deductions, should be reduced to present value using a factor of 0.438233. The parties contested whether the amount ordered by the Orphans' Court to be repaid to the estate should be deducted from the value of the claim. The estate also argued that the value of the claim should be reduced by an amount allocable to the heirs' claim against the law firm.

The Tax Court initially noted that the parties stipulated to the use of the settlement amount as the starting point for valuing the claim. It further noted that the settlement was drafted nine years after the valuation date. It stated, "While normally we would not attach such importance, if any, to an event or transaction occurring almost 9 years after decedent's death in determining a date-of-death value for an asset owned by a decedent, in this case we do so because of the parties' stipulation."

The Tax Court next considered whether the attorneys' fees ordered returned to the estate should be deducted from the value of the claim. The Court found that while the settlement agreement did not allocate any amounts between any of the claims against the law firm, the amount ordered repaid to the estate should be deducted because the settlement agreement released all claims of the estate which included the amount ordered by the Orphans' Court. Since the Orphans' Court order was enforceable against the law firm, it should be set off against the settlement. It further reasoned, "Were we not to make this allocation, decedent's gross estate would be increased by the repaid fees, which in essence would cause the $247,500 to be taxed twice." Thus, it permitted the deduction for the repaid attorneys' fees.

The Court also considered whether the agreement to apportion 60% of the recovery to the heirs should correspondingly reduce the amount of the claim. The Tax Court found that since the Pennsylvania courts dismissed the heirs' claims because the heirs lacked standing, no portion of the settlement award should be allocated to the heirs' claims and thus, deducted when valuing the claim.

Therefore, the Tax Court valued the claim starting with the settlement amount, less repaid attorneys' fees and attorneys' fees expended in connection with the settlement. It then reduced that sum to present value using a factor of 0.438233, leaving $130,962 as the value of the claim.

This abstract originally appeared in *Valuation Case Digest*, authored by John J. Stockdale, Jr.

Okerlund v. United States (I)

Citation: 53 Fed. Cl. 341, 2002 U.S. Claims LEXIS 221
Court: United States Court of Federal Claims
State/Jurisdiction: Specialty Federal
Date of Decision: August 23, 2002
Judge: Wilson

The issue in this consolidated case was the fair market value of two minority nonvoting stock interests in Schwan's Sales Enterprises, Inc. (SSE), one as of December 31, 1992 (date of gift), and the other as of December 31, 1994 (date of charitable contribution).

Daubert challenge rejected

The first issue addressed by the court in this opinion is the plaintiffs' challenge of the qualifications and admissibility of the government's expert witness, Herbert Spiro. The court thoroughly reviewed his qualifications and methodologies in light of the *Daubert* factors, and concluded that his testimony and report were admissible. Notably, he used the same methodologies—market approach and income approach—as did plaintiffs' own expert, Shannon Pratt. These methods have been generally accepted in the business appraisal community and by the courts for many years.

1992 date uses guideline companies, DCF

For the 1992 valuation, both experts used a guideline public company method and a discounted cash flow method. In the guideline public company method, Spiro used valuation multiples near the medians, while Pratt used valuation multiples below the medians. In the discounted cash flow method, Spiro used a discount rate of 15.93% and Pratt used a discount rate of 16.5%.

The court concluded:

> In sum, although the risk factors identified by both experts are not insignificant, the totality of the circumstances an economic indicators considered by the Court...weigh in favor of Dr. Spiro's pricing multiples, which more closely conform to the guideline company medians.

For the same reason, the court accepted Spiro's discount rate in the income approach.

Site visit after valuation date

Pratt visited the company headquarters and interviewed management, which Spiro did not. However, Pratt's visit was after the 1992 valuation date and after the death of Marvin Schwan, who had been the CEO. In addressing the significance of the management interviews, the court stated:

> The Court is not persuaded that this methodological difference is as significant as plaintiffs suggest, at least with respect to the identification of enterprise level risks in 1992. Dr. Pratt's interview with SSE management on site in Marshall, Minnesota, occurred after the death of Marvin Schwan, which poses the risk of "20/20 hindsight" with respect to the weight given to the risk factor of management succession and the companys reliance on a key figure. To the extent that the interviews revealed characteristics of the company not accessible through other sources, the Court finds that this information is more relevant to the assessment of shareholder risks rather than enterprise risks, and therefore, impacts the discount for lack of marketability to a greater extent than the value of shares on a freely traded basis under various methods.

Thorough analysis of DLOM credited

Spiro opined to 30% discount for lack of marketability, and Pratt opined to 45% on both dates. The court found that a 40% discount should be applied for the December 31, 1992 valuation date, and 45% for December 31, 1994.

Additionally, both experts agreed on an additional 5% discount for nonvoting stock, which the court accepted and applied additively, making the total discount 45% for the 1992 gifts and 50% for the 1994 gifts.

The following are relevant excerpts from the court's opinion:

> Both experts relied on two sources of empirical data for aid in quantifying the discount for lack of marketability: (1) discounts on sales of restricted shares of publicly traded companies; and (2) discounts on private transactions prior to initial public offerings (IPOs). . .Based on these studies, and an examination of the perceived risks facing a potential investor in SSE stock, Dr. Pratt concluded that a 45% discount for lack of marketability was appropriate, and Dr. Spiro concluded that a 30% discount was justified.
>
> Dr. Pratt's expert reports contain a far more detailed analysis of the empirical studies of trading prices of restricted shares and pre-initial public offering transactions than the AVG Report. The eight independent studies of restricted stock transactions reviewed in the Willamette Reports reported average discounts ranging from 25 to 45%. According to Dr. Pratt, the two most important factors in determining the size of the discount were the amount of dividends paid (more dividends are associated with a lower discount for lack of marketability) and the perceived holding period (the longer the holding period the greater the discount for lack of marketability). (Tr. at 71-72.) The second major line of studies, involving pre-IPO transactions, observed discounts averaging approximately 45 to 47%. n18 (Tr. at 74.) Unlike the AVG Report, the Willamette Report considered the pre-IPO studies more relevant for the purpose of determining the appropriate discount for lack of marketability. According to Dr. Pratt, the discounts observed in restricted stock studies reflect the existence of a public market for the stock once the

> temporary restrictions lapse. For a variety of reasons, . . .purchasers of restricted stock "generally expect to be able to resell the stock in the public market in the foreseeable future." (J. Ex. 508, at 78.) Pre-IPO discounts, on the other hand, are based on purely private transactions before a company enters the public market, a situation more comparable to closely held companies such as SSE. (Tr. at 205.). . .
>
> The Court finds Dr. Pratt's analysis of the relevant empirical studies and the shareholder risks more persuasive than the AVG reports rather truncated analysis.

1994 charitable contribution evidence unrefuted

For the 1994 valuation, the government did not present independent valuation evidence, but relied on the plaintiffs original charitable contribution filing of $12.51 per share. Plantiffs had made an amended filing at $19.77, which the government previously accepted.

The court stated:

> Although the Court may choose not to accept the second Willamette appraisal even if it is uncontradicted, [citation omitted] the Court finds the methodological approaches and conclusions of the 1994 report persuasive. The report constitutes both credible evidence under 26 U.S.C. § 7491(a)(1) [see sidebar], and, together with Dr. Pratt's testimony at trial, sufficient evidence to satisfy plaintiff's burden of proof under the preexisting general rule.

Estate of Theodore Thompson v. Commissioner (I)

Citation: T.C. Memo 2002-246, 2002 Tax Ct. Memo LEXIS 254
Court: United States Tax Court
State/Jurisdiction: Specialty Federal
Date of Decision: September 26, 2002
Judge: Jacobs

The issue in this case was whether decedent's gross estate included the value of interests in two family limited partnerships: The Thompson Turner Family Limited Partnership ("Turner Partnership") and the Thompson Family Limited Partnership ("Thompson Partnership").

Facts

On April 21, 1993, decedent, his two children, and his son-in-law agreed to form two family limited partnerships and two corporations to serve as the general partners. Decedent contributed to the partnership approximately $1,286,000 in securities, plus notes receivable due from his daughter's children. Decedent died on May 15, 1995.

Decedent's estate reported that decedent held:

- a) 87.65% interest in the Turner Partnership ($875,811),
- b) 54.12% interest in the Thompson Partnership ($837,691),
- c) 490 shares of Turner Corp. stock valued at $5,190, and
- d) 490 shares of Thompson Corp. stock valued at $7,888.

The reported values were determined by applying a 40% combined discount for minority interest and lack of marketability to the net asset value of the partnerships' assets.

The IRS determined a $707,054 deficiency in estate taxes, based on:

- a) the value of decedent's interest in the Thompson Partnership was $1,396,152,
- b) the value of decedent's interest in the Turner Partnership was $1,717,977,
- c) the value of decedent's 490 shares of Thompson Corp. was $13,977, and
- d) the value of his 490 shares of Turner Corp. was $4,094.

Consequently, the IRS increased decedent's taxable estate by $1,400,627 for decedent's interest in the partnerships, and $4,993 for the value of decedent's shares. In addition, the IRS disallowed both the minority and lack of marketability discounts applied by the estate.

Partnerships had economic substance

The IRS first argued that the partnerships should be disregarded for estate tax purposes because they lacked "economic substance and business purpose." The Tax Court disagreed because both partnerships were validly formed, and "[p]otential purchasers of decedents assets would not disregard the partnership. Thus the partnerships had sufficient substance to be recognized" for estate tax purposes.

Decedent retained economic benefit

Alternatively, the IRS argued that "because decedent retained the economic benefit and control of the transferred assets, section 2036(a) applies so that the date-of-death value of the assets decedent transferred to the partnerships is includable in decedents gross estate." This time the Tax Court agreed:

> Here, decedent's outright transfer of the vast bulk of his assets to the partnerships would have deprived him of the assets needed for his own support. Thus, the transfers from the partnerships to decedent can only be explained if decedent had at least an implied understanding that his children would agree to his requests for money from the assets he contributed to the partnerships, and that they would do so for as long as he lived.
>
> In light of decedent's personal situation, the fact that the contributed property constituted the majority of decedent's assets, including nearly all of his investments, the establishment of the partnership is far more consistent with an estate plan than with any sort of arms-length joint enterprise between partners.

The court concluded that decedent retained enjoyment of the contributed property within the meaning of 2036.

Partnerships merely 'recycled value'

The estate then argued that decedent's transfer of his assets to the partnerships was a "bona fide sale for an adequate and full consideration," thus falling within the exemption to 2036(a). The Tax Court rejected this contention:

> [N]one of the individual partners in either of the partnerships was involved in the conduct of an active business. Additionally, it is clear that [decedent's son, daughter, and son-in-law] did not actually pool their assets with those of decedent. To the extent the partnerships could have generated income resulting from their separate activities, they arranged matters so that any such income went to them directly, and not to the partnerships. . . They, like decedent, merely "recycled" their property through the partnership form. . .
>
> In the final analysis, neither decedent nor his family conducted the partnerships in a business-like manner. None of the parties involved in the partnerships joined together with the intent to either form business enterprises or otherwise to conduct any trade or business. The partnerships did not engage in transactions with anyone outside the family; loans and gifts were made to family members only. The lending activities of the partnerships lacked any semblance of legitimate business transactions. This exclusivity might be consistent with decedents generosity towards his family members, but it was inconsistent with any valid business operation. In reality, these loans were testamentary in nature, using decedents money as a source of financing for the needs of individual family members, not for business purposes.

The court thus held that the full date-of-death value of the assets that decedent transferred from his trusts to the partnerships was includable in his gross estate pursuant to section 2036(a).

Rauenhorst v. Commissioner

Citation: 119 T.C. No. 9 (2002)
Court: United States Tax Court
State/Jurisdiction: Specialty Federal
Date of Decision: October 7, 2002
Judge: Ruwe

In *Gerald A. and Henrietta V. Rauenhorst v. CIR*, 119 T.C. No. 9 (2002), the full Tax Court considered whether the anticipatory assignment of income doctrine should be applied to recharacterize the transfer of warrants to four charitable organizations. The petitioners were the only partners of a partnership that held warrants to purchase 772.14 shares in a corporation for $1 per share. On September 28, 1993, the corporation received a letter of intent to acquire the outstanding stock and warrants of the corporation from a second corporation. The corporation's officers who signed the letter of intent in their official capacity, collectively held 92.7% of the corporation's outstanding stock. The corporation's Board of Directors authorized negotiations with the second corporation on October 22, 1993. On November 9, 1993, the partnership transferred portions of its warrants to four charitable organizations, retaining warrants to 2.14 shares of the corporation's stock. On November 16, 1993, the corporation offered to repurchase the warrants for $7,598.48 per share. The donees agreed to the sale. On November 22, 1993, the corporation announced its agreement to sell all its outstanding stock to the second corporation. The sale of corporate stock closed on December 22, 1993.

The petitioners had the warrants valued for charitable deduction purposes, and claimed a deduction of $5,304,530 in connection with the transfer of the warrants. The IRS contested the deduction. It applied the anticipatory assignment of income doctrine to recharacterize the gift. It claimed that as of November 9, 1993, the warrants had ripened into a right to receive income as a result of the pending acquisition of the corporation, and thus the petitioners should have included the fair market value of the warrants in their income for income tax purposes.

Before the Tax Court, the petitioners argued that the anticipatory assignment of income doctrine could not be applied in this case. They relied upon Rev. Rul. 78-197 for this position. Rev. Rul. 78-197 provides that the proceeds of a stock redemption will only be treated as income to the donor if the donee is legally bound or can be compelled to surrender its shares for redemption. The IRS argued that the issue was not whether the donees were compelled to sell their warrants on the date of transfer, thus disavowing Rev. Rul 78-197. Rather, it argued that the warrants had ripened into a right to receive income by way of the certainty of the then pending acquisition.

In addressing the contentions of the parties, the Court stated, "This Court has not adopted the 'bright-line' test stated in Rev. Rul. 78-197 ..., as the test for resolving anticipatory assignment of income issues, and instead we have considered the donee's control to be merely a factor, albeit an important factor." However, the Court refused to permit the IRS to disavow Rev. Rul 78-197. It noted that the IRS has not modified or disavowed Rev. Rul. 78-197 and that revenue rulings have been treated as concessions by the Tax Court and other courts. It reasoned, "No doubt taxpayers have referred to that ruling in planning their charitable contributions, and, indeed, petitioners submit that they relied upon that ruling in planning the charitable contributions at issue. Under the circumstances of this case, we treat the Commissioner's position in Rev. Rul. 78-197 ... as a concession."

The Court then considered whether the donee's could be compelled to sell the transferred warrants. The petitioners presented affidavits from the donees that stated the donees had not entered into any agreement to sell the warrants as of the date they received the warrants. The IRS argued that the letter of intent and the Board of Director's authorization to negotiate a sale of the company made the sale a practical certainty. It further presented a valuation report, attached to the petitioner's tax return, which indicated that there was little chance of the acquisition not closing prior to the end of 1993. The Tax Court rejected this evidence. It stated, "Those items might be particularly relevant for determining whether the stock warrant purchase ripened to a practical certainty; however, none of those items alone, or in combination, show that the donees were legally bound, or could be compelled, to sell their stock warrants." The Tax Court ruled in favor of the petitioners. It found that the IRS failed to present any evidence regarding the degree of control the donees held over the warrants justifying the application of the anticipatory assignment of income doctrine.

This abstract originally appeared in *Valuation Case Digest*, authored by John J. Stockdale, Jr.

Estate of Atkinson v. Commissioner

Citation: No. 01-16536 (11th Cir. 2002)
Court: United States Court of Appeals
State/Jurisdiction: 11th Circuit Federal
Date of Decision: October 16, 2002
Judge: Per Curiam

In *Estate of Melvine B. Atkinson v. CIR*, No. 01-16536 (11th Cir. October 16, 2002), the U.S. Court of Appeals for the Eleventh Circuit considered whether an estate may make a charitable deduction for an amount passing from a charitable remainder annuity trust (CRAT) to a charity. The CRAT was formed in 1991 and funded with stock having a value of $4 million. The CRAT was required to pay the decedent $200,000 annually during her lifetime. Following her death, the annuity would pass to four beneficiaries in equal amounts for the remainder of their lives provided the beneficiaries paid their share of any estate taxes due upon the decedent's death. After the four beneficiaries died, any remaining trust assets would pass to a charity.

All the requirements were met in the formation of the CRAT. However, the CRAT never paid the decedent the required annual annuity payment. Following the decedent's death, all the beneficiaries disclaimed their remainder interest under the terms of the agreement. One beneficiary brought suit to receive the annuity interest without paying her share of the estate tax, based on a promise from the decedent. "The estate claimed a charitable deduction in the amount of $3,894,535, representing the present value of the remainder interest in the annuity trust as of the date of Atkinson's death, measured under the assumption that ... [the litigating beneficiary], whose claim against the estate had not been settled at that time, would prevail on that claim and be entitled to an annuity from the trust for the balance of her lifetime and, correlatively, that the charities would not take their remainder interest in the trust until ... [the beneficiaries] death." The IRS rejected the charitable deduction.

Before the Tax Court, the estate argued that it was entitled to the charitable deduction for the remainder interest in the CRAT. The Tax Court agreed with the IRS's position and disallowed the charitable deduction. It reasoned that the CRAT, while validly formed, was not adhered to in practice. Therefore, the deduction was inappropriate. The estate appealed.

The Eleventh Circuit affirmed the Tax Court. It stated, "To preserve the estate's ability to claim a charitable deduction for a remainder interest in property, the trust must not only be set up as a CRAT, but it must also comply with the CRAT statutory requirements from its formation to the final disposition of the trust's assets." The Eleventh Circuit noted that the annual payments required under the CRAT were not made during the decedent's life. It ruled, "... since the CRAT regulations were not scrupulously followed through the life of the trust, a charitable deduction is not appropriate." The court concluded, "Despite the certain charitable donation in this case, the countervailing Congressional concerns surrounding the deductibility of charitable remainders in general counsel strict adherence to the Code, and, barring such adherence, mandate a complete denial of the charitable deduction."

This abstract originally appeared in *Valuation Case Digest*, authored by John J. Stockdale, Jr.

Estate of Dailey v. Commissioner (II)

Citation: T.C. Memo 2002-30, 2002 Tax Ct. Memo LEXIS 322
Court: United States Tax Court
State/Jurisdiction: Specialty Federal
Date of Decision: December 9, 2002
Judge: Foley

The issue in this case was whether the taxpayer was entitled to recover litigation and administrative costs, including appraiser and attorney fees, under Internal Revenue Code section 7430 and Tax Court Rule 231. The court is authorized to award costs to the petitioner (taxpayer) in cases in which the respondent (IRS) is not substantially justified in maintaining its position against the petitioner because it "did not have a reasonable basis in law and fact" for its position.

In this case, the IRS conceded that it was not substantially justified in maintaining its position that the taxpayer's FLP should be disregarded for valuation purposes. However, the IRS argued that it was substantially justified in adopting its own expert's valuation analysis and maintaining its position that the taxpayer's valuation, including significant discounts, was not correct.

Although the taxpayer ultimately won on the valuation issue, the court found that the IRS was substantially justified in maintaining its own valuation position.

The values of family limited partnership interests are difficult to determine. [citation omitted] Respondent's expert began with the net asset value of the FLP, then made adjustments reflecting minority and marketability discounts. Regarding the minority discount, he compared the FLP to closed-end mutual funds. Regarding the marketability discount, he relied on studies relating to the value of common stock with legal restrictions impairing transferability (i.e., Restricted Stock Studies) and a study relating to the value of closely held company shares prior to initial public offerings (i.e., Pre-IPO Study).

Problems with the expert's analysis were not revealed until petitioners' counsel conducted voir dire and cross-examination. With respect to the valuation of the FLP interests, this Court held that, "although neither expert was extraordinary, petitioners expert provided a more convincing and thorough analysis than respondents expert."

The taxpayer was allowed costs only on the issue of whether the FLP should be disregarded. In reviewing the affidavits submitted with the taxpayers motion, the court concluded that only 20% of the appraisers and attorneys time was spent on this issue versus the valuation issue, and awarded costs accordingly.

Succession of Helis v. United States (II)

Citation: No. 97-190T (Fed. Cl. 2003)
Court: United States Court of Federal Claims
State/Jurisdiction: Federal Claims
Date of Decision: January 8, 2003
Judge: Bruggink

In *Succession of Betty Felix Helis v. United States,* No. 97-190T (Fed. Cl. January 8, 2003), the Court of Federal Claims considered how interest paid to the IRS, but later refunded, should be accounted for in calculating the value of the estate. The estate held an interest in a closely held company holding gas and oil rights. The IRS disputed the valuation of the interest. The estate paid the additional estate taxes of $19.4 million under sec. 6166, which permitted the estate to pay the tax over a fifteen-year period. Over that period, the estate paid $16.7 million of interest to the Government. The estate deducted the amount of interest paid under sec. 6166 as an administrative expense. The estate further contested the IRS's valuation of the business and prevailed. The Court of Federal Claims, in an earlier ruling, determined that the value of the interest as reported on the estate's tax return was correct. Thereafter, the parties contested the proper treatment of the interest refund.

The IRS argued that the refunded interest should not be deducted as an administrative expense under sec. 2503, because that interest was not in fact incurred by the estate. The estate disagreed. It argued that there was no legal reason to assume that the payments were anything other than final payments at the time they were made, and that if the defendant's argument is acceptable then the amount of liability may be subject to a theoretically infinite set of adjustments.

The Court of Federal Claims considered and accepted the IRS's position. It noted, "The estate is created at death, but it can be affected by events in succeeding calendar years. Determination of the final amount of the taxable estate is therefore an open-ended process which may take years to finalize." It then reasoned, "So long as the recovery or gain, in this case the cancellation of interest, is more properly attributable to the creation of the estate, as opposed to subsequent income of the estate, it is appropriate to fold the recovery into the estate tax calculation. That is particularly so when the estate elected to take the deduction under estate rather than income tax laws." It further reasoned, "The economic reality to the estate is that it will not be diminished beyond what it would have consisted of in the event plaintiff's figure had been used from the beginning."

This abstract originally appeared in *Valuation Case Digest*, authored by John J. Stockdale, Jr.

Kimbell v. Commissioner (I)

Citation: 244 F.Supp. 2d 700, 2003 U.S. Dist. LEXIS 523
Court: United States Tax Court
State/Jurisdiction: Specialty Federal
Date of Decision: January 15, 2003
Judge: Buchmeyer

After decedent's death, her estate filed returns listing the value of decedent's 99% partnership interest as \$1.257 million. The IRS audited the returns and found the value of decedent's interest to be \$2.463 million. The estate paid the additional taxes and brought this action seeking a refund of \$837,089 for the IRS's overvaluation of the estate. The government moved for partial summary judgment, as did the estate. The district court found that the estate failed to prove either of the exceptions to IRC section 2036(a) and thus the partnership's assets were included in the decedent's gross estate. It granted the government's motion and denied the estate's.

Facts

At decedent's death, she held interests in three entities: (1) the R.A. Kimbell Living Trust (Trust); (2) the R.A. Kimbell Management Co., LLC ("LLC"); and (3) the R.A. Kimbell Property Co., Ltd. ("Partnership").

The Trust was fully revocable by decedent prior to her death. The LLC was owned 50% by the Trust, 25% by decedent's son, and 25% by decedent's daughter-in-law. The LLC contributed 1%

of the capital to the Partnership and was its general partner, and the Trust contributed 99% of the capital and was a limited partner.

District court findings

The question before the court was how the decedent's transfer of assets into the Partnership should be treated under section 2036(a) of the Internal Revenue Code. That section of the statute provides that the gross estate includes all property the decedent transferred at any time, unless the transfer qualifies for the "bona fide sale exception" or the "retained income or rights exception."

Bona fide sale exception

The estate argued that the decedent's transfer of assets to the Partnership was a bona fide sale meeting the Tax Court's two requirements: (1) an arm's-length transaction; (2) for adequate and full consideration. The district court disagreed, holding that the decedent's transfer failed both requirements.

First, the court said that it could not even find two parties, much less two parties conducting an arm's-length transaction. The Partnership was owned by two entities: 99% by the Trust, which was wholly owned by the decedent, and 1% by the LLC, 50% of which was owned by the Trust. "Therefore, Decedent not only 'stood on both sides of the transaction, but, for all intensive purpose, was both sides of the transaction."

Second, the court stated that the meaning of full and adequate consideration did not include "paper transactions such as the one at issue." Through the Trust, the decedent contributed 99% of the capital for the Partnership and in exchange received no consideration, other than the interest in the Partnership. The district court quoted *Estate of Harper v. Commissioner* and found that, similar to that case, there was merely a "recycling of value" and not a transfer of consideration.

Retained income or rights exception

The District Court said that the estate also failed to meet the retained income or rights exception, because the Partnership Agreement reserved for any 70% partner the right to remove the general partner, who in turn had sole discretion to make distributions of income. Through the Trust decedent owned 99% of the Partnership. Thus she could remove the general partner at any time and substitute herself or anyone of her choice, thereby retaining the power to benefit personally from the Partnerships income.

The estate claimed that decedent had "irrevocably" transferred her assets to the Partnership. The court rejected this argument because decedent could select a new general partner who would distribute the income back to decedent.

Finally, the estate argued that there were issues of material fact as to whether decedent and her son/executor had an express or implied agreement to retain income or rights for decedent. The court rejected this claim as a "red herring," stating that there was no need to look any further than the Partnership Agreement itself.

The court granted the governments motion for partial summary judgment and denied the estate motion for partial summary judgment.

Schott v. Commissioner (II)

Citation: No. 02-70007 (9th Cir. 2003)
Court: United States Court of Appeals
State/Jurisdiction: 9th Circuit Federal
Date of Decision: February 18, 2003
Judge: Noonan

In *Patricia A. Schott, et al. v. CIR*, No. 02-70007 (February 18, 2003), the U.S. Court of Appeals for the Ninth Circuit determined whether interest from grantor retained annuity trusts (GRATs) qualified as dual-life annuities for gift tax purposes. The Schotts created individual, identical GRATs containing nonvoting common stock for the benefit of their children. The GRATs provided that the grantor would receive annual payments of 11.54% of the initial fair market value during the GRATs 15-year term. The grantor's spouse would receive the annuity payments upon the grantor's death, unless the spousal interest was revoked by the grantor. Otherwise, the GRATs were irrevocable. On their gift tax returns, the Schotts claimed that the retained interests were qualified interests under IRC sec. 2702 and should be valued as dual-life annuities according to the annuity tables of sec. 7520.

Before the Tax Court, the IRS argued that the interest from the Schotts' trusts was not a qualified interest under sec. 2702 because the dual-life annuity was contingent on the date of a spouse's death, and therefore, not a fixed date. The Schotts noted that because the holder had the power to revoke the trust and the trust had a term of 15 years, the interest from the GRATS was a qualified interest as described in sec. 2702. The Tax Court ruled in favor of the IRS. It stated, "an annuity measured by two lives was unqualified because the annuity could extend beyond the life of the 'term holder.'" The Schotts appealed.

On appeal, the Ninth Circuit found in favor of the Schotts and reversed the Tax Court's decision. It found that the IRS's argument regarding the contingency of the date of the spouse's death "merely restates an unfounded objection to life annuities. As the end of the grantor's life can be ascertained with acceptable probability by an annuity table, so can the date and duration of the spouse's annuity be ascertained with acceptable probability." The Ninth Circuit concluded, "A two-life annuity, based on the lives of the grantor and spouse with a limit of fifteen years, falls 'within the class of easily valued rights' that Congress meant to qualify."

This abstract originally appeared in *Valuation Case Digest*, authored by John J. Stockdale, Jr.

Estate of Costanza v. Commissioner

Citation: No. 01-2207 (6th Cir. 2003)
Court: United States Court of Appeals
State/Jurisdiction: 9th Circuit Federal
Date of Decision: February 19, 2003
Judge: Gilman

In the *Estate of Duilio Costanza v. CIR*, No. 01-2207 (February 19, 2003), the U.S. Court of Appeals for the Sixth Circuit considered whether a self-canceling installment note (SCIN) was a bona fide transaction within the meaning of IRC sec. 2001(b). In 1993, Costanza sold his commercial properties and a restaurant business located thereon to his son, in exchange for a SCIN. The note required monthly payments over 11 years and was secured by a mortgage on the properties. It also contained a cancellation-upon-death provision.

Costanza died unexpectedly from surgery complications in May 1993. Due to the cancellation-upon-death provision, Costanza's son reported that the SCIN had no value on the estate's federal tax return. Before the Tax Court, the IRS argued that the sale for the SCIN was not a bona fide transaction "or in the alternative, the transaction was a 'bargain sale' that would increase the estate's adjusted taxable gifts." The Tax Court found that the transaction was not a bona fide sale because the payments had not been made monthly as called for in the note, rather only one quarterly payment had been made. Furthermore, because the decedent's death occurred only three months following the SCIN transaction, the Tax Court determined that the transaction was completed in anticipation of the decedent's demise. Because the Tax Court determined that the transaction was not a bona fide sale, it did not address the IRS's bargain sale argument. The estate appealed.

On appeal, the Sixth Circuit noted that intrafamily sales are "presumed to be a gift" and therefore, not bona fide transactions within the meaning of IRC sec. 2001(b). It noted however, "this presumption may be rebutted by an affirmative showing that there existed at the time of the transaction a real expectation of repayment and intent to enforce the collection of the indebtedness." The Sixth Circuit found that Costanza's son testified that he and his father had made an oral arrangement to submit the monthly payments quarterly, to make banking easier for his father. It also found that upon the formation of the SCIN, medical experts had set Costanza's life expectancy to be between 5 and 13.9 years. Therefore, it determined that the estate had adequately "rebutted the presumption against the enforceability of an intrafamily SCIN." Thus, the Sixth Circuit reversed the Tax Court's decision and ruled that the transaction was a bona fide sale within the meaning of sec. 2001(b). It then remanded the issue to the Tax Court to consider the IRS's alternative argument regarding whether the transaction was a bargain sale.

This abstract originally appeared in *Valuation Case Digest*, authored by John J. Stockdale, Jr.

Estate of Leichter v. Commissioner

Citation: T.C. Memo 2003-66, 2003 Tax Ct. Memo LEXIS 66
Court: United States Tax Court
State/Jurisdiction: Specialty Federal
Date of Decision: March 6, 2003
Judge: Gerber

The issue in this estate tax matter was the fair market value of all 20,000 outstanding shares of Harlee International, Inc., a family-owned S corporation that was an importer and wholesale-distributor of futon and waterbed frames. The Tax Court considered the testimony of three experts, as well as three other valuation conclusions, and ultimately concluded that Harlee was worth $2,091,750 as reported on the estate tax return.

The business

Decedent's husband, Harvey Leichter, started Harlee in 1981. Harvey predeceased the decedent by three months, at which time decedent took over as president of Harlee.

For some time Harlee was in the business of importing and distributing waterbed frames and liners. When the waterbed market decreased, Harlee began to transition into the futon frame market. At the time of decedent's death, the business consisted of 40% waterbed sales and 60% futon sales.

The business was dependent on its relationships with Asian representatives who dealt directly with Asian manufacturers to supply its products. For various reasons, this required Harlee to keep at least a three- to four-month inventory supply at all times.

The business was also dependent on its customer relationships with U.S. distributors, which generated most of the companys revenue. Harlee was required to continually seek out new distributor customers because when a distributor got big enough it tended to cut out Harlee as the middleman and create its own overseas relationships.

The Tax Court outlined Harlee's sales and other financial information in detail:

> For the 4 years preceding decedent's death (1991 through 1994), Harlee had total sales of $ 2,426,721, $ 1,896,895, $ 2,778,872, and $ 3,894,587, respectively. In each of the 2 years preceding death, Harlee's sales increased more than 40% from the prior year. For that same period, Harlee's cost of goods sold averaged in the mid-to-high 70-percent range in relation to total sales, and its operating expenses averaged approximately 18% of total sales. Harlee's adjusted net income for the 4 years preceding decedent's death was generally increasing, as follows: $40,194, $ 83,640, $ 77,570, and $ 113,191. Similarly, for Federal tax purposes, Harlee reported generally increasing amounts of ordinary income culminating in $163,121 for its 1994 taxable year.

Tax return and notice of deficiency

On the estate tax return, the estate listed the fair market value of Harlee as $2,091,750, based upon the appraisal report of Lawrence F. Sherman. Two years after the return was filed, the IRS issued a notice of deficiency claiming that the fair market value of Harlee was $2,718,358.

At trial, the estate did not present Sherman as a witness and argued that Sherman's appraisal was erroneous and should be disregarded. The Tax Court found that most of the errors that the estate alleged invalidated Sherman's appraisal were merely orthographic.

Only two of the alleged errors appeared to be substantive: (1) that Sherman overstated by $900,000 the company's excess working capital; and (2) that Sherman did not consider $90,000 in liabilities. First, the Tax Court found that Sherman's estimate of excess working capital was not overstated and was consistent with the IRS expert's opinion. Second, the Tax Court found that the $90,000 in liabilities was "unknown and unforeseeable at the time of decedents death." Therefore, Sherman's appraisal was not erroneous.

The Tax Court considered the Sherman appraisal not only as evidence of the fair market value of Harlee, but as an admission of value by the estate because it was filed with the estate tax return.

Probate proceedings

The Tax Court also considered valuation evidence from a probate proceeding involving the administration of decedent's estate. That proceeding concerned a dispute between the decedent's two sons, Jeffrey and Steven, arising from decedent's disinheritance of Steven from her will. Steven had worked in the family business for many years before being fired by the decedent. He also took over Harlee's operations after decedent's death. Jeffrey had no direct involvement with the business.

The probate court appointed an independent referee to inventory and value the assets of the estate. The referee, Joseph D. Bua, valued Harlee at $2,261,713. The probate court adopted this value and ordered that Harlee be distributed to Steven, and the remainder of decedent's estate be distributed to Jeffrey.

Court assessment of estate experts

At trial, the estate offered two expert witnesses, Burdette Garvin and John McCallum. Both experts testified that the value of Harlee was less than half what the estate had claimed on its estate tax return.

Garvin reached his $863,000 fair market value figure by determining the company's adjusted book value and by using several other methods, including the discounted earnings method, the guideline company method, and the industry market ratios method.

In determining adjusted book value, Garvin included a $1,254,408 note payable that had been converted to equity prior to the decedent's death. The Tax Court found that this was clear error. Garvin also increased noncurrent liabilities by $1,400,000 for what he termed negative goodwill. The Tax Court criticized this calculation because Garvin had also made substantial discounts to the value of Harlee's assets and inventory.

After reaching a weighted value based on the other three methodologies, Garvin discounted that value first by an unspecified amount for the loss of Harvey Leichter as a key person and then by another unspecified amount for lack of marketability. The Tax Court found that these two discounts were duplicative because they were taken for the same reasons.

McCallum's conclusion that Harlee was worth $400,000 was supported by a brief valuation report. Without detailing his methodology, the Tax Court found that:

> his conclusions and analysis are brief and cursory in nature. . . . Mr. McCallum's 'Observations as to Conditions of Harlee is less than 10 sentences. [He] provides no explanation of the Leichter's role at Harlee in concluding that a 15-percent discount should be applied for the lack of continuity of management. We accord no weight to Mr. McCallum's report because of the lack of adequate explanation in support of his conclusions.

IRS experts guideline companies not similar

The IRS expert, John Thomson, opined that Harlee was worth $2,150,000, significantly less than the IRS's deficiency notice position. The Tax Court described Thomson's valuation methodology:

> Primarily, Mr. Thomson used two methods in arriving at his value. Through the market approach, he compared Harlee to five publicly traded firms, discounted the value of Harlee to match more accurately the comparables to the subject and added both a 15-percent control premium and an excess working capital value of $900,000. Through the income method, Mr. Thomson forecasted Harlee's sales for the subsequent 5 years and used a net discounted cashflow method to value those sales at present value. In so doing, Mr. Thomson looked at Harlee's previous 5 years of operation and then discounted the future cashflow by 17%.

The Tax Court found that Thomson's conclusion was "within a reasonable range" and was supported by the facts of the case as presented at trial. Nonetheless, there were some weaknesses in his analysis, most notably his use of guideline companies that were not similar to Harlee.

Tax Court holding

Because (1) the estate failed to present satisfactory evidence of a lower value at trial; (2) the value reported on the estate tax return was close to the value determined by the probate court; (3) there was no evidence that a hypothetical seller would sell at going concern value rather than liquidation value since liquidation value was higher; and (4) the IRS failed to meet its burden of proof that the value was higher than reported on the estate tax return, the Tax Court concluded that the fair market value of Harlee was $2,091,750, as reported on the estate tax return.

McCord v. Commissioner (I)

Citation: 120 T.C. No. 13, 2003 U.S. Tax Ct. LEXIS 16
Court: United States Tax Court
State/Jurisdiction: Specialty Federal
Date of Decision: May 14, 2003
Judge: Vasquez

Petitioners Charles T. and Mary S. McCord gifted interests in McCord Interests, Ltd., L.L.P. (MIL) to their four children, trusts for the benefit of the children, and two charitable organizations by way of assignment agreements. The issues in this gift tax matter were (1) the extent of the rights assigned by the petitioners, and (2) the fair market value of the gifts.

MIL was a family owned holding company that held "stocks, bonds, real estate, oil and gas investments, and other closely held business interests." Of these assets, 65% were marketable securities and 30% were real estate limited partnership interests.

Rights assigned

Petitioners argued that the gifts assigned were only assignee interests, and not full partnership interests, because they had not received written consent to the assignment from all partners as required by the partnership agreement. The IRS argued that full partnership interests were transferred, so that the assignees became full partners. The experts agreed that if the petitioners were correct then the value of the gifted interests would be less.

Distinguishing *Kerr v. Commissioner*, 113 T.C. 449 (1999), in which the court had found that full partnership interests had been transferred, the Tax Court in this case agreed with petitioners. Unlike the parties in *Kerr*, the parties in this case had previously adhered to the partnership agreement requirement of written consent of all partners. In addition, the agreement in this case did not contain language referring to the transferred interests as full partnership interests. The court found that the petitioners did not intend to transfer all their rights, but only to transfer assignee interests that consisted of the economic rights of the partnership interests.

Valuation evidence

Both parties presented the valuation report and testimony of an expert witness on the issue of the fair market value of the gifted interests in MIL. Petitioners presented William H. Frazier, who also provided the appraisal required by the assignment agreement. The IRS presented Mukesh Bajaj. The court accepted both as experts in the valuation of closely held entities such as MIL.

The parties agreed that net asset value of MIL was $17,673,760, broken down as shown by the court in Table 1.

TABLE 1	
Asset Type	**Value**
Equities portfolio	$3,641,956
Bond portfolio	$8,040,220
Bond portfolio	$5,194,933
Real estate	$581,553
Oil and gas interests	$215,098
Total	$17,673,760

The primary disagreements between the experts were the appropriate minority and marketability discounts to be applied to the net asset value of MIL. The discount and fair market value opinions of the experts, and the court's ultimate conclusions with respect to each, are shown in Table 2.

TABLE 2			
	Minority Discount	**DLOM**	**FMV**
Frazier	22%	35%	$3,684,634
Bajaj	8.34%	7%	$6,202,429
Court	15%	20%	$4,941,916

Calculation of minority discount

Both experts agreed that the minority discount should be calculated as the weighted average of the discounts determined for each type of asset that MIL held. They differed, however, in the specific discounts determined for each asset type because they used different measurement dates, sample comparables, and selected discounts within the range of discounts indicated by the comparables.

The court used Bajaj's measurement dates, because they were closer to the valuation date. The court reviewed the selection of comparables by both experts and determined its own pool of comparables. The court then considered the experts' reasoning for their selection of specific discounts.

Frazier argued that higher than average discounts were warranted based upon his regression analysis and consideration of various factors. Bajaj argued that lower than average discounts were warranted based upon a "new fund" analysis because MIL was a relatively new entity. The court rejected the reasoning of both experts and selected the average discount based upon the chosen comparables.

The court's detailed review of the expert's analysis in calculating the minority discount is thorough and instructive.

Marketability discount

The experts disagreed on the appropriate marketability discount to be applied to MIL on an "entity-wide" basis, and also on the appropriate method for determining the discount.

Frazier opined that a 35% marketability discount was appropriate based on his analysis of the restricted stock studies, including the SEC study, the Silber study, the Standard Research Consultants (SRC) study, and the Hertzel & Smith study. He also testified that pre-IPO studies, including the Willamette Management Associates study and the Emory studies, supported this discount.

Bajaj opined that a 7% marketability discount was appropriate based on an analysis of his own private placement study, as well as the Wruck study and the Hertzel & Smith study.

Court rejects pre-IPO studies

Bajaj opined that the pre-IPO study marketability discount "may reflect more than just the availability of a ready market" for two reasons. First, the pre-IPO price is likely to be a bargain price offered to insiders of the company as a form of compensation. Second, the discount reflects the risk that the IPO may not occur or may occur at a lower price.

Persuaded by Bajaj's testimony criticizing the pre-IPO studies as a useful source of marketability discount data, the court rejected Frazier's opinion to the extent that he relied on the pre-IPO data.

Court rejects restricted stock analysis

The court reviewed Frazier's restricted stock study analysis, and found a number of flaws in his reasoning and methodology. Because of these errors, the court rejected Frazier's restricted stock analysis. The court did not completely reject the restricted stock studies as a source of marketability discount data, but concluded that Frazier had not adequately analyzed the data from the studies in reaching his 35% discount.

Private placement studies average discount

The court then considered the private placement studies used by Bajaj and his analysis of the data from those studies. Bajaj testified that the data indicates that factors other than illiquidity are included in the discount. In his analysis, Bajaj sought to factor out the effect of assessment and monitoring costs on the level of the discount, so that pure liquidity was the only element of the resulting marketability discount.

The court accepted the private placement study done by Bajaj as a useful source of data to quantify the marketability discount. However, the court rejected Bajaj analysis of the data.

> "Dr. Bajaj has indeed been helpful in focusing our attention (and Mr. Frazier's attention) on the distinction between illiquidity and other factors (e.g., assessment and monitoring costs) that contribute to private placement discounts. However, his apparent confusion regarding the nature of the discount for lack of marketability (i.e., whether such discount can be explained purely in terms of illiquidity or whether other factors may be involved) is troubling. In his direct testimony, Dr. Bajaj is fairly clear that assessment and monitoring costs associated with private placements are outside the realm of the marketability discount. In his rebuttal testimony, however, he indicates that such costs may contribute to the marketability discount for a closely held entity. That leads us to question whether other "negative characteristics" (in the words of Mr. Frazier) associated with closely held entities may contribute to the appropriate marketability discount for an assignee interest in MIL. Therefore, while we are impressed by portions of Dr. Bajaj's analysis, he has not convinced us that the appropriate marketability discount in this case can be inferred from the illiquidity cost associated with private placements."

The court concluded that the appropriate marketability discount was 20% based on the average of the middle 29 discounts from the total of 88 private placements in Bajaj's study.

Estate of Strangi v. Commissioner (III)

Citation: T.C. Memo 2003-145
Court: United States Tax Court
State/Jurisdiction: Specialty Federal
Date of Decision: May 20, 2003
Judge: Cohen

The sole issue for decision on remand was whether the value of the property transferred by the decedent to the Strangi Family Limited Partnership and Stranco, Inc. was includable in his gross estate pursuant to section 2036(a) of the Internal Revenue Code. The Tax Court ruled that 2036 applied and that the full amount of the assets-which amounted to 98% of decedent's assets-must be included in his gross estate.

Right to income and possession or enjoyment

Under the first prong of the test, the court determined that the documents governing the transfer contained no restrictions that would preclude decedent or his agent from receiving income from SFLP and Stranco. The court also found an implied agreement for retained possession or enjoyment. "[D]ecedent as a practical matter retained the same relationship to his assets that he had before formation of SFLP and Stranco."

Although the court acknowledged that the parties took steps to abide by the formal terms of the structure created, it also maintained that such steps did not preclude decedent from retaining economic benefit for the purposes of 2036(a)(1). "[T]he crucial characteristic is that virtually nothing beyond formal title changed in decedent's relationship to his assets."

Right to designate other persons to possess or enjoy

Alternatively, the Tax Court found that decedent retained a right to designate who could enjoy property and income from SFLP and Stranco under 2036(a)(2). "[I]t is immaterial whether we characterize the pertinent documents and relationships as creating rights exercisable by decedent alone, in conjunction with other Stranco shareholders, or in conjunction with Stranco's president."

Decedent also retained the right to designate who could enjoy the transferred SFLP property itself. No independent trustee was interposed as a decision maker, rather, all decisions ultimately were made by decedent's attorney in fact.

No consideration for transfer

Having concluded that 2036(a) applied, the court then determined that decedent's transfer of property to SFLP and Stranco did not qualify for the "bona fide sale" exception because it was not an arm's-length transaction. Decedent essentially stood on both sides of the transaction. The court also found that there was no full and adequate consideration, merely a "recycling" of value through a partnership. The court required that the full amount of the transferred assets be included in decedent's gross estate.

Estate of Deputy v. Commissioner

Citation: T.C. Memo 2003-176
Court: United States Tax Court
State/Jurisdiction: Specialty Federal
Date of Decision: June 13, 2003
Judge: Gerber

The decedent, Helen Deputy, formed a family limited partnership comprised 99% of a limited partnership interest retained by Deputy and two 0.5% general partnership interests, one held by Deputy and one held by her son. Before her death, Deputy transferred her remaining shares in Godfrey Conveyor Co., Inc., a boat building business, to the FLP. The FLP owned a 19.99% interest in Godfrey at the time of her death. The primary issue at trial was the fair market value of the Godfrey shares. The values opined by the experts at trial and determined by the court are shown in Table 1.

TABLE 1: DISCOUNTED FMV OF GODFREY SHARES			
	Dorman for Estate	Burns for IRS	Tax Court
Undiscounted FMV	$17,341,379	$30,740,869	$24,000,000
X 19.99%*	$3,466,427	$6,145,100	$4,797,441
X discount	44% = $1,525,228	25% = $1,536,275	30% = $1,439,232
Discounted FMV	$1,941,000 (rounded)	$4,608,825	$3,358,209

* Note: The parties reached their undiscounted fair market values for the FLP's 19.99% interest differently. The IRS expert simply multiplied his undiscounted FV by 19.99%. The estate's expert and the Tax Court divided their undiscounted FMV by 938 (the number of Godfrey shares outstanding) to arrive at a per-share value, which they then multiplied by 187.5 (the number of Godfrey shares held by the FLP). Note that although the experts' discounts differed by nearly 20%, their absolute discount amounts were separated by little more than $11,000.

The estate's tax return reported that the fair market value of the Godfrey shares held by the FLP was $2,246,500, based on an appraisal by Michael Dorman, and that Deputy's interest in the FLP was worth $2,589,000. The IRSs deficiency notice determined that Deputy's interest in the FLP was $4,835,300. The estate filed an amended return valuing the Godfrey shares at $1,941,000, based on a revised appraisal, again prepared by Dorman, who also served as the estate's expert witness at trial.

Valuation evidence presented by the estate

Dorman discussed all three primary valuation approaches in his report but ultimately relied solely on the asset approach and arrived at a fair market value for Godfrey of $17,341,379. He rejected the market approach because he could not find what he believed were comparable companies. Of six possible comparables, he rejected four because they were unprofitable, unlike Godfrey. He decided against using the remaining two because he thought that they alone would not provide a reliable indicator of comparable data.

Under his asset approach, Dorman began with shareholders equity of $17,160,705 and deducted $126,806 to account for a partial year. He then converted book values to fair market values, resulting in a $2,392,916 increase of fair market value over book value. Dorman then deducted $1,919,869 for environmental liabilities and $165,566 for capital gains tax. He arrived at an adjusted net asset value of $17,341,379. (See Table 2).

TABLE 2: ESTATE'S EXPERT-ASSET APPROACH		
+	Shareholder equity	$17,160,705
-	Partial year	($126,806)
+	Excess of FMV over book value	$2,392,916
-	Environmental liabilities	($1,919,869)
-	Capital gains taxes	($165,566)
	Net asset value	$17,341,379

Under the income approach, Dorman arrived at normalized annual earnings of $1,846,793 and a 17.5% capitalization rate. As shown in Table 3, the primary difference between the experts capitalization rates was in the industry risk premium component. Dorman stated that he arrived at his 3% industry adjustment after listing six general categories and noting that Godfrey was a small company. Dorman concluded a $10,553,101 capitalized value for Godfrey, almost $7 million less than his net asset value for the company. (See *Table 4*). He discarded the income approach and concluded that Godfreys fair market value was $17,341,379, as determined by the asset approach.

TABLE 3: CAPITALIZATION RATES		
Item	Dorman	Burns
Treasury bond (risk-free) rate	6.14%	6.56%
Premium for equity risk	7.90%	7.50%
Premium for small stock risk	5.78%	5.78%
Company/industry risk	3.00%	-5.20%
Total	22.82%	14.64%
Less: Growth	-5.50%	-4.63%
Capitalization rate	17.50%	10.01%
*Round to the nearest 0.5.		

Valuation evidence presented by the IRS

The IRS's expert, Francis Burns, also considered the three main valuation approaches and concluded that Godfrey's fair market value was $30,740,869. He rejected the net asset approach because he said that Godfrey was an established and successful operating company. He thought the asset approach was inappropriate because it limited the company's value to its tangible assets.

Burns valued the company under the market approach using 15 public companies in the same general industry as Godfrey. He admitted that none of the 15 were "perfect comparables" but believed that they were sufficiently similar to "indicate acceptable valuation multiples." Burns determined a value range of $34,700,000 to $51,500,000 under this approach, but he ultimately relied solely on the income approach.

Under the income approach, he determined normalized earnings of $3,077,161 and a capitalization rate of 10.01%. (See Table 3). Burns derived his 5.2% industry adjustment from Ibbotson data. He concluded a fair market value for Godfrey of $30,740,869. (See Table 4).

TABLE 4: INCOME APPROACH - BOTH EXPERTS & TAX COURT			
	Dorman for Estate	Burns for IRS	Tax Court
Normalized earnings	$1,846,793	$3,077,161	$23,958,808
Diveded by capitalization rate	17.50%	10.01%	10.00%
Capitalization value	$10,553,101*	$30,740,869	$24,000,000
*Note: Dorman ultimately discarded this in favor of his results under the asset approach.			

Tax Court findings on undiscounted fair market value

The Tax Court began by stating that because the FLPs largest asset was an interest in Godfrey, the fair market value of Godfrey was the primary issue. The court also noted that the parties agreed to the discounts to be applied *to the FLP, but not to the Godfrey shares.*

The court first discussed Dormans report, stating that it found his reasons for rejecting the market approach "somewhat curious because, in spite of the comparable companies losses, [the IRSs] experts calculations with similar comparables resulted in the potential for values that were two to three times the value reached by use of the approach advanced by Mr. Dorman." The court also thought Dorman did not sufficiently explain why he believed the companies he rejected would not be "reliable." In the end, however, neither expert relied on the market approach in their final conclusion of value, and the court concurred with this decision.

The court also found Dorman's reasoning under his asset approach to be "inadequate and without meaningful explanation." Moreover, the court agreed with Burns that the asset approach was inappropriate in valuing a "long-established, financially successful operating company." Although the estate claimed that it was customary for businesses in Godfrey's industry to be acquired for net asset value, the court noted that most of those acquisitions involved financially troubled companies. The estate attempted to argue that Godfrey did not have intangible assets protected by intellectual property laws, but the court was not convinced:

> The estate's arguments, however, do not explain away Godfrey's long-established financial successes, good worker relationships, extensive and loyal dealer marketing relationships, and good reputation for product and service. Although neither party

> attempted to isolate or separately value those aspects, they represent some of the reasons for Godfrey's past success and, likewise, reasons for the potential for future success. The long-established ability of the entity to earn income and profit render inappropriate the use of a net asset approach to value Godfrey.

Having established that the income approach was most appropriate for valuing Godfrey, the court adopted Burns capitalization rate because of his industry risk premium:

> Ultimately, we accept Mr. Burns' explanation that there is a premium in the industry, on the basis of his analysis of publicly held companies. We note that there is no meaningful universe of information available for closely held companies or Godfrey's particular boat manufacturing niche. Although the 5.2-percent premium was based on some data from years subsequent to 1997, we are satisfied that the 5.2% is within a reasonable range. In part, we base our conclusion on Godfrey's tendency to generally outperform the industry and economy, so that the 5.2-percent premium may be on the conservative side. Moreover, we are more comfortable with Mr. Burns' methodology, for which he has provided explanations supporting his conclusions and assumptions. On the question of industry risk, Mr. Dorman's figures are without empirical support or explanation and appear to be purely subjective.

The court, however, did not adopt the normalized income determined by either expert, but instead recalculated the amount on its own, as shown in *Table 5*. The court disliked that Burns relied solely on normalized 1997 earnings, which left out the reduced income levels of earlier years. It also criticized Dorman for emphasizing the recessionary period and leaving out the income increases in 1997. The court used Dorman's annualized 1997 income and incorporated the amounts for the preceding three years.

TABLE 5: COURT'S NORMALIZED INCOME

Year	Income	Weight	Weighted Income
1997	$3,085,615	4	$12,342,460
1996	$2,497,222	3	$7,491,666
1995	$1,082,997	2	$2,165,994
1994	$1,958,688	1	$1,958,688
		Total	$23,958,808
Divided by weight factor of 10 and rounded			$2,400,000

Using Burns 10% capitalization rate and normalized earnings of $2,400,000, the court found that Godfrey's undiscounted fair market value was $24 million on the valuation date.

Expert testimony on discounts

Burns did not apply a minority discount because he concluded that minority interests would receive the same percentage return on their investment as a majority interest. He did, however, apply a 25% marketability discount, relying on *The FMV Restricted Stock Study*™ and the *Management Planning, Inc.* restricted stock study.

Dorman applied a 44% combined minority and marketability discount, derived from a matrix table created by his company to "replicate an investors decision process." The matrix used by Dorman is shown in *Table 6*. Although Dorman discussed various studies in his report, including those referenced by Burns, as well as one by Professor Steven E. Bolten, he ultimately relied solely on the matrix devised by his firm.

TABLE 6: DORMAN'S DISCOUNT MATRIX							
	Percent (%) of discount based on condition						
	Good	Above Average	Average	Below Average	Poor	Doorman's Rating	Court Rating
Information availability & reliability	1	2	3	4	5	2	0
Investment size	1	2	4	6	8	6	6
Company outlook, management & growth	2	4	6	8	10	4	0
Ability to control	0	5	10	15	20	10	10
Any restrictions on transferability, anticipated holding period & company's redemption policy	2	5	8	11	14	8	5
Dividend payout history & outlook	2	5	8	11	14	14	8
Total	8	23	39	55	71	44	29

Tax Court findings on discounts

The Tax Court disagreed with Burns that no minority discount should be applied. It also preferred Dorman's approach because it "focuses more specifically on Godfrey's unique attributes and therefore provides a more direct approach to evaluate the interest in Godfrey." The court was reluctant to accept Dorman's conclusions outright, however, because "no foundation or background is provided to support the indexing in each category in the matrix" and because the matrix was created by Dorman's company and was therefore "obviously subjective." Notwithstanding these statements, the court went on to discuss each category in the matrix and use it as a guide to analyze the facts. Despite its criticism, the court apparently accepted the underlying structure of the matrix and also agreed with several of Dorman's discount conclusions.

The first category rates the availability and reliability of financial information. Although Dorman selected an above-average rating, the court saw no reason why any discount should apply "where the subject has ample quality financial information available." In the second category, Dorman assigned six discount points to account for the relatively large investment necessary to buy the FLPs shares in Godfrey, and the court agreed.

The court found the third and sixth categories duplicative. In the third category, which addresses financial outlook, management, and growth potential, the court found Dorman's evaluation too conservative, because the record reflected a "much more positive picture of Godfrey's financial record and prospects." So even though Dorman assigned Godfrey an above-average rating for the this category, the court assigned no discount for this factor.

Regarding ability to control, the fourth category, the court agreed with Dorman's 10 discount points. He reasoned that the FLPs 19.99% block would not have control but was the second largest holding and therefore "would enjoy swing power, and have a strong voice in the day-to-day operations and decision making of the company."

In the fifth category, concerning restrictions on transfer and anticipated holding period, Dorman assigned eight discount points, based on a likely holding period of five years or more. The court agreed that restrictions would likely delay a sale of the interest, but it found no basis in the record for a five-year holding period or "any particular difficulties in connection with the Deputy family." The court thought five discount points was more appropriate.

The last category deals with dividend payout history, which Dorman assigned the poorest rating of 14 because Godfrey had not paid any dividends to date and was unlikely to pay any in the future. The court said, however, that "the actual payment of dividends is not the sole measure. The potential to pay dividends must also be considered. A return may also be expected in the form of increase in the value of the investment or potential for capital gain. In other words, prospective earning power is important." The court found that Dorman's analysis inappropriately ignored any potential for gain due to increase in value, given Godfrey's "financial performance and future prospects." Combining the lack of dividends with potential capital appreciation, the court found that Godfrey's potential returns were "more in the middle range" and that eight discounts points were more appropriate.

The court thus arrived at a 29% combined discount, which it rounded to 30%, compared with Dorman's 44%, using the matrix categories as the structure for analysis. Accordingly, the court held that the 187.5 Godfrey shares held by the FLP had a discounted fair market value of $3,358,209.

Hackl v. Commissioner (II)

Citation: 2003 U.S. App. LEXIS 13936
Court: United States Court of Appeals
State/Jurisdiction: 7th Circuit Federal
Date of Decision: July 11, 2003
Judge: Evans

This opinion is the Seventh Circuit Court of Appeals' ruling on appeal from the Tax Court opinion of *Hackl v. Commissioner*, 118 T.C. 279 (U.S. Tax Ct. 2002).

In 1995 the Hackl's bought two tree farms and contributed them, along with cash and securities, to Treeco, LLC. Shortly afterwards, the Hackl's began annual transfers of Treeco stock to their family members. By 1998, the family members held 51% of the companys voting shares. The Hackl's believed the gifts qualified for the gift tax exclusion, but the IRS disagreed, claiming that the transfers were ineligible gifts of future interests. The couple disputed the $400,000 gift tax deficiency, but the Tax Court sided with the IRS.

On appeal, the Hackl's argued that the future interest exception applies only if the donee received "something less than the full bundle of legal property rights." Because the Hackl's gave up all of their property rights to the shares, they asserted that the shares were excludable gifts. The IRS interpreted the exclusion more narrowly, arguing that "any transfer without a *substantial present economic benefit* is a future interest and ineligible for the gift tax exclusion." (Emphasis added.)

The Seventh Circuit agreed with the IRS and the Tax Court, holding that the restrictions on transfer in Treeco's operating agreement meant that the gifted shares were "essentially without immediate value to the donees." The court reminded the parties that tax exclusions "are matters of legislative grace that must be narrowly construed."

Hess v. Commissioner

Citation: T.C. Memo 2003-251
Court: United States Tax Court
State/Jurisdiction: Specialty Federal
Date of Decision: August 20, 2003
Judge: Ruwe

Hess Industries, Inc. (HII) manufactures metal processing machines and automation systems for the automotive industry. In November 1995, Johann and Johanna Hess gave 10 shares of HII common stock (a 10% stockholder interest) to an irrevocable trust established for their daughter. The sole issue was the fair market value of the stock for gift tax purposes.

Income adjustment not foreseeable

The taxpayers' expert, Gregory Heebink, used the discounted cash flow (DCF) method and the guideline public company method. He determined that the fair market value of the stock was $128,000 per share.

In both of his appraisal methods, Heebink adjusted HII's historical earnings because management indicated that the company's cost of sales had been understated in the most recent fiscal year. The Tax Court said that this adjustment should not have been made because the existence of a misstatement had not been established, and the adjustment wasn't reasonably foreseeable on the valuation date.

The court noted that HII's financial statements and tax returns had never been amended to account for the understatement of expenses. In addition, the court found that "the alleged understatement was not discovered or quantified until 1997, almost 2 years after the gift of HII stock and after the audit of petitioners' gift tax returns."

Because Heebink's valuation methods reflected this improper adjustment to earnings, the Tax Court concluded that "Mr. Heebink's valuation analysis significantly understates the value of HII stock."

Income approach should be considered

The IRS's expert, Eric Engstrom, relied on four valuation methods in his appraisal. He used the net asset value method and the guideline public company method. He also used a prior transaction involving HII's common stock and a valuation formula that was contained in a stockholder agreement. In his final analysis, Engstrom determined the fair market value of the common stock to be $269,000 per share.

Engstrom also performed a DCF analysis. However, he did not assign any weight to this method because HII's future income was difficult to predict, and small changes in certain assumptions resulted in large changes in the implied value of the common stock.

The Tax Court concluded that less weight should be assigned to the DCF method when a company's future income is relatively unpredictable, or when the valuation conclusions are highly sensitive to small changes in assumptions. However, the court stated that the method should still be considered in the valuation process.

Prior transaction overstates value

The Tax Court's most significant criticism of Engstrom's analysis related to a prior transaction involving HII common stock. Engstrom assumed that the purchase price was entirely attributable to the purchase of the stock. However, in connection with the sale of stock, the selling stockholder had also signed a covenant not to compete with HII. Although the parties did not assign any value to this agreement, the Tax Court believed that "at least some portion of the purchase price was attributable to the 8-year covenant."

The court did not reach a conclusion regarding the value of the covenant. It simply indicated that the covenant had some value and, therefore, "the value of HII stock was less than the value that Mr. Engstrom derived from that transaction."

Discounts

The Tax Court accepted the testimony of both experts that a 15% minority interest discount should be applied under certain valuation methods. However, the court criticized Heebink for applying a discount under the guideline public company method, because the conclusions of this method already reflected a minority discount.

Heebink applied a 30% marketability discount, whereas Engstrom applied a 25% discount. The court accepted Engstrom's opinion because Heebink appeared to commingle issues of control into his selection of a marketability discount.

Tax Court splits the difference

In its final analysis, the Tax Court concluded that "the value of HII stock falls somewhere in the middle" of the range of values presented at trial. Without any further explanation, it determined that the gifted shares had a fair market value of $200,000 per share.

It is interesting to note that the Tax Court's conclusion is almost exactly the midpoint between the conclusions of Heebink ($128,000) and Engstrom ($269,000).

Estate of Gribauskas v. Commissioner

Citation: No. 01-4189 (2nd Cir. 2003)
Court: United States Court of Appeals
State/Jurisdiction: 2nd Circuit Federal
Date of Decision: August 26, 2003
Judge: Van Graffeiland

In the *Estate of Paul C. Gribauskas v. CIR*, No. 01-4189 (2nd Cir. August 26, 2003), the U.S. Court of Appeals for the Second Circuit considered whether annual lottery payments should be valued using the annuity tables in IRC sec. 7520 for estate tax purposes. On the date of death, the decedent held the right to receive one-half of 18 remaining annual payments from the Connecticut Lotto jackpot he won in 1992. The future annual payments could not be assigned or transferred to third parties under state law. Nonetheless, a gray market developed for the payments. On that market, the right to the future payments trade at a significant discount to account for the restrictions on transferability. The estate valued the remaining lotto payments, inclusive of a discount for lack of marketability based on the gray market. That valuation resulted in a value that was $900,000 less than the valuation of the payments using the annuity tables.

The IRS contested that valuation. It claimed that the remaining lotto payments should be valued using the annuity tables in sec. 7520. However, it stipulated that a gray market for the transactions existed, and if deviation from the annuity tables was warranted, then the estate correctly valued the payments. The matter proceeded to the Tax Court, which ruled in favor of the IRS. The estate appealed.

Before the Second Circuit, the estate argued that a deviation from the annuity tables was warranted in this case. The Second Circuit noted that a deviation from the annuity tables is warranted when the application of the tables would produce "a substantially unrealistic and unreasonable result." The court then noted that the Ninth Circuit permitted deviation from the annuity tables in a factually similar matter, which the Tax Court dismissed as "anomalous." *Shackleford v. U.S.*, 262 F.3d 1028 (9th Cir. 2001). Moreover, it noted that the IRS stipulated that restrictions on transferability adhering to the lotto prize reduced the marketability and the value of that prize by some $900,000. After considering the case law and the stipulation, the Second Circuit reversed the Tax Court and permitted deviation from the annuity tables in valuing the lotto prize in this case. In doing so, it rejected the IRS's argument that "the need for efficiency and consistency ... justifies] the application of the standardized tables." The Second Circuit stated, "The law sufficiently accounts for such policy concerns by placing the burden on the party challenging the application of the tables to prove that the tables yield a substantially unreasonable or unrealistic result." Thus, the court permitted the application of a lack of marketability discount in arriving at the fair market value of lotto payments in this case.

This abstract originally appeared in *Valuation Case Digest*, authored by John J. Stockdale, Jr.

Lappo v. Commissioner

Citation: T.C. Memo 2003-258
Court: United States Tax Court
State/Jurisdiction: Specialty Federal
Date of Decision: September 3, 2003
Judge: Thornton

The only issue in this case was the fair market value of gifted family limited partnership (FLP) interests.

Facts

On October 20, 1995, taxpayer Lappo and her daughter formed the Lappo Family Limited Partnership, and on April 19, 1996, they transferred to the FLP marketable securities and real estate with appraised values of $1,318,609 and $1,860,000, respectively. On April 19, 1996, Lappo gifted a 66.81% interest in the FLP to her daughter as trustee of the Lappo Generation Trust and a 0.67% interest to each of her four grandchildren ("April gifts"). On July 2, 1996, Lappo gave her remaining 29.22% interest in the FLP to her daughter as an individual ("July gift").

On her gift tax returns, Lappo valued the April gifts at $1,040,000 and the July gift at $423,871. The IRS filed a notice of deficiency in the amount of $998,508. The IRS initially raised but later withdrew challenges based on the following theories: (1) lack of economic substance; (2) restriction on right to use or sell; and (3) gift on formation.

Valuation evidence

The parties agreed on the net asset values (NAVs) of the real estate ($1,860,000 at all times) and the marketable securities ($1,296,882 for the April gifts and $1,379,531 for the July gift). The only disputed issues were the magnitudes of discounts for lack of control (DLOC) and marketability (DLOM) to be taken.

Robert P. Oliver testified for the taxpayer. Both experts used publicly traded real estate investment trusts (REITs) as the starting point to determine the DLOC for the FLP's real estate holdings. Oliver started with 400 REITs and eliminated all but seven as being insufficiently comparable. Considering a number of factors that he said differentiated the FLP from his guideline companies, he made certain upward adjustments to the NAVs of his guideline companies and determined a 35% DLOC for the April gifts and a 30% DLOC for the July gift.

For the marketable securities component of the FLP interests, he concluded a 7.5% DLOC. Later, however, the taxpayer agreed to use the IRS's 8.5% DLOC for the marketable securities, which the court accepted.

To determine the DLOM, Oliver relied on the Management Planning, Inc. restricted stock study. Of the original 197 transactions, he identified a guideline group of 39 with a median discount of 29.3%. He adjusted this upward by 5.7% and applied a 35% DLOM to both gifts.

Dr. Alan C. Shapiro testified for the IRS. For the real estate component, he started with 62 real estate companies and eliminated 10 that were not REITs. To adjust for the inherent liquidity premium in REIT data, Dr. Shapiro used Dr. Bajaj's private placement study and determined a 7.5% liquidity premium. From this figure, he concluded an 8.5% DLOC.

In determining the DLOM, Dr. Shapiro again relied on the Bajaj private placement study, which showed an average DLOM of 7.2%. He adjusted this upward to 8.3% after considering a number of other factors.

Tax Court findings

The Tax Court rejected most of Oliver's valuation, using his conclusions only as a check against the court's own conclusions. Although it accepted Shapiro's empirical data, the court did not accept his ultimate conclusions, but rather drew its own conclusions using the raw data from the studies he relied on.

Minority interest discount

Regarding the real estate component, the Tax Court was not persuaded that Oliver's guideline group was "sufficiently large or made up of companies sufficiently comparable." On the other hand, the court found Dr. Shapiro's sample "sufficiently large to make tolerable any dissimilarities between the partnership and the REITs in his guideline group."

The court also concluded that Oliver's analysis supporting his adjustments fell short. Its reasoning sheds light on what the court expects in such an analysis:

Mr. Oliver has inadequately explained how he derived the NAVs that are critical to his computation of the price-to-NAV discounts. The record does not adequately reflect the management disclosures that led to Mr. Oliver's upward adjustments.... Moreover, Mr. Oliver has failed adequately to explain the apparent volatility in his recommended price-to-NAV discounts over less than 3 months....

Moreover, we are unconvinced of the appropriateness of the upward adjustments Mr. Oliver made to this volatile guideline company data to account for factors specific to the partnership. He does not explain how he quantified each factor, how the factors were netted, or why the net effect should result in an upward adjustment to the median guideline company discounts, rather than a downward adjustment or a wash.... It seems most likely that Mr. Oliver's upward adjustments are, to some extent, plug numbers used to justify his ultimate, very round minority interest discount figures of 35% and 30 percent...."

Some of these upward adjustments are very large. For instance, in determining a \$25,928,000 NAV for Shopco as of July 2, 1996, Mr. Oliver started with a reported book value of \$4,862,000 and adjusted it upward by \$21,066,000.

Turning to Dr. Shapiro's analysis, the court agreed that some adjustment for the liquidity premium inherent in REIT data prices was necessary, but it hesitated "to rely on a single academic study—particularly one that Dr. Shapiro did not participate in preparing and could not elaborate upon first hand." So the court averaged the average discounts from the Bajaj study, the Wruck study, and the Hertzel & Smith study, which were 14.09%, 17.6%, and 13.5%, respectively. The average of those figures was about 15%, yielding a liquidity premium of 17.6%.

Using that liquidity premium, the court arrived at a DLOC of 18.4% for the April gifts and 16.12% for the July gift, which the court rounded to 19% for all of the real estate component of the FLP. Together with the stipulated 8.5% DLOC for the marketable securities component, the court concluded an overall DLOC of 15%.

Marketability discount

The Tax Court criticized Oliver's guideline group because 13 of the 39 were high-tech companies—their high discounts reflecting high risk. The court was unpersuaded that these companies were comparable to the FLP. After removing them from Oliver's group, the median discount of the remaining 26 companies was 19.45%, instead of the original 29.3%

Citing to *McCord v. Commissioner*, the court said that, in this context, it preferred Dr. Shapiro's private placement approach (i.e., the Bajaj study) over Oliver's "more narrow" restricted stock approach. "Absent further explication of the Bajaj study by Dr. Shapiro, however, and without the benefit of other empirical studies that would tend to validate the conclusions of the Bajaj study, we are unpersuaded that a 7.2-percent discount is an appropriate quantitative starting point for determining the marketability discount applicable to the gifted interests in this case."

Using the raw data from the private placement study, the court observed that the average discount was 22.21%. Averaging this with the 20.14% average discount from the Hertzel & Smith study yielded an unadjusted DLOM of 21%. The court noted that this figure was very close to the 19.45% discount it determined from Oliver's data. Looking at the other factors considered by the experts, the court decided that a 3% upward adjustment was appropriate to capture the characteristics specific to the FLP. The result was a DLOM of 24%.

Peracchio v. Commissioner

Citation: T.C. Memo 2003-280
Court: United States Tax Court
State/Jurisdiction: Specialty Federal
Date of Decision: September 25, 2003
Judge: Halpern

The primary issues in this gift tax case were the appropriate discounts for lack of control (DLOC) and lack of marketability (DLOM) to apply to gifted and sold interests of a family limited partnership (FLP).

Facts

On November 25, 1997, taxpayer Peter Peracchio and his wife created the Peracchio Family Trust. The same day, Peracchio, his son, and the trust executed an agreement of limited partnership forming Peracchio Investors, L.P. Peracchio contributed cash and securities worth $2,013,765, and his son and the trust each contributed $1,000. Also on that day, Peracchio gifted a 45.47% interest in the FLP to the trust and sold a 53.48% interest to the trust for $646,764. The FLP's assets consisted entirely of cash and marketable securities.

On his gift tax return, Peracchio claimed a combined DLOC and DLOM of 40%. The IRS rejected the discount and determined a deficiency of $328,317. By trial, the IRS had modified its position that no discounts were warranted to allow a 4.4% DLOC and a 15% DLOM. Applied serially, these yielded a combined discount of 18.74%.

Valuation evidence

Taxpayer presented two experts, Timothy R. Dankoff and Charles H. Stryker. Francis X. Burns testified for the IRS. The experts' discount conclusions, as well as those of the Tax Court, are shown in Table 1.

TABLE 1: DISCOUNTS APPLIED BY EXPERTS AND TAX COURT

	Dankoff (TPI)	Stryker (TP2)	Burns (IRS)	Tax Court
DLOC	7.7%	5.0%	4.4%	6.0%
DLOM	35%	40%	15%	25%

Both Dankoff and Stryker considered the *Mandelbaum* factors and other empirical studies to derive the DLOM. Dankoff determined his benchmark or "quantitative starting point" from *Mandelbaum* and Stryker determined his from restricted stock studies.

Tax Court findings

The court several times expressed its dissatisfaction with all the experts' analyses and appeared to accept the IRS's expert's conclusions as the lesser of two evils. Primarily, the court was displeased with the experts' use of benchmark averages and their failure to tailor the empirical data to the case at hand. But it also criticized the experts for making estimates not supported by empirical evidence.

Minority interest discount

The court rejected Stryker's testimony on the DLOC because "his methodology is comparatively imprecise (his 5-percent discount is not statistically derived from observed discounts) and incomplete (he considers only domestic equity funds)."

The court also was not persuaded by Dankoff's 5% discount on the cash, noting that this figure was "judgmentally determined." Although similarly unhappy with Burns' 2% "estimate," the court nonetheless accepted his testimony as a concession that a 2% DLOC would be appropriate.

Dankoff's use of the median discount instead of the mean confused the court, as the only reason he gave was to exclude outliers, which he had already done. The court thought it more straightforward to "account for obvious outliers by excluding them from the samples in question" and then use the mean discount. On its own, the court also excluded some funds that traded at unusually high premiums. It concluded a total discount factor of 6% for the cash and marketable securities.

Marketability discount

The Tax Court had a scathing rebuke for Dankoff's reliance on *Mandelbaum* as establishing a legal standard for the DLOM:

> To the extent Mr. Dankoff believes that the benchmark range of discounts we utilized in *Mandelbaum v. Commissioner*, supra, is controlling in this or any other case, he is mistaken. Nothing in *Mandelbaum* suggests that we ascertained that range of discounts for any purpose other than the resolution of that case. To the contrary, we specifically stated that we were using the upper and lower limits of that range "as benchmarks of the marketability discount for the shares at hand." If, instead, Mr. Dankoff simply believes that such range of discounts is equally appropriate under the facts of this case, he offers no justification whatsoever for that view. We believe he would be hard pressed to do so; the entity at issue in *Mandelbaum*, an established operating company, bears little resemblance to the partnership.

The court also had no kind words for Stryker, whose use of the average DLOM indicated by restricted stock studies it rejected:

> While restricted stock studies certainly have some probative value in the context of marketability discount analysis, see, e.g., *McCord v. Commissioner*, 120 T.C. at 390-393, Mr. Stryker makes no attempt whatsoever to analyze the data from those studies as they relate to the transferred interests. Rather, he simply lists the average discounts observed in several such studies, effectively asking us to accept on faith the premise that the approximate average of those results provides a reliable benchmark for the transferred interests. Absent any analytical support, we are unable to accept that premise, particularly in light of the fundamental difference between an investment company holding easily valued assets (such as the partnership) and the operating companies that are the subject of the restricted stock studies.

Having rejected both the taxpayer's experts DLOM analyses, the court was left unenthusiastically with Burns' "brief analysis of six [unnamed] factors 'that may influence the size of the marketability discount.'" Burns suggested that a negotiation between buyer and seller would produce a

DLOM in the range of 5 to 25%, and he believed a "fair outcome" of such negotiations would yield about a 15% discount.

The court was not persuaded by his discount range and was "even less impressed by his arbitrary selection of the midpoint of that range (15 percent) as his suggested discount." However, under duress to determine a DLOM, the court treated Burns' range as a concession that a discount of up to 25% would be appropriate.

Estate of Stone v. Commissioner

Citation: T.C. Memo 2003-309, 203 Tax Ct. Memo. LEXIS 312
Court: United States Tax Court
State/Jurisdiction: Specialty Federal
Date of Decision: November 7, 2003
Judge: Chiechi

The only issue in these consolidated cases was whether assets owned by each of five family limited partnerships (FLPs) were includible in the gross estates of Mr. and Mrs. Stone under I.R.C. section 2036(a). The Tax Court held that the transfers to the FLPs were bona fide, arm's-length transfers for full and adequate consideration and thus were not includible in the estates.

Facts

In 1933, Mr. and Mrs. Stone founded several ventures in the apparel industry. At some point before 1976, those ventures became Stone Manufacturing Co., a global manufacturer and distributor of sports apparel. In 1976, Mr. Stone formed Stones, Inc., as a holding company of Stone Manufacturing.

In the early 1990s, litigation developed between the Stones' four children involving some family trusts. The children were also concerned about the management of their parents' assets, which posed potential grounds for additional litigation among the children. The Stones shared their children's concerns, as they no longer wanted to actively manage their assets and wished their children to take over for them.

To that end, the Stones and their children formed five different FLPs in 1996, with different children (and/or spouse) named general partner of each FLP. The Stones had valuations performed for all of their assets, and in 1997 contributed most of their assets, including their stock in Stones, Inc., to the FLPs. They retained sufficient assets, however, to maintain their current standard of living. After the transfers of property, the children settled their litigation.

Mr. Stone died in 1997, and Mrs. Stone died in 1998. Mr. Stone's estate tax return showed a net estate tax of $4,031,260, and Mrs. Stone's return showed net estate tax of $861,972. The IRS issued a notices of deficiency in the amount of $8,491,090 for Mr. Stone's estate and $688,385 for Mrs. Stone's estate.

Tax Court findings

The IRS challenged the transfers under I.R.C. 2036(a), claiming that they were not bona fide sales for adequate and full consideration. The IRS relied primarily on the *Estate of Harper, Estate of Reichardt,* and *Estate of Thompson*, arguing that there was no evidence in the record indicating that the Stones intended to conduct a "joint enterprise for the mutual profit of their children and themselves." The estate, on the other hand, claimed that the Stones' transfers of property to the FLPs were bona fide sales for full and adequate consideration. In support of its position, the estate pointed out that the Stones received pro rata ownership in the FLPs in return for their contributions.

The Tax Court agreed with the estate, distinguishing the instant case factually from Estate of Harper and the others. It rejected the IRS's argument that because the Stones did not actively participate in the children's negotiations regarding the various assets, the transfers were not bona fide, arm's-length transfers. The court laid out the facts weighing in favor of the estate:

Each member of the Stone family was represented by his or her own independent counsel and had input into the decision-making as to how each of the Five Partnerships was to be structured and operated and what property was to be transferred to each such partnership. The Stone family understood that Mr. Stone and Ms. Stone would not be bound by any agreements that the children were able to reach as a result of the children's negotiations and that Mr. Stone and Ms. Stone would make the ultimate decision as to which, if any, of their respective assets to transfer to each of the Five Partnerships. In this connection, although Mr. Stone and Ms. Stone agreed to form the Five Partnerships, they did not intend to, and did not, transfer all their respective assets to such partnerships. Instead, they retained sufficient assets to enable them to maintain their respective accustomed standards of living. Mr. Stone and Ms. Stone did not accept the children's recommendations resulting from the children's negotiations regarding the structure, funding, and operation of the Five Partnerships without thought, comment, or question.

The court found that, unlike in *Harper* and other cases, the Stones did substantially more than just change the form of the contributed property. The court found that the FLPs had economic substance and "operated as joint enterprises for profit through which the children actively participated in the management and development of the respective assets of such partnerships during their parents' lives (and thereafter)." The court concluded by saying that the transfers in this case did not constitute a "recycling of value" as found in some previous Tax Court cases.

Estate of Cook v. Commissioner (II)

Citation: No. 02-61011 (5th Cir. 2003)
Court: United States Court of Appeals
State/Jurisdiction: 5th Circuit Federal
Date of Decision: November 13, 2003
Judge: Duhe

In the *Estate of Gladys J. Cook v. CIR*, No. 02-61011 (5th Cir. November 13, 2003), the U.S. Court of Appeals for the Fifth Circuit considered whether a deviation from the annuity tables of IRC sec. 7520 was warranted when valuing lottery payments. The decedent and her sister formed a family limited partnership, through which they purchased lottery payments. Each sister held a 48% limited partnership interest and 2% general partnership interest. In 1995, the partnership won a $17 million Texas lottery. The lottery winnings were payable in 20 equal installments and were not transferable. In late 1995, after receiving only one lottery payment, the decedent died.

Her estate hired an appraiser to value the limited partnership interest. The expert utilized a discounted cash flow method and applied a lack of marketability discount in determining the value of the 19 remaining lottery payments. He concluded that the remaining lottery payments had a value of $4.575 million and the decedent's interest in the FLP had a value of $1,579,749. The estate reported this amount on its estate tax return. The IRS contested the valuation of the lottery payments. It claimed that the payments should have been valued using the annuity tables. The matter proceeded to trial.

Before the Tax Court, the parties stipulated that there was no market for the lottery payments. Both parties presented expert testimony regarding the fair market value of the remaining payments, and both experts applied lack of marketability discounts to the value of the payments. However, the IRS primarily argued that the lottery payments were a private annuity and should be valued under the annuity tables. The Tax Court agreed. It found that deviation from the annuity tables was not warranted because the lottery payments were akin to private annuities. The estate appealed.

On appeal, the estate argued that the Tax Court erred in valuing the lottery payments using the annuity tables in sec. 7520 because the annuity tables failed to take into account the effects of marketability. In support for its position, the estate noted that the Second and the Ninth Circuits have reached the opposite decision on this question. See *Gribauskas v. CIR*, No. 01-4189 (2nd Cir. 2003), and *Estate of Shackelford v. CIR*, 262 F.3d 1028 (9th Cir. 2001). A majority of the Fifth Circuit rejected the estate's claim. The majority determined that deviation from the annuity tables is only warranted when the underlying assumptions – interest rate and mortality – are shown to be "unreasonable or unrealistic." With regard to its sister jurisdictions, it stated, "The holdings in *Shackleford* and *Gribauskas* depart from the longstanding trend based on the premise that the right to alienate is fundamental to the valuation of <u>any</u> property. [Emphasis in original. Internal citations omitted.] We agree that the right to alienate is necessary to value a capital asset; however, we think it unreasonable to apply a non-marketability discount when the asset to be valued is the right, independent of market forces, to receive a certain amount of money annually for a certain term of years." Thus, it affirmed the decision of the Tax Court and created a split in the circuits.

One judge dissented. This judge stated, "I would follow the well-reasoned decisions of the 2nd and 9th Circuits' holding that in arriving at an alternative fair market value to compare with the table value a court can consider non-marketability or any other legitimate factor that affects the fair market value of the annuity."

This abstract originally appeared in *Valuation Case Digest*, authored by John J. Stockdale, Jr.

Estate of Green v. Commissioner

Citation: T.C. Memo 2003-348, 2003 Tax Ct. Memo LEXIS 348
Court: United States Tax Court
State/Jurisdiction: Specialty Federal
Date of Decision: December 29, 2003
Judge: Thornton

At decedent's death, she owned 3,276 shares of Royal Bancshares, Inc. (RBI), or 5.09% of the outstanding RBI shares. Decedent had the fifth largest holding of 62 shareholders, but no one individual owned a controlling interest.

The estate tax return valued the 3,276 shares at $163,800. The IRS determined that the fair market value of the shares was $1,048,320. By the time of trial, however, the IRS claimed that the shares were worth $860,000, or $262.52 per share, and the estate contended that they were worth $655,200, or $200 per share.

Valuation evidence

Gary L. Schroeder testified for the estate, and William C. Herber was the expert for the IRS. Both experts used an income approach and arrived at very similar values. Schroeder determined a value of $23,370,000 for RBI on a controlling interest basis, and Herber concluded a value of $23,300,000. The IRS accepted the estate's value conclusion. Both experts also used market approaches, and again arrived at similar values under the guideline publicly traded company method. Schroeder concluded a value of $28,330,000 for RBI, and Herber determined a value of $28,000,000. Again, the IRS agreed to the estate's value conclusion.

The experts differed slightly in their values derived from the guideline merged and acquired company method. Schroeder identified five banks in his transaction analysis, compared with Herber's nine. But the primary difference was Schroeder's consideration of a potential significant pending loan impairment. Because he selected transaction multiples between the median and the low end of the range, Schroeder concluded a value of $25,920,000 for RBI, compared with $28,500,000 determined by Herber, who did not consider any possible loan impairment.

Experts' discounts

The experts disagreed only slightly on their discounts for lack of control. Using *Mergerstat Review*, Schroeder calculated a control premium of 20% and an implied lack of control discount of 20%. Herber relied partially on a study by Christopher Mercer in Quantifying Marketability Discounts that showed an average discount of 19%. He also conducted his own study of control premiums in banking company transactions and concluded an average discount range of 18.4% to 19.6%.

Herber then considered additional factors that led him to reduce the discount to 15%: (1) decedent's "substantially larger interest" than typical minority interests in banks; (2) lack of concentration of ownership in RBI stock; (3) the highly regulated and "transparent" banking industry; and (4) RBI's solid capitalization, high returns on equity and assets, high rating compared with other banks, and favorable dividend payout.

The experts disagreed widely on their discounts for lack of marketability. Schroeder relied on restricted stock studies indicating discounts ranging from 31.2% to 45%, with an overall average discount of 34.9%. He also relied on pre-IPO studies that indicated an average discount ranging from 43% to 45.7%, with an overall average discount of 44.4%. Schroeder also considered several other factors, including, again, the potential loan impairment, and seven prior transactions involving RBI stock. He ultimately concluded a discount of 40%.

Herber also relied on restricted stock studies, primarily the Management Planning, Inc. (MPI) study, which indicated a discount range from 26.2% to 32.7%, compared with the 24% to 45% range of other studies. Herber also considered the *Mandelbaum* factors and RBI's stability of earnings, dividend payout history, and low company risk. He concluded that a 25% discount was appropriate.

Tax Court findings

The Tax Court accepted the estate's values for the income approach and guideline publicly traded company method, as the IRS had already conceded to them. Under the guideline merged and acquired company method, the court said it was unclear to what extent the potential loan impairment affected Schroeder's appraisal, so it rejected his conclusion but concluded its own value of $27,500,000.

The court gave equal weight to each of the three methods, arriving at an undiscounted value for RBI of $26,266,667, as shown in Table 1.

Table 1	
Approach	Value
Income approach	$23,300,000
Market approach guideline publicly traded company method	$28,000,000
Guideline merged and acquired company method	$27,500,000

Tax Court discounts

The Tax Court was unpersuaded by either expert's discount for lack of control analysis. It found Herber's adjustments down to 15% not well supported, and stated that he had not convinced the court that the discount should be less than 17%. Accordingly, the court held that a 17% discount for lack of control was appropriate.

The court wasn't entirely satisfied with the discounts for lack of marketability, either. It believed that Schroeder's "double counting" of the potential loan impairment and his consideration of the prior transactions caused him to overstate his recommended discount. As for Herber's discount, the court pointed out that his discount was at the "rock bottom" of the range, rather than at the "slightly lower end," as Herber recommended. The court also questioned his 24% lower range limit, noting that he himself admitted that most of the studies showed median discounts from 30% to 35%.

Moreover, the court criticized Herber's analysis of the MPI study, in which only two transactions involved companies with revenues comparable to RBI's relatively small revenues. Those transactions had an overall average discount of 43%. Citing *Valuing a Business*, 4th edition, the court noted that the MPI study indicates a "clear correlation between the size of a company's gross income and the size of the lack of marketability discount."

So the court rejected Herber's 25% discount and concluded a 35% discount, which was at the higher end of Herber's range and "consistent with the average discount that Mr. Schroeder derived from the restricted stock studies."

On a final note, the court said that although it believed the pre-IPO studies Schroeder used were "entitled to some consideration," it did not find that they justified a discount greater than 35%.

Conclusion

The court concluded a fair market value for decedent's shares of $721,297 ($220.18 per share), as shown in Table 2.

Table 2	
Total aggregate value of RBI stock	$26,266,667.00
5.09% of value of stock	$1,336,973.00
Less: 17% discount for lack of control	($227,285.00)
	$1,109,688.00
Less: 35% discount for lack of marketability	($388,391.00)
FMV of decedent's shares	$721,297.00
FMV per share (3,276 shares)	$220.18

Estate of Trompeter v. Commissioner (III)

Citation: T.C. Memo. 2004-27, 2004 Tax Ct. Memo LEXIS 31
Court: United States Tax Court
State/Jurisdiction: Specialty Federal
Date of Decision: February 4, 2004
Judge: Laro

One of the main issues before the Tax Court was the value of 1533.48 shares of preferred stock of Sterling Holding Co. owned by the decedent. The stock was subject to a redemption agreement requiring Sterling to repurchase it at a future date.

Appellate court ruling

The case was remanded to the Tax Court to clarify: (1) how the Tax Court arrived at $4.5 million as the value of the omitted assets, (2) the reasoning and explanation of the 4% discount rate for the preferred stock, and (3) the use of the "well accepted present value formulae." Only the second issue is discussed in this abstract.

Tax Court opinion

The Tax Court previously applied a 4% discount rate to the preferred stock to reflect the time value of money. In its supplemental opinion, the court addressed the Ninth Circuit's concerns and raised the discount rate to 12.5% to take into account the risk that Sterling might not fulfill its contractual obligation.

To justify the higher discount rate, the Tax Court used the rate of compensation that a holder of the preferred stock would receive if a redemption was untimely. The court also stated that the new discount rate was approximate to the rate that was payable on the subordinate series B stock, to which the preferred stock could be converted.

On remand, the estate argued that a 20% discount rate should be applied. The Tax Court disagreed and stated that the discount rate suggested by the estate does not take into account that the stock holder would receive daily dividends at a 12.5% annual rate. In addition, the court stated "The estate's rate ignores the solid history of Sterling in honoring its contractual obligations."

Lack of marketability

On remand, the estate also argued that the series A preferred stock should be discounted for lack of marketability. The court stated that "[w]here as here the value determined for shares of stock is not the freely traded value of those shares, a lack of marketability discount is inappropriate."

Estate of Abraham v. Commissioner (I)

Citation: 2004 Tax Ct. Memo LEXIS 41
Court: United States Tax Court
State/Jurisdiction: Specialty Federal
Date of Decision: February 18, 2004
Judge: Ruwe

The issue in this estate tax case was whether three family limited partnerships (FLPs) should be respected for estate tax purposes.

The decedent, Abraham, had numerous properties that were placed in three FLPs for purposes of estate planning. Decedent continued, by way of her appointed guardian, to benefit from those properties until her death, exclusive of the other partners, who were her children.

The estate engaged Michael Lipof, a real estate consultant, to value the FLPs for the estate tax return. In doing so, Lipof applied a discount of 30% to 40 % to the asset value of each FLP to determine the fair market value of the FLPs.

The IRS filed a notice of deficiency, claiming that most of the assets held by the FLPs should be included in Abraham's gross estate under Section 2036.

The Tax Court noted that the decedent by definition violated Section 2036 by continuing to enjoy the property held by the FLPs. "Possession or enjoyment of the property transferred is retained where there is an express or implied understanding among the parties at the time of the transfer, even if the retained interest is not enforceable."

The Tax Court concluded that the FLPs were "merely a testamentary vehicle employed to shift her assets to future generations while maintaining her continued right to benefit from the FLP interests transferred. This is precisely the type of situation for which Section 2036 was created." The Tax Court disregarded the FLPs and valued the property held in the FLPs at full fair market value.

Estate of Hillgren v. Commissioner

Citation: T.C. Memo 2004-46
Court: United States Tax Court
State/Jurisdiction: Specialty Federal
Date of Decision: March 3, 2004
Judge: Cohen

The issues in this estate tax case were whether the court should disregard a family limited partnership (FLP) under IRC Section 2036(a), and the fair market value of the assets of the partnership.

Facts

Decedent suffered from depression, and following her failed first attempt at suicide, she formed an FLP with her brother, Mark Hillgren, and transferred all of her income-producing real estate to the FLP. Hillgren did not contribute any property to the FLP, but rather contributed his services. He was to receive 25% of the profits of the FLP under the partnership agreement. Decedent committed suicide several months later.

After formation of the FLP, the decedent's relationship to the real property that had been transferred to the FLP did not change. The same management company continued management of the properties in the same manner. Hillgren continued to deal with the properties in the same manner he had before, pursuant to a business loan agreement (BLA) that decedent and Hillgren had previously entered into. All of the FLP's income was distributed to decedent and used for her personal living expenses. Thus, the partnership form was completely disregarded by decedent and Hillgren.

FLP disregarded under § 2036(a)

The Tax Court ruled that because decedent and Hillgren did not respect the FLP entity, and decedent's relationship to the property did not change after formation of the FLP, the entity would be disregarded for estate tax purposes. Therefore, the real estate held by the FLP was included in the decedent's gross estate.

Valuation of the real estate

Although the FLP was disregarded, several parcels of the real estate were still subject to the BLA. Therefore, in determining the value of the real estate, the expert for the estate, Carsten Hoffman, opined that the following discounts should be applied in valuing the University property: 25% for Hillgren's interest under the BLA, 50% for a combined discount for lack of marketability and lack of control, and 5% for a discount for lack of voting rights. Hoffman based the latter two discounts on a comparison of real estate limited partnerships. He presented a similar analysis for the other properties subject to the business loan agreement.

The experts for the IRS, Raynor Klaris and John A. Thomson, discounted only the University property because the IRS attorney mistakenly told them that it was the only property subject to the BLA. Klaris and Thomson agreed with the 25% discount to account for Hillgren's interest under the BLA. In calculating a 35% discount for lack of marketability and a 10% discount for lack of control, they used a comparison of closed-end equity funds and real estate investment trusts. They also considered six restricted stock studies in the DLOM calculation.

The Tax Court accepted the values opined by Hoffman as "reasonable" and "not contradicted by reliable evidence."

Okerlund v. United States (II)

Citation: 2004 U.S. App. LEXIS 6970
Court: United States Court of Appeals
State/Jurisdiction: Federal
Date of Decision: April 9, 2004
Judge: Gakarsa

At issue in this appeal was the use of subsequent events in valuing the closely-held stock of Schwan's Sales Enterprises, Inc. (SSE). The Court of Appeals concluded that the Court of Claims did not commit reversible error and upheld the decision.

Taxpayers contended that actual results for the two years following the valuation date should be considered to show that the IRS' expert's projections were overoptimistic and taxpayer's expert's projections were more reasonable. The appellate court noted that it reviewed for errors of law and for clear errors on finding of fact.

The appellate court stated, "Plaintiffs did not point to a single case suggesting that the failure to consider subsequent events constitutes legal error." It noted that the trial court's assessment of the risks at the valuation date was a factual matter, and "consideration of post valuation financial results here would be improper."

Although taxpayer's expert visited the facility and interviewed management after two of the risk factors had materialized, neither visited the premises *before* the fact. Had a management interview been conducted before the risk factors actually affected the company adversely, the potential impact of the risk factors might have carried more weight with the court.

In the original decision, discounts for lack of marketability of 40% on one gift date and 45% on another gift date were found based on a combinate of restricted stock and pre-IPO data, in addition to a 5% discount for nonvoting stock. These discounts were not an issue on appeal.

Polack v. Commissioner (II)

Citation: 2004 U.S. App. LEXIS 8612
Court: United States Court of Appeals
State/Jurisdiction: 8th Circuit Federal
Date of Decision: May 3, 2004
Judge: Loken

The issue in this case was the value of Zip Sort, Inc. shares gifted by taxpayer to his children. The Tax Court's valuation of 88 cents a share was upheld by the Eighth Circuit.

Facts

Polack gifted 1,040,000 shares of nonvoting common stock of Zip Sort to his children. Zip Sort prints bulk mailings and prepares them for mailing. On his 1992 gift tax return, Polack relied on Gerald Gray's opinion that the value of the shares was $0.50 each. The IRS valued the shares at $1.65 and assessed a deficiency. Polack then petitioned the Tax Court for a redetermination. At trial, the IRS lowered that amount to $0.88 based on the opinion of Brad Cashion.

Valuation evidence

The appraisals by Gray and Cashion differed on three key points: future net VARI (value added refund income), future capital expenditures, and whether to include a non-operating asset.

Gray projected that Zip Sort's net VARI would equal 3.89% of its future sales after relying on Polack's statement that Zip Sort would retain only 25-35% of future VARI. Gray predicted that for 1993-1995 Zip Sort's future capital expenditures would be $200,000 per year and $150,000 per year after 1995. Gray also excluded a $170,000 non-operating asset on Zip Sort's unaudited financial statement, because Polack stated that it was offset by a $150,000 debt to himself.

Cashion prepared his report six years later, based on a tour of Zip Sort's facilities and his conversation with Dana Rhoads, president of operations. Cashion projected that, as of the 1992 valuation date, Zip Sort's gross VARI would equal 18% of future sales and that Zip Sort would retain 50% of its VARI receipts resulting in net VARI of $810,000 in 1993. Cashion predicted Zip Sort's annual capital expenditures to be $100,000, and he included the $170,000 non-operating asset.

Tax Court findings

The Tax Court found Cashion's appraisal to be more credible.

> With respect to net VARI, the court found that Cashion reasonably relied on what Rhoads told him, that Cashion's projection of 50% VARI retention was consistent with Zip Sort's retention of other USPS [United States Postal Service] discounts, and that

Gray's "bald projection of $350,000" was not based on credible evidence. With respect to capital expenditures, the court found Cashion's projections "reliable and probative of [Zip Sort's] value" because they were based on Rhoads' statements and Zip Sort's operational history. With respect to the non-operating asset, the court rejected Polack's uncorroborated testimony of an offsetting debt "in the face of the evidence that the asset was listed on [Zip Sort's] balance sheet at a value approximating $170,000."

Holding on appeal and rationale

The Court of Appeals affirmed the decision because it determined that Polack's offer of proof, the 1993 and 1994 unaudited financials, were irrelevant, and that the Tax Court's determination of fair market value was not clearly erroneous.

Estate of Blount v. Commissioner (I)

Citation: T.C. Memo. 2004-116
Court: United States Tax Court
State/Jurisdiction: Specialty Federal
Date of Decision: May 12, 2004
Judge: Gale

The issue in this estate tax case was the value of decedent's interest in a closely held company on the date of his death. The U.S. Tax Court disregarded an ESOP repurchase liability and a buy-sell agreement, but included the full value of company-owned life insurance, and valued the company at $9.9 million.

At the time of his death on September 21, 1997, decedent owned 83.2% or 43,080 shares of BCC (Blount Construction Company). BCC was in the business of construction and street repair for various clients and at the time of death was owned by decedent and BCC ESOP.

In 1981, prior to the formation of the BCC ESOP, decedent and the only other shareholder, Jennings, entered into a shareholders' buy-sell agreement with BCC. The agreement restricted the transfer of stock during the lifetime of the shareholder and at death,and set the per-share purchase price as BCC's book value at fiscal yearend immediately preceding the deceased shareholder's death.

In 1992, BCC adopted the BCC ESOP. The Tax Court noted that "BCC made annual cash contributions to the ESOP, and the ESOP obtained shares of BCC stock either from decedent ... or from the company, making it a third, minority shareholder. In addition, the company took out life insurance policies for $3 million on each of the stockholders. In early 1996, Jennings passed away and BCC redeemed his shares. Consequently, decedent and BCC ESOP remained as the BCC's only shareholders.

Then, in October 1996, decedent discovered that he was terminally ill with cancer, which prompted him to enter into a new buy-sell agreement with BCC. The new agreement was operative only upon his death and set a fixed, lump-sum purchase price of $4 million. Decedent signed the agreement in his individual capacity and on behalf of BCC as its president.

After decedent's death, the IRS challenged the valuation of his interest in BCC. BCC had Business Valuation Services (BVS) perform an annual independent valuation of BCC ESOP to determine the per-share value of the stock. BVS had arrived at $8,041,126 or $86.73 per share value as of January 31, 1996, and $8,491,321 ($164.01/share) as of January 31, 1997. The IRS valued decedent's BCC stock at $7,921,975.

John T. Grizzle testified for the estate. He concluded that the buy-sell agreement was similar to other such agreements negotiated at arms length. He asserted that in the industry, a construction company is typically valued by applying a multiple of four to the entity's cash-flow adjusted for non-operating and non-recurring items. Applying this income approach, he concluded that the buy-sell price for decedent's BCC shares represented a 4.25 multiple of its adjusted cashflow.

Grizzle also looked at three comparable company sales. The court criticized his reasoning stating: "Mr. Grizzle did not contend that the sale prices of the companies he examined were determined by using a multiple of adjusted cashflow. Rather, he backed into the multiples after the fact by comparing the sale prices to the adjusted cashflows. He compared those multiples to the multiple of cashflow implicit in the purchase price designated in the 1996 Agreement to conclude that the price term was comparable to what unrelated parties have negotiated at arm's length."

In neither approach did Grizzle consider the value of BCC's nonoperating assets, because he contended that in actual sales, the seller usually retains those assets. On the basis of his analysis, Grizzle concluded that the fair market value for BCC was $4,541,678, and decedent's 43,080 BCC shares had a fair market value of $3,778,676 as of the valuation date.

Gerald M. Fodor, also testified for the estate. Fodor used a blend of income and asset-based approaches to value BCC. For the income approach, he used a capitalization of earnings model. In his projection of BCC's "net free cash flow capacity" Fodor used historical earnings. Fodor adjusted the earning capacity downward by $200,000 to account for annual contributions to the ESOP. "He also adjusted for depreciation, capital investment, and retained working capital. He concluded that BCC would have $234,060 in net free cash flow capacity." Fodor used a capitalization rate of 32.94% and a growth rate of 4% and arrived at capitalized earnings of $809,896. He added approximately $5.6 million to reflect net working capital and the difference between BCC's book value and fair market value, and subtracted $750,000 to reflect the obligation to repurchase BCC shares held by ESOP participants.

"Mr. Fodor weighted the income-based value of $5.8 million at 75% and the asset-based value of $7.9 million at 25%, to yield a final blended value of $6 million. ... Multiplying this value by decedent's 83.2-percent interest in BCC resulted in a corresponding $4,992,537 fair market value for decedent's 43,080 shares." He neither included the life insurance proceeds received by BCC (he reasoned they were offset by BCC's obligation to redeem decedent's stock) nor applied any discounts or premiums.

James R. Hitchner testified for the IRS. Hitchner's testimony was similar to Fodor's, except that he used a 5% growth rate and a 20% capitalization rate resulting in a net capitalization rate of 15%. Hitchner did not, however, deduct for the ESOP repurchase liability.

"Mr. Hitchner used two different approaches to determine BCC's asset-based value: The adjusted book value approach and the modified adjusted book value approach... As with the income approach, Mr. Hitchner did not reduce the asset-based value to reflect any ESOP repurchase obligation. He also did not indicate a final value under either approach." Hitchner gave greater weight to the modified adjusted book value approach and arrived at a "concluded" value of $7 million. To this he added the value of the life insurance proceeds, for a total value of BCC of approximately $10 million.

The Tax Court found that the 1996 buy-sell agreement was a modified version of the 1981 agreement, and ignored the agreement's set value because decedent had the unilateral ability to modify it, thus failing to satisfy the requirement that it be binding during life. The court also disregarded the agreement under § 2703, which requires that to be included in a valuation, a buy-sell agreement's terms must be "comparable to similar arrangements entered into by persons in an arm's length transaction." Here, the court concluded that the parties were "related" and had not engaged in arm's-length bargaining.

Additionally the court included the full amount of the insurance proceeds. The court determined that such proceeds are includable as nonoperating assets, and also concluded that because the buy-sell agreement had been disregarded, the issue of whether BCC's obligation under that agreement to redeem decedent's stock should offset the proceeds was not before the court.

The court essentially sustained the IRS's determination, making only a $200,000 downward adjustment to the value the IRS had placed on BCC.

Kimbell v. Commissioner (II)

Citation: 2004 U.S. App. LEXIS 9911
Court: United States Court of Appeals
State/Jurisdiction: 5th Circuit Federal
Date of Decision: May 20, 2004
Judge: Davis

In this estate tax case, the Fifth Circuit vacated and remanded the district court's granting of summary judgment to the Commissioner on the grounds that that the transfer under IRC §2036 was a bona fide sale for full and adequate consideration.

Facts

In January 1998, the decedent's living trust, along with her son and daughter-in-law, formed an LLC. The trust contributed $20,000 for a 50% interest, while the son and daughter-in-law contributed $10,000 each for a 25% interest. Later that month the decedent's living trust and the newly formed LLC formed a limited partnership. The living trust contributed $2.5 million worth of cash and assets in exchange for a 99% limited partnership interest. The LLC contributed $25,000 for a 1% general partnership interest. The decedent's son managed both the LLC and the limited partnership. Decedent continued to hold approximately $450,000 in assets for living expenses outside of the LLC and limited partnership.

Valuation evidence

The estate's federal return claimed a 49% combined minority and lack of marketability discount. The tax return concluded that the fair market value of the decedent's interest in the limited partnership was $1.2 million and the fair market value of the LLC interest was $17,000.

The IRS audited the estate and concluded that the assets were subject to IRC §2036(a), which recaptures certain assets prior to death.

Trial court findings

At trial, the IRS successfully argued that the transferred assets could be recaptured because the transaction was not a bona fide sale for full and adequate consideration. The district court, which defined an arm's-length transaction as one involving "two parties who are not related...," concluded that the transaction was not at arm's length because the parties were related and therefore the transaction was not bona fide.

The District Court accepted the IRS's conclusion, and granted partial summary judgment on that rationale.

Holding on appeal and rationale

In its opinion vacating the District Court's opinion, the Fifth Circuit stated, "[t]he government's inconsistency argument ... is a classic mixing of apples and oranges: The government is attempting to equate the venerable "willing buyer-willing seller" test of fair market value (which applies when calculating gift or estate tax) with the proper test for adequate and full consideration under § 2036(a). This conflation misses the mark: The business decision to exchange cash or other assets for a transfer-restricted, non-managerial interest in a limited partnership involves financial considerations other than the purchaser's ability to turn right around and sell the newly acquired limited partnership interest for 100 cents on the dollar. Investors who acquire such interests do so with the expectation of realizing benefits such as management expertise, security and preservation of assets, capital appreciation and avoidance of personal liability. Thus there is nothing inconsistent in acknowledging, on the one hand, that the investor's dollars have acquired a limited partnership interest at arm's length for adequate and full consideration and, on the other hand, that the asset thus acquired has a present fair market value, i.e., immediate sale potential, of substantially less than the dollars just paid—a classic informed trade-off."

The Court of Appeals concluded that the facts of the case supported the contention that the transaction was bona fide. They included:

> (1) Mrs. Kimbell retained sufficient assets outside the Partnership for her own support and there was no commingling of Partnership and her personal assets... (2) Partnership formalities were satisfied and the assets contributed to the Partnership were actually assigned to the Partnership... (3) The assets contributed to the Partnership included working interests in oil and gas properties which do require active management... (4) David Kimbell and Michael Elyea advanced several credible and unchallenged non-tax business reasons for the formation of the Partnership that could not be accomplished via Mrs. Kimbell's Trust...

Specifically, the court found that a living trust would not provide legal protection from creditors as a limited partnership would, because with the partnership, all the capital assets could be pooled, thereby reducing administrative costs and keeping all accounting functions together.

The Court of Appeals concluded that the transaction was bona fide for full and adequate consideration as a matter of law and remanded to the circuit court the issue of whether Mrs. Kimbell's interest in the Partnership was an assignee interest or limited partnership interest.

Sidney E. Smith, Jr., v. United States (I)

Citation: 2004 U.S. Dist. LEXIS 14839
Court: United States District Court
State/Jurisdiction: Western District of Pennsylvania
Date of Decision: June 30, 2004
Judge: Baxter

This case was an order resulting from motions for summary judgment. At issue in this estate tax case was the recognition of certain restrictions set out in the partnership agreement. If the restrictions were recognized and declared valid, the partnership interest would be subject to a significant marketability discount which would result in a dramatic lowering of the estate's tax burden.

In 1997, the decedent and the plaintiffs formed a family limited partnership (FLP) under Pennsylvania law. The only asset of the FLP was the entire stock of an operating company known as Erie Navigation Company.

In 1998, Mr. Smith made two gifts to his children Sidney and Jill (the plaintiffs). The IRS disputed the value of the gifts. Mr. Smith died prior to this litigation, so his estate assumed his role in the matter.

In the partnership agreement, the parties agreed to limit the price and terms in which the partnership would be required to pay a partner for their limited partnership interest if the partnership exercised its right of first refusal.

Valuation evidence

The plaintiff's valuation report reflected a marketability discount based on the limitations in the partnership agreement. However, the IRS disregarded the limitations in the partnership agreement, based on its reading of 26 U.S.C. § 2703(a), which states:

a. General Rule. - For purposes of this subtitle [governing estate, gift, and generation-skipping transfer taxes], the value of any property shall be determined without regard to -

1. any option, agreement, or other right to acquire or use the property at a price less than the fair market value of the property (without regard to such option, agreement, or right), or

2. any restriction on the right to sell or use such property.

Holding and rationale

Both parties filed motions for summary judgment. The magistrate judge concluded that the restrictions set out in the partnership agreement were subject to § 2703(a), but that it had complied with the exception that was required by § 2703(b)(1) (bona fide business arrangement test). The magistrate judge did not grant summary judgment to either party on the issue of whether the restrictive provision satisfies § 2703(b)(2) (testamentary device test). That issue remained for trial.

Senda v. Commissioner (I)

Citation: T.C. Memo. 2004-160
Court: United States Tax Court
State/Jurisdiction: Specialty Federal
Date of Decision: July 12, 2004
Judge: Cohen

In *Mark W. Senda and Michele Senda v. CIR*, T.C. Memo. 2004-160, the U.S. Tax Court considered whether the gift tax should be based on the value of limited partnership interests or the value of publicly held stock transferred to those family limited partnerships (FLPs). Between 1996 and 1998, the Sendas received approximately $6 million in MCI WorldCom stock as a result of Mark Senda's employment.

In 1998, the Sendas formed SFLP I with their three minor children. The SFLP I agreement required the annual preparation of financial statements and annual partner meetings. The Sendas transferred 28,500 MCI shares to the SFLP I and received a 10% general partnership interest and an 89.89% limited partnership interest. Each child contributed an oral accounts receivable for a .010% limited partnership interest. The oral accounts receivable were not reduced to writing, had no repayment terms and have never been paid. On the same day SFLP I was formed, the Sendas transferred a 29.94657% limited partnership interest to each child.

In 1999, the Sendas formed SFLP II, which was identical in respect to SFLP I. The Sendas transferred 18,477 MCI shares to SFLP II and received a 1% general partnership interest and a 98.97% limited partnership interest. The children received a .01% limited partnership interest in exchange for their contribution of an oral accounts receivable. On the same day as SFLP II was formed, the Sendas transferred a 17.9% limited partnership interest to each child.

The partnership formalities required under the SFLP I and II agreements were not followed. The only records maintained by the general partner were partnership tax returns and brokerage account statements. The funds expended to form the FLPs were not reflected as a liability of the partnership. Moreover, delays occurred between the gifts and the issuance of certificates of ownership.

The Sendas prepared gift tax returns for the 1998 and 1999 gifts of limited partnership interests. The gifts were valued using the pro rata value of the MCI stock less discounts for lack of marketability and minority interest. The IRS contested the values listed on the 1998 and 1999 gift tax returns. It argued that the capitalization of the FLPs and the transfer of limited partnership units to the children on the same date were indirect gifts to the children. Therefore, it sought the gift tax on the value of the MCI stock without reference to discounts. The matter proceeded to the Tax Court.

The Tax Court initially noted, "Section 25.25111(h)(1), Gift Tax Regs., provides that a transfer of property by a taxpayer to a corporation represents a gift by the taxpayer to the other shareholders of the corporation to the extent of their proportionate interests in the corporation." It further noted that it is not dispositive of an indirect gift that the contributions to the partnership and gifts of partnership units occur on the same day. Looking at the facts of this case, the Court determined that because the partnership formalities were not followed, it was unclear whether the Sendas' initial contributions to the FLPs were ever allocated to their capital accounts. Further, Mark Senda's evasive testimony regarding the contributions and limited partnership transfers showed that "petitioners were more concerned with ensuring that the beneficial ownership of the stock was transferred to the children in tax-advantaged form than they were in the formalities of FLPs." It concluded, "As a result [of the informality], however, petitioners have presented no reliable evidence that they contributed the stock to the partnerships before they transferred the partnership interests to the children. At best, the transactions were integrated ... and, in effect, simultaneous." Thus, the Tax Court concluded that the contributions of MCI stock to the FLPs were indirect gifts of the stock to the children for the purposes of sec. 2501 and 2511, and the gift tax should be levied on the value of the stock rather than the value of the limited partnership units.

This abstract originally appeared in *Valuation Case Digest*, authored by John J. Stockdale, Jr.

Estate of Josephine Thompson v. Commissioner (I)

Citation: 2004 Tax Ct. Memo LEXIS 180
Court: United States Tax Court
State/Jurisdiction: Specialty Federal
Date of Decision: July 26, 2004
Judge: Swift

The issue in this estate tax case was the value of a 20% interest in Thomas Publishing Company (TPC), a producer and seller of industrial and manufacturing business guides and directories.

Valuation evidence

Both parties presented the testimony of expert witnesses. Estate's experts, George E. Goerig, Esq., and Paul M. Wichorek, CPA, determined the value of decedent's 20% interest at the time of death was $1,749,709 or $3.59 per share. Estate's experts noted that no proper comparables were available, so they used the capitalization of income method. The experts downplayed TPC's past substantial income due to the expected downturn that would be caused by the Internet and other new technologies. Estate's experts calculated that a capitalization rate of 30.5% would be proper. See Exhibit 1.

EXHIBIT 1: ESTATE'S CAPITALIZATION RATE CALCULATION	
Risk factors	Percentage
Risk-free rate of return	6
Corporate equity risk	7.8
Small stock risk	4.7
Internet and management risk	12
Total capitalization risk	30.50%

Estate's experts then applied the 30.5% capitalization rate to the estimated after-tax sustainable income of $7,864,000, which resulted in an entity value of $25,784,000.

The experts took the undiscounted 20% interest of $5,304,000 and applied a 40% minority discount and a 45% discount for lack of marketability. Estate's experts based their minority discount percentage on a general reading of valuation texts. The discount for lack of marketability was based on four factors. (1) TPC had no interest in going public; (2) the absence of sales for prior 10 years; (3) the inability of an existing stockholder to gain control by purchasing the estate's 20% interest; and (4) inability for the potential buyer of the 20% interest to force a liquidation of the company.

IRS estimation of value

Brian C. Becker, the Commissioner's expert, determined that the date-of-death value for the 20% interest was $32.4 million. In his valuation, Becker used two methods; the discounted cash-flow (DCF) method and the comparable public company method.

Under the comparable public company method, the Commissioner's expert identified 11 companies that were appropriate comparables. Those guidelines required that the company be under SIC codes #2731 (Books: Publishing, or Publishing and Printing) or #2741 (Miscellaneous Publishing) and that they had positive cashflows for 1995-1997.

Becker took reported financial information for each company and created four ratios: stock price to net income, stock price to cashflow, stock market value to tangible and intangible assets and stock price to revenue. He calculated the median ratio for the comparables and applied the medians to TPC's averages over a 5 year period.

Under the DCF method, Becker used a 2.4% annual income growth rate and applied that to the actual net cashflow for 1997 to estimate the subsequent 5 years.

Becker then applied multiple calculations that changed with each new report. The changes were not limited to corrections in calculations. The court detailed the changes and the fact that each report contained new errors and that the changes were, "suspect, not sufficiently explained and not persuasive."

Ultimately, Becker valued the estate's 20% undiscounted interest at $46,282,500. Becker then applied a 30% discount for lack of marketability based on six factors; "(1) TPC was not publicly traded; (2) historically, TPC was profitable; (3) investment risks associated with TPC were moderate; (4) TPC had consistently paid cash dividends; (5) as of May 2, 1998, TPC held more than $137 million in net liquid assets; and (6) the estate owned the single largest block of TPC stock." This resulted in a discounted value of $32,393,000

Becker stated that he did not apply a minority discount because a minority interest is inherent when using DCF.

Holding and rationale

The court criticized both experts for their lack of experience and for the general credibility of their valuations. The court revalued the company noting that the correct valuation, "[S]hould be based on a capitalization of TPC's estimated sustainable net income for 1998-2002 calculated as an average of TPC's 1993-97 income with an additional $10 million per year in expenditures relating to projected Internet—and technology-related expenditures." The court also added $68 million of nonoperating assets.

The court also adjusted the estate's expert's capitalization rate, noting that the Internet and management presented no risk. See Exhibit 2.

EXHIBIT 2: COURT'S CAPITALIZATION RATE CALCULATION	
Risk factors	Percentage
Risk-free rate of return	6
Corporate equity risk	7.8
Small stock risk	4.7
Internet and management risk	0
Total capitalization risk	18.50%

The court then applied a 15% minority discount and a 30% discount for lack of marketability to the 20% interest resulting in a value of $13,535,240 or $27.75 a share. The court did not assess an accuracy-related penalty as was requested by the Commissioner. A comparison of the different valuations is presented in Exhibit 3.

EXHIBIT 3: VALUATIONS COMPARED		
Party	Value of 20%	Value per share
Estate	$1,749,709	$3.59
Commissioner	$32,393,000	$66.49
Court	$13,535,240	$27.75

Estate of Theodore Thompson v. Commissioner (II)

Citation: 2004 U.S. App. LEXIS 18473
Court: United States Court of Appeals
State/Jurisdiction: 3rd Circuit Federal
Date of Decision: September 1, 2004
Judge: Scirica

This appeal to the 3rd Circuit from the Tax Court, *Estate of Thompson v. Commissioner*, T.C. Memo. 2002-246, is another of the ongoing litigation efforts of IRS to destroy Family Limited Partnerships (FLPs) as an estate planning plan. If successful generally, this would be adverse to the use of business valuation appraisers in FLP situations since the use of IRC Sec. 2036(a) in essence eliminates the entity and thus the entity equity interest-based valuation discounts developed from acceptable valuation methodology.

The issue before the Third Circuit

The case involved the application of Section 2036(a)(1)(the IRS raising on brief 2036(a)(2) being disregarded by the appellate court), namely whether the decedent, in establishing two FLPs, retained lifetime control and enjoyment of the transferred assets, via an implied agreement or understanding, such that the asset value at date of death (not the FLP interests) would be includable in the decedent's estate.

Further, the question was raised as to whether 2036(a) should be inapplicable on the ground that the transfers of assets to the FLPs were "bona fide sales for full and adequate consideration in money or money's worth" and thus excluded from 2036(a) consideration. Essentially, Mr. Thompson, age 95, transferred most of his assets to two FLPs, one for each of his children and their children, in exchange for pro-rata limited partnership interests. The value conclusion of the estate's appraiser (Mr. Thompson died a couple of years later) was that his limited partnership interests should be on an Net Asset Value (NAV) basis with a 40% combined marketability and lack of control discount.

Insufficient retained assets

The Tax Court determined that 2036(a)(1) applied, and thus that no discount from NAV was permissible and the 3rd Circuit affirmed the Tax Court, noting that there was not error in interpreting the law and no clear error in the Tax Court's factual analysis and determination. Once again, as in *Harper*, T.C. Memo. 2002-121, *Estate of Reichardt*, 114 T.C. 144, and several other cases, "bad facts" contributed to the court's determination that, in substance, a testamentary plan was involved (especially with the Texas "Fortress Plan" marketing program as adopted by the decedent and his family), which is just what 2036(a) is designed to thwart in the sense of its public policy.

As the 3rd Circuit stated, "substance and not form" guides our analysis (fn 16). Plus, see *McNichol v. Commissioner*, 265 F.2d 667(1959), pointing out that the existence of formal legal structures which prevent de jure retention of benefits of the transferred property does not preclude an implicit retention of such benefits.

The Tax Court had found that the 95-year old decedent did not retain sufficient assets to support himself, that his children obtained assurances that decedent would be able to (and in fact did) withdraw assets from the FLPs to continue cash gift programs to his family, and that, if decedent ran short of funds to take care of himself, the FLPs would provide the "infusion" of money to cover his expenses, and indeed this occurred.

Thus, under the "bad facts" cases, as cited above, *Thompson* qualifies as another one. So, it appears clear that 2036(a)(1) properly was applied; but then there is the "bona fide sale" exception to 2036(a), given some "legs" by *Church*, W.D. TX, 1/18/2000, affid w/o pub. op. 268 F.3rd1063(5th Cir. 2001), Stone, T.C. Memo. 2003-309, and, of course, the recent 5th Circuit reversal of the Texas District Court in *Kimbell*, 371 F.3rd 257(2004).

The Thompson court not only referred to its own precedent on this issue in the *Estate of D'Ambrosio v. Commissioner*, 101 F.3d 309(1996), but also pointed out the differences between the cited cases and the *Thompson* case. Essentially, what the *Thompson* court determined was that the facts evidenced a solely testamentary plan, promoted by the Fortress Plan group, and thus that the "bona fide sale" exception does not apply, without however stating that it cannot apply in other better fact situations.

What does this say to tax advisors and appraisers? I believe this is a challenge to all advisors, including appraisers, that the use of pass-through entities must be real, multi-purposed, and filled with the appropriate documentation and operational monitoring that our clients should expect of advisors that are competent, communicative and careful.

Smith, John David v. United States

Citation: No. 04-20194 (5th Cir. 2004)
Court: United States Court of Appeals
State/Jurisdiction: 5th Circuit Federal
Date of Decision: November 15, 2004
Judge: King

In *John David Smith v. United States of America*, No. 04-20194 (5th Cir. November 15, 2004), the U.S. Court of Appeals for the Fifth Circuit considered whether retirement accounts should be discounted for potential future income taxes. The decedent, Louis R. Smith, held two retirement accounts through his employer at the time of his death. The accounts were funded with tax-deferred contributions and held marketable securities and bonds. Furthermore, the accounts, by their own terms, could not be sold.

The estate reported the value of the retirement accounts as of March 7, 1997, the date of death, on the estate tax return based on the account statements for that date. The accounts had a collective value of $768,358. The estate paid the tax due in full at that time. In October 1999, the estate requested a refund related to the overvaluation of the retirement accounts. On its supplemental tax return, the estate applied a 30% discount to the value of the retirement accounts to account for the income taxes that would be paid by the beneficiaries upon distribution of the retirement accounts. The IRS denied the refund. It concluded that, "[n]o discount for taxes due, now or in the future, is allowable in valuing the assets in dispute." The matter proceeded to trial before a district court, which agreed with the IRS's position and denied the refund. The estate appealed to the Fifth Circuit.

Before the Fifth Circuit, the estate argued that the District Court erred when it concluded that the inherent income tax liability that will be borne by the beneficiaries should not be taken into account when valuing the retirement accounts. It likened the inherent tax liability of the retirement account to the built-in capital gains tax liability permitted by the IRS in the valuation of closely held stock. The Fifth Circuit rejected the IRS's claims.

It initially noted that because of the tax deferred status of the retirement accounts, income tax will be due upon the eventual distribution of the retirement accounts because it is income in respect to a decedent. However, the tax liability will be offset to a degree under sec. 691 by the estate taxes paid on the value of the retirement account. The Fifth Circuit then found that the application of the "inherent" tax liability arising from the eventual distribution of the retirement accounts violated the willing buyer-willing seller standard by identifying the willing buyer as the actual beneficiary. It noted, "A hypothetical buyer would pay the value of the securities as reflected by the applicable securities exchange prices. A hypothetical seller would likewise sell the securities for that amount. Correctly applying the willing buyer-willing seller test demonstrates that a hypothetical buyer would not consider the income tax liability to a beneficiary on the income in respect of a decedent since he is not the beneficiary and thus would not be paying the income tax." It further noted that the discount size was not tied to the tax rate of the beneficiaries because the tax rate was dependent upon when the beneficiaries received the accounts. The court noted, "The Estate's argument is exactly the kind of beneficiary-specific inquiry, with the added feature of speculation on the future, that the hypothetical willing buyer-willing seller test precludes."

The court next considered the estate's argument that the tax liability here was similar to the built-in capital gains tax discount permitted when valuing closely held companies. The Fifth Circuit did not find this argument convincing. It noted that (1) the underlying assets were different (retirement accounts holding marketable securities versus closely held companies holding appreciated assets), (2) the built-in capital gains tax will be due in the hands of the hypothetical buyer while the tax liability at issue here will only arise in hands of a beneficiary, and (3) sec. 691 provides partial relief to the beneficiary while there is not a partial relief provision for the hypothetical buyer of the closely held stock. Therefore, the court concluded that the tax liability arising upon distribution of the retirement account to the beneficiaries was not similar to the capital gains tax liability attached to certain assets of closely held companies.

The Fifth Circuit concluded that no discount for potential future taxes arising from the beneficiaries' receipt of the retirement accounts should be taken into account when calculating the fair market value of the retirement accounts for estate tax purposes. In reaching this determination, the court declined to consider the estate's argument that a lack of marketability discount should apply in this case because the retirement accounts could not be sold. It declined to entertain this argument because it was not made before the district court.

This abstract originally appeared in *Valuation Case Digest*, authored by John J. Stockdale, Jr.

Estate of HA True v. Commissioner (II)

Citation: 2004 U.S. App. LEXIS 24844
Court: United States Court of Appeals
State/Jurisdiction: 10th Circuit Federal
Date of Decision: December 2, 2004
Judge: Seymour

The U.S. Court of Appeals for the Tenth Circuit considered whether the Tax Court erred when it found that the value of interests in several companies for estate tax purposes was not established by the price terms of those companies' buy-sell agreements. The decedent operated many businesses in the oil and gas and ranching industries during his life. On the date of his death, June 6, 1994, he held several interests in closely held family-owned companies. Each company had a buy-sell agreement in place. The buy-sell agreements required the active and continue participation of the stockholder or partner, prohibited a stockholder or partner from encumbering the interest, and established the price at which the interest would be redeemed should a terminating event occur. The redemption price was based on the companies' tax book value.

Two historical occurrences are relevant to the resolution of this action. The first involved a 1970s gift tax matter between the decedent and the IRS. In that action, the IRS contested the valuation of stock in two companies at issue here for gift tax purposes. The value of the stock was determined using the buy-sell agreements. The U.S. District Court of Wyoming determined that the price used in the buy-sell agreements was determinative of the value of the stock for gift tax purposes. It based its decision on *Brodrick v. Gore*, 224 F.2d 892 (10th Cir. 1955), which held "where a property interest was burdened by specific contractual provisions, and such provisions equally bound all parties to the contract in life and death, the value of such property for estate tax purposes would be based on the terms in the contract, rather than the property's fair market value."

The second significant event was the 1984 redemption of the decedent's daughter's interests in the True companies. The daughter's interests were redeemed pursuant to the terms of the buy-sell agreements for a total price of $8.6 million. Thereafter, the decedent revised his will and excluded this daughter because she had been provided for during his lifetime.

The estate reported the value of the True companies for estate tax purposes by reference to their value under the buy-sell agreements. The IRS contested those valuations. It argued that the buy-sell agreements were not determinative of the value of the interest for estate tax purposes. The matter proceeded to trial before the U.S. Tax Court. T.C. Memo. 2001-167. The Tax Court applied the price control test (also known as the *Lauder* test). If the buy-sell agreement meets all the factors of this test, it will control for estate tax purposes. The factors are "(1) the price is determinable from the agreement, (2) the terms of the agreement are binding throughout life and death, (3) the agreement is legally binding and enforceable, and (4) the agreement was entered into for bona fide business reasons and is not a testamentary substitute intended to pass on the decedent's interests for less than full and adequate consideration." The Tax Court agreed with the IRS and found that the True companies' agreements floundered on the fourth factor. It then valued the decedent's interests in the companies based on expert valuation testimony presented to it at trial. The estate appealed to the Tenth Circuit.

On appeal, the estate argued that the Tax Court erred when it concluded that the formula price in the buy-sell agreements did not establish the value of the interest for estate tax purposes. It specifically claimed that the Tax Court placed too great an emphasis on whether the agreements were testamentary devices and too little emphasis on full and adequate consideration. The estate further argued the Tax Court erred when it ignored the precedent established in *Brodrick* in favor of the price control test. It lastly argued that the IRS was collaterally estopped from challenging the determinative value of the buy-sell agreement by virtue of the 1973 decisions in the gift tax action. Alternatively, the estate argued that even if the price terms did not control in this case, the Tax Court erred when it disregarded the remaining restrictive terms in the buy-sell agreements when it determined the fair market value of the True companies.

The Tenth Circuit began with the fourth prong of the price-control test. It noted that the requirements were conjunctive and therefore, the agreement must not be a testamentary device and must represent adequate and full consideration. It noted that there was little case law interpreting this prong.

However, it provided a non-exclusive list of factors from which an inference regarding testamentary intent may be drawn. They included (1) health or age of the decedent when the agreement was entered, (2) lack of regular enforcement of the agreement, (3) the exclusion of significant assets from the agreement, (4) the arbitrary manner in which the price terms was selected, including the failure to obtain appraisals or seek professional advice, (5) the lack of negotiation between the parties in reaching the terms of the agreement, (6) whether the agreement provided for adjustment or revaluation of the price terms, and (7) whether all the parties were equally bound by the terms. Moreover, the court noted, "courts often ask whether the terms of the agreement, and the manner in which those terms were established, reflect an agreement reached by parties operating at arm's length." The Tenth Circuit determined that the terms of the agreements here were unilaterally set by the decedent without the assistance of appraisals or professional advice. It further agreed that the use of tax book value removed significant assets from the valuation equations, specifically the value of the companies' proven reserves. It also drew a negative inference from the lack of a revaluation or adjustment clause in the agreements. The Tenth Circuit found the manner in which the decedent wrote his daughter out his will following the redemption of her interest in the companies indicative of the finding that the agreements were a testamentary device. In doing so, it specifically pointed to the decedent's admission that his daughter's inheritance had been satisfied by the redemption of her interest in the companies. Thus, it found that the Tax Court was justified in drawing a negative inference from the factors in arriving at its determination that the agreement represented a testamentary device.

The Tenth Circuit then considered whether the agreement represented full and adequate consideration. It noted that even in the face of testamentary intent, the price of a buy-sell agreement will be upheld if it represents adequate and full consideration, i.e. fair market value. The estate argued that the Tax Court ignored the Tenth Circuit's precedent in *Brodrick*. The Tenth Circuit disagreed. It found that *Brodrick*, which analyzed only the binding in life and death and legal enforceability of the agreement within the context of the 1939 tax code. Sec. 2031 of the code was promulgated in 1958 and applied to estates of decedents dying after 1954. The court noted, "In the almost fifty years since sec. 20.2301-2(h) was issued, neither its construction nor its validity has ever been adversely challenged in the courts" and taxpayers frequently cite to and rely upon it. The court further noted that since the *Brodrick* decision, the Tax Court and tax law has evolved as illustrated by the price control test. It ruled, "In light of the foregoing analysis, *Brodrick* is overruled to the extent it holds that the terms in a buy-sell agreement are wholly controlling for estate tax purposes when the agreement's restrictive terms bind all parties equally at life and death. For us to constrain our analysis on this equation to the approach employed in *Brodrick* would run counter to the last fifty years of development in this area of the law."

The estate next argued that the 1973 District Court of Wyoming decision in a gift tax action collaterally estopped the IRS from challenging the buy-sell agreements. In that action, the district court determined that the price in the buy-sell agreements was determinative of the value of the interests for gift tax matters under *Brodrick*. The court found that the IRS was not estopped from making this argument because the earlier action did not address whether the buy-sell agreements served as testamentary substitutes. Thus, it found that the 1973 action did not have a preclusive effect on this action.

The Tax Court lastly considered whether the Tax Court adequately determined that the price in the buy-sell agreements did not present full and adequate consideration at the time the agreements were entered. They particularly argued that the Tax Court erred in considering only the unrestricted fair market value of the interest in answering the full and adequate consideration question. The Tenth Circuit disagreed It noted, "To allow the non-price terms in the agreements to automatically depress the value of the transferred interests for the purpose of determining whether they were transferred for adequate consideration would re-validate the controlling force of the restrictions from which a testamentary inference has already been draw. Proceeding in such a manner would presume the viability of the agreements whose validity is at issue for valuation purposes." However, the Tenth Circuit noted that the Tax Court permitted a lack of marketability discount when determining the fair market value of two of the companies even though "the [Tax] court did not specifically attribute the discount to any of the terms in the buy-sell agreements." The discounts were based on an expert report prepared near in time to when the agreements were entered. The Tenth Circuit concluded, "Through its use of a lack-of marketability discount the tax court appropriately gave weight to taxpayers' intent to keep these companies within the family." A discount for lack of marketability was not applied to the remaining companies because the "taxpayers did not present to the tax court any evidence regarding the four remaining buy-sell agreements to prove they represented adequate consideration at the time the True family members entered into them."

Lastly, the estate argued that the Tax Court's valuation of the True companies failed to adequately take into account the non-price terms of the buy-sell agreements. The Tenth Circuit noted, "After determining the price terms in the True company buy-sell agreements did not control the values of the True companies, the tax court also held the 'restrictive provisions of the buy-sell agreements (including but not limited to the formula price) are to be disregarded' for estate and gift tax valuation purposes." The Tenth Circuit noted, "This case law does generally indicate that the restrictive impact of a buy-sell agreement should be considered as a factor in valuing the interests for estate and gift tax purposes even if its specific price terms are held not to be controlling. We agree that the existence of such a restrictive agreement and the bona fide business reasons supporting it should be acknowledged when determining the fair market value of an interest. A willing buyer and a willing seller with knowledge of all the relevant facts surrounding the exchange would certainly take this approach. Despite the tax court's seemingly ardent language to the contrary, however, we are not convinced the court ignored the restrictive nature of the True company buy-sell agreements in the course of valuing the interests at issue here." It found that the court applied a lack of marketability discount when it valued each True entity, which considered the family's commitment to family control as well as the depressive effect of state partnership law. The Tenth Circuit conclude, "Where a court's task is to determine the value of interests on which a willing buyer and willing seller would agree, its analysis would be distorted by giving explicit weight and recognition to buy-sell restrictions whose testamentary purpose has been established." Therefore, it found, "The tax court's application of a general marketability discount adequately took such limitations into account." Thus, it affirmed the Tax Court's valuations.

This abstract originally appeared in *Valuation Case Digest*, authored by John J. Stockdale, Jr.

Estate of Noble v. Commissioner

Citation: 2005 Tax Ct. Memo LEXIS 3
Court: United States Tax Court
State/Jurisdiction: Specialty Federal
Date of Decision: January 6, 2005
Judge: Laro

The issue in this estate tax case focuses on the value of decedent's share of a bank. At the date of death, September 2, 1996, decedent owned an 11.6% interest in Glenwood State Bank. On decedent's estate tax return, the estate valued the interest, as of the date of death, at $903,988. The IRS sent a notice of deficiency asserting the interest was worth $1.1 million.

Judge Laro, in his opinion, commented on the lack of factual testimony submitted, noting that:

> Neither party called a fact witness to testify at trial. (Each expert who testified at trial testified solely as an expert and not as both a fact witness and an expert witness.) Nor did either party introduce at trial any exhibit other than the expert reports, the two stipulated exhibits, and a statement listing one of the expert's qualifications. Most of the facts which we find in this case come from the stipulation of facts and the two accompanying exhibits. While the parties invite the Court to find additional facts solely from data relied upon by the experts in forming their expert opinions, we decline to do so.

Valuation evidence

On its estate tax form, the estate valued the shares as of their book value. Decedent owned 116 shares out of 1000 shares outstanding. The book value for each share, minus a 45% minority interest discount, equaled $903,988. The rest of the shares were owned by the Glenwood Bancorporation, which was controlled by the Dean family (a 69% interest). The Dean family did not share any family relationship with the decedent.

Prior to the valuation date, Glenwood Bancorporation had bought two blocks of stock paying $1,000 per share for ten shares and $1,500 per share for seven shares. The court opinion did not elaborate as to the circumstances surrounding these two sales.

On December 31, 1996, which was after the death of the decedent and after the valuation date, a member of the Dean family offered to buy the shares for $878,004. The estate declined the offer. On October 24, 1997, the estate sold the shares to Glenwood Bancorporation for $1.1 million.

The Dean family based its initial offer on an appraisal prepared by Dennis R. Hein on behalf of Seim Johnson. Hein discounted his value of the shares with a 29% minority interest discount and a 35% discount for lack of marketability to arrive at the offered price of $878,004.

IRS's expert

After overcoming some evidentiary hurdles, the IRS proffered the testimony of their expert William C. Herber, whose report was referred to as the Shenehon report. Herber valued the shares by considering four methods of valuation: (1) book value, (2) discounted cash flow, (3) public guideline market method, and (4) the private guideline market method (transaction method). Herber then applied a 15% minority discount and a 30% discount for lack of marketability. Judge Laro summarized Herber's testimony (see Exhibit 1):

> The book value method reflected Glenwood Bank's reported equity as of June 30, 1996, the most current data available as of decedent's date of death. The discounted cashflow method applied a 14.5-percent discount rate to Glenwood Bank's projected annual income for each of the years during a 10-year period ending in December 2005 and an 11.5-percent rate to the bank's residual value. The public guideline market method reflected prices paid for companies which were engaged in a business similar to Glenwood Bank's and whose stock was actively traded in a public market. The private guideline market method reflected transactions involving acquisitions of privately held banks comparable to Glenwood Bank.

EXHIBIT 1: HERBER VALUATION

	Book value	Discounted cash flow	Public guide-line market	Private guide-line market
Value before discounts	$14,135,000	$11,100,000	$14,000,000	$18,200,000
15% minority interest discount	$2,120,250	n/a	n/a	$2,730,000
Marketable minority interest value	$12,014,750	$11,100,000	$14,000,000	$15,470,000
30% lack of market-ability discount	$3,604,425	$3,330,000	$4,200,000	$4,641,000
Nonmarketable minor-ity interest value	$8,410,325	$7,770,000	$9,800,000	$10,829,000
Subject percentage interest	11.6	11.6	11.6	11.6
Resulting value of subject interest	$975,598	$901,320	$1,136,800	$1,256,164
The average of the resulting values is: $1,067,470.50 [($975,598 + $901,320 + $1,136,800 + $1,256,164)/4].				

Estate's experts

Hein's report was presented by the taxpayer as evidence of value. Hein reaffirmed his report stating that his valuation in 1996 was still his opinion at the time of trial. The estate presented the report of Janet M. Labenz as a rebuttal to Herber's report. The Labenz report "addressed the differences between the Shenehon report and the Seim Johnson report."

Christopher Mercer also submitted a report on the behalf of taxpayer. The Mercer report concluded that the fair market value of the 11.6% interest was $841,000. Judge Laro summarized Mercer's approach. See Exhibit 2 for the resulting values derived under these five methods.

> The Mercer report generally arrived at this fair market value through a two-step process. First, the Mercer report ascertained the marketable minority value for Glenwood Bank by considering five methods (a transaction value method, a net asset value method, a discounted future earnings method using a 10-percent earnings growth and a 20-percent earnings growth, and two guideline company methods, one using a regional peer group, the other a high-equity assets group, and both using capitalized earnings and capitalized book value). The transaction method recognized the two sales of Glenwood Bank stock happening before the valuation date and reflected the $1,500-per-share price paid in the more recent second sale. The net asset value method reflected Glenwood Bank's reported equity as of June 30, 1996, as adjusted to take into account an unrealized $128,000 gain in bond portfolio and a 38-percent related tax adjustment ($48,640). The discounted future earnings method reflected earnings growth rates of 10% and 20% and a present value rate of 14.1%. The guideline company methods reflected a regional group of 11 financial institutions similar to Glenwood Bank and a nationwide group of 19 banks that reported total assets of less than $1 billion and an asset/equity ratio of greater than 12%.
>
> The Mercer report gave no weight to the transaction value method, the net asset value method, or the discounted future earnings method, and ascertained the value of the marketable minority interest to be $12,721,000 by averaging the other four amounts ($8,306,000 + $17,174,000 + $8,543,000 + $16,860,000)/4 = $12,720,750) and rounding the resulting average to the nearest thousand. The Mercer report as a second step in the valuation process then ascertained the applicable fair market value of decedent's 11.6-percent interest by applying a 43-percent lack of marketability discount to the marketable minority interest value of $12,721,000 ($12,721,000 x 43% = $5,470,030) and multiplying the resulting rounded number of $7,251,000 ($12,721,000 - $5,470,030 = $7,250,970) by 11.6%.

EXHIBIT 2: MERCER VALUATION	
Method	**Resulting Value**
Transaction value	$1,500,000
Net asset value	$14,124,000
Discounted future earnings:	
10% earnings growth	$11,364,000
20% earnings growth	$14,224,000
Guideline company regional peer group:	
Capitalized earnings	$8,306,000
Capitalized book value	$17,174,000
Guideline company high/equity assets group:	
Capitalized earnings	$8,543,000
Capitalized book value	$16,860,000

The Mercer report applied a 43% discount for lack of marketability. This amount was derived from Mercer's quantitative marketability discount model that the court noted was "adopted and advocated by Mercer."

Mercer noted that he ignored the post-death event because a hypothetical investor would not have known about it at decedent's death.

Holding and rationale

Judge Laro, after an extensive review of the law and different methods of valuation, valued the interest at its post-death sale price, minus inflation. The court noted that there had not been any material change in circumstances between the sale date and the date of death. The court reasoned that, "An event occurring after a valuation date, even if unforeseeable as of the valuation date, also may be probative of the earlier valuation to the extent that it is relevant to establishing the amount that a hypothetical willing buyer would have paid a hypothetical willing seller for the subject property as of the valuation date. Unforeseeable subsequent events which fall within this latter category include evidence, such as we have here."

Estate of Bongard v. Commissioner

Citation: 124 T.C. 95, 2005 U.S. Tax Ct. LEXIS 8
Court: United States Tax Court
State/Jurisdiction: Specialty Federal
Date of Decision: March 15, 2005
Judge: Goeke

In this estate tax case, there were two issues: whether pursuant to IRC Sections 2035(a) and 2036(a), (b) the gross estate should have included:

1. shares Wayne Bongard (decedent) transferred to a holding company and

2. the holding company's membership units Bongard transferred to a family limited partnership (FLP).

Bongard was a successful businessperson who started Empak, Inc. (Empak). He transferred all his shares in Empak to WCB Holdings, LLC (WCB Holdings). Bongard then transferred his WCB Holdings membership units to the Bongard Family Limited Partnership (BFLP) for a 99% limited partnership interest therein.

From its inception until Bongard's death, BFLP did not perform any activities, never acted to diversify its assets, or make any distributions. The WCB Holdings membership units in BFLP were nonvoting, and Bongard determined whether the Empak shares held by WCB Holdings would be redeemed. WCB Holdings did not redeem any of its class B membership units held by BFLP before his death.

The IRS claimed a deficiency of $52,878,785. It determined, among other things, that the 5,134,629 shares of Empak stock decedent transferred to WCB Holdings were includable in Bongard's gross estate because he had retained sections 2035(a) and 2036(a) and/or (b) rights and interests in the transferred property.

The court found that Bongard received an interest that represented adequate and full consideration reducible to money value, and that the transaction was motivated by a legitimate and significant nontax purpose—positioning the company so that it could obtain additional capital through either a public or private offering ("corporate liquidity event"). Therefore, the court ruled that this transfer had satisfied the bona fide sale exception of Section 2036(a).

The court rejected the IRS's argument that an arm's-length transaction cannot occur between related parties, noting that the bona fide sale exception has not been limited to transactions involving unrelated parties.

The court also rejected the argument that the formation of WCB Holdings was not a bona fide sale because there was not a true pooling of assets. In stead, the court concluded that when WCB Holdings was capitalized, the members' capital accounts were properly credited and maintained, WCB Holdings's funds were not commingled with Bongard's, and all distributions during his life were pro rata.

For these reasons, the court determined that the transaction resulted in a true pooling of assets.

However, because the court found that estate tax savings did play an important role in motivating the second transfer—the transfer of Bongard's membership units in WBC Holdings to BFLP—and because the court found that an implied agreement existed that allowed Bongard to retain the enjoyment of the property held by BFLP, the court held that under Section 2036(a)(1), Bongard's gross estate included the value of the membership units.

The court rejected the estate's contention that BFLP had been established to provide another layer of credit protection for Bongard (the holding company provided this already) and to facilitate gift-giving. The court focused on the fact that the partnership made only one gift, never diversified its assets during Bongard's life, never had an investment plan, and never functioned as a business enterprise or otherwise engaged in any meaningful economic activity.

Thus, the transfer did not satisfy the bona fide sale exception, but did come within Section 2036(a)'s test for an implied agreement based on the retention of benefits of the transferred property.

Estate of Bigelow v. Commissioner (I)

Citation: T.C. Memo 2005-65, 2005 Tax Ct. Memo LEXIS 65
Court: United States Tax Court
State/Jurisdiction: Specialty Federal
Date of Decision: March 30, 2005
Judge: Colvin

In this estate tax case, the issue was whether the value of real property transferred to a family limited partnership (FLP) was included in Bigelow's (decedent's) gross estate.

Prior to her death, Bigelow established a trust, which transferred real property—but not liabilities totaling $450,000 secured by the property—to Spindrift Associates, Ltd., an FLP that Bigelow formed with her children right after she had a stroke. The trust was the FLP's sole general partner. After the transfer, Bigelow was left with an insufficient amount of income to meet her living expenses or to satisfy her liability for the indebtedness. Her sole purposes in establishing the FLP were to facilitate gift giving and to reduce estate tax.

The court held that the value of the property should be included in Bigelow's gross estate under IRC Section 2036.

The court found that Bigelow's use of partnership income to replace the income lost as a result of the transfer of the property to the FLP showed that there was an implied agreement between Bigelow and her children that she would retain the right to the income from the property.

In determining that the FLP transaction did not constitute a bona fide sale for adequate and full consideration, the court determined that the transfer of the property was not made in good faith, because it left Bigelow unable to meet her financial obligations or to pay expenses. Additionally, the FLP's failure to respect partnership formalities evidenced a lack of good faith.

Finally, the transfer did not provide and had no potential to provide any non-tax benefit to Bigelow, because management of the assets did not change as a result of the transfer, there was no pooling of assets, and, as the FLP's sole general partner, the trust did not get any additional protection from creditors. The court found that the fact that the transfer facilitated Bigelow's ability to make gifts to her children and grandchildren was not a bona fide purpose under § 2036 for establishing the FLP.

Estate of Korby v. Commissioner (I)

Citation: T.C. Memo 2005-103; 2005 Tax Ct. Memo LEXIS 102
Court: United States Tax Court
State/Jurisdiction: Specialty Federal
Date of Decision: May 10, 2005
Judge: Goeke

In this estate tax case, the issue was whether the value of assets contributed to a family limited partnership (FLP) was includable in the decedent's gross estate; the Tax Court held it was.

The FLP

Austin (decedent) and Edna Korby had four sons. Dennis, one of the sons, along with Austin, were trustees of the Korby's living trust, which gave Austin and Edna the authority to control and direct payments from the living trust, add or remove living trust property, and amend or revoke the living trust. Most of the Korby's assets were transferred to the trust.

After the living trust was formed and funded, Korby Properties, A Limited Partnership (KPLP), an FLP, was established. All Korby family members signed the partnership agreement, along with the living trust, which served as the general partner. The KPLP agreement provided for management fees to be paid to the general partner, which also had the power to determine the amount of such fees. The KPLP agreement also required KPLP to reimburse the general partner for "all reasonable and necessary business expenses incurred in managing and administering the partnership."

Austin contributed 58.46% of KPLP's assets, Edna contributed 38.26% of KPLP's assets, Austin and Edna's sons contributed 1.28% of KPLP's assets, and the living trust contributed 2% of KPLP's assets. After the transfers to the living trust and KPLP, Austin and Edna did not have any bank accounts open in their own names. Edna was suffering from dementia, and Austin had had a stroke, so they incurred significant medical expenses.

The living trust paid many of the Korby's household expenses, medical expenses, some living expenses, and occasional cash payments to Austin . To pay all these expenses, the living trust received cash payments from KPLP and the Korby's Social Security payments. KPLP paid the utility and heating bills, property taxes, and insurance for the Korby's residence and paid for subscriptions to newspapers and periodicals.

After Austin's death, the IRS issued a deficiency notice to the estate, claiming that the full values of the assets held by KPLP and the living trust were includable in the gross estate under IRC sections 2036 and 2038. The Tax Court agreed.

Holding and rationale

The court concluded that an implied agreement existed between Austin, on his own behalf and on behalf of Edna, and the sons, that after the assets were transferred to KPLP, income from the assets would continue to be available to Austin and Edna for as long as they needed income. The court based this opinion on the fact that Austin and Edna could have been expected to incur significant medical expenses in the future, but only retained relatively insignificant assets to provide for such expenses, as well as regular living expenses. Also a factor in the court's opinion was that KPLP distributed significant percentages of its income to the living trust, which totaled at least 52.6% of the Austin and Edna's income.

The court rejected the argument that these were management fees because: they were not used by Dennis (as co-trustee); no management contract had been executed; the fees were disproportionately large to the services rendered; and no self-employment income was reported for the fees. The court also used many of these factors, as well as Austin's unilateral decisions surrounding the establishment and operation of KPLP, to arrive at its conclusion that the bona fide sale exception to Section 2036 was not met.

The court held that 58.46% of KPLP's value was includable in the gross estate.

Estate of Abraham v. Commissioner (II)

Citation: 2005 U.S. App. LEXIS 9540
Court: United States Court of Appeals
State/Jurisdiction: 1st Circuit Federal
Date of Decision: May 25, 2005
Judge: Lynch

The First Circuit affirmed all aspects of a Tax Court determination unfavorable to the *Estate of Ida Abraham* (the Estate).

The Tax Court, applying IRC Section 2036, had ruled that (1) the Estate had underreported estate taxes due because the decedent had an interest in certain property purportedly transferred to her three children by gift and purchase in three family limited partnerships (FLPs), (2) the purchase of the decedent's interests by the children were not bona fide sales for adequate and full consideration, and (3) that the decedent retained rights in the income from the total property.

Michael Lipof had valued the FLPs by applying a 30% to 40% discount to the asset value of each FLP. The Tax Court ignored these discounted values, and, instead, included in the gross estate the underlying fair market value of the commercial real estate held by each FLP.

The Court of Appeals found that the Tax Court correctly placed the burden of proof on the Estate because the IRS's Notice of Deficiency had not failed to describe the basis on which the IRS relied to establish a deficiency. One of the Estate's arguments in this regard was that the Notice failed to explain how the IRS valued the FLP interests at the fair market values of the underlying real estate.

The court found that although the Notice did not explain, step-by-step, why the IRS wanted to include in the gross estate the total value of the underlying real estate, it was clear that the Estate understood the IRS's theory. The Estate's own computations began with, and then applied discounts to, the fair market value of the underlying real estate. The court reasoned that read in this context, the clear implication of the Notice was that (1) the IRS sought to include 100% of the FLPs in the gross estate, and (2) the IRS valued the FLPs at the value of the underlying real estate, as the Estate itself did in its computations.

Accordingly, the court concluded that since the IRS's valuation was based on the Estate's own appraisal, it was entitled to a presumption of correctness, and that to the extent that any discounts might have been appropriate due to the fact that the assets were in the form of FLPs, the burden was on the Estate to show the appropriateness of such discounts.

The court affirmed all other aspects of the Tax Court decision.

Estate of Schutt v. Commissioner

Citation: T.C. Memo 2005-126; 2005 Tax Ct. Memo LEXIS 126
Court: United States Tax Court
State/Jurisdiction: Specialty Federal
Date of Decision: May 26, 2005
Judge: Wherry

Schutt, I, Business Trust (Schutt I) and Schutt, II, Business Trust (Schutt II), both Delaware business trusts, were formed in 1998. The trusts were capitalized by the contribution thereto of stock by Charles Porter Schutt (decedent) through a revocable trust and by Wilmington Trust Company (WTC) as trustee of various trusts created for the benefit of decedent's children and grandchildren. At his death in 1999, decedent held through the revocable trust a 45.236% interest in Schutt I and a 47.336% interest in Schutt II.

As of the valuation date, the underlying asset value of Schutt I was $65,273,495, of which the revocable trust's proportionate share was $29,527,314. The underlying asset value of Schutt II was $28,504,626, of which the revocable trust's proportionate share was $13,493,064. The value reported for the gross estate was $61,590,355.08, which included $15,837,295.45 and $7,237,104.56 for the revocable trust's interests in Schutt I and Schutt II, respectively.

The IRS issued a notice of deficiency, determining that the discounts applied in valuing the interests in Schutt I and Schutt II were excessive. The IRS also asserted that the full market value of the underlying assets contributed by the revocable trust to Schutt I and Schutt II should be included in decedent's gross estate under IRC Sections 2036(a) and 2038.

Holding and rationale

The Tax Court held that the transfers of stock to Schutt I and Schutt II were bona fide sales for adequate and full consideration within the meaning of Sections 2036(a) and 2038, such that the value of the transferred assets did not have to be included in decedent's gross estate under these statutes.

Transfers made for non-tax reasons

A key finding by the court was that decedent's transfer was made for other than estate tax advantage, namely, to ensure the perpetuation of decedent's "buy and hold" investment philosophy for the purpose of protecting his family's wealth. The court also found significant that by using the business trusts, decedent was able to apply this philosophy to the stock of the WTC trusts. Decedent's motives were well-documented by his estate planning advisers.

Despite this evidence of decedent's motives, the IRS maintained that tax savings through valuation discounts constituted the dominant reason for formation of Schutt I and II. The IRS characterized the issue of valuation discounts as having "dominated" the early discussions concerning the formation of a new entity. The IRS also noted that decedent and his advisers initially contemplated only transferring stock from the revocable trust to a business trust, and emphasized that the subsequent decision to involve the WTC trusts served a tax purpose of making available minority, as well as marketability discounts.

The court rejected these assertions, finding that although it was clear that estate tax implications were recognized and considered in the initial stages of the planning process, the record failed to reflect that such issues predominated in decedent's thinking and desires. What may have originally been approached as a relatively routine estate planning transaction, rapidly developed into an opportunity and vehicle for addressing decedent's more fundamental concerns.

Bona fide sale

Finally, the court also determined that other factors indicative of a bona fide sale were that the contributed property was actually transferred to Schutt I and II in a timely manner; that entity and personal assets were not commingled; that decedent was not financially dependent on distributions from Schutt I and II, retaining sufficient assets outside of the business trusts amply to support his needs and lifestyle; and that decedent did not effectively stand on both sides of the transactions.

Adequate consideration

Given these circumstances, the court also held that the discounted value attributable to entity interest valuation principles was not per se to be equated with inadequate consideration, and rejected the IRS's contention that the transactions featured prohibited value recycling. The key here, the court reasoned, was that others contributed more than half of the property funding the entities, and that, therefore, decedent was not merely recycling his shareholdings.

Estate of Jelke v. Commissioner (I)

Citation: T.C. Memo 2005-131, 2005 Tax Ct. Memo LEXIS 128
Court: United States Tax Court
State/Jurisdiction: Specialty Federal
Date of Decision: May 31, 2005
Judge: Gerber

The issues in this estate tax case were whether built-in capital gains tax liability should be discounted (indexed) to account for time value, and the appropriate discounts for lack of marketability and control.

Facts

Jelke's (decedent's) gross estate included a 6.44% interest in a closely held corporation, Commercial Chemical Co. (CCC), the assets of which consisted primarily of marketable securities. CCC had been in existence for many years, was well managed, and had a relatively high rate of return in the form of annual dividends coupled with capital appreciation of approximately 23% annually for the 5-year period before Jelke's death. Also during this 5-year period, there was no intent to completely liquidate CCC, and its securities turnover (sales) averaged approximately 6% annually.

At the time of Jelke's death, the securities had a market value of approximately $178 million and a built-in capital gain tax liability of approximately $51 million if all of the securities were to be sold on the valuation date. The net asset value of CCC without consideration of the effect of the built-in capital gain tax liability was approximately $188 million.

The estate contended that the $188 million value should be reduced by the entire $51 million before considering discounts for lack of control and marketability. The IRS contended that the built-in capital gain tax liability should be discounted (indexed) to account for time value because it would be incurred in the future rather than immediately. Under the IRS approach, the reduction for built-in capital gain tax liability would be approximately $21 million.

The parties also disagreed about the discounts for lack of control and marketability. The estate applied 20% and 35% additional discounts to Jelke's stock interest for lack of control and marketability, respectively.

Holding and rationale—built-in gains treatment

The court's guiding principle was that the determination of the fair market value of a closely held company may be effectively established by reference to arm's-length sales of the company within a reasonable time before or after the valuation date. Absent an arm's-length sale, fair market value is normally determined using the hypothetical willing buyer and seller model. Implicit in that model is the axiom that the seller would attempt to maximize profit and the buyer to minimize cost.

The estate attempted to support its position through its expert, William Frazier, who purported to use a net asset approach to valuation, which the estate contended requires an assumption of liquidation on the valuation date. The IRS attempted to support its position through its expert, Israel Shaked, who contended that an assumption of liquidation was not appropriate and that the reduction should be calculated on the basis of CCC's established history of securities turnover.

The court agreed with the IRS. After a comprehensive review of case law on this issue, the Tax Court found that a hypothetical buyer of CCC would, in most respects, be analogous to an investor/buyer of a mutual fund, especially given that the investor here would be a 6.44% investor who, inherently, would be unable to cause liquidation.

Also significant was that the record evidenced no intention on any of CCC's holders to liquidate it. Thus, the court concluded that the hypothetical seller of CCC shares would not accept a price that was reduced for possible tax on all built-in capital gain knowing that CCC sold or turned over only a small percentage of its portfolio annually. For these reasons, the court held that an assumption of complete liquidation on the valuation date was inapplicable.

Frazier contended that irrespective of the unlikelihood of liquidation, there should be a dollar-for-dollar decrease for the built-in capital gain tax liability, representing the present value of that liability because the liability would increase over time. In that regard, the estate argued that Shaked incorrectly assumed that the stock would not appreciate.

In addressing this argument, Shaked explained that the need to discount the built-in capital gain tax liability is analogous to the need to discount carryforward losses because they cannot be used until years after the valuation year. Shaked's approach was to calculate the built-in capital gain tax liability by determining when it would likely be incurred.

The court agreed with Shaked's approach of discounting the built-in capital gain tax liability to reflect that it would be incurred after the valuation date. Accordingly, the court agreed that the tax liabilities would have to be indexed to account for the time value of money.

The court found that Shaked's asset turnover rate reasonably predicted the period over which CCC's assets would be disposed of and thus built-in capital gain tax liability would likely be incurred.

Based on this turnover rate, the court found it appropriate to use a 16-year period of recognition for the tax liability attributable to the built-in capital gain, and concluded that a 13.2% discount rate was reasonable. This holding resulted in an 11.2% reduction in value for built-in capital gain tax liability.

Discounts for lack of control and marketability

Frazier discounted decedent's CCC interest by 25% for lack of control; Shaked applied a 5% discount. Frazier based his discount on the assumption that CCC was most like a closed-end and not widely traded investment fund holding publicly traded securities. In contrast, Shaked's analysis began with an average discount (8.61 percent) for closed-end funds, and reduced this because he claimed that CCC outperformed the comparables used by Frazier. The court adopted a 10% lack of control discount.

Frazier used a 35% discount for lack of marketability, and Shaked used a 10% discount. Frazier considered studies of operating companies with a minimum restriction on resale of at least two years.

Shaked based his analysis on the *Mandelbaum* factors. He believed that CCC's well-diversified portfolio resulted in low price volatility and was a factor in applying a low discount for marketability. In addition, since CCC's assets were marketable securities, it would be easier to find a willing buyer for this company than for a riskier company whose performance was more speculative.

The court disagreed with both experts and applied a 15% discount for lack of marketability.

Estate of Baird v. Commissioner (II)

Citation: 2005 U.S. App. LEXIS 13905
Court: United States Court of Appeals
State/Jurisdiction: 5th Circuit Federal
Date of Decision: July 11, 2005
Judge: Jolly

In this estate tax case, the issue was whether the IRS's position in applying discounts to fractional, non-controlling interests in timberland was justified for purposes of determining whether taxpayers were entitled to administrative and litigation costs. The Tax Court had ruled that the IRS's position was justified so that taxpayers were not entitled to their costs.

John Baird's estate included a 14/65 undivided interest in a Louisiana trust that held 2,957 acres of timberland in 16 noncontiguous tracts, and his wife's estate included a 17/65 interest in the same trust.

Both estates claimed a 50% fractionalization discount from the pro rata fair market value of the timberland. A fractionalization discount accounts for the fact that the sum of all fractional interests in property is worth less than the whole. It also takes into account the restrictions on sale or transfer of the property when more than one person or entity holds undivided fractional interests in the property.

The IRS took the position that the only discount allowable when valuing the estates' non-controlling fractional interests was the cost of partitioning the property based on the estimated costs of a hypothetical partition in kind in an IRS forester's report, which amounted to approximately three percent. The estates protested this position, criticizing the forester's use of transactions involving sales of controlling interests, and explaining the risks and difficulties involved with partitioning the 16 tracts. Reports by James A. Young, Lewis C. Peters, and James C. Steele, III, pointed out that the IRS position was not in line with a substantial body of data suggesting that the discounts for undivided interests should be significantly higher than the pro rata share of the estimated cost of partition.

In a prior decision, the Tax Court held that the taxpayers established 55% as the average amount by which non-controlling fractional interests in Louisiana timberland were discounted and that an additional five% discount was appropriate due to peculiar circumstances with respect to the decedents' remaining family members (for a total of 60%).

The Fifth Circuit reversed and remanded on the issue of costs. It found that before the IRS issued the notices of deficiency, the taxpayers had provided enough information to the IRS to alert it to the fact that the in-kind partition described in the forester's report was not viable. The court also concluded that the IRS's estimate of the costs of a hypothetical in-kind partition was speculative and unsupported.

The Fifth Circuit, therefore, concluded that the Tax Court abused its discretion by determining that the IRS satisfied its burden of proof of substantial justification for its position.

Estate of Strangi v. Commissioner (IV)

Citation: 2005 U.S. App. LEXIS 14497
Court: United States Court of Appeals
State/Jurisdiction: 5th Circuit Federal
Date of Decision: July 15, 2005
Judge: Jolly

In this last installment of the *Strangi* case, which has been going back and forth between the Tax Court and the Fifth Circuit, the Fifth Circuit affirmed the Tax Court's decision on remand that Strangi had retained enjoyment of the assets he had transferred to Strangi Family Limited Partnership (SFLP) and Stranco, Inc. through an implied agreement, and, thus, that the transferred assets were properly included in his estate under IRC Section 2036(a) for estate tax purposes. The Fifth Circuit also upheld the Tax Court's determination that the bona fide sale exception to § 2036(a) was inapplicable.

Implied agreement

The benefits retained by Strangi included periodic payments made prior to Strangi's death on his behalf, his continued use of the transferred house, and the post-death payment of various debts and expenses. The Tax Court concluded that Strangi and the other shareholders of Stranco, i.e., the Strangi children, had an implicit agreement by which Strangi would retain the enjoyment of his property after the transfer to SFLP.

The Tax Court found that SFLP's distribution of over $100,000 to pay for funeral expenses, estate administration expenses, specific bequests and various personal debts that Strangi had incurred provided strong circumstantial evidence of an understanding between Strangi and his children that "partnership" assets would be used to meet Strangi's expenses. The Fifth Circuit agreed, noting that the "possession or enjoyment" of one's assets is the assurance that they will be available to pay various debts and expenses upon one's death, which is what Strangi received.

The Tax Court also found "highly probative" Strangi's "continued physical possession of his residence after its transfer to SFLP." The Estate argued that SFLP charged Strangi rent on the home. Although the rent charge was recorded in SFLP's books in 1994, the Estate made no actual payments until 1997. The Fifth Circuit found that even assuming that the belated rent payment was not a post hoc attempt to recast Strangi's use of the house, such a deferral, in itself, provided a substantial economic benefit. Therefore, it concluded that the Tax Court did not err in considering Strangi's continued occupancy of his home as evidence of an implied agreement.

Finally, the Fifth Circuit concluded that the Tax Court did not err in finding an implied agreement based on evidence that Strangi lacked liquid assets—other than $762—but had $17,000 in monthly expenses; the court believed some arrangement to meet his expenses must have been made. As the court said:

> In sum, upon creation of SFLP, Strangi retained assets barely sufficient to meet his own living expenses assuming he was never required to pay rent, estate administration costs, outstanding personal debts, funeral expenses, or taxes. At the same time, Strangi began receiving substantial monthly payments out of SFLP's coffers. Given these circumstances, we cannot say that the Tax Court clearly erred in holding that Strangi and his children had some implicit understanding by which Strangi would continue to use his assets as needed, and therefore retain "possession or enjoyment" within the meaning of § 2036(a)(1).

No bona fide sale exception

Section 2036(a) provides an exception for any transfer of property that is a "bona fide sale for an adequate and full consideration in money or money's worth." The Tax Court held that Strangi's transfer of assets to SFLP lacked a substantial non-tax purpose, and, that, therefore, the bona fide sale exception did not apply.

The Fifth Circuit again found that the Tax Court's ruling was not clearly erroneous. The appellate court found that none of the five non-tax rationales proffered by the Estate were supported by the evidence. These rationales were: (1) deterring potential tort litigation by Strangi's former housekeeper; (2) deterring a potential will contest (3) persuading a corporate executor to decline to serve; (4) creating a joint investment vehicle for the partners; and (5) permitting centralized, active management of working interests owned by Strangi.

The Fifth Circuit emphasized that it was receiving the case after a full trial on the merits, and that the Tax Court had presented a litany of circumstantial evidence to support its conclusions. Because it was bound to review the Tax Court only for clear error, the Fifth Circuit could not disturb the Tax Court's findings of fact unless it was convinced that the Tax Court had made a mistake. Finding no clear mistakes, the court affirmed.

Sidney E. Smith, Jr., v. United States (II)

Citation: No. 02-264-ERIE (W.D. PA 2005)
Court: United States District Court
State/Jurisdiction: Western District of Pennsylvania
Date of Decision: July 22, 2005
Judge: Baxter

In *Sidney E. Smith, III, et al. v. United States of America,* No. 02-264 ERIE (W.D. PA July 22, 2005), a magistrate for the U.S. District Court of the Western District of Pennsylvania considered a second motion for summary judgment regarding the application of sec. 2703 to disregard decrements to marketability from a buy-sell agreement. The plaintiff is the executor of his father's estate. In 1997, the father and the plaintiff established a family limited partnership (FLP) and transferred 100% of their stock in a closely held company to the FLP. The FLP contained a provision governing the purchase and sale of FLP interests. Under the agreement, the FLP held a right of first refusal on the transfer of an interest in itself. Furthermore, the agreement provided the FLP, in the event it enforced its right of first refusal, a below fair market value purchase price payable over fifteen years and carrying interest at the AFR for long-term debt on the date of closing.

In 1998, the decedent made two gifts of limited partnership units to his children. The value reported on the gift tax return included a discount for lack of marketability that was in part attributable to the favorable price terms of the buy-sell provision. The IRS contested the lack of marketability discount based on sec. 2703, which permits the IRS to disregard buy-sell provisions that permit the repurchase of stock at less than fair market value or restrict the right to sell or use the property. It argued that the favorable terms of the buy-sell provision fit within that definition.

In 2004, the magistrate held that sec. 2703 applied to buy-sell provisions written into an FLP agreement. However, it declined to award summary judgment to either party because the record did not conclusively show that this arrangement was or was not like agreements entered into at arm's-length by third parties as required under the sec. 2703 (b)(3) exclusion. After subsequent discovery, the magistrate was again presented with cross-motions for summary judgment on this issue.

The magistrate granted the IRS's motion for summary judgment. In reviewing the record in this case and the evidence, the court noted that sec. 2703 was intended to supplement the pre-existing law. The pre-existing law is summarized in *Estate of Lauder v. CIR*, T.C. Memo. 1992-736. It requires that (1) the price be fixed and determinable under the agreement, (2) the agreement be binding in life and death upon the parties, and (3) the agreement have a bona fide business purposes. Sec. 2703(b) added the requirement that the agreement be similar to those entered into at arm's-length by unrelated third parties. The court noted that it did not address the issue of whether the agreement was binding upon the decedent in life and death in its earlier decision.

The court then considered whether the decedent had the unilateral right during life to alter or amend the buy-sell provision. It noted that the FLP agreement provided the power to alter or amend upon the vote of the majority of the general partnership units without the consent of the limited partners. The court found that the decedent held at all time two-thirds of the general partnership units and after the gifts at issue held 53.96% of the limited partnership units. Therefore, the decedent had the power to unilaterally alter or amend the buy-sell provision during his life. Since the decedent could unilaterally alter the agreement in life, the buy-sell provision should be disregarded when determining value for gift tax purposes. Thus, it granted the IRS's motion for summary judgment and held that sec. 2703 applied to look through the buy-sell provision.

This abstract originally appeared in *Valuation Case Digest*, authored by John J. Stockdale, Jr.

Keller v. United States

Citation: No. V-02-62 (S.D. Tex. 2005)
Court: United States District Court
State/Jurisdiction: Southern District of Texas
Date of Decision: September 30, 2005
Judge: Rainey

In *Rayford L. Keller, et al. v. United States of America*, No. V-02-62 (S.D. Tex. September 30, 2005), the U.S. District Court for the Southern District of Texas considered whether summary judgment was appropriate in this family limited partnership (FLP) action. The plaintiff is the executor of the estate of Maude O'Conner Williams (decedent). The decedent owned two trusts at the time of her death, the value of which were includible in her estate for estate tax purposes. The trusts had an aggregate value in excess of $300 million, which was invested in mutual funds and stocks. Additionally, the decedent had the power to invade the corpus of the trusts and appoint who would enjoy the benefit of the trusts. On May 9, 2000, the decedent, in her individual capacity and as trustee of the trusts, established an FLP and a corporate general partner. The corporate general partner held a 0.1% general partnership interest and the trusts each held a 49.95% limited partnership interest. It is undisputed that the FLP and corporate general partner were not capitalized until August 2001. The decedent died on May 15, 2000.

On her estate tax return, the estate reported the full value of the funds held by the trusts and FLP. Her estate later amended the tax return and reported a lower value for the FLP by taking discounts for the FLP. The estate filed this refund suit. The IRS brought this motion for summary judgment arguing that sec. 2036 applied to the facts of this case, among other issues.

The District Court initially noted that sec. 2036 applies to recapture the value of assets transferred by a decedent during her life over which she retains benefit of or the power to appoint who will enjoy the benefit thereof. Sec. 2036 has a built in exception for transfers that are bona fide sales for adequate and full consideration. The District Court looked to *Kimbell v. United States*, 371 F.3d 257 (5th Cir. 2004) and *Strangi v. Commissioner*, 417 F.3d 468 (5th Cir. 2005) for guidance. It noted that *Kimbell* held that a bona sale may occur between related parties, as here, but is subject to heightened scrutiny. *Kimbell* further found that a bona fide sale occurs where "the partnership was in actual possession of the assets transferred, partnership formalities were satisfied, [grantor] ... retained sufficient assets outside of the partnership to meet her personal needs, some of the assets contributed were active business assets, and ... [grantor] had non-tax business reasons for creating the partnership." The District Court contrasted *Kimbell* with *Strangi*, which focused on the substantial non-tax purpose of the FLP, including that of active management of jointly contributed assets. The *Strangi* court emphasized that simply because the assets could have been actively managed, but were not, did not post hoc create a substantial non-tax purpose.

The District Court then concluded that summary judgment was inappropriate under the facts of this case because the Fifth Circuit through *Kimbell* and *Strangi* require a case-by-case analysis of the facts to determine whether the sec. 2036 exception should be applied. However, it noted that the plaintiff's burden to show a substantial non-tax purpose would be heavy.

This abstract originally appeared in *Valuation Case Digest*, authored by John J. Stockdale, Jr.

Estate of Kelley v. Commissioner

Citation: T.C. Memo 2005-235; 2005 Tax Ct. Memo LEXIS 236
Court: United States Tax Court
State/Jurisdiction: Specialty Federal
Date of Decision: October 11, 2005
Judge: Vasquez

In April 1999, Webster Kelley and his daughter and son-in-law ("the Loudens") formed Kelley-Louden Business Properties, LLC (KLBP LLC), and Kelley-Louden, Ltd., a family limited partnership (KLLP). Kelley contributed $1,101,475 cash and certificates of deposit to KLLP, and the Loudens contributed $50,000 cash. Kelley died in December 1999, at which time he owned 33.33% of the LLC, and 94.83% of the family limited partnership (FLP). On the date of death, KLLP held assets totaling $1,226,421, which consisted of $807,271 cash and $419,150 in certificates of deposit, and had no liabilities.

The estate hired Appraisal Technologies, Inc. (ATI), to prepare a valuation of decedent's interests in these closely held entities. ATI concluded that a 53.5% valuation discount was applicable. Accordingly, the estate filed estate tax returns reporting Kelley's KLLP interest at a value of $521,565 and his interest in KLBP LLC at a value of $1,833.33. The IRS issued a notice of deficiency, determining that the discounts claimed by the estate were too high and that lower discounts were appropriate, i.e., a 25.2% discount.

Valuation evidence

At issue was the fair market value of Kelley's interests. ATI's president, Ron Lint, ASA, and his associate, Jeff Mills, ASA, used both a NAV and an income approach, and gave 80% weight to the NAV approach and 20% weight to the income approach.

The IRS expert, Dr. Raymond Widmer, used the NAV approach and valued the interests using a 25.2% valuation discount. Applying this discount, Dr. Widmer determined a value of $869,970 for the 94.83% limited partner interest in KLLP and $3,055 for the one-third interest in KLBP LLC.

Holding and rationale

Because the entities involved were investment companies, the court found that the net asset value (NAV) approach was most applicable, as NAV is best suited for valuing nonoperating entities.

Minority discount

The court found that a minority discount was appropriate, and that such a discount could be determined by reference to general equity closed-end funds. ATI determined that KLLP would be most comparable to the closed-end funds in the fourth quartile (funds with least demand) with price to NAV discounts of 21.8% to 25.5%. It based its discount on KLLP's size, and two studies by Partnership Profiles, Inc. (PPI), which suggested that discounts for comparable publicly registered but nontraded partnerships should be in the 27-29% range.

Dr. Widmer calculated a minority discount of 12% by calculating an arithmetic mean of the entire data set for closed-end funds, not only the fourth quartile. Dr. Widmer determined that it is essential to use the whole array of closed-end funds as this calculation will remove the marketability element in the discounts or premiums.

The court rejected ATI's discount methodology, ruling instead that Dr. Widmer's approach was better because shareholders in all closed-end funds lack control. The court also concluded that in using only the fourth quartile, ATI combined elements of the lack of marketability discount with the minority discount because the funds in the fourth quartile had the lowest demand and therefore the highest marketability discount. Using this approach, the court held that a 12% minority discount was correct.

Discount for lack of marketability

The court agreed that a discount for lack of marketability was appropriate in valuing the interests in KLLP, as there is not a ready market for partnership interests in a closely held partnership. In determining the marketability discount, ATI used the restricted stock approach. After considering numerous barriers to marketability of a limited partnership interest in KLLP, ATI determined that a 38% marketability discount should apply to KLLP. Dr. Widmer determined a 15% discount for lack of marketability on the basis of a study by Dr. Mukesh Bajaj.

The court, again, was not persuaded by ATI's approach. It found that the restricted stock studies examined mostly operating companies, and that "there are fundamental differences between an investment company holding easily valued and liquid assets (cash and certificates of deposit), such as KLLP, and operating companies." However, it was also not persuaded by Dr. Widmer's discount, saying that his conclusion based on the Bajaj study "is not entirely accurate."

Because it declined to use either party's DLOM, the court conducted its own DLOM analysis, finding that a 20% initial marketability discount was appropriate. The court based this discount on the approach used in *McCord v. Commissioner*[1], where the court focused on the Bajaj study and found that a 20% marketability discount was appropriate for interests in an FLP classified as an investment company. It further found that an upward adjustment of 3% was proper, based on the approach used in *Lappo v. Commissioner*[2], to incorporate characteristics specific to the partnership, thus concluding that a total DLOM of 23% applied.

---

1. *McCord v. Commissioner,* 120 T.C. No. 13, 2003 U.S. Tax Ct. LEXIS 16, (May 14, 2003). See the July 2003 issue of *Business Valuation Update*™ for coverage of this case.
2. *Lappo v. Commissioner,* T.C. Memo 2003-258 (September 3, 2003). See the November 2003 issue of *Business Valuation Update*™ for coverage of this case.

Davenport v. United States

Citation: No. G-03-923 (S.D. Tex. 2005)
Court: United States District Court
State/Jurisdiction: Southern District of Texas
Date of Decision: October 18, 2005
Judge: Froeschner

In *Gordon E. Davenport v. United States of America*, No. G-03-923 (S.D. Tex. October 18, 2005), the U.S. District Court for the Southern District of Texas determined whether an appraisal should be admitted into evidence. This action originates in a 1980 transfer by gift of 537 shares in a closely held oil drilling business. Davenport's aunt made three gifts of stock that year in equal amounts to three beneficiaries including Davenport. However, a gift tax return was not filed in connection with the gifts. Upon the aunt's death in 1991, the oversight was discovered and gift tax returns were filed along with the estate tax return. For estate tax purposes, the government and the estate stipulated to the value of the stock at $2,000 per share. The gift tax has not been paid, and the government has sought to hold the donees liable for the tax.

Before the Tenth Circuit, the donees including Davenport successfully argued that they should not be held bound by the stipulation to the value of the stock in the estate proceeding. The Tenth Circuit agreed because the parties in the estate action were different from the parties in the donee liability action. *Botefuhr v. United States*, No. 01-5133 (10th Cir. October 31, 2002). This action arises from the valuation of the stock for donee liability purposes.

The government engaged a well-credential business appraiser to determine the value of the stock on the date it was gifted in 1980. He concluded that the stock had a fair market value of $2,665 per share. Underlying his valuation was the assumption that the donor had "good and legal" title to the stock. Davenport contested that assumption.

The donor received the stock from the estate of her sister, who died in 1979. However, the sister's estate was subject to litigation over the value of the stock that was ultimately transferred to Davenport. Therefore, Davenport argued that the title to the stock gifted to him was clouded by the government's litigation, which was not resolved until 1984. The government's expert acknowledged the defect in title. Furthermore, the expert indicated that his valuation would not apply under this fact situation and "he was unaware of any methodology to permit calculation of the stocks' value under these circumstances that would not be speculative."

The District Court concluded that the expert's valuation was inadmissible. It reasoned, the expert's "failure to consider the devaluative effect of the cloud on ... [the donor's] ownership interest in the stock invalidates a basic foundation of his opinion and renders it inadmissible: his methodology simply does not 'fit' the undeniable facts of this case." Thus, it granted Davenport's motion to strike this expert.

This abstract originally appeared in *Valuation Case Digest*, authored by John J. Stockdale, Jr.

Estate of Blount v. Commissioner (II)

Citation: 428 F.3d 1338, 2005 U.S. App. LEXIS 23502
Court: United States Court of Appeals
State/Jurisdiction: 11th Circuit Federal
Date of Decision: October 31, 2005
Judge: Birch

The issue in this estate tax case was the value of George Blount's (decedent's) interest in a closely held company on the date of his death. The U.S. Tax Court disregarded an ESOP repurchase liability and a buy-sell agreement, but included the full value of company-owned life insurance, and valued the company at $9.9 million.

Blount owned 83.2% or 43,080 shares of Blount Construction Company (BCC). In 1981, prior to the formation of the BCC ESOP, he and the only other shareholder, entered into a shareholders' buy-sell agreement with BCC. The agreement restricted the transfer of stock during the lifetime of the shareholder and at death, and set the per-share purchase price as BCC's book value at fiscal yearend immediately preceding the deceased shareholder's death.

Then, in 1996, Blount as the only remaining shareholder entered into a new buy-sell agreement with BCC. The new agreement was operative only upon his death and set a fixed, lump-sum purchase price of $4 million. He signed the agreement in his individual capacity and on behalf of BCC as its president. Additionally, there was a life insurance policy owned by the company that provided about $3.1 million to pay off the mandated buy-out of the shares.

The Tax Court found that the 1996 buy-sell agreement was a modified version of the 1981 agreement, and ignored the agreement's set value because Blount had the unilateral ability to modify it, thus failing to satisfy the requirement that it be binding during life. The court also disregarded the agreement under IRC Section 2703, which requires that to be included in a valuation, a buy-sell agreement's terms must be "comparable to similar arrangements entered into by persons in an arm's length transaction." Here, the court concluded that the parties were "related" and had not engaged in arm's-length bargaining. The Tax Court included the full amount of the insurance proceeds as nonoperating assets, and also concluded that because the buy-sell agreement had been disregarded, the issue of whether BCC's obligation under that agreement to redeem decedent's stock should offset the proceeds was not before the court.

The Eleventh Circuit affirmed the Tax Court's decision that the buy-sell agreement could not set the value of BCC for estate tax purposes, but reversed on the inclusion of the insurance proceeds as nonoperating assets.

The Appellate Court determined that the exception to the rule that the value of the taxable estate generally is the fair market value of the decedent's property at the date of death, codified by the Omnibus Budget Reconciliation Act of 1990, Pub. L. 101-508, 104 Stat. 1388 (OBRA), was inapplicable because the stock-purchase agreement in this case was unilaterally changeable during Blount's lifetime, and thus violated the exception's requirement that the buy-sell agreement must be binding during the life of the decedent.

The court came to the same conclusion under the different theory that the agreement did not satisfy the exception's requirement that the buy-sell agreement must be comparable to similar arrangements entered into at arm's length, because it found that the Tax Court had not erred in its determination that the agreement had not been made at arm's length.

As to the insurance proceeds, the appellate court ruled that the Tax Court had erred because those proceeds had already been taken into account in the determination of net worth. The court noted that even when a buy-sell agreement is inoperative for purposes of establishing the value of the company for tax purposes, the agreement remains an enforceable liability against the valued company, if state law fixes such an obligation—which it had in this case. Here, the insurance proceeds were offset dollar-for-dollar by BCC's obligation to satisfy its contract with the decedent's estate. The court thus concluded that such nonoperating "assets" should not be included in the fair market valuation of a company where, as here, there is an enforceable contractual obligation that offsets such assets.

Estate of Kahn v. Commissioner

Citation: 125 T.C. No. 11 (2005)
Court: United States Tax Court
State/Jurisdiction: Specialty Federal
Date of Decision: November 17, 2005
Judge: Goeke

In the *Estate of Doris F. Kahn v. CIR*, 125 T.C. No. 11 (November 17, 2005), the full Tax Court considered whether a discount was properly applied to an individual retirement account (IRA) to account for the built-in gains that would be taxable to the estate or beneficiaries upon their distribution. The estate held two IRAs at the time of the decedent's death in 2000. Each IRA had an undiscounted value in excess of $1 million, and the IRAs were non-transferable. The underlying assets in each IRA were marketable securities. The estate reported the fair market value of each IRA by including discounts of 21 and 22.5% respectively. The IRS contested the application of the discounts, and the matter proceeded to trial before the Tax Court.

The estate put forward several arguments supporting the application of a discount to the IRAs. The Tax Court initially noted that an IRA is a trust for the benefit of an individual or his beneficiaries, and that distributions from an IRA are taxable as income to the beneficiary whenever made. Moreover, an IRA is an asset includible in the gross estate of a decedent. Furthermore, in order to account for potential double taxation under the estate and income tax regimes, sec. 2036 of the Code permits an offset to the distributee of an amount equal to the estate taxes paid on that asset.

The Tax Court then set about rejecting all the estate's positions. It noted that while the IRAs themselves are not marketable, the underlying assets- the marketable securities-are. It reasoned that since the IRAs are not marketable, the tax liability associated with the gain on the underlying assets stays with the decedent or his beneficiaries. Therefore, a willing buyer would negotiate a sale of the underlying assets without reference to the tax liability of the seller. It stated:

> The tax or marketability burden on the IRAs must be borne by the seller because the IRAs cannot legally be sold and therefore their inherent tax liability and marketability restrictions cannot be passed on to a hypothetical buyer. Therefore, there is no reason a hypothetical buyer would seek to adjust the price of the marketable securities that are ultimately being purchased. By the same token, a hypothetical seller would not accept a downward adjustment in the value of the securities for a tax liability that does not survive the transfer of ownership of the assets. A hypothetical buyer would not purchase the IRAs because they are not transferable. The buyer would purchase the IRAs' marketable securities and would obtain a tax basis in the assets equal to the buyer's cost.

By applying the above reasoning, the Tax Court rejected analogies of the IRAs to unassignable lottery payments, closely held stock, stock subject to resale restrictions, and real property subject to cleanup or rezoning costs. Thus, the Tax Court concluded that the IRAs should be included in the estate at their undiscounted value, and any potential double taxation issues would be resolved through application of sec. 691 upon distribution of the underlying assets.

This abstract originally appeared in *Valuation Case Digest*, authored by John J. Stockdale, Jr.

Davis v. United States (I)

Citation: 2005 U.S. Dist. LEXIS 34372
Court: United States District Court
State/Jurisdiction: New Hampshire
Date of Decision: December 19, 2005
Judge: McAuliffe

What are the odds that a lottery winner can persuade a federal court that the present value of his right to receive future lottery payments warrants a discount for lack of marketability?

The New Hampshire lottery winner had died before receiving the last ten of his annual payments of $209,000. By referring to IRS annuity tables, his estate valued his right to these payments at about $1.6 million, and then discounted it for lack of marketability by half, or to roughly $800,000.

The IRS challenged the discount, claiming that the "present value" contained in the annuity tables was controlling; and moreover, that this value was equivalent to fair market value for estate tax purposes. Federal tax regulations specifically provide that in estate valuations, "the fair market value of annuities . . . is their present value" as determined by the tables.

The estate agreed that the right to receive annual lottery payments constituted an "annuity" within the meaning of applicable provisions of the tax code (IRC §§ 2039 and 7520(a)), as well as estate tax regulations (§ 20.7520-3(b)(1)(i)(A)). The estate also agreed on the general rule "that the annuity must be valued by reference to IRC annuity tables," unless it could show that the result would be so "unrealistic or unreasonable" that an alternative valuation should apply.

"The estate's claim appears to be this," the Court observed: "a well-informed buyer would be willing to pay substantially less for an identical annuity that he or she could not sell or assign than that same buyer would be willing to pay for an identical annuity that could be sold or assigned." And more critically, the estate claimed that the IRC tables fail to take into account the diminished market value of a non-transferable annuity.

The federal courts are divided on the narrow legal question of how to value a non-transferable right to receive lottery winnings in the form of guaranteed, annual payments. The Davis court reviewed the precedent—and then extended the divide a bit further by considering the valuation of all non-marketable annuities.

The problem, according to the Court, is that the IRC annuity tables consider only two factors: time and a discount interest rate. Consequently, they provide only a present valuation—which for a marketable annuity is "roughly equivalent to its 'fair market value.'" The tables also provide "a cost-effective, efficient, and, generally speaking, reliable means by which to calculate an annuity's fair market value," the Court said, "without the need to call upon . . . valuation experts," whose opinions sometimes produce "wide variations." (Note to analysts: The wider gap between opinions may win points with clients—but not always with judges.)

More importantly, however, the annuity tables' many attributes fall into doubt when dealing with non-assignable annuities, as "by virtue of their structure and assumptions," the tables fail to consider that "a hypothetical buyer would naturally be willing to pay less for a non-marketable annuity than . . . a marketable one," which he or she could convert immediately into a lump sum for reinvestment or "any number of uses."

"The right to transfer is one of the most essential sticks in the bundle of rights that are commonly characterized as property," the Court declared, citing precedent from the Ninth Circuit, which has joined the Second Circuit on this issue (and disagreed with the Fifth Circuit's finding that no discounts apply). "It is axiomatic that if an asset's marketability is restricted, it is less valuable than an identical marketable asset."

Having determined that the IRC annuity tables: (1) do not account for lack of marketability; and (2) that the fair market value of a non-marketable annuity is some degree less than its present value; and (3) that the IRC tables are not necessarily an accurate measure of fair market value—the Court next determined whether the estate had carried its burden to prove, as a matter of law, that an alternate valuation must be used. "It has not."

At this juncture, all the Court could conclude was that the "present value" of the non-marketable annuity was likely to be higher than its "fair market value." Use of the IRC tables might be inappropriate—but they might not, depending on the case, warrant the conclusion that the IRC tables produce an "unrealistic and unreasonable" value. That is factual matter which the parties must resolve at hearing (this case came on their cross motions for summary judgment).

You can't win 'em all, perhaps—but our bet is that the next call both parties made was to their valuation experts, and also their attorneys. Because in its conclusion, the Court explained that its determination turned on defining the interest as an annuity, instead of a "right to receive defined cash payments of a defined period," for which a present value can readily (and accurately) be expressed, as in the cases of reducing an individual's lifetime earnings to a lump sum, present value. "A 'marketability' factor simply has no place in that kind of calculation," the Court said, giving a nod to the jurisdictions that have declined to discount the present value of annual lottery payments, and perhaps a nudge to the IRS to review its definitions of the same.

Estate of Hughes v. Commissioner

Citation: T.C. Memo. 2005-296
Court: United States Tax Court
State/Jurisdiction: Specialty Federal
Date of Decision: December 27, 2005
Judge: Colvin

In the *Estate of Winifred Hughes v. CIR*, T.C. Memo. 2005-296, the Tax Court determined that the estate was not entitled to deduct amounts due under a promissory note as a sec. 2053 claim against the estate. Since the death of the decedent's husband in 1996, she solely owned, but was not actively involved in, her husband's businesses. His business associate, McBride, was the decedent's attorney-in-fact and the sole director and officer of Advanced Leasing, an auto sales and leasing business owned by the decedent.

Advanced Leasing was valued as of April 10, 1996 at zero dollars for the decedent's husband's estate tax return. Advanced Leasing frequently borrowed money from a limited partnership, whose limited partners were the decedent's children and grandchildren. At all relevant times, Advanced Leasing was insolvent and, with the exception of 1997, was unprofitable. In 1997, Advanced Leasing earned a pre-tax profit of $29,000.

In 1997, McBride, acting in his capacity as decedent's attorney-in-fact and as a representative of Advanced Leasing, executed a stock subscription agreement. The agreement transferred 4,000 newly issued shares of Advanced Leasing to the decedent for a $400,000 demand note. Advanced Leasing was not appraised in connection with this transaction, which was not reported to its accountants nor listed in its financial records. No payments were made under the demand note during the decedent's life, and Advanced Leasing closed after her death in 2000.

After the decedent died, her estate transferred $400,000 to Advanced Leasing, which was used to retire debt owed to the limited partnership. This amount was deducted on the estate's tax return under sec. 2053 as a claim against the estate. Additionally, Advanced Leasing was valued at zero dollars on the estate tax return because its liabilities exceeded its assets. The IRS denied the deduction, and the matter proceeded before the Tax Court.

The Tax Court initially noted, "An estate may deduct the value of a claim based on a decedent's promise to pay only if the liability was contracted bona fide and for full and adequate consideration in money or money's worth."

The Tax Court first determined that the decedent did not receive full and adequate consideration in exchange for her promise to pay.The Court noted that the business had no value on the decedent's 2000 date of death or her husband's 1996 date of death, and was insolvent at all times, regardless of whether the $400,000 was included or not. While acknowledging that the business's fortunes were improving at the time of the transaction and it earned a modest profit in 1997, the

Court stated, "We do not believe that the value of Advanced Leasing's stock increased from zero on April 10, 1996 (as reported on the estate tax return for ... [the decedent's husband and signed by the decedent's executor]) to $400,000 on April 29, 1997, and then fell to zero on July 25, 1999...." Therefore, the Court concluded that the stock had no value on the date of the transaction and the transaction did not occur for full and adequate consideration.

The Court next considered whether the transaction was "contracted bona fide," which it defined as "in good faith and bargained for at arm's length." The Court determined that the transaction was not arm's length because McBride stood on both sides of the transaction in his respective capacities as manager of the business and conservator of the decedent. It further noted that McBride did not obtain a valuation of Advanced Leasing in connection with this transaction; an attorney, who gave advice regarding the transaction, indicated that business had no value; and the corporate accountants were unaware of the transaction. Moreover, the dealership made no demand for payment during the decedent's life. Therefore, the Court concluded that the transaction was not bona fide.

Since the transaction was not bona fide and was not made for adequate and full consideration, the amount paid under the note to the dealership was not a deductible claim under sec. 2053. Rather, the Court found that this transaction was a testamentary disposition for the benefit of the decedent's children and grandchildren since the post-death payment under the demand note was funneled to a partnership owned by the decedent's children.

This abstract originally appeared in *Valuation Case Digest*, authored by John J. Stockdale, Jr.

W.G. Anderson v. United States

Citation: 2005 U.S. Dist. LEXIS 39573
Court: United States District Court
State/Jurisdiction: Western District of Louisiana
Date of Decision: December 28, 2005
Judge: Hicks

What do valuation analysts most like to hear from a court? How about: The expert made "an impressive witness," followed by the adoption, in large part, of that expert's analysis.

Of the four witnesses who appeared in this case, none impressed the Court to the others' exclusion. Name and credentials do count for a lot—the rebuttal witness was, after all, *Business Valuation Update*™ emeritus Shannon Pratt, (Shannon Pratt Valuations, LLC, Portland). But most outstanding were the experts' selection, at different points in their analyses, of solid data and accurate comparables, as specific to the subject company as possible.

Discounts as certain as death, taxes

The 1997 death of Mrs. Gertrude Anderson generated over $14 million in estate and gift taxes. After an IRS audit, the Government assessed an additional $3 million-plus. The disputed difference related primarily to the fair market value of the Estate's minority interests in four LLCs, whose assets consisted largely of mineral and oil exploration rights.

All experts relied on the report of the same petroleum engineer to derive the baseline value of the mineral interests. In prior orders, the Court ruled that it would accept both the NAV and market approaches, but would give the former a 2:1 weight over the latter. In calculating the NAV, the parties would apply a minority discount of 10%, lack of marketability discount of 40%, and a 10% liquidation cost to the stipulated baseline value.

The Court also held the parties to a 40% marketability discount in their market approach analysis—which predictably became the only consistent element, due to the inherent difficulty in equating the value of public corporations with interests in a family-held oil and gas business. The experts also disagreed on the best method to calculate starting values for the LLCs, but neither had challenged the other's selections of comparable publicly-owned companies. The Court thus treated the comparables as "equally valid"—although not necessarily of equal weight.

Measures and multiples critical in market approach

In adjusting the comparables to reflect the economic realities of the subject LLCs, the Estate's expert, Charles Stryker (Trenwith Group, LLC, New York City) used two primary measures: price-to-pretax cash flow and price-to-appraised worth. John Thomson (Klaris Thomson Schroeder, Inc., Los Angeles), the Government's expert, used three: price-to-cash flow for the 12 months prior to valuation; price-to-cash flow for the prior fiscal year; and price-to-a-3-year cash flow average. While rebuttal expert Pratt found no significant difference in the start values that rose from the various measures, he agreed with all experts that, at a minimum, price-to-cash flow is an acceptable measure of value for an oil and gas company. The Government argued that by including price-to-appraised worth, the Estate would be double-counting the value of LLC assets. But the Estate countered that appraised value simply provided another comparison point between the LLCs and the comparables—and the Court agreed, ordering the parties to use the Government's three measures, plus price-to-appraised worth.

Next, the experts used the financial measures to create a range of multiples, which they'd apply to the comparable companies to come up with the LLCs' value. "Perhaps more than any other determination," according to the court, "the selection of a range of multiples ... is a judgment call by a qualified expert." Both Thomson and Stryker chose multiples below the statistical median of the range derived from the comparables, but varied significantly on how far below the median to go.

Based on the LLC's smaller size, lower operating margins, non-operator status, and other factors, Stryker felt that the lower range was more appropriate. Thomson agreed that the LLCs were both smaller and less diverse than the comparables, but their overall financial conditions—including lack of debt, history of distributions, and profit margins—suggested a higher range of multiplies. Thomson analyzed Mergerstat data on public- versus privately-held companies to derive his range—which at first blush appeared "sound," according to the court. However, the data did not provide sufficient detail to allow specific comparison to the acquisition values of the LLCs. As rebuttal witness, Pratt preferred the Estate's approach, suggesting that the Government's range would have been more reliable if it had used a larger downward adjustment from the median values.

The Court agreed, deeming the Estate's range of multiples to be the more accurate in the market approach. But because the LLCs were more likely to be liquidated than held for public sale, the Court adopted the Government's allocation of a 33.3% weighted market approach and 66.7% weighted net asset approach. And though the Court cited with approval Pratt's credentials—for some reason (and lest readers be confused) the opinion refers to him as "Carl," which just goes to show that in the end, the name doesn't count as much as the numbers.

Senda v. Commissioner (II)

Citation: No. 05-118 (8th Cir. 2006)
Court: United States Court of Appeals
State/Jurisdiction: 8th Circuit Federal
Date of Decision: January 6, 2006
Judge: Benton, Jr.

In *Mark W. Senda v. CIR*, No. 05-1118 (8th Cir. January 6, 2006), the U.S. Court of Appeals for the Eighth Circuit determined that the Sendas made an indirect gift of publicly traded stock to their children, rather than a gift of limited partnership interests. Therefore, the entire value of the gifted stock was subject to the gift tax, rather than the discounted value attributable to the limited partnerships. In 1998 and again in 1999, the Sendas formed a limited partnership with their children. The children each contributed oral accounts receiveable valued at $200, in exchange for a 0.01% limited partnership interest. The Sendas contributed $2 million in stock for the remaining limited and general partnership units. Immediately thereafter, the Sendas gifted limited partnership units to their children. (The 1999 transaction was substantially similar to the 1998 transaction discussed above). The Sendas reported the gifts on their gift tax return based on the value of the limited partnership units, including discounts for lack of marketability and lack of control.

The IRS contested the values of the stock. It argued that the transaction was an indirect gift to the children of the underlying stock. It claimed that the formation of the limited partnership and gifts to the children were simultaneous and should be treated as one transaction for gift tax purposes.

The Tax Court agreed with the IRS. It noted that the Sendas were required to prove that they capitalized the FLPs before making the gifts. The Tax Court concluded that "[a]t best, the transactions were integrated ..., and, in effect, simultaneous" because the Sendas lacked any documentary support and presented equivocal testimony regarding the timing of the formation and gift. It then applied the step transaction doctrine and concluded that an indirect gift had been made of the underlying public stock. This decision mooted the issue of applicability of discounts for lack of control and lack of marketability.

The Sendas appealed to the Eighth Circuit, which initially noted, "This sequence [of the transactions] is critical, because a contribution of stock *after* the transfer of partnership interests is an indirect gift to the partners (to the extent of their proportionate interest in the partnership)." (Emphasis in orginial). The Eight Circuit affirmed the Tax Court's decision that the transactions were effectively simultaneous. It found that Senda's testimony conflicted with his documentary evidence making both unreliable.

Moreover, it affirmed the application of the step transaction doctrine to this case. It defined the doctrine: "In some situations, formally distinct steps are considered as an integrated whole, rather than in isolation, so federal tax liability is based on a realistic view of the entire transaction." The court found that Senda's testimony indicated that he was concerned that the transactions occurred on the same day and not with the order of the transactions. Therefore, the court affirmed the Tax Court's characterization of the transactions as simultaneous under the step transaction doctrine.

This abstract originally appeared in *Valuation Case Digest*, authored by John J. Stockdale, Jr.

Robertson v. United States

Citation: 2006 U.S. Dist. Lexis 1167
Court: United States District Court
State/Jurisdiction: Northern District of Texas
Date of Decision: January 13, 2006
Judge: Kaplan

The U.S Magistrate sounds a bit testy when handing down a recent decision on the fair value of limited partnership interests. Perhaps it was the time of the year: Who isn't a bit stressed after the holidays? Or perhaps he found the testimony of three different experts in this estate tax case to be more complicated than necessary—and not always careful enough, tossing out a report by one of the taxpayer's experts because the "methodology was difficult to follow, and the Government effectively impeached [its] credibility by pointing out several errors in [its] calculations."

The main issue wasn't all that complicated: The Government was suing to collect generation skipping transfer (GST) taxes from several beneficiaries of charitable lead non-exempt trusts, who had each received nearly $10 million in distributions, primarily in partnership units from a trust-owned LP. As there was no dispute regarding liability, the date of valuation, or the net asset value (NAV) of the partnership assets, the sole issue was the valuation of the limited partnership units.

The Court was even-handed in its sharp-eyed (and sharp-tongued) review. After rejecting a taxpayer report, the Court dismissed the Government's market approach—because all of the experts, including presumably its own, had specifically disavowed this approach in their analyses (A good reminder for all parties on the same side to get on the same page.) Finally, the Magistrate made short shrift of the Government's "right of first refusal" NAV analysis, finding it "speculative" because it assumed certain hypothetical buy-back scenarios *without any evidentiary support*. (Our emphasis added, as another reminder how important it is to back up your assertions with reliable analysis and data.)

This left the Government's expert, Francis X. Burns (CRA International, Chicago) with a sole remaining net asset value approach, using the NAV of the partnership units discounted by a combined lack of marketability and lack of control discount of 17.925%. Similarly, the taxpayer's remaining expert, Peter J. Phalon (Waterview Advisors, Dallas) applied an NAV analysis, but posited a combined effective discount of 41.5%.

Discounts must rely on good data

Although both experts compared the partnership assets to closed-end funds, the Court found Phalon's analysis and data to be "more thorough." For example, Phalon properly determined a discount for a partnership account based on World Equity Closed-End fund data, but Burns had mistakenly included the same account in his equities classification and used General Equity Closed-End Fund data to determine a discount for that account. Moreover, Burns analyzed closed-end funds using a mean rather than a median approach, which exaggerated the impact of outliers. Phalon used the median approach, which the Court found more indicative of market factors—and therefore allowed an 8% discount for lack of control based on his closed-end analysis.

Phalon then examined the partnership structure for additional discounts, comparing closed-end funds versus publicly traded partnerships, both investing in real estate. He attributed another 22% discount to structural differences between investment companies and limited partnerships; of that amount, he conservatively estimated that 50% of the difference, or an additional 11% was due to lack control.

On the Government's side, its expert "employed no such analysis." Nor did he offer any "compelling reason" why the Court should reject the taxpayer's upward adjustment. The Court accepted Phalon's numbers up to this point—but it found that an additional 3% discount was unwarranted, as Phalon had based this on six factors unique to the partnership, none of which was empirically quantifiable—and many of which he may have already factored into his closed-end fund analysis.

Both experts properly referred to restricted stock studies for their DLOM analysis; and both agreed on the general downward trend in restricted stock studies since 1990, due to the removal of restrictions on the stock's purchase and sale. But on this issue, they flip-flopped on who'd been the more careful. This time, the Government's Burns relied on academic research and available data to determine a 12.5% discount rate for lack of marketability. But the taxpayer's Phalon used subjective factors, not supported by any empirical data, in advocating a 25% lack of marketability discount. And when the Court inquired, Phalon couldn't adequately explain how he arrived at that percentage, and admitted that it was vulnerable to upward and downward adjustment. Thus Burns won on this point, with his 12.5% discount.

But reading between and into the lines: What really won the day was careful, methodical analysis, based on "hard" data that wasn't (too) hard to follow.

Estate of Disbrow v. Commissioner

Citation: T.C. Memo. 2006-34
Court: United States Tax Court
State/Jurisdiction: Specialty Federal
Date of Decision: February 28, 2006
Judge: Laro

In the *Estate of Lorrain C. Disbrow v. CIR*, T.C. Memo. 2006-34, the Tax Court determined that sec. 2036(a) applied to recapture the value of a residence transferred to a general partnership and leased to the decedent. In late 1993 and on the advice of her attorney, the decedent, her children, and their spouses formed a general partnership. No person contributed any capital to the partnership upon its formation. Shortly thereafter in 1993, the decedent transferred her residence to the partnership for no consideration. On January 1, 1994, the decedent gifted her remaining 28.125% interest in the partnership to her children and their spouses in pro rata amounts.

From 1994 through 2000, the decedent and the partnership annually executed a rental agreement for the residence. The rental agreement was a standard form contract prepared by the attorney who created the partnership. The agreement was modified by redlining several provisions limiting the decedent's use or modification of the residence. Further, the agreement required the decedent to maintain the residence and required her to pay below market rent. The rent payments were not consistently received and the partnership made no effort to enforce its rights to collect rent or eject the decedent.

The decedent died on February 9, 2000. Her estate did not include any amount representing the value of the residence. The IRS disagreed with this assessment. It applied sec. 2036(a)(1) to recapture the value of the residence. Sec. 2036(a)(1) applies to recapture the value of inter vivos transfers where the decedent retains the use, enjoyment, or income from the transferred property and where the transfer was not a bona fide sale for adequate consideration in money or money's worth.

Before the Tax Court, the estate argued that the decedent relinquished her entire interest in the residence, and her continued occupancy was pursuant to a lease agreement. The Tax Court disagreed. It noted that whether a decedent completely parted with her interest in the transferred property is analyzed in light of the facts and circumstances, considering the decedent's post-transfer relationship to the property. Under the facts here, the court stated, "While the presence of a lease may sometimes lead to a finding of a lack of retention for purposes of section 2036(a)(1) . . . such is not true where, as here, the tenant pays less than FRV [fair rental value] as to the lease of the property." The court concluded, "Decedent's rights under the lease agreements to the exclusive possession and enjoyment of the residence triggers the application of section 2036(a)(1) to the residence in that the decedent did not pay FRV for that possession and enjoyment.

Moreover, the Tax Court found that "the annual lease agreements were a subterfuge to disguise the testamentary nature of the transfer." Five factors led the Court to this conclusion: (1) the partnership carried on no business and made no profit throughout its existence; (2) the decedent and the partnership did not respect the landlord-tenant relationship insofar as payments were consistently late and no action was taken by the partnership to remedy that problem; (3) at the time of the transfer, the decedent was 72 years old and in poor health; (4) a partner testified that the partnership wanted the decedent to remain in the home for as long as she was able; and (5) the transaction was entered into with the advice of counsel, who indicated that removal of the residence from the estate was a primary consideration.

Therefore, the court agreed with the IRS and found that the decedent retained an interest in the residence she transferred to the partnership. It applied sec. 2036(a)(1) to recapture the value of the residence for estate tax purposes.

This abstract originally appeared in *Valuation Case Digest*, authored by John J. Stockdale, Jr.

Temple v. United States

Citation: 2006 U.S. Dist. LEXIS 16171
Court: United States District Court
State/Jurisdiction: Eastern District of Texas, Lufkin Division
Date of Decision: March 10, 2006
Judge: Heartfield

No analytical model can "fix" flawed assumptions; and no study—no matter how valid the data—can overcome a flawed application. That seems to be the lesson the *Temple* court hammers home in its discussion and determination of discounts for lack of marketability and control. The discussion won't end with this case, however, as the decision leaves a couple of key questions on models and methods open for debate.

Valuations of $34 million gifts requires an army of appraisers

After developing a $2 billion timber company in Texas, Arthur Temple and his wife transferred over $34 million in assets to their children and grandchildren, using four family-owned entities: (1) Ladera Land, Ltd. ("Ladera"), which owned a ranch; (2) Boggy Slough West, LLC ("Boggy

Slough"), which operated a winery; (3) Temple Interests, L.P. and (4) Temple Partners, L.P., identical partnerships that held publicly-traded securities (collectively, the "Temple Partnerships").

In valuing the gifts for his taxes, and without consulting an appraiser, Temple applied a 40% discount to Ladera and Boggy Slough. (The opinion doesn't mention initial discounts for Temple Partnerships). After its audit, the IRS declared that Temple had undervalued all gifts, and assessed an extra $3.54 million in taxes and interest.

Temple challenged the deficiency and hired a team of experts. Their first step—arriving at a net asset value for each entity, went as smoothly as a stroll on a Texas prairie. But the second—determining the appropriate discounts, put the experts in a Texas twister. To clear the dust from the data, the Court examined the analysis for each:

1. *Ladera.* Temple's expert, Nancy Czaplinski CPA, ASA, CFA (American Appraisal Associates, Inc.; Milwaukee), combined a 25% minority discount and a 45% discount for lack of marketability (DLOM) for a total 58.75% discount. For the minority discount, she used "the inverse of the premium for control" from a Mergerstat study. But a second Temple expert, Charles Elliot Jr., ASA, CFA (Houston), was forced to admit that the Mergerstat data involves sales from publicly-held companies and not the purchase of specific percentage interests; and that he'd never used the control premium study to compute a lack of control discount.

For the DLOM, Czaplinski used the Quantitative Marketability Discount Model (QMDM). Her inputs included a 10-15 year holding period and a 3% expected appreciation of property assets. As to the first, the Court found no holding period requirement in the controlling agreement; however, "under the [QMDM], the longer the holding period, the higher the discount." The Court also noted that Czaplinski had derived the 3% expected appreciation from a "conversation with someone in her firm's real estate department" without an effort to tie the rate to Texas or other market comparables.

The holding period assumptions were "enough, in the absence of a holding period requirement... to concern the Court with the reliability of that aspect of Czaplinski's calculations." It also noted that she'd derived her remaining assumptions "without talking to anyone associated with Ladera."

On the other side, the government's expert, Francis Burns, ASA (InteCap, Inc.; Chicago), had examined average discounts for limited partnerships holding primarily real estate, which were similar to Ladera. "Burns's analysis allows for numerous data points and assists the Court in arriving at a reasonable discount," which it determined was a 33% combined discount for lack of control and marketability, plus an additional 7.5% incremental lack of marketability discount for a total discount of 38%.

2. *Boggy Slough.* Temple had transferred a 76.6% non-managing membership to one child, and several 1.6% interests to the grandchildren. To value these gifts, Czaplinski applied the same discounts (25% lack of control and 45% DLOM) as with Ladera. This time, the Court found more

support for her calculations from fellow expert William Lyon, MAI, who took a sales comparison approach; he also considered the "numerous problems" associated with "absolute lack of control any individual [interest] has with respect to the property" and its dissolution. Given that any action required unanimous consent (and California entity law did not mandate dissolution), the Court concluded that a 60% discount was appropriate for the majority (76.6%) interest.

Surprisingly, the minority interests warranted a lower rate; the Court applied the same 38% combined lack of control/marketability discount to these as it had the Ladera gifts.

3. *Temple Partnerships.* For these identical investment holding companies, both parties' experts (Elliot and Burns) used closed-end funds to determine the minority discount and restricted stock studies to determine the DLOM. (The Court rejected a third Temple expert who calculated a DLOM that depended on a 50-year holding period.)

Once again the Court favored the more comprehensive Burns, who had not excluded any funds from his minority discount analysis, as Elliott had. Burns had also used the average discount of closed-end funds as opposed to Elliott, the Court said, who "simply chose the discount" from the 75th percentile without providing sufficient explanation or support. Applying the government's analysis to three valuation dates, the Court applied minority discounts in a range of 3.3% to 10.1%.

As for the DLOM, Burns had not only looked to the restricted stock studies but also to: academic research; costs of going public; secondary market transactions; asset liquidity; partnership interest transferability; and historic distributions. This "fuller" analysis persuaded the Court to adopt his 12.5% lack of marketability discount.

A gift to the taxpayer—more grist for analyst's discount mill

After applying the Court's discounts, the plaintiff did receive a $7 million refund of taxes and interest—proving that his army of experts paid off. But in its support for better substantiated detail and data; its questions on holding period requirements in the QMDM; and its application of a larger discount for a controlling interest, the Temple decision does keep the industry debate on discounts churning.

Koblick v. Commissioner

Citation: T.C. Memo. 2006-63
Court: United States Tax Court
State/Jurisdiction: Specialty Federal
Date of Decision: April 3, 2006
Judge: Goeke

In *Ian G. Koblick and Tonya A. Koblick v. CIR*, T.C. Memo. 2006-63, the Tax Court determined the fair market value of a minority interest in a company donated to a charitable organization, which was part of a plan by all shareholders of the company to donate all the stock to the non-profit organization. The taxpayers held a 45% interest in Jules Verne Undersea Lodge, Inc. (JUL), which had two other shareholders owning 45% and 10% respectively.

JUL's by-laws imposed restrictions on the shareholders' ability to transfer their interests. JUL had the absolute right to stop a sale or transfer. Furthermore, it had the right, but not the obligation, to purchase the stock of a shareholder who desired to transfer his interest.

JUL owned a submersible barge and two dive bells. The barge was located in a Florida lagoon. The barge was originally constructed as a research station, but was obtained by JUL from a salvage yard and outfitted to be a 5-bed hotel. It primarily received revenue from its hotel operations, but also received 10% of its income from research.

JUL was not a profitable operation. It incurred annual losses between $5,434 and $21,067 during its operations for the four years preceding the 1994 donation. While it did not have any liabilities on the date of donation, it had no equity and had never declared a dividend.

The shareholders, collectively, donated their stock in JUL to a charitable organization on December 19, 2004. The barge was valued by a consulting engineer for the charitable organization and that value was reported to the taxpayers. The taxpayers also obtained their own independent appraisal from a marine surveyor as to the value of the barge. Both appraisers valued the assets of the business using a replacement value method. Based on the appraisal, the taxpayers reported the value of their charitable contribution at $720,000 ($810,000 less $90,000 the charitable organization gave to the donors). The IRS revised the value of the donation to $360,000 and issued a notice of deficiency.

Two issues underlying the fair market value of the donation came before the Tax Court: the value of the barge and the size of discounts for lack of marketability and minority interest.

The Tax Court valued the barge based on the replacement cost analysis performed by the charitable organization because the author of the analysis had helped build the barge in 1977. However, it adopted the useful life and depreciation analysis performed by the taxpayers' expert. This resulted in a value of the barge, dive bells and associated equipment at $1.06 million.

The Court then considered whether a discount for minority interest or lack of control should be applied. The IRS's expert applied a 22% discount while the taxpayers' expert argued that no discount should be applied. The Court reasoned that while the taxpayers' 45% block had swing vote characteristics, a hypothetical buyer would have difficulty implementing changes to the company's by-laws.

The taxpayers argued that no minority interest discount should be applied. It reasoned that since their donation was part of an agreed-upon plan by all the shareholders to transfer the entire company, their minority interest should be viewed as a controlling interest. The Tax Court noted the taxpayers' position was supported by *N. Trust Co. v. Commissioner*, 87 T.C. 349 (1996), which involved a prearranged transfer of a company to a trust by its four equal shareholders that resulted in the court's reduction of the size of the minority interest claimed by the taxpayers from 90% to 25%. Applying the *N. Trust Co.* reasoning, the Tax Court reduced the minority interest discount applicable here from the 22% argued by the IRS to 10%.

Since the Court's resolution of the valuation of the taxpayer's block of stock resulted in a valuation less than the value determined by the IRS in its notice of deficiency, the Tax Court fixed the value of the donated stock at the amount determined in the notice of deficiency.

This abstract originally appeared in *Valuation Case Digest*, authored by John J. Stockdale, Jr.

Estate of Manship v. United States

Citation: No. 04-CV-92-M2 (E.D. La. 2006)
Court: United States District Court
State/Jurisdiction: Eastern District of Louisiana
Date of Decision: April 13, 2006
Judge: Noland

In the *Estate of Douglas L. Manship v. United States of America*, No. 04-CV-91-M2 (M.D. La. April 13, 2006), the U.S. District Court for the Eastern District of Louisiana considered whether documents disclosed by an appraiser, who obtained them from the estate's attorney, were covered by the work product or attorney-client privilege. The estate engaged a credential business appraiser to value three closely held businesses for estate tax purposes. The appraiser's report was attached to the estate tax return and submitted to the IRS. A revised appraisal report was attached to a later administrative claim that sought a $26 million refund in estate taxes.

The appraiser was listed as the estate's testifying expert. The IRS issued a subpoena duces tecum to the appraiser that requested documents relating to his valuation of the businesses. The appraiser timely responded to the subpoena and privilege was not raised as an objection to any of the sought documents at the time. The IRS's attorney contacted the estate's attorney indicating that several of the documents produced may have been subject to the attorney-client privilege, but that as a result of their production the privilege was waived. The estate then sought to recover the documents as privileged work product or under the attorney-client privilege. The IRS opposed the motion.

The District Court determined that any claim the estate may have had under the attorney-client or work product privilege was waived. It reasoned that (1) the estate waived the privilege by voluntarily disclosing the documents; (2) by listing the appraiser as a testifying expert, F.R.C.P. 26(a)(2)(B) permitted the government to discover "all documents 'considered' by those experts in rendering their valuation opinions" "regardless of when those materials were received, generated, reviewed and/or used;" and (3) the estate failed to object within 14 days of the subpoena duces tecum as required by F.R.C.P. 45 (c)(2)(B). "As a general rule, when a party fails to object timely to interrogatories, production requests, or other discovery efforts, objections thereto are waived." The court also noted that since the estate placed the valuation in issue and intended to rely on it at trial, any privilege connected with the reports and related documents submitted by the estate in connection with the estate tax return and the administrative claim was waived. Lastly, the court noted that the IRS would be unable to adequately cross-examine or present rebuttal expert testimony without full access to the documents that the estate's appraiser considered in forming his opinion of value. Therefore, the District Court rejected the estate's assertion of privilege and permitted the IRS to review the documents obtained by it from the estate's expert that were considered by the appraiser in forming his valuation conclusion.

This abstract originally appeared in *Valuation Case Digest*, authored by John J. Stockdale, Jr.

Estate of Amlie v. Commissioner

Citation: 2006 Tax Ct. Memo LEXIS 76
Court: United States Tax Court
State/Jurisdiction: Specialty Federal
Date of Decision: April 17, 2006
Judge: Gale

Sometimes the squeaky wheel does get more out of the will. Rod Amlie was one of several prospective heirs to his mother's assets, which consisted of Iowa farm land as well as a 13.6% common stock interest in a bank. In 1986, his mother struck Rod from her will—but then established a spendthrift trust for him. A couple of years later, she voluntarily accepted a court-appointed conservator, who spent the next decade attempting to secure a guaranteed buy-sell option for Mrs. Amlie's minority stake in the bank, his efforts largely thwarted by Rod's legal objections.

Key factor is hiring valuator

Concerned that such a substantial portion of the Amlie assets were tied up in a minority interest, the conservator negotiated a 1991 agreement that fixed a price and buyer for the stock as well as a guarantee that her minority shares would receive the same price as those of the controlling interest, in the event the majority stakeholder sold.

In 1994, the majority owner (David Hill) sold his interest to First American Bank Group, Ltd. (FABG), receiving shares in FABG as determined by certain book value ratios of the merged banks. Per the 1991 guarantee, the conservator negotiated an exchange of Amlie's interest for FABG common stock at the same ratios received by Mr. Hill, which turned out to be close to $118 per share; and—in a move that turned out to be critical later on—retained a valuation consultant to determine whether this was a fair price for the FABG stock together with the price guarantee, or what became known as the "Hill Rights."

To reach this opinion, the (unnamed) valuation specialist reviewed merger multiples for appropriate M and A comparables in the banking industry, and concluded that Mrs. Amlie's minority interest, coupled with the Hill Rights as well as the right to defer capital gains taxes until after death, was fairly priced at $118 per share. The conservator submitted this 1994 agreement for court approval, contending that it established a further hedge against the risks of Mrs. Amlie's post-merger, minority interests.

Rod Amlie was the sole heir who objected, claiming that the $118 price failed to compensate for the Hill Rights by up to $500,000, as determined by his valuation expert (also unnamed). For various reasons, the district court rejected the 1994 agreement, which sent the parties back to negotiating a fair price for the FABG stock.

The squeaky wheel could have been right

The family negotiations culminated in a 1995 agreement whereby all of Mrs. Amlie's bank stock would be sold to Rod's trust at the $118 price. The trust could then pursue whatever price it could obtain, while the remaining heirs would have received a fixed price without incurring the risks of continued litigation and lack of liquidity.

Within two years, the trust had negotiated with FABG to redeem all of the stock at $217.50 per share plus 4% per year compounded semiannually until Mrs. Amlie's death, thus securing a premium for the Hill Rights. When she died a year later, her bank interests sold at the negotiated price, and Rod (as executor) received $993,757 for the estate's share at the $118 price, plus an additional $495,968, which then passed to his trust at the premium value.

Estate valuation turns on 'arms length' aspect

On its tax returns, the estate valued the minority bank interests at $993,757; while on its fiduciary income tax return, Rod's trust reported the $495,968 as capital gains. Not surprisingly, the IRS assessed a deficiency of $495,968 against the estate's return, claiming that the value of the bank stock should equal the price that FABG paid for it following Mrs. Amlie's death. The estate claimed that the buy-sell agreement fixing the price at $118 should be controlling.

To prevail, the estate would have to show that the buy-sell agreement was binding on all parties during life and after death; the restrictions had a bona fide business purpose, and were not substitutes for a testamentary disposition. In addition, the Tax Court said that under Section 2703(b)(3), a 1990 amendment to the Code, the agreement must be comparable to similar "arms length" arrangements.

Until this case, no court had found a buy-sell agreement to comply with §2703(b)(3). But in reviewing each of the requirements, the Court found:

Fixed price. The 1995 agreement fixed the $118 price as a ceiling (and floor) on the value of Mrs. Amlie's FABG stock, thereby passing all the risk of subsequent loss (or gain) to Rod's trust; it was irrelevant that the precise portions of the trust's bequest wouldn't be known until after Mrs. Amlie died and the rest of her estate valued.

Bona fide business purpose. "We are persuaded that the conservator, in securing the [buy-sell agreement], was seeking to exercise prudent management of decedent's assets by mitigating the very salient risks of holding a minority interest in a closely held bank, consistent with the conservator's fiduciary obligations."

Not a testamentary device. This finding turned on the fairness of the consideration received, which was "significant," given the risks of "substantial litigation hazards." Notably, the conservator had only agreed to the $118 price "after receiving professional advice that it was a fair price."

Comparable arms-length terms. Here, too, the estate's employment of a valuation specialist to establish market comparable prices for the buy-sell agreement was persuasive. Additionally, while §2703 favors multiple comparables for this purpose, the regulations "delineate more of a safe harbor than an absolute requirement."

The fact that Rod Amlie later secured a $217 price per share "raises questions" whether the $118 was comparable to similar, arms-length arrangements. But in the end, the agreement by his siblings to a lower price simply convinced the Court that the parties disagreed over the potential risks and rewards:

> In the circumstances, the other prospective heirs struck a bargain for the proverbial 'bird in the hand' of a guaranteed price, transferring to Rod the benefits and burdens of the pursuit of the possible 'two in the bush.' It may have been a bad bargain in hindsight, but we are persuaded it was arm's length when made.

Huber v. Commissioner

Citation: 2006 Tax Ct. Memo LEXIS 97
Court: United States Tax Court
State/Jurisdiction: Specialty Federal
Date of Decision: May 9, 2006
Judge: Goeke

To support the taxpayers' claims that gifts of closely-held stock among family members were "arms length" transactions, sufficient to support a 50% discount for lack of marketability (DLOM), it helps that nearly 250 shareholders of the closely-held company, all of them related to some degree, also accepted the same discounted value. When you've got a pool of friends and family that large—executing about 90 transactions during the relevant time period—you've nearly created your own fair market for comparables.

When a private company acts public

The taxpayers were shareholders of JM Huber Corporation—one of the largest family-held businesses in the country, then reporting over $500 million in annual sales. According to the Tax Court, Huber "emulated public companies" by maintaining high levels of communication with its 250 shareholders, who were generally family members (and also family-owned trusts). Pursuant to its by-laws, Huber could redeem stock from its shareholders, but there was no public market for the shares. To measure the financial performance of the company, set Board compensation (including CEO stock options), authorize redemptions, etc., Huber had employed Ernst and Young (E&Y, New York) since 1993 to provide an annual valuation.

To value Huber shares, E&Y had consistently used a publicly-traded market comparable methodology; and had consistently applied a 50% marketability discount. During the years in question (1994-2000), about 90 sales or exchanges of Huber stock had taken place between shareholders, including immediate family members, distant cousins, and trustees. All of these sales had taken place at the E&Y discounted value.

Those 90 transactions included Petitioners' gifts of Huber stock to family, which they valued according to E&Y reports. The IRS agreed with E&Y's assessment of the freely-traded value of the shares, but challenged the 50% marketability discount. According to its expert, Appraisal Economics, Inc. (Paramus, NJ), a 25%-40% DLOM was more appropriate, rejecting the E&Y discount because the sales at those values were not "arms-length" transactions.

IRS 'ignored' the evidence

Relying on such key cases as *McCord v. Commissioner* (2003) and *Estate of Bongard v. Commissioner* (2005), the IRS urged the court to closely scrutinize the family transactions for failure to maintain "arms-length." The Service also argued that the E&Y reports were not reliable because they were aged eight months to a year by the time the transactions took place.

But the Tax Court criticized the IRS for "focusing on isolated sales that took place between closely-related family members as if they were the only sales." The Service had ignored the 90-plus transactions involving an "amalgam of relationships," in which the parties were fully informed regarding Huber's finances, with sufficient independent knowledge to assess the E&Y valuations.

As examples, the taxpayers offered two sales: One took place when a Huber family executor had to raise money to pay estate tax (he was also a Stanford MBA, ran a private equity firm, and served as a nonvoting Huber director). In the second, a Huber family trustee needed to satisfy trust expenses, and sold to one of its beneficiaries, the sister of the Huber CEO and also a nonvoting board member.

These parties were under no compulsion to make/receive the gifts of stock (as in *McCord*); any family relationships between them were effectively "neutralized" by the distance of these relationships, as well as their fiduciary obligations to obtain the best price. The variety of these relationships was, according to the Court, "a positive indicator of the existence of arm's length sales."

In other words, "we reject [the IRS'] suggestion that almost 250 shareholders would harmoniously accept an artificially low valuation of the Huber stock so that a few people who may or may not be related to them can pay less estate tax."

The Court also rejected the "hypothetical" notion that offering the stock for public sale would have garnered a higher price. "Courts have long recognized the rights of shareholders in closely held companies to remain private." As there was "no basis to suggest" an available market where a potential buyer would purchase Huber shares at higher than the E&Y values, these values—including the discounts—were the "best reference" available, and confirmed the estate's valuation.

Estate of Rosen v. Commissioner

Citation: 2006 T.C. Memo LEXIS 116
Court: United States Tax Court
State/Jurisdiction: Specialty Federal
Date of Decision: June 1, 2006
Judge: Laro

When Lillie Rosen's son-in-law attended a seminar on family limited partnerships (FLPs) in 1994, the federal Tax Court had yet to develop its "economic substance approach" to transfer tax cases. So by the time this case reached Judge David Laro, a notable authority on the subject, he was able to produce a primer on "what not to do" when trying to form an FLP to fall within the exception of IRC Section 2036.

A 'simple change in form' is not enough

It's hard to read the facts of the Rosen case, given all that BV appraisers know today. After his seminar, the son-in-law consulted with the family attorney, who advised him that "simply changing the form in which the decedent's assets were held from a trust to a limited partnership would generate significant tax savings," and that these savings were a "major and significant reason" to form an FLP. On the basis of his "general" understanding of FLPs and his discussions with the son-in-law—but without meeting with any other family members, the attorney determined who among them would be the general and limited partners, the percentage amount each would contribute, and which assets would fund the FLP. He never spoke about forming an FLP with Lillie Rosen, who was ill and aged at the time, suffering from what would become "full blown" dementia by the time the documents were done in 1996.

Only one family member signed the documents in the presence of the attorney. None of them knew (or had calculated) the dollar amount of their capital calls until a couple of months later, even though the documents required contribution at the time of execution. The stated purpose of the FLP was the "business of making, protecting, enhancing, and otherwise investing. . . in any type of security," which amounted to $2.4 million in cash and marketable securities in a Merrill Lynch account, transferred from the family trust to the FLP, with the trust becoming the 99% limited partner. After the opening of a new Merrill Lynch account in the FLP name, "there was no material change in the manner in which the . . . assets were managed."

Over the next four years, the FLP provided living expenses for the ailing Mrs. Rosen, and continued her gift-giving program to many family members, characterizing these withdrawals from the Merrill Lynch account as "loans" supported by two demand notes. But no other partner took similar loans; and one of the notes was prepared after her death in 2000, back-dated to the day she died. By this time, the FLP had given away 64% of the limited partnership interests; it then redeemed the trust's interest to pay decedent's legal fees, funeral expenses, and other bequests.

For tax purposes, the IRS sought to bring all of the FLP's assets back into her gross estate, pursuant to §2036(a)(1). Per that same provision, the estate claimed exemption because the transfers were a "bona fide sale for full and adequate consideration," and that the decedent did not retain full possession and enjoyment of the assets. (It also argued that §2035(a) limited the estate because Ms. Rosen had given away a 48.5% limited partnership interest more than three years before her death, from 1996-1998. "To state the obvious," the Court said, the 1998 gifts "were not more than three years before her death in 2000.")

The law on FLP's is also obvious—now

Citing the (by now) well known case law of *Estate of Thomson* (2004), *Estate of Abraham* (2004), *Estate of Strangi* (2005), and *Estate of Bongard* (2005) (copies of full-text court opinions available for subscribers of the *BVLaw*™ database at BVLibrary.com), the Court explained that to fall within the 2036(a)(1) exception for a bona fide transfer, the FLP must have: (1) served a legitimate, non-tax purpose; and (2) bestowed on each transferor a partnership interest proportionate to the fair market value of the transferred property. Given its findings on the first prong, the Court didn't need to discuss the second.

Despite its stated purpose, the Rosen FLP "conducted no business activity and had no business purpose for its existence," according to Judge Laro, "other than the avoidance of Federal estate (and gift) tax." A legitimate, significant non-tax reason is "one that actually motivated the formation of [the] partnership from a business point of view." A "theoretical justification" won't suffice.

To support its holding, the Court also compiled the following "laundry list" of factors—a comprehensive summation which could help current practitioners avoid the fate of the Rosen FLP:

- It conducted minimal and mostly passive investment activity.
- It failed to follow "commonplace" business procedures such as maintaining books of account, making proper capital calls, holding formal partnership meetings, etc.
- None of the FLP partners negotiated its original terms, and decedent's daughter stood "on all sides of the transaction" as general partner, trustee of the largest limited partner interest, and decedent's attorney-in-fact.
- Compared to the decedent's contribution, the children's contributions were "de minimus," and given her contemporaneous gifts to the children, decedent arguably funded the FLP on her own.
- The management of the assets was the same before and after the transfer.
- During the first four years of the FLP (and the last four years of her life), decedent gave away almost 65% of her limited partnership interest.
- After forming the FLP, decedent was unable to meet her personal living expenses and gift giving program, which required withdrawal of FLP funds, which also went to meet her death expenses.
- The assets of the FLP consisted solely of marketable securities and cash. (Note: "the mere holding of an untraded portfolio of marketable securities weight against the finding of a non-tax benefit for a transfer of that portfolio to a family entity.")

- Decedent was 88 years old and in failing health when the FLP was formed.
- The FLP provided no more meaningful protection from her creditors than the former family trust.
- Decedent enjoyed the FLP assets and their income during her lifetime, receiving distributions when and as she needed them—just as she had from the trust. This arrangement could be implied from her age and condition at the formation of the FLP, the transfer of all her assets, and the failure of the loans to qualify as bona fide debts.

In the Matter of the Estate of Norman B. Hjersted (I)

Citation: 2006 Kan. App. LEXIS 517
Court: Court of Appeals
State/Jurisdiction: Kansas
Date of Decision: June 2, 2006
Judge: Sundby

If you're unwilling to suffer the financial consequences of divorce later in life—then don't expect to escape them at death. That appears to be the "life" lesson of the *Hjersted* case; the valuation lesson concerns the application of discounts to an FLP that one spouse creates to disinherit the other.

Apparently, the late Mr. Hjersted wanted to cut his wife out of his will. In 1997, after nearly twenty years of marriage, he created a family limited partnership (FLP) to hold all the outstanding shares of his company; he became a 2% general partner and a 96% limited partner of the FLP, and his son by a prior marriage a 1% general partner and 1% limited partner. Three years later, in March 2000, he transferred his 96% limited partnership interest to his son as part gift/part sale. He also set up his will to "pour over" the remaining probate assets into a trust, for which his son was trustee. A year later Mr. Hjersted died, and his wife sought her spousal elective share of the estate.

Elective share prevents decedent from disinheriting wife

As with most states, Kansas adopted its elective share statute from the Uniform Probate Code, which gives a surviving spouse the right to elect a percentage of the augmented estate (to which certain uncompensated, non-probate transfers have been added) based on the length of the marriage. The purpose is to prevent one spouse from disinheriting the other, and the rationale is based on similar "partnership" and "support" theories which underlie the uniform dissolution of marriage laws: During their lives together, both spouses have contributed to the accumulated estate, and each owes the other a duty of support. These duties continue after death, as the survivor's claim on the estate.

In this case, the statutory scheme required the district court to analyze the FLP as a non-probate, uncompensated transfer. The son argued that only the gift portion qualified, worth $675,000 (which was the maximum tax-free transfer as of March 2000). The son had purchased the remainder of the 96% limited partnership interest by a down payment and promissory notes, in amounts determined by an appraisal. Because the sole asset was 100% of the company stock, the (unnamed) appraiser first determined the stock to be worth $4,500 per share, and then applied a combined 32.5% discount for lack of marketability and control.

By contrast, the wife's appraised value of the company stock reflected only a 10% discount for lack of marketability; and found the 96% interest to be worth over $2.55 million. Reducing this value by the promissory notes ($744,000) and the son's down payment ($39,000), the wife urged the court to pull back over $1.770 million into the estate. With a minor exception, the court agreed with the wife, finding that although the FLP "was a valid and existing limited partnership at the time of the gift. . . and continues to be so," its entire value, without discounts, should augment the estate because the wife had not consented to the transfer. Her elective share exceeded $1.175 million.

Consent is not the issue; uncompensated transfer is

The Appeals Court found that consent was irrelevant; the "paramount" determination was valuing the gift at the time of transfer. "Here, the transfer was a 96% limited partnership interest in [an FLP] on March 1, 2000." The augmented estate must include the value to the extent it was not supported by consideration.

But despite the district court's focus on consent, it had weighed the expert appraisals and decided that the wife's was better supported by more recent data (concerning the increase in pre-tax income in early 2000) and an on-site investigation. The son's appraisal suffered an "inherent bias to minimize value." Competent evidence thus supported the court's finding that 500 shares of the company were worth $2.66 million.

The only question left was whether the court erred by valuing the company shares without discounting for the limited partnership interest. The appeals court analyzed the transfer, and found that not only had the son received the 96% limited partnership interest and 1% general partnership interest—but he would also receive the remaining 2% general partnership interest from the trust due to "pour over" provisions of the will. "Discounts for lack of control and lack of marketability were unnecessary in these circumstances for several reasons," the Court said:

- Discounts for individual interests inject speculation into the appraisal.
- Discounts are not appropriate where the transaction effectively unifies all of the partnership interests in one individual.
- The partnership performed no management functions (citing *Estate of Bongard*).

- The partnership disregarded standard procedures, including requiring capital calls and filing state/federal returns; and the company paid dividends directly to the father and son rather than the partnership. A legal but "artificial" entity does not merit the same discounting that might otherwise apply to "real" partnership interests.

Last, but not the least, among valuation lessons: Discounts in these cases could help create "layers of illusory ownership for non probate transfers, each with the potential for additional discounting, and all for the purpose of insulating the true value of assets transferred, in furtherance of a scheme to disinherit a spouse."

Kohler v. Commissioner

Citation: 2006 Tax Ct. Memo LEXIS 156
Court: United States Tax Court
State/Jurisdiction: Specialty Federal
Date of Decision: July 25, 2006
Judge: Kroupa

The stars must have been aligned during the *Kohler* decision, because everything went right for the taxpayer. First, lawyers for the Kohler estate won key legal victories on the burden of proof and the valuation date; then the expert for the IRS made a critical miscalculation in his report (the kind you'd never wish on anyone, even the opposition). Finally, the Tax Court (Judge Kroupa) not only considered both Kohler experts to be "thoughtful and credible," giving significant weight to their reports—but also found that between them, the more advantageous valuation ruled the day.

Of course, the taxpayer could have wished that the IRS had never assessed deficiencies in the first place, but then the business valuation and legal community would be without this "textbook" case, brought to you by two of the leading authorities in the field, on how to value a large, closely-held business.

A household name

Kohler is one of the leading manufacturers of kitchen and bath products; separate divisions also manufacture small industrial engines, household furnishings, and operate hospitality services. Despite public renown, Kohler has always been a privately-held family business since its founding in 1887. It has also paid annual dividends since 1900. In fact, Kohler's stated policy was to reinvest at least 90% of its annual earnings in the business, paying out 7% to 10% as dividends even during recessions (even if it had to cut back on retained earnings). Shareholders depended on dividends as the sole source of ROI—and often as their only source of income, without any active market for sale or appreciation of the shares.

Kohler also issued two business plans: A management plan, which was a realistic projection of achievable targets, given current economic realities; and an operations plan, which was a theoretical, "best case" projection of what could happen in a perfect world. Kohler regularly updated its management plan for lenders, insurance companies, etc.; its operations plan was for internal use only.

Reorganization in 1998

To recapture the 4% of stock held by non-family members, Kohler effected a tax-free reorganization (under §368(a) IRC) in May of 1998. Under its terms, non-family shareholders could either accept a cash-out price of $52,700 per share, or exercise dissenters' rights—which some did with varying success, settling for up to $135,000 per share, including claims for breach of fiduciary duty.

During the reorganization, on March 4, 1988, Frederic Kohler died. Before reorganization, Kohler's estate owned 12.85% voting stock; afterwards, it owned 14.45%. To value the taxable interest, the estate hired Robert Schweihs ASA, CBA (Willamette Management Associates, Chicago), who had performed periodic valuations for the company and knew its operations well. Schweihs was (and still is) a household name in business valuation, having co-authored a leading text (Valuing a Business, Fourth Edition) with Shannon Pratt and Robert Reilly.

Schweihs appraised the fair market value of the estate's Kohler holdings as of September 4, 1998 at $47.01 million. He also appraised the value of the estate at Frederic's death six months earlier at $50.115 million. Pursuant to §2032 IRC, the estate elected the alternate date—six months after the decedent's death, to value its holdings, and filed its return with the $47.01 million appraisal. After an extended audit, during which the estate withheld certain documents until the court denied its motion to quash, the IRS determined the fair market value of the Kohler holdings on the alternate date to be $144.5 million, based on an appraisal by Richard May (founder of Valuemetrics Advisors, Inc., now with Duff & Phelps, Chicago). (The decision does not mention whether the IRS used May's appraisal during the subsequent litigation).

The valuations were, needless to say, nearly $100 million apart.

A critical shift in taxpayer's favor

In most cases, it's up to the taxpayer to prove that IRS deficiency notices are incorrect. This burden of proof shifts to the IRS if the taxpayer can show well-maintained, substantiated records and cooperation with the IRS. In this case, the Kohler estate had "legitimate" concerns about turning over sensitive corporate records—but after an unsuccessful motion to quash, the company complied with all IRS requests. The deluge of documents made the burden of proof "a meaningful issue, rather than simply an academic one." (A good lesson for lawyers and taxpayers: the more you turn over, the more likely you can show credible records and compliance.) Accordingly, the Tax Court placed the burden on the IRS to prove that the taxpayer was liable: an important shift, which became critical to the taxpayer victory.

The IRS also lost a bid to value the Kohler estate on the date of Frederic's death, because it missed a procedural deadline for amending its pleadings. The question still remained whether, on the alternate valuation date, the Kohler stock should be valued before or after the reorganization; the IRS tried to "backdoor" its argument by claiming the Court should either: (a) value the pre-organization stock on the alternate valuation date; or (b) ignore the transfer restrictions and purchase option in valuing the post-organization stock. The taxpayer won on this point, too, primarily because the Court recognized that pursuant to §2032(a) and the accompanying Estate Tax Regulations, a qualified, tax-free reorganization is not a "distribution, sale, or exchange" or other substantial change in form—or value.

The narrow question then became the fair market value of the post-reorganization Kohler stock on the alternate valuation date, including the transfer restrictions and purchase option. Given its decision on burden of proof, the Court first considered the IRS expert report by Scott Hakala, Ph.D., CFA (CBIZ Valuation Group, LLC).

How important is a USPAP certification?

The Court considered the expert's credentials before his substantive appraisal, noting that although he had a doctorate and a CFA, he was neither a member of the ASA nor the Appraisal Foundation. The Court also noted that his report had omitted "the customary USPAP certification" regarding the appraiser's compliance with standards and independence. (An interesting observation, as not all appraisers regularly include the USPAP language, even though their reports qualify.)

In its more detailed discussion of the expert's income approach, the Court indicated that Hakala had declined to use a dividend based method, preferring a discounted cash flow (DCF) instead—but then he'd opted not to use Kohler-provided projections, making his own expense assumptions "without first discussing them [with] anyone at Kohler." He created two DCF models, one using revenues from the company's management and the other from its operations plan, giving the former a 20% weight versus 80% for the latter, because he believed the "aspirational" plan was the more likely scenario. The Court disagreed, saying he weighted the results "inconsistent with reality of the business."

The IRS expert had also made a last-minute correction to his income approach values, which had overvalued the Kohler stock by $11 million—"not a minor mistake" according to the Court, and which—no matter how it was made—seemed to be one from which the Service couldn't recover. The Court noted for the record its market approach, using the guideline company method (80% weight) as well as the transaction method (20%), averaging the two and applying a 25% discount for lack of marketability. But in the final analysis, it found that: (1) the IRS had declined to use a dividend approach for a private company with a long and consistent dividend policy; (2) it had weighted a theoretical operations plan over a realistic management plan; and (3) it had failed to use management projections. These facts were sufficient to hold that the IRS had failed in its burden of proof. "Accordingly, we find the value of the estate's stock to be [as] reported on its return, $47,009,625."

Discussion of taxpayer's appraisal academic

The Court completed its record with high praise for the taxpayer's valuation reports by Schweihs and also Roger Grabowski, ASA (Duff & Phelps). It noted their respective credentials and professional experience, including extensive teaching experience and publications. Their reports provided "thoughtful, credible valuations strongly supporting the value the estate reported on its tax return."

The Court's discussion of their income and market approaches reads like a textbook case study on how to value a closely-held business, and is worthwhile reading for all business appraisers (and their attorneys). Highlights include:

Schweihs report

- Schweihs was "very familiar" with company management and operations, having performed periodic valuations before.
- His income approach used a discounted dividend method and also a dividend capitalization method, "important indicators of value where dividends represent the best, if not the only opportunity for minority shareholders to receive a cash return on...investment."
- His market approach used only the guideline company method, because he was unable to find sufficient comparables for the transaction method.
- He did not use prior sales of Kohler stock, because they included a premium for being a stockholder in a prominent, privately-held company, which could not be quantified.
- He applied a 45% discount for lack of marketability under the DCF and capital market methods, and a 10% DLOM to the dividend methods because they more directly reflected the value of shares.
- He applied a 26% lack of control discount in his DCF.
- He assigned a 20% weight to the DCF and capital market methods, 30% to dividend methods.
- He concluded a value for Kohler stock of $47.01 million at the alternate valuation date ($50.115 million at the date of death).

Grabowski report

- Grabowski spent 3 ½ days at the company interviewing 12 employees, including considerable time with the president and the general counsel/executor of the estate.

- He used the management plan, including its projections, in his DCF and discounted dividend analysis.
- For his guideline public company analysis, he identified publicly-traded companies in each market segment in which Kohler operated, and applied valuation multiples to these entities, weighting the valuation conclusion of each segment based on the relative portion of Kohler's business that each comprised.
- Each of his methods resulted in fairly close values; after assessing the strengths and weaknesses of each, he decided the adjusted discounted dividend method was the most appropriate, "because it reflected the actual cash flows a shareholder would expect to receive," and also the remote possibility that Kohler could be sold or go public.
- He applied a 35% DLOM, a 25% discount for lack of control, for a bottom line fair market value of Kohler stock on the alternate valuation date of $63.385 million.

Janis v. Commissioner

Citation: No. 04-74624 (9th Cir. 2006)
Court: United States Court of Appeals
State/Jurisdiction: 9th Circuit Federal
Date of Decision: August 21, 2006
Judge: McKeown

In *Conrad Janis v. CIR*, No. 04-74624 (9th Cir. August 21, 2006), the U.S. Court of Appeals for the Ninth Circuit considered the fair market value of an inherited art collection for partnership basis purposes. The taxpayer's father operated an art gallery, which held a significant number of artworks from a variety of artists. The taxpayer was the executor of his father's estate. He engaged Sotheby's to value each artwork for estate tax purposes. It determined that the collection had an aggregate value of $36.636 million. The taxpayer then applied a blockage discount to reduce the value of the collection to $12 million.

A blockage discount is commonly applied when valuing the collections of artists at the time of their death. When valuing a gallery's collection, a blockage discount may also be appropriate after considering several factors: (1) prominence of the artists; (2) types of works in the collection; (3) the distribution of the works by artist, types, and quality; (4) the number of similar type items on the market; (5) the market response on the valuation date; (6) the number and sale price of comparables near the time of death; (7) the annual sales of the gallery; (8) the length of time needed to liquidate the collection; (9) the earning capacity of the gallery; and (10) the tangible and intangible assets, including goodwill, reputation and provenance of the gallery. The IRS and the estate agreed to a fair market value of the collection of $14.4 million, including a blockage discount.

After the estate closed in 1991, the collection and business of the gallery was transferred to a partnership operated by the taxpayer and his brother. Thereafter, they restated the cost of goods sold to the undiscounted value of the collection. This had the effect of making the partnership unprofitable.

The IRS contested the taxpayer's revision of the cost of goods sold to the undiscounted value of the collection and argued that the value reflected on the estate tax return was the appropriate value. The Tax Court agreed and the taxpayer appealed.

On appeal, the taxpayer argued that the Tax Court's conclusion as to the valuation of the partnership was not binding on the Ninth Circuit. It claimed that because the IRS and the taxpayer stipulated to the facts, the Tax Court's valuation decision was a conclusion of law, which is reviewed de novo. The Ninth Circuit disagreed and affirmed the valuation as a finding of fact, subject to the clearly erroneous standard. After considering the Tax Court's decision, the Ninth Circuit affirmed the valuation of the collection.

The taxpayer additionally argued that he did not owe a duty of consistency to use the same value on the estate and his individual tax returns. The Ninth Circuit noted that the duty of consistency is found where (1) the taxpayer makes a representation, (2) on which the IRS relies, and (3) the taxpayer attempts to change his position after the statute of limitations has run such that the IRS is harmed. The Ninth Circuit held that the taxpayer made a representation to the IRS when he entered into a Form 890 settlement with the IRS as to the value of the collection in his capacity as executor of the estate. Furthermore, in that capacity, the taxpayer had "an incentive to *minimize the value of the collection*" and after the distribution of the estate, he "had an incentive to *maximize the value of the collection*." (Emphasis in original). Moreover, it found that the IRS relied on Form 890 in closing the estate. Therefore, the taxpayer had a duty of consistency to use the value reported on the estate tax return as the value of the collection on the taxpayer's individual tax return.

This abstract originally appeared in *Valuation Case Digest*, authored by John J. Stockdale, Jr.

McCord v. Commissioner (II)

Citation: 2006 U.S. App. LEXIS 21473
Court: United States Court of Appeals
State/Jurisdiction: 5th Circuit Federal
Date of Decision: August 22, 2006
Judge: Wiener

In one of the biggest upsets in business valuation law, the Fifth Circuit Court of Appeals overturned *McCord v. Commissioner*, 2003 U.S. Tax Ct. LEXIS 16 (2003)(*McCord I*). Most analysts know the 117-page McCord I for its determination of marketability discounts, where—in a splintered majority, with dissents by Judge David Laro among others—the Tax Court rejected the taxpayer's restricted stock analysis, conducted by William Frazier, ASA (HFBE, Houston), and endorsed the criticism of pre-IPO studies by Dr. Mukesh Bajaj (LECG, Emeryville, CA) without adopting his final conclusions.

The original opinion generated extensive controversy in the BV profession. In the *Business Valuation Update™'s* "2003 in review," former editor-in-chief Shannon Pratt critiqued the Tax Court's conclusions regarding the marketability discounts, and hoped that the appeal would set the record straight. At the time, Dr. Pratt also recognized that the legal and tax issues caused as much debate as the valuation issues—and indeed, in its recent rejection of *McCord I*, the 5th Circuit focuses more on the Tax Court's violation of an "immutable rule" of valuation evidence as well as its "palpable hostility to...the defined value gift clause."

Key *McCord* facts revisited

In January 1996, the McCord family transferred all of their interests in a limited partnership to exempt and non-exempt donees by an Assignment Agreement. Rather than use percentage interests, however, they conveyed dollar amounts of the net fair market value of the partnership interests pursuant to a sequentially structured "defined value clause." (A common provision to make sure that conveyances come within allowable tax exemptions, as it provides that donors are conveying only so much of the gift/interest that equals the exemption amount.)

In conjunction with the Assignment Agreement, Frazier's appraisal calculated that each donee would receive $89,505 for each 1% of limited partnership interest at the time of the gifts. The donees had access to legal counsel, and had the express right to review the Frazier appraisal and/or obtain an independent appraisal as well as arbitrate any disputes regarding the valuation.

Although one donee's counsel did review the valuation (and ultimately agreed with Frazier's conclusions), there was no evidence of any agreement between the taxpayers and the exempts—"not so much as an implicit, 'wink-wink' understanding," according to the 5th Circuit—that any donee "was expected to or in fact could accept a percentage interest...with a value less than the full dollar amount" conveyed. (The lone exception was the Tax Court's footnote in *McCord I*, stating that "it is against the economic interest of a charitable organization to look a gift horse in the mouth,"—a by-now familiar comment which the 5th Circuit calls a "gratuitous generalization.")

Approximately two months later, the donees entered into a separate Confirmation Agreement, which translated the dollar value of each gift under the Assignment Agreement's defined value formula into percentages of interests in the partnership.

A procedural anomaly intervenes

The taxpayers used Frazier's appraisal to calculate their gift tax returns, including a 35% discount for lack of marketability based on his analysis of restricted stock studies as well as supporting data from pre-IPO studies.

But the IRS assessed over $4 million in deficiencies, claiming that the taxpayers had: (1) understated the fair market value of the donated limited partnership interests; and (2) erred in discounting those values. The Commissioner's fair market valuation of a one-percent limited partnership interest was $171,749—or nearly twice that of the taxpayers'—and was based on Dr. Bajaj's by-now famous rejection of pre-IPO studies, including his assessment that a 7% marketability discount was appropriate.

The parties originally tried the dispute before Judge Maurice B. Foley, primarily through a joint stipulation of facts as well as a stipulation that the Commissioner carried the burden of proof. The Commissioner also attacked the "defined value gift clause," claiming that it violated public policy and "form-over-substance" doctrines. Based on these stipulations, Judge Foley held that the Commissioner had failed to meet its burden of proof on any contested issue and could not prevail.

Two years later, however, the Tax Court's Chief Judge issued an unusual order that retroactively took the case away from Judge Foley and re-assigned it to what resembled an en banc panel. This uncommon proceeding ultimately produced McCord I from an eight-judge majority, with concurring and dissenting opinions from five other justices (including J. Foley). The majority did not base its holdings on any of the Commissioner's equitable arguments. Instead, the majority "crafted its own interpretation" of the Assignment and Confirmation agreements, according to the 5th Circuit, "all based entirely on a theory the Commissioner had never espoused."

> At the core of the novel methodology thus conceived and implemented, sua sponte, by the Majority is the consistently rejected concept of postponed determination of the taxable value of a completed gift...until two months [later]...Stated differently, the Majority in essence suspended the valuation date of the property that the Taxpayers donated in January [per the Assignment Agreement] until the date in March on which [per the Confirmation Agreement] the disparate donees acted, post hoc, to agree among themselves on the Class B limited partnership percentages that each would accept as equivalents of the dollar values irrevocably and unconditionally given by the Taxpayers months earlier.

This "unique methodology violated the immutable maxim that post-gift occurrences do not affect, and may not be considered in, the appraisal and valuation processes...The flip side of the maxim," the Court continues, betraying its frustration with the Tax Court, "is that subsequent events are off limits."

As a result of this critical legal error, the majority's independent valuation of the donated property—which fell precisely halfway between those of Mr. Frazier and Dr. Bajaj—"becomes irrelevant to the amount of the gift taxes owed by the Taxpayers."

The feature that most 'fractionated' the Tax Court

One possible explanation for the wresting of the original case away from Judge Foley was the "aggressive and sophisticated" tax planning by the McCords, which the Tax Court panel viewed "with palpable hostility," according to the 5th Circuit. "The feature that most fractionated the Tax Court was the Taxpayer's use of the dollar-formula, or 'defined value clause' specified in the Assignment Agreement" to quantify the gifts in dollars rather than percentages.

The result was, as Judge Foley pointed out in his *McCord I* dissent, a "tortured" analysis of the Assignment Agreement that required the taxpayers to use the majority's valuation to determine the dollar value of the transferred interest, but Frazier's appraisal to determine the percentage interests transferred. "There is no factual, legal, or logical basis for this conclusion."

The 5th Circuit agrees with Judge Foley's conclusion that the taxpayers completed their gifts on the date of the Assignment Agreement; and that these gifts had an "ascertainable value," despite their expression in dollars instead of percentage interests. The value was not varied by the donees' Confirmation Agreement—in which the taxpayers took no part, and which took place two months after the transfer of gifts.

But in the end, the 5th Circuit uses a "process of elimination" to determine the applicable fair market values of the gifts. As the Tax Court had correctly rejected the Commissioner's valuation—but incorrectly applied its own "imaginative" methodology "out of whole cloth"—the values left were those which Frazier had reached in his original report, and which the taxpayers used on their returns. Affirming without discussing Frazier's calculation of marketability discounts, the 5th Circuit allots the remainder of its analysis to the Tax Court's final legal error—its failure to apply a discount for the present negative value of the donees' assumption of estate tax liability under IRC Section 2035.

Harsh words for the Service

In its notation that the IRS deficiency notices were "almost double the Frazier values," the 5th Circuit observes that not even Bajaj had agreed with them, valuing all the gifts at $1.7 million less than the asserted deficiencies. "This exemplified a practice of the IRS that we see with disturbingly increased frequency," the Court says in a footnote, "e.g., a grossly exaggerated amount asserted in a notice of deficiency." It cites the recent *Caracci* case as an example.

It's anyone's guess whether the IRS will heed such reprimand. But for business appraisers, this reversal means that *McCord I* has lost most of its precendential value; and though the appellate decision is binding only on the 5th Circuit, analysts and attorneys are likely to cite it as support for traditional valuation approaches.

Dallas v. Commissioner

Citation: 2006 Tax Ct. Memo LEXIS 216
Court: United States Tax Court
State/Jurisdiction: Specialty Federal
Date of Decision: September 28, 2006
Judge: Colvin

The *Dallas* case bears enough factual resemblance to *Gross v. Commissioner* (originally decided by the Tax Court in 1999, confirmed by the 6th Circuit in 2001), to alert most appraisers of the issues as well as the outcome—which adds yet another tax-affecting and discount case to the IRS arsenal.

In the Dallas family, the father "sold" about 55% of non-voting stock in a private S corporation to his sons' trusts, in exchange for cash and self-canceling notes. At the time, a third party appraiser ascertained the fair market value of the stock using a capitalization of income approach, discounted by a 40% tax-affected rate, 15% for lack of control and 35% for lack of marketability.

In auditing a Dallas son, the IRS deemed the transfers gifts, to which it applied lesser discounts and no tax-affected rate; it also determined the notes held less than face value because of their self-canceling provisions. On review, the Tax Court quickly agreed that the inter-family transfers were "bargain gifts," and turned to the "tax affecting" issue and the application of discounts.

As George Hawkins, ASA, CFA and Michael Pascall, ASA, CFA (Banister Financial, Atlanta) observed about Gross for the January 2002 *Business Valuation Update™*, "[the IRS] picked a great fact pattern to argue" the tax-affecting issue. They identified five factors that bolstered the IRS position—four of which are largely present in the Dallas case:

1. The S Corp had stable and profitable operations;

2. The S Corp consistently paid out enough dividends for shareholders to pay their pro-rata, "pass through" income tax;

3. There was no evidence that the company's corporate status would change; and

4. A minority interest was at stake.

One note: In *Gross*, the S Corp had a consistent annual 100% pay-out to shareholders; in *Dallas*, the company used retained earnings to expand—a fact that failed to persuade the *Dallas* court to distinguish the two cases. "Our analysis [in *Gross*] did not depend on the proportion of corporate income distributed":

We said that, in determining the present value of an expected stream of earnings, any tax-affecting to reflect the shareholder-level tax burden should be done equally (or not at all) to both the discount rate and the expected cash flows, with the result that, in either case, the present value determined would be the same. That analysis is independent of earnings distributed.

The fifth factor in *Gross*—restrictive agreements that made it difficult to break the S Corporation status, is not present in *Dallas*. But the Tax Court did find "the assumptions of the [taxpayer's] witnesses that a hypothetical buyer and seller would assume without any supporting evidence that those events would occur,"—i.e., a change in corporate status or dividend practice—"detracts from the credibility of their opinions."

The taxpayer's case also suffered when its second appraiser apparently lifted passages "verbatim" from the original appraisal, and was "substantially unfamiliar" with his own report. "We give [his] testimony little weight," the Court said.

The original appraisal, which valued the S Corp shares at the transfer, didn't fare much better. In providing his reasons for tax-affecting, the appraiser testified that: (1) he had always tax-affected; (2) an informal poll at (an unnamed) conference suggested that 90%-95% of attendees tax-affected; (3) the ASA rejected certification unless applicants tax-affected; (4) bankers, investment bankers, and business brokers tax-affect S Corp sales; and (5) his company had tax-affected ESOP valuations for the Department of Labor.

The Tax Court found this analysis "unconvincing." Likewise, the taxpayer failed to persuade the Court to adopt the Delaware Chancery's tax-affecting rationale in the recent *Delaware Open MRI Radiology Assoc., Inc. v. Kessler* (see the July 2006 *BVU*). "The issue in [*Del. Open MRI*] was whether minority stockholders...received fair value of the going concern in a merger," the *Dallas* Court said. The fair market value standard, however, must consider the price a willing hypothetical buyer and seller would negotiate—and in this case, the Court found "insufficient evidence" that the hypothetical parties would tax-affect the S Corp's earnings.

The Tax Court also quickly resolved the disputes on discounts:

1. *Lack of voting power.* The taxpayer's second appraiser had specifically valued a non-voting minority interest, and so did not apply a lack of control discount. He did apply a 5% discount for lack of voting power, as non-voting stockholders couldn't pool their votes as might minority shareholders. In denying the discount, the Court said that any anticipation of pooling votes was "speculative."

2. *Minority interest.* The taxpayer didn't dispute the 15% minority discount for non-operating assets; however, it argued that the IRS' 20% minority discount for operating assets was too low, because it used a formula based on the control premium, adjusting for excessive executive compensation. But the Court found "no indication" of this basis, and no reason to increase the discount.

3. *Lack of marketability.* The taxpayer had examined restricted stock studies over several time periods, selecting the 34.2% mean DLOM from pre-1990 studies and adjusting this to 40% to account for the company's weak prospects of going public. But the Court ratified the 20% DLOM by the IRS, saying the taxpayer should have used studies from the time period in which the transfers took place—in which the median DLOM was 13.2% (suggesting, perhaps, that the discount could have been lower).

4. *Fair market value of the notes.* The taxpayer had executed the self-canceling notes in 1999; after learning from an IRS reviewer that these provisions reduced the notes' face value, the taxpayer deleted them from like notes in a 2000 stock transfer. The taxpayer claimed at trial that the 1999 notes had been a "drafting mistake," but the Tax Court held the "unambiguous," self-canceling notes to the lesser face value.

Like many family-run, private corporations, the Dallas father and sons held executive positions for which they received "unreasonable" compensation, according to the IRS. It argued for increasing the company's projected net income—as any sale to unrelated investors would allegedly reduce the salaries.

But the IRS had failed to provide customary "reasonable compensation" evidence to the Tax Court. In addition, "we have no more reason to assume changes in [the company's] executive compensation policies than we have to assume changes in dividend paying policies or a change in its S corporation status." In the final analysis, the Tax Court's holding in *Dallas* remains internally consistent if not consistent with *Gross*; whether either is "correct" on tax-affecting is still open to debate.

Langer v. Commissioner

Citation: 2006 Tax Ct. Memo LEXIS 235
Court: United States Tax Court
State/Jurisdiction: Specialty Federal
Date of Decision: October 30, 2006
Judge: Haines

By cooperating yet remaining independent, taxpayer's legal counsel and appraisers served the Langer estate well. Together, their effective estate planning followed by adept negotiations during the audit and litigation phases led to a nearly 50% combined valuation discount of an LLC interest—without any Section 2036 attack by the Service, or a trial on the discount.

Diligence pays off

Since 1879, the Langer family had owned and farmed land located in Sherwood, Oregon, just outside of Portland. As the surrounding population and commercial development increased, farming became impractical. The family decided to "go with the flow" of Sherwood's development, actual and potential, through estate planning.

In 1995, the family created an 8-Phase PUD (planned unit development) for their properties and received approval from the town council. Three years later, they formed the Langer Family LLC, bringing together the family members' respective farm holdings under a single manager's control. Maximizing land values was an important goal, as was managing the development process, including dealing with the local city council. And of course, preserving maximum value, net of income and estate tax, for family members was an imperative for the family LLC.

Legal counsel guided the family throughout the process, including tax attorney John Draneas (Draneas & Huglin, P.C.; Lake Oswego, OR), who would eventually represent the estate in audit negotiations with the IRS as well as in the Tax Court litigation. When F. Wallace Langer, one of the family patriarchs, died in 2000, Draneas helped the estate obtain qualified appraisal assistance to complete its federal tax return (Form 706). Thus, there were five years of careful planning before the IRS intervened.

Most pre-trial issues resolved in estate's favor

On advice of counsel, the estate selected Steven Kam, ASA (Cogent Valuation, San Francisco), to prepare the valuation report of the decedent's non-managing, minority interest (29.19%) in the Langer Family LLC. In his conclusions, Kam first developed combined discounts for lack of control and marketability of more than 63%, in large part due to Wallace Langer's non-managerial role and minority interest in the LLC.

A concerted team effort by Kam and the estate's attorney successfully resolved most of the pre-trial issues in the estate's favor. Notably, the Service settled on 47.5% combined discount, and dropped a §2036 challenge to the viability of the LLC, due to proof of its overriding business purpose. The parties also reached stipulations on the values of five of the PUD parcels.

Only two real estate values remained in dispute

By the time the matter reached trial, the valuation of just two out of seven PUD phases were in dispute (the LLC had sold one phase prior to Langer's death). Through their respective expert real estate appraisers, both the IRS and the estate accepted the "highest and best use" value for the real estate, which—given the facts surrounding Sherwood's growth and the impetus for the LLC, was clearly commercial retail development.

Both experts also agreed to use the comparable sales methodology; however, in advancing specific comparables and considering PUD risks (market uncertainties and costs), they came up with different conclusions of value.

On the valuation of PUD phase 2, the experts were $100,000 apart in their appraisals (not much considering the decedent's 29%-plus interest in the LLC and the stipulated 47.5% discount). The Tax Court agreed with the IRS appraisal of $620,000, based on its "detailed and reasonable comparison of each comparable to Phase 2." The Court did not find that *all* of the expert's comparables were reliable indicators of value, particularly those located outside of the Sherwood area. However, the elimination of these outlying values "would not have a significant impact on the final value determination," the Court said, and it accepted the overall determination.

But on PUD Phase 5, the experts were substantially farther apart: The IRS appraiser opined a value of $3.4 million, while taxpayer's appraiser came up with a $2.1 million value. (Keep in mind that for the value of decedent's interest, the divergence was barely $200,000, meaning that a little over $100,000 in estate tax was at issue, plus interest over the years since the filing of the return). Yet it seems that the eleven hours of trial—completed in a single day, according to attorney Draneas—was well worth it, as the Tax Court came up with a $2.8 million value for Phase 5.

Insights from the litigation

In its final opinion, the Tax Court also provided a number of insights for appraisers and client advisors in its determinations of Phase 5 value:

1. *DCF analysis does not apply appropriate valuation date.* The estate's real property appraiser, while paying lip service to the comparable sales method, essentially employed a discounted cash flow (DCF) analysis, relying on his opinion that any sale required three-years of extended marketing and due diligence. The Tax Court disagreed, for two reasons.
   - First, the date of death is the applicable valuation date for estate tax purposes (unless the allowable alternate valuation date is selected). Instead of determining the price at which Phase 5 would change hands between a willing buyer and seller on the date of death, however, the estate's expert had determined the price at which it would change hands three years later, discounted by 12% annually.
   - Second, the appropriate sales comparables should account for any uncertainties such as offsite improvement costs, changing city and resident views on commercial development, and possible oversupply of commercial properties. "A further discount is not necessary," the Court said.

2. *Relevancy of sales comparables.* The Tax Court accepted only two of the estate's comparables, as the remaining two had occurred three year after the date of death. But the Court rejected five of the IRS comparables, fixing on the same two that it had accepted from the estate. A good reminder that the Tax Court is likely to play the "pick and choose" game with appraisals, so the better the report, the more likely the trier of fact will choose its elements for the ultimate determination of fair market value.

3. *Weighing Comparable Sales.* The Tax Court listed five factors in considering relevant comparable sales: location, exposure, configuration, accessibility, and zoning. Two of these—location and exposure—were the most significant in this case. Given Phase 5 was less-desirably located than the court-selected comparables and had an "awkward configuration," the Court concluded that a 25% discount from the average sales price per square foot of the comparables was appropriate.

Estate of Korby v. Commissioner (II)

Citation: 2006 U.S. App. LEXIS 30087
Court: United States Court of Appeals
State/Jurisdiction: 8th Circuit Federal
Date of Decision: December 8, 2006
Judge: Bye

After retiring with a modest estate, the Korbys attended a free estate planning seminar given by an attorney, who later helped them transfer about $1.88 million in assets to a living trust, and from there to a family limited partnership. The living trust retained a 2% general partnership interest, while the Korbys eventually gifted the 98% limited partnership (LP) interest in four equal parts to their four sons, who each declared a 43.61% combined discount for lack of control and marketability on the gifts. (The case does not address these gifts.)

When the elder Korbys died, both their estates listed the general partnership interests on their respective returns—but excluded the gifted LP interests. The IRS assessed deficiencies against both estates totaling over $2.1 million, asserting that the Korbys had retained the "possession and enjoyment of" the full value of the FLP assets.

Three strikes against the FLP

At trial, the Tax Court upheld the deficiencies, citing three issues against the Korbys. First, the Court found they had "an implied agreement" to retain all rights to the FLP's assets, to use as income for as long as they needed it, upon request and without scheduled disbursements. Over time, the FLP had made distributions to the living trust ostensibly as "management fees" (which had gone toward the Korbys' living and medical expenses). But there was no written management agreement or regularly scheduled disbursements; the husband had not tracked his "management" fees for the FLP assets or reported any fees on his personal income tax returns.

Second, the Korbys "essentially stood on all sides of the partnership," having formed the partnership for tax avoidance rather than credit protection or any other independent business purpose.

Finally, as Mrs. Korby had predeceased her husband, her estate claimed a marital deduction, arguing that all her rights to the FLP assets had passed to her husband under the terms of the living trust. In answer to this claim, the IRS had pointed out that pursuant to the gift transfer to the sons, the husband had never received any rights to the FLP income or assets. In the estate/gift action, the Korby's trustees contended this statement by the IRS constituted a "judicial admission" that the Korbys had lacked control over the FLP assets.

But the Tax Court rejected the argument, and the Court of Appeals confirmed (as it did all major aspects of the opinion), noting the IRS had always maintained that both Korbys retained an interest in the FLP assets. "Such a claim is not inconsistent with contending the interest did not pass from [wife to husband] at the time of her death via the terms of the living trust."

Estate of Gimbel v. Commissioner

Citation: 2006 T.C. Memo LEXIS 274
Court: United States Tax Court
State/Jurisdiction: Specialty Federal
Date of Decision: December 19, 2006
Judge: Swift

This case is a "must-read" on the valuation of a large block of restricted public shares, including the Tax Court's conclusions regarding the appropriate methodologies, marketability discounts, and consideration of post-valuation events.

Estate owned 13% of outstanding stock

On her death in June of 2000 (the valuation date), Georgina Gimbel owned more than 3.6 million shares in Reliance Steel and Aluminum Company (Reliance), a publicly traded "metal services center" with over 4000 employees and $997 million in assets.

The decedent's block of shares represented nearly 13% of the company's outstanding stock—enough that her estate was considered an affiliate; and nearly all of its holdings were subject to restrictions under applicable federal securities laws.

Specifically, SEC Rule 144 limited the estate's sale of the restricted stock during any three-month period to the greater of 1% of the outstanding stock or the average weekly trading volume for the previous four weeks. (The estate had already satisfied Rule 144's one-year holding requirement.) Pursuant to these "dribble out" provisions, it would have taken the estate at least thirty-nine months to sell its 3.6 million shares.

Although Reliance had conducted an IPO in 1994, the parties (and the Court) agreed that as of the valuation date, the company probably would not have approved a second public offering of the estate's shares, as (among other reasons) it would have had to disclose a large pending acquisition, which was subject to a confidentiality agreement.

A private market also did not exist, as strategic investors were not likely to purchase the estate's minority interest, especially given the "industry trends toward acquisition of entire companies," the Court said.

Repurchase was a possibility

Reliance had instituted a formal stock repurchase plan since 1994, which allowed it to repurchase up to 6 million shares. But through the 2000 valuation date, Reliance had repurchased only 1.37 million shares (2.7 million after adjustment for a stock split); the largest repurchase had been in 1998, of about 430,000 shares (646,000 adjusted).

Just ten days before Gimbel died, the CEO reported a "record year," and announced Reliance would consider repurchasing shares at about $19 per, as it had in the past. After her death, the estate tried unsuccessfully to find strategic buyers for the 13% block of shares. Nearly five months later, after the company had secured an additional $50 million line of credit, it agreed to repurchase 63% of the estate's shares at $19.35. (Thought the record is unclear, the Board may have derived this figure from its investment bankers, who advised a 10-15% discount to the stock's publicly traded price.)

Estate takes a 21% discount

In preparing the estate's tax return, Gregory Range (Duff and Phelps, San Francisco) valued its Reliance shares at the valuation date average trading price ($20.8), discounted by 20.72% for lack of marketability and liquidity related to the block's size and sales restrictions.

On audit, the IRS asserted an 8% discount, assessing a $9.5 million deficiency. (The notice did not indicate how the Service had calculated the discount.)

At trial, both parties retained new valuation experts. For the estate, Curtis Kimball, ASA, CFA (Willamette Management Associates, Atlanta) concluded a 17% discount was appropriate. For the IRS, Ken Nunes, CFA (Caliber Advisors, San Diego) assessed a 9% discount. The key difference: whether it was "reasonably foreseeable" that Reliance would repurchase some portion of the estate's stock at the valuation date. The estate's expert did not believe any repurchase was foreseeable; the IRS expert did.

Nunes believed that in June of 2000, Reliance would have repurchased 50% of the estate's shares. (The record does not specifically indicate how he reached the 50% figure.) To calculate the discount, Nunes first considered several factors: 1) the 10%-15% suggested discount by the company's investment bankers at the actual repurchase date (October 2004); 2) the CEO's testimony that the company would have relied on its bankers' advice on the valuation date (June 2004); and 3) the lack of material change to the company's financial status from June to October 2004. From these, Nunes chose a 12.5% midpoint for an initial discount to 50% of the estate's shares.

As a second step, Nunes estimated the holding costs during the three months (or so) to repurchase the shares, and increased the discount from 12.5% to 13.9%.

Court found some repurchase foreseeable

Given the company's policy and historic practice—and the CEO's public announcement just 10 days prior to the valuation date—the Court concluded repurchase was foreseeable, but concluded 20% was the more likely figure.

As, "neither of the estate's experts provided a distinct methodology for estimating a repurchase discount," the Court applied the Service's 13.9% discount to 20% of the estate's shares, for a total repurchase value of just about $12.9 million.

For the remaining shares, the Court adopted the "dribble-out" valuation analysis. Although all three experts had agreed on the SEC-imposed liquidation period, they had disagreed on accounting for the time value of money and the measures that a buyer would take against possible price fluctuations:

Range report. In preparing the estate's tax return, Range had multiplied the estate's 3.6 million shares by the valuation date closing price to reach the gross sale proceeds, discounted to a present value using a risk-free rate of return. Range had also assumed any hypothetical investor would purchase put options to maintain the valuation date price throughout the dribble-out period; he subtracted this estimated cost from the sales proceeds to reach a final value of about $55.5 million, reflecting a 24.5% discount from the overall valuation date trading price.

Kimball report. Kimball also multiplied all of the estate's shares at the valuation date trading price, but then added over $1 million in estimated dividends during the liquidation period. He used a 13.2% discount to reflect the expected rate of return on equity, for a total value of about $62 million, or a 17.4% overall discount from the public price.

Nunes report. Nunes valued 50% of shares remaining after repurchase at the valuation date trading price, but then subtracted the estimated cost for hedging contracts ("cashless collars" and "prepaid variable forward contracts") that a hypothetical investor would use to protect against the price decreases during the dribble-out period. This resulted in net sale proceeds of $35.6 million, reflecting a 5% discount from the public price; when combined with the 50% of repurchased shares, the overall discount calculated by the IRS was 9.5%.

Risk prevention measures questionable

On review, the Tax Court did not believe the hedging contracts, put options, and other risk-avoiding measures would have been available for the estate's sizeable block of restricted stock, which lacked both liquidity and marketability.

Kimball's dribble-out methodology "was more reasonable and generally accepted," it said, applying it to the 80% of estate shares (remaining after the Court-posited 20% repurchase), to reach a total gross value of about $60.7 million, discounted by Kimball's 13.2% rate for a $51.4 million value.

Adding this to the $12.9 million for the 20% repurchased shares, the Court's final value for the estate's shares was approximately $64.3 million, reflecting an overall discount of 14.2%—which was just about the midpoint between the IRS' original 8% discount, assessed in the notice of deficiency, and the estate's 20.72% discount in its original return.

Estate of Berry v. Commissioner

Citation: 2007 Pa. Commw. LEXIS 182
Court: United States Tax Court
State/Jurisdiction: Specialty Federal
Date of Decision: April 24, 2007
Judge: Flaherty

The Berry FLP was formed in 1998 through a mother's contribution of over $6.78 million in marketable securities and cash in return for a 1% general partnership interest and 97% limited partnership interest. The mother later gifted a 15% limited partner interest to each of her two children, and made substantial withdrawals of cash for additional gifts and expenses. When she died in 2003, her estate filed federal and state tax returns; the IRS accepted the estate's calculation of a 33% combined discount on the FLP, for lack of control and marketability.

But the Pennsylvania Department of Revenue disallowed the discounts, asserting that—given the nature of the partnership and assuming no compulsion to sell—a partner would not have disposed of his or her interest at a discount.

After losing an agency and lower court appeal, the taxpayer reached the state court, which examined both the business purpose of the FLP and whether the IRS's allowance of the discounts was dispositive. As to the latter, the Court did not explain why the IRS had permitted the discounts, but it did acknowledge there were no state regulations pertaining to FLPs, and that typically, the Department of Revenue would defer to "criteria that mirror those of the Internal Revenue Service." A local estate tax statute, for example, specifically provided that where the state had no rules pertaining to the value of a life interest, "the regulations in effect for Federal Estate tax purposes shall apply."

Although all parties agreed that IRS regulations applied to the case, the Court found that the Service's conclusions regarding taxable value did not. There was no statutory or legal authority requiring the state Department of Revenue to be bound by the federal agency when making an assessment of local inheritance tax.

At the same time, when it came to deciding the FLP's purpose, the Court looked to the language of IRC §2036 and established federal law. It also reviewed testimony by the family accountant, who listed the standard estate planning objectives: to shield assets from liability, preserve the estate, and save taxes. (The partnership agreement reflected these as well.) The FLP's only activity consisted of selling stock to distribute funds to the decedent, who retained unfettered access to the assets throughout her lifetime.

Under these facts, the Court found the FLP served no legitimate business purpose, and affirmed the state's denial of estate tax discounts.

Estate of Erickson v. Commissioner

Citation: T.C. Memo. 2007-107
Court: United States Tax Court
State/Jurisdiction: Specialty Federal
Date of Decision: April 30, 2007
Judge: Kroupa

In the *Estate of Hilde E. Erickson v. CIR*, T.C. Memo. 2007-107, the U.S. Tax Court considered whether assets transferred by a decedent to a family limited partnership shortly before her death should be included in her gross estate under IRC § 2036. The decedent held significant assets in stock and bonds as well as rental property. In the late 1990s, she transferred control over her assets to her financially savvy daughter under a power of attorney. The daughter's control over the assets was made permanent when the decedent was besieged by Alzheimer's disease. In her capacity as attorney-in-fact, the daughter established a family limited partnership (FLP) in May, 2001. The decedent's two daughters were the general partners of the FLP. The FLP agreement contemplated a contemporaneous transfer of assets to the partnership. The decedent transferred $2.1 million in assets to the FLP, but the bulk of those assets were transferred within two days of her death in late September, 2001. After the FLP was fully capitalized, the decedent gifted limited partnership interests to her grandchildren. The decedent held a 24.18% interest after the gifts.

Several important events occurred following the decedent's death. First, her estate was left with insufficient funds to pay the estate taxes. The FLP redeemed some limited partnership units and purchased the decedent's home to provide the needed funds. Secondly, the FLP shifted its investment strategy from bonds to real estate. However, its property managers and investment advisors did not change between the periods before decedent's disease and after her death. Third, the FLP made unsecured loans to the decedent's children and grandchildren. While the loans were repaid, the FLP adjusted the interest rates when the borrower could obtain a lower rate at a bank. Lastly, the IRS audited the decedent's estate tax return. The IRS determined that that the full value of the assets to the FLP should be included in the decedent's gross estate. The estate contested the estate tax deficiency and the matter proceeded before the Tax Court.

The Tax Court noted that § 2036 applies to recapture the value of assets transferred by the decedent when the decedent retained the enjoyment of the assets either directly or indirectly, unless the assets are transferred for full and adequate consideration in money or money's worth. The court first considered whether the decedent retained the transferred assets' economic benefit.

The court listed some factors indicating when a decedent impliedly retained the economic benefit: (1) commingling of FLP and personal funds; (2) history of disproportionate distributions; (3) the arrangement's testamentary characteristics; (4) whether the transfer comprises of all or substantially all of the decedent's assets; (5) unilateral formation of the partnership; (6) type of assets transferred; and (7) the decedent's personal situation. The court found that the decedent impliedly retained the economic benefit from the transferred assets because the business form was not respected insofar as there was a several-month delay between formation and capitalization, which was not contemplated by the FLP agreement; the estate lacked sufficient funds to pay its post-death obligations and received the needed funds from the FLP regardless of the FLP's characterization of the transactions; and the FLP was formed while the decedent was on her deathbed.

The Tax Court then considered whether the decedent received adequate and full consideration when she transferred the assets. The court noted, "[T]he bona fide sale exception applies if the record shows that a family limited partnership was formed for legitimate and significant nontax reason and that each transferor received a partnership interest proportionate to the fair market value of the property." It further noted several factors indicated no legitimate nontax purpose: (1) the taxpayer stood on all sides of the transaction; (2) the taxpayer's financial dependence on the FLP; (3) commingling of partnership and personal funds; and (4) the taxpayer's failure to transfer money to the FLP. Here it found that the decedent, through her daughter as attorney-in-fact, stood on all sides of the transaction and no other partner received legal guidance with respect to the formation and capitalization of the FLP. Furthermore, it noted that besides the vehicle holding the assets, nothing changed with respect to those assets because they continued to be managed by the same people and in the same matter as before the FLP's capitalization. Lastly, it found that the decedent was financially dependent on the FLP as shown by the transfer of funds, characterized as redemption of limited partnership units and purchase of her home, to pay the estate tax. Therefore, the Tax Court held that the bona fide sale exception did not apply and the assets transferred to the FLP should be included in the value of the decedent's gross estate under § 2036.

This abstract originally appeared in *Valuation Case Digest*, authored by John J. Stockdale, Jr.

Stone v. United States (I)

Citation: 2007 U.S. Dist. LEXIS 38332
Court: United States District Court
State/Jurisdiction: Northern District of California
Date of Decision: May 25, 2007
Judge: Henderson

In *Robert Grove Stone v. United States of America*, No. C06-0259 TEH (N.D. Cal. May 25, 2007), the U.S. District Court for the Northern District of California determined whether an undivided minority interest in a collection of paintings should be valued inclusive of a fractional interest discount for federal estate tax purposes. Stone represented the estate of a decedent that owned the collection, which consisted of an undivided 50% interest in 19 paintings by well-known and desirable fine artists.

The estate had the collection appraised by an auction house, Soetheby's. The appraisal was brief and did not explain the methodology used to arrive at the paintings' value. The estate engaged a business appraiser to determine the fractional interest discount applicable to the estate's collection. Since the appraiser was unable to identify any comparable transactions of fractional interests in fine art, the appraiser used fractional interest transactions in real estate and real estate holding companies as a proxy. He concluded that a 44% fractional interest discount was appropriate for the decedent's 50% undivided interest in the collection. Thus, the estate reported a value of the decedent's interest in the collection at $1.42 million.

The IRS audited the return. It concluded that two of the paintings were undervalued and disallowed the fractional interest discount altogether. The IRS valued the decedent's interest in the collection at $2.76 million, the pro rata value of the entire collection. The estate paid the tax and brought this refund action.

The first question before the District Court was the value of the two paintings. The IRS had the paintings appraised by its Art Advisory Panel. This independent panel valued the paintings based on comparable sales. The court found that the Art Advisory Panel correctly valued the paintings. In doing so, it emphasized the independent nature of the panel and the inadequacy of the Soetheby's appraisal. Further, it rejected the price at which the paintings actually sold in 2005 as reflective of the 1999 value because the valuation date and the transaction date were too temporally distant.

The second question presented to the District Court was whether a fractional interest discount should be applied, and if so, what was the appropriate size of that discount. The court first acknowledged that the IRS's experts on this issue had significant experience in the art market while the estate's expert was a business appraiser and lacked experience in the art market. The court credited the IRS's experts' testimony, which noted that while sales of fractional interests had occurred in the art market, they did not occur at a discount. The IRS's expert stated, "The art market differs from the real estate or business market. Art is simply not fungible." Thus, the court held, "[A] hypothetical willing seller of an undivided fractional interest in art would likely seek to sell the entire work of art and split the proceeds, rather than seeking to sell his or her fractional interest at a discount. At a minimum, because an undivided interest holder has the right to partition, a hypothetical seller under no compulsion to sell would not accept any less for his or her undivided interest than could be obtained by splitting proceeds in this manner." Further, "The hypothetical willing seller would know that he or she had the right to partition and would therefore not accept any less for his or her undivided interest than could be obtained via partition."

The court then considered how much of a discount was appropriate for the costs to partition and sell the art collection. The estate's business valuation expert determined that the cost of partition amounted to a 51% discount from the fair market value. This discount assumed that the partition would occur as a result of a court-ordered sale that would take 3 years to complete. He deducted $50,000 in legal fees, $5,000 in appraisal fees, and 2% in sales commissions. He further assumed growth of 3% annually, but discounted to present value using a 28% discount rate, which was based on the rate of return for micro cap companies plus 10% for illiquidity. The IRS's expert agreed that a 2% sales commission was appropriate, but found that the appraisal costs would be waived by the selling auction house.

The court rejected the costs to partition determined by the estate. It found the discount rate was improperly calculated. It noted that there was a disconnect between the assumed growth rate and the discount rate, and the discount rate based on micro cap companies was not comparable to art. The court adopted the position of the estate's expert that the appraisal fees would be waived by the selling auction house. It further agreed that the legal fees needed to be deducted because it assumed that the willing seller would file a court action to partition the property. Lastly, it adopted the 2% selling costs charged by an auction house as appropriate. The court then provided the parties with an opportunity to resolve the discount size and return to court if they could not do so.

This abstract originally appeared in *Valuation Case Digest*, authored by John J. Stockdale, Jr.

Negron v. United States

Citation: 2007 U.S. Dist. LEXIS 40412
Court: United States District Court
State/Jurisdiction: Northern District of Ohio
Date of Decision: June 4, 2007
Judge: Aldrich

In *Carol Negron v. United States of America*, No. 1:05CV2305 (N.D. Ohio June 4, 2007), the U.S. District Court for the Northern District of Ohio considered whether lottery payments should be valued using the annuity tables in IRC § 7520 for federal estate tax purposes. Negron is the executor of two estates that shared an Ohio Super Lotto prize with a third person. At the time the decedents died in 2001, 15 annual payments remained unpaid. The lottery payments were non-assignable and could not be collateralized. Negron elected to have the remaining payments paid to the estates in lump sums. The value of the remaining payments was computed by the estate using a 9% discount rate, which resulted in each estate receiving a $2.275 million payment. The estates reported this amount as the value of the remaining payments on their respective estate tax return.

The IRS audited each estate's return. It revised the value of the remaining lottery payments using the value calculated by reference to the § 7520 tables. The estates paid the outstanding tax due and sought a refund.

On a motion for summary judgment before the District Court, the estates argued that the valuation of the lottery payments by reference to the annuity tables was inappropriate. While acknowledging that the Sixth Circuit Court of Appeals had not passed on the issue, the Second and Ninth Circuit agreed with this position, but the Fifth Circuit relied on the annuity tables. The District Court noted that there is a presumption that the value indicated by the annuity tables is the correct value unless the proponent shows that (1) the value ascribed by the tables is unreasonable and unrealistic and (2) a more realistic and reasonable means to value the payments exists. The District Court determined that the reasoning of the Second and Ninth Circuit made "economic sense that the transferability of an annuity would affect its fair market value." However, it noted that the estate did not present any evidence of a more realistic and reasonable value for the annuity. Therefore, the court granted the estate's motion for summary judgment in part, found that the annuity tables produced an unrealistic and unreasonable result in this case, and allowed the case to continue to decide whether there was a more realistic and reasonable method for valuing the annuity.

This abstract originally appeared in *Valuation Case Digest*, authored by John J. Stockdale, Jr.

Davis v. United States (II)

Citation: 2007 U.S. Dist. LEXIS 43432
Court: United States District Court
State/Jurisdiction: New Hampshire
Date of Decision: June 13, 2007
Judge: McAuliffe

In *Mary C. Davis, Executrix v. United States of America*, No. 04-cv-273-SM (D. N.H. June 13, 2007), the U.S. District Court for the District of New Hampshire determined that a non-transferable right to annual lottery payments was properly valued by reference to the annuity tables. The decedent won the Massachusetts lottery in 1989. He elected to receive his prize in 20 equal payments of $209,220. The decedent was not permitted to transfer or assign his right to the future payments. The decedent died with 10 payments remaining. His estate initially reported the value of the remaining payments as determined under the § 7520 annuity tables at $1.58 million.

After paying the estate tax, the estate determined that the lottery payments should not have been valued by reference to the annuity tables. It obtained an expert appraisal from a credentialed business appraiser. The expert applied a 50% discount to the value determined under the annuity tables. He reasoned that hypothetical buyer would demand the discount because of the risks involved in obtaining the payments annually from the estate. He concluded that the right to the lottery payments had a fair market value of only $800,000. The IRS denied the refund and the estate brought this refund action.

The District Court held that the value determined under the annuity tables was the proper value of the lottery payments. The court rejected the assumption used by the estate's expert. It found that "[t]he question here is not how much a hypothetical buyer would pay the estate for its 'used' lottery ticket. Instead, the question is how much that hypothetical buyer would pay to stand in the shoes of the estate." Restated, the court considered the price a hypothetical willing buyer and seller would agree to purchase a non-transferable annuity. The court credited the IRS's two financial experts, who determined that the value of a similarly restricted annuity was only, at most, 5% less than the value determined under the annuity tables.

The District Court then considered whether a 5% difference between the fair market value and the value determined under the annuity tables was "sufficiently substantial to render the IRC [annuity table] figure 'unrealistic and unreasonable,'" requiring deviation from those tables. After considering cases, which had values at least 25% lower than the annuity table value and where the annuity tables were not used, the court found that the facts in those cases were substantially different from the facts of this case. Further, it found that a relatively minor deviation of 5% did not support a deviation from the tables. Thus, the court denied the estate a refund, basing the value of the remaining lottery payments on the annuity tables.

This abstract originally appeared in *Valuation Case Digest*, authored by John J. Stockdale, Jr.

Stone v. United States (II)

Citation: 2007 U.S. Dist. LEXIS 58611
Court: District Court
State/Jurisdiction: United States
Date of Decision: August 10, 2007
Judge: Henderson

Appraisers may remember this recent case, *Stone v. United States*, concerning the estate tax valuation of a fractional (50%) interest in nineteen paintings, including several acclaimed masterpieces.

In the first phase of proceedings, the federal district court rejected the IRS' contention that no discount applied to this or any fractional interest in artwork. At the same time, the Court ruled that estate's proposed 51% discount, calculated by an accredited business appraiser, was unpersuasive. "Art is simply not fungible," it said, in finding that transactions data for fractional interests in real estate simply did not translate to the volatile art market, especially when well-known and frequently sold works are involved.

The Court could have calculated a discount from the available evidence—but instead gave the parties the opportunity to negotiate an appropriate discount for the costs to partition, drawing from their available expertise. It simply reminded them that the estate held the burden of proof—and that so far, the Court had not found the estate's assumptions credible.

Taxpayer urges acceptance of methodology

In this second phase of proceedings, the parties returned to court, having been unable to reach an agreement. In re-briefing the issue, the estate proposed a 35% discount, based on the same valuation methodology but with varied assumptions. Specifically, the estate still assumed that the artwork would appreciate by 3% annually, but in calculating net present value, instead of assuming a discount rate of 28% (18% plus a 10% illiquidity premium), the estate proposed reducing the discount rate to 20%.

The argument was unsuccessful:

> This Court continues to fail to find persuasive a model that assumes that investors who would choose to invest in art, which is expected to appreciate at an annual average rate of 3% (and some of which, in this case, actually appreciated at an annual average rater of approximately 4%) would expect to receive significantly higher returns if they invested their money elsewhere.

"Put another way," the Court said, "an investor seeking a 20% or 28% return would not choose to invest in art that is expected to return only a fraction of those percentages." Even if the Court accepted the estate's methodology—its assumptions were still unreasonable, and the estate failed to provide any alternative evidence by which the Court could determine a reasonable expected rate of return from art investors.

Burden of proof determines outcome

The IRS maintained that no discount was appropriate—but conceded that it would accept a 5% discount, "in a spirit of compromise." This included a 2% sales fee and $50,000 in legal fees, which the Court had already accepted in the prior proceeding as reasonable costs-to-partition. Thus, the IRS' proposed 5% discount included "only an approximate 1.2% discount for the uncertainties involved in waiting for [a] partition action to be resolved."

The 5% discount was "relatively low," according to the Court. But the estate bore the burden of proof, and it needed to provide some reliable basis for a larger discount or persuade the Court that a hypothetical buyer would refuse to purchase the estate's 50% interest without the greater discount. The estate failed on both points, and as a result, any finding by the Court that exceeded the IRS discount would be "impermissibly arbitrary." Having given the parties the opportunity to avail themselves of their own expert resources—and having failed to receive persuasive evidence, the Court permitted the estate to take a 5% discount for its 50% interest in the art collection.

Estate of Josephine Thompson v. Commissioner (II)

Citation: 2007 U.S. App. LEXIS 20066
Court: Court of Appeals
State/Jurisdiction: United States
Date of Decision: August 23, 2007
Judge: Jacobs

Recent federal appeals court decisions have highlighted the importance of the allocation of burden of proof in Tax Court valuation cases. In last year's *JPMorgan Chase & Co. v. Commissioner*, for example (see Oct. 2006 *Business Valuation Update*™), the Seventh Circuit all but threw out the Tax Court's exhaustive opinion on valuation principles and methodology. The valuation analysis (by Judge David Laro) wasn't inaccurate, according to the higher court. But having rejected the valuation position by the taxpayer, who carried the burden of proof, the Tax Court should have deferred to the IRS' position. This year, the Second Circuit cited *JPMorgan* in upholding a bankruptcy court's "mark-to-market" valuation of a company's consumer debt portfolio, finding:

> Once the bankruptcy court rejected the debtors' method as failing to clearly reflect income, it was not the court's task to determine *de novo* whether the Commissioner's method did....Unless the IRS interpretation is clearly unlawful or arbitrary, a court must defer to its method of calculating fair market value.

These decisions are placing more pressure on the party with the burden of proof in a tax appraisal case to carry that burden with a highly credible appraisal—or risk losing it all to the other side's expert opinion.

Taxpayer retains inexperienced experts

Appraisers may recall the first incarnation of this case, *Estate of Thompson v Commissioner*, 2004 Tax Ct. Memo LEXIS 180, for its findings on marketability and minority discounts. At stake was a 20% interest in a century-old, closely held company that published business-to-business directories. For several years before the decedent's death (in May 1998), the company's operating income remained steady at about $25 million. But with the advent of the Internet, print subscriptions and sales fell. Rising expenses led to an overall decline in operating income, and by 2002, the company was barely breaking even.

To prepare its valuation of the New York publishing company, the estate hired an attorney and accountant—both from Alaska. The reason, according to the Tax Court, was to avoid an audit by IRS staff in New York and receive a more favorable audit from the Alaska office. The attorney, who had limited appraisal experience, also served as estate administrator, a role the Tax Court regarded as "somewhat in tension with his role as a purported independent valuation expert for the estate." The accountant was not a credentialed business appraiser, having undertaken "occasional" small business valuations. Although the Tax Court received the estate's valuation reports into evidence, it viewed them as "marginally credible." Likewise, the Alaska experts were "barely qualified" to value a million-dollar New York business.

These findings helped persuade the Tax Court to disfavor the estate's valuation, which used a capitalization of income approach to value the decedent's 20% shares at $1.75 million. In particular, the estate's reliance on a 12% "Internet and management" risk factor in calculation of a 30.05% capitalization rate was improper, as was its omission of certain non-operating assets. Last but not least, the Tax Court found the estate's 40% discount for minority ownership and 45% discount for lack of marketability to be inflated.

Errors in IRS valuation, too

The IRS expert, a credentialed business appraiser, used both the comparable public company method and the discounted cash flow (DCF) method to conclude a $225 million value for the publishing company. The estate's 20% interest yielded $46.3 million, discounted 30% for lack of marketability for a final value of $32 million. The IRS contended these values more accurately reflected the company in 1998, when there was "no reason to think" that the Internet would have such a dramatic and deleterious effect.

The Tax Court rejected the Commissioner's values; its market approach lacked sufficiently similar comparables and its DCF analysis contained "significant errors" and "suspect" recalculations. As neither side had produced anything but "deficient and unpersuasive" valuations, the Tax Court cobbled its own, employing the capitalization of income method and the taxpayer's cap rate, minus the 12% Internet and management risk factor. To redress another perceived error by the estate, the Tax Court added $68 million in short-term investments (which it considered non-operating assets, but the estate characterized as operating assets), to arrive at a total $111 million value for the company, or $22.7 million for the 20% shares. After applying a 15% minority discount and a 30% marketability discount, the Tax Court reached a final value for the estate's interest of $13.5 million.

Burden of proof: all or nothing?

In its appeal to the Second Circuit, the taxpayer argued that pursuant to the applicable provision of the Internal Revenue Code (§ 7491), once it submitted a credible appraisal, the burden shifted to the Commissioner to prove valuation. (Notably, the parties stipulated that the estate submitted "credible evidence.") When the Tax Court rejected the Commissioner's values, the estate argued, it should have adopted the estate's values.

The Second Circuit disagreed:

> [The allocation of the burden of proof] does not require the Tax Court to adopt the taxpayer's valuation, however erroneous, whenever the Court rejects the

> Commissioner's proposed value; the burden of disproving the taxpayer's valuation can be satisfied by evidence in the record that impeaches, undermines, or indicates error in the taxpayer's valuation.

In this case, the IRS not only presented evidence in support of its valuation, it also successfully rebutted the estate's valuation by identifying its errors and inconsistencies. Notwithstanding the Code's allocation of the burden of proof in § 7491, the "Tax Court is not bound by the formulas and opinions proffered by expert witnesses. It may reach a determination of value based upon its own analysis of all the evidence in the record." The Second Circuit affirmed the Tax Court's valuation in all but one respect: After adding the $68 million in non-operating assets to the company's capitalized income, the Tax Court included the income produced by the $68 million in its projections, thus double-counting this amount. The case was remanded to the Tax Court to correct the double-counting, and to retain all other respects of its valuation analysis.

Estate of Bigelow v. Commissioner (II)

Citation: 2007 U.S. App. LEXIS 22030
Court: Court of Appeals
State/Jurisdiction: 9th Circuit Federal
Date of Decision: September 14, 2007
Judge: Gould

Add *Bigelow* to the ever-growing list of "bad facts" cases concerning family limited partnerships (FLPs). An eighty-five year-old widow owned California beach property, worth about $1.45 million. Given her health concerns, she transferred the property to a trust and then to an FLP. The trust became the sole general partner and a limited partner, in exchange for $500. Her two children each contributed $100 to become limited partners.

The beach property was encumbered by a mortgage, for which Mrs. Bigelow remained personally liable; the FLP did not assume this debt. During her lifetime, however, the FLP used partnership funds to make substantial monthly payments on the loan. As her revenue sources dwindled and her expenses increased, the FLP also covered the shortfall. It characterized these payments as "advances" on her partnership account, but never received a note or other interest-bearing obligation in return. Only after the widow died, in 1997, did the partnership reduce her capital account to reflect these and other payments. The FLP sold the property for $1.475 million and distributed the proceeds to the remaining partners and her estate. Until then—and notwithstanding the "advances" to the decedent, the FLP had made no distributions.

Implied agreement to enjoy FLP income

After she died, the widow's estate filed its tax return, including a 37% discount for lack of control and marketability to its interest in the FLP. The IRS assessed a deficiency of over $200,000, based on the full value of the beach property, minus the remaining mortgage obligation but excluding any discounts. The Tax Court upheld the deficiency, finding an implied agreement between the widow and her children that she would retain the right to the FLP income to meet her living expenses. Further, the transfer of the property to the FLP did not meet the "good faith, bona fide sale" exception of IRC §2036(a), as the transfer would have "impoverished" the widow but for the implied agreement to use partnership funds to meet her financial needs.

On review, the Ninth Circuit Court of Appeals agreed with both findings. The partnership's payments on the widow's personal loan obligations, without receiving any obligation in return or deducting the amounts from her partnership account until after her death, supported the implied agreement. "A key problem with the conveyance of the...property to [the FLP] is, for estate tax purposes, that the...debt that was secured by the property was not also transferred." Another problem: The FLP deducted only the payment of principal from the widow's capital, not the interest. These facts indicated the FLP paid the debt in the widow's stead and that she retained the use of nearly $2,000 in monthly income from the FLP.

The FLP also failed to observe partnership formalities, and lacked any legitimate business purpose. It did not shield the partners from potential liability, and although the FLP may have facilitated gifts to her heirs, "gift-giving is considered a testamentary purpose," the Court ruled, "and cannot be justified as a legitimate, non-tax business justification."

Ninth Circuit declines to adopt 'per se' rule

Finally, although the estate contended that the widow received a proportionate number of limited partnership shares in exchange for the fair market value of the property, it also claimed a substantial discount in valuing the property for estate tax purposes. The Commissioner argued that these positions were inconsistent, but the Ninth Circuit Court declined to adopt the "per se" rule.

We agree with the Third and Fifth Circuits and the Tax Court that an *inter vivos* transfer of real property to a family limited partnership, which inherently reduces the fair market price of the resultant partnership interests does not *per se* disqualify the transfer from falling under §2036(a)'s exception.

To avoid the reach of §2036(a) in this case, the estate needed to demonstrate "more than a proportional exchange" between the fair market value of the property (at $1.45 million) and the $100 limited partnership units. The estate also needed to show a "genuine" pooling of assets and the related potential for creating intangible value from the amassing of assets. "The validity of the adequate and full consideration prong cannot be gauged independently of the non-tax-related business purposes involved in making the bona fide transfer inquiry," the Court held, and given the facts of this case, affirmed the Tax Court's decision in all respects.

Estate of Jelke v. Commissioner (II)

Citation: 2007 U.S. App. LEXIS 26477
Court: Court of Appeals
State/Jurisdiction: United States
Date of Decision: November 15, 2007
Judge: Hill

The 2005 *Jelke v. Commissioner* decision has been described as "poor" for the taxpayer (by Shannon Pratt in the *Business Valuation Update*™) and frustrating for the appraiser. The Tax Court declined to follow the leading case, *Estate v. Dunn* (5th Cir. 2002), and adopt a dollar-for-dollar discount for a holding company's built-in capital gains tax liability. After receiving the disappointing result in *Jelke*, the taxpayers almost did not want to appeal, according to their original appraiser, Will Frazier. "Their advisors and I had to beg them."

But they ended up hiring attorney John Porter (Baker Botts, Houston), "a good choice on their part," Frazier said. (Porter led the reversal of *McCord v. Comm'r* by the Fifth Circuit in 2006.) The effort evidently paid off, as the Eleventh Circuit opinion provides an exhaustive but excellent review of precedent in support of its decision. We've abstracted the case in some detail to give appraisers a full understanding of the context for the *Jelke* decision and its ultimate findings.

A long, slow path to 'economic reality'

After a brief recitation of the facts—the decedent owned a minority (6.44%) interest in a closely held investment company that owned marketable securities—the Court began with Revenue Ruling 59-60, "the focal point for the proper method of valuing closely held securities." Given the close relationship between the values of the stock of a holding company and the underlying assets, Rev. Ruling 59-60 recommends the net asset value method, which in turn relies on the "venerable willing buyer-willing seller test."

The Court turned to tax law next. Prior to the Tax Reform Act of 1986, the federal tax code and case law permitted C corporations to distribute appreciated property to shareholders without incurring income tax at the corporate level. Courts generally did not permit a discount for built-in capital gains tax liability unless a sale or liquidation was either planned or imminent, deeming the discounts to be too speculative.

The Tax Reform Act made "dramatic" changes, requiring the recognition of corporate-level gains on distributions of appreciated property. Because an individual shareholder/taxpayer would no longer receive a step-up in basis to fair market value on the valuation date (e.g., at a decedent's death for estate tax purposes), the Court explained, "it now became more important than ever for a taxpayer to be able to quantify his or her loss in value of the stock due to inherent capital gains tax liability in the corporation."

But despite tax reform, the IRS steadily refused to allow a capital gains discount. Courts, while recognizing the "possibility" that a discount for the capital gains taxes could be allowed, adhered to the "rigid" position that the highly speculative nature of the tax mandated that its present value be zero. Then along came *Estate of Davis* (1998). Citing Rev. Ruling 59-60 and "economic reality theory," the Tax Court held that a hypothetical buyer and seller would take some account for imbedded capital gains tax. Rather than permit a separate discount, however, the Tax Court attributed approximately one-third of the allowed marketability discount to the contingent capital gains liability.

IRS position 'beginning to erode'

Davis "set the stage" for other courts to being to make inroads into the IRS position. In the 1998 *Estate of Eisenberg*, the Second Circuit concluded that a willing buyer and seller would negotiate a discount to account for the tax liability, despite no imminent liquidation or sale.

> [T]here is simply no evidence to dispute that a hypothetical willing buyer...would likely pay less for the shares of a corporation because of [the] buyer's inability to eliminate the contingent tax liability. ...Further, we believe...a tax liability upon liquidation or sale for built-in gains is not too speculative.

But language in *Eisenberg* and *Estate of Welch* (6th Cir. 2000) suggested that while a discount was permissible, it need not be on a dollar-for-dollar basis. While neither circuit court "seemed keen on offering a 100% discount," the *Jelke* opinion observed, each failed to prescribe a specific approach to calculate its magnitude. Disputes between the IRS and taxpayers began to focus on the appropriate valuation method and amount of the reduction. In *Estate of Jameson* (2001), the decedent owned 98% of a closely held interest that operated both a timber and an investment company. Applying a net asset valuation, the Tax Court allowed a partial discount for the capital gains tax liability on the timber property, incurred over the timber harvest. But it permitted no discount on the investment property, assuming a hypothetical buyer would continue operations.

On appeal, the Fifth Circuit disagreed with the presumption that a strategic, not a hypothetical, buyer would continue to operate the company for timber production. An "economically rational buyer" would account for the consequences of the unavoidable, substantial built-in tax liabilities, especially given the company's low basis in the investment property. It instructed the Tax Court to reconsider the amount of capital gains on the timber operations and to calculate a discount for the contingent liability on the investment property.

Dunn ushers in new valuation era

A year later, the Fifth Circuit went a step further in *Estate of Dunn*. The decedent owned a majority (62.2%) interest in a family corporation that rented heavy equipment, but lacked a supermajority, two-thirds interest that could force liquidation under Texas law. Because the family also planned to keep running the company, the Tax Court approved a 5% discount for built-in capital gains, reflecting the "small" possibility that a hypothetical buyer would liquidate.

This time, the Fifth Circuit disagreed "emphatically." A hypothetical buyer and seller must always be assumed to liquidate the corporation immediately upon the valuation date, triggering a tax on the built-in gains. The "likelihood is 100%," the Fifth Circuit said, and the appropriate amount for the discount was equal to 100% of the capital gains liability, dollar for dollar.

This decision substantially altered the Tax Court's fair market value test, according to the *Jelke* opinion. "An era of valuation certainly had begun." While the Fifth Circuit declined to extend *Dunn* to the valuation of imbedded tax liability in a decedent's IRA, it approved discounts for contingent estate taxes related to gifted partnership interests in *Estate of McCord* (2006).

Majority favors practicality, precision

This evolving case law provided the backdrop for the questions in the *Jelke* appeal. Given the minority interest at stake and the unlikelihood of liquidation, the IRS urged the Eleventh Circuit to ratify the Tax Court's acceptance of a present value of the $51 million capital gains liability, indexed over a sixteen-year period (the likely time when the assets would be sold), or $21 million. The estate claimed this approach was both inconsistent and incomplete, given the likelihood that the underlying securities would change over time. It urged the application of *Dunn* and the certainty of a dollar-for-dollar discount—and the Court agreed.

> In our case, why would a hypothetical willing buyer...*not* adjust his or her purchase price to reflect the entire $51 million? The buyer could just as easily venture into the open marketplace and acquire an identical portfolio of blue chip domestic and international securities...without any risk exposure to the underlying tax liability.

The Tax Court's distinction between the majority interest at stake in *Dunn* and the minority interest in *Jelke* was not persuasive. "We are dealing with hypothetical, not strategic, willing buyers and sellers," the Court observed. This led to its threshold, "arbitrary" assumption that a liquidation takes place on the date of death, freezing all assets and liabilities at that time. Whether a majority or minority interest is present "is of no moment."

The Court also rejected any distinction based on *Dunn's* consideration of an interest that held operating as well as investment assets, which led the Fifth Circuit to apply an earnings-based valuation to the operations side (weighted 85%), and a net asset valuation to the investment side (15%). In *Jelke*, the company was solely an investment holding company, so the *Dunn* analysis applied only to the net asset valuation with no need for weighting. More importantly, the Tax Court's present value approach was "fluidly ethereal," requiring courts to "gaze into a crystal ball, flip a coin, or at the very least, split the difference" between the respective approaches of the taxpayer and the IRS.

"We think the approach set forth by the Fifth Circuit in [*Dunn*] is the better," the Court held, in a two-to-one decision. By calculating the estate tax based on a "snapshot of valuation" on the date of death, the simple, logical *Dunn* rationale provides "practical certainty to taxpayers, appraisers and financial planners alike." It is a "welcome road map for those in the judiciary," the Court added, "not formally trained in the art of valuation." Finally, the dollar-for-dollar approach relieves courts from spending time and resources having to "wade through a myriad of divergent expert witness testimony, based on subjective conjecture and divergent opinions."

Notably, the Court declined to rule on the Tax Court's determination of discounts, finding no error in the assessment of a 15% lack of marketability discount and 10% for lack of control.

A strong dissent

Like the *Dunn* panel, the *Jelke* majority anticipated that critics in the business appraisal community might call their methodology unsophisticated and overly simplistic. In assuming this risk, it quoted the Fifth Circuit's observation in *Dunn* that opposite oversimplification on the methodology spectrum lies "over-engineering."

> [Our] economic reality approach mimics the marketplace and places a practical, transactional overlay upon the proverbial willing buyer-willing seller analysis. It allows the issue to conform to the reality of the depressing economic effect that the lurking taxes have on the market selling price.

A lone dissenting judge decried the adoption of the "rule of least effort." "The majority gives in to the judicial equivalent of the doctrine of ignoble ease," the dissent wrote, citing Theodore Roosevelt's philosophy on the "strenuous life." The Tax Court's "real value approach" may not be perfect, and it depends on certain arguable assumptions—such as past rates of liquidation. But it produces a more accurate result than the majority's arbitrary assumption method, the dissent argued, "because it more closely reflects the economic interests of those who control the company."

Rector v. Commissioner

Citation: 2007 Tax Ct. Memo LEXIS 384
Court: Court of Appeals
State/Jurisdiction: United States
Date of Decision: December 13, 2007
Judge: Laro

The valuation of interests in Family Limited Partnerships (FLPs) and Limited Liability Companies (LLCs) has been a significant source of engagements for BV appraisers. But as recent cases attest, the IRS continues to use Internal Revenue Code Section 2036(a)(1) to, in effect, destroy the entity and render valuation of the entity interests irrelevant, leaving only the valuation of the underlying assets. Further, appraisers are now faced with the new IRC Section 6695A penalty provisions. Field efforts by the IRS will now focus on making sure that the taxpayer's appraisers have: 1) developed a true understanding of relevant facts; 2) exercised reasonable due diligence in reviewing legal and tax assumptions; and 3) created a reasonable, credible report.

More difficult to find 'good facts' FLPs

Two cases last year tested the continued viability of FLP and LLC planning. *Erickson v. Commissioner,* a Tax Court decision and *Estate of Bigelow v. Commissioner*, the Ninth Circuit's confirmation of a Tax Court ruling, were both "bad facts" cases in which the courts had little difficulty concluding that Section 2036(a)(1) applied. The courts also found no "bona fide sale" exception, as there was no evidence in either case that the FLP had any substantial, nontax business or investment purpose. In *Bigelow*, for example, these findings permitted the court to disregard the appraiser's 37% combined discount (for lack of control and marketability) for the FLP interests.

The latest Tax Court case continues this unfortunate trend. In *Rector v. Commissioner,* Judge David Laro once again delves into the 2036(a) arena. The facts are fairly typical: Ms. Rector was ninety-two and actively in control of her wealth when she and her two sons, with assistance of counsel, formed an FLP in 1998, funding it with nearly $9 million in cash and marketable securities. She was also, directly and through her living trust, the only partner contributing assets to the entity. The Tax Court fixed upon this absence of any "pooling of assets" among the FLP partners as well as the following negative facts:

- Decedent and her sons did not negotiate the terms of the FLP and did not retain independent counsel.
- The FLP was not funded until three months after its formation.
- The decedent transferred most of her accessible wealth to the FLP, leaving her with insufficient liquid assets to pay her living expenses.
- The FLP failed to follow such formalities as issuing financial statements and holding regular meetings.
- The FLP operated without a business plan or an investment strategy, and it neither traded nor acquired assets.
- The FLP functioned only to manage its own accounts, pay decedent's personal expenses, and make distributions, but it failed to follow a strictly pro rata distribution policy (the decedent's sons became partners via gifts).

After forming the FLP, the decedent continued to receive monthly distributions from an irrevocable trust, which held over $2.5 million in liquid assets. But Judge Laro found that the trust corpus was not "realistically available" to the decedent, given its specific language and the "implied understanding" among decedent and her sons not to invade the trust corpus. More importantly, when the FLP was formed, they knew that her annual income from the trust would be insufficient to cover decedent's annual expenses, which were nearly three times what she received from the trust.

Finally, "at all relevant times, decedent held both a majority interest in [the FLP] and the powers incident to serving as [the FLP's] general partner." The FLP agreement gave her the right, first as direct general partner and then indirectly, through the revocable trust, "to do anything reasonably connected with [the FLP] assets." Given all these facts, it's not surprising that the Court found under Section 2036(a)(1) an implied understanding among decedent and her sons that she retained the right to income and economic benefit from the FLP assets.

Laro sets high hurdle for 2036(a) exception

The estate contended that Section 2036(a)'s exception for a "bona fide sale for an adequate and full consideration" applied, but the Court dispensed with this argument as well. "The formation of [the FLP] entailed no change in the underlying pool of assets or the likelihood of profit." Without such potential for profit, the transfer of decedent's assets for partnership interests could not have been accompanied by sufficient consideration. As to its alleged nontax, business purposes, the Court considered and rejected the following:

- *Estate tax savings.* "The estate's stated goal of gift-giving is a testamentary purpose and not a significant non-tax business purpose."
- *Managing/diversifying assets.* The FLP did not require any active management, and it did not have any strategy to alter/diversify investments from its pre-transfer plan.
- *Asset protection.* Decedent did not have any legitimate concern about liabilities. Notably, the FLP failed to protect her assets from creditors while she (and her revocable living trust) remained general partner.

Judge Laro appears to be setting out a difficult test for establishing a "significant nontax business purpose" for an FLP or LLC. In particular, *Rector* indicates that the wealthy individual establishing the entity should *not* also be its general partner. At a minimum (and as *Bigelow* also suggests), the FLP's general partner should be an LLC or possibly a Subchapter S corporation. In the Court's discussion of the decedent as general partner (as further evidence of an "implied understanding" of asset control) it did not discuss a GP's fiduciary obligations to the partnership, which could mitigate such a finding. An LLC or S Corp as a general partner, with owners other than just the decedent, might also help.

In conclusion, Judge Laro adopted a "step transaction" approach, finding that decedent's transfer of assets to the FLP and her subsequent gifts of the limited partner interests were part of a "single plan" to minimize her Federal estate tax without entailing a significant nontax business purpose or a genuine pooling of assets.

What makes for a 'good' FLP

In light of these findings, as well as the *Bigelow* and *Erickson* cases, the key question for appraisers is what might constitute a "good facts" FLP case, one which will have a better chance of passing muster by the IRS and the courts. Clearly, due diligence is a must. An appraiser who is retained at the preparation and filing of a gift or estate tax return concerning FLP or LLC interests must determine the true facts upon which to base the appraisal and conclusions of value. This may entail going beyond mere statements of the client or legal counsel.

For example, where the agreement purportedly transferred FLP interests to assignees, the appraiser should obtain and review the actual transfer documents to make certain they track the agreement. The appraiser should also review these documents to determine: the actual date of transfer; the timeliness of transfer documents; the purposes of the entity; the involvement of the partners in discussions or negotiations; and the sources of support for the senior person(s) after funding the partnership or limited liability company.

Of course, it's preferable to bring the BV appraiser in at the planning stage for an FLP/LLC. That way, the appraiser can assist the estate owner's advisors and attorneys by explaining the valuation process and suggesting plan designs to maximize opportunities for the entity's success and the appraisal's usefulness. These suggestions may include:

- keeping a substantial portion of the value of the estate owner's assets outside the FLP;
- having an LLC or S corporation as the general partner of the FLP;
- having clear language in the relevant agreement that only assignee interests can be transferred;
- providing for periodic meetings; and
- making outright gifts or other transfers to family members with which they can become founding partners ("pooling of interests") of the FLP.

This abstract was written for the *Business Valuation Update*™ by Owen G. Fiore, JD, Fiore Wealth Planning Consulting, www.owenfiore.com.

In the Matter of the Estate of Norman B. Hjersted (II)

Citation: 2008 WL 269013
Court: Supreme Court
State/Jurisdiction: Kansas
Date of Decision: February 1, 2008

In deciding *Estate of Norman B. Hjersted*, the Kansas Court of Appeals held that discounts for lack of marketability and control did not apply to a family limited partnership (FLP), particularly when its purpose was to disinherit Mr. Hjersted's wife of nearly twenty years, to the benefit of his son by a prior marriage. (The case abstract appeared in the August 2006 *Business Valuation Update*™.) The son appealed to the Kansas Supreme Court.

Discounts create 'illusory layers of ownership'

To recap: Prior to his death, Mr. Hjersted created an FLP to hold all the outstanding stock (500 shares) of his closely held company. He became a 96% limited partner of the FLP and a 2% general partner; the remaining 2% belonged to his son. Three years later, Hjersted transferred his 96% limited partnership interest to the son as part gift/part sale. The transaction stipulated that the gift was worth $675,000, the then-maximum allowable without incurring federal income tax. To carve out this gifted portion, an appraiser valued the 500 shares at $4,500 per share and the company at $2.25 million. He then subjected the 96% limited partnership interest to combined, layered discounts for lack of marketability and control equaling 32.5%, for a total fair market value of approximately $1.46 million.

When Hjersted died a year after the transfer, his wife sought her statutory elective share of the estate. At trial, her valuation expert determined the fair market value of the company's 500 shares as of the transfer date; he was not asked to—nor did he consider—its value "as contained within" the FLP. He valued the company at $2.66 million, to which he applied a 10% marketability discount. Accordingly, the 96% interest was worth just over $2.55 million. For the most part, the trial court agreed; although the FLP was valid, it said, the wife had not consented to the transfer. After reducing the 96% interest by the son's cash and loan contributions, the court valued the wife's elective share at $1.175 million, and the son appealed.

The appellate court found that the wife's consent was "irrelevant," but it upheld her expert valuation. Discounts injected too much speculation into the appraisal, the court said, and were inappropriate when the transaction unified ownership into one individual. Moreover, applying discounts could help create "layers of illusory ownership for non-probate transfers...in furtherance of a scheme to disinherit a spouse."

Supreme Court offers 'contours of guidance'

On further review, the Supreme Court focused on a fine legal distinction: As a rule, an appellate court "does not weigh conflicting evidence, pass on the credibility of witnesses, or redetermine questions of fact." That is the trial court's role—but in this case, the appellate court overstepped its bounds. In rejecting the discounts used by the son's appraiser, its analysis revealed a "de novo" review and resulting legal conclusion. However, it did not subject the wife's appraiser and his 10% discount to a similar review, but "apparently embraced the propriety of his discount within the 'factual' determination" of the lower court. This despite the appraiser's admission at trial that he did not value the FLP interest—only its sole asset, the 500 shares of company stock.

> Consequently, the Court of Appeals' decision ultimately made case-dispositive a valuation that made no pretense of addressing that court's paramount issue: value of the [FLP] interest on [the transfer date].

The trial court found that the FLP was a valid transfer, and rejected the wife's argument that its nature was illusory or for a non-business purpose. Accordingly, the Court of Appeals could not revisit this conflicting evidence and then rely on the purported artificiality of the FLP to conclude that the combined discounts were unnecessary, the Supreme Court held.

The higher court reversed the appellate holding. The valuation of the FLP interest was "best left" to the trial court, which would—at a minimum—address the validity of the combined 32.5% discounts in the original appraisal. The court could adjust, compromise, or even reject one or both discounts. "We cannot prognosticate all the factors that the...court could decide to consider in this value determination," the court said. At the same time, it offered "some general contours of guidance," and then discussed in considerable detail the four areas that invoke application of lack of marketability and control discounts: estate and gift tax, dissenting shareholder cases, spousal elective share, and divorce.

Policy on discounts 'at odds'

In particular, tax courts have allowed combined discounts for FLP interests "ranging from 25% to 35% and sometimes even more." These decisions usually turn on findings of legitimate business and estate planning interests; similar findings might permit application of discounts to the Hjersted FLP in the context of an augmented estate.

On the other hand, courts generally do not apply discounts in dissenting shareholder actions, because they penalize minority shareholders while unfairly enriching the majority; and Kansas is among the majority of states to disallow discounts in this context. On remand, the trial court should consider whether the wife's situation was comparable to a minority shareholder and entitled to an undiscounted value, the Supreme Court said. As part of its analysis, the court should consider that it previously accepted the 10% marketability discount—which could be contrary to the "outright rejection" of discounts in the state's dissenting shareholder case law.

In fact, the Court of Appeals relied on this case law when rejecting the 32.5% combined discounts, in part because they unified the partnership interests in the son. The Supreme Court directed the trial court not to consider this factor, however. In reality, the control of the FLP did not reside in the son's 96% limited partnership interest, the court observed, but in the general partnership interest, of which he owned only 1%. The son didn't inherit the entire interest until his father's death.

Likewise, in the probate area, the trial court could find that the FLP represented "legitimate steps toward a legitimate estate planning and business objective." Or it could find (as it did during the original trial) that the appraisal at the time of the transfer suffered from an "inherent bias," because it sought to minimize the tax consequences—a purpose inconsistent with that of the spousal elective share.

Finally, the trial court could find parallels in state divorce law, which did not clearly prohibit application of discounts. Overall, the many sides of the debate further supported the district court re-taking this decision, "so it may continue addressing, if not balancing, competing considerations" and the often "at odds" public policy considerations of the spousal elective share statute.

Mirowski v. Commissioner

Citation: T.C. Summ. Op. 2008-74
Court: United States Tax Court
State/Jurisdiction: Specialty Federal
Date of Decision: March 26, 2008
Judge: Chiechi

In this case, Tax Court Judge Chiechi delivered a welcome boost to BV appraisers who try to determine acceptable discounts for fractional interests transfers in family limited partnerships (FLPs) and limited liability companies (LLCs). The Judge was obviously well aware of recent "bad facts" FLP cases, in which taxpayers suffered defeats under IRC §2036(a), the entities were rejected, and appraiser valuations became irrelevant.[1] The IRS will continue to scrutinize these entities; however, *Mirowski* provides a basic primer for good planning and effective presentation of an FLP or LLC case in Tax Court, at least where there is a responsive judge.

Mirowski facts—a formula for success

Mrs. Mirowski's husband, a physician, co-developed an implantable cardioverter defibrillator (ICD) in the 1960s, which became quite lucrative through patents and licensing agreements after his death in 1990. The Mirowskis had three daughters (each with two children), and were close-knit. As sole heir to her husband's estate, Mrs. Mirowski embarked upon a program of making gifts to family members, friends, and a family foundation. As the court noted, Mrs. Mirowski was a "careful, deliberate and thoughtful decision maker, especially with respect to financial matters."

She was committed to having family members work together and "valued the family cohesiveness that joint management of a family business can foster."

In 1992, Mrs. Mirowski created an irrevocable trust for each of her daughters, appointing all three as co-trustees of each trust, gifting substantial interests in the pacemaker patent licensing agreements and royalties to the trusts. She retained a majority (51.09%) interest in the patent and licensing agreements for herself. Mrs. Mirowski retained Goldman Sachs as her principal investment advisor, and eventually developed a diversified investment plan. By then, the royalties amounted to millions of dollars each year.

In 2000, U.S. Trust suggested planning an LLC and Mrs. Mirowski's long-time legal counsel drafted the documents. Because the family preferred making significant decisions at its annual retreats, they delayed review of the proposed LLC (Mirowski Family Ventures, or MFV) until August of 2001. By then Mrs. Mirowski, a diabetic, developed a foot ulcer, but it was not life-threatening at the time.

Events moved quickly, including: 1) Mrs. Mirowski executed final LLC documents on August 22nd and they were filed on August 30th; 2) over $60 million in assets (including the 51.09% interest in patent and licensing agreements and marketable securities) were transferred to MFV between September 1st and 7th; and 3) on September 7th, she gave each of her daughters' trusts a 16% member interest in MFV, for a total of 48%. On September 10th, her foot ulcer deteriorated suddenly, and she died on September 11, 2001.

Facts assist appraisers before trial

Given these strong facts, the parties first agreed on substantial valuation discounts for both gift and estate purposes, as determined by the taxpayer's appraiser, Curtis R. Kimball, ASA (Willamette Management Associates) and his IRS counterpart, David Fuller (VALUE Incorporated). According to Kimball, the two valuations were not that far apart. Notably, the assistance the family received from its appraisal as well as its legal and tax advisors significantly helped in preparing for litigation and preserving the entity formation, to the point that the valuation discounts were not an issue at trial.

Judge Chiechi made substantial factual findings, which form the basis for the Tax Court's decision, including: 1) at no time before September 10, 2001 did the decedent, her family, or her physicians expect her to die so suddenly; 2) the testimony of two daughters (the third suffered chronic epilepsy) was clear, credible and convincing; and 3) the real and significant non-tax business purposes met the §2036(a) criteria to apply the "bona fide sale" exception to the transfers creating MFV. As to those purposes, Judge Chiechi found the following reasons valid and supported by the evidence:

1. The daughters (and their children) were to jointly manage the family assets.
2. The bulk of the assets were pooled, to allow for continued investment opportunities, which would not have been available if the daughters (or their trusts) had received separate, portioned gifts.

3. Each of the daughters (and their children) shared the assets equally.

The IRS tried to analogize these to the "bad facts" cases, but Judge Chiechi dismissed the arguments, distinguishing this case on its facts.

Tax Court analysis—take heed!

At all relevant times, including after decedent's death, MFV was a "valid functioning investment operation and has been managing the business matters relating to the ICD patents and...license agreements, including related litigation," the court held. Because the "bona fide sale" exception in §2036(a) applied, MFV was a successful vehicle for substantial valuation discounts, even though the gifts were but a few days prior to Mrs. Mirowski's death.

As to the gifts, there was no implied agreement of retained income or enjoyment until death, and Mrs. Mirowski's position as sole manager of MFV was not fatal, given the detailed provisions and imposed fiduciary obligations of the operating agreement. Also, certain other Code sections were not problematic for MFV (namely §2038(a)(1) and §2035).

Other Tax Court judges may differ with Judge Chiechi's analysis; therefore, analysts still need to consider all the decisions in the FLP/LLC area. The importance of structuring FLPs and LLCs in a careful manner, funding the entities properly, and then operating them according to the controlling legal documents cannot be overstated. Appraisers can review the pertinent valuation and funding issues with families and their advisors. For example, contribution of the patent and licensing interests to MFV by the daughters' trusts and Mrs. Mirowski could have strengthened the taxpayer's "pooling of assets" argument.

As always, lessons to be learned

Mirowski is quite similar by its facts and outcome to *Estate of Stone v. Commissioner*, (T.C. Memo. 2003-309). In both cases the Tax Court found credible evidence of non-tax purposes. However, these Tax Court Memorandum Decisions are fact specific and have limited precedent value. Thus the IRS will continue to challenge FLPs/LLCs where the facts are in dispute or where the entities are created primarily for tax avoidance purposes. As independent professionals with knowledge of the relevant facts and law—as well as valuation standards, methodology and analysis—appraisers will continue to render helpful advice in structuring FLP and LLC plans, and in developing appropriate strategies for supporting valuation discounts.

---

1. Such cases include *Estate of Bigelow v. Comm'r*, (9th Circuit, 2007), abstracted in the Nov. 2007 *BVU*; *Estate of Erickson v. Comm'r* (July 2007 *BVU*) and *Estate of Rector v. Comm'r* (Feb. 2008 *BVU*), both Tax Court decisions.

This abstract was written for the *Business Valuation Update*™ by Owen G. Fiore, JD, Fiore Wealth Planning Consulting, www.owenfiore.com.

Astleford v. Commissioner

Citation: T.C. Memo 2008-128
Court: United States Tax Court
State/Jurisdiction: Specialty Federal
Date of Decision: May 5, 2008
Judge: Swift

"In order to calculate the fair market value of limited partnership interests [the] petitioner transferred as gifts," the Tax Court begins, in a nice preface to the issues presented in *Astleford v. Commissioner*:

> ...we must determine the fair market value of 1,187 acres of Minnesota farmland, whether a particular interest in a general partnership should be valued as a partnership interest or as an assignee interest, and the lack of control and lack of marketability discounts that should apply to the limited and to the general partnership interests.

In a lengthy opinion, the Tax Court considers the testimony of six appraisal experts, four for the taxpayer and two for the Internal Revenue Service. (The court does not name the business and real estate appraisers, referring to them simply as experts for either party.) It also considers the comparability of data from sales of publicly traded REITs (real estate investment trusts) to data from sales of registered RELPs (real estate limited partnerships) and—while declining to declare one dataset superior to the other—the court does examine which set of sales transaction data applies more to the facts and circumstances of the various Astleford family interests.

Analytical note. Of particular interest to appraisers: There are two "pearls" in the Astleford *opinion. The first relates to the adoption of a fairly significant combined discount for lack or marketability and control related to a 50% general partnership interest. The second relates to the Tax Court's acceptance of a significant "tiered" discount for the multiple ownership levels inherent in the real estate partnership/limited partnership interests.*

Wealthy developer leaves all to wife

When M.G. Astleford died in 1995, he owned interests in over forty real properties located primarily in Minnesota. All of these passed through a marital trust to his wife, who formed the Astleford Family Limited Partnership (AFLP) in 1996 to "facilitate the continued ownership, development, and management" of the real estate interests and to facilitate gifts to the couple's three adult children. At the time of its formation, Mrs. Astleford retained a 10% general partnership interest in AFLP and gave each of the children a 30% limited partnership (LP) interest. The limited partners made no capital contributions at the time of any gifts and received no voting rights; no outside party could join AFLP without the consent of the general partner, who also controlled all rights regarding the sale/transfer/partition of the partnership assets.

Mrs. Astleford initially funded the AFLP in 1996 with an eldercare facility (stipulated value of nearly $900,000). In 1997, she transferred to AFLP her 50% general partnership interest in the Pine Bend Development Company (Pine Bend), which owned 3,000 acres of land, including 1,187 acres dedicated to farming (the Rosemount property). She gifted additional LP shares in AFLP to her children to keep the 30-30-30 ownership configuration while maintaining herself as 10% general partner (GP) in AFLP.

In her 1996 and 1997 federal gift tax returns, Mrs. Astleford declared certain values and discounts related to her respective gifts to the children. On audit, the IRS found higher fair market values for several of the properties that funded AFLP and a higher net asset value (NAV) for the entire partnership. The IRS also decreased some of the marketability and lack of control discounts related to the gifted AFLP limited partnership interests. The taxpayer's versus the IRS's assessments are shown in the table below.

	Taxpayer's gift tax returns		IRS audit determinations	
Year	Taxable gifts	Gift tax liability	Taxable gifts	Gift tax liability
1996	$277,441	$79,581	$626,898	$127,619
1997	$3,954,506	$2,005,689	$10,937,268	$3,997,288

Through various pre-trial stipulations—and as the Tax Court neatly summarized at the start of its opinion, the parties disputed only three issues related to AFLP and its assets: 1) the fair market value of the Rosemount farmland; 2) whether the 50% Pine Bend interest should be valued as a GP or assignee interest; and 3) the applicability and amount of discounts for lack of control and lack of marketability to the gifted AFLP limited partnership interests.

'Market absorption' discount appropriate?

The taxpayer's real property appraiser considered the 1,187-acre Rosemount property to be "extraordinarily large and unique." In his market approach, he compared eighteen similar properties based on date of sale, location and size, and calculated an initial value for the Rosemount farmland of nearly $3.7 million. But a sale of the entire property would flood the local market, he believed, reducing the per-acre price for farmland and requiring a market absorption discount. Assuming the property would sell over the course of four years and would appreciate 7% per year—and using a 25% discount rate to present value the expected cash flows, which was derived from a real estate development study—the expert's final fair market value for the farm property came to $1,817 per acre for a total of $2.16 million.

The IRS appraiser also used the market approach—comparing 125 Minnesota farmland properties and personally visiting twelve. He ultimately chose two comparables, adjusted only for dates of sale (because the properties were so similar to the subject), and arrived at a fair market value for the Rosemount farmland of $3,500 per-acre or nearly $4.16 million total, almost twice as much as the taxpayer's appraiser. The IRS expert further concluded that a market absorption discount was not appropriate. The Pine Bend partnership originally purchased the 1,187 acres in a single transaction, and thus (he believed) it could also sell the tract in its entirety. Even if an absorption discount was appropriate, the IRS expert considered the 25% present-value discount rate excessive. He cited a 1997 Minn. farm business management study that showed farmers in the region earning an average rate of return on equity of 9.2%.

The Tax Court found the IRS expert to be "particularly credible and highly experienced," possessing a "unique knowledge" of the area. The court adopted his initial $3,500 per-acre finding, but believed that due to the size of the property, a sale of all 1,187 acres in a single year merited a market absorption discount. The taxpayer's discount was "unreasonably high," however, because it relied on a 25% rate of equity return that real estate developers expected to earn. In another nod to the IRS expert, the court held that his 9.2% rate of return was based on what farmers in the area were "actually earning." Rounding this figure up to 10%, applied over four years, the court found the farmland to be worth $2,786 per acre for a total fair market value of nearly $3.31 million.

Analytical note. The court indeed felt that it would be difficult for the surrounding market to absorb the 1,187 acres and applied the absorption discount. The court took exception, however, to the 25% discount rate because it was based on developers' rates of return, which contemplate greater risk. But was the 9.2% rate (which the court rounded to 10%) plucked from the IRS expert the right *rate? It was said to be based upon "the return on equity which farmers in the area were actually earning." An alternate source would be the "going in discount rate" on agricultural property in the region available from a number of surveys published by national real estate consulting firms. That rate (with a slight increment for the risk of an uncertain time horizon and appreciation rate) might have resulted in a supportable discount rate somewhere between the 10% adopted by the court and the taxpayer's 25%. Footnotes to the transcript reveal that experts for both sides accounted for transaction costs and periodic property taxes in their absorption analysis.*

Discounts for a 50% GP *and* LP interests?

The taxpayer treated the 50% Pine Bend interest as an assignee interest, based primarily on the other 50% owner's failure to consent to the transfer to the AFLP. Because, under Minn. law, an assignee would only have rights to Pine Bend's profits—and no management control—the taxpayer's expert, as a preliminary matter, discounted the assignee interest by 5%.

But the AFLP partnership resolution treated the Pine Bend transfer as one of all the taxpayer's rights and interests, the IRS pointed out. Further, as AFLP's sole general partner, the taxpayer was essentially in the same management position whether she transferred a GP or assignee interest. The substance of the transfer should trump its form, the IRS argued—and the court agreed, finding the taxpayer funded AFLP with a 50% general partnership interest.

To determine the discounts for lack of marketability and control for the 50% GP interest, the taxpayer's expert examined comparable data from sales of registered real estate limited partnerships (RELPs). He identified trading discounts (differences between unit/share trading prices and unit/

share NAVs) in 17 RELP comparables and established a range of 22% to 46% for a combined lack of marketability and control discount. But then, "without explaining further," according to the court, the expert "abruptly concluded" that a 40% combined discount applied to the 50% interest.

The IRS expert believed that because the 50% GP interest was "simply an asset of AFLP," the discounts he applied at the entity level obviated the application of discounts to the 50% interest. But in an interesting footnote, the court observed that in previous cases, the IRS (as well as the Tax Court) had applied layered discounts where a taxpayer held a minority interest in an entity that in turn owned a minority interest in another entity. "The 50-percent Pine Bend interest constituted less than 16% of AFLP's NAV and was only 1 of 15 real estate investments" that AFLP held at the time of the transfer, the court said. "[L]ack of control and lack of marketability discounts at both the Pine Bend level and the AFLP parent level are appropriate."

The court eliminated four of the RELP comparables that the taxpayer's expert selected because their data came from the wrong year (1999 instead of 1997, the year of the gift). The remaining data showed median and mean trading discounts of 30% to 36%, and a 1997 sample of 130 RELPs showed a 28.7% median and 30% mean discount. Thus the court concluded that a 30% combined discount applied to the 50% GP interest that the taxpayer transferred to the AFLP, valued at nearly $1.3 million.

Analytical note. An interesting methodology disconnect occurs here. The discounts for lack of control and lack of marketability related to the Pine Bend GP interest are estimated and applied on a combined basis, whereas on the overall AFLP interest discussed below, they are estimated and applied separately.

The BV profession has frequently struggled with the concept of lack of control and marketability discounts for 50% interests. Such interests generally do not enjoy control, but they clearly do not experience the same lack of control suffered by lesser interests. With little empirical data to go on, many experts have opined that the discounts do apply to a 50% interest, just to a lesser degree. Given this, the resulting 30% would appear relatively high, especially when compared to the combined discounts for lack of control and marketability of 34% applied to the subject 30% LP interest in AFLP.

It is at this point the court first discusses the appropriateness of discounting an entity inside an entity or "tiered" discounts. This has been another challenge for our profession. Many experts have put forth that if such a discount applies it must certainly be reduced. The justification frequently appears to be no more than their concern for letting the taxpayer get away with too much of a good thing. Here it seemed important to the court that Pine Bend was not the primary asset of AFLP, and it did not explicitly limit its discount based on the tiered structure of the entities.

LP discounts turn on selected comparables

In determining discounts for gifts of the limited partnership interests in AFLP, the taxpayer's expert first looked at nine RELP comparables, which had an average trading discount of 38%.

Of these, four RELPs were "most comparable," with trading discounts ranging from 40% to 47%. Ultimately the expert settled on a lack of control discount for the LP interests of 45% for the first gift year (1996) and 40% for the second (1997).

But the expert's nine RELP comparables were "significantly more leveraged," the court observed, demonstrating debt-to-NAV ratios of 82% to 205% compared to AFLP's more moderate leverage of 52% debt-to-NAV. Of his selected four comparables—which he considered most similar—two had NAV's approximately five times AFLP's NAV, and the other two were "even more leveraged." Because AFLP held less debt and was inherently less risky than the comparables, the court found the taxpayer's 45% and 40% discounts "unlikely." Moreover, because AFLP's cash distribution rate was significantly higher than the average rate of the RELPs—10% versus 6.7%—the court found that under his own approach, which conceded less risk to companies with higher cash distributions—the expert's discounts should be lower than the 38% average that he observed among the comparables. The RELP comparables were "too dissimilar" to AFLP to warrant the reliance that the taxpayer's expert placed on them, the court ruled, and his combined discounts for the LP interests were "excessive."

Rather than "[sift] through the RELP data looking for more appropriate RELPs to serve as comparables," the court turned to the IRS expert, who examined comparability data from sales of REITs. It declined to declare either the REIT or RELP data superior to the other, since prior courts have accepted expert valuations derived from both. In considering the facts of this case, the court found that RELPs more closely resembled AFLP and also the Pine Bend partnership in size, marketability, management, distribution requirements, and taxation. The low trading volume of RELPs on the secondary market also did not disqualify their data.

By comparison, the abundance of REIT sales "tends to produce more reliable data," the court noted. Any differences between REITs and the subject partnerships could be minimized by having a larger pool of REIT comparables from which to choose, and by subjecting the comparables to a methodology that accounts for their greater liquidity. In analyzing REIT data in this context, the court explained, it is appropriate to back out of their trading prices any liquidity premiums, resulting in lack of control discounts.

Taking this approach, the IRS expert obtained sales data for 75 REIT comparables, which showed that in 1996 they traded at a median 0.1% premium over per-share NAV and a 1.2% discount under per-share NAV in 1997. Using regression analysis, he concluded that REITs generally traded at a 7.79% liquidity premium over private real estate partnerships. He combined this observed premium with the respective 1996/1997 trading data to arrive at a lack of control discount for the AFLP limited partnership interests of 7.14% in 1996 and 8.34% in 1997.

Method was misapplied

The court agreed with the IRS expert's method but held that on their face, his discounts appeared unreasonably low. Moreover, other studies cited by the expert suggested that the applicable liquidity premiums were nearly two times the levels he used.

A better method to derive liquidity premiums is to look at the difference in average discounts observed in private placements of registered and unregistered stock, since a public market is available to the former but not the latter. According to two studies cited by the IRS expert, this difference amounted to approximately 14%, which resulted in a general liquidity premium of 16.27% inherent in publicly traded assets and also applicable to REITs. (If an illiquid asset trades at a discount of 14% relative to a liquid asset, then the liquid asset is trading at a relative 16.27% premium, or 1/[1 - 0.14]-1 = 0.1627.)

The court eliminated or backed out this 16.27% liquidity premium from the median REIT trading data provided by the IRS expert, subtracting the .1% in 1996 and adding the 1.2% in 1997 to arrive at a lack of control discount for the AFLP partnership interests of 16.17% and 17.47%, respectively.

Analytical note. A number of interesting things can be observed here. First the Court states that it has no opinion whether RELP or REIT data are more representative for purposes of estimating the discounts appropriate for an FLP. Then it says that RELPs more closely resemble the attributes inherent in AFLP. But it also observes that the capital structure of the RELPs selected by the taxpayer's expert are dissimilar to that of AFLP and reject them. With an insufficient number of remaining RELPs to work with, the Court resorts to using the REIT data largely because there is so much of it.

This reasoning first appeared in McCord v. Comm'r *(2003): that an absence of comparable data can be overcome by an abundance of incomparable data. With the move to the REIT data comes the need to uncouple the REIT discount or premium from the liquidity premium inherent in the REIT market prices. (Analyst's tip: There are less cumbersome ways to utilize REIT data to estimate a discount for lack of control. Hint: The* Mergerstat®/BVR Contol Premium Study™ *includes REIT takeover transactions.)*

The discounts computed in this way by the IRS expert are rejected by the court merely because they "appeared unreasonably low." That's all. Too low. The court then performed its own analysis of privately placed registered and unregistered stock to derive a liquidity premium. You can't help but wonder whether the court had some unstated benchmark lack of control discount in mind hovering in the plus or minus 20% range.

Final conclusions of value

As a final matter, the Tax Court compared the taxpayer's estimate of a 15% marketability discount for the 1996 limited partnership gifts to the IRS's 21.23% and saw "no reason" not to adopt the higher discount. The parties stipulated to a 22% marketability discount for the 1997 gifts and the court adopted these as well. In conclusion, it found that the fair market value of each of the taxpayer's three gifts of 30% limited partnership interests to her children were worth $172,525 in 1996, for a total taxable gift of $517,575; and that the fair market value of each 1997 gift of a 30% limited partnership interest was worth $2,188,404, for a total gift value of $6,565,215.

Analytical note. We are not told how either the taxpayer or the IRS computed their lack of marketability discounts of 15% and 21.23%, respectively. We only know that without discussion of the relative merits of either's methodologies, the court could "perceive no reason not to use [the IRS's] higher marketability discount" and rounded it up to 22%. Maybe 15% was unreasonably low.

In summary, we can take away that the discounts related to both 50% interests and tiered entities are not necessarily restricted relative to other holdings and that in the final analysis, courts make their decisions based as much on their perception of reasonableness as rigorous analysis. Overall, however, this analyst thinks the Tax Court pretty much got this one right.

The analytical notes in this abstract were provided by Theodore D. Israel, CPA/ABV, CVA, Eckhoff Accountancy Corporation, www.eckhoff.com.

Holman v. Commissioner

Citation: 130 T.C. No. 12
Court: United States Tax Court
State/Jurisdiction: Specialty Federal
Date of Decision: May 27, 2008
Judge: Halpern

The IRS has aggressively—and for the most part, effectively—challenged the efficacy of Family Limited Partnerships (FLPs) as tax avoidance devices, particularly through the application of Internal Revenue Code (IRC) Section 2036(a). Now, with the "regular decision" (and thereby having precedential value) of the United States Tax Court in *Holman v. Commissioner*, the IRS resurrects §2703 of the IRC in its scrutiny of FLPs to disregard transfer restrictions, and the court addresses discounts for lack of control and lack of marketability—including an interpretation of the holding period component that has already prompted significant debate in the appraisal community.

Four reasons for formation

The Holmans—husband and wife—formed the Holman Limited Partnership (HLP) on November 2, 1999, designating themselves as both general and limited partners (GP and LP) and Mr. Holman's mother as a limited partner, in her dual capacity as trustee and custodian for interests related to their four children. On the same day, the Holmans transferred over $2.8 million of Dell Computer stock to the HLP, receiving proportional shares of HLP interests. Six days later, they gifted limited partnership interests to each child through the trustee/custodian, leaving themselves with a minor GP interest and the LPs owning a substantial majority. The Holmans made smaller gifts of Dell stock in 2000 and 2001, each time causing reconfiguration of the partnership so that by 2001, they owned 12.3% while the remaining LPs owned 87.7%.

The Holmans had four reasons for forming the HLP: 1) long-term growth; 2) asset preservation; 3) asset protection; and 4) educating the children on wealth and business management. Accordingly, the partnership agreement contained substantial restrictions on the transfer of LP shares, including a "buy-back" provision in the event of a non-permitted transfer. (This provision became a major focus in the avoidance of transfer restrictions and determination of discounts, discussed below.)

In filing their gift tax returns (Form 709) for each of the three transfers, the Holmans relied on an independent appraisal that applied an overall 49.25% discount to the fair market value of the LP transfers. In its challenge, the IRS claimed that the first (1999) transfer was an indirect gift; that §2703 voided the transfer restrictions; and that the discounts were excessive.

Analytical note. Advisors and appraisers working together on FLP planning should take note of the discussion of the "indirect gift"/step transaction issue raised by the IRS. While in Holman *the argument was rejected, the court was careful to indicate that each case requires fact-specific analysis to determine if the FLP formation and funding has independent significance from gifts made thereafter. The Tax Court's May decision in* Astleford(abstracted in the June 2008 *BVU*) *seemed to side-step this issue even though the FLP funding and gifts all occurred on the same day.*

Indirect gift turns on timing

Pursuant to IRC §2512, the IRS argued that the 1999 transfer of Dell stock to the HLP was an indirect gift to the limited partners. It relied on two prior decisions: *Shepherd v. Commissioner* (11th Cir. 2002) and *Senda v. Commissioner* (8th Cir. 2006), in which the court found that a partner's transfer of stock (and real estate, in *Shepherd*) to a partnership were indirect transfers to the other partners.

The court, however, distinguished the two cases on their facts. In particular, in *Senda* the taxpayers transferred shares of stock to two FLPs on the same day they transferred LP interests to their children. But here, the Holmans first transferred Dell Stock to the HLP, for which they received proportional partnership interests. They didn't gift the LP units to the children until six days later:

> [The taxpayers] did not first transfer LP units to [the Trustee] and then transfer Dell shares to the partnership, nor did they simultaneously transfer Dell shares to the partnership and LP units to [the Trustee].

Under the "step transaction" doctrine, the IRS argued that because the HLP formation and the LP gifts were so close in time, the court should treat them as a single transaction, resulting in an indirect gift. But to make such a ruling, the court would have to find that "the legal relations created by one transaction would have been fruitless without a completion of the series," it said.

Given the six-day passage of time between formation and funding, the court could not find that the HLP was of no legal consequence absent the 1999 gift. "Indeed, [the IRS] does not ask that we consider either the 2000 gift (made approximately 2 months after formation…) or the 2001 gift (made approximately 15 months [later]…) to be indirect gifts of Dell shares." Moreover, the taxpayers assumed the risk that stock values would change, even in the six days between events. These facts gave enough "independent significance" to the transactions for the court to find there was no indirect gift.

Notably, the court declined to draw any "bright line" concerning the amount of time necessary to deem a series of events independent for purposes of the step transaction doctrine. In this case, six days was sufficient.

Analytical note. Even though the Shepherd *and* Senda *cases used the indirect gift theory to find asset transfers rather than gifts of partnership interests,* Holman *is the first gift tax case to discuss this issue in detail, where there was a time gap between the donors' transfers to the FLP and the gifts of partnership interests. The volatility of the Dell Computer stock saved the day for the taxpayers on the six-day time gap, given the very real risk of loss for such a publicly traded stock. The court may very well look differently on entities with less volatile stock or real estate holdings.*

Transfer restrictions must serve business purpose

Under IRC §2703(a), "the value of any property transferred by gift is determined without regard to any right or restriction relating to the property." Under §2703(b), however, the value will include the restrictions if: 1) they comprise a bona fide business arrangement; 2) they are not devices to make transfers for less than full and adequate consideration; and 3) their terms are similar to those in arm's-length transactions.

The HLP partnership agreement contained one particular restriction (paragraph 9.3) that, in the event of a non-permitted assignment of an LP interest, allowed the partnership to buy-back the interest from the assignee at fair market value based on the assignee's pro rata, distributional share. In attempting to disregard this restriction under §2703, the IRS argued that it could not be part of a bona fide business arrangement because the HLP's primary goals were not business but personal—i.e., to preserve the taxpayers' wealth and "disincentivize" their children from spending it.

The taxpayers argued that the creation of a mechanism—including a buy-sell agreement—to ensure family control of a family business satisfied the bona fide requirement. But the court disagreed, largely because in this case, "we do not have a closely held business." From its formation, the HLP had simply held Dell stock and its transfer restrictions served principally to discourage the LPs' dissipation of assets.

Further, in the event of an unpermitted transfer, the restriction would prevent an assigning LP from realizing the difference in the fair market value of her LP units (which would include discounts) and the units' proportional share of the net asset value (NAV)(undiscounted). Under paragraph 9.3, the partnership could dissolve and redistribute that difference to the remaining partners, increasing their interests and effectively resulting in a transfer for less than adequate consideration.

Because the transfer restrictions did not meet the first two requirements of §2703(b), the court did not need to rule on the third. However, it did note that the IRS offered "colorful" if not convincing expert evidence that no independent investor would ever agree to "get into this deal" given its overall limitations and assets.

Analytical note. In reviewing corporate cases involving active business operations, the court in Holman *concluded that a true business purpose was required to meet the first of the three tests for the §2703(b) "safe harbor." The court assumed the transfer restrictions in the FLP agreement were a "device" for transferring assets at less than full and adequate consideration (even though partnership interests were transferred by gift, not the Dell stock). So, the interesting evidence on the third requirement—comparability to arm's-length, negotiated transactions—was dismissed without decision. However, the FLP entity itself was accepted, with only the single, optional "buy-back" restriction disregarded under §2703(a). It remains to be seen what practical impact this will have on the level of valuation discounts. The FLP interests gifted still possess no or limited control, and are generally non-marketable.*

Experts clash on discounts

Both the IRS and the taxpayers presented qualified business appraisers, who agreed that the NAV of the partnership on the date of the 1999 gift was $2.81 million, based on the number of Dell shares and their publicly traded values. The experts disputed NAV as of the two subsequent gifts. Relying on gift tax regulations, the IRS used averages of the high and low prices of Dell stock on the date of the gifts. Claiming that the rules didn't apply to gifts of partnership interests, the taxpayers used closing values of Dell stock. But the taxpayers cited no authority for disregarding the rules, the court said. Because the NAV of the partnership turned "exclusively" on the values of the publicly traded Dell stock, it adopted the IRS' net asset values for the 2000 and 2001 gifts.

In determining the applicable discount for lack of control, both experts relied upon data from closed-end investment funds, and each used three samples—one for each gift—of similar size. (In fact, they used many of the same samples.) But although the IRS relied solely on general equity funds, finding them the most comparable to the HLP, the taxpayers' expert used seven specialized funds. The IRS calculated median, mean, and interquartile mean discounts for each of his samples; the taxpayers' expert computed only the median, and adjusted these an additional 10% upward to account for the HLP's qualitative factors (lack of diversification, etc.). Their conclusions for the discount for lack of control were:

	1999 gift	2000 gift	2001 gift
Taxpayer expert	14.4%	16.3%	10.0%
IRS expert	11.2%	13.4%	5.0%

At trial, the taxpayers' expert admitted that the specialized funds resembled HLP only in their singular focus, and he agreed there was no correlation between the funds' quantitative factors and the discounts at which they traded. He further admitted his report failed to explain why he included the specialized funds in his samples.

The court calculated the median discounts from this subset of specialized samples (17.1% and 17.8%) and compared them to the medians from the full sample (12% and 13%), and found the differences "significant," enough to disregard the data and adopt the more reliable general equity fund data. It constructed samples for each valuation date from the data common to both experts, resolving outliers by "following...the lead" of the IRS expert and using the interquartile mean. Overall, the court found the IRS expert's approach "more thoughtful," while the taxpayers' expert "failed to convince us" that his cited qualitative factors justified an increased adjustment to the obtained averages. Accordingly, the court applied minority interest discounts of 11.32%, 14.34%, and 4.63% to the three respective gifts.

Holding period—little or no influence?

Bothexperts used restricted stock studies to calculate the marketability discount. From his samples, the taxpayers' expert calculated median and mean discounts of 24.8% and 27.4%, respectively. He analyzed the "investment quality" of the LP units and found they had "virtually no ready market," and that a willing buyer would have "no real prospects" of publicly selling those interests for full value. Based on all factors, the expert concluded that the DLOM should be "at least" 35%.

The IRS expert examined restricted stock studies for three distinct periods and calculated the average discounts for each:

1. Before the SEC adopted Rule 144A (pre-1990), when there was no resale market for restricted stock; the average discounts were 34%.

2. The seven years after 144A, which permitted limited access to a resale market; average discounts were 22%.

3. The two years following the 1997 amendment of 144A, which reduced the required holding period from two to one year; average discounts were 13%.

Based on this evolution, he isolated two components that influenced investors in restricted stocks: limited liquidity and the holding period. In particular, he concluded that the 12% decline in discounts between pre- and post-144A was due to the opening of a limited resale market and represents the "charge" or incremental level of discounts that investors demanded before 1990, when the market became more liquid. The other 22% (of the 34%) was attributable to holding period restrictions and other factors. For private holding companies such as the HLP, which are not subject to legally imposed holding periods or the risks attendant to restricted stock, he said, the discount for lack of marketability was closer to 12%.

Adopting this baseline, the IRS expert analyzed HLP-specific factors—its failure to make distributions, diversify from Dell stock, and its transfer restrictions. The last two increased marketability, he said—specifically because Dell is freely tradable and the buy-back provision permitted the partnership to dissolve and redistribute the assets to the remaining partners. The withdrawing LP would benefit because, in the event she wanted to make an impermissible assignment, given the minority and marketability discounts that would apply to her proportional share of NAV, it would be in her economic interest, as well as the partnership's, to negotiate some price between the discounted value of the units and the dollar value of the units' proportional NAV share.

A reasonable buyer would request (and likely receive) a discount ranging from 10% to 15%, the IRS expert concluded. Given his baseline of 12%, he applied an overall DLOM of 12.5% for the LP interests. He made little, if any, adjustment for the holding period, believing that in this case, it had "little, if any, influence."

More credible expert

Once again, the court found the IRS expert's approach more persuasive. The court "lack[ed] confidence" in the marketability discounts that the taxpayers' expert calculated. His assertion that the LP units lacked any available market could conceivably lead to a DLOM of 100% and a value of zero for the gifts. At any rate, the expert failed to persuade the court that his "stopping point" at 35% was "anything but a guess." The court also believed that the IRS expert correctly considered the partnership buy-back scenario; even if it ran counter to the HLP's stated purpose—to preserve family assets—the purpose might well yield to economic self-interest of the partners. Finally, the court agreed that the holding period, in this case, carried little weight. In light of the available expert evidence, "we cannot determine any better estimate of an appropriate marketability discount" than the estimate by the IRS expert of 12.5%.

Analytical note. The discussion of the holding period issue, and the possibility of a buy-back by the FLP or its partners would seem to violate the basic FMV standard of a hypothetical buyer-seller. And while both parties' appraisers were accepted as experts, the court's detailed discussion of discounts shows a clear belief that the IRS expert was more thorough in his use of databases and valuation proxies, and the level of support for his valuation conclusions. The taxpayers' appraiser was unable to explain with credibility his analysis and conclusions. In the end, the court lacked confidence in the taxpayers' expert, and his DLOM of "at least" 35%. The result: the court was left with the IRS expert's more credible conclusion of 12.5%—which the court adopted.

The analytical notes in this abstract were provided by Owen G. Fiore, JD, FioreWealthPlanningConsulting, www.owenfiore.com.

Alan Baer Revocable Trust v. U.S., Inc.

United States District Court Cites Noble in Considering Subsequent Events

Case name: Alan Baer Revocable Trust v. U.S.
Citation: 2009 WL 1451577(D. Neb.)
Date of decision: May 18, 2009
Country: US
State or Federal: State
State/Jurisdiction: Nebraska
Court: United States District Court
Type of action: Malpractice (Appraisal)
Experts: George Rebensdorf (taxpayer)
Judge: Bataillon
SIC: 4813 Telephone Communications, Except Radiotelephone (except resellers)

The owner of stock in a private, closely held, telecommunications company died in 2002. He left his shares to 23 beneficiaries through a trust, contingent on the trustee selling the stock for a profit and realizing $1.34 million for the bequests. After payment of these contingent bequests, the trustee would pour the remainder of the shares—plus additional assets—into a qualified residual interest trust (QTIP trust) for the spouse, and for which the estate claimed a marital deduction of over $60 million. Of this amount, approximately $41.7 million represented the value of partnerships that held the decedent's stock—minus the contingent bequests—based on an appraisal performed at the time of death.

As for the contingent bequests, the estate's representative noted on the tax return that they "may never be paid out," but if they were, they would take six years to complete. Accordingly the estate present-valued the $1.34 million contingent bequests to $997,663, using a six-year term and a discount rate of 5%. After all the deductions, it paid federal estate taxes on only $457,804.

The IRS calls the appraisal 'incomprehensible.' On review, the IRS reduced the marital deduction by nearly $2 million, based on its finding that the "41+ million" appraisal was "overvalued," most likely to obtain an "artificially high basis for future write-off" of the decedent's investments. Although his personal representative "made a legitimate effort, pending spouses [date of death], to have all of the estate values reasonably determined through commercial appraisals," the IRS also noted that the appraisal of the partnerships that held the telecom stock "was so complex as to be incomprehensible."

Both parties agreed that the decedent's basis in the stock was just over $4.8 million. The estate also found fault with the original appraisal, saying that it was premised on a "speculative valuation" of a start-up company with no earnings. An appraisal performed for the tax proceedings (in 2006) showed that at the date of death in 2002, the company was worth only $3 million. The appraiser who performed both valuations ascribed the substantial difference to the status of a joint venture agreement (the partnership's principal asset), which he did not realize at during the 2002 evaluation was in breach. In 2006, after receiving no royalty payments on the agreement since the breach, it was only "possible" the partnership could increase in value, the appraiser said.

Setting the stage for subsequent proceedings. The IRS filed a motion for summary judgment, arguing that by its terms, the trust provided "a possibility the [contingent] bequests will be funded and paid to beneficiaries other than [the] surviving spouse." The proper inquiry was whether the contingent bequests qualified for the marital deduction, it said. "The underlying value of the stock relative to decedent's investment is irrelevant."

The estate argued that the contingent bequests essentially had no value, because the contingency—that the stock would sell at a profit—could not be realized. The stock's value was therefore directly at issue, because at the date of death, it amounted to less than the decedent's $4.8 million basis. Given this material factual dispute, the estate claimed that summary judgment was improper.

The federal district court (Nebraska) agreed that the value of an estate for federal tax purposes is a factual inquiry in which the court must weigh all relevant evidence. Specifically, when valuing unlisted stock, the applicable Treasury Regulations 20.2031-2(f) provide:

...where selling prices are unavailable because actual sale prices and bona fide bid and asked prices are lacking, the fair market value is to be determined by taking into consideration....in the case of shares of stock, the company's net worth, prospective earning power and dividend-paying capacity, and other relevant factors....

The other relevant factors include the goodwill of business; the economic outlook in the particular industry; the company's position in the industry and its management; the degree of control of the business represented by the block of stock to be valued; and the value of securities of corporations engaged in the same or similar lines of business which are listed on a stock exchange.

As a general matter, the court added, a fair market value determination does not include events subsequent to the valuation date, unless those events were reasonably foreseeable at the time.

An event occurring after a valuation date is not necessarily irrelevant to a determination of fair market value as of that earlier date...if the event was reasonably foreseeable...or, even if unforeseeable as of the valuation date, it may be probative of the earlier valuation to the extent that it is relevant to establishing the amount that a hypothetical willing buyer would have paid a hypothetical willing seller for the subject property as of the valuation date. *Estate of Noble v. Commissioner*, T.C. Mem. 2005-2, 2005 WL 23303, *10 (Jan. 6, 2005).

The rule against subsequent events is simply that, the court said, "a rule of evidence" (citing *Noble* again). In a valuation case, the essential question regarding any evidence is whether its admission would make an asserted fair market valuation more or less probable.

In this case, the government was incorrect in asserting that value was irrelevant. The estate presented evidence (the 2006 appraisal) that the date-of-death value of the company, on which the IRS based its deficiency, was overstated. Even the IRS admitted that the estate's 2002 appraisal was "incomprehensible," the court said. "The issue is whether [the company's] value can be ascertained with fair certainty, and if so, what that value is." If the estate can show that at the date of death, the contingency on which the bequests depends (selling the stock at profit during the spouse's lifetime) will never occur, then their value could be extinguished for federal estate tax purposes.

Accordingly, the court denied the IRS motion for summary judgment. Further, it restated the *Noble* standard, finding that in future proceedings, it would limit the introduction of subsequent events to those that are relevant to the amount that a hypothetical willing buyer and seller would negotiate for the closely held assets as of the valuation date.

Estate of Black v. Comm'r

A 'Facts too Good to be True' Family Ltd. Partnership Case?

Case name: Estate of Black v. Comm'r
Citation: 133 T.C. 15
Date of decision: Dec. 14, 2009
Country: US
State or Federal: Federal
State/Jurisdiction: Federal Circuit
Court: United States Tax Court
Type of action: Federal Taxation
Judge: Halpern

This latest family limited partnership (FLP) case is a good reminder (as Steve Akers wrote in the February 2010 *BVU*) that it helps to have a "good" client—and to tell a good story to the Tax Court. In this case, Judge Halpern recognized not only the humble beginnings of Samuel Black Jr., but also his dedication to work, marriage, and family. These traits helped Mr. Black build substantial wealth and business success over a life that spanned nearly a century, and they may have helped his heirs win a solid legal victory after his death.

Born into poverty. Samuel Black was born in 1902 and began work at the age of 11 selling bread and newspapers on the streets of his Pennsylvania hometown. In 1925, he began work for Erie Indemnity Co., a local automobile insurance agency, working out of his "home office" at the YMCA. By the 1990s Erie had grown into a multiline national insurance company, and Mr. Black had become its second largest shareholder, retiring as senior vice president but maintaining his seat on the board until he was 95.

Mr. Black was "bullish" on his own company but a conservative subscriber to the "buy and hold" investment philosophy. He and wife of 70 years had a single son and two grandsons. The son was in a difficult marriage and the grandsons lacked jobs and ambition. To pool, protect, and prolong his family's wealth, in 1993 Mr. Black formed a family limited partnership (FLP) with the help of longtime financial and legal advisors. He held a 1% general partnership interest as the managing partner, and the limited partnership interests were dispersed among his son and his grandsons' trusts. The partnership agreement imposed substantial stock transfer and other restrictions on the LPs and even on the managing partner (other than Mr. Black). Mr. Black was 91 years old, active, and in good health at the time the FLP was formed.

The FLP was funded entirely with Erie stock, using all of the Blacks' holdings; the son contributed all the stock he held in his own right and as executor for his sons' trusts, excluding only 125,000 shares that he'd pledged as collateral for a loan. These contributions were credited at fair market value to the partners' respective accounts. Between 1993 and 2001 the net asset value of the FLP rose from $80 million to $318 million. During that time, the FLP acquired and operated commercial real estate, distributed 92% of the dividends it received on the Erie stock (with appropriate negative adjustments to the partners' capital accounts), and purchased shares in the son's insurance business. In addition to the distributions from the FLP, Mr. and Mrs. Black received sufficient income from other sources to maintain their personal lifestyle.

Mr. Black died in 2001 and Mrs. Black followed soon after. After receiving the Blacks' estate tax returns, the IRS assessed four notices of deficiencies totaling over $83 million. Notably, the parties resolved all the valuation issues prior to trial, leaving only the Sec. 2036(a) issue—that is, whether the Blacks' contributions of stock to the FLP constituted bona fide transfers for adequate consideration, sufficient to value the FLP interests at fair market value (with discounts) for estate tax purposes.

Unique circumstances. The taxpayer claimed the following factors in support of the FLP's bona fide, legitimate, non-tax purpose:

- The FLP adhered to Mr. Black's buy-and-hold investment philosophy, increasing its net asset value nearly fourfold;

- The transfer restrictions prevented Mr. Black's son from selling or encumbering his contribution of $11 million in Erie stock, and they prevented his grandsons from reaching their stock, even when their trusts terminated;

- The Black family's consolidated position allowed it to maintain a seat on the Erie board of directors; and

- The FLP protected the son's stock during a costly divorce, during which his wife received only the 125,000 shares the son had pledged for personal loan.

The taxpayer also relied primarily on a 2005 case, *Estate of Schutt v. Comm'r* (see the July 2005 *BVU*), in which the Tax Court acknowledged that the "mere holding of an untraded portfolio in marketable securities" is a negative factor in its assessment of an FLP's non-tax purpose—particularly when one person contributes the stock. But in that case, which concerned substantial contributions of DuPont and Exxon stock to the FLP, the court also recognized "unique circumstances"—primarily the taxpayer's desire to pool and protect the assets from dissipation by his heirs, including their trusts, by perpetuating his "buy and hold" investment philosophy in the FLP.

The IRS tried to distinguish *Schutt* by contending that the taxpayer's desire to protect his Erie holdings was either "ill-founded" or insignificant. The court was more persuaded by the precedent and the "unique" facts of this case, however. Testimony showed that the FLP had prevented Mr. Black's son from "funding" his entire divorce with Erie stock (other than the shares released by the bank) and prevented his unemployed grandsons from reaching the assets. Mr. Black's desire to preserve the Erie holdings within his family was a sufficient legitimate, non-tax reason to form the FLP and satisfied the "bona fide" portion of the 2036(a) exception.

Adequate and full consideration. The second prong requires the transferors to receive "partnership interests proportionate to the value" of the transferred property, the court explained. In this case, the IRS stipulated that the FLP limited partners received interests proportionate to the value of their stock contributions, thus effectively conceding the issue. The court also pointed out that the FLP properly credited the stock contributions to the transferors' capital accounts and adjusted for any distributions. These facts also satisfied the prior Tax Court precedent (*Schutt* and also *Estate of Bongard* (2005)) that the taxpayer's transfer of Erie stock was made for full and adequate consideration.

Accordingly, "the fair market value of Mr. Black's partnership interest in Black LP, rather than the fair market value of the Erie stock that he contributed thereto, is includable in his gross estate," the court concluded.

Heckerman v. Commissioner

IRS Challenges Family LLC As Indirect Gift, Including 58% Marketability Discount

Case name: Heckerman v. Commissioner
Citation: 2009 WL 2240326 (W. D. Wash)
Date of decision: July 27, 2009
Country: US
State or Federal: Federal
State/Jurisdiction: Washington
Court: United States District Court
Type of action: Federal Taxation
Judge: Coughenour

Whether transfers to a family limited partnership or limited liability company (LLC) survives an IRS challenge as an indirect gift to minority interest holders pursuant to IRC Sec. 2501 comes down to three critical considerations: 1) type of assets transferred; 2) timing of the transfers; and 3) receipt of adequate consideration.

Wealthy Californians want children to "work for the money." In the fall of 2001, the Heckermans—a couple owning substantial real estate and securities—wanted to pass property to their young children that would make them "work for their money," without triggering a gift tax. Following the advice of legal and financial advisors, they established two trusts for the children and three corporate entities: an Investments LLC and a Real Estate LLC, which were solely owned by a Family LLC.

The Heckermans subsequently transferred a $2 million Malibu beach home to the Family LLC. On January 11, 2002, they transferred $2.85 million in mutual funds to the Investments LLC. Notably, they also did the following:

- Transferred 1,217.65 units in Family LLC to each of their children on January 11, 2002;
- Signed gift documents stating that the assignments were effective on that date;
- Provided the IRS with a document stating that the children's trusts were admitted as members to the Family LLC, effective January 11, 2002; and,
- Provided an appraiser with the valuation (gift transfer) date of January 11, 2002.

The appraiser determined a $511,000 fair market value for each child's minority interest in the Family LLC, and then applied a 58% discount for lack of marketability ($706,650 on the total $1.02 million). The Heckermans reflected the discounted values of the LLC transfers on their tax returns, concluding that no gift tax was due.

The IRS disagreed. According to the IRS, the cash transfers were "really...indirect gift[s] of the proportionate amount of cash...to each child's trust," and they valued each gift at $511,000. Alternatively, under the step-transaction doctrine, because the transfers of cash and LLC units took place on the same day, they "were merely part of an integrated action indeed to pass cash to [the taxpayers'] children in a tax advantaged form." The Service assessed a gift tax, the taxpayers' appealed, and the IRS filed a motion for summary judgment on the issues of indirect gift.

Real estate transfers not at issue. Importantly, the IRS did not argue that the taxpayers' contribution of real estate to the Family LLC in December 2001, one month prior to the cash transfers, constituted indirect gifts. Thus the type of asset and timing appears to have helped these transfers escape a Sec. 2501 challenge.

The cash transfers posed a different problem for the taxpayers, who needed to show that they contributed the assets to the Family LLC before they gifted the LLC units to their children. The federal district court (W.D. Wash.) cited the following three leading cases to "delineate the contours" of the taxpayers' burden:

- In *Shepherd v. Commissioner* 115 T.C. (RIA) 376, 389 (2000), *aff'd by* 283 F.3d 1258 (11th Cir.2002), the Tax Court held that "a transfer to a partnership for less than full and adequate consideration may represent an indirect gift to the other partners." In that case, however, the taxpayer's same-day transfers of real estate and stock to a family partnership were allocated to his and his children's capital accounts according to their respective partnership shares, and were not indirect gifts.

- Likewise, in *Estate of Jones v. Commissioner*, 116 T.C. 121 (2001), all of the taxpayer's contributions to the family entity were properly reflected in the capital accounts.

- In contrast, in *Senda v. Commissioner*, T.C.M. (RIA) 2004-160 *aff'd by* 433 F.3d 1044 (8th Cir.2006), the taxpayers simultaneously transferred stock to a family partnership and then to minority ownership interests in the partnership to their children. In finding indirect gifts, the court noted that the taxpayers failed to present any reliable evidence that they 1) contributed the stock before they transferred the partnership units; and 2) properly allocated the transfers among the capital accounts. The timing was critical, the court said, but the "formality" did not matter in this case, because under the step-transaction doctrine, it considered the transfers as an integrated whole.

'Plethora of evidence' substantiates sequencing. The taxpayers tried gamely to show that the cash transfers to the LLC units took place before the transfers of LLC units to the children—but the court cited the "plethora" of objective evidence that all transfers took place on January 11, 2002, including the documentation provided to the IRS and their appraiser.

The taxpayers also failed to persuade the court that they increased their capital accounts by their cash contributions at the time of the transfers, which would have offered proof of adequate consideration. In fact, their attorney wrote a letter to the IRS stating that "no initial capital contribution...was designated in the LLC operating agreement; ...and no contemporaneous capital accounts were maintained reflecting the account as an asset of the LLC." Under these facts, the court found the transfers similar to those in *Senda* and unlike those in *Shepherd* and *Jones*, and declared them indirect gifts.

The court was also persuaded by *Senda* and the IRS's alternative argument. Under the step-transaction doctrine, the cash transfers to the Investments LLC and the gifting of Family LLC units "were, at best, integrated, and, in effect, simultaneous." The taxpayers' clear intent was "to convey property to their children while minimizing their tax liability, pursuant to which they crafted, with the help of their attorneys and advisors, a scheme consisting of pre-arranged parts of a single transaction." The taxpayers did not delay the gifts after funding or bear any economic risk that the LLC units' value would decline (as in *Holman v. Commissioner*, 130 T.C. 12 (2008), in which a six-day delay between transfer of securities and family partnership units helped avoid application of the step-transaction doctrine). As such, the doctrine applied to the transfers in this case, and the court granted the IRS's motion for summary judgment.

*Note: Copies of *Shepherd*, *Jones*, *Senda*, and *Holman* are available at *BVLaw*™.

Estate of Jorgensen v. Commissioner

Terrible FLP Facts Preclude Analysis of Discounts

Case name: Estate of Jorgensen v. Commissioner
Citation: 2009 WL 7920771 (U.S. Tax Ct.)
Date of decision: March 26, 2009
Country: US
State or Federal: Federal
Court: United States Tax Court
Type of action: Federal Taxation
Judge: Haines
SIC: 6733 Trusts, Except Educational, Religious, and Charitable (personal trusts, estates, and agency accounts)

There are "bad facts" cases concerning the formation and funding of limited family partnerships (FLPs). Then there are cases like this one, in which the estate could not persuade the U.S. Tax Court to find a single legitimate (non-tax) business purpose for the FLP. It did not help that one of the family's attorneys wrote a letter outlining the need to hire a valuation expert to appraise the FLP assets, "to have any chance of justifying the discounted value...if a gift tax or estate tax return is audited."

A frugal widow saves roughly $2 million. During their long marriage, an army colonel and his wife saved considerably and invested wisely. Consequently, by 1995 they were able to form and fund a family limited partnership with roughly $500,000 of marketable securities. They each became limited partners (LPs) along with their six grandchildren. The colonel and his two children were named general partners. The stated purpose of the FLP was to "pool certain assets and capital for...investing in securities." None of the couple's children or grandchildren contributed to the FLP, and the colonel made all decisions regarding its investments.

When the colonel passed away in 1996, his estate attorney recommended that the widow transfer all of their brokerage accounts into the FLP, so that "hopefully your limited partnership interest... will qualify for the 35% discount." "Obviously, no one can guarantee that the IRS will agree to a discount of 35%," he added, but even if the IRS agreed to "only" a 15% discount, the widow and her children would save in gift and estate taxes.

The attorney also recommended that she form a second FLP, funded with some $1.8 million in marketable securities. She retained an 80% LP interest, the colonel's estate held the remaining 20% interest, and the children and grandchildren were once again listed as LPs. This time, the two grown children became general partners, in large part because their mother rejected any active management role. Over the next few years, the widow transferred LP percentage interests (between 1% and 7%) to her children and grandchildren. In 1998—and per the advice of counsel quoted above, one of the children requested an appraisal of a 1% LP interest in the second FLP. (The court opinion does not reveal the outcome). Overall, on her gift tax returns, the widow valued the transfers from 1999 through 2002 using discounts ranging from 42% to 50% discount, to remain within then-applicable annual gift tax exclusion ($10,000).

During the remainder of the widow's life, the FLPs held passive investments only. Neither one operated a business. At one point, one of her grown children tried to access "some of this money that's mine," as he put it, and was surprised that he could only obtain a loan (with interest) against his partnership interest. (He later testified that "it took a while to get my head around the fact that [the FLP] wasn't just like a bank account you can get money out of.") He borrowed $125,000 from the FLP but made only two interest payments; he also received a $48,500 "loan" from the FLP to buy a Cadillac, but his mother later forgave the loan, without reporting it as a gift. She also drew on the funds to make cash gifts to family members and to pay taxes and other personal expenses.

After she died in 2002, her son repaid the first loan to the FLP, acting on his sister's advice to "clean up the Partnership" and "be real straight on who borrowed what...so [it] looks legit." Presumably, their mother's estate applied minority and marketability discounts to the FLP assets when filing its tax return. (The court opinion does not detail the estate's valuation of the FLPs.) On audit, the IRS assessed nearly $800,000 in deficiencies, and the estate appealed.

Looking for a legitimate, significant nontax purpose. The estate claimed that the transfer of assets to the FLPs were "bona fide sales for adequate consideration," sufficient to keep them from the value of her gross estate (per I.R.C. Sec. 2036(a)(1)). But, "whether a sale is bona fide is a question of motive," the Tax Court said. "We must determine whether [the decedent] had a legitimate and significant nontax reason...for transferring her property." It examined each of the purposes claimed by the estate:

1. *Management succession.* Because the colonel's widow did not want responsibility for fund assets, the FLP's primary purpose was to maintain control and authority over their management. However, to provide a credible nontax purpose, an FLP's management must be both efficient and active, the court said. Although the colonel took an active investment role, his widow and children "were not nearly as knowledgeable or interested." The accounts seldom traded and the FLPs were largely passive. "[T]he mere holding of an untraded portfolio of marketable securities weighs against the finding of a nontax benefit for [its] transfer...to a family entity," the court held.

2. *Financial education and family unity.* Similarly, there was no evidence that the colonel "actually taught his children much about investing," it said, adding that they "faced a steep learning curve" after his death, and let the investment adviser make most decisions. Further, the promotion of family unity was "no more than a theoretical purpose," especially when one child was a spendthrift and the other frugal.

3. *Perpetuation of investment philosophy.* Under these facts, the court held that "perpetuation of a 'buy and hold' strategy for marketable securities is not a legitimate or significant nontax reason for transferring the bulk of one's assets to a partnership."

4. *Pooling of assets.* Because the FLPs served in part as gift-giving devices, the pooling of their assets permitted economies of scale and lower operating costs, the estate claimed. But the family's adviser testified that transferring the accounts directly could have accomplished the same gift-giving purposes, without adding any significant expense or oversight. In fact, the formation and funding of the FLPs most likely created more expense for the family, the court observed.

5. *Spendthrift concerns.* The FLPs protected the LPs against creditors, potential divorce claims, and spendthrift tendencies, the estate said. Even the profligate child served as general partner to both, the court pointed out. He also continued to access the funds for "loans," indicating no curb to his tendencies.

6. *Giving equal gifts.* Facilitating and simplifying gift giving, alone, does not amount to a legitimate nontax purpose, the court held.

Finally, the estate argued that the FLPs were not mere tax-avoidance devices, because the colonel and his widow did not use discounts to value the initial transfers, from 1995 through 1998. However, discounts were taken after his death, the court noted, and around this time, the widow's advisors discussed the advantage of discounts and potential for an IRS audit.

Assets and lack of arm's length are key. The widow and her children failed to treat the FLPs as separate, formal partnership entities, the court added. Neither FLP maintained books and records, other than an unreconciled checkbook and brokerage statements. There were no formal meetings or partnership minutes. Although the widow was not dependent on FLP funds for her livelihood, she drew on them for gifts and personal expenses; she also permitted substantial loans to her son. After her death, the estate paid its tax and other obligations with FLP funds. Under all these facts, the court concluded that the FLP lacked any legitimate nontax business purpose.

"We find especially significant that the transactions were not at arm's length and that the partnerships held a largely untraded portfolio of marketable securities," it said, in finding that I.R.C. Sec. 2036(a)(1) pulled the FLP assets back into the value of the decedent's gross estate.

Keller v. United States

Another Taxpayer Win: Court Accepts 47.5% Discount for Formed (but not Funded) FLP

Case name: Keller v. United States
Citation: 2009 WL 2601611 (S.D.Tex.)
Date of decision: August 20, 2009
Country: US
State or Federal: Federal
State/Jurisdiction: Texas
Court: United States District Court
Type of action: Federal Taxation
Experts: Robert Reilly (taxpayer); Alan Shapiro (IRS)
Judge: Rainey

With the aid of longtime financial and legal advisors, a wealthy Texas widow established a family limited partnership (FLP), to be funded with $250 million in corporate investment bonds. One of her daughters had recently been through an expensive divorce, and she wanted to protect the family's wealth from similar dissolutions. She set up a limited liability company as the .1% general partner (GP), intending to fund it with $300,000 from her personal accounts. The limited partners (LPs) would consist of two family trusts, each holding a 49.95% interest. Initially, she would own all of the GP, transferring her interests to family members after her death.

Although her health was declining, the 90 year-old widow was sharp enough to give her advisors "marching orders" to complete the FLP. (For instance, her accountant urged her to allocate an additional $110 million to the FLP, but she rebuffed him.) In May 2000, the widow was diagnosed with cancer. Neither her doctors nor her advisors believed her death was imminent, but just days after signing the papers—and before she could effectively transfer the assets or capitalize the GP interest, the widow died. Her advisors "stood down," believing the failure to fund was fatal to the FLP.

One year later, a Texas federal court decided in *Church v. U.S.*, 2000 WL 206374 (W.D. Tex) (available at *BVLaw*™) to recognize an FLP even though the founder died days before funding. Believing *Church* breathed new life into their own efforts, the family advisors completed the transfer of the FLP assets on behalf of the deceased widow. Her estate paid taxes on the assets' full value by borrowing $114 million from the FLP, which was backed by a promissory note. The estate subsequently filed an amended return using discounted values and claimed a tax refund for the difference.

A bona fide business purpose. At trial, the federal district court (S.D. Tex) found that despite her failure to fund, the widow intended the $250 million in corporate investment bonds to be partnership property, and the $300,000 check she'd cut before her death (but had not deposited) was intended to capitalize the GP. As for the loan to pay the estate taxes, the FLP had already reported $30 million in interest payments (at 5.07% per year). The court found this was "an actual and necessary administrative expense" and allowed the estate to deduct the interest. Thus the FLP became valid under state (Texas) law prior to the widow's death and its assets became partnership property.

Based on the same evidence, the partnership transfers fell squarely within the exceptions of both IRC Sec. 2036(a) and 2038(a) as a "bona fide sale for adequate and full consideration." The clear purpose of the FLP was to consolidate, manage, protect, and pass along the family's wealth. "Any estate tax savings that resulted from these partnerships were...merely incidental," the court observed. The widow was not trying to avoid federal estate taxes or create a sham transaction to disguise gifts to her heirs. Her team of advisors conveyed her intent "with notable consistency" in forming the FLP. Finally, she retained well over $100 million to support her personal living expenses.

After her death—and in accordance with the partnership agreement—the transfers to the LP trusts became assignee interests, proportionate to their respective contributions and as reflected in their capital accounts. Accordingly, their fair market values would reflect not the decedent's share of all the assets, but the value of the LP interests, including discounts for lack of control and lack of marketability.

The court expressly commended the taxpayer's expert for using "the correct standard in determining the fair market value" of the transferred assets. By contrast, the government's expert "violated several of the tenets of the hypothetical buyer and seller standard, including considering the true identities of the buyer and seller, speculating as to events occurring after the valuation date, and aggregating the interests of different owners." Without detailing the experts' calculations or approaches, the court adopted the taxpayer's appraised values in full, including a combined 47.5% discount.

In a resounding victory for the estate and its appraiser **Robert Reilly** (Willamette Management Associates), the federal district court in *Keller v. U.S.*, 2009 WL 2601611 (S.D. Tex.) (Aug. 20, 2009) approved the FLP and discounted its assets for lack of marketability and lack of control at a combined rate of 47.5%. The court also discredited the government's undiscounted appraisal, finding that it violated several tenets of the fair market value (FMV) standard by considering "real" (rather than hypothetical) buyers and sellers and speculating as to subsequent events.

Estate of Litchfield v. Comm'r

New Tax Court Decision on Discounts and Embedded Taxes Hinges on Experts

Case name: Estate of Litchfield v. Commissioner
Citation: 2009 WL 211421 (U.S. Tax Court)
Date of decision: Jan. 29, 2009
Country: US
State or Federal: Federal
Court: United States Tax Court
Type of action: Federal Taxation
Judge: Swift
SIC: 6733 Trusts, Except Educational, Religious, and Charitable (personal trusts, estates, and agency accounts)

With about $26.4 million in assets, the Litchfield estate consisted primarily of minority stock interests in two closely held, family owned companies, Litchfield Realty Co. (LRC) and Litchfield Securities Co. (LSC). The Internal Revenue Service (IRS) and the estate agreed on the net asset values (NAV) of the estate's interests. However, they aggressively disputed the discounts related to built-in capital gains taxes, lack of control, and lack of marketability.

Marjorie Litchfield died in 2001. At that time, her estate owned a 43.1% interest in LRC, which held Iowa farmland and marketable securities along with a farming subsidiary. LRC earned a marginal profit, but the company was not performing up to management expectations. Its farm holdings, for example, yielded less than 1% net annual income compared to Midwestern farmland generally, which yielded about 4% of NAV annually. Historically, the company had sold portions of its farm holdings to raise cash.

To increase profitability and shareholder returns, LRC converted from a C corporation to an S corporation in January 2000. However, for the 10 years following conversion, if the company sold any of its former C Corp assets then it would incur corporate-level tax on the sale (per IRC Sec. 1374). The company also postponed switching from share-lease agreements with its farmers to straight cash leases, which would have been more profitable and produced more taxable corporate income. As of the valuation date, LRC's total NAV of $33.174 million included $28.762 million in built-in capital gains—or 86.7% of NAV. Just over $19.789 million of the built-in capital gains taxes related to its farm holdings and $8.972 million to its marketable securities.

To prepare the estate's tax return in connection with LRC, its expert appraised the estate's 43.1% interest in the company at a fair market value of $6.475 million—after application of discounts for the built-in capital gains taxes, lack of control, and lack of marketability. On audit, however, the IRS valued the estate's interest in LRC at just over $10 million and assessed a deficiency of approximately $3.825 million. *The chart below shows the breakdown of the parties' respective valuations for LRC:*

	Estate expert	IRS expert
NAV (estate's 43.1% interest)	$14.298 million	$14.298 million
Discount for capital gains tax	17.4%	2.0%
Discount for lack of control	14.8%	10.0%
Marketability discount	36.0%	18.0%
Ultimate fair market value	$6.475 million	$10.069 million

The estate also owned some 23% of Litchfield Securities Co. (LSC), a C corporation that held "blue chip" marketable securities as well as partnership and other equity investments for a combined NAV of $52.824 million. Like LRC, none of the LSC stock had ever been publicly traded, and its stock transfer policies generally restricted redemptions or sales outside of the Litchfield family. Its investment strategy focused on maximizing cash dividends to its shareholders, and these had increased consistently over the years.

In the late 1990s, however, the directors became concerned that elderly shareholders in both LRC and LSC would not have adequate cash reserves to pay for estate taxes and other obligations on their deaths. Consequently, management contemplated sales of LRC and LSC corporate assets to finance stock redemptions for those shareholders. After the death of Mrs. Litchfield, LRC sold its farm services subsidiary and, due to mergers and acquisitions of the public companies in its portfolio, LSC realized a significant appreciation of its holdings.

As of the valuation date, LSC's NAV included $38.984 million in built-in capital gains, or 73.8% of its total NAV. Note: The capital gains tax applicable to both companies ranged from 35.5% to 39.1%. The estate's expert discounted its 22.96% stock interest in LSC by capital gains tax as well as lack of marketability and control, but on audit, the IRS determined a deficiency of over $3.014 million. *Their respective valuations broke down as follows:*

	Estate expert	IRS expert
NAV (estate's 22.96% interest)	$12.133 million	$12.133 million
Discount for capital gains tax	23.6%	8.0%
Discount for lack of control	11.9%	5.0%
Marketability discount	29.7%	10.0%
Ultimate fair market value	$5.748 million	$9.565 million

The court considered discounts for capital gains first. At trial, U.S. Tax Court Judge Swift found that the built-in capital gains associated with the total assets of both companies were "substantial." *In particular:*

A hypothetical buyer would be willing to pay fair market value for the LRC and LSC stock, which would take into account and...reflect the millions of dollars in untaxed appreciation over the years in the values of LRC's and LSC's underlying assets. Knowledgeable buyers, however, also would negotiate discounts in the price of the stock to estimate, on the basis of current tax laws, the corporate capital gains tax liabilities due on that very same appreciation when the assets are sold or otherwise disposed of by the corporation. In other words, if a valuation of...corporate stock in a hypothetical sale is significantly affected by the untaxed appreciated value of the underlying corporate assets, the stock valuation ...should reflect the corporate capital gains tax liabilities that the appreciated assets carry with them and that will be paid by the corporation upon sale or other disposition of the assets.

In this context, the court considered the two experts' valuations in turn:

1. Built-in capital gains taxes. In calculating his discount for built-in capital gains tax related to both entities, the estate's expert not only reviewed historic asset sales but also board meeting minutes. He also spoke with current management about their plans for future sales. He then estimated asset turnover rates, projecting a 5-year holding period for LRC and 8 years for LSC. After estimating appreciation and applying capital gains tax at the projected sale dates, discounted back to present values, he reached his discounts of 17.4% and 23.6%, respectively.

By contrast, the IRS expert did not talk to management, and he used turnover rates based solely on historical asset sales. For LRC, he used a 1.86% turnover rate to project an asset-holding period of over 53 years. Because LRC had elected S Corp status, the expert did not include any capital gains tax liability beyond 2009 (ten years following conversion). For LSC, he used a 3.45% asset turnover rate, resulting in a 29-year holding period. By applying similar calculations to each entity (multiplying capital gains tax by gains on asset sales as of the valuation date, discounted by a ratable portion over the relevant holding periods), he reached his 2% discount for LRC's NAV and 8% for LSC.

The court's findings: Given the "highly appreciating non-operating investment assets" that both companies held, the court considered it likely that a hypothetical buyer and seller would negotiate "significant" discounts related to the built-in capital gains tax liability. Further, the assumptions by the estate's expert related to asset turnover rates were based on more accurate data, especially his conversations with management and review of current sales. The IRS expert, on the other hand, did not account for appreciation during the holding periods and looked only at historic data. For these reasons, the court accepted the estate's expert's discounts for built-in capital gains tax, without adjustment.

2. Lack of control. To determine the discount for lack of control (DLOC) for LRC's securities holdings, the estate's expert used closed-end funds, observing a median 7.16% discount among the data. He used REITs (real estate investment trusts) and RELPs (real estate limited partnerships) in relation to the firm's farm holdings and found an average 25.5% discount.

The estate's expert then looked at factors particular to LRC and assigned each a value between -1 (poor investor rights) and 1 (excellent rights). For instance, a 43.1% stakeholder in LRC would have some ability to force liquidation and change operating policies, and these factors received a zero (neutral) value. The company's historical returns were substantially below those of similar investments, and this received a -1 value. Using these factors, weighted for LRC's combined asset classes, he calculated a 14.8% DLOC for the estate's interest.

For its interest in LSC, the estate's expert used closed end funds and observed the mean, median, and standard deviation of the discounts. He then assigned values from -1 to 1 to each of the factors that he also used to assess LRC; for example, because a 22.96% stakeholder would have little influence on operations or liquidation, this factor received a -0.5, but the company's financial efficiency and historical returns received a 0 value. After determining a DLOC of 12.23%, unweighted by asset class, the expert reduced this to account for LSC's small percentage of cash and short-term investments, resulting in an 11.9% DLOC.

According to the IRS expert, a DLOC is generally required "only if" the buyer intends to change the entity's operations. Because LRC's assets were performing well, a buyer would not expect a large discount for lack of control. Notably, in considering the entity's securities holdings, the IRS expert did not break down his analysis by asset class, but looked at closed end funds to find an average 3.4% discount. Since the standard deviation was 17%, he "trimmed the mean" (removed the top and bottom 10%), resulting in a "trimmed" 5.2% average discount. Given the estate's sizeable 43.1% interest in LRC, the IRS expert believed that a DLOC below 5% was appropriate for its marketable securities.

When considering the entity's farmland holdings in LRC, the IRS expert reviewed a variety of data, including Mergerstat™, and noted a range of 17% to 20% DLOC. Nevertheless, because discounts for public takeovers are generally higher than those for "normal" sales activity, LRC's farming assets merited a DLOC lower than the Mergerstat range, or 15%. Even though the farmland comprised the bulk of the firm's NAV, he averaged the two findings (5% and 15%) to conclude an overall DLOC for the estate's 43.1% interest in LRC of 10%.

For LSC, the IRS expert once again used the 5.2% "trimmed mean" from the closed-end funds. Because the estate's 22.96% interest was the single largest block of stock, its returns were good—and a purchaser would not want to change operations, a hypothetical buyer "would place no value on control," he believed and a "nominal" DLOC of 5% was appropriate.

The court's findings: The court noted that both experts calculated similar DLOC for LRC's farming assets (15.7% vs. 15%), and both used lower-than-average discounts for its securities; and both averaged the respective discounts in their overall determination of DLOC. But only the taxpayer's expert used a weighted average to account for LRC's more significant holdings of farm property, while the IRS expert used a straight average. "A straight average would have been appropriate if LRC's farmland and securities holdings were roughly equivalent," the court said, in determining that the estate's expert's 14.8% DLOC was more appropriate.

With regard to the DLOC for the estate's LSC stock interest, the IRS expert used the same 5% discount as he did for LRC's marketable securities, without accounting for the estate's much smaller interest in LSC. The estate's expert accounted for the size difference, and once again, the court adopted his 11.9% DLOC for the 22.96% interest in LSC.

3. Marketability discount. To calculate LRC's discount for lack of marketability (DLOM), the estate's expert looked at restricted stock studies and observed a range from 10% to 30% for larger, profitable companies and a 30% to 50% range for smaller, riskier companies. Once again, he assigned average investor values of -1 to 1 to each class of LRC's assets (e.g., its farmland was -0.5 and its marketable securities -0.125) to reach a DLOM for the estate's 43.1% interest of 36%.

He also used the same restricted stock studies for the LSC interest. After assigning average values to its assets classes, such as cash and short term investments (-0.5) and marketable securities (0), he concluded a DLOM for the estate's 22.96% interest in LSC of 29.7%

The IRS expert looked at restricted stock studies, including three from the 1990s that the estate's expert did not consider, and observed an average 25% DLOM. Because he believed the data did not account for liquidity and "corporate distress," he also looked at private placement studies (more indicative of a "true" discount, he said), and observed discounts ranging from 7.23% to 17.6%. He then adjusted for entity-specific factors, such as LRC's dividend-paying policy, the estate's sizeable interest, and stock transfer restrictions, to determine an 18% DLOM for the estate's 43.1% interest.

He reviewed the same studies with reference to LSC, and because these assets were more readily ascertainable and saleable, its earning history was consistent and its management competent, he determined a lower than average discount of 10% for the estate's 22.96% interest.

The court's findings: The court considered it appropriate to weigh the assets of both entities by class, but believed that both of the estate's expert's DLOMs were too high, particularly when combined with his discounts for lack of control. Some of the restricted stock data the estate's expert used were aged, and his discounts were higher than the average benchmark studies that included "all components of a lack of marketability discount," according to the court. Finally, the estate's expert had performed a valuation for the same entities in connection with a 2000 gift estate tax return, in which he determined a "significantly lower" discount for the estate's interest in LSC (21.4% in 2000 vs. 29.7% in 2001). As a result, and without further discussion, the court concluded DLOM for the estate's respective interests in LRC and LSC of 25% and 20%.

Overall, the court found that the fair market value of the estate's 43.1% interest in LRC was $7.546 million, and its 22.96% interest in LSC was worth $6.530 million.

Estate of Malkin v. Commissioner

'Sham' Funding plus Pledging FLP Assets for Personal Debt Adds up to Taxpayer Loss

Case name: Estate of Malkin v. Commissioner
Citation: 2009 WL 2958661 (U.S. Tax Ct.)
Date of decision: Sept. 16, 2009
Country: US
State or Federal: Federal
State/Jurisdiction: Federal Circuit
Court: United States Tax Court
Type of action: Federal Taxation
Judge: Halpern

After the recent series of "good" cases for the taxpayer in the family limited partnership and LLC arena, along comes the *Malkin* decision, in which the U.S. Tax Court (Judge Halpern) delved into a highly complex estate plan—and came up with shovels full of shadowy financing and false intent.

Publicly traded stock worth over $16 million. The former CEO of a Mississippi timber company acquired over 1 million shares in his public company, and wanted to pass on a significant portion to his two children while restricting their ability to sell. With the help of financial advisors, he created a family limited partnership (FLP) in 1998, retaining the general partnership interest and funding it with $16.8 million of the stock, distributing limited partnership units to the children's trusts. In return, the trustees contributed cash and interest-bearing, self-cancelling installment notes (SCINs). They also executed agreements permitting the founder to pledge the LP interests as security.

During the life of the FLP, interest payments on the SCINs came from "unidentified sources" or directly from the father's personal accounts. He also pledged the bulk of FLP assets to secure personal bank debts. Although he paid the FLPs a fee and executed personal guaranties in connection with the pledges, he was diagnosed with pancreatic cancer in 1999 before making any repayments.

After his diagnosis, the father set up a second FLP, funding it with more stock and his interest in four LLCs, which he controlled with his son. Notably—before transferring stock to this FLP, the founder pledged them as collateral for a personal loan. Shortly thereafter, the founder died, leaving all his wealth in the FLPs and his estate insolvent. After an audit of the estate's return, however, the IRS assessed over $6 million in deficiencies, claiming 1) the FLP stock transfers failed as a bona fide transfer under Sec. 2036(a) and 2) the FLP LLC transfers constituted indirect gifts to the children.

Estate argues legitimate business purpose. At trial, the estate denied any express or implied agreement between the FLP trustees to permit the decedent to retain the economic benefits of the stock. For example, his pledge of the FLP stock as security for his debts was not only backed by his personal guaranties but was "an investment decision made at arm's length, in the best interests of the [FLPs]." The estate even tried to argue that his pledge of stock *before* transferring them to the second FLP indicated that he did not specifically use FLP assets as collateral.

The court disagreed, finding the decedent "applied all the ...stock he transferred to the FLPs toward the discharge of his legal obligations." The situation was strikingly similar to *Estate of Bigelow v. Comm'r* (T.C. Memo 2005, *aff'd* 9th Cir. 2007) (see Nov. 2007 *BVU*), in which an FLP founder transferred real property without also transferring the underlying debt, retaining the right to apply FLP assets to pay it off. Further, the estate offered no evidence that the fees paid in connection with the pledges were reasonable and provided no explanation "what business purpose [the] decision served." The estate's assertions were "baseless," the court said, citing the government's argument:

The decedent's relationship to his [company stock] never changed. He controlled them before and after the transfer to the [FLPs]...The trusts...had no role in the affairs of the partnerships. Neither the trustees nor decedent's children objected to his use of the stock obtain personal loans.

Thus the court ruled the decedent retained the use and enjoyment of the FLP stock assets during his lifetime. It also found "no legitimate and significant nontax reason for creating either of the FLPs" sufficient to fall within the bona fide sale exception of Sec. 2036(a)(1). There was no pooling of family wealth—just the holding of an untraded portfolio of marketable securities, which weighed against a finding of an independent purpose. (See *Estate of Rosen v.* Comm'r (T. C. Memo 2006) and the August 2006 *BVU*). "The property the FLP passively held was simply decedent's wealth," the court concluded, and "favorable estate tax treatment was the aim of the change in form." Accordingly, it pulled the full value of the stock transfers back into the estate.

LLC transfers were indirect gifts? As to the transfer of LLC interests, these constituted indirect gifts to the children, the government argued, citing *Shepherd v. Comm'r* (T.C. Memo 2000, *aff'd* 11th Cir. 2002) (see April 2002 *BVU*). In both cases, the FLP founders effectively transferred the partnership assets on the same day they created and exchanged the partnership units on behalf of their children. "Thus, at the time of the transfer, the [FLP] trusts were already limited partners, and they acquired interests in the [LLCs] by virtue of their status as limited partners."

The estate tried to distinguish *Shepherd*, asserting the trusts purchased the second FLP interests for "fair market value," as evidenced by the SCINs. The court, however, found the father was terminally ill when he executed the contracts; there was no evidence he ever expected repayment—and in fact, he had already made interest payments in connection with the first FLP. The estate offered no reason for these actions other than the father's "generosity and donative intent." As in *Shepherd*, the purported sale of LLC interests to the partnership were "a sham," the court held, and constituted indirect gifts to the children through their trusts.

Estate of Miller v. Comm'r Internal Revenue

New FLP Case: Taxpayer's First Asset Transfer Merits Discount, But Not Second

Case name: Estate of Miller v. Commissioner
Citation: T.C. Memo 2009-119, 2009 WL 1472208 (U.S. Tax Ct.)
Date of decision: May 27, 2009
Country: US
State or Federal: Federal
Court: United States Tax Court
Type of action: Federal Taxation
Judge: Goeke
SIC: 6733 Trusts, Except Educational, Religious, and Charitable (personal trusts, estates, and agency accounts)

This latest decision by the U.S. Tax Court—which follows several "bad facts" cases concerning family limited partnerships (FLPs), including *Estate of Jorgensen* and *Estate of Hurford*—contains an interesting "split" decision for the taxpayer, in which one FLP asset transfer successfully escapes the pull of IRC Sec. 2036, but the other does not. (For *Jorgensen* and *Hurford* case abstracts, see the June and February 2009 issues of BVU, respectively).

A long-time family investor. The father of the Miller family researched and invested in marketable securities using a specific method of charting stocks for the 26 years following his retirement. When he died in 2000, Miller's stock portfolio was worth roughly $7.6 million.

On the advice of their estate planner, Miller's 86 year-old widow decided to form an FLP with a portion of the assets. In November 2001, she filed the appropriate paperwork with the state of Indiana and at year's end the per-unit value of the FLP was appraised for gift tax purposes, even though it had yet to hold any assets. The widow's son, who was designated general manager of the FLP, provided the appraiser with detailed statements concerning the assets to be transferred.

The December 2001 appraisal valued the FLP's marketable securities at just over $3.8 million on a net asset value basis, and then applied a 35% discount for lack of marketability, resulting in a $2,265 per-unit value. However, the widow, her son, and three other children did not sign the partnership agreement for more than a year, and assets weren't transferred into the FLP's brokerage accounts until April 2002. The stated purpose of the FLP was to "buy, sell, and trade in securities of any nature..." and to acquire similar assets and investments to further this goal. As general partner, the eldest son worked 40 hours per week for a monthly fee to manage the FLP securities according to his father's charting method.

About a year later, the widow fell and broke her hip. Within a month she was diagnosed with congestive heart failure, and in early May 2003, her son caused her to sign a letter transferring all of her remaining assets (abut $900,000) into the FLP. By the end of the month, she was dead and the FLP used some assets to pay her estate taxes. In 2004, her estate tax return valued the FLP assets at $2.59 million, after application of the 35% marketability discount. The IRS assessed over $500,000 in deficiencies, which the estate paid and then sued for a refund.

Focused on finding a legitimate, non-tax purpose. The IRS did not contest the 35% discount; instead, it argued that the full value of the FLP assets should be pulled back into the estate because their transfer did not constitute a "bona fide sale for adequate and full consideration" per IRC Sec. 2036(a). The FLP served no legitimate and substantial, non-tax purpose, it said, citing *Estate of Stone v. Comm'r*, (2003) and *Estate of Bongard v. Comm'r* (2005). Factors that supported its argument included:

- The FLP's lack of a functioning business operation;
- The significant delay between its forming and funding;
- The type of assets transferred (marketable securities);
- The widow's age (86) when she formed the FLP, and that she stood on both sides of the transaction;
- She failed to retain sufficient non-FLP assets for personal expenses; and
- The stated purpose of the FLP was not sufficient to qualify as legitimate.

The estate claimed that the FLP served the legitimate, non-tax business purposes of asset protection, management succession, centralized management, and continuation of the family's investment strategy. The marketable securities were never actually transferred to the FLP (but into its brokerage accounts); and were never commingled with the widow's personal assets. In addition, the FLP observed partnership formalities, including active management by the son/general partner.

Of all these, the court focused on the family's investment purpose. Citing *Estate of Mirowkski v. Comm'r* (2008), another FLP case that featured a family with a specific investment strategy, the court found that the widow "established and funded [the FLP] to ensure that her assets continued to be managed according to Mr. Miller's investment philosophy." The court was also persuaded by credible testimony from the family and its estate attorney that Mr. Miller had passed his particular stock-charting method directly to his eldest son, who as general manager continued to monitor the stock market daily, actively discuss the FLP's trades with his family, and provide them with financial advice.

"[An FLP's] activities need not rise to the level of a 'business' under the Federal income tax laws in order for the exception under section 2036(a) to apply," the court held. Nor is the type of assets conclusive in a 2036(a) determination. "The non-tax purpose behind formation of [the FLP] was to continue Mr. Miller's investment philosophy and to apply it to family assets." This goal could not have been met had the FLP not received his marketable securities. In addition, at the time of the first funding, the widow was in general good health, and she retained sufficient assets (over $1 million) outside of the FLP to pay for daily living expenses.

The second transfers were a different story. The "driving force behind the May 2003 transfers was the precipitous decline in [the widow's] health in the weeks before the transfers," the court observed. Moreover, any argument that the contributions would continue the family's investment philosophy was undercut by the widow's failure to include them in her initial transfers. Had she wanted all of her assets managed according to her husband's strategy, "there would have been no reason to wait until the last weeks of her life," the court said.

Instead, these second transfers were driven by the desire to reduce her taxable estate, as they "completely depleted" the widow's resources, including any funds to pay living her expenses or estate tax liabilities. Although the son testified that had his mother recovered, he would not have used FLP funds for his mother's expenses or health needs, the court found this "inconceivable." Accordingly, the second transfer of assets did not qualify for the Sec. 2036(a) exception, it held, and included their full, fair market value in the widow's estate, without any discount.

Murphy v. U.S.

Major Victory for Taxpayer & Appraiser in Classic FLP Case

Case name: Murphy v. U.S.
Citation: 2009 WL 3366099 (W.D. Ark.)
Date of decision: Oct. 2, 2009
Country: US
State or Federal: Federal
State/Jurisdiction: Arkansas
Court: United States District Court
Type of action: Estate and Gift Taxation
Experts: Donald Barker (estate); Francis Burns (IRS)
Judge: Barnes

In a textbook example of how to form, fund, and operate a family limited partnership—sufficient to value various assets (including publicly traded securities, real estate, and restricted holdings) at substantial discounts for federal estate tax purposes—the *Murphy* case makes excellent reading for appraisers, attorneys, and financial advisors alike.

Total estate exceeds $135 million. The Murphy Oil Corp. grew from a small family-owned business into an international conglomerate with over $2 billion in market cap. The Murphy family also owned substantial holdings in a timber and banking company. During the 1990s, the CEO and controlling stockholder set out to preserve his extensive holdings for his children. He did not want to leave the assets outright for fear that the children might dissipate them through poor investment decisions and divorce.

Accordingly, he established a family limited partnership (FLP) to pool and grow the family's wealth over the long-term. He created an LLC as the general partner, taking a 49% non-controlling interest for himself and giving two of his more responsible children a combined 51% interest, which permitted them to make day-to-day decisions concerning partnership operations and investments. He transferred nearly $89 million in Murphy Oil stock to the FLP along with timber and banking securities and real estate holdings. (Importantly, the transfer represented only 50% of his total wealth, leaving sufficient personal assets to pay his living expenses and estate taxes after death.) After all was formed and funded, the father owned a 95.2% limited partnership interest in the FLP.

For the next five years, the FLP purchased and sold assets, hired and managed employees, prepared monthly statements, and sent quarterly statements to the partners. The partners met several times a year to discuss FLP business and respected the entity's separate form; for instance, the father never mixed his personal assets with the FLP's. The partnership made two distributions, one to cover the partners' pro rata tax liabilities and a second to give additional shares of the timber company to the father, with appropriate adjustments to each partner's capital accounts.

In 2002 the father died unexpectedly. The estate paid over $46 million in taxes—but the IRS cited $34 million in deficiencies, most of which related to the FLP transfers. Not surprisingly, the estate lacked sufficient liquidity to pay the additional assessment because its only remaining assets were tied up in the FLP's non-controlling, non-marketable interests. It borrowed from the children's trusts and sued the IRS for a $41 million refund.

Legitimate non-tax business purpose proves critical. After hearing from several witnesses at trial, the court found that the FLP was created to accomplish the following:

- Pool the family assets for investment according to the father's philosophy;
- Pass the management responsibility to the next generation;
- Enable the father to make lifetime gifts of interests in the FLP while ensuring that the voting of the underlying assets stayed under central management;
- Educate the father's descendants about wealth acquisition, management, and preservation; and
- Protect the family assets from creditors, failed marriages, and dissipation by future generations.

Moreover, the older children had actively managed the FLP assets according to the father's philosophy and they respected partnership formalities at all times. Based on these strong facts, the court summarily concluded that the partners established the FLP "in good faith and for legitimate and significant non-tax purposes," sufficient to exclude its assets from the father's gross estate pursuant to IRC Sec. 2036(a)(1)(bona fide sale exception for adequate consideration).

The court turned next to the more complicated questions of valuation. Both the estate and the IRS offered experienced, credentialed experts to establish the fair market value of Mr. Murphy's 95.2% limited partnership interest in the FLP. Both experts applied the net asset value approach to the underlying assets (Murphy Oil, timber, and banking stock) and then applied Rule 144 and blockage discounts as well as discounts for lack of control and lack of marketability. Not surprisingly, the bulk of the parties' dispute (and the court's opinion) focused on the appropriate size of the discounts.

Publicly traded stock. In valuing the Murphy Oil stock, the estate's expert considered not only the size of the block relative to its daily trading volume but also qualitative factors such as: 1) the stock's volatility; 2) actual price changes under varying market conditions; 3) the company's financial outlook and earnings trend; 4) the stock's pricing and performance trend; and 5) transfer restrictions. Based on these factors, the expert believed a 5% Rule 144/blockage discount was appropriate. By contrast, the IRS's expert did not assess these additional qualitative factors or the effect of SEC sales restrictions to reach his1.9% blockage discount. The court found his analysis to be less credible, and adopted the estate's expert's 5% Rule 144/blockage discount.

Similarly, the estate's expert applied a qualitative analysis to the FLP's unrestricted shares in the timber company and reached a 5% blockage discount. For the remaining shares, subject to Rule 144 restrictions (which could only be sold in private transactions), he used a Black Scholes/put option approach to determine a discount of 12.7%. He then calculated a weighted average discount for the entire block of timber company stock to be 10.6%. The court preferred this analysis over that of the IRS expert, who did not consider any market- or company-specific factors in determining a blockage discount and used an option collar approach to determine a Rule 144 discount. (Notably, the Federal Court of Claims also rejected the IRS's option collar approach to valuing Rule 144 discounts in *Litman v. U.S.*; see the November 2007 *BVU*.)

The experts differed by only .1% in their Rule 144/blockage discounts for the FLP's bank holdings—but because the estate's expert applied a broader and more qualitative approach, the court adopted his 1.3% figure versus the IRS's 1.2%. (In fact, the only instance in which the court found the IRS expert to be more credible than the estate's expert was in connection with the FLP's timberland and farm holdings, for which the parties enlisted real estate appraisers.) Taking the value of the Murphy Oil stock, the timber company shares and the bank shares, plus the real estate and other assets and then subtracting liabilities, the court found the Murphy FLP was worth just over $132 million on the valuation date. Multiplying this by Mr. Murphy's pro rata share reached a net asset value of roughly $126 million for his 95.2% LP interest.

Discount for lack of control (DLOC). Both experts divided the FLP's assets into separate asset categories to determine appropriate discounts for each. For the first (equity securities), both experts relied on data from closed end funds, but only the estate's expert screened the funds to select the 19 that were most similar to the FLP's holdings. He concluded an 11% DLOC compared to the IRS expert, who used data from 30 funds to reach a 6.9% DLOC.

To determine the DLOC for cash/cash equivalents, the estate's expert factored in the partnership's abnormally large cash balance, reasoning that it could be invested in equities or real estate in line with the FLP's long-term goals. "He also considered...that an investor...would have no control over this cash," the court observed. "The [IRS expert] did not consider this," it added. "Rather, he based his determination on the fact that discounts generally decline as the asset category moves down the scale of investment risk" to reach a 2% DLOC for this asset category.

Finally, in determining a DLOC for the partnership's real property, each expert relied Partnership Profiles studies and their data on secondary sales of limited partnership real estate interests. Interestingly, the IRS concluded that a 35% discount was appropriate—but the estate's expert believed a portion of the discount was derived from data that included a lack of marketability discount, and he thought a 26.3% DLOC was more appropriate.

After calculating a weighted average of all the discounts, the estate's expert determined a 12.5% discount compared to the IRS's 10%. Once again, the court found the analysis by the estate's expert to be more credible, and it adopted his 12.5% DLOC.

Discount for lack of marketability (DLOM). Both experts considered restricted stock studies. The estate's expert relied on three studies, including FMV Opinions, comparing the data to the holding period, relative risk, distribution policy, and transfer restrictions on Mr. Murphy's LP interest. In particular, the holding period for the Murphy holdings was substantially longer (one to two years) than that of the restricted stocks in the studies, and the estate's expert determined a 32.5% DLOM.

The IRS expert also looked at restricted stock sales prior to amendments to Rule 144, which eased the trading of these shares among qualified buyers. "These studies showed a 12% decline in the average discount after the enactment of Rule 144A," according to the expert, who said the decline reflected the "discount that investors require for having virtually no resale market" and believed a 12.5% DLOM was appropriate.

The expert did not consider the longer holding period for the Murphy shares, however. For a fifth and final time, the court was persuaded by the estate's expert, and it adopted his 32.5% DLOM. After applying all of the estate's determinations and discounts, the court found the fair market value of the Murphy 95.2% LP interest to be $74.5 million—and ordered a complete tax refund consistent with its calculations.

Pierre v. Commissioner

Tax Court Split 9-to-6 on Preserving Family LLC for Gift vs. Income Tax Purposes

Case name: Pierre v. Commissioner
Citation: 2009 WL 2591652 (U.S. Tax Ct.)
Date of decision: Aug. 24, 2009
Country: US
State or Federal: Federal
State/Jurisdiction: Federal Circuit
Court: United States Tax Court
Type of action: Federal Taxation
Experts: James F. Shuey (taxpayer)
Judge: Wells

Single-member limited liability companies (LLCs) are peculiar entities, retaining some features of a corporation (personal liability) and some of a partnership (management flexibility and pass-through income). To clarify the tax treatment of such hybrids, in 1996 the U.S. Treasury promulgated what's become known as "check-the-box" regulations (Sections 301.7701-1 through 301.7701-3, Proced. & Admin. Regs.):

Whether an organization is an entity separate from its owners for federal tax purposes is a matter of federal tax law and does not depend on whether the organization is recognized as an entity under local law.

Under these provisions, the entity form of a single-member LLC is disregarded for federal income tax purposes. In what appears to be a new and creative effort to undermine family LLCs, the IRS argued in this recent case that the same regulations require a single-member LLC, validly formed under state law, to be disregarded for federal gift tax purposes.

A generous gift. Nine years ago, a taxpayer received $10 million from a friend. Wanting to provide for her son and grandchild but concerned about keeping the wealth intact, she organized a single-member family LLC under New York law. (Under the regulations, she did not elect to treat the LLC as a corporation, and thus agreed with the IRS that the entity form should be disregarded for federal income tax purposes.)

The taxpayer then formed two trusts for her children and transferred $4.25 million in marketable securities to the LLC. Twelve days after funding, she exchanged her entire interest in the family LLC for the trusts, giving each a 40.5% membership in return for two promissory notes of $1.09 million. An appraiser arrived at these amounts after valuing a 1% interest in the LLC at $26,965, including a 30% combined discount for lack of marketability and lack of control. (Note: The appraiser later admitted an error, having used a 36.5% discount when valuing the underlying assets.)

On her gift tax return, the taxpayer used the discounted values to conclude that no tax was due. The IRS disagreed, assessing deficiencies of over $1.13 million. Under its interpretation of the check-the-box regulations, the IRS argued that the transfer of LLC interests to the children's trusts were transfers of proportionate shares of the underlying LLC assets to be assessed at fair market value without the application of discounts.

A court divided. In a majority opinion signed by nine federal tax court judges and written by Judge Wells, the U.S. Tax Court first discussed the respective roles of federal and state law in valuing asset transfers. In particular, the U.S. Supreme Court has held that an interest validly created under state law will be respected by the courts but is subject to federal estate and gift laws. "State law determines the nature of property rights, and Federal law determines the appropriate tax treatment of those rights."

Thus the taxpayer did not have a property interest in the LLC's underlying assets because New York law recognized the entity separate and apart from its member. "There was no State law 'legal interest or right' in those assets for Federal law to designate as taxable, and Federal law could not create a property right in those assets," the Tax Court held. Consequently, the taxpayer's gift tax liability is determined "by the value of the transferred interest in [the family LLC], and not by a hypothetical transfer of the underlying assets."

The court next turned to whether the check-the-box regulations preempted this precedent. Interestingly, the IRS cited *Shepherd v. Comm'r* (11th Cir. 2002) and *Senda v. Comm'r* (8th Cir. 2006) to support its arguments. (Both cases are available at *BVLaw*.™) The court distinguished these cases on their facts, however. "Both *Shepard* and *Senda* stand for the proposition that a transfer of property to a partnership for less than full and adequate consideration may represent an indirect gift to the other partners."

By contrast, this taxpayer transferred the cash and securities to the family LLC prior to the trusts receiving the assets and their 40.5% interests. "Neither the check-the-box regulations nor the cases cited by respondent support compel a conclusion that the existence of an entity validly formed under applicable State law must be ignored in determining how the transfer of a property interest in that entity is taxed under Federal gift tax provisions."

Moreover, in the past, when Congress has found the "willing buyer, willing seller" fair market value standard inadequate in valuing certain transfers, it has enacted IRC provisions (Sections 2701, 2703, e.g.) to disregard valid state law restrictions. "By contrast, Congress has not acted to eliminate entity-related discounts in the case of LLCs or other entities generally or in the case of a single-member LLC specifically," the court observed. Until then, the IRS cannot seek to "overrule" the federal gift tax regime and substantial precedent. Accordingly, for federal gift tax purposes, the court valued the taxpayer's transfers to the trusts as transfers of interests in the family LLC and not as transfers of a proportionate share of the underlying assets.

A delayed decision. Notably, the court will address the valuation issues, including the application and magnitude of discounts, in a separate opinion. It will also decide if the step transaction doctrine will collapse the separate transfers to the trusts. (The parties have already briefed and argued these issues, so all that remains is the court's decision—though there is no indication of how long this will take.)

Also notable in this case: six Tax Court judges dissented in two separate opinions. "Where the property transferred is an interest in a single-member LLC that is validly created and recognized under State law, the willing buyer cannot be expected to disregard that LLC," Judge Halpern wrote in the first dissent. Congress has not yet enacted a "targeted substitute" in this context—but that simply leaves the courts in the familiar role of interpreting the "complexity, breadth, and vagueness" of the applicable IRC provisions (Sec. 2501). "The check-the-box regulations put the choice of entity classification in the hands of the taxpayer," Judge Halpern concluded. "That the taxpayer bears any burden along with the benefits seems only fair."

In the second dissent, Judge Kroupa criticized the majority for failing to discuss "what it means for an entity not to be 'separate' from its owner," and for providing a "false" distinction between an entity's "classification" and its "valuation." The check-the-box regulations provide that the owner of a disregarded entity is to be treated as the owner of its assets. This "plain language" requires the court to disregard the family LLC as an entity separate from its owner for purposes of assessing federal gift tax liability.

Given the divisiveness of the opinion and the substantial federal interest at stake, the IRS may appeal this issue, especially if it loses its argument to apply the step transaction doctrine and preclude discounts.

Index for Section 3

www.ingramcontent.com/pod-product-compliance
Lightning Source LLC
LaVergne TN
LVHW062242200926
848484LV00006B/1593
* 9 7 8 1 9 3 5 0 8 1 2 9 6 *